®

ott Larsen

Osborne **McGraw-Hill**

Berkeley   New York   St. Louis   San Francisco
Auckland   Bogotá   Hamburg   London
Madrid   Mexico City   Milan   Montreal
New Delhi   Panama City   Paris   São Paulo
Singapore   Sydney   Tokyo   Toronto

Osborne/**McGraw-Hill**
2600 Tenth Street
Berkeley, California 94710
U.S.A.

For information on translations or book distributors outside the U.S.A., or to arrange bulk purchase discounts for sales promotions, premiums, or fund-raisers, please contact Osborne/**McGraw-Hill** at the above address.

Maximizing Corel® WordPerfect® 8

1234567890 AGM AGM 901987654321098

ISBN 0-07-882451-6

Publisher: Brandon A. Nordin
Editor-in-Chief: Scott Rogers
Acquisitions Editor: Joanne Cuthbertson
Project Editor: Heidi Poulin
Editorial Assistants: Gordon Hurd, Stephane Thomas
Technical Editor: Roger Gagon
Copy Editor: Gary Morris
Proofreader: Stefane Otis
Indexer: Valerie Robbins
Computer Designer: Roberta Steele
Illustrator: Arlette Crosland
Series Design: Michelle Galicia
Cover Design: Regan Honda

PART I

Power Tools for Creating Documents

CONTENTS

PART II

Power Tools for Formatting Documents

PART III

Power Tools for Automating Tasks

PART IV

Power Tools for Working with Other People and Programs

Foreword

Maximizing Corel WordPerfect 8 is the latest title in the Corel Press series of books. The titles in this series provide readers with the tools needed to take advantage of the solutions contained in the Corel software products they have purchased. The authors, along with the staff at Corel, have spent many hours working on the accuracy and features included in this book and we think you'll appreciate their efforts.

This book is designed to help you get the most out of WordPerfect 8—so that you can take full advantage of its most powerful features. It is intended for the user who already has a grasp of the basics, and wants to learn how to become even more proficient. This book focuses on power tools for creating and formatting documents, automating tasks, and for working with other people and programs. We believe we have created a package that will maximize your productivity as you work in WordPerfect 8.

The Corel Press series represents a giant step in the ability of Corel to disseminate information to our users through the help of Osborne/McGraw-Hill and the fine authors involved in the series. Congratulations to the team at Osborne who have created this excellent book, and to the team at Corel who supported the creation of this book!

Dr. Michael C. J. Cowpland
President & CEO
Corel Corporation

Acknowledgments

Whenever you tackle a project as comprehensive as this book, it makes all the difference in the world to have a reliable, hard-working group of people behind you. We were fortunate to have an outstanding team at all levels help us complete this book, and they are well deserving of our thanks and praise.

We'd like to thank acquisitions editor Joanne Cuthbertson, project editor Heidi Poulin, and editorial assistant Gordon Hurd, who all helped keep the project on track and headed in the right direction. Thanks also to technical editor Roger Gagon, copy editor Gary Morris, proofreader Stefany Otis, indexer Valerie Robbins, and designer Roberta Steele for lending their expertise to the book.

Our thanks also go to Elden Nelson for his insight into the concept and direction of the book, and to Howard Collett for spearheading the initial stages of the project. We'd also like to thank Tisha Flora, Heather Carr, and Robert Raleigh for their initial work on a few of the book chapters. WordPerfect wouldn't be where it is today without Corel Corporation, and our thanks especially to Cindy Howard, Michelle Murphy Croteau, and Richard Whitehead, for their support and assistance.

Finally, we couldn't have completed this project without the love and support of our families, who were behind us all the way and sacrificed much while we were buried in chapters. So to Brian (who belongs to Gayle) and to Cori (who belongs to Scott)—you have our eternal gratitude.

Introduction

Take heart, WordPerfect enthusiasts! Corel's WordPerfect 8 is stronger than ever in the marketplace and packed with so much power you won't believe what you can easily accomplish. This book is dedicated to helping you take advantage of everything WordPerfect 8 has to offer—pushing your WordPerfect skills to the limit in the process. Whether you've been using WordPerfect for a few months or for several years, you're bound to find ways to get your work done faster and easier than ever before.

We've loaded this book with as many tips, tricks, and shortcuts as we could find to help you increase your WordPerfect productivity—much of it not documented anywhere else. In addition, we've included lots of hands-on sections to guide you step-by-step through specific tasks, such as creating a letterhead template (complete with custom prompts and macro triggers), formatting a newsletter with QuickStyles, and adding an "image map" navigation graphic to a Web page. You'll also find invaluable reference information in an easy-to-read format—from table formula functions, to common merge commands, to supported graphics formats.

And to top it all off, we've put together a companion CD that's chock full of macros, templates, sample files, and utilities to save you even more time. We've even thrown in the trial versions of Corel's WebMaster Suite and WordPerfect Suite 8.

Who Should Read this Book?

If you want to improve your WordPerfect skills and learn ways to get your work done faster and easier, then this book is for you. Because we've got so much great information to cover in this book, we don't spend much time on the basics. If you're reading this book, you should already know how to find your way around WordPerfect. For example, you should know how to open and save a file, create a basic document, and print a document. In addition, you should be familiar with Windows and know how to start and exit programs, minimize program windows, and navigate around dialog boxes and file folders.

Which Version Do You Need?

In order to follow all of the instructions in this book, you need to have Corel WordPerfect version 8 installed, which is part of the Corel WordPerfect Suite 8 for Windows 95/Windows NT. If you purchased the initial release of Corel WordPerfect Suite 8, your package included a voucher for CorelCENTRAL 8, a communication and scheduling program that wasn't complete when the suite started shipping. By calling the telephone number on the voucher, you should have received a CD with CorelCENTRAL 8, as well as an updated version of WordPerfect Suite 8. This updated version fixes some minor bugs from the initial release and adds a few enhancements.

This book assumes that you're using the updated version of WordPerfect 8. If you come across information in this book that is missing or works incorrectly in your version, make sure that you have the updated version. You can check which version you're using by choosing Help | About Corel WordPerfect from within WordPerfect. If your version is 8.0.0.153 (the original release), then you should update it. If you are a registered user, the updated version (with CorelCENTRAL) can be obtained for a small shipping and handling fee. Call Corel at 1-800-77COREL (1-800-772-6735) to order the update.

NOTE: *Corel offers two editions of WordPerfect Suite 8: the standard edition and the Professional edition (which includes additional products such as Paradox 8 and Corel Time Line). The Professional edition also includes the updated version of WordPerfect 8.*

What's Covered in this Book?

We've divided this book into four sections of "power tools" that can help you maximize your WordPerfect skills. Each chapter focuses in-depth on a WordPerfect feature (or features)—starting with a basic overview, and then moving into the more advanced capabilities, all in an easy-to-understand format. Along the way, we've thrown in lots of tips, secrets, and hands-on projects.

Power Tools for Creating Documents

Part I explores those WordPerfect features that can help you create documents faster than ever. Chapter 1 shows you how to create and edit templates that instantly set up your document's formatting and even prompt you for custom information. In Chapter 2, you'll learn how to use the Merge feature to set up customized mass mailings. Chapter 3 uncovers some of the shortcuts available with WordPerfect's "Quick" features, including QuickCorrect, QuickWords, and QuickLinks. And Chapter 4 reveals some common tips, tricks, and traps for features such as headers/footers, columns, tabs, and the Spell Checker.

Power Tools for Formatting Documents

Part II focuses on some of the tools WordPerfect offers for formatting your documents. Chapter 5 teaches you how to use styles, and Chapter 6 delves into the many tools for creating tables, including table formula functions. In Chapter 7, you'll learn how to insert and manipulate graphics images. Chapter 8 shows you how to quickly sort information in your documents, and Chapter 9 explores the reference tools, such as Table of Contents, Index, and Cross-Reference.

Power Tools for Automating Tasks

In Part III, you'll learn how to automate your WordPerfect tasks so you can get your work done in a flash. Chapters 10 and 11 concentrate on WordPerfect's powerful macro language, taking you from the basics of recording and playing macros to the steps for creating your own advanced macros. In Chapter 12, you'll learn how to add hyperlinks to your documents that can jump to an Internet site or start a macro with a single click. Chapter 13 shows you how to easily customize WordPerfect's toolbars, Property Bars, and keyboards to put your favorite features and macros within easy reach.

Power Tools for Working with Other People and Programs

Part IV highlights the many different ways that WordPerfect can help you communicate and interact with other people and programs. Chapter 14 shows you how to easily publish your documents on the Internet, even incorporating such things as image maps and Java applets. In Chapter 15, you'll learn how to customize the

Address Book to store and use information about your contacts, and in Chapter 16, we'll show you how to manage your files and keep track of different document versions. Chapter 17 explains how to use OLE to link and embed information from other programs right in a WordPerfect document. In Chapter 18, you'll learn how WordPerfect can interact with the other programs in Corel's WordPerfect Suite 8, such as Quattro Pro and Presentations. Chapter 19 provides helpful information for those who need to develop programs that work with WordPerfect, using a programming language such as Visual Basic or Delphi. And finally, Chapter 20 highlights some of the bonus tools and utilities that are included with WordPerfect Suite 8.

Appendixes

This book also includes two appendixes. Appendix A contains an alphabetical listing of WordPerfect's searchable codes and corresponding numeric values that can be used when searching with OLE Automation commands. Appendix B describes the contents of the companion CD included with this book.

What's On the Companion CD?

The companion CD included with this book is a valuable resource that's loaded with macros, templates, utilities, and other files to help you maximize your productivity in WordPerfect 8, as well as in Windows 95/Windows NT. Appendix B gives a complete description of all the files on the CD, which includes:

- Trial versions of Corel's WebMaster Suite and Corel's WordPerfect Suite 8

- Shareware utilities, including Client Manager 3.2 from Software Studios, WinZip, Net Timer Pro, Java applets, and much more

- Loads and loads of WordPerfect macros, including macros that correspond with chapters in this book, as well as macros from third party vendors, such as Software Studios and IVY International Communications (publishers of *WordPerfect Suite Magazine*)

- Close to 100 sample templates, macros, merge files, documents, and other files that work hand-in-hand with the information provided in this book

Conventions Used in this Book

We realize that you probably won't sit down and read through this entire book in one sitting, but instead will more likely use it as a reference as you're working on a project. To help you find the information you need quickly and easily—as well as highlight the many useful tips and shortcuts at the same time—we've used several different icons and sidebars throughout the book:

NOTE: *These paragraphs provide additional bits of information about the current topic.*

TIP: *Pay special attention to these helpful shortcuts, which point out little known secrets and faster ways to accomplish tasks.*

CAUTION: *Watch out for potential problems with the information provided in these warnings.*

Sample files on the companion CD that correspond to the current section are highlighted in these paragraphs (as well as in the "On the CD" sidebars).

Power Tip   The Power Tip sidebars provide specific steps and instructions for advanced tips, tricks, and shortcuts that will increase your WordPerfect productivity.

On the CD   The On the CD sidebars highlight some of the bonus macros, templates, and other tools included on the companion CD, and also give brief instructions for using them.

How To   Complete a project step-by-step with the hands-on information provided in a "How To" section.

Quick Reference   The Quick Reference sections provide easy-to-use reference material that you won't easily find documented elsewhere.

What Do You Think?

We've done our very best to pack as much WordPerfect information into an easy-to-read format as we could. We'd love to hear your thoughts on the book, including your success stories, as well as any other WordPerfect tips and shortcuts that we might have missed. Feel free to e-mail your comments to us at: **bgh@comwerx.net** (Gayle Humpherys) or **scott@studio2.com** (Scott Larsen). Long live WordPerfect!

PART I

Power Tools for Creating Documents

Chapter
1

Instant Documents with Projects and Templates

It used to be that whenever you needed to create a new document, you'd start from a blank document screen and add all the formatting and text from scratch—even if it was the same formatting you'd just used in a document the day before. Then along came the Template and Project features in WordPerfect to end this time-consuming cycle of repetitive document creation. Now, when you need to create a new document, templates and projects set up the entire document formatting in an instant and can even prompt you for custom information with which to fill in the document.

In this chapter, you'll learn how to get the most out of projects and templates. We'll start with an overview of using them, and then show you how to edit them to meet your needs. You'll also learn how to create your own custom templates that combine the power of automated prompts, macros, and more.

Projects and Templates Overview

Projects and templates are the ultimate document creation power tools. They set up your entire document formatting in an instant, automatically insert text to customize the document, and place all the tools and features you need for that task right at your fingertips. Projects and templates are basically the same, with the difference being that projects include the PerfectExpert panel, which has additional tools and features. For example, the business card project in WP 8 gives you options for instantly changing the card's style or text, adding graphics, and even quickly printing an entire sheet of ten cards. The PerfectExpert panel only appears with projects included with WP 8—it isn't part of the custom templates that you create. In this chapter, we'll use the terms "project" and "template" interchangeably.

NOTE: *Corel WordPerfect Suite 8 comes with projects for all of its major applications, including WordPerfect, Quattro Pro, and Presentations.*

Selecting a Project

Selecting a new project is as easy as choosing File | New. From the New dialog box (see Figure 1-1), you can select a project to create a new document or you can select one of the last nine documents you had opened in WP to continue working on. The projects are grouped by category, and the icon next to the project name indicates which Suite program the project is for. If you want to see a list of all the projects for a particular program, select the option in square brackets at the top of the drop-down list, such as [Corel WordPerfect 8]. When you're ready to begin, select the project you want and choose Create.

Select one of the last
nine documents you
had open

Drop-down list of
project categories

Last four projects selected

Select a new
project

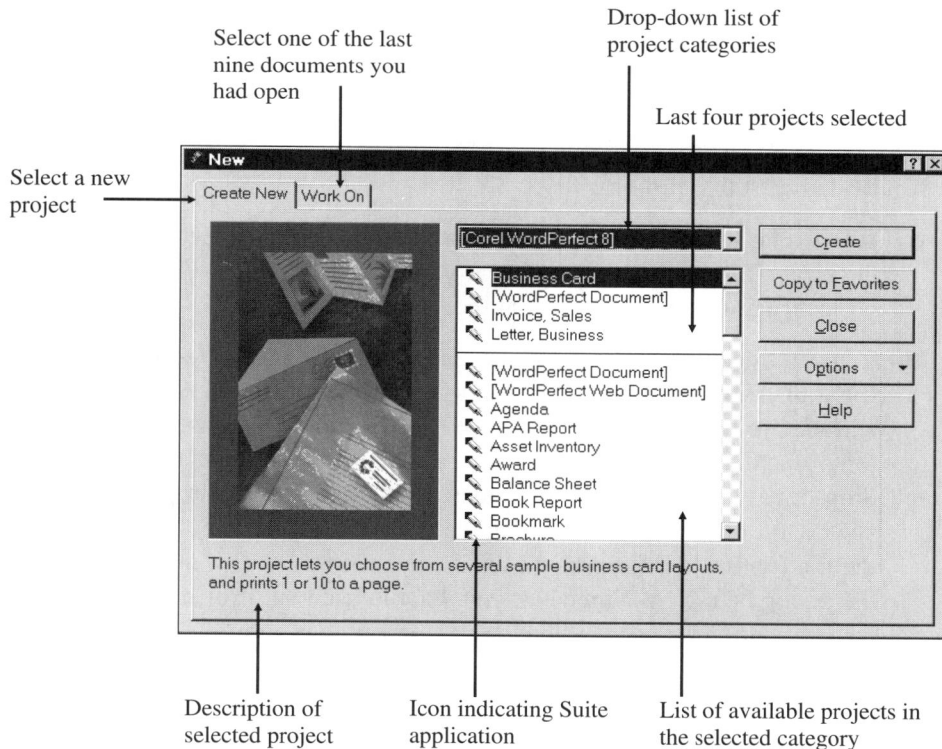

This project lets you choose from several sample business card layouts, and prints 1 or 10 to a page.

Description of
selected project

Icon indicating Suite
application

List of available projects in
the selected category

FIGURE 1-1   The New dialog box is where you organize and select your projects and templates

NOTE: *Only eight of the 79 projects included with WordPerfect are actually copied to your hard drive during a typical installation (see the "Projects Installed with WP" section). Before selecting a project that isn't already on your hard drive, make sure you have the WP Suite 8 CD in the drive so the project can be loaded.*

Shortcuts for Selecting a Project

If you use projects and templates frequently, try some of these shortcuts for quickly selecting a project:

- You can have the New dialog box automatically appear each time you start WP. To do this, choose File | New, then from the Options pop-down button, select Show This Dialog at Startup. Choose Close.

- You can select a new project before WordPerfect has been loaded. Click the Start button on the Windows taskbar, and then choose Corel WordPerfect Suite 8 | Corel New Project. The New dialog box appears. When you select a project, the corresponding Suite program is automatically loaded with that project.

- WP displays the last four projects you used in each category at the top of the project list in the New dialog box (see Figure 1-2). To use one of these projects again, simply select it at the top of the list and choose Create.

- You can bypass the New dialog box altogether by adding toolbar buttons for your favorite projects. To do this, right-click the toolbar you want to add the project button to and choose Edit. Click the Programs tab at the top of the dialog box, and then choose Add Program. From the File Type drop-down list, select WP Templates. Using the Look In drop-down list, switch to the directory containing the project file you want to add, select the file (with a WPT extension), and choose Open. Choose OK to close the dialog box. Now, whenever you want to use your project, just click the new button on your toolbar. (See Chapter 13 for more information on how to customize the button text or icon.)

Quick Reference ▸▸▸ Projects Installed with WP

WP 8 comes with 79 WordPerfect projects (plus several more for Quattro Pro and Presentations). During a typical installation, eight projects are copied to your hard drive:

Calendar, Monthly	Letter, Business	Memo	Resumé
Fax Cover Sheet	Letter, Personal	Newsletter	Sign

To use any of the other projects, you need to have your WP 8 CD in the drive or copy the project onto your hard drive. If you use a project frequently and want to copy it to your hard drive, copy *both* the WPT and AST file for that project from the \Corel\Suite8\Template directory on your CD to the \Corel\Suite8\Template directory on your hard drive.

PROJECTS TOOLBAR: *The companion CD contains a toolbar with custom buttons to select the eight installed projects. See the "How to Copy Toolbars Between Templates" section later in this chapter for instructions on using this toolbar.*

■ If you want to simply create a new document from a blank screen, you could choose File | New and select the [WordPerfect Document] project in the [Corel WordPerfect 8] category. A faster method is to click the New Blank Document button on the WordPerfect toolbar or press CTRL-N.

TIP: *When you create a new blank document, your default template (WP8US.WPT) determines what initial formatting is applied, as well as what toolbars, menu bars, and keyboards are available. If you want to change the default template, choose Tools | Settings and double-click Files. Select the Template tab, then set the Default Template Folder to the directory containing the new template. In the Default Template text box, enter the filename of the template or use the file folder icon to select it. Choose OK, and then choose Close when you're finished.*

Using Projects and Templates

When you select a project, WP inserts the document formatting and either displays a dialog box customizing the new document or a PerfectExpert with options. These options allow you to do such things as select names from the Address Book or set up some of the document's formatting.

The very first time you use a project, WP prompts you to select or create an Address Book entry with information about yourself, called the "Personal Information." Many templates include an option in the dialog box to select a new personal information entry. You can also change the personal information from the New dialog box by choosing Personal Information from the Options pop-down button. The new personal information is used for every template you create from that point forward, until you select a different entry.

TIP: *If you change the personal information and the new entry isn't used in the template you select, exit WordPerfect and start it again. This causes WP to reread the registry key containing the personal information so the correct entry is used.*

Once the template has been filled in with any custom information, you're free to edit, save, and print the document as you would any other document. If it's displaying, the PerfectExpert panel has many options for formatting the document quickly.

NOTE: *After closing the document, the PerfectExpert panel remains displayed with the WordPerfect "Home" options. If you want to close the PerfectExpert, click the "X" in the upper-right corner of the panel. You can also close it by choosing Help and deselecting PerfectExpert, or by clicking the PerfectExpert button on the Toolbar.*

Managing the Project List

WordPerfect provides several tools for managing your projects and project categories in the New dialog box. In this section, you'll learn tips for such tasks as creating new project categories, moving and copying projects between categories, and using your 6.1 and 7 templates in WP 8.

Power Tip▸▸▸ Customizing the PerfectExpert

The PerfectExpert panel can be displayed along the left or right side of the screen, as well as in a "floating" palette. To move the PerfectExpert to the right side of the screen, move the mouse pointer over the border area of the PerfectExpert panel until it turns into a four-sided arrow. Then click and drag the panel to the right side of the screen. To have the PerfectExpert display in a floating palette, click and drag the PerfectExpert to the center of the screen. Once there, you can click and drag the title bar to move it where you want on the screen.

You can also change the size of the PerfectExpert. To do this, move the mouse pointer over the border separating the PerfectExpert with the document window until it turns into a two-sided arrow. Click and drag until the panel is sized as you want.

Creating and Removing Project Categories

The New dialog box comes set up with over 20 project categories, from Business Forms to Hobbies to Time Management. The categories simply serve to organize and group your templates and projects. The same template can appear in several different categories. You can manage your categories in any of the following ways. Each option assumes that you've already displayed the New dialog box by choosing File | New.

Adding a Category

To create a new project category, from the Options pop-down button choose Create Category. In the Display Name text box, type a name for the new category and choose OK. Once you've created a category, you can copy and move projects and templates into that category as explained in "Copying, Moving, and Removing Projects."

Renaming a Category

To change the name of a project category, first use the project category drop-down list to select the category you want to rename. Then choose Options | Rename Category. Type the new name for the category and choose OK.

Deleting a Category

To delete a category from the New dialog box, select the category from the project category drop-down list. Choose Options | Remove Category and choose OK to verify the deletion. Only the category information is removed from the New dialog box—the actual template files are not deleted.

Adding New Projects

When you create a new template by choosing Options | Create WP Template in the New dialog box, it's automatically added to a project category when you save it. If you have other templates or documents that aren't currently listed in the New dialog box, you can add them in one of two ways:

■ Copy the template or document file into your Custom WP Templates directory, usually \Corel\Suite8\Template\Custom WP Templates. This also applies to any templates from WP 7 that aren't in the additional template folder (see the Power Tip "Using the Additional Template Folder"). Once the files are in the directory, you can select them from the Custom WP Templates category, or copy them into other categories as explained in the next section.

NOTE: *WP 6.1 templates need to be converted before you can use them in WP 8. For instructions, see the Power Tip "Using 6.1 Templates in WP 8."*

■ Choose Options | Add Project from the New dialog box. This displays a series of dialog boxes that walk you through adding a new PerfectExpert project (a file with an AST extension) or a regular document.

TIP: *Corel periodically adds new PerfectExpert projects to their Web site (www.corel.com) that can be downloaded and added to your project list.*

PERFECTEXPERT PROJECTS: *The companion CD contains thre PerfectExpert projects from Corel—one each for WordPerfect, Presentations, and Quattro Pro. See Appendix B for more information.*

Copying, Moving, and Removing Projects

Once a template or project has been added to the New dialog box, you can copy it into additional project categories, move it from one category to another, or remove it from a category. To copy or move a project, switch to the category and select the

Power Tip►►► Using the Additional Template Folder

Generally, only those templates in your template directory (usually \Corel\Suite8\Template) are displayed in the New dialog box. However, if you have templates in a different directory, such as your templates from WP7, you can use the additional template folder to include those templates in the New dialog box. If you want to use your 6.1 templates, see the Power Tip "Using 6.1 Templates in WP 8" later in this chapter.

To select the additional template folder, choose Tools | Settings and double-click Files. Select the Template tab. In the Additional Template Folder text box, type the path where the templates are stored or use the file folder icon to select the folder. Choose OK, and then Close.

Now when you choose File | New, a new project category should be listed. The category uses the same name as the last subdirectory in the path to the additional template folder. For example, if the additional template folder is C:\Corel\Office7\Template\Publish, a new project category named Publish is added. You can rename this category if you want.

project you want to move or copy. From the Options pop-down button, choose Copy Project or Move Project, and then select the new category. To remove a project from a category, select the project and choose Options | Remove Project. Choose OK to confirm the action.

NOTE: *If you want to delete the actual template file, remember that removing it from the New dialog box doesn't affect the file itself. To delete the template, you can choose File | Open, switch to your template directory, select the file, and choose File | Delete.*

TIP: *If you want to see what template filename is associated with a project in the New dialog box, select the project, right-click it, and choose Project Properties. The File Name text box shows the path and filename to the project.*

When you copy, move, and remove projects, the actual template file is not affected—only the information displayed in the New dialog box changes. This information (the project categories, names, and descriptions) is stored in a file called PROJECTS.USR. If the project information doesn't display correctly, such as duplicate project names or missing projects, you can delete or rename the PROJECTS.USR file. Doing this will cause WP to rebuild the PROJECTS.USR file the next time you choose File | New. If you're including projects from the WP 8 CD, the rebuilding process can take several minutes to complete.

CAUTION: *When you delete the PROJECTS.USR file, you lose any customization that you've made to the New dialog box, such as projects that you've moved or copied into different categories. Also, if you don't have your WP 8 CD in the drive when the list is rebuilt, the projects on the CD that haven't previously been copied to your hard drive will no longer be listed in the New dialog box.*

NOTE: *Typically, the PROJECTS.USR file is stored in the \Windows \Personal\Corel User Files directory under Windows 95 or the \WinNT \Profiles\"UserName"\Personal\Corel User Files directory under Windows NT (where "UserName" is the profile folder of the user currently logged in). However, on some computers the Corel User Files directory may be in a different location, such as \My Documents.*

Editing Projects and Templates

The templates included with WP can save a lot of time, but what if the formatting isn't quite what you need? Perhaps you'd like the fax cover sheet footer in a slightly larger font or your company logo added to the work schedule. Or maybe you just need larger margins. If you find yourself making certain formatting changes each time you use a particular template, you can speed up your work by editing the template itself. In this section, you'll learn how to add text and graphics to existing templates, change the default formatting, and even modify the template prompts.

Power Tip➤➤➤ Using 6.1 Templates in WP 8

You can use templates from WP 6.1 in WP 8. However, if the 6.1 templates use automated prompts, they first need to be converted. (WP 6.1 templates that don't use prompts only need to be copied into your Custom WP Templates directory before you can access them.)

To convert a 6.1 template, follow these steps:

1. Make sure you have the TCONVERT.WCM macro in your default macros directory. This macro is included on the WP 8 CD, but it isn't installed during a typical installation. If you don't have this macro in your macros directory, copy the TCONVERT.WCM file from the \Corel\Suite8\Macros \WPWin directory on the CD to the default macros directory on your hard drive (usually the same directory).

2. Copy the 6.1 templates you want to convert into your Custom WP Templates directory, usually \Corel\Suite8\Template\Custom WP Templates.

3. Choose File | New. From the project category drop-down list, select Custom WP Templates.

4. Select the 6.1 template you want to convert in the list of templates and choose Options | Edit WP Template.

5. When the template opens, a dialog box appears asking if you want to convert the template. Choose Yes.

6. The template is converted and you're asked if you want to overwrite the file with the new version or save it under a new name. Choose Yes unless you need to keep a copy of the original 6.1 template.

7. Choose the Close button on the Template Property Bar. Now you can use your templates in WP 8 by selecting them from the Custom WP Templates directory in the New dialog box.

On the CD... Project List Clean-Up

The history list, categories, names, and descriptions for projects in the New dialog box are stored in a file called PROJECTS.USR. If there are errors in your project list (such as duplicate project names), you can delete or rename the PROJECTS.USR file. The companion CD includes a macro called PROJECT CLEANUP.WCM that automatically renames the PROJECTS.USR file so WP will build a new one. Remember that when you delete the PROJECTS.USR file, you lose any customization that you've made to the New dialog box, such as projects that you've moved or copied into different categories.

To use this macro, choose Tools | Macro | Play. Select the PROJECT CLEANUP.WCM macro, and choose Play. If the PROJECTS.USR file isn't found in the typical directory, you're prompted for the location. Type in the path or use the file folder icon to select the PROJECTS.USR file from the directory where it's saved. Choose OK and the macro renames the PROJECTS.USR file to PROJECTS.OLD. The next time you choose File | New, the project list is rebuilt. Remember that if you want the projects from the WP 8 CD included in the project list, you need to have the WP 8 CD in the drive before choosing File | New. If you're including projects from the CD, the rebuilding process can take several minutes.

If you want to restore your previous project list with any customized categories, rename the PROJECTS.OLD file to PROJECTS.USR.

Adding and Deleting Text or Graphics

Suppose you want to add your company name or logo to one of the templates included with WordPerfect. Here's how you can do it:

1. Choose File | New. Switch to the category containing the template you want to edit and select that template in the list. Templates that appear in square brackets, such as [WordPerfect Document], can't be edited. From the Options pop-down button, choose Edit WP Template.

2. The template opens into a document window with the Template Property Bar displaying at the top of the screen.

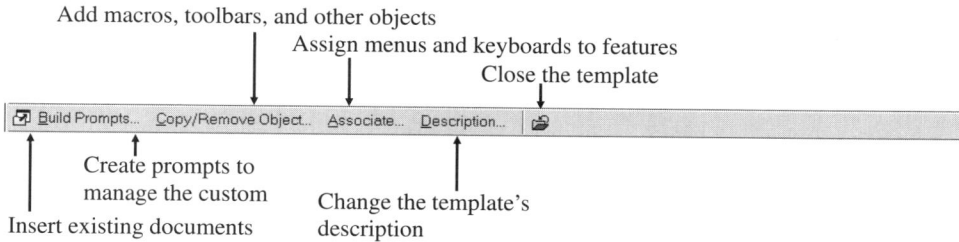

Add macros, toolbars, and other objects

Assign menus and keyboards to features

Close the template

| Build Prompts... | Copy/Remove Object... | Associate... | Description... | |

Create prompts to manage the custom

Insert existing documents

Change the template's description

3. To add text or graphics, simply type in the text or insert a graphics image in the desired location, as you would in any document. You can also edit any existing text. Some of the template text might be formatted with a style or even inserted as part of an embedded template macro. If you don't see the text you want to change in the main document window, try following the steps under the "Changing the Formatting" section.

4. If there is any text that you want to delete from the template, delete it as you normally would. Be careful that you don't delete text in square brackets, such as [Company Name], or angle brackets, such as <Name>. These are prompts that correspond to special bookmark codes. To remove the prompts and codes, follow the steps under the "Modifying Prompts" section.

5. If you're finished making changes, click the Close button on the Property Bar and choose Yes to save your changes.

NOTE: *If you're editing a template on the WP 8 CD that hasn't been copied onto your hard drive and try to save your changes, WP informs you that you don't have access rights (since you can't save onto the CD). The Save Template dialog box appears, where you can save your revised template on the hard drive (without affecting the original template on the CD). See the "Saving and Naming Templates" section later in the chapter for more information.*

Changing the Formatting

When you're editing a template, you can modify much of the document formatting as you would in any regular document. For example, you can usually select a new document font, change the margins, and so on. However, there are a couple of places where formatting codes might be hidden, such as in styles and template macros. Making these changes requires a little more skill.

Editing Styles in Templates

To see if the template you're editing contains any custom styles, choose Format | Styles to display the Style List dialog box. The five heading styles appear in every document and most likely are not being used by the template. The DocumentStyle also appears in every document, and it often contains formatting codes. Any other styles in the list are custom styles that are probably being used for formatting the template.

> **TIP:** *The fax cover sheet and letter templates let you select between different appearances, such as contemporary and traditional. These appearances are formatted by styles named _Style1, _Style2, and so on. To find out which style corresponds to a particular document appearance, select a style in the list. A description at the bottom of the dialog box indicates which document appearance that style formats.*

To edit a style, select the style and choose Edit. The Styles Editor dialog box appears with the formatting codes for that style (Figure 1-2). To edit a code, double-click it and make the changes you want. To delete a code, click and drag it out of the Contents text box. (If you accidentally delete a code, press CTRL-Z to restore it.) To add new formatting, use the menus in the Styles Editor dialog box to insert the new formatting. (For more information on styles, see Chapter 5.)

> **TIP:** *The "From the Desk Of" information in the fax cover sheet template is inserted with a footer in each of the four appearance styles (_Style1 and so on). To edit the formatting used for this text (for example, to select a larger font size), edit the style for the appearance type you want to modify and double-click the FooterB code. Select the Reveal Codes checkbox so you can see the codes in the footer. Make the changes you want for the text inserted at the bottom of the cover sheet and choose OK. The actual "From the Desk Of" text is inserted as part of an embedded macro.*

When you've finished making formatting changes to a particular style, choose OK. You can repeat this process to edit other styles in the list. Choose Close to return to the template document.

> **CAUTION:** *Be careful that you don't delete any [Named Region] codes within a style. These codes are needed for the PerfectExpert tools to work correctly.*

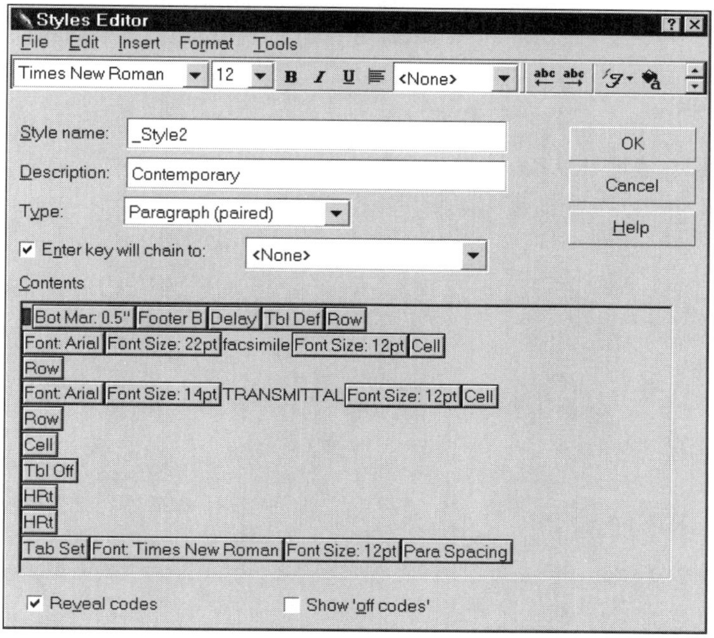

FIGURE 1-2 Many templates are formatted with styles

Editing Macros in Templates

A few templates, such as the letter and fax cover sheet templates, contain embedded macros that also affect some of the template's formatting. These macros are set to play automatically as soon as you select the template. While you should generally avoid making major changes to these macros, you can edit them to change some of the minor formatting, as well as the wording of text displayed in that template's initial dialog box.

To edit a template macro, after editing the template, choose Tools | Template Macro | Edit. Any macros embedded in the template are listed in the dialog box. Select the macro you want to edit and choose Edit. The macro opens in a separate document window, with the Macro toolbar displaying.

In most cases, the text you can safely edit in a template macro is formatted with the redline font attribute, so it appears in red. Usually this is text that appears in a dialog box or is inserted into the document. For example, you can change the complimentary letter closing options listed in the Letter PerfectExpert dialog box.

Or you can change the names of the different letter and fax cover appearances if you don't like "Contemporary" or "Cosmopolitan."

Power Tip... Editing the Default Template

WordPerfect uses a template for *every* document—including new, blank documents. By default, new documents are formatted with the WP8US.WPT template. You can change the formatting used in all the new documents you create by editing this template. For example, you can change the default margins, line spacing, or justification. Or you can even add text that you want to appear in every document, such as adding the path and filename code in a footer.

To make changes to your default template, follow these steps:

1. Choose File | New.

2. From the project category drop-down list, select Custom WP Templates.

3. Select the "Create a blank document" project and choose Options | Edit WP Template.

4. Make the changes you want for all your new documents, such as changing the margins, tab settings, or line spacing. You can add headers, footers, or other text that you want to appear automatically in every new document.

5. When you're finished, choose the Close button on the Template Property Bar and choose Yes to save your changes.

Now, every time you create a new document, your new settings are automatically in place. If you create a document from a specific template, such as a fax cover sheet, your new settings *won't* appear unless you've also added them to those individual templates.

You can also change the formatting for all your new documents by editing the default DocumentStyle. For more information, see Chapter 5.

CAUTION: *If you're editing text in quotation marks, make sure that you don't delete the quotation marks themselves.*

When you're finished making changes to the macro, click the Save & Compile button on the Macro toolbar. After the macro has correctly compiled, choose Options | Close Macro to return to the Template Editing window.

Modifying Prompts

There are several different ways that templates get the custom information they fill in the template with. Some templates use embedded macros to display dialog boxes, while others use PerfectExpert buttons. Perhaps the most common method is with template prompts. Unlike embedded macros and PerfectExpert buttons, template prompts can be easily modified. The easiest way to tell which method a specific template uses is to select the template. If the title of the initial dialog box is "Template Information," you know that template prompts are being used.

Template Information		
Personal information:	[ ] Teresa L. Davis	OK / Cancel / Next Field / Help
Recipient information:	[ ]	
Name :		
Address :		
City :		
State :		
ZIP Code :		
Greeting :		

You can add, edit, or delete the prompts in those templates that use prompts. First, edit the template as explained in the preceding section so the Template property bar is displaying. Then choose the Build Prompts button on the Property Bar.

TIP: *If the insertion point is in a structure such as a table, header, or footer while editing a template, the Template Property Bar is replaced with the Property Bar for that feature, such as the Table Property Bar. To display the*

Template Property Bar again, place the insertion point in a location not affected by these features. One method that works in almost all cases is to press either CTRL-HOME or CTRL-END to place the insertion point at the top or bottom of the template.

When you choose the Build Prompts button, the Prompt Builder dialog box displays, which lists any prompts that are already in the template (Figure 1-3). From here you can do one of four things:

- *Add New Prompts*   To add a new prompt to the template, choose Add. In the Prompt text box, type the prompt as you want it to appear in the Template Information dialog box and choose OK. Then click outside the dialog box and place the insertion point in the template where you want the prompt information inserted. Choose Paste and the prompt is inserted in square brackets.

- *Edit Prompt Names*   To change the text of a prompt, select the prompt in the Prompt Builder dialog box and choose Edit. Type the new prompt and choose OK. The prompt text is automatically updated each place it's used in the template.

- *Change Prompt Order*   To change the order the prompts are displayed when you're filling in the template, select a prompt and use the Move Up and Move Down buttons to position it where you want.

- *Delete Prompts*   To remove a prompt from the template, select the prompt in the Prompt Builder dialog box and choose Delete. Choose Yes to confirm the deletion. The prompt is deleted from the dialog box list, as well as from each location it was inserted in the template.

When you're finished making changes to the prompts, choose OK in the Prompt Builder dialog box. WP displays a message box as it updates the prompts in the template. Then close and save the template.

TIP: *You can also add prompts that insert your personal information in a template. Personal information prompts aren't displayed in the Template Information dialog box when you select the template, but an Address Book icon is added so a new personal information entry can be selected. To add a personal information prompt, choose Personal in the Prompt Builder dialog box. Place the insertion point in the template where you want the prompt included; then select the desired personal information field and choose Paste.*

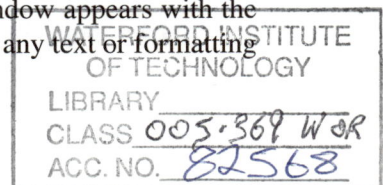

FIGURE 1-3 The Prompt Builder dialog box helps you customize template information

MESSAGE.WPT: *The companion CD contains a message pad template that uses prompts for the message information and also automatically inserts the current date and time, as well as your name as the message-taker. To use this template, copy the MESSAGE.WPT file from the CD to your Custom WP Templates directory. Choose File | New, switch to the Custom WP Templates category, and select the Automated Message Pad template.*

Creating a New Template

Sometimes even editing an existing template won't easily give you the results you want. That's why WordPerfect gives you access to the same powerful tools used in its shipping templates so you can create your own custom templates. In this section, you'll learn how to set up a new template, embed custom macros and toolbars, and add triggers to automatically play macros.

Setting Up

To begin creating a new template, choose File | New. From the Options pop-down button, choose Create WP Template. A blank document window appears with the Template Property Bar displaying. At this point you can add any text or formatting that you want to have automatically set up each time you create a document with this template.

If you've already created a document that contains some of the formatting you want in your template, you can insert that document and then edit it if needed. This saves you from having to redo all the formatting you've already spent time setting up. To insert an existing document, choose the Insert File button on the Template Property Bar.

Switch to the directory containing the document you want to insert, select that file, and choose Insert. WP inserts a copy of the document into the template, so any changes you make won't affect your original file. Once you've inserted the document, you can add any new text or formatting, delete text that you don't want included as part of the template, or change text to template prompts, as explained in the following sections.

Adding Text and Formatting

When you're creating a template, you can use any formatting feature that's available in regular documents. For example, you can change the paper size, subdivide the page, insert tables and graphics, and so on. Here are a few tips you might find useful:

- Consider using a header or footer to make sure text is always positioned at the top or bottom of your document, no matter what custom text is later inserted. If you want the header/footer information to appear only on the first page, use the Delay Codes feature (Format | Page | Delay Codes) to have a Header/Footer Discontinue code take effect on the second page. Or, if you don't want the header/footer information to begin until the second page, use the Suppress feature (Format | Page | Suppress) to suppress the header/footer on the first page.

- If you need the text to appear in a fixed position on the page (and don't want to use a header or footer), place the text in a graphics text box. You can customize the text box border—even remove it completely—as well as determine how the document text wraps around the box (see Chapter 7 for more information). Try to avoid using the Advance feature to position text as this can make it difficult to later position other text correctly.

- If you don't want a part of the template changed by those who use the template, format it in a table cell and then lock that cell. Locked cells also speed table entry because pressing TAB to move through the table skips over them. Table lines can be removed if needed.

■ If you want your template to include the current date or time, make sure you select the Automatic Update option before inserting the date/time code. Otherwise, the template will always use the date and time of when it was originally created. (If you want to insert the current date as *text* when you use the template, see the Power Tip "Date, Text, and Templates" later in the chapter.)

Inserting Template Prompts

By now you've probably noticed that many of the templates included with WordPerfect prompt you for custom information, and then automatically fill that information in the template. WP lets you customize your own templates in the same way with template prompts. For example, if your template creates a memo, you can be prompted for the recipient's name, memo subject, and file reference. In previous versions of WordPerfect, each template was limited to 12 prompts. But now in WP 8, you can add as many prompts as you need. If you have more prompts than will display at once in the Template Information dialog box, WP adds a scroll bar so you can see and enter the remaining prompts.

You can create three types of template prompts:

■ *Standard Prompts*   Standard prompts are displayed in the Template Information dialog box when the template is selected. The user enters the information, which is then automatically inserted in the correct locations in the template. When you're creating or editing a template, these prompts appear in square brackets, such as [Street Address].

■ *Address Book Prompts*   Address Book prompts look and work the same as standard prompts, with the added functionality of being linked to an Address Book field. This allows the user to select an Address Book entry and have the appropriate information automatically inserted into the Template Information dialog box and then into the template. Prompts linked to the Address Book can also be manually typed in the Template Information dialog box, just like standard prompts.

■ *Personal Information Prompts*   Prompts that are linked to the personal information do *not* appear in the Template Information dialog box. They are linked to fields in the current personal information entry and are automatically inserted when the template is selected. The Template Information dialog box does indicate which personal information entry is currently selected and has an icon allowing you to select a different entry if needed. Personal information prompts appear in angle brackets, such as <First Name>.

To add prompts to your template, choose the Build Prompts button on the Template Property Bar. The Prompt Builder dialog box appears (see Figure 1-4). To add a standard or Address Book prompt, choose Add. In the Prompt text box, type the prompt text as you want it to appear in the Template Information dialog box.

NOTE: *WP automatically displays a colon after the prompt in the Template Information dialog box, so you don't need to include one when you name the prompt.*

To link this prompt to an Address Book field, select the corresponding field from the Link to Address Book Field drop-down list. For example, if you're creating a prompt for the street address, select the Address field.

TIP: *If you've created custom Address Book fields and want to link a prompt to one, select the Show All Available Fields checkbox.*

Choose OK to add the prompt to the prompt list. You can continue to add the remaining prompts for your template before pasting them in the document, or you can paste them as you go. When you're ready to insert a prompt into the document, click outside the Prompt Builder dialog box. Then click the insertion point a second time to place it where you want the prompt inserted and choose Paste in the Prompt Builder dialog box to insert the prompt in the template. It will appear in square brackets, such as [Name]. Continue this process to add and paste the additional prompts where you want them inserted in the document. You can paste the same prompt more than one time in a document and you can also have several prompts on the same line. The prompts can be formatted with different fonts and font attributes if desired.

TIP: *If you accidentally paste a prompt in the wrong location and you haven't yet closed the Prompt Builder dialog box, simply delete the prompt text and brackets from the document, and then repaste the prompt in the correct location. If you've already closed the Prompt Builder dialog box and processed the prompts, choose Build Prompts again and use the Delete button to remove the prompt, and then re-add it to the list and paste it in.*

Power Tip→→→ Using the Same Prompt Multiple Times

If you want to include the same prompt more than once in your template, you don't need to paste it each time from the Prompt Builder dialog box. After adding the prompt to the Prompt Builder dialog box, you can simply type the prompt name in square brackets into the template document each place you want it inserted. Make sure you type the prompt name as it appears in the Prompt Builder dialog box, and don't include any spaces between the text and the brackets, such as **[First Name]**.

When you choose OK to close the Prompt Builder dialog box, WP formats each occurrence of the prompt with the necessary bookmarks so it will be correctly filled in when the template is used. If you add the prompt text after closing the Prompt Builder dialog box, simply choose Build Prompts and choose OK to process the new prompts.

To insert a personal information prompt, choose Personal in the Prompt Builder dialog box. Click outside the dialog box and click a second time to place the insertion point where you want the prompt inserted. Select the personal information field you want from the dialog box and choose Paste. The prompt is inserted using angle brackets, such as <Name>. Repeat this to paste in any other personal information prompts. When you're finished, choose Close.

The order in which the prompts are listed in the Prompt Builder dialog box is how they will appear in the Template Information dialog box when you later use the template. If you want the prompts to appear in a different order, use the Move Up and Move Down buttons to rearrange them. Changing the order in the dialog box doesn't affect the prompts inserted in the document.

When you're finished adding and inserting prompts, choose OK in the Prompt Builder dialog box. WP takes a few seconds to process the prompts in the template. When this step has finished, you can turn on Reveal Codes (View | Reveal Codes) and see that each prompt has unique bookmark codes placed around it. These codes tell WP where to insert the custom information when you later fill in the template.

QuickMarks

If you've inserted prompts of any kind into your template, you can also tell WP where to place the insertion point after the template has been filled in. This is done by setting a QuickMark. After displaying the Template Information dialog box and filling in the template, WP searches for a QuickMark code. If one is found, it moves to that location, leaving the insertion point ready for you to begin typing into the template document. To insert a QuickMark while editing a template, place the insertion point where you want it located after filling in the template and choose Tools | Bookmark; then choose Set QuickMark.

CAUTION: *If you've selected the option to automatically insert a QuickMark each time you save a document (under Tools | Bookmark | Set QuickMark on File Save), make sure you position the insertion point correctly just before closing and saving your template. Otherwise, the QuickMark will be moved to the location of the insertion point when the template was last saved.*

Embedding Template Objects

One of the more powerful aspects of templates is the ability to embed macros, toolbars, styles, and other objects. Once embedded, these objects can be "triggered" by certain events or associated with different features, as you'll learn in the next section. Embedded objects help make sure that everything you need for a template is located in one place, so you don't have to worry about keeping track of several different files.

There are six types of objects that can be saved within a template: menu bars, toolbars, keyboards, macros, styles, and QuickWords (formerly known as Abbreviations).

■ *Menu Bars, Toolbars, and Keyboards*   When you create or edit a menu bar, toolbar, or keyboard from a blank document window, your changes are saved in the default template, usually WP8US.WPT. These custom objects are also available when you select other templates. The advantage to saving them within a specific template is that you can then remove them from your default template so they're *only* available in the template where you need them. If you use a lot of different toolbars and keyboards, this helps keep your default template from becoming cluttered.

■ *Macros*   There are two types of macros in WP: template macros and macros on disk. Template macros are available only when the associated template is selected, while regular macros (saved on a disk) can be accessed at any time. If you want to use an existing macro on your hard drive in a template as a trigger, you must first copy that macro into the template (as explained later). Once the macro has been embedded in the template, any changes you make to the original macro won't affect the macro in the template. To update the template macro, you must either edit the macro from within the template or recopy the macro on disk into the template.

■ *Styles*   When you create a new style, it is usually only saved in the current document. You can also save a style into a file and then retrieve it into other documents. Or you can copy the style to your default template. If you want to use a style you've created in another template, you need to copy the style first to your default template and then into the specific template.

■ *QuickWords*   QuickWords is a new feature in WP 8 that replaces the Abbreviations feature from previous versions of the program. QuickWords are used to expand abbreviated text into longer text that can contain formatting and even graphics. The QuickWords are stored in their own template— QW8EN.WPT. This template is listed as <WP QuickWords File> in the Custom WP Templates project category. QuickWords are listed as an available object in other templates only to allow copying abbreviations from older templates into the QuickWords template.

Creating Template Objects

If you haven't yet created the custom toolbar, keyboard, or other object that you want to use in your template, you can create it directly within the template. If it's already been created and is part of your default template, you can copy it to your new template as described in the following section.

■ To create a new toolbar, menu bar, or keyboard while you're editing or creating your template, choose Tools | Settings and double-click Customize. Select the tab at the top of the dialog box for the item you want to create, such as Menus. Choose Create and type a name for your custom item.

NOTE: *If you want this item to be available from your default template, before choosing OK, choose Template, select Default Template, and choose OK.*

Choose OK and begin creating your toolbar, menu bar, or keyboard. For more information on creating these objects, see Chapter 13.

■ To create a new style in your template, choose Format | Styles and create the style as you normally would. (See Chapter 5 for more information.)

■ To create a macro for your template, begin by recording at least part of the macro. Then you can edit the macro and add additional macro commands if needed. Choose Tools | Template Macro | Record. Record at least one section of your macro, and when you're finished, click the Stop button on the Macro toolbar.

If you want to edit the macro and add additional commands to it, choose Tools | Template Macro | Edit. Select your macro and choose Edit. (See Chapter 10 for more information.)

■ QuickWords cannot be created within a specific template, but must be created from the default template. They are then available from within any selected template. (See Chapter 3 for more information on creating QuickWords.)

Copying Template Objects

If you've already created a toolbar, menu bar, keyboard, style, or macro and want to copy it into a specific template, choose the Copy/Remove Object button on the Template property bar. The Copy/Remove Template Objects dialog box appears (Figure 1-4). From the Templates to Copy From drop-down list, select the template currently containing the object you want to copy (most often the default template). From the Object Type drop-down list, select the type of object you want to copy, such as Toolbars. Then select the specific object name in the Source list on the left. Choose Copy to copy the item into the current template, or choose Copy All to copy all the objects.

Power Tip>>> Date Text in Templates

If you want a template to insert the current date whenever it's used, you can include a date code while creating or editing the template. However, this also means that if a document created by the template is saved and later opened, the date doesn't accurately reflect the creation date of the document. To avoid this, you can embed a macro in the template that automatically plays when the template is selected and replaces the date code with date *text*.

The companion CD includes a macro called TEMPLATE DATE.WCM that you can use in your templates to do this. This macro also includes the Template Fill macro command so it automatically fills in any prompts in the template (you can also use this macro in templates that don't use prompts). To use this macro in a template, follow these steps:

1. Choose File | New. Select the template you want to edit and choose Options | Edit WP Template.

2. Choose Copy/Remove Object from the Template Property Bar.

3. From the Object Type drop-down list, select Macros on Disk.

4. Click the file folder icon to the right of the Source text box, select the TEMPLATE DATE.WCM macro, and choose Select.

5. Choose Copy to copy the macro into your template, and then choose Close.

6. Choose Associate on the Template Property Bar and select Triggers.

7. Select Post New in the Items to Associate list box; then from the Macros drop-down list, select Template Date (this replaces the <dofiller> macro if your template uses prompts). Choose OK.

8. Choose Close on the Property Bar; then choose Yes to save your changes.

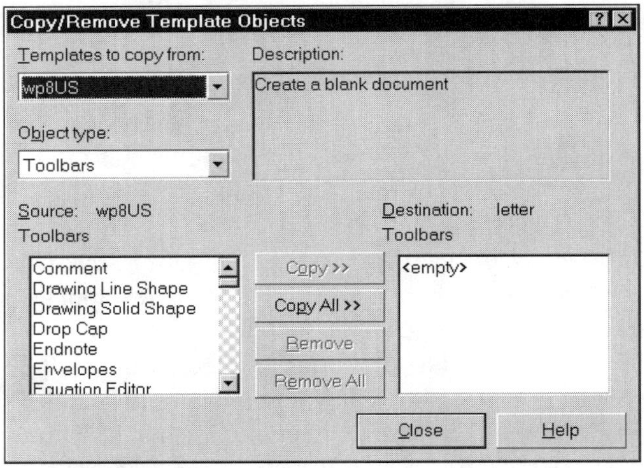

FIGURE 1-4   Use this dialog box to copy and remove objects from your template

NOTE: *The template file you're copying from must be saved in your Custom WP Templates directory or it won't be listed in the Templates to Copy From drop-down list.*

For practice copying a toolbar, follow the steps in the "How to Copy Toolbars Between Templates" section. For practice copying a macro on disk, see the Power Tip "Date Text in Templates."

If you want to remove an object from a template, select the object in the Destination list on the right of the Copy/Remove Template Objects dialog box and choose Remove. Or choose Remove All to remove all of the objects at once.

How to ▸▸▸ Copy Toolbars Between Templates

Many people wonder how they can copy a specific toolbar from one computer to another. For example, you might have a custom toolbar at work that you'd also like to use at home. Since toolbars are stored within templates, you can use the template editing tools to copy the toolbar from one computer to another.

How to... **Copy Toolbars Between Templates**
(continued)

The companion CD contains a toolbar with custom buttons created to select the eight projects that are copied to your hard drive during a typical installation of WP 8. The following steps will walk you through copying this toolbar from the TOOLBAR.WPT template on the CD to your default template. The steps will also indicate how you can copy toolbars from one computer's default template to another computer.

1. Copy the template containing the toolbar you want to copy into the same directory on your hard drive as your default template (WP8US.WPT), which is likely \Corel\Suite8\Template\Custom WP Templates. For example, copy the TOOLBAR.WPT file from the companion CD to your Custom WP Templates directory.

   If you're copying the WP8US.WPT toolbar from another computer (e.g., from your work computer to your home computer), before you copy it into the second computer's Custom WP Templates directory, rename the template file to something like WP8OLD.WPT so you don't replace the existing default template. However, rename it *after* you've transferred it to a floppy or temporary directory so you don't rename the original file on the first computer.

2. Choose File | New. From the project category drop-down list, select Custom WP Templates.

3. Select your default template in the list, which is labeled "Create a blank document." If you have two entries listed as "Create a blank document," you need to determine which one is the WP8US.WPT template. To do this, select one of the entries, right-click it, and choose Project Properties. Scroll to the end of the File Name text box and check which file is selected. If you selected the WP8US.WPT template, choose OK. If you selected the other template (such as the WP8OLD.WPT template), choose OK and select the other "Create a blank document" entry.

4. From the Options pop-down button, choose Edit WP Template.

5. Choose Copy/Remove Object from the Template Property Bar.

6. From the Templates to Copy From drop-down list, select the template you copied, such as TOOLBAR or WP8OLD.

How to...   **Copy Toolbars Between Templates**
(*continued*)

7. Make sure the Object Type drop-down list is set to Toolbars.

8. In the Source list on the left, select the custom toolbar that you want to copy over, such as Projects. Choose Copy. If your template already has a toolbar by that name, you're asked if you want to replace it.

9. When you're finished, choose Close, and then choose the Close button on the Template Property Bar. Choose Yes to save your changes.

10. If needed, right-click the toolbar from a blank document window and select the newly copied custom toolbar.

These steps can also be used to copy toolbars from your WP 6.1 and WP 7 templates into your WP 8 default template.

Associating Objects

Another powerful template tool is the ability to associate specific macros, keyboards, and menus with different situations or events. For example, when you're creating a document from a template, you can have a custom menu bar appear when you're at the main document window or working in a table. This is called *associating an object with a feature,* and it works with menu bars and keyboards. Or you can set a macro to automatically play at a certain time, such as just after selecting the template or just before printing. This is called a "trigger" and is only available with macros.

NOTE: *Toolbars can no longer be associated with different features in WP 8 templates, although you can still copy them into a template and then select them by right-clicking the toolbar.*

Selecting Features

Follow these steps to associate a menu bar or keyboard with a particular feature:

1. Edit the template, if you haven't already, so the Template Property Bar is displaying.

2. Choose Associate to display the Associate dialog box:

3. In the Item to Associate list box, select the feature that you want to connect to the menu or keyboard. For example, to have a custom menu bar automatically displayed from the main document screen after the template is selected, select Main in the list. Or, to have a special keyboard selected when a graphic is selected in the document, select Graphics.

4. From the appropriate drop-down list, select the menu or keyboard that you want connected to this feature. Only those objects that you have either created within the template or copied into the template are available to select.

5. Choose OK when you're finished.

Setting up Triggers

To trigger a macro to a certain event in the template, such as just after the template is selected or just before printing, follow these steps:

1. Edit the template if you haven't already, and choose Associate from the Template Property Bar.

2. Select Triggers at the top of the dialog box.

3. In the Item to Associate list box, select the time or event when you want the macro to play. Table 1-1 gives a list of each trigger option and a description of when the macro is played with that trigger selected.

4. From the Macros drop-down list, select the macro to play at the selected time. The macro must be copied into the template before it can be set up as a trigger.

5. Choose OK when you're finished.

Trigger Event	Macro is Played...
Post Close	After the template document is closed
Post New*	Immediately after the template document is opened into a document window
Post Open	After a template document that has been saved is later opened
Post Print	Just after the template document is printed
Post Startup	Right after WordPerfect is loaded (this only works when triggered in the default template, usually WP8US.WPT)
Post Switch Doc	After you switch back to the template document from another document window
Post Tables	Just after a table structure is created in the template, but before any text can be added
Pre Close*	After you choose File | Close to close the template document, but before the document is actually closed
Pre New	Before you open another document
Pre Open	After you choose File | Open to open another document, but before that document is opened
Pre Print*	After you choose File | Print, but before the printer actually prints the template document
Pre Switch Doc	Before you switch to another document window
Pre Tables	After you select the option to create a table, but before the table structure is actually inserted into the document

*Indicates most commonly used triggers

TABLE 1-1 Template Triggers

TIP: *If your template uses prompts, the <dofiller> macro is already assigned to the Post New trigger. If you want to assign a different macro to the Post New trigger (so it plays as soon as the template is opened), add the TemplateFill ( ) macro command to your macro. This way, WP will still fill in the prompt information correctly. Add this command in your macro where you want the Template Information dialog box to appear and prompt the user for the custom information. Also, if your template includes a QuickMark to indicate where you want WP to leave the insertion point after filling in the template, you can include a QuickMarkFind ( ) command at the end of your Post New trigger macro.*

On the CD ▸▸▸ Spell-Check Reminder

The companion CD includes the SPELL REMINDER. WCM macro that you can use with template triggers to remind you to spell check a document just before you print or close it. By setting up a trigger for this macro in your default template, each time you create a document and then either print or close it, you're asked if you want to spell check the document first. To set up this macro trigger, follow these steps:

1. Choose File | New and switch to the Custom WP Templates project category. Select "Create a blank document" and choose Options | Edit WP Template.

2. Choose Copy/Remove Object. From the Object Type drop-down list, select Macros on Disk. Click the file folder icon to the right of the Source text box, select the SPELL REMINDER.WCM macro on the CD, and choose Select.

3. Choose Copy, and then Close.

4. Choose Associate from the Property Bar, and select Triggers at the top of the dialog box.

5. In the Item to Associate list box, select Pre Print to spell check before printing, or select Pre Close to spell check just before closing a file.

> **6.** From the Macros drop-down list, select Spell Reminder. Choose OK.
>
> **7.** Choose the Close button from the Property Bar, and choose Yes to save the changes.
>
> Now, each time you create a new document and print or close it, a dialog box appears asking if you want to perform a spell check. If you choose No, the document is printed or closed normally. If you choose Yes, a message first reminds you to press ENTER after closing the Spell Checker. Then the Spell Checker begins, prompting you to correct misspelled words as normal. If you see the "Preparing Document" message box, click the cancel button in the upper-right corner to close it. After the Spell Checker has finished, choose Yes to close it, and then press ENTER and the document is printed or closed.

Saving and Naming Templates

When you're finished creating your new template, you're ready to save it and place it in a project category. Choose the Close button on the Template Property Bar, and then choose Yes to save your changes. The Save Template dialog box appears, as shown in Figure 1-5.

In the Description text box, type a description of your template as you want it to appear in the New dialog box. In the Template Name dialog box, type the filename you want to use for the template—WP automatically adds the WPT extension. Finally, select the project category you want the template placed in from the Template Group list box.

CAUTION: *If you forget to select a template group, your template is automatically placed in the first group in the list, which is usually the Auto category. This can make it difficult to find your template later on.*

Choose OK to save and close the template.

FIGURE 1-5 The Save Template dialog box lets you specify where you want to save your template

NOTE: *The actual template files are saved in subdirectories under your template directory that correspond to the project category. For example, a template placed in the Hobbies category would be saved in the \Corel\Suite8\Template\Custom WP Templates\Hobbies directory.*

On the CD ⟩⟩⟩ Letterhead Template

The companion CD contains a sample letterhead template that includes the following elements: prompts for the recipient's name and address (linked to the Address Book); a macro that automatically changes the date code to date text; and a custom menu containing options for finishing the letter, including printing, spell checking, and inserting bullets.

To use this template, copy the LETTER.WPT file from the CD to your Custom WPT directory. Choose File | New. From the project category drop-down list, select Custom WPT Templates. Select

Letterhead in the list and choose Create. The Template Information dialog box appears. If you want to change the personal information for the letterhead, click the Address Book icon to the right of Personal Information and select new entry. To select an entry from the Address Book for the letter recipient information, click that Address Book icon and select the entry you want. Otherwise, type the requested information. Choose OK.

The template is filled in and the macro automatically plays to convert the date code to date text. The insertion point is positioned for you to begin typing the letter. As you're typing the letter, you can choose Letter | Bullet to insert a bullet. When you're finished, you can use the other options on the Letter menu to spell check, save, and print your letter.

Summary

Templates and projects give you great ease and flexibility when it comes to setting up and formatting new documents. WordPerfect takes care of most of the formatting automatically, and even prompts you for custom information that's inserted in the right locations. The dozens of projects included with WP 8 make use of the PerfectExpert feature to give you all the tools you need right at your fingertips.

WordPerfect also gives you the power to create your own custom templates, which can be customized with prompts, toolbars, keyboards, macros, and other objects. You can set up template triggers that automatically play a macro when the template is opened, printed, closed, and so on. With the help of projects and templates, creating new documents has never been faster and easier!

In Chapter 2, you'll learn how the Merge feature can help you quickly perform mass mailings and create customized documents.

Chapter 2

Mass Mailings and More with Merge

It's 4:30 on Friday afternoon and you've just been given the assignment to prepare a monthly summary letter (with envelopes) for each of your company's 200 clients—before you go home. Any clients with an overdue balance should receive a modified letter listing the appropriate late charges. In addition, those clients in Los Angeles should have a note added to the end of their summary reminding them of the local conference next month. Should you cancel your weekend plans? Not if you have WordPerfect 8's Merge feature!

The Merge feature handles the creation of customized documents—especially on a large scale—with power and ease. The available merge options and commands give you control and flexibility over the final output you receive. In this chapter, you'll learn how to put the power of the Merge feature to work for you, from setting up merge data and form documents to inserting advanced codes that automate the merge process. We'll show you how to merge with different data sources, including the Address Book and other database programs, and how to select which records in a data file are merged. The end of the chapter contains some handy merge tricks, such as merging directly into a table and creating duplicate copies.

Merge Overview

The Merge feature helps you quickly create new documents by combining the information in a form document with data from another source. For example, if you have a database that contains customer names and addresses, you can create a form document with the basic text and formatting of a letter you want each customer to receive, and then merge that letter with the database information. WP creates a new letter for each record in the database, customizing it with the customer's name, address, and any other information you want included. As you'll learn later in this chapter, you can use a variety of merge commands and options to further customize and control the documents that are created during a merge.

Merge Terms

A merge has two basic parts: the data source and the form document. Once these two components are in place, you can merge them together to create new documents. But what exactly *is* a data source or a form document? Understanding the merge terms is the first step in unleashing the power of the Merge feature. In this section, we'll give you a brief description of the merge terms used throughout this chapter.

- *Data Source*   A data source supplies the individual pieces of information that customize a form document during a merge, such as a name or address. A data source can be a WordPerfect data file, an Address Book, a database file from a program such as Paradox, an ODBC data file, an ASCII delimited file, a spreadsheet file, or input from the keyboard.

- *Data File*   A data file is one type of data source that can be used for a merge. A data file is a WordPerfect file that can be in either a text or table format. It contains information separated into fields and records with ENDFIELD and ENDRECORD codes in text format, or cells and rows in table format. Data files were known as secondary files in older versions of WordPerfect.

- *Form Document*   A form document contains the main text and formatting for the final merged document, along with merge field codes that tell WP where to insert information from the data source. Form documents can also contain other advanced merge codes that control the final output of the merge. In previous versions of WordPerfect, form documents were called *primary files* or *form files*.

- *Field*   A field is one piece of information in a data source, such as a last name or phone number. A field can contain one character or several words. In WP data files, fields are separated with ENDFIELD codes or table cells.

- *Record*   A record is a group of related fields in a data source. Each record contains the same fields. For example, a data source might have a record for each client with fields for the client's name, address, and account number. In WP data files, records are separated with ENDRECORD codes or table rows.

Setting Up a Data File

One of the most common data sources for a merge is a WordPerfect data file. Data files are most often in text format, where the information is separated with ENDFIELD and ENDRECORD codes (see Figure 2-1).

Data files can also be formatted as a table, where cells and rows separate the fields and records (see Figure 2-2). You can create a new data file with the help of the Quick Data Entry feature, or you can import a file from another database or spreadsheet program as a merge data file. In this section, you'll learn how to create new data files, import data files from other programs, and edit the information in a data file.

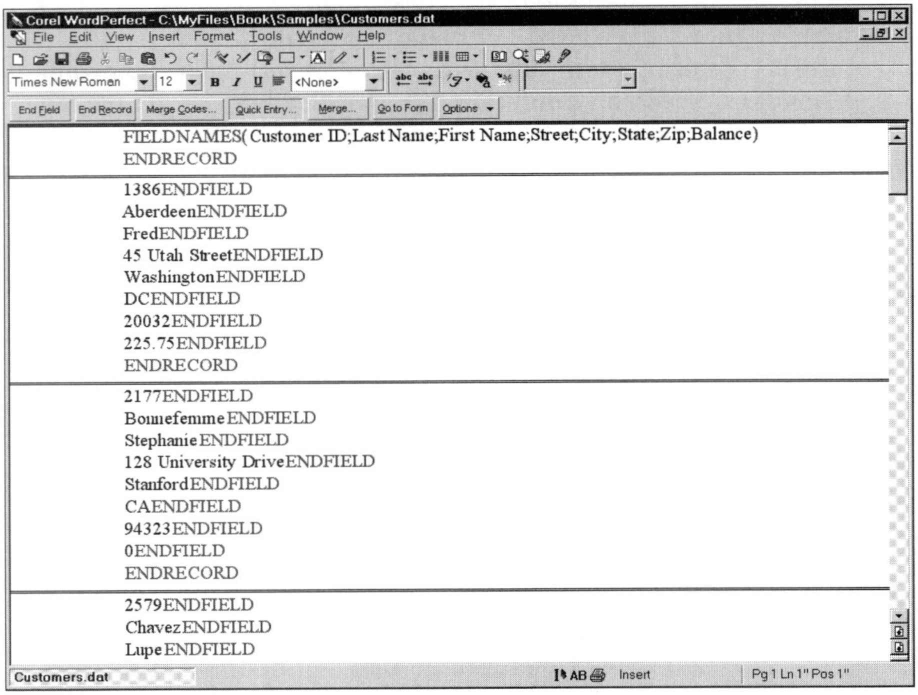

FIGURE 2-1   Merge data files use ENDFIELD and ENDRECORD codes to organize your information into records

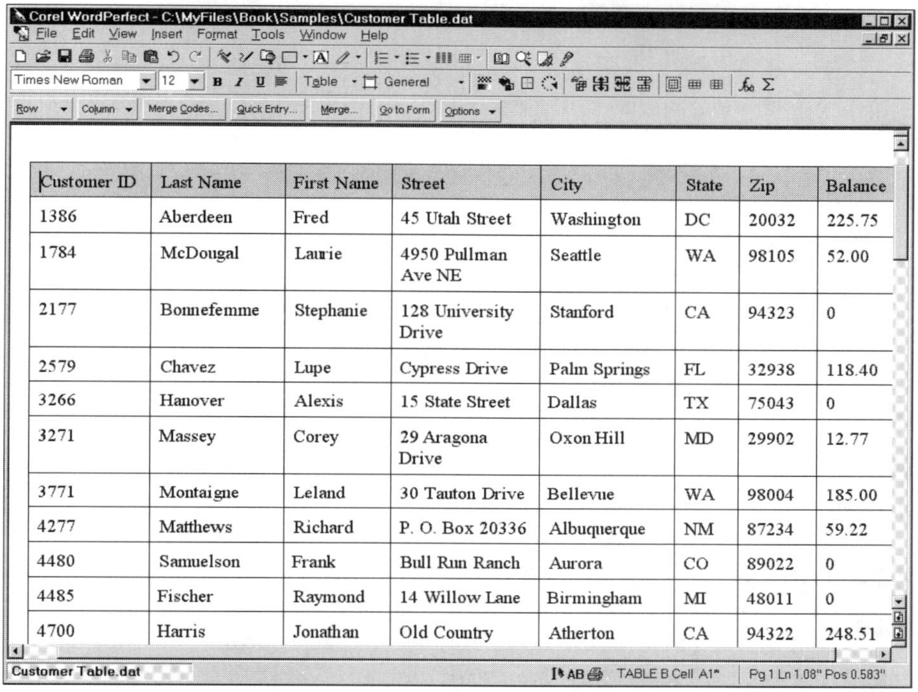

Customer ID	Last Name	First Name	Street	City	State	Zip	Balance
1386	Aberdeen	Fred	45 Utah Street	Washington	DC	20032	225.75
1784	McDougal	Laurie	4950 Pullman Ave NE	Seattle	WA	98105	52.00
2177	Bonnefemme	Stephanie	128 University Drive	Stanford	CA	94323	0
2579	Chavez	Lupe	Cypress Drive	Palm Springs	FL	32938	118.40
3266	Hanover	Alexis	15 State Street	Dallas	TX	75043	0
3271	Massey	Corey	29 Aragona Drive	Oxon Hill	MD	29902	12.77
3771	Montaigne	Leland	30 Tauton Drive	Bellevue	WA	98004	185.00
4277	Matthews	Richard	P. O. Box 20336	Albuquerque	NM	87234	59.22
4480	Samuelson	Frank	Bull Run Ranch	Aurora	CO	89022	0
4485	Fischer	Raymond	14 Willow Lane	Birmingham	MI	48011	0
4700	Harris	Jonathan	Old Country	Atherton	CA	94322	248.51

FIGURE 2-2 A merge data file in table format

Using Quick Data Entry

To create a new merge data file from scratch, go to a blank document window and choose Tools I Merge; then choose Create Data to display the Create Data File dialog box. The first step is to name the fields you want each record in your data file to contain. The field names describe the type of information in each field, such as Last Name or ID Number. In the Name a Field text box, type a name for the first field you want in each record of your data file, and then choose Add or press ENTER. The field name is added to the list box. Continue typing and adding field names until you've named all the fields you want to have in each record.

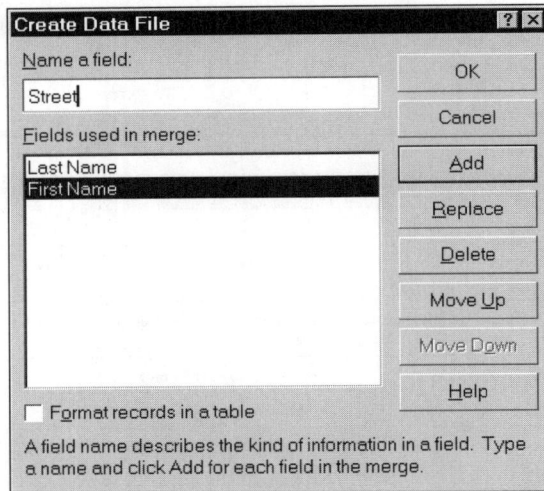

TIP: *The more you can break down the fields, the more flexibility you'll have when you later merge with this data file. For example, instead of creating a single field called Name, create separate fields for the First Name, Last Name, and Greeting. Similarly, create separate fields for the City, State, and ZIP Code, instead of placing them all in a single field.*

You can change the order of the fields by using the Move Up and Move Down buttons, or you can delete a field you've added by selecting it and choosing Delete. If you want to format the data file as a table, select the Format Records in a Table option. Choose OK when you're finished.

The Quick Data Entry dialog box appears next with a text box for each of the field names (see Figure 2-3). Type the information for each field of the first record. If you need to insert a hard return within a field, such as for a two-line address, press CTRL-ENTER. When you're finished, choose New Record or press ENTER. WP inserts the information into the document with the appropriate ENDFIELD and ENDRECORD codes.

NOTE: *You can move between the field text boxes in the Quick Data Entry dialog box by pressing TAB, pressing ENTER, or choosing Next Field.*

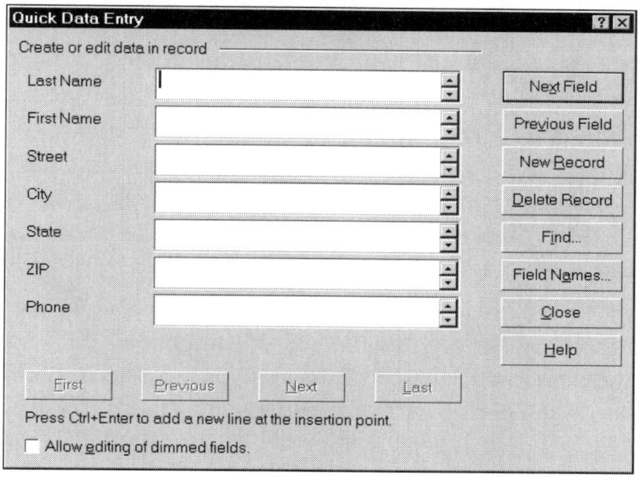

FIGURE 2-3 The Quick Data Entry dialog box shows the fields in each record

After the first record has been inserted in the document, the Quick Data Entry dialog box is cleared so you can create a new record. Type the information for the next record, choose New Record to insert it, and continue this process to create each record in your data file. When you're finished, choose Close, and choose Yes to save the changes. Type a filename for your data file using a DAT extension, and then choose Save.

TIP: *If you want to convert a table to an existing text data file, select the entire table, right-click it, and choose Delete. If the first row of your table has headings that you want to use for the field names, select Convert Contents to Merge Data File (Use Text in First Row as Field Names). Otherwise, select Convert Contents to Merge Data File. Choose OK to convert the table.*

Importing a Data File

If you already have data stored in another database or spreadsheet program, you can use that information in a merge by importing it into a WP data file. To import a file, go to a blank document window and choose Insert | Spreadsheet/Database | Import. From the Data Type drop-down list, select the type of file you're importing, such as Paradox.

NOTE: *If your database program isn't listed on the Data Type drop-down list, you can use your database program to export the data in ASCII delimited format, and then import the ASCII delimited file into WP.*

TIP: *You don't have to import the database or spreadsheet information into a WP data file to be able to use it in a merge. Instead, you can merge directly from the file by selecting it as the data source when performing the merge. See the "Performing a Merge" section later in this chapter for more information.*

From the Import As: drop-down list, select Merge Data File. In the FileName text box, type the path and filename of the file you want to import, or use the file folder icon to select it. Then press TAB to move out of the FileName text box.

CUSTOMER.DB: *If you want to practice importing a database file, the companion CD contains a sample Paradox database file named CUSTOMER.DB.*

If you're importing a database file, the Import Data dialog box shows a list of the available fields in the file (see Figure 2-4). If you don't want to include certain fields in the WP data file, deselect them in the list. If you're importing an ASCII delimited file, change the field and character delimiters if needed. If you're importing a spreadsheet, you can select a named range in the spreadsheet to import, or you can specify the specific range of cells that you want included. (For more information on importing spreadsheets and database files, see Chapter 17.)

When you've selected the options you want, choose OK to import the data. WP creates a new merge data file using the information in the selected file. Choose File | Save, and type a filename for the data file.

NOTE: *If you import a database file, the field names are automatically included. If you import a spreadsheet or ASCII delimited file, you can add field names as described in the "Editing a Data File" section next.*

Editing a Data File

Once you've created or imported a data file, you can edit any of the information, change the fields used in each record, or add and delete entire records. You can make changes to the data file information directly from the document screen or by using

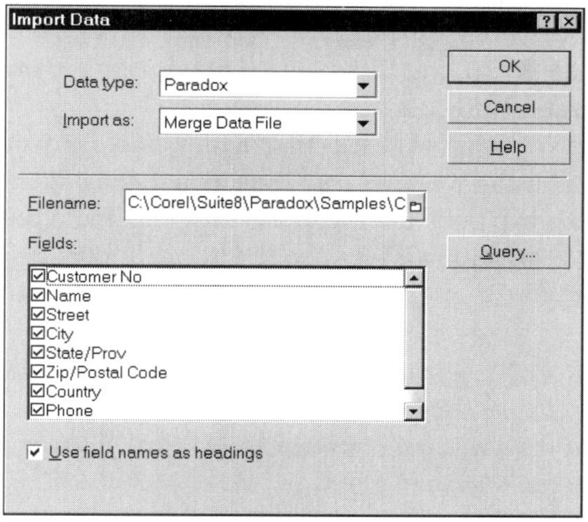

FIGURE 2-4 The Import Data dialog box shows the available fields in a database file

the Quick Data Entry dialog box. This dialog box lets you easily scan through the records in the data file one at a time, and ensures that each record has the same number of fields.

NOTE: *If you make changes directly from the document window, you can insert ENDFIELD and ENDRECORD codes from the Merge toolbar or by pressing ALT-ENTER for ENDFIELD or ALT-SHIFT-ENTER for ENDRECORD.*

The Quick Data Entry feature works best with data files that use field names. If your data file doesn't have a FIELDNAMES code at the top, follow the steps in the "Adding Field Names to a Data File" Power Tip to add them. Then choose Quick Entry on the Merge toolbar. The current record in the data file is displayed in the Quick Data Entry dialog box. From here, you can make changes to the records or field names, as described in the following sections.

Editing Records

To make changes to a record, use the Previous and Next buttons in the Quick Data Entry dialog box to locate the record you want to modify. You can also use the First and Last buttons to jump to the first or last record in the data file. To search for a specific record, choose Find, type the text you want to find, and choose Find Next or Find Prev to locate the record. If the record found isn't the one you want, choose Find again and repeat the process.

Once the record you want to edit is displaying, make any changes you want to the field information, using the scroll bar if needed to view the additional fields. To move between fields, use the Next Field and Previous Field buttons. You can also press TAB and SHIFT-TAB to move between fields, or simply click the insertion point in the field you want to edit.

NOTE: *If a field text box is dimmed and not available to edit in the Quick Data Entry dialog box, the field contains formatting such as a font code or style. If you want to keep the formatting in the field, you need to make any changes directly from the document window. To remove the formatting from the field and make changes in the dialog box, select the Allow Editing of Dimmed Fields option. Choose OK when the message box appears, and then make the changes you want.*

Adding and Deleting Records

To add a new record to the data file, use the Previous and Next buttons until the record that you want to insert the new record immediately after is displayed. If you want to add the new record to the end of the data file, choose Last. Then choose New Record and type the information for the new record.

Power Tip▸▸▸ Adding Field Names to a Data File

If your data file was imported from a spreadsheet or ASCII delimited file and doesn't yet have field names, you can easily add them. To do this, place the insertion point at the top of the data file and choose Merge Codes on the Merge toolbar. Select FIELDNAMES in the Insert Merge Codes dialog box and choose Insert. When the Create Data File dialog box appears, type a name for each field in your data file, choosing Add after each one. Choose OK when you're finished, and then choose Close in the Insert Merge Codes dialog box.

To delete an entire record from the data file, use the Previous and Next buttons to display the record you want to delete and choose Delete Record.

Changing Field Names

To add or delete fields within each record of the data file, choose Field Names from the Quick Data Entry dialog box. The Edit Field Names dialog box displays a list of the current field names (see Figure 2-5). To add a new field name, select the existing field that's in the position where you want the new field inserted; then replace the text in the Field Name text box with the new field name. Choose Add to insert the new field just *after* the selected name, or choose Add Before to insert it immediately before.

To delete a field from each record in the data file, select the field name you want to delete and choose Delete. Choose OK to delete that field and its contents from each record in the data file. To change the name of a field, select the field in the list and type the new name in the Field Name text box; then choose Replace. When you're finished making changes to the field names, choose OK. Each record in the data file is updated with the new field information. If you added a new field, you need to go through each existing record and add the information for that field.

To return to the data file, choose Close in the Quick Data Entry dialog box, and then choose Yes to save the changes you made.

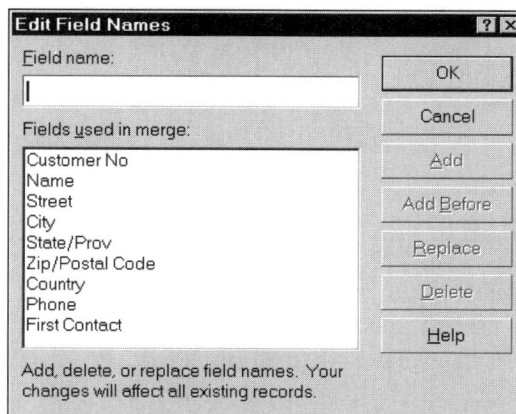

FIGURE 2-5 The Edit Field names dialog box lets you add or delete fields from every record in your data file

TIP: *You can quickly print your data file in a list format without page breaks between each record. To do this, first choose the Options pop-down button on the Merge toolbar and select Hide Codes to keep the ENDFIELD and ENDRECORD codes from printing. Then choose Options | Print from the Merge toolbar and choose OK. When the file has printed, choose Options and select Display Codes.*

Creating a Form Document

An essential element of any merge is the *form document,* which contains the text and formatting for the final merged document, as well as codes that instruct WP where to insert field information from the data source. Form documents can also contain other advanced merge codes that perform a variety of tasks, such as prompting the user for information or playing a macro.

To create a new form document, go to a blank document window, choose Tools | Merge, and then choose Create Document. WP displays the Associate Form and Data dialog box shown below. This is where you tell WP where to find the data information that you want to use with this form document. You can specify a data file, an Address Book, an ODBC data source, or no association (for keyboard input).

To select a data file, type the path and filename of the data file in the text box, or use the file folder icon to select it. To use an Address Book, select Associate an Address Book, and then select the Address Book from the drop-down list (for more information on the Address Book, see Chapter 15). The ODBC data source option is for files from ODBC (Open Database Connectivity) database programs, such as MS Access, dBASE, and Excel. To use this option, you must already have the correct ODBC drivers loaded for your database (refer to your database program manual for more information). Select Associate an ODBC Data Source, choose Select ODBC Data Source, and select the file. If you don't want to associate a data source with this form file, select No Association.

You can use a database or a spreadsheet file as your data source, such as a Paradox file, without having to convert it to WP's data file format. Just select the file in the Associate Data File text box.

After selecting the data source, choose OK. WP displays the Merge toolbar at the top of the document window:

| Insert Field... | Date | Merge Codes... | Keyboard... | Merge... | Go to Data | Options ▼ |

These buttons help you insert merge codes, such as FIELD codes that indicate where information from the data source should be included. You can also use the toolbar buttons to begin the merge, switch to the associated data file, or change the way merge codes are displayed.

Add any text and formatting that you want to include in each merged document. At the locations where you want custom information inserted from the data source, such as a name and address, insert FIELD codes as explained in the following "Inserting FIELD Codes" section. Figure 2-6 shows a sample merge form letter with text and FIELD codes.

As you're creating the form document, keep these tips in mind:

- If you want to use the text and formatting from an existing document, choose Insert | File, select the document you want, and choose Insert. Or, before you begin creating the form document, open the existing document, choose Tools | Merge, and then choose Create Document. Make sure Use File in Active Window is selected and choose OK. Then select the data source, choose OK, and add any other formatting or merge codes.

- To have the current date inserted whenever the form document is merged, choose Date on the Merge toolbar. The inserted date will use the document's current date format. To change the date format, place the insertion point at the top of the document and choose Insert | Date/Time. Select the format you want and choose Apply Format, then choose Close.

- The QuickCorrect feature—including SmartQuotes—is automatically turned off whenever a merge document is open in a document window. If you want to have SmartQuotes or other QuickCorrect options available as you're creating the form document, choose Tools | QuickCorrect. To turn SmartQuotes on, select the SmartQuotes tab and select the options you want. Use the tabs at the top of the dialog box to turn on any other options you want, and choose OK when you're finished.

■ If your form document is longer than one page and you want to include page numbering in the final merged document, make sure you set the page number to one at the top of the form document. Otherwise, the merged documents will use continuous page numbering rather than starting over with page one for each new record. To insert this code, place the insertion point at the top of the form document and choose Format | Page | Numbering. Choose Set Value, type **1,** and choose OK twice.

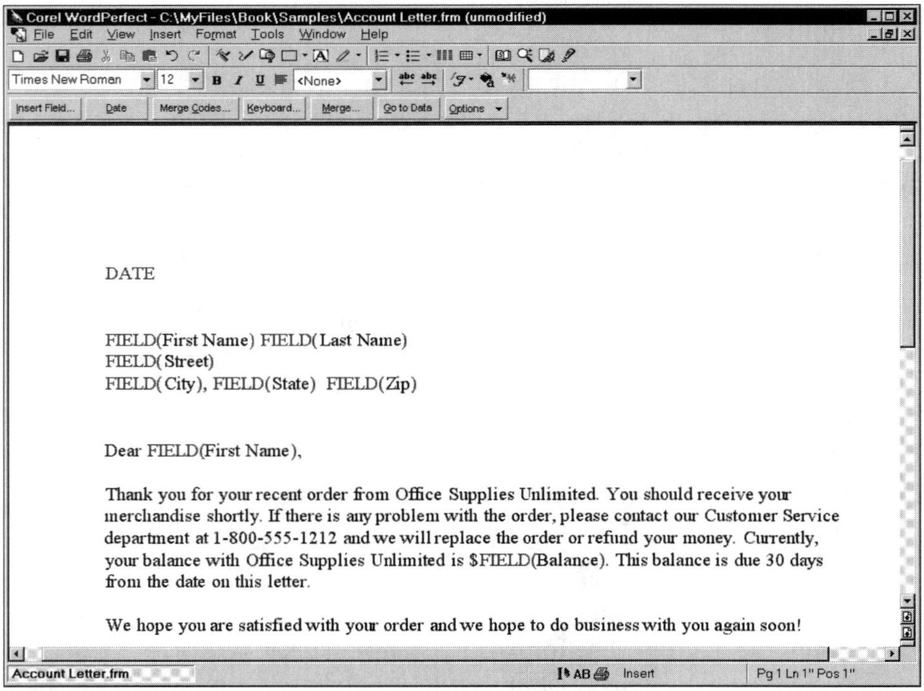

FIGURE 2-6 A merge form document with text and FIELD codes

Inserting FIELD Codes

One of the things that makes a merge form document different from a regular document is the presence of merge codes. The most common merge code is a FIELD code, which tells WP where to insert a piece of information from the associated data source when the document is merged. For example, in Figure 2-6, the FIELD codes indicate where the customer's name and address should be inserted, as well as the account balance. When this form document is merged with a data file like the one shown in Figure 2-1, the result is the document in Figure 2-7.

You can insert FIELD codes anywhere in a form document, including in headers and footers. To insert a FIELD code, place the insertion point in the form document

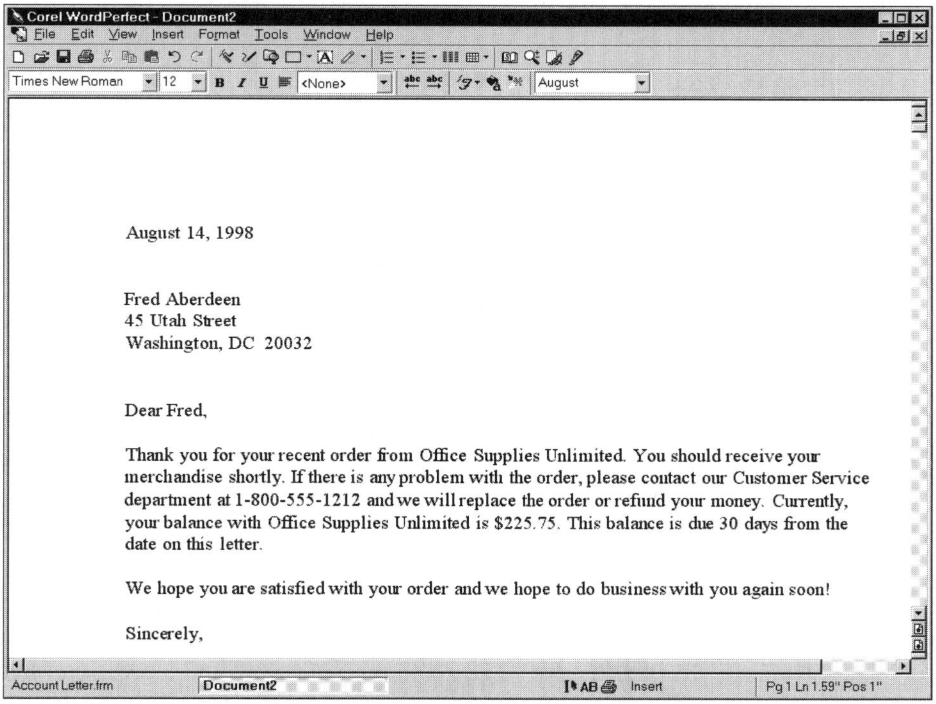

FIGURE 2-7 The resulting document after merging the form document in Figure 2-6 with the data file in Figure 2-1

where you want information from the data source inserted. Choose Insert Field on the Merge toolbar. The Insert Field Name or Number dialog box shows a list of the available fields in the associated data source. Select the field you want to insert and choose Insert and Close.

```
Insert Field Name or Number                               ? X

  Filename:     Customers.dat                    [   Insert    ]

  Field Names:                                   [ Insert and Close ]

  Customer ID                      ▲            [ Data Source  ▼ ]
  Last Name
  First Name                                     [   Close    ]
  Street
  City                                           [   Help     ]
  State
  Zip                              ▼
```

If there isn't a data source currently associated with the form document, you can select one by choosing the Data Source pop-down button and then selecting the option you want, such as Data File or My Addresses. Or you can type a field name or number directly in the Field text box. If you type a field name and the data source you later use doesn't contain a field with that name, no data will be inserted at that location. If you type a field number, the corresponding field in the data source is inserted. For example, if you type **2** to insert a FIELD(2) code, the information in the second field of each record in the data source is inserted at that location when you merge—no matter what the field name is.

NOTE: *If the form document doesn't currently have an associated data source, the data source you select the first time you merge with this form document becomes associated with it.*

You can continue to insert as many FIELD codes as you want into the form document. You can insert the same FIELD code in several places if you want the same information included more than once. When you're finished adding FIELD codes, choose File | Save and save your document using a filename with an FRM extension.

Using Merge Commands

The FIELD code is just one of over 80 merge commands available in WP 8. You can use merge commands to create truly customized documents by doing such things as prompting the user for information, deciding what text to include or exclude, or playing a macro. Both form documents and data files can contain merge codes (for example, the ENDFIELD and ENDRECORD codes in a data file are merge codes). In this section, you'll learn how to add power to your merges by inserting merge codes. We'll explain how to use some common merge commands and give you a quick reference chart with descriptions of more than half of WP's merge commands.

Merge Code Basics

Merge codes display in red in the document window. They can't be directly typed into the document, but must be inserted through the buttons on the Merge toolbar, such as the Merge Codes and Insert Field buttons. Many merge commands require "parameters" that are included between the parentheses of the code and are separated by semicolons. The parameters supply the specific information to the merge command and can be anything from text to another merge command. For example, the FIELD code parameter is the name of a specific field, such as FIELD(ZIP Code). The parentheses also display in red, since they are part of the merge code. If you delete one of the parentheses, the entire merge code is deleted.

TIP: *You can hide merge codes in a form or data document so they don't display by choosing Options on the Merge toolbar and then selecting Hide Merge Codes. You can also have the merge codes display as a diamond marker to indicate the location of each merge code by choosing Options | Display as Markers. To display the codes again, choose Options | Display Codes.*

In a form document, you can insert FIELD, DATE, and KEYBOARD codes by choosing their corresponding button on the Merge toolbar. To insert any other merge code, choose Merge Codes on the Merge toolbar to display the Insert Merge Codes dialog box:

Insert Merge Codes

Merge codes

ASSIGN(var,expr)
ASSIGNLOCAL(var,expr)
BEEP
BREAK
CALL(label)

Insert

Close

Help

Assign a value to a global variable

When you select a merge code in the dialog box, a brief description displays at the bottom of the dialog box. Select the code you want to use and choose Insert. Some codes are inserted directly into the document. Other codes display a second dialog box prompting you for the parameters. If the parameter information is text, you can type it in the dialog box and choose OK. If you need to use other merge codes for the parameters, leave the dialog box blank and choose OK to insert the code into the document. Then make sure the insertion point is placed inside the parentheses correctly and type any text or insert the additional merge codes using the Merge toolbar.

When you're adding merge codes to a form document, any spaces, hard returns, tabs, or other formatting you insert *outside* of the merge code parentheses become part of the form document. For example, if you insert several merge codes in a row and press ENTER after each one to place them on separate lines, those extra hard returns will show up in the final merged document. To avoid this, you can use the CODES merge command. This command tells WP to ignore any text or formatting between its parentheses that's not part of another merge code. This allows you to place multiple merge codes on separate lines without having to worry about the formatting affecting the merged document. You'll see examples of the CODES merge command in the following sections as we cover some of the more common merge commands.

Merge Commands to Interact with the User

When you're performing a merge, it's often useful to be able to interact with the person performing the merge by asking for additional information or displaying prompts. For example, if the data file you're using doesn't contain a piece of information needed in the merge, you can have WP prompt the user for that information. There are three different merge commands you can use to ask the user for information during a merge: KEYBOARD, GETSTRING, and CHAR.

The KEYBOARD Command

The KEYBOARD command pauses the merge and prompts the user to type information into the document from the keyboard. For example, suppose you want to send each customer a letter informing them of the sales representative they should contact with questions, but the data file you're using doesn't contain a field with the sales representative's name. You can use the KEYBOARD command to prompt the user to type in the representative's name for each letter as it's merged (see Figure 2-8).

NOTE: *The KEYBOARD command is commonly used with form documents that don't involve a data file at all, in a process called a "keyboard merge." For more information, see the "Keyboard Merges" section later in this chapter.*

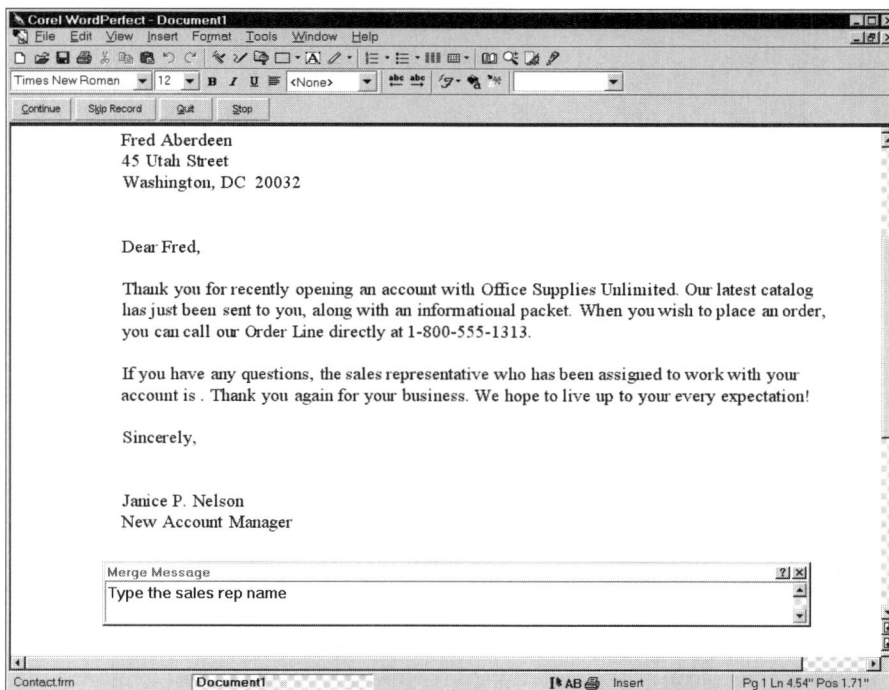

FIGURE 2-8 The KEYBOARD command prompts the user to type in information from the keyboard

To insert a KEYBOARD code, place the insertion point in the form document where you want the information to be typed in when the document is merged. Choose Keyboard on the Merge toolbar. In the Enter Prompt text box, type the prompt that you want to display and choose OK. If you don't want to use a prompt, simply leave the text box blank and choose OK. When you perform the merge, WP pauses at each KEYBOARD command and displays the prompt. The requested information can then be typed directly into the document. After typing the information, choose Continue on the Merge toolbar to continue with the merge.

TIP: *If you don't want the document text after the KEYBOARD command to display in the document screen as the information is being typed, insert the DISPLAYSTOP command where you want the display to stop. This helps direct the user's attention to the location in the document where the text is being inserted.*

If you want to remind the user which record is currently being merged, you can include information from the data file within the prompt message. For example, adding FIELD codes for the first and last name changes the prompt to look like this:

Merge Message	? ☒
Type the sales rep name for Fred Aberdeen	▲ ▼

To do this, insert the KEYBOARD code as previously explained, typing any text you want to include in the prompt. After the code has been inserted in the document, place the insertion point in the message text where you want the field information included and use the Insert Field button on the toolbar to insert the field codes. The final code might look something like this:

```
KEYBOARD (Type the sales rep name for FIELD(First Name)
    FIELD(Last Name).)
```

The GETSTRING Command

The GETSTRING command is similar to the KEYBOARD command, but it prompts the user to type information into a dialog box instead of directly into the document. In addition, the text typed into the dialog box is assigned to a variable, so it can be used in multiple locations throughout the document. For example, if you want to prompt the user for the sales representative's name and then insert that name in several places throughout the document, you could use the GETSTRING command to display a dialog box similar to this:

```
┌─────────────────────────────────────────────────┐
│ Sales Rep                               [?][X]    │
│                                                   │
│  Enter the sales rep name           ┌───────────┐ │
│                                     │    OK     │ │
│  ┌───────────────────────────────┐  ├───────────┤ │
│  │                               │  │  Cancel   │ │
│  └───────────────────────────────┘  └───────────┘ │
└─────────────────────────────────────────────────┘
```

To use GETSTRING, place the insertion point in the form document where you want to prompt the user. The text isn't actually inserted here—only the dialog box appears requesting the information. Then choose Merge Codes on the Merge toolbar, select GETSTRING, and choose Insert. A dialog box appears asking for three parameters: the variable, prompt, and title. In the Variable text box, type a name for the variable that will hold the information entered by the user. The variable name can be any text you want (up to 30 characters), such as **RepName**. In the Prompt text box, type the prompt text that you want to appear in the dialog box, such as **Enter the sales rep name**. In the Title text box, type the text you want to appear in the title of the dialog box, such as **Sales Rep**. Choose OK to insert the code.

NOTE: *If you want to add FIELD codes to the prompt text so information from the current record is displayed in the dialog box, place the insertion point in the prompt text where you want the information included and insert the FIELD codes. Make sure you insert them before the semicolon separating the prompt and title text.*

The GETSTRING command prompts the user for information but it doesn't actually insert it into the document. To do this, you need to use the VARIABLE command. Place the insertion point in the form document where you want the text inserted. Choose Merge Codes, select VARIABLE, and choose Insert. In the Enter Variable text box, type the variable name you used, such as **RepName**. Choose OK. Repeat this to insert a VARIABLE code each place in the form document where you want the information inserted.

NEW ACCOUNT.FRM: *The companion CD contains a sample form document named NEW ACCOUNT.FRM that uses both the KEYBOARD and GETSTRING commands. You can open this document to see another example of using these commands. You can merge this form document with the CUSTOMERS.DAT sample data file on the companion CD.*

The CHAR Command

The CHAR command is almost identical to GETSTRING, with the exception that it allows the user to type only a single character in the dialog box. This is useful if you want to ask a "Yes" or "No" question. Whatever character is pressed is assigned to the variable name used. The variable can then be inserted into the document or evaluated to determine what action to take next. To insert the CHAR command, follow the steps given earlier for GETSTRING, but select the CHAR command instead. For an example of using the CHAR command, see the "How to Set Up a Continuous Keyboard Merge" section later in this chapter.

Merge Commands to Make Decisions

One of the more powerful aspects of merge commands is their ability to make decisions based on certain conditions. For example, you can have WordPerfect check to see if a specific field is blank or matches a certain value and if so, perform a specific action. This is possible with the help of the IF commands and the SWITCH command.

The IF Commands

Three related commands—IF, IFBLANK, and IFNOTBLANK—can help WP make decisions during a merge. The IF command lets WP evaluate a certain condition and then perform a set of actions if that condition is true. For example, if your data file has a field containing an account balance, you can use IF to determine whether the balance is greater than zero. If it is, you can insert a paragraph into the document requesting that the remaining balance be paid by a specific date.

The IFBLANK and IFNOTBLANK commands can be used to determine whether a specific field in the data file is blank or not, and then perform a set of actions accordingly. For example, if your data file contains separate fields for the first name, middle initial, and last name, you can use IFNOTBLANK to determine whether the middle initial should be inserted, as shown by these commands:

```
FIELD(First Name) IFNOTBLANK(Initial)FIELD(Initial)
ENDIF FIELD(Last Name)
```

The command above first inserts the information found in the First Name field, followed by a space. Then the IFNOTBLANK command evaluates the contents of the Initial field. If it is *not* blank, the Initial field is inserted, followed by another space. The ENDIF command indicates the end of the commands associated with IFNOTBLANK, so the contents of the Last Name field are inserted in either case.

Each of the IF commands must always be used with an ENDIF command. The ENDIF command tells WP where the conditional commands stop. Any commands after the ENDIF command are executed no matter what the outcome of the IF evaluation. You can also use the ELSE command to tell WP which actions to perform if the evaluation condition is *not* met. For example, these commands check to see if a data file field named Balance equals zero, and then insert text into the document depending on the result.

```
CODES(
IF (FIELD(Balance)=0)
    INSERT (Thank you for paying your balance in full.)
ELSE
    INSERT (Please pay your remaining balance of
 $FIELD(Balance) within 30 days.)
ENDIF
)
```

The CODES command tells WP to ignore any of the hard returns, spaces, or tabs used to format the codes between its parentheses. Because any text within the CODES command is ignored, you need to use the INSERT command to tell WP to type text into the document. The IF command evaluates the Balance field for the current record and if it equals zero, a sentence is typed into the document thanking the person for paying off the balance. If the field *doesn't* equal zero, the ELSE command causes WP to insert a sentence asking the person to pay the remaining balance. The ENDIF command marks the end of the evaluation section, so any commands after this point are executed. Notice the final closing parenthesis on the last line—this belongs to the CODES command on the first line, indicating that the section of merge codes has ended.

The SWITCH Command

Another command that can be used to make decisions during a merge is the SWITCH command. Like the IF command, the SWITCH command evaluates a condition and then performs a different set of actions based on the result. But while the IF command checks for a true or false condition, the SWITCH command looks at the contents of a specific variable or field and then searches through a series of CASEOF statements until it finds one that exactly matches the contents. When a match is found, the commands associated with that CASEOF statement are executed.

For example, if your data file has a field named Major that contains a college major, you can use a SWITCH statement like this:

```
CODES(
SWITCH(FIELD(Major))
   CASEOF (Education)
      INSERT (The Education offices are in the
Johnson Building.)
   CASEOF (Engineering;Biology;Chemistry)
      INSERT (The Science offices are in the Smith Building.)
   CASEOF (Business;Accounting)
      INSERT (The Business offices are in the
Peterson Building.)
   DEFAULT
      INSERT (Please contact your counselor for
further information.)
ENDSWITCH
)
```

This set of commands also uses the CODES command to ignore any hard returns or formatting within the group of codes. The SWITCH command looks at the contents of the Major field in the data file. The CASEOF statements list the different possible values, which allows WP to find one that matches and then perform the associated actions. For example, if the Major field contains "Education," information about the Education offices is inserted. If the Major field contains "Engineering," "Biology," or "Chemistry," the second CASEOF statement is executed and information about the Science offices is inserted. The DEFAULT command on the last line tells WP what to do if none of the CASEOF statements match the field. For example, if the Major field contained "English," or was left blank, the DEFAULT command would cause WP to insert the statement about contacting the counselor.

As with the IF commands, the SWITCH command must have an ENDSWITCH inserted at the end of the CASEOF statements. WP only performs the commands between the matching CASEOF statement and the next CASEOF statement in the list. After those commands have been processed, WP jumps to the first command after the ENDSWITCH command to continue with the merge. You can insert more than one command between CASEOF statements if you want.

TIP: *If you want WP to process the commands in the matching CASEOF statement as well as those in the next CASEOF statement, insert the CONTINUE command at the end of the CASEOF statement.*

STUDENT DATA.FRM: *For another example of a form document that uses the IF and SWITCH commands, open the STUDENT DATA.FRM on the companion CD. You can merge this form document with the STUDENTS.DAT sample data file on the CD.*

Merge Commands to Access Other Form and Data Files

Since you usually don't just work with *one* data file or form document, WP makes it easy to use multiple files during a merge. For example, if you've broken a large data file into several smaller files, you can still use all the data files in the same merge. Or you can have WP select a different form document based on the contents of a field in the data file. WP provides three techniques for working with other form documents and data files: chaining, nesting, and substituting.

Chaining Files

The CHAINDATA and CHAINFORM commands tell WP to use a different data file or form document as soon as the current merge has ended. The CHAINDATA command is inserted in the actual data file, while the CHAINFORM command is placed in the form document. These codes can appear anywhere within the data file or form document, since WP doesn't begin using the new file until the current merge has ended.

For example, if you've broken down a large data file into two smaller data files, you can use CHAINDATA to link the smaller files together so they're both used during the same merge. To do this, insert the CHAINDATA command at the top of the first data file, after the FIELDNAMES command. The codes might look something like this:

```
PROCESSON CHAINDATA(names2.dat) PROCESSOFF
```

The PROCESSON and PROCESSOFF codes are used to make sure that WP executes the CHAINDATA command. When you merge this data file with a form document, as soon as the last record has been merged, the same form document is merged with the records in the NAMES2.DAT file.

CAUTION: *When you chain data files, make sure that each data file uses the same field names for those fields inserted in the form document.*

The CHAINFORM command allows you to process the records in a data file with two separate form documents. For example, if you have two form documents—one that creates a letter and one that creates address labels—you can use CHAINFORM to merge the same data file with both form documents. After the letters are merged, WP automatically uses the labels form document to create labels for the same addresses. The CHAINFORM command can be inserted anywhere in the first form document, and it indicates the filename of the second form document, as shown here:

```
CHAINFORM(c:\myfiles\labels.frm)
```

As soon as WP has completed merging the first form document with all the records in the data file, the second form document is merged with those same records.

Nesting Files

The two nesting commands—NESTDATA and NESTFORM—work generally like the two chaining commands. The main difference is that NESTDATA and NESTFORM start using the new data file or form document immediately, instead of waiting until the end of the current merge. When the nested merge has finished, WP returns to the original merge and picks up where it left off.

The NESTDATA command is most useful when you want to insert information from a second data file during a merge. For example, suppose you have two data files with customer information—one with the customer number, name, and address, and the other with the customer number and current balance. You can set up a form document that uses the first data file to create a letter containing the customer's name and address. Then, in the body of the form document, you can insert merge codes to access the second data file, locate the record that matches the current customer number, and insert the appropriate balance. This process is repeated for each record in the data file.

For practice using the NESTDATA command to access a second data file during a merge, see the "How to Use Two Data Files in One Merge" section.

The NESTFORM command can be used to specify which form document is merged with each record in a data file. For example, the following commands evaluate the information in a field named Conference. If the conference field contains "Los Angeles," the current record is merged with a form document named LA.FRM, which provides registration details and schedules for the Los Angeles conference. If the conference field contains "New York," the NY.FRM form document with the New York conference information is merged with that record instead. Or, if the conference field is blank, the record is merged with a form document named INFO.FRM, which provides general information about both conferences.

```
CODES(
SWITCH(FIELD(Conference)
   CASEOF (Los Angeles)
      NESTFORM(c:\myfiles\conf\la.frm)
   CASEOF (New York)
      NESTFORM(c:\myfiles\conf\ny.frm)
   DEFAULT
      NESTFORM(c:\myfiles\conf\info.frm)
ENDSWITCH
)
```

When you use NESTFORM in this way, you need to create a separate form document that contains the merge commands like those in the previous example. This merge document serves to "direct" WP to the right form document for each record. The text and formatting for the actual letters is contained in the nested form documents. When the merge has finished, you're left with a document containing a mixture of the three letters, depending on what the conference field for each record contained.

SPECIAL OFFER.FRM: *The companion CD contains a sample form document named SPECIAL OFFER.FRM that you can open for an example of the NESTFORM command.*

How to... Use Two Data Files in One Merge

The NESTDATA command gives you the ability to access a second data file during a merge, find the record that matches a field in the first data file, and insert any information from that data file before continuing with the merge. In order to use this technique, you need to have two data files with at least one field in common, such as a name, customer number, or category. The common field serves as the link between the two data files during the merge.

For example, suppose you have a data file that contains the name, address, and a field indicating the type of information requested by that person. The beginning of your data file might look like this:

```
FIELDNAMES(First Name;Last Name;Address;City;State;ZIP;Category)ENDRECORD

SusanENDFIELD
LowryENDFIELD
1920 Holly Springs Dr.ENDFIELD
MinneapolisENDFIELD
MNENDFIELD
52109ENDFIELD
PhotographersENDFIELD
ENDRECORD
```

A second data file might contain the names and addresses of different companies and the categories they fall under, such as this one:

```
FIELDNAMES(Category;Company;Address;City;State;ZIP;Phone)ENDRECORD

BakeriesENDFIELD
The Best BakeryENDFIELD
3443 James Ave.ENDFIELD
MinneapolisENDFIELD
MNENDFIELD
52109ENDFIELD
(612) 555-9663ENDFIELD
ENDRECORD
```

Use Two Data Files in One Merge (continued)

Since these two data files share a common field—the category—you can access them both in the same merge. For example, you can set up a form document that creates a letter addressed to each person in the first data file, with the body of the letter listing the name and address of the company in the category they requested. That way, if a record in the first data file contains "Florists" in the Category field, the merge would look through the second data file until a record was found that also had "Florists" in the Category field. Then the address and phone number of that company would be inserted into the letter. The form document for this type of merge would look something like this:

```
ASSIGN( Request;FIELD( Category))

FIELD(First Name) FIELD(Last Name)
FIELD( Address)
FIELD(City), FIELD(State)  FIELD(ZIP)

Dear FIELD(First Name),

Thank you for contacting Wedding Referral Services. You indicated that you would like more
information regarding TOLOWER(FIELD(Category)). We highly recommend the following
companies in your area. You can contact them directly for further information.
CODES(
NESTDATA( companies.dat)
WHILE("FIELD( Company)"<>"XXX")
      IF("FIELD(Category)"="VARIABLE(Request)")
INSERT(
      FIELD(Company)
      FIELD(Address)
      FIELD(Phone)

)NEXTRECORD
ELSE  NEXTRECORD
ENDIF
ENDWHILE
)Please let us know if we can help any further.
```

And the final merged letter might look like this:

How to... Use Two Data Files in One Merge
(*continued*)

Susan Lowry
1920 Holly Springs Dr.
Minneapolis, MN 52109

Dear Susan,

Thank you for contacting Wedding Referral Services. You indicated that you would like more information regarding photographers. We highly recommend the following companies in your area. You can contact them directly for further information.

Picture Perfect Photography
5208 University Ave.
(612) 555-2987

Please let us know if we can help any further.

Sincerely,

Wedding Referral Services

To set up this type of merge, follow the general guidelines next. The companion CD contains two sample data files—NAMES.DAT and COMPANIES.DAT—as well as a sample form document called COMPANY INFO.FRM with the merge codes already included. You can use these documents to follow along with the explanations here.

1. First, the *second* data file needs to have a "dummy" record as the last record. This record is needed so WP can tell when it has reached the end of the second data file and return to the original merge. The COMPANIES.DAT file on the companion CD already has this dummy file added. To add a dummy record to another data file, open the second data file, place the insertion point at the end, and use the Quick Entry feature to create a new record with **XXX** in each of the fields. Close and save the data file when you're finished.

2. Once you have both data files created, you can modify the form document. The next several steps will explain the various merge commands needed in the form document, without giving the specific instructions for inserting each code. The codes can all be inserted by choosing Merge Codes on the Merge toolbar, selecting the code, and following the given guidelines to insert the parameters.

How to... **Use Two Data Files in One Merge**
(*continued*)

3. Use the ASSIGN command at the top of the form document to assign a variable name to the field in the first data file that contains the same information as a field in the second data file. For example, the following command assigns the information in the Category field to a variable named Request:

```
ASSIGN(Request;FIELD(Category))
```

4. Insert any formatting, text, or FIELD codes from the first data file that you want at the top of the form document. In the previous example, the name and address fields are inserted, along with the first paragraph of the letter text.

5. When you're ready to pull information from the second data file, insert the NESTDATA command to tell WP which data file to use, such as:

```
NESTDATA(companies.dat)
```

You can use the CODES command as shown in the previous example to format the merge codes on separate lines without having the hard returns inserted into the final merged document.

6. Use a WHILE loop to have WP repeat the next set of commands for each record in the second data file until the end is reached. For example, this command begins a WHILE loop that has WP repeat the commands between WHILE and ENDWHILE for each record in the second data file, until the Company Field contains the text "XXX" (the dummy record indicating the end of the second data file). As soon as that occurs, the loop is stopped.

```
WHILE ("FIELD(Company)"<>"XXX")
```

How to... Use Two Data Files in One Merge (continued)

7. Next, use an IF statement within the WHILE loop to determine if the field in the current record matches the variable assigned earlier in the form document (which contains the contents of a field in the first data file). For example, this command checks to see if the Category field in the second data file matches the contents of the variable named Request:

```
IF ("FIELD(Category)"="VARIABLE(Request)")
```

8. Within the IF statement, tell WP what fields and text to insert into the form document when a matching record is found in the second data file. In the previous example, the fields containing the company name, address, and phone number are inserted. To insert fields from the second data file, choose Insert Field on the Merge toolbar, and then choose Data Source | Data File. Select the second data file and choose Close; then select and insert the fields you want from that data file.

   If you're using the CODES command as shown in the previous example, make sure you use the INSERT command for any hard returns, tabs, or other formatting that you want included in the merged document.

9. At the end of the text and FIELD commands that you want included when the second data file has a matching record, insert a NEXTRECORD command so WP moves to the next record in the data file and doesn't get stuck in an infinite WHILE loop.

10. Use the ELSE command followed by a NEXTRECORD command to have WP move to the next record in the data file if the current record *doesn't* match the variable assigned in the form document.

11. Finally, end both the IF statement and WHILE loop with the ENDIF and ENDWHILE commands.

How to... Use Two Data Files in One Merge *(continued)*

When you merge with this form document, make sure you select the first data file as your data source. WP inserts the fields and formatting from the first record in the first data file, and then opens the second data file when it reaches the NESTDATA command. The WHILE loop searches through the second data file until a record is found that matches the common field information, or until the end of the data file is reached. If a matching record is found, the commands in the IF statement are processed to insert fields from that record into the document. After the end of the second data file has been reached, WP returns to the original data and form document and repeats the process for the next record in the first data file.

Substituting Files

The SUBSTDATA and SUBSTFORM commands are very similar to the NEST commands described previously. These commands immediately substitute the specified data file or form document in place of the current file. However, unlike the NEST commands, SUBSTDATA and SUBSTFORM do not return to the original data file or form document when they're finished. As soon as the SUBSTDATA or SUBSTFORM command is encountered, WP switches to the substituted data file or form document file, starts at the beginning, and continues until the end is reached.

Quick Reference ▶▶▶ Common Merge Commands

WordPerfect 8 has over 80 merge commands that you can use in your merge data files and form documents. This chart contains descriptions of some of the more common commands, grouped according to category. For a complete listing and explanation of all the available merge commands, select the Merge Programming Commands document in the Reference Center on the WP Suite 8 CD.

The text in parentheses after command names indicates the type of parameters for that command. Any parameters listed in square brackets ([]) are optional.

Variables and Prompts

ASSIGN(var;expr)	Creates a variable with the given name (var) and assigns to it the value in the given expression (expr). For example, ASSIGN(Name;FIELD(Last Name)) creates a variable called Name and assigns the contents in the Last Name field to it. The variable is global and can be accessed in any nested form documents, data files, or macros. The variable contents can be inserted into the document with the VARIABLE command.
CHAR (var[;prompt][;title])	Displays a dialog box prompting the user to type a single character, such as **Y** or **N**. The key pressed is assigned to the given variable name (var). For an example of CHAR, see the "How to Set Up a Continuous Keyboard Merge" section later in this chapter.
GETSTRING (var[;prompt][;title])	Prompts the user to type information into a dialog box. The text typed is assigned to the given variable name (var). For an example of GETSTRING, see the "Merge Commands to Interact with the User" section earlier in the chapter.
KEYBOARD ([prompt])	Pauses the merge and displays a message so the user can type information from the keyboard into the document. For an example of KEYBOARD, see the "Keyboard Merges" section later in the chapter.
PROMPT(message)	Displays a message to the user, such as instructions or a status counter. If you want the prompt to appear for a specific amount of time, use the WAIT(10ths second) command immediately following the PROMPT command.

| VARIABLE(var) | Accesses the contents of the given variable. If the command is used by itself, the variable contents are inserted into the document. Or the VARIABLE command can be used within another merge command. For example, the command PROMPT(VARIABLE(Balance)) displays the contents of the variable Balance in a prompt. |

Working with Other Files and Macros

CHAINDATA (filename)	Continues the merge with the records in the specified data file (filename) as soon as the end of the current data file is reached. This command is generally placed within data files to link smaller data files together. For an example of CHAINDATA, see the "Merge Commands to Access Other Form and Data Files" section earlier in the chapter.
CHAINFORM (filename)	Continues the merge with the specified form document (filename) as soon as the current merge has ended. The new form document is merged with the same data file. For an example of CHAINFORM, see the "Merge Commands to Access Other Form and Data Files" section earlier in the chapter.
CHAINMACRO (macroname)	Plays the specified macro (macroname) one time when the current merge has ended. The CHAINMACRO command can appear anywhere in the form document.
DOCUMENT (filename)	Inserts the specified document (filename) into the merged document at the location of the DOCUMENT command. This command is useful for inserting different paragraphs to "build" a document.

EMBEDMACRO (macro statements)	Allows you to embed macro commands directly within a merge. The macro commands are compiled and processed when the merge is run. For more information on EMBEDMACRO, see the "Macros in Merges" section later in this chapter.
NESTDATA(filename)	Interrupts the current data file and begins using the specified data file (filename) instead. When the nested data file has finished, the merge returns to the original data file. For an example of using NESTDATA, see the "How to Use Two Data Files in One Merge" section earlier in the chapter.
NESTFORM(filename)	Interrupts the current merge and begins using the specified form document (filename). The new form document begins at the location of the NESTFORM command. When the form document has been processed for the current record, the merge returns to the original form document and continues with the next command. For an example of using NESTFORM, see the "Merge Commands to Access Other Form and Data Files" section earlier in the chapter.
NESTMACRO (macroname)	Runs the specified macro (macroname) as soon as the NESTMACRO command is encountered. After the macro has finished, the merge continues with the next command in the form document. For more information on NESTMACRO, see the "Macros in Merges" section later in the chapter.

Making Decisions

IF(expr), ELSE, and ENDIF	Executes a set of commands if the given condition (expr) is true. If ELSE is included, the commands between IF and ELSE are executed if the condition is true; otherwise the commands between ELSE and ENDIF are executed. The ENDIF command must always be included at the end of the statements. For an example of using IF, see the "Merge Commands to Make Decisions" section earlier in the chapter.

IFBLANK(field)	Executes a set of commands if the given field name (field) is blank. An ENDIF command must be included at the end of the statements. The ELSE command can also be used.
IFNOTBLANK(field)	Executes a set of commands if the given field name (field) is *not* blank. An ENDIF command must be included. For an example of using IFNOTBLANK, see the "Merge Commands to Make Decisions" section earlier in the chapter.
IFEXISTS(var)	Executes a set of commands if the specified variable (var) has been defined. An ENDIF command must be included at the end of the statements.
SWITCH(expr) and ENDSWITCH	Evaluates the given information (expr) and executes a different set of commands based on the results. The CASEOF and DEFAULT commands are used to determine which commands are executed if the contents match. For an example of the SWITCH command, see the "Merge Commands to Make Decisions" section earlier in the chapter.
CASEOF (expr[;...;expr])	Used with the SWITCH command to specify the commands that should be executed when the SWITCH expression matches one of the values in the CASEOF expression (expr). Multiple expressions are separated by semicolons and are case-sensitive.
CONTINUE	Used at the end of a CASEOF statement to execute the commands in the next CASEOF statement as well.
DEFAULT	Used with the SWITCH command for any conditions not covered by previous CASEOF commands. If the expression in the SWITCH expression does not match any of the CASEOF values, the commands between DEFAULT and ENDSWITCH are executed.

Loops and Subroutines

CALL(label) and RETURN	Transfers execution of the merge to the specified subroutine label name (label). The RETURN command must be used at the end of the label subroutine to direct the merge back to the statement after the CALL command.
FOREACH (var;expr1;...exprN) and ENDFOR	Repeats a set of commands for each specified expression (expr1...exprN), assigning the next expression to the variable (var) each time through the loop. The set of commands must end with the ENDFOR command. For example, the following FOREACH loop inserts the abbreviated days of the week into the document:

```
FOREACH(WeekDay; Sun; Mon; Tue; Wed; Thu; Fri; Sat)
   INSERT (VARIABLE(WeekDay) )
ENDFOR
```

FORNEXT (var;start;stop[;step])	Repeats a set of commands a specified number of times. The given variable (var) begins at the start value (start) and is incremented by the specified amount (step) until it reaches the stop value (stop). If no step value is given, the variable is incremented by one. Each time through the loop, the commands between FORNEXT and ENDFOR are repeated. In the next example, the variable Count begins with the start value of 1. Each time through the loop, the variable Count increases by 1 and the commands are repeated until Count is equal to 10, so the loop repeats ten times. The commands in the loop use the variable Count to insert a list of numbered steps into the document.

```
FORNEXT(Count;1;10;1)
   This is a step number VARIABLE(COUNT).
ENDFOR
```

GO(label)	Transfers execution of the merge to the subroutine with the given label name (label). The GO command lets you skip part of a merge, or it can be used to create a loop by returning to a label name at the beginning of the form document. When the execution is transferred to the subroutine, it does not return to the location of the GO command when finished, as the CALL command does.
LABEL(label)	Marks a location in the form document with the given name (label) so that the merge execution can be transferred to that location with the CALL or GO command.
WHILE(expr) and ENDWHILE	Repeats a given set of commands as long as the given expression (expr) is true. The ENDWHILE command must be included to mark the end of the loop. For an example of using the WHILE command, see the "How to Use Two Data Files in One Merge" section earlier in the chapter.

Formatting Text

DATE	Inserts the current date in the document's date format. Each time the document is merged, the current date (set by the computer's clock) is inserted as text.
FIELD(field)	Inserts the contents of the specified field name (field) from the current record in the data file. The FIELD command can also be used within other merge commands to evaluate the contents of the specified field.
INSERT(text)	Inserts text or formatting inside a CODES command. Since WP doesn't recognize hard returns, tabs, or spaces within the CODES command, you can use the INSERT command to have these codes included in the merged document. For an example of using the INSERT command, see the "How to Use Two Data Files in One Merge" section earlier in the chapter.

PAGEOFF	Eliminates the hard page break between each merged document. This is useful when you want to place the items of a data file in a list format.
PAGEON	Turns the hard page breaks back on after PAGEOFF has been used in a document. This command is only needed if PAGEOFF is used earlier in the form document.
POSTNET(string)	Inserts the POSTNET bar code for the specified ZIP code (string). The given string can either be a specific ZIP code or the field name where the ZIP code is located. For an example of using POSTNET, see the "Creating Labels" section later in the chapter.
TOLOWER(expr)	Converts the specified expression (expr) to all lowercase letters. For example, the command TOLOWER(FIELD(Name)) would convert the text in the Name field to all lowercase letters.
TOUPPER(expr)	Converts the specified expression (expr) to all uppercase letters.

Miscellaneous

CODES(merge codes)	Allows you to insert merge codes in the form document and have any formatting such as hard returns, spaces, or tabs ignored. This lets you easily insert a group of merge codes in a document and format them on separate lines. Any merge codes inside the CODES parentheses are executed, but all text and formatting is ignored. You can use the INSERT command to insert text and formatting within the CODES command.
COMMENT(comment)	Allows you to include comments that are ignored by the merge and not inserted into the form document. WP ignores anything between the parentheses, including formatting such as hard returns.

| NEXTRECORD | Moves the merge to the next record in the data file. If the next record is not found, the merge is ended or control is returned to the previous data file if the current data file was nested. For an example of using NEXTRECORD, see the "How to Use Two Data Files in One Merge" section earlier in the chapter. |
| REPEATROW | Inserts a new row in a table for each record in the data file. This command lets you easily merge information into a table and have the table expand to fit the number of records in the data file. For an example of using REPEATROW, see the "Merging into Tables" section later in the chapter. |

On the CD ▶▶▶ Sample Merge Files

The companion CD contains several sample merge form documents and data files that use a variety of WP's merge commands. You can open these documents to view the commands in them, and you can also try merging the form documents and associated data files to see how the merge behaves.

Each sample form file has a comment at the top that indicates which sample data file it is intended to work with. In addition, comments are included throughout the form documents to give a brief explanation of what the merge commands are doing.

The sample form documents include:

ACCOUNT LETTER. FRM	COMPANY INFO.FRM	PHONE MESSAGE.FRM
ADDRESS BOOK LABELS.FRM	KEYBOARD MEMO.FRM	SPECIAL OFFER.FRM
CLASS SPACE ROLL.FRM	NEW ACCOUNT.FRM	STUDENT DATA.FRM

Keyboard Merges

While most merges involve two files—a form document and a data source—you can also perform a merge with only the form document. This type of merge is commonly called a "keyboard merge," since any custom information is typed directly from the keyboard instead of being inserted from a data source. A keyboard merge is useful for documents that you typically create one at a time, such as a memo.

NOTE: *Keyboard merges have a similar function as templates and projects. For more information on templates, see Chapter 1.*

To create a keyboard merge, follow these steps:

1. Go to a blank document window and choose Tools | Merge; then choose Create Document. Select No Association and choose OK.

2. Add any text and formatting you want for the document.

3. To indicate where you want information typed in from the keyboard, insert a KEYBOARD code. The KEYBOARD command pauses the merge and prompts the user to type information into the document (see Figure 2-8). Place the insertion point where you want the information inserted and choose Keyboard on the Merge toolbar.

4. In the Enter Prompt text box, type the message that you want to appear in the prompt, such as **Type the Memo Subject**. Choose OK and the code is inserted into the document.

5. Repeat this process to insert a KEYBOARD code in each location where you want information inserted. Figure 2-9 shows a sample keyboard merge document that prompts the user for the heading information for a memo.

6. When you've added all the KEYBOARD commands, choose File | Save and type a name for the form document using an FRM extension. Then follow the steps in the "Performing a Merge" section later in the chapter to merge the form document with information typed from the keyboard.

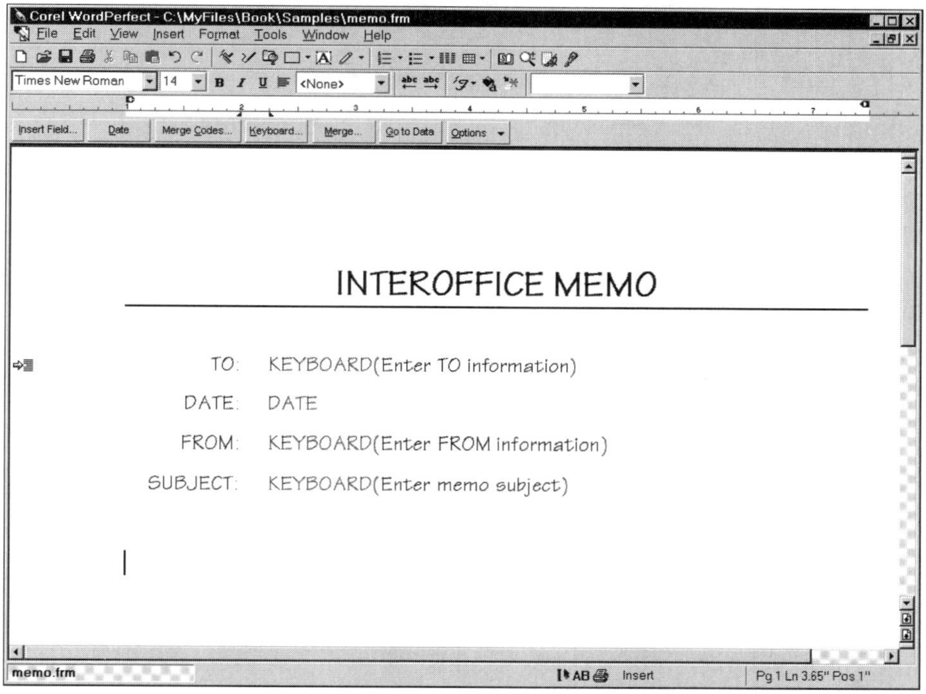

FIGURE 2-9 A keyboard merge uses KEYBOARD commands and no data file

KEYBOARD MEMO.FRM: *The companion CD contains a sample keyboard merge form document named KEYBOARD MEMO.FRM that you can open for an example of a keyboard merge.*

You can add other merge commands to the keyboard merge that control its behavior. For example, after a keyboard merge has been completed, you can have WP ask the user if the merge should be repeated to create a second document. For the steps on how to do this, see the "How to Set Up a Continuous Keyboard Merge" section.

How to▸▸▸ Set Up a Continuous Keyboard Merge

Normally, a keyboard merge creates only one document. However, you can add commands to the end of a keyboard merge form document that ask the user if the merge should be repeated. If the user presses **Y**, the keyboard merge starts a second time to create a new document in the same document window.

Repeat Merge	? ✕
Do another merge? (Y/N)	Cancel
|	

To set up your keyboard form document to do this, follow the steps here. The companion CD contains a sample form document called PHONE MESSAGE.FRM that you can open as an example of creating a continuous keyboard merge.

1. Create your form document with KEYBOARD codes as explained in the "Keyboard Merges" section.

2. Place the insertion point at the end of the form document and press CTRL-ENTER to insert a page break.

3. With the insertion point on the new page, you'll enter the commands shown below:

```
CODES(
    CHAR(Answer;Do another merge? (Y/N);Repeat Merge)
    IF (TOLOWER(VARIABLE(Answer))=y)
        CHAINFORM(c:\myfiles\letter.frm)
    ENDIF
)
```

How to... Set Up a Continuous Keyboard Merge *(continued)*

4. To insert these commands, choose Merge Codes on the Merge toolbar. Select the CODES command and choose Insert. Press ENTER twice; then press UP ARROW to place the insertion point on a blank line between the parentheses of the CODES command.

5. Select CHAR in the dialog box and choose Insert. In the Variable text box, type **Answer**. In the Prompt text box, type the prompt you want to use, such as **Do another merge? (Y/N)**. In the Title text box, type the title for the prompt dialog box, such as **Repeat Merge**. Choose OK.

6. Press ENTER to move to a new line, select IF in the dialog box, and choose Insert. Leave the Enter Expression text box empty and choose OK.

7. Select the TOLOWER command and choose Insert. Choose OK.

8. Select the VARIABLE command and choose Insert. Type **Answer** in the Enter Variable text box and choose OK.

9. Press RIGHT ARROW once, and then type **=y** to add the condition for the IF statement. Press END; then press ENTER to move to a new line.

10. Select the CHAINFORM command and choose Insert. In the Enter File Name text box, type the path and filename for the keyboard form document that you want to have repeated, or use the file folder icon to select it. Choose OK.

11. Select the ENDIF command and choose Insert.

12. Save and close your form document.

When you merge with this document, the first document is created normally, prompting you at the location of any KEYBOARD commands. After the merge has finished, a dialog box appears asking if you want to perform another merge. If you press Y, the form document repeats to create a new document. If you press any other letter, the merge quits. Make sure you don't have the form document open in a document window when you begin the merge, or the CHAINFORM command won't be able to use it again if you answer "Yes" to the prompt.

Performing a Merge

Once you have the form document and data source in place, you're ready to merge the two together. When you perform a merge, you can set several options for things such as where the merged output is sent, whether envelopes are created, which records from the data source are included, and how page breaks and blank fields are handled.

If you have either the form document or the data file that you want to merge with currently open in a document window, you can start a merge by choosing Merge on the Merge toolbar. Otherwise, choose Tools | Merge, and then choose Perform Merge. The Perform Merge dialog box appears:

Perform Merge	? X
Form document ▾ Current Document	Merge
	Cancel
Data source ▾ C:\MyFiles\customer.dat	Reset
Select Records...	Envelopes...
Output ▾ New Document	Options...
All Records	Help

If you started the merge with a document open in the current document window, the Form Document option displays Current Document, indicating that the current document will be used in the merge. If you don't want to merge the document in the current window, choose File on Disk from the Form Document pop-down button and select the filename of the form document you want to use. If the Form Document option displays a text box, type the path and filename of the form document you want to use (or use the file folder icon to select it).

After you select the form document, the Data Source text box should display the data source that's associated with that form document. If you want to select a different data source, choose the Data Source pop-down button, and then choose the option you want, such as File on Disk or Address Book. If you're performing a keyboard merge, choose None. The ODBC option is for files from ODBC database programs, such as MS Access, dBASE, and Excel. To use this option, you must already have the correct ODBC drivers loaded for your database (refer to your database program manual for more information). After choosing ODBC from the Data Source pop-down button, choose Select ODBC Data Source and select the file you want to use.

When you choose File on Disk from the Data Source pop-down button, you can select a WP merge data file, a database file (such as a Paradox file), or a spreadsheet file (such as a Quattro Pro file).

The next step is to tell WP what to do with the merged documents. For example, you can have them inserted in a new document window, in the current document window, sent directly to the printer, or even e-mailed. Choose the Output pop-down button; then select the option you want. Choose File on Disk to have the merged documents automatically saved in a file with the filename you specify. For the steps on e-mailing the merged documents, see the Power Tip "Merging to E-mail."

Power Tip... Merging to E-mail

If you have e-mail access, you can merge a form document and data source and have the resulting documents automatically e-mailed to each recipient as a message attachment. In order to do this, you must use the Address Book or a data file that contains a separate e-mail address field as your data source.

You need to set up your e-mail program in Windows 95 before you can merge to e-mail in WordPerfect (unless you're using Novell GroupWise 4.1). To do this, from the Windows taskbar choose Start | Settings | Control Panel and double-click the Mail and Fax icon. Choose Show Profiles; then with Corel 8 Settings selected, choose Properties. If there isn't an option in the list for your e-mail service, choose Add. Select the appropriate option, such as Internet Mail, and choose OK. Set the options to configure the service and choose OK. If the list of information services doesn't contain a Personal Folders option, choose Add, select Personal Folders; then choose OK. Switch to the directory where you want the messages stored, type a filename, such as mailbox.pst, and choose Open. Choose OK; then Close.

When you're ready to merge a form document to e-mail, follow these steps:

1. Open the form document and choose Merge from the Merge toolbar.

2. Make sure the Data Source option shows the correct data file or Address Book.

3. From the Output pop-down button, choose E-mail. The Merge to E-mail dialog box appears.

4. From the Select Field Name of E-mail Address drop-down list, select the field in the data file or Address Book that contains the e-mail address for each record.

5. In the Subject Line text box, type the subject text you want to use for each message.

6. Choose OK; then choose Merge to begin the merge. The form document is merged and the e-mail messages are automatically sent to each recipient.

Creating Envelopes

WordPerfect makes it easy to create envelopes for your merged documents. When you use this option, an envelope is created for each record during the merge, and all of the envelopes are placed together at the end of the merged document. If you're merging directly to the printer, the envelopes are printed immediately after the merged documents.

To have envelopes created during a merge, choose Envelopes from the Perform Merge dialog box. The Envelope dialog box appears. To set up the envelope, type the return address you want to use, or select it from the Address Book. Then place the insertion point in the Mailing Addresses text box. Choose Field at the bottom of the dialog box and the Insert Field Name or Number dialog box appears with a list of the available fields in the selected data source. Select the field that you want to appear on the first line of the envelope address, such as Name or First Name and choose Insert and Close.

If you want to insert a second field on the same line, press SPACEBAR to insert a space, and choose Field again. Select the next field, such as Last Name, and choose Insert and Close. Press ENTER to move to the next line of the address. Repeat this process to insert the remaining fields for the envelope address (see Figure 2-10).

If you want to include bar codes on the envelope, the ZIP code must be in a separate field in the data source. Choose Options and select the bar code location you want, such as Position Bar Code Below Address; then choose OK. Place the insertion point in the POSTNET Bar Code text box and choose Field. Select the field containing the ZIP code and choose Insert and Close.

When you've set all the options for the envelopes, choose OK to return to the Perform Merge dialog box.

Selecting Merge Records

If you don't want to include *every* record from your data source during the merge, WP makes it easy to select which records are used. You can either select records that meet certain criteria, such as all those with a specific ZIP code, or you can mark the individual records that you want to include.

To select which records should be merged, first select the data source from the Data Source pop-down button in the Perform Merge dialog box. Then choose Select Records. If you're selecting records from a data file, the Select Records dialog box appears. To select records in a certain range or that match certain conditions, select Specify Conditions (see Figure 2-11). To mark individual records, select Mark Records (see Figure 2-12).

FIGURE 2-10 You can create envelopes by selecting fields from the data file

If you're selecting from the Address Book, the Address Book dialog box appears. Select an address you want to use in the list and choose Select Address. You can quickly select multiple addresses by holding down CTRL as you select each address,

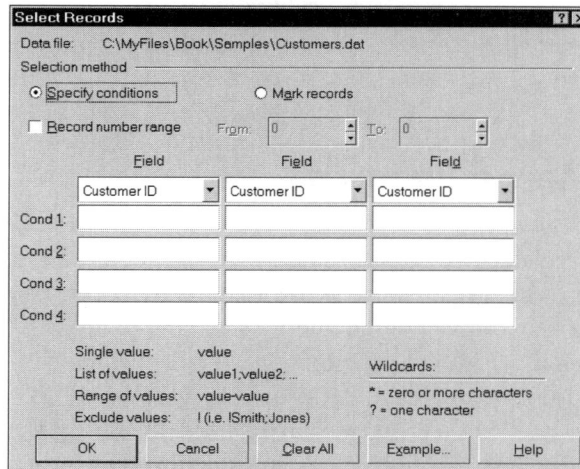

FIGURE 2-11 WP can merge only those records that match specified conditions

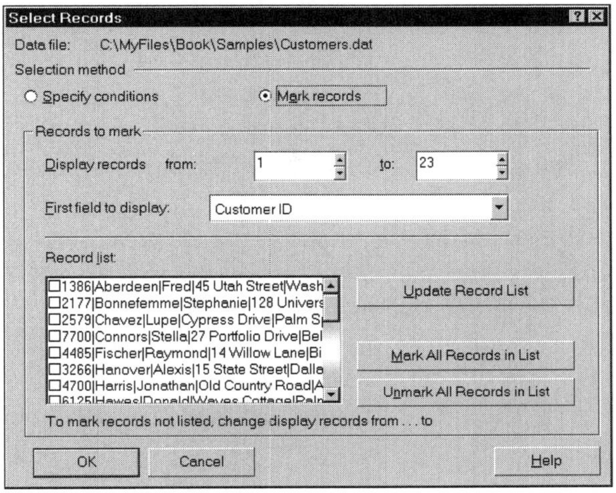

FIGURE 2-12   You can mark individual records to merge

and then choose Select Address to add each address to the list. Choose OK when you're finished.

Selecting a Range

If you want to merge a certain range of records in the data file, such as the first 20 records or records 50-75, select Record Number Range in the Select Records dialog box, and then type the range numbers in the From and To text boxes. You can further narrow the records in the range by specifying conditions, as explained in the "Specifying Conditions" section next. If you want to merge all the records in the range, choose OK to return to the Perform Merge dialog box.

Specifying Conditions

If you have the Specify Conditions option selected, WP lets you select records based on the contents of certain fields (see Figure 2-11). For example, you can select those records with a certain ZIP code, those from a specific state, or those with last names in the first half of the alphabet. You can specify up to four conditions for selecting the records. Records that meet any one of the four conditions will be included in the merge. In addition, each condition can evaluate up to three different fields.

To specify a condition for the records you want to include, use the first Field drop-down list to select the field in the data file that you want to evaluate, such as the ZIP Code field or Last Name field. Then, in the Cond 1 text box, type the value or list of values that the matching records should contain. To include a list of matching values, separate each possible match with a semicolon. For example, to include those records that contain a ZIP code of 77187 *or* 77532, select the ZIP Code field from the Field drop-down list, and type **77187;77532** in the Cond 1 text box. If you want to further narrow the selection, use the second column to specify another condition. For example, to include only those records in the two specified ZIP codes that have a last name beginning with A-M, from the Field drop-down list over the second column, select the Last Name field. Then, in the Cond 1 text box for the second column, type **A*-M***. The asterisk is a wildcard character that represents one or more characters. The hyphen indicates a range of values. Your field conditions should look like this:

Field	Field
Zip	Last Name
Cond 1: 77187;77532	A*-M*

For more examples of how you can set up conditions to select records, choose Example and the Examples of Selecting Records dialog box appears (see Figure 2-13). The settings in this dialog box would merge records in a data file that match any of the four given conditions. To see additional examples, choose More.

When you've set the conditions for the merge records you want to use in the current merge, choose OK to return to the Perform Merge dialog box.

NOTE: *You can also select merge records that match certain criteria by using the Sort feature on the merge data file before beginning the merge process. For more information on the Sort feature, see Chapter 8.*

Marking Records

If you want to select individual records to include in the merge, select Mark Records at the top of the Select Records dialog box (see Figure 2-12). This option lets you select records that don't necessarily have anything in common.

The Record List shows the records in your data file. Each field in the record is separated with a pipe symbol (|). If you want to change which field is displayed

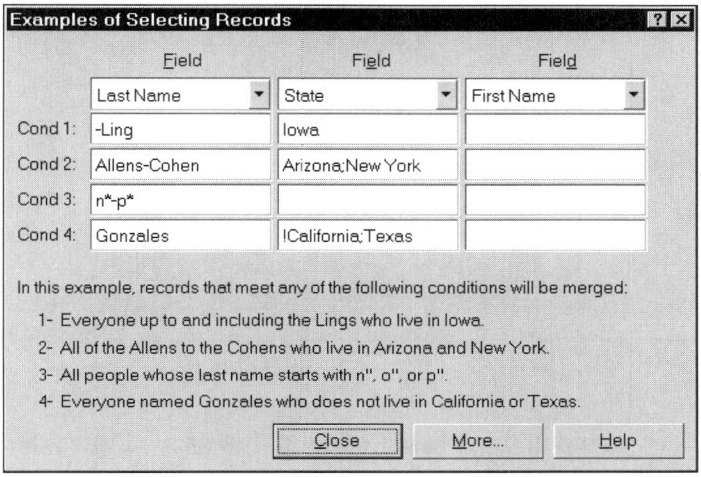

FIGURE 2-13 Examples of selecting merge records that match conditions

first for each record, from the First Field to Display drop-down list, select the field you want. Then choose Update Record List. The Record List is updated to show the selected field information for each record, as well as any fields in the record *after* that field.

NOTE: *If all the records in your data file aren't listed, change the Display Records From and To amounts.*

To mark the records you want to include, simply select the checkbox next to each record. You can choose Mark All Records in List to mark all the records in the current list, or you can choose Unmark All Records in List to unmark each record. When you've marked the records you want, choose OK to return to the Perform Merge dialog box.

Other Merge Options

To set additional options for the merge, choose Options from the Perform Merge dialog box. The Perform Merge Options dialog box appears (see Figure 2-14). If you don't want each merged document to be separated with a hard page break, deselect that option. You can also set the number of merged copies that you want

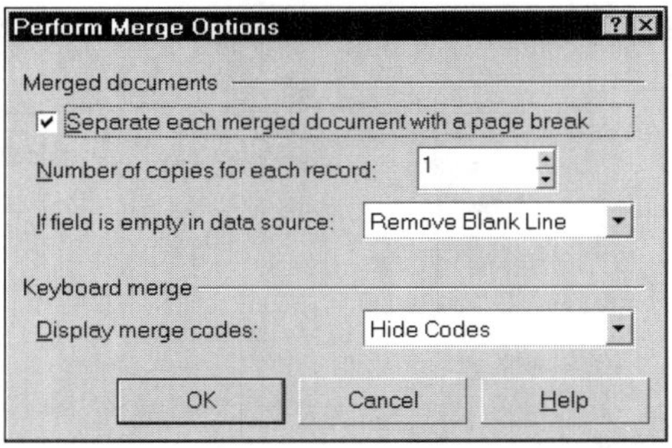

FIGURE 2-14 The Perform Merge Options dialog box

created for each record in the data file. This option is useful for creating duplicate labels, as described in the "Merge Tips and Tricks" section later in the chapter.

If your form document references a field in the data source that's empty, you can determine how WP handles any blank lines. For example, if you're creating a letter, you might insert the following field codes at the top of the letter.

```
FIELD(First Name) FIELD(Last Name)
FIELD(Company)
FIELD(Address)
FIELD(City), FIELD(State) FIELD(ZIP Code)
```

However, there might be some records that don't have a company name. With the If Field is Empty in Data Source option set to Remove Blank Line, WP automatically removes the extra hard return when there is no company name in the previous example. If the record *does* contain a company name, it is inserted on a separate line. If you don't want the blank line removed, select Leave Blank Line from the drop-down list.

Finally, if your form document contains KEYBOARD codes, you can select whether WP displays those codes as the user is typing information into the document. If you want the user to be able to see the location of any merge codes in the document as they type text, choose Show Codes from the Display Merge Codes drop-down list.

Choose OK when you're finished to return to the Perform Merge dialog box. If you've modified any of the options for the merge, such as selecting records or creating envelopes, WP indicates those changes at the bottom of the Perform Merge dialog box. If you perform a second merge with the same form document and data source, the settings remain in effect. If you've modified any settings by choosing the Options button, those changes apply to *any* form document that you later merge during the current session of WP. If you want to reset all of the options to the default settings, choose Reset.

When you're ready to merge, choose Merge in the Perform Merge dialog box and WP begins the merge process. If the form document contains any KEYBOARD codes, WP pauses and displays the message prompt. Type the text into the document and choose Continue on the Merge toolbar or press ALT-ENTER to move to the next prompt. When the merge has finished, the merged documents appear in the document window, unless you selected a different output option, such as printing or e-mailing. If you created envelopes with the merged document, the envelopes are inserted at the bottom of the merged documents.

Merge Tips and Tricks

The possibilities for using the Merge feature are practically endless. While we can't cover everything in one chapter, we can show you a few helpful merge tips and tricks, such as merging into a table, using macros within a merge, and creating duplicate copies.

Merging into Tables

WP makes it easy to insert information from a data source in a table format, such as an attendance list or class roll (see Figure 2-15). The secret is to use the REPEATROW merge command, which automatically creates a new table row for each record in the data file. To create a form document that merges information into a table, follow these steps:

1. Go to a blank document window and choose Tools | Merge; then choose Create Document.

2. Select the data source that you want to use. For example, if you're using a data file, select Associate a Data File, and then type the path and filename of the data file or use the file folder icon to select it. Choose OK.

3. In the new document, set up the formatting that you want for the document, such as the page size, margins, and font. Type and format a title at the top of the page, as well as any other text you want included

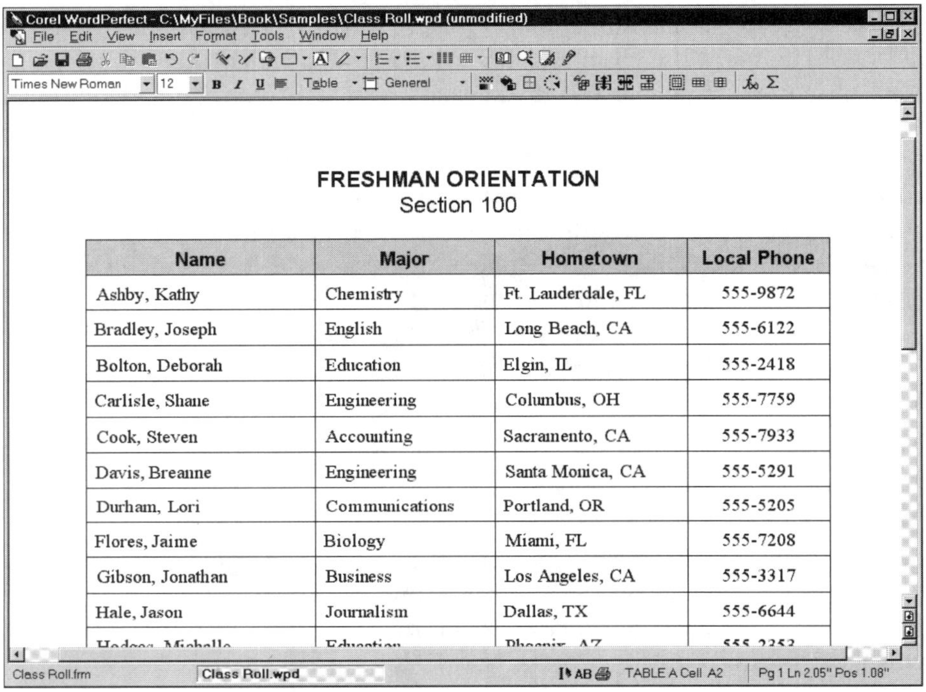

FRESHMAN ORIENTATION
Section 100

Name	Major	Hometown	Local Phone
Ashby, Kathy	Chemistry	Ft. Lauderdale, FL	555-9872
Bradley, Joseph	English	Long Beach, CA	555-6122
Bolton, Deborah	Education	Elgin, IL	555-2418
Carlisle, Shane	Engineering	Columbus, OH	555-7759
Cook, Steven	Accounting	Sacramento, CA	555-7933
Davis, Breanne	Engineering	Santa Monica, CA	555-5291
Durham, Lori	Communications	Portland, OR	555-5205
Flores, Jaime	Biology	Miami, FL	555-7208
Gibson, Jonathan	Business	Los Angeles, CA	555-3317
Hale, Jason	Journalism	Dallas, TX	555-6644

FIGURE 2-15 Merge commands help you easily merge information into a table

before the table. You can insert fields from the data source by choosing Insert Field on the Merge toolbar.

4. When you're ready to create the table, place the insertion point where the table should begin and choose Insert | Table. In the Columns text box, type the number of columns you want in the table, such as **5**. In the Rows text box, type **2**. Choose Create.

5. In the first row of the table, type and format the headings you want for each column. (For more information on formatting tables, see Chapter 6.)

6. The second row of the table is where you insert the merge codes. Place the insertion point in the second row of the table where you want information from the data source inserted and choose Insert Field from

the Merge toolbar. Select the field you want inserted in that cell and choose Insert and Close.

7. Repeat this to insert FIELD codes in any of the other table cells in the second row. Don't worry if the field names wrap to a second line.

8. After you've inserted all the FIELD codes, place the insertion point in the last cell of the second row, after any FIELD codes or text in that cell. Choose Merge Codes on the toolbar. Select REPEATROW and choose Insert; then choose Close. Your form document might look something like this:

FRESHMAN ORIENTATION
Section 100

Name	Major	Hometown	Local Phone
FIELD(Last Name), FIELD(First Name)	FIELD(Major)	FIELD(City), FIELD(State)	FIELD(Local Phone) REPEATROW

9. Save your form document. When you're ready to merge, choose Merge on the toolbar, set any merge options you want and choose Merge. The merge automatically creates a new table row for each record in the table.

CLASS ROLL.FRM: *The companion CD contains a sample merge form document named CLASS ROLL.FRM that you can open for an example of merging into a table.*

Merging into Floating Cells

In addition to merging information into a table, you can merge into a floating cell. If your data file contains fields with currency amounts, such as a balance due, you don't need to worry about including the formatting with the number, such as the dollar sign, commas, and two decimal places. Instead, you can use floating cells, which automatically format the number correctly. For example, if you merge a field with the number 3645.5 into a floating cell, it would be automatically formatted as $3,645.50. Floating cells can be placed anywhere in a form document, such as in the body of a letter.

However, you can't simply create the floating cell in the form document, since the amounts are not automatically reformatted when the document is merged. Instead, you can use the EMBEDMACRO command to place macro commands within the form document that create the floating cell for each merged record "on the fly." Then the numbers are formatted correctly within the floating cell.

To create floating cells during a merge, open or create the form document that you want to use and place the insertion point where you want the formatted number to appear. Insert the following merge codes into your form document using the Merge Codes and Insert Field buttons on the toolbar:

```
CODES(
ASSIGN(X;FIELD(Balance))
EMBEDMACRO(
    X:=StrNum(X)
    FloatingCellCreate ( )
    FloatingCellNumberFormat (Currency!)
    Type (X)
    PosLineEnd ( ))
)
```

For the FIELD(Balance) code, insert the field name in your data source that contains the numbers you want to format. The codes after EMBEDMACRO can be typed from the keyboard. These commands assign the value in the specified field to the variable *X*. Then the macro commands convert that string to a number format, creating the floating cell and format it with the currency format. The number value is inserted into the floating cell and the insertion point moves outside the floating cell codes.

ACCOUNT LETTER.FRM: *The companion CD includes a sample form document called ACCOUNT LETTER.FRM that shows an example of using an embedded macro to create floating cells in a letter.*

Now when you merge with this form document, the embedded macro inserts the numbers in floating cells so they use the correct formatting.

TIP: *You can have the embedded macro format the floating cell with a different numeric format by changing the parameter of the FloatingCellNumberFormat command. For example, you can use* **Commas***! to format the numbers with commas only and no dollar signs. Or you can use* **DateFormat***! to automatically format dates, such as formatting 4/16/98 as April 16, 1998.*

Macros in Merges

WP gives you several options for playing macros during a merge. Follow these guidelines if you want to use a macro during a merge:

- If you want the macro to play one time at the end of the merge, use the CHAINMACRO command. This command can be placed anywhere in the form document, since the macro doesn't play until the merge has finished. Open the form document and choose Merge Codes from the Merge toolbar. Select CHAINMACRO and choose Insert. Type the macro name in the text box or use the file folder icon to select it, and then choose OK. Choose Close in the Insert Merge Codes dialog box. The macro you selected will play one time immediately after the merge has finished.

- If you want the macro to play for each merged document, use the NESTMACRO or EMBEDMACRO command. The NESTMACRO command can be used to play a macro that has already been created. The EMBEDMACRO command lets you type macro commands right into the merge form document. To use these commands, open the form document and place the insertion point where you want the macro to play. Choose Merge Codes on the toolbar. To use an existing macro, select NESTMACRO and choose Insert; then type the macro name (or use the file folder icon to select it) and choose OK. If you want to type macro commands into the form document, select EMBEDMACRO and choose Insert. Type the macro commands between the parentheses of the EMBEDMACRO code. Choose Close from the Insert Merge Codes dialog box. When you merge with this form document, the macro is played for each record in the data source. (See Chapter 10 for more information on macros.)

TIP: *By using the EMBEDMACRO command, you can perform math calculations on numbers from the data source. First, use the ASSIGN command to assign the contents of the field containing the number to a variable, such as ASSIGN(X;FIELD(Balance)). Then use the EMBEDMACRO command to manipulate that variable with macro commands, such as EMBEDMACRO (X:=X*0.25) to determine 25 percent of the variable X. The VARIABLE(X) command would insert the result into the document.*

- If you want to use a macro during a keyboard merge pause, you can simply play the macro as you normally would. For example, you can choose Tools | Macro | Play, select the macro, and choose Play. Or, if you have the macro assigned to a toolbar button or keystroke, you can press the button or keystroke to play the macro. The merge remains paused until you press Continue on the Merge toolbar or press ALT-ENTER.

Creating Duplicate Copies

You can use the Merge feature to quickly create copies of documents that don't even contain any merge codes. For example, you can quickly fill a sheet of labels with the same address (see Figure 2-16), or copy the text and formatting on a subdivided page to the other subdivided sections.

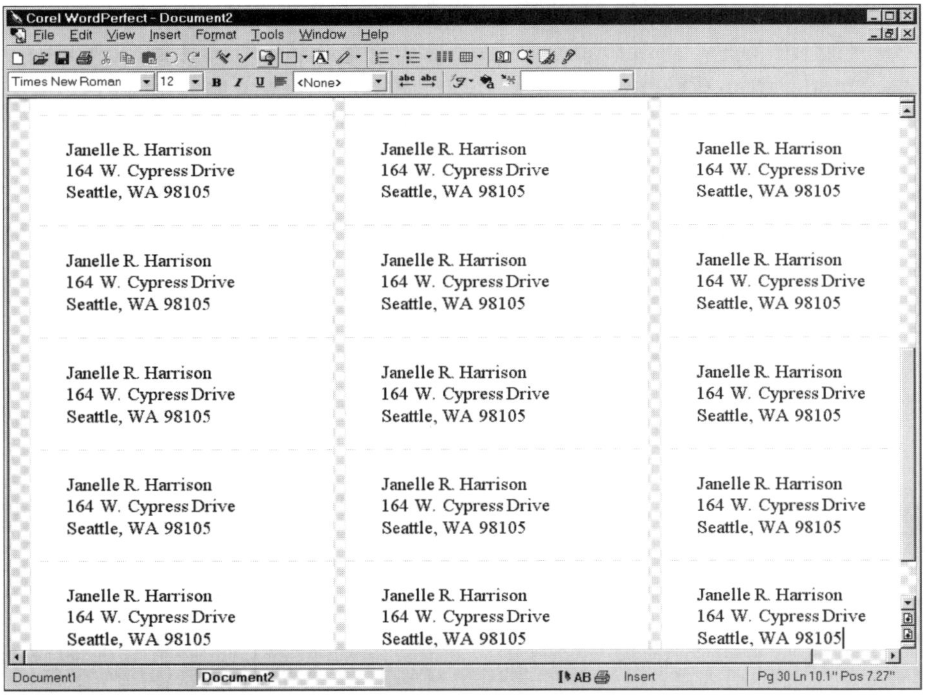

FIGURE 2-16 The Merge feature can create duplicate copies of a label

To do this, format a document with the label type (Format I Labels) or subdivide page options (Format I Page I Page Setup I Divide Page) that you want. Then type and format the text for the first label or subdivided page. When you have one label or "page" created, choose Tools I Merge, and then Perform Merge. Make sure the Form Document option is set to Current Document. From the Data Source pop-down button, choose None.

Choose Options in the Perform Merge dialog box. In the Number of Copies for Each Record text box, type the total number of labels or subdivided pages that you want to create, such as **30** for a sheet of 30 labels. Choose OK, and then choose Merge to begin the merge. WP repeats the label or page you created the specified number of times, separating each label or subdivided page with a hard page break. When the merge has finished, you can print or save the merged document.

CAUTION: *If you merge another document in the same session of WP, make sure you set the Number of Copies for Each Record option back to 1.*

Creating Labels

The Merge feature gives you lots of options for merging information onto labels. For example, you can include bar codes on the labels or automatically have the label address formatted in all uppercase letters:

FRED ABERDEEN
45 UTAH STREET
WASHINGTON, DC 20032

To create labels for the information in a data file or the Address Book, follow these steps:

1. Go to a blank document window and choose Tools I Merge; then choose Create Document.

2. If you want to create labels for the information in a data file, select Associate a Data File and type the path and filename of the data file. If you want to create labels for entries in the Address Book, select Associate an Address Book, and then select the Address Book you want from the drop-down list. Choose OK.

3. Choose Format | Labels. Select the type of labels you want to use, such as Avery 5163 Address, and choose Select.

4. If you want the label address to be formatted in all uppercase letters, choose Merge Codes on the toolbar, select TOUPPER, and choose Insert. Choose OK, and then Close.

5. Now use the Insert Field button on the Merge toolbar to insert the fields for the first line of the address. If you inserted the TOUPPER code, make sure the FIELD codes are included between the parentheses. After you've inserted the fields for the first line, press END to move outside the closing parentheses, and then press ENTER to move to the next line.

NOTE: *The merge codes and length of the field names might cause the field information to wrap on more than one line or even onto a second label. Don't worry about the wrapping of the fields, since the merge codes won't be included in the final merged document.*

6. Continue this process to insert the field codes for each line, using spaces and punctuation to format the fields. Each line of the label must have its own TOUPPER command if you want the address to be formatted in uppercase letters.

7. If you want to include bar codes on the label, the ZIP code must be in a separate field in the data source. To insert bar codes, place the insertion point on the label where you want the bar code inserted and choose Merge Codes on the toolbar. Select POSTNET, choose Insert, and then Close. Choose Insert Field on the toolbar, select the field containing the ZIP code, and choose Insert and Close.

Your finished label form document might look something like this:

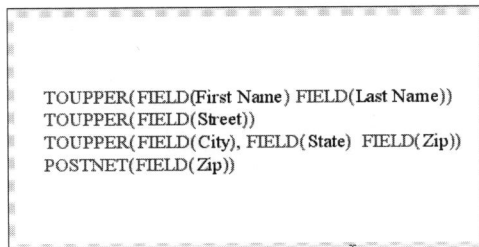

```
TOUPPER(FIELD(First Name) FIELD(Last Name))
TOUPPER(FIELD(Street))
TOUPPER(FIELD(City), FIELD(State)  FIELD(Zip))
POSTNET(FIELD(Zip))
```

ADDRESS BOOK LABELS.FRM: *The companion CD contains a merge form document named ADDRESS BOOK LABELS.FRM that you can open as an example of merging onto labels. This form document is set up to use fields from the Address Book.*

If you want to use this label format in the future, choose File | Save and save the form document with a filename such as **labels.frm**. To merge the labels, choose Merge on the toolbar. If you want to create labels for only a few records in the data file or Address Book, choose Select Records and follow the guidelines in the "Selecting Merge Records" section earlier in the chapter to select the records you want. Choose Merge to begin the merge.

Summary

WordPerfect's Merge feature is packed with power and gives you the tools you need to quickly create customized documents. The Merge feature can easily perform mass mailings of documents that are personalized with information from a data source such as the recipient's name and address. In addition, you can use advanced merge commands to interact with the user, make decisions, play macros, and access other form documents and data files. The Merge feature works with information from a variety of data sources, including the Address Book, ODBC database files, and other database programs. You can easily select which records from the data source are included during a specific merge, as well as quickly create envelopes and labels.

The Merge feature gives you practically unlimited control and flexibility over the documents you create. You'll be amazed at what you can do with a little understanding of how the Merge feature and commands work!

In Chapter 3, we'll explore some of the shortcuts available with WordPerfect's "Quick" features, such as QuickCorrect, QuickWords, and QuickLinks.

Chapter
3

The QuickCorrect and other "Quick" Features

Everybody likes to find shortcuts, whether it's a faster route to work or a more efficient method of budgeting. And we're the same when it comes to using WordPerfect—we want to find the easiest, fastest way to accomplish our task. Fortunately, WordPerfect has *lots* of shortcuts to choose from. Some of the most simple shortcut tools are the "Quick" features— QuickCorrect, QuickWords, QuickLinks, and so on. The "Quick" features take something you've typed into your document— usually an abbreviation of some sort—and automatically expand it into what you *really* had in mind. This basic concept goes a long way in getting you to the end result faster.

In this chapter you'll learn how to push the "Quick" features to their limits and make them work for you. We'll show you how features like QuickCorrect and QuickWords can dramatically reduce the time it takes to insert text and formatting in your documents. We'll give you lots of ideas for customizing these features to do more than you thought possible. You'll also learn how to effortlessly link your documents to the Internet with QuickLinks and correct your work instantly with the Proofreading tools.

QuickCorrect

If you've been using WordPerfect for a while, you're undoubtedly familiar with QuickCorrect. QuickCorrect does just what its name implies—it quickly corrects the mistakes you make as you type them, such as changing "teh" to "the." But it also does a whole lot more. You can use QuickCorrect to automatically expand abbreviated text—such as changing "ssn" to "Social Security Number"—as well as fix capitalization errors, create bulleted lists, insert SmartQuotes, and more. In this section, you'll learn how to get the most out of these capabilities of QuickCorrect.

Traditional QuickCorrect

The best-known aspect of QuickCorrect is its ability to correct mistakes and expand abbreviations on the fly, or right as you type into a document. Here's a brief review of QuickCorrect:

- To use QuickCorrect, simply type a misspelled word or abbreviation into your document. If the word is found in the QuickCorrect word list, as soon as you press SPACEBAR or ENTER, WordPerfect automatically replaces it with the new word.

- To see a list of the words that WP corrects, choose Tools | QuickCorrect. In the QuickCorrect dialog box, the words along the left are the misspelled words or abbreviations that will be replaced with the words on the right (Figure 3-1).

- To add a new QuickCorrect item, in the Replace text box, type the misspelled word or the abbreviation that you want to have replaced, such as **freind** or **ssn**. In the With text box, type the text as you want it to appear in the document, such as **friend** or **Social Security Number**. Choose Add Entry.

- To remove words from the QuickCorrect list, select the entry in the list, choose Delete Entry, and then choose Yes to confirm the deletion.

- If you need to make changes to an entry, select it in the QuickCorrect dialog box, and then edit the Replace and With text boxes as you want. Choose Replace Entry to save your changes.

- To turn QuickCorrect off, deselect the Replace Words as You Type option. Once you turn QuickCorrect off, it remains that way for all of your documents until you turn it on again.

QuickCorrect Facts and Features

Here are a few helpful facts about the QuickCorrect feature, including some of its new capabilities in WP 8:

- WordPerfect 8 comes with a list of 161 common spelling and grammar errors that it will automatically replace in your documents.

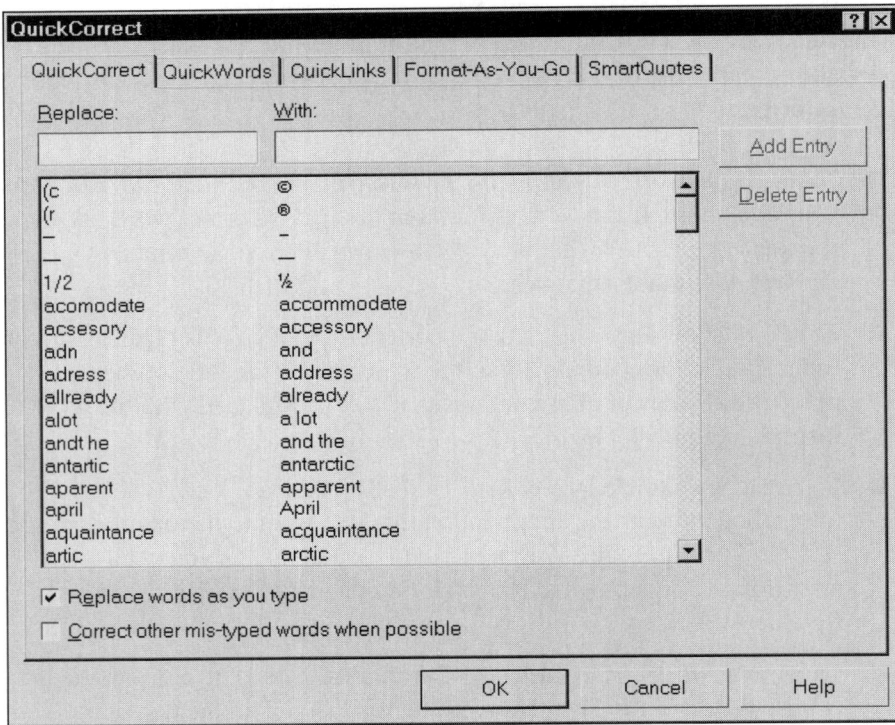

FIGURE 3-1 The QuickCorrect dialog box shows the automatic
                replacements for abbreviations and misspelled words

■ The QuickCorrect entries are stored in the WT80US.UWL file. This file
    also contains your Spell Checker user word lists, or those words that you
    add during a spell check. Typically, the WT80US.UWL file is stored in
    the \Windows\Personal\Corel User Files directory under Windows 95 or
    the \WinNT\Profiles\"UserName"\Personal\Corel User Files directory
    under Windows NT (where "UserName" is the profile folder of the user
    currently logged in). However, on some computers the Corel User Files
    subdirectory might be in a different location. If the WT80US.UWL file is

deleted, the next time you start WordPerfect, a new file is created with only the default word list. If you've spent time customizing your QuickCorrect list, it's a good idea to occasionally back up this file. See the On the CD section for a macro that helps you quickly back up some of your WP 8 customization files.

On the CD ... Backing Up QuickCorrect and QuickWords

WordPerfect lets you customize many of its aspects so that you can work the way you like, including changing your default settings and adding entries to QuickCorrect and QuickWords. If you've made a lot of customization changes and then later need to reinstall WP for some reason, it can be a time-consuming chore to set everything back up just like you had it.

The companion CD includes a macro called BACKUP SETTINGS.WCM that helps you back up four of the main files that contain your custom WP settings and word lists. The macro backs up the following files:

- WT80US.UWL   This file contains entries that you've added to the QuickCorrect list, as well as words that you've added during a spell check.

- QW8EN.WPT   This template contains all of your QuickWord entries.

- WP8US.WPT   This template contains your custom toolbars, keyboards, and menu bars, as well as some of your custom settings.

- PROJECTS.USR   This file contains an index of the project categories, names, and descriptions displayed in the New dialog box.

To use the backup macro, choose Tools | Macro | Play. Select the BACKUP SETTINGS.WCM macro and choose Play. In the dialog box that appears, select those files you want to back up and change the path for them if needed. Choose OK. The macro makes a copy of each file in the same directory where the original file is located using a BAK extension. If you need to restore these files, simply rename the backup file to use the original filename. (For more information on templates and projects, see Chapter 1.)

- QuickCorrect doesn't include any formatting (such as fonts and font attributes) with the replacement text it inserts. If you need the text formatted a certain way, use QuickWords as explained later in this chapter.

- WP now corrects and expands QuickCorrect entries when they're typed with any sort of punctuation. For example, if you type **(febuary)** and press SPACEBAR or ENTER, it's automatically changed to (February). You can include periods, parentheses, quotation marks, and other punctuation when you type QuickCorrect words in your document and they're still replaced correctly.

- You can use two words for the QuickCorrect replacement word, such as replacing "tot he" with "to the."

- QuickCorrect is automatically turned off for *all* open documents when you have a merge file or a macro open in any document window. Since macro and merge files require specific formatting, including straight quotes instead of SmartQuotes, WP disables the entire QuickCorrect feature so you don't have to remember to turn it off and then back on again.

TIP: *If you want to use QuickCorrect in a merge file or macro, such as to insert SmartQuotes in a merge form file, you can turn QuickCorrect back on manually by choosing Tools | QuickCorrect and selecting the options you need. If you do this frequently, consider recording a macro that selects your QuickCorrect options, and then adding that macro to a toolbar button so you can easily play it. (See Chapter 10 for more information on recording macros and Chapter 13 for information on toolbars.)*

- You're limited to 128 characters, including spaces, for the text you type as the replacement text.

QuickCorrect Tips

Here are some tips about QuickCorrect that perhaps you didn't know before:

- WordPerfect can automatically correct some misspelled words that *aren't* in the QuickCorrect list. If you choose Tools | QuickCorrect and select the Correct Other Mis-Typed Words When Possible option, WP automatically fixes words that have only one suggestion in the Spell Checker dictionary as a correct replacement. For example, if you type **fortunatly** in your document, WP automatically corrects it to "fortunately," even though that word isn't in the QuickCorrect list.

CAUTION: *If you select the option to correct other misspelled words, make sure that your documents don't contain unusual proper nouns or words with unique spellings that haven't been previously added to your Spell Checker user word list. Since these words are more likely to have a single replacement suggestion (if they have any at all), they might be automatically replaced with something you don't want.*

- If you don't want a word replaced for a particular occurrence, you don't need to delete that entry or turn QuickCorrect off. Instead, type and expand the word normally in the document. Press CTRL-Z to undo the QuickCorrect action; then press RIGHT ARROW to move past the space or hard return that you originally inserted and continue typing the document text. If you press SPACEBAR or ENTER a second time, the word is simply expanded again.

- If you type the abbreviation text in all lowercase letters, WP expands it with the capitalization that you originally used when you added the entry. However, if you type the abbreviation in all uppercase letters, the replacement text is also inserted in all uppercase letters.

- If the text you want to use as a replacement for a new QuickCorrect entry is already typed into your document, you don't need to retype it. Instead, select the replacement text and choose Tools | QuickCorrect. The selected text is automatically inserted in the With text box and you can simply type the abbreviated text.

NOTE: *When you select text in the document to use as a QuickCorrect replacement, only 63 characters are inserted into the dialog box, even if you selected more than that in the document. You can add to the replacement text (up to 128 characters) by clicking in the With text box and typing any additional text.*

- You can use special characters and symbols in the replacement text by pressing CTRL-W and selecting the symbol you want. For example, you can use QuickCorrect to replace accented words and names, such as replacing "resume" with "résumé." Or you can add QuickCorrect entries for all the common fractions.

- You can add new entries to your QuickCorrect list during a spell check. When the Spell Checker stops on a word that you frequently misspell, make sure the correct replacement is selected in the Replacements list box and choose Auto Replace. The misspelled word and correct replacement are added to your QuickCorrect list so WP automatically fixes that word as you type it in future documents.

Format-As-You-Go

Another part of the QuickCorrect feature is called *Format-As-You-Go*. With Format-As-You-Go, WordPerfect corrects such things as capitalization and the number of spaces between sentences, along with automatically inserting bullets, symbols, and graphics lines. To set the Format-As-You-Go options, choose Tools | QuickCorrect and select the Format-As-You-Go tab at the top of the dialog box (Figure 3-2). Select the options you want and deselect those you don't. Here's a brief description of each option:

- *Sentence Corrections*   These options help make sure that your sentences use correct capitalization and spacing.

- *CapsFix*   CapsFix corrects words that are typed in improper mixed case, such as tHIS, when CAPS LOCK is turned on. WP automatically corrects the word to use an initial uppercase letter and even turns CAPS LOCK off for you.

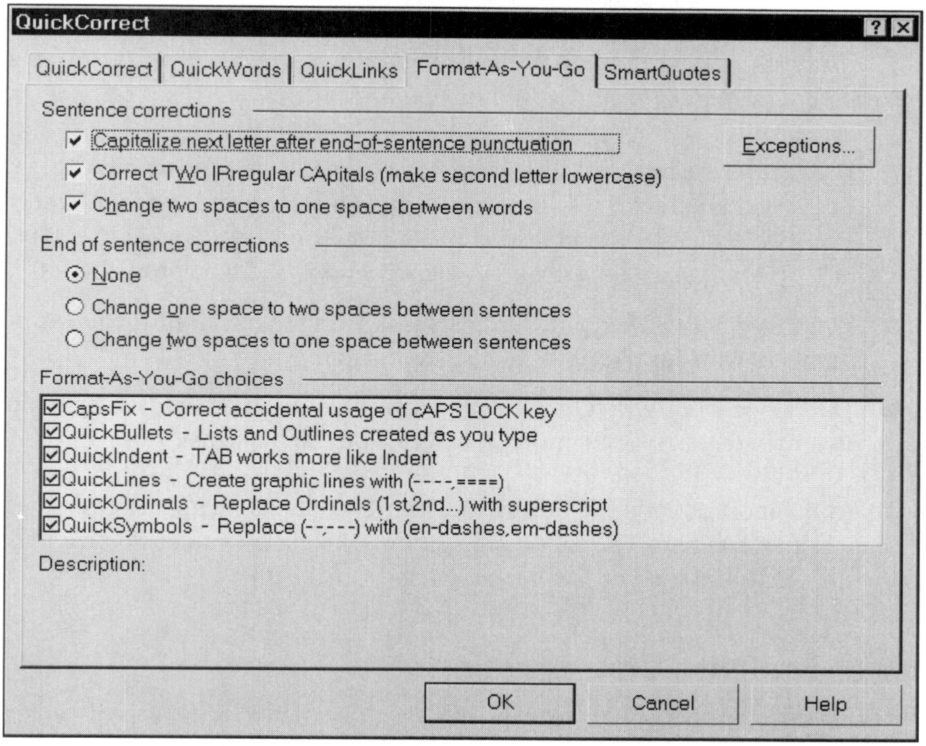

FIGURE 3-2 The Format-As-You-Go options help you correct capitalization, insert bullets, and more

NOTE: *CapsFix only works when text is typed with CAPS LOCK turned on. If you type text in improper case simply by holding down the SHIFT key, the CapsFix feature won't correct it.*

■ *QuickBullets* Use QuickBullets to create a simple numbered, lettered, or bulleted list. If you type an asterisk, letter, or number, and then press TAB, WP changes the tab to an indent and begins a new list. When you press ENTER, WP automatically inserts the next number or letter in the list.

■ *QuickIndent* QuickIndent helps you indent a paragraph after you've typed several lines. When you press TAB at the beginning of any line in a paragraph other than the first line, the entire paragraph is automatically indented.

TIP: *You can use QuickIndent to create paragraphs with hanging indents, where all but the first line is indented. Make sure the first line of the paragraph doesn't already begin with a tab, and then press TAB at the beginning of any line in the paragraph except the first.*

- *QuickLines*   The QuickLines feature helps you insert full-width horizontal graphics lines. To insert a single line, type at least four hyphens in a row, such as ----, and then press ENTER. To insert a double line, type at least four equal signs in a row, such as ====, and then press ENTER.

- *QuickOrdinals*   The QuickOrdinals feature automatically formats ordinal numbers with superscript text, such as changing 1st to 1st.

- *QuickSymbols*   With QuickSymbols, you can insert an en-dash by typing two hyphens (--), or an em-dash by typing three hyphens (---).

To get the most out of these Format-As-You-Go options, there are several ways you can customize them. The following sections explain how to customize two of the options: End-of-Sentence Capitalization and QuickBullets.

End-of-Sentence Capitalization

If you've selected the option to capitalize the next letter after end-of-sentence punctuation, be aware of the Exception List. The Exception List indicates those words containing periods that will *not* cause WP to automatically capitalize the next letter. Words in the Exception List are words such as "Inc." and "vs.," which are frequently included in the middle of sentences.

To see the Exception List, choose Exceptions in the Format-As-You-Go dialog box (Figure 3-3). You can add or delete words from this list if you want. Choose Close when you're finished. If you type an exception word in your document, WP does not automatically capitalize the next letter following it.

NOTE: *If you type three or more spaces between an exception word and the following word, WP will still capitalize the following word, even though the word is on the Exception List.*

TIP: *You can add new words to the Exception List directly from the document screen. First, make sure the Add Exceptions When You Correct Them in the Document option is selected at the bottom of the Exception List*

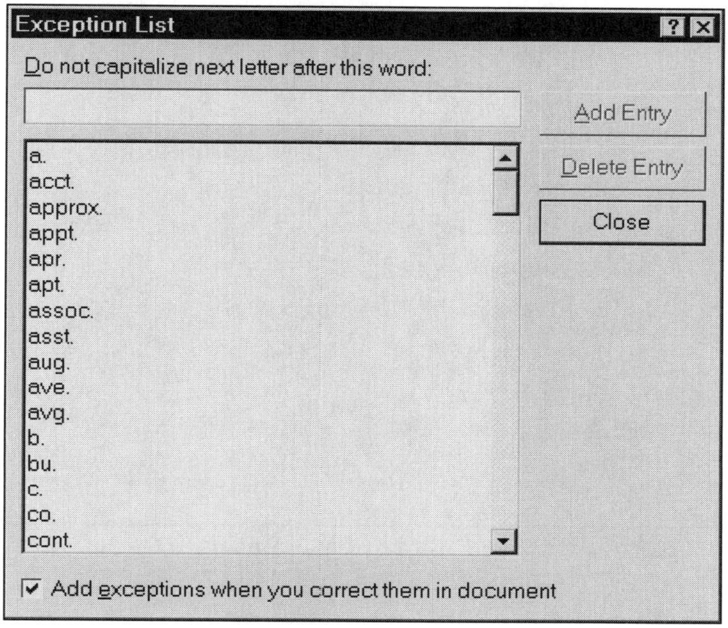

FIGURE 3-3 The Exception List dialog box displays words with punctuation that don't cause WP to capitalize the next letter

dialog box. Then, when you type a word containing punctuation in the middle of a sentence and WP automatically capitalizes the next word, simply correct the capitalized letter in the document screen. When you do this, WP adds the word containing the punctuation to the Exception List.

QuickBullets

With the QuickBullets feature, you can easily create lists using numbers, upper- or lowercase letters, upper- or lowercase Roman numerals, and six different types of bullets. Simply start by typing the first letter, number, or bullet "trigger" character, and then press TAB. Table 3-1 shows which keys will start each type of list.

NOTE: *If you're creating a numbered or lettered list, make sure you include a period after the number or letter, or the QuickBullets feature will not activate.*

Key	Type of List Created
1.	Numbers
A.	Uppercase letters
a.	Lowercase letters
I.	Uppercase Roman numerals
i.	Lowercase Roman numerals
* or o	Small Round Bullet ●
O	Large Round Bullet one of the six ●
>	Triangle ◣
^	Diamond ◆
-	Straight Line –
+	Star ★

TABLE 3-1 Characters Recognized by QuickBullets to Create a List

If you want to use a bullet character that's not listed in Table 3-1, you can format your list to use a different character from the Symbols dialog box. See the "Changing the Bullet Character" Power Tip for steps on how to do this.

Power Tip... **Changing the Bullet Character**

Several different bullet options are available for creating lists with the QuickBullets feature (see Table 3-1). If you want to use a different bullet character, follow these steps:

1. Create the list normally using one of the available bullets. You can do this either with the QuickBullets feature or by choosing Insert | Outline/Bullets & Numbering.

2. After you've created the list, place the insertion point anywhere in the list and choose Insert | Outline/Bullets & Numbering.

3. Select the Bullets tab at the top of the dialog box; then choose More Bullets.

4. Select the new bullet character you want to use from the Symbols dialog box, and choose Insert and Close.

5. Choose OK and your list is updated to use the new bullet.

If you frequently use a bullet that's not one of the default options, you can create a new bullet style and copy it to your default template so you can use it in all your new documents. However, the new bullet style will only be available through the Bullets & Numbering feature and not through QuickBullets. To do this, choose Insert | Outline/ Bullets & Numbering, and then select the Bullets tab. Choose More Bullets, select the new bullet character from the Symbols dialog box, and choose Insert and Close. From the Options pop-down button, choose Copy. Select Default Template and choose OK. If you're asked if you want to overwrite existing styles, choose Yes. Choose Cancel to close the dialog box.

To use your new bullet, choose Insert | Outline/Bullets & Numbering. Select the Bullets tab, and then select your new bullet style in the list and choose OK to insert the first bullet into your document.

Here are a few tips for using QuickBullets:

■ To end your list, press ENTER to move to a new line; then press BACKSPACE to delete the bullet or number that was inserted. If you need to continue a numbered or lettered list later in the document, place the insertion point where you want to begin the continue list and choose Insert | Outline/Bullets & Numbering. If the type of list you used previously isn't already selected, select it from the available options. Make sure Resume Outline or List is selected and choose OK.

■ If you want to change the amount of spacing used between the bullet or number and the text, just add a new tab setting or change the current tab setting. This is easily done with the Ruler (View | Ruler).

■ If the bullets appear as hollow squares, it indicates that the fonts used for the WP symbols have not been correctly installed. To reinstall the symbol fonts, run the Corel WordPerfect Suite 8 Setup. Follow the prompts to perform a custom installation, and then deselect all of the options. Select Required Components in the list and choose Components; then select Perfect Fit and choose Components. Select Symbol Fonts and choose OK twice. Choose Next to continue with the installation.

SmartQuotes

WP's SmartQuotes feature inserts "curly" quotation marks (" ") into your documents as you type. To configure this feature, choose Tools | QuickCorrect and select the SmartQuotes tab. Here are a few SmartQuotes tips:

- If you want to use a different symbol for a quotation mark that's not listed in the drop-down list, click in the appropriate text box and press CTRL-W to display the Symbols dialog box. Select the symbol you want to use and choose Insert and Close.

- Sometimes you might need to insert curly quotes in a document after a number, such as "Chapter 12." In these cases, you don't need to change the settings in the QuickCorrect dialog box. Instead, type the number, followed by a "dummy" letter, then the quotation mark, such as "**Chapter 12x**." Then simply go back and delete the dummy letter so the curly quote remains. Similarly, if you need to insert straight quotes with text, use numbers as the dummy characters so straight quotes are inserted, and then delete the numbers.

- Remember that if you're working on a macro or merge document, the QuickCorrect feature—including SmartQuotes—is automatically turned off. If you need to include curly quotes in a merge form file, simply open the QuickCorrect dialog box and reselect the SmartQuotes options you want.

- If you open a document that doesn't use SmartQuotes, you can quickly replace the straight quotes with curly quotes by using the Find and Replace feature. Simply type a quote mark in both the Find and Replace With text boxes—WP automatically uses the correct curly quotes.

QuickWords

QuickWords could be considered the power version of QuickCorrect. Like QuickCorrect, the QuickWords feature is designed to speed up your work by automatically expanding abbreviated text as you type in a document. Unlike

QuickCorrect, however, QuickWords lets you insert much, much more than plain text. You can use QuickWords to automatically replace abbreviated text with entire formatted paragraphs, graphics, tables, hyperlinks, and more. In this section, you'll learn how to create and expand QuickWords, as well as get lots of ideas for the different ways that you can put QuickWords to work.

NOTE: *If you created custom abbreviations in WP 6.1 or 7, you can convert these abbreviations to QuickWords in WP 8. In order to do this, you must have the default 6.1 or 7 template available that contains the abbreviations (STANDARD.WPT in 6.1 or WP7US.WPT in 7). Then follow the steps in the "Copying Abbreviations into WP 8" Power Tip to copy the abbreviations into your WP 8 QuickWords list.*

Power Tip→→ Copying Abbreviations into WP 8

Similar to abbreviations in WP 6.1 and 7, QuickWords in WP 8 are stored in a template (QW8EN.WPT). If you have a WP 6.1 or 7 template that contains abbreviations, you can copy those abbreviations into the QuickWords template in WP 8. Follow these steps:

1. Copy the template containing the abbreviations into your Custom WP Templates directory (usually \Corel\Suite8 \Template\Custom WP Templates). The default 6.1 template is STANDARD.WPT and the default WP 7 template is WP7US.WPT.

2. Choose File | New and switch to the Custom WP Templates category.

3. Select <WP QuickWords File> and from the Options pop-down button, choose Edit WP Template.

4. Choose Copy/Remove Object on the Template Property Bar.

5. From the Templates to Copy From drop-down list, select the template you copied, such as WP7US.

6. From the Object Type drop-down list, select QuickWords.

7. To copy all the abbreviations, choose Copy All. Otherwise, select an individual abbreviation in the Source list and choose Copy. Repeat this to copy other abbreviations.

8. When you're finished, choose Close. Click the Close button on the Template Property Bar and choose Yes to save the changes.

The new QuickWords are now available for any WP 8 document. To see a list of the QuickWords, choose Tools I QuickWords.

Expanding QuickWords

Since QuickWords is a new feature in WP 8, we'll go into a little more detail on the basics of using it. QuickWords are expanded the same way as QuickCorrect entries. Simply type the abbreviated text in your document and press SPACEBAR or ENTER to expand the text automatically to the formatted version. Try this: type \opening in a document window and press ENTER (this is one of the sample QuickWords included with WP 8). WP automatically inserts the text "Dear Sir or Madam."

NOTE: *QuickWords are not case sensitive, so typing \opening will expand the same QuickWord as typing \Opening or \OPENING.*

If you don't want QuickWords to expand automatically as you type them, choose Tools I QuickWords and deselect the Expand QuickWords as You Type Them option. When this option is turned off, you can expand all the QuickWords in a document at the same time by playing the EXPNDALL.WCM macro included with WordPerfect. This macro isn't copied onto your hard drive during a typical installation, so first copy it from the \Corel\Suite8\Macros\WPWin directory on the CD to the default macros directory on your hard drive (usually the same directory). Then choose Tools I Macro I Play, select the EXPNDALL.WCM, and choose Play to have all the QuickWords in your document expanded.

You can also have QuickWords expand as plain text. To do this, choose Tools I QuickWords. From the Options pop-down button, select Expand as Plain Text, and then choose OK. Now when a QuickWord is expanded, the text is inserted without any formatting, graphics, tables, and other elements.

Creating QuickWords

To create a new QuickWord, type and format the text you want the QuickWord to contain in a document window. You can include multiple paragraphs or even entire documents, along with such elements as graphics, tables, fonts, hyperlinks, and drop caps.

TIP: *If you're including a graphic, attach the box to a character or paragraph if you want it to move with the text around it. If you always want it to appear in a certain location on the page, attach it to the page. (For more information on graphics, see Chapter 7.)*

After formatting the QuickWord text, select it. Make sure you've included any codes at the top or bottom of the text that you want to be included in the QuickWord. If you're including graphics, tables or other codes, it's a good idea to turn on Reveal Codes (View | Reveal Codes) and make sure you've selected the correct codes. With the text selected, choose Tools | QuickWords. In the text box, type the abbreviation for this QuickWord (one or two words). Choose Add Entry to add it to the QuickWord list.

TIP: *The QuickWord samples that are included with WP 8 all begin with a back slash, such as \cheetah. You don't have to use a back slash when you name your QuickWords, but we suggest that you use some symbol in the name, such as an asterisk or exclamation point. This not only helps you identify QuickWords as you type them into your documents, but it lets you use the text of the QuickWord name (such as "cheetah") normally in a document without having it expand every time.*

Here are just a few ideas for things you can insert with QuickWords:

- Your company logo and address
- Tables with formulas already inserted
- Custom shapes drawn with the shape tools
- Boilerplate paragraphs

- A graphics file with your scanned signature
- Hyperlink buttons that play macros (see "How to Include Macros in QuickWords" for more information)

How to... Include Macros in QuickWords

You can't have a macro automatically play when you expand a QuickWord. However, you *can* have the QuickWord insert a hyperlink which, when clicked, plays a macro. To see how this works, this section will take you through the steps of adding a macro hyperlink to a simple table invoice and then creating a QuickWord of the invoice. When inserted, the QuickWord will look like this:

INVOICE

Description	Quantity	Unit Price	Total
			$0.00
			$0.00
			$0.00
		Sales Tax (6.5%)	$0.00
		Shipping	$3.00
		TOTAL DUE	$3.00

Change Sales Tax Rate

To speed up the process of creating this QuickWord, we've included a document on the companion CD called INVOICE TABLE.WPD, as well as a macro called INVOICE.WCM. The file contains a blank invoice table set up with formatting and math formulas. The macro works with this table to change the sales tax rate used in the table. You'll learn how to add the macro as a hyperlink and create a QuickWord entry for this table in the next steps.

Follow these steps to create a QuickWord that inserts an invoice table and hyperlink macro:

1. Choose File | Open; select the INVOICE TABLE.WPD file from the companion CD and choose Open.

2. Press CTRL-END to move the insertion point to the bottom of the document.

How to... **Include Macros in QuickWords**
(*continued*)

3. To create a hyperlink, type **Change Sales Tax Rate**, which will be the text of the hyperlink button.

4. Select the text you just typed and choose Tools | Hyperlink.

5. Click the file folder icon to the right of the Document/Macro text box and select the INVOICE.WCM macro. (If you link the text to the macro on the companion CD, the CD must be in the drive whenever you click the hyperlink button to play the macro.)

6. Select the Make Text Appear as a Button option, and then choose OK. Your document should now look like the previous illustration.

7. To create a QuickWord for the table and hyperlink, press SHIFT-CTRL-HOME to select the entire document.

8. Choose Tools | QuickWords. In the Abbreviated Form text box, type **\invoice**. Choose Add Entry.

9. Choose File | Close to close the document and choose No when asked if you want to save the changes.

Now, whenever you need to insert a simple invoice into any document, just type **\invoice** and press ENTER. The invoice table is inserted, along with the hyperlink button. You can type text in the invoice and the formulas in the table automatically calculate the totals. To change the sales tax rate, click the Change Sales Tax Rate button. The macro plays and you're prompted for the new tax rate. (For more information on hyperlinks, see Chapter 12. For more information on macros, see Chapter 10.)

Managing QuickWords

To see a list of the QuickWords you have available, choose Tools | QuickWords. If you select a QuickWord in the list, the dialog box shows you a preview of what is contained in that QuickWord (see Figure 3-4).

NOTE: *You can also get to the QuickWords list by choosing Tools |*
QuickCorrect and selecting the QuickWords tab.

To change the name of a QuickWord, select the QuickWord you want to rename
and from the Options pop-down button, choose Rename Entry. Type the new name
for the QuickWord and choose OK. To delete a QuickWords entry, select the
QuickWord in the list and choose Delete Entry; then choose Yes to confirm the
deletion.

If you want to change the text or formatting inserted by a QuickWord, select the
QuickWord and choose Insert in Text. (You can also close the dialog box and type
the QuickWord so the text is expanded into a document window.) Make any changes

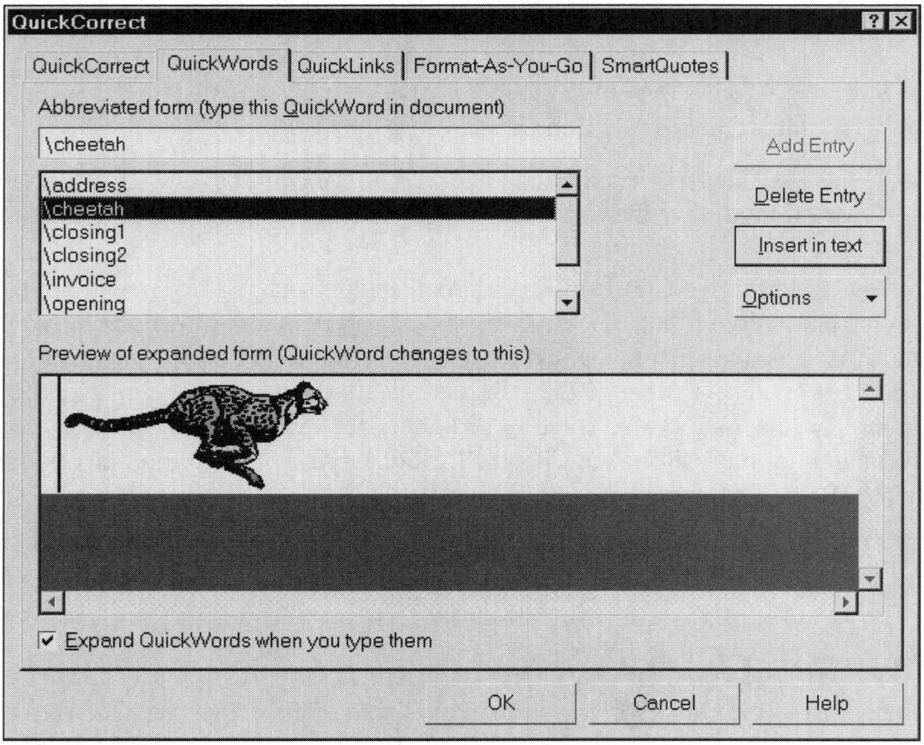

FIGURE 3-4   The QuickWords dialog box shows you a preview of your
QuickWords

you want to the text or formatting, and then reselect the portion that you want as part of the QuickWord. Make sure you select all the codes you need (turn on Reveal Codes to help). Then choose Tools | QuickWords. Select the QuickWord name in the list that you're editing; and from the Options pop-down button, choose Replace Entry, and then choose Yes to confirm the replacement.

QuickLinks

QuickLinks could be considered QuickWords for the Internet. With QuickLinks, you can easily create links in your documents to Internet sites or e-mail addresses. QuickLinks are actually hyperlinks that point to a specific Internet site, so when you click the hyperlink in your document, your Web browser is opened to the corresponding site. (For more information on the Hyperlinks feature, see Chapter 12.)

There are two different kinds of QuickLinks: automatic hyperlinks that create a link to specific Internet addresses when they're typed in a document, and regular QuickLinks that expand abbreviated text to a hyperlink pointing to an Internet site. In this section, you'll learn how to use both types of links.

Automatic Hyperlinks

When you type an Internet address into a WordPerfect document, the QuickLinks feature automatically converts it to a hyperlink. For example, if you type **www.corel.com**, it's converted to a hyperlink that appears in blue, underlined text (the default hyperlink formatting). If you then click on this link, your Web browser opens and automatically takes you to that Web site.

NOTE: *In order for Internet hyperlinks to work, you must have an Internet browser installed, such as Netscape, and a connection to an Internet service provider.*

WordPerfect recognizes and converts the following Internet formats:

- www.corel.com or http://www.corel.com
- ftp://ftp.corel.com
- john@corel.com, mailto:john@corel.com, or sendto:john@corel.com

For each format, you can substitute any valid Internet site or e-mail address in place of "corel.com" or "john@corel.com."

NOTE: *Currently, WordPerfect doesn't recognize the format ftp.corel.com as a valid Internet link. For FTP sites, you must use the ftp:// prefix, such as ftp://ftp.corel.com.*

To turn off this feature so Internet addresses aren't automatically formatted as hyperlinks, choose Tools | QuickCorrect; select the QuickLinks tab; and then deselect the Format Words as Hyperlinks When You Type Them option. Choose OK.

Creating QuickLinks

If you frequently insert specific Internet sites or e-mail addresses into your documents, you can use QuickLinks to avoid having to type the full address each time. QuickLinks converts abbreviated text, such as @Corel, to a hyperlink that points to the corresponding Internet site (such as www.corel.com). The full Internet site address doesn't appear in the document; instead the link is formatted with the abbreviation name, such as Corel.

To create a QuickLink to a common Internet site, follow these steps:

1. Choose Tools | QuickCorrect. Select the QuickLinks tab at the top of the dialog box (see Figure 3-5).

2. In the Link Word text box, type the abbreviation for the site, using the capitalization as you want it to appear in your document, such as **Osborne**.

3. In the Location To Link To text box, type the full Internet site address or e-mail address, such as **www.osborne.com**.

4. Choose Add Entry. WP adds the entry to your QuickLinks list and automatically inserts the @ symbol before the name, such as @Osborne.

5. Choose OK.

To insert an Internet hyperlink in your document, just type the abbreviated text with the @ symbol, such as **@Corel** or **@Osborne**. When you press SPACEBAR or ENTER, QuickLinks changes your text to a hyperlink and removes the @ symbol. If you click on this link, WP opens your Web browser and goes to the corresponding site.

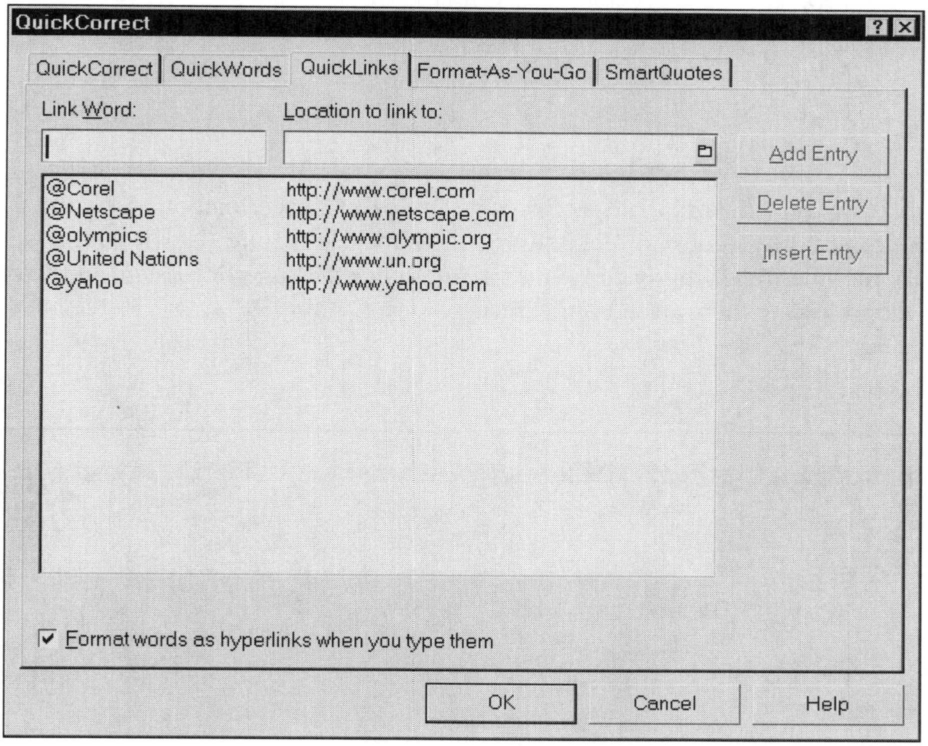

FIGURE 3-5 You can create QuickLinks to common Internet sites

TIP: *To have your link appear as a button instead of blue, underlined text, right-click the link and choose Edit Hyperlink. Select the Make Text Appear as Button option and choose OK.*

Proofreading Tools

One of the great things about the "Quick" features is that they work on the fly—making changes right as you type text into your documents. This in itself is a shortcut, because it keeps your fingers on the keyboard instead of continually searching through the menus. WordPerfect's other on-the-fly features are found in the Proofreading tools: Spell-As-You-Go, Grammar-As-You-Go, and Prompt-As-You-Go. These tools flag spelling and grammar mistakes as you type and put the dictionary and thesaurus right at your fingertips. To select these tools, choose Tools | Proofread; and select the options you want.

NOTE: *When you have Grammar-As-You-Go selected, Spell-As-You-Go still flags misspelled words. But when only Spell-As-You-Go is selected, the Grammar-As-You-Go feature is disabled.*

Spell-As-You-Go

When you type a word that's not part of the Spell Checker dictionaries and that's not corrected by QuickCorrect, the Spell-As-You-Go feature flags it with a wavy red underline. When this occurs, you can right-click the underlined word and do one of the following things (see Figure 3-6):

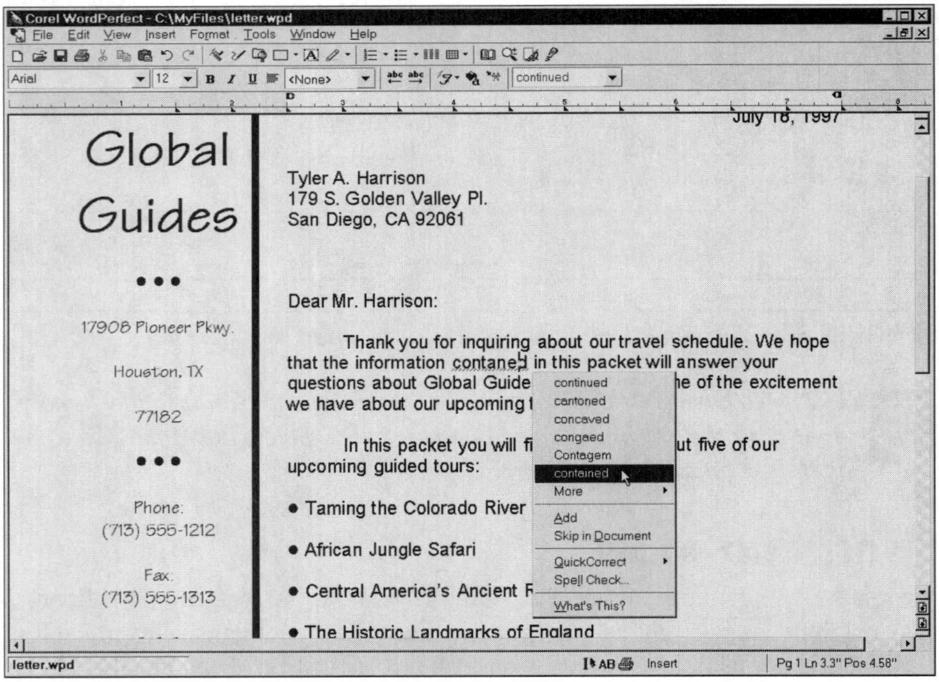

FIGURE 3-6 Spell-As-You-Go gives you immediate options for correcting a word

- Select the correctly spelled word from the suggested replacements (if there are more suggestions than will display on the menu, choose More).

- Add the word to your Spell Checker user word list so it is always recognized during future spell checks.

- Tell WP to skip that particular spelling any time it appears in the current document.

- Add the word to your QuickCorrect list by choosing QuickCorrect, and then selecting the correct replacement from the list. When you do this, the next time you misspell the word the same way, WP automatically replaces it.

- Start the Spell Checker.

Grammar-As-You-Go

Grammar-As-You-Go is similar to Spell-As-You-Go in that it flags potential problems in the document. In addition to spelling errors (still flagged in red), grammatical problems such as incorrect verb tense are flagged with a wavy blue underline. If you right-click the flagged word, the pop-up menu indicates the category of the problem, such as Capitalization or Tense Shift, and offers suggestions for fixing the error. You can select a correction, tell WP to skip that particular occurrence, or start Grammatik.

Prompt-As-You-Go

Prompt-As-You-Go is a tool that displays on the default Property Bar:

Prompt-As-You-Go text
box and drop-down list

It can serve as a dictionary, usage guide, or thesaurus, depending on the current word in the document. Generally, the Prompt-As-You-Go text box displays the word that the insertion point is currently located in. (For many smaller words, Prompt-As-You-Go doesn't offer any suggestions, so the text box is blank.) The color of the word in the text box indicates the type of information being offered.

If the Prompt-As-You-Go text box shows the word in red, that indicates the current word is not recognized by WP's Spell Checker dictionaries. This feature works even if you have Spell-As-You-Go turned off. If the spelling needs to be corrected, select the correct spelling from the words suggested on the drop-down list.

If the word in the text box is blue, that indicates a grammatical problem. The drop-down list then offers replacement suggestions to correct the problem. If the word appears in black, then there are no spelling or grammar errors. Rather, the Prompt-As-You-Go drop-down list offers synonym suggestions from the Thesaurus. This is a speedy tool for diversifying the vocabulary in your document.

```
brochure                  ▼
brochure
booklet
folder
leaflet
pamphlet
```

Summary

WP is loaded with shortcuts for getting your work done faster. The "Quick" features take care of much of your document formatting for you. With features like QuickCorrect and the Proofreading tools, your common mistakes are flagged and corrected for you as you type in your document. QuickWords and QuickCorrect let you expand abbreviations into longer text and—in the case of QuickWords—into completely formatted sections of your document. The QuickLinks feature helps you link your documents to the Internet.

In Chapter 4, you'll learn some more shortcuts and neat tips and tricks for a host of WordPerfect features that help you create and format better documents.

Chapter

4

Tips, Tricks, and Traps

If there's one thing we've learned about WordPerfect users over the years, it's that they *love* tips—can't get enough of 'em. And for good reason, too. Tips highlight all the shortcuts and "hidden" aspects of a program that can help you work even faster and easier. The more tips you know, it seems, the better off you are.

The good news is that WordPerfect 8 is loaded with so many features, the tips are practically endless. The bad news is that because there are so many features and tips, it's impossible to cover them all in depth. We've devoted chapters to the major features such as tables, graphics, templates, merge, and macros. But that doesn't mean the minor features don't also have great tips associated with them. That's why this chapter was included—to give you some power tips for those features that aren't covered elsewhere, such as headers/footers, footnotes/endnotes, and Spell Checker.

We've grouped the features covered in this chapter into three sections: document elements, such as headers/footers, columns, and footnotes/endnotes; document formatting features, such as fonts, tabs, and special characters; and document tools, such as Spell Checker, Reveal Codes, and Find and Replace. We figure that if you're reading this book, you probably already know *how* to use these features, so we won't be covering the basic steps of creating a header, for example. Instead, you'll find an assortment of tips and tricks, along with a few traps to watch out for.

Document Elements

WordPerfect documents often contain several different "elements," or sections other than the main body text. For example, you can add headers, page numbers, and footnotes to your documents. In this section we'll cover four of these elements: headers/footers, columns, footnotes/endnotes, and page numbers. For each, you'll learn a few tips for getting the most out of that feature, some tricks to try that you might not have thought of before, and some traps to watch out for.

Headers and Footers

Headers and footers allow you to place information at the top or bottom of your documents. You only need to type the header or footer once and it automatically

appears on each page. You can create headers and footers by choosing Insert |
Header/Footer. Here are some tips, tricks, and traps for using headers and footers.

Header/Footer Tips

As you're working with headers and footers, you can save time with these useful
tips and shortcuts:

- If you want the header or footer to appear on all the pages in your
  document *except* the first page, use the Suppress feature to suppress
  the header/footer on the first page. Or you can create the header/footer
  in a Delay Code on the first page so it won't go into effect until the
  second page.

- If you want the header or footer to appear *only* on the first page, place a
  Header/Footer Discontinue code in a Delay Code (Format | Page | Delay
  Codes) on the first page that will take effect on the second page. This
  ensures that the Header/Footer Discontinue code always goes into effect
  on the second page, no matter what document text is later added or
  deleted. If you place the Header/Footer Discontinue code at the top of the
  second page instead of in a Delay Code, it might later move to a different
  page as the document is edited.

- Headers and footers are created within the top and bottom page margins,
  which means that your document margins are reduced when you create a
  header/footer. To move the header/footer closer to the edge of the page
  and increase the margins for the document text, change the page margins.
  If you want to change the amount of space between the header/footer and
  the document text, edit the header/footer and use the Header/Footer
  Distance button on the Header/Footer Property Bar to specify the amount.

CAUTION: *If you decrease the page margins, make sure that your header or footer doesn't extend into the "unprintable zone," which is an area close to the page edges where laser and inkjet printers can't print. The size of the unprintable zone varies depending on the type of printer. If your header/footer appears in Page view but doesn't print, it's likely that it extends into the unprintable region. Check your printer manual to determine your printer's minimum margin settings.*

- If your document uses columns and you also want the header or footer to appear in columns, you can turn columns on within the header/footer (see Figure 4-1). This allows you to have a separate header/footer for each column (which is useful for parallel columns). If you want the same header/footer to appear with each column, you need to repeat the header/footer text for each column.

- You can edit the header/footer text and only have your changes appear from that page forward in the document. See the "Editing Headers/Footers for Subsequent Pages" Power Tip for step-by-step instructions on doing this.

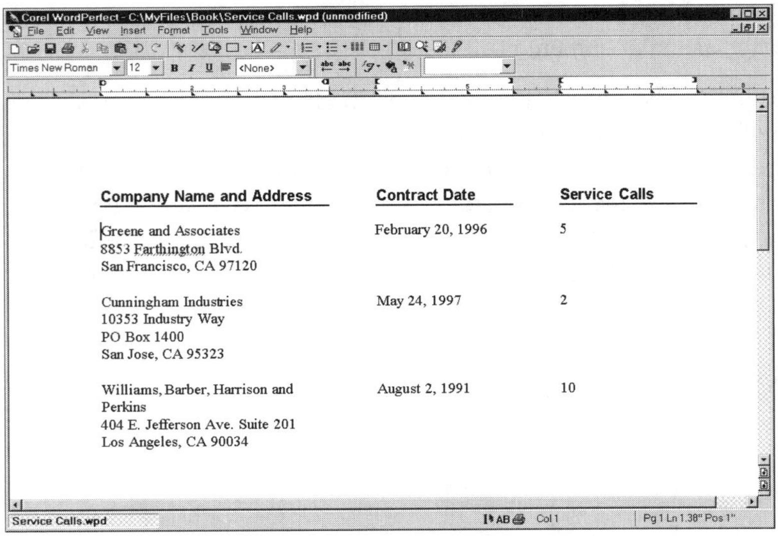

FIGURE 4-1 You can create headers/footers over parallel columns

Power Tip... Editing Headers/Footers for Subsequent Pages

When you edit a header or footer, your changes usually take effect on the first page where that header/footer appears—even if you make the changes by clicking in the header/footer on a page in the middle of your document. That's because WP edits the most recent header/footer *code* in the document, which is often several pages prior to where you make the change. If you want to change a header/footer in the middle of your document, here's a technique you can follow to have the edited header/footer appear only from the current page forward:

1. Place the insertion point on the page where you want the new header/footer to begin.

2. Click the insertion point inside the header/footer text. (If you can't see the header/footer text, choose View | Page.) Make a note of which header or footer you're using, such as Header A, as indicated in the title bar of WP.

3. Select the entire header/footer text by choosing Edit | Select | All. Then press CTRL-C to copy it to the Clipboard.

4. Click the insertion point back in the document text (on the page where you want the new header/footer to start).

5. Now create a new header/footer by choosing Insert | Header/Footer; selecting the *same* header or footer you're already using, such as Header A; and choosing Create.

6. Press CTRL-V to paste in your existing header/footer text. Make any changes you want and click back in the document text when you're finished.

Because you created a new header/footer, your changes appear in the document only from that page forward. Your original header/footer still appears on the previous pages. If you need to make further changes later in the document, simply repeat these steps to create another new header/footer on the page where you want the changes to begin.

Header/Footer Tricks

Don't limit yourself to just including the date or page number in your headers and footers. Here are some great ideas that you might want to try.

- Use headers to quickly create a sheet of duplicate labels. All you need to do is select the label paper size, create a header on the first label, and then insert enough hard page breaks to place the header on the remaining labels.

TIP: *A fast way to insert multiple hard page breaks is with the Repeat feature. Choose Edit | Repeat Next Action; type the number of page breaks you want; and choose OK. Then press CTRL-ENTER, and WP instantly repeats it the number of times you specified.*

- When you're creating a header or footer in a merge form document, don't forget that you can insert field codes into the header or footer to include custom information when the document is merged. For example, in a multiple-page merge form letter, you can create a second-page header that includes a field code for the recipient's name.

- Add a footer to your default document style that includes a path and filename code so this information automatically appears in every new document. See the "How to Automatically Insert the Path and Filename" section for more information.

How to... Automatically Insert the Path and Filename

If you want each document's path and filename appear at the bottom of the page, you can add a footer to your default document style so this information automatically appears in every new document you create. Follow these steps to set this up:

1. Choose File | Document | Current Document Style.

2. From the Styles Editor dialog box, choose Insert | Header/Footer. Select Footer B and choose Create. (Footer B is used so you can still create footers in your documents using Footer A without accidentally replacing the path and filename footer.)

How to... Automatically Insert the Path and Filename (*continued*)

3. Select the Reveal Codes checkbox so you can easily see the codes you're inserting.

4. Choose Format | Font; select the font you want for the path and filename, such as Arial 8-point; and choose OK.

5. If you want the path and filename information to appear flush right, press ALT-F7.

6. Choose Insert | Other | Path and Filename to insert the code that displays the current document's path and filename.

7. Select the Use as Default checkbox, and then choose OK. Choose Yes to apply your style to all new documents.

Now each time you create a new document, its path and filename appear in a footer (after you first save the document). If you want to remove the path and filename from a specific document, place the insertion point at the top and choose Insert | Header/Footer; select Footer B; and choose Discontinue. To permanently remove the path and filename from all new documents, repeat the previous steps to edit the document style and delete the footer code, and then save your changes as the default.

Header/Footer Traps

If you run into problems with your headers and footers, check to see if one of these "traps" is the source of your headaches.

■ The two available headers (Header A and Header B) use the exact same space at the top of the page. Similarly, the two footers (Footer A and Footer B) share the same space at the bottom of the page. If you use both of the headers or footers on every page, the text in them can overlap. When this happens, you can combine the text into the same header/footer, insert a hard return in one of the headers/footers so the text appears on a different line, or format the header/footer text using tabs, spaces, or line justification to avoid overlap.

NOTE: *WP provides two different headers and footers so you can easily create different headers/footers for odd and even pages.*

- Headers and footers use the left and right margins set in the document style. To change the margins for the header/footer text, insert the margin settings in the document style (File | Document | Current Document Style). If you want to use different margins for the document text, set those margins at the top of the document.

- If the font for your headers and footers doesn't match your document text font, set the default document font (File | Document | Default Font). You can still change the font used within the document text by inserting regular font codes.

Columns

The powerful Columns feature in WordPerfect gives you many options for quickly formatting your text in newspaper or parallel columns. Newspaper columns make long lines of text easier to read, and parallel columns group corresponding sections of text into "rows" down the page. Whether your column format is simple or complex, this section will speed up your work by giving you lots of useful tips and tricks and by pinpointing traps that can cause potential problems.

Column Tips

If your document format calls for columns of any type, don't forget these tips:

- The easiest way to turn on columns is with the Columns button on the toolbar. If you want to change the number of columns in your document, place the insertion point where the columns begin and select the new number of columns from the Columns Toolbar button.

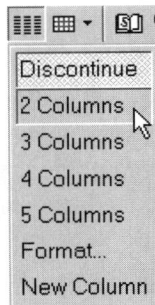

Discontinue
2 Columns
3 Columns
4 Columns
5 Columns
Format...
New Column

■ To add a vertical line between all the columns in your document, choose Border/Fill in the Columns dialog box to display the Column Border/Fill dialog box, and then select the Column Between border line (you may need to scroll down the list):

■ Pressing CTRL-ENTER in columns inserts a column break and moves the text to the next column.

■ You can also create newspaper columns with the Subdivide Page feature (Format | Page | Page Setup | Divide Page). This feature divides your entire document into smaller "pages."

■ Use the Parallel Columns with Block Protect option when you want to make sure that the corresponding columns in each "row" automatically appear together on the same page.

■ You can create headlines that span more than one column (see Figure 4-2) by placing the heading in a text box and positioning the text box across the desired columns. See the Power Tip "Spanning Columns" for more information.

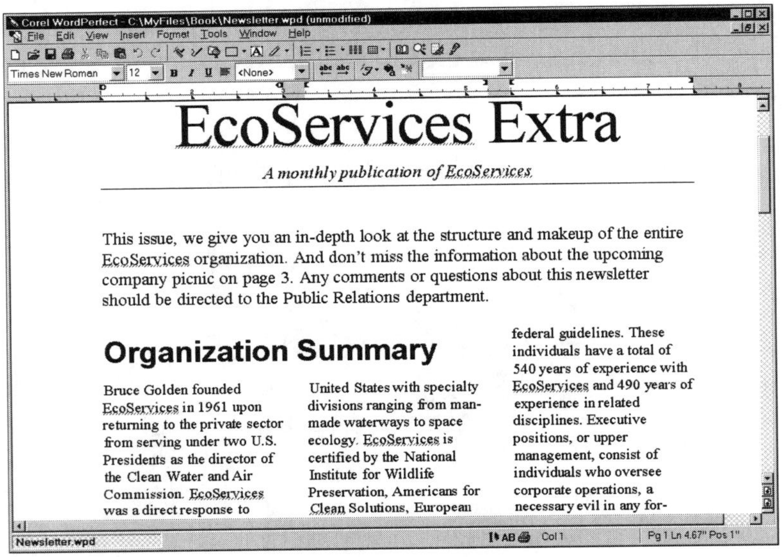

FIGURE 4-2 You can use a text box to span columns with a heading

Column Tricks

Columns can be set up to give you a wide variety of document formats. Here are a few ideas you might not have thought of before.

- If your document uses a narrow table, format it in columns so you can utilize the entire page space (see Figure 4-3).

- Use parallel columns instead of tab and indent codes when you need to format a document with headings in a narrow left column and longer, descriptive paragraphs on the right (such as a résumé).

- If you frequently use a particular column layout with custom column widths and borders, create a style that contains the column definition code. Then you can quickly format a document with your custom column layout by simply selecting the style. (For more information on styles, see Chapter 5.)

Power Tip▸▸▸ Spanning Columns

Follow these steps to have a heading span two or more columns in a document (see Figure 4-2):

1. Format the columns in your document as you normally would.

2. Choose Insert | Text Box. Type and format the heading text, selecting a larger font if desired. Click outside the text box in the document when you're finished.

3. Right-click the text box and choose Position. From the Attach Box To drop-down list, select Page.

4. From the Horizontal drop-down list, select Left Column.

5. In the Across Columns text boxes, specify which columns you want the text box to span, such as 1 to 3, or 2 to 4.

6. Choose OK.

7. Right-click the text box again and choose Size. To have the text box fill the entire width of the columns you specified, select Full for the Width and choose OK.

8. To change or remove the border line, right-click the text box and choose Border/Fill; then select the border option you want from the Available Border Styles list box and choose OK. To remove the border, click the blank option in the upper-left corner.

Column Traps

As with any feature in WordPerfect, there's always a chance that your columns won't turn out quite the way you expected. Here are a few known trouble spots:

- If you've selected balanced newspaper columns and your columns don't appear to be balanced correctly, make sure you don't have any extra hard returns at the bottom of the last column. Also, make sure you don't have any hard column breaks or block protect codes within the column text.

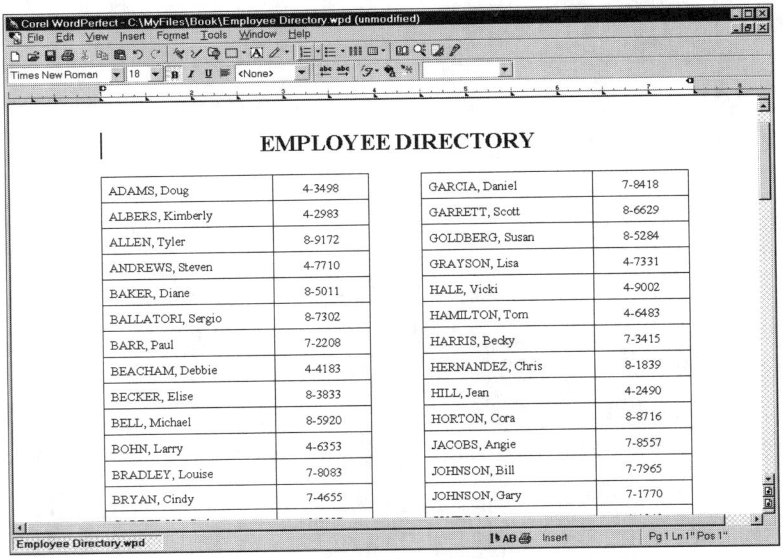

EMPLOYEE DIRECTORY

ADAMS, Doug	4-3498	GARCIA, Daniel	7-8418
ALBERS, Kimberly	4-2983	GARRETT, Scott	8-6629
ALLEN, Tyler	8-9172	GOLDBERG, Susan	8-5284
ANDREWS, Steven	4-7710	GRAYSON, Lisa	4-7331
BAKER, Diane	8-5011	HALE, Vicki	4-9002
BALLATORI, Sergio	8-7302	HAMILTON, Tom	4-6483
BARR, Paul	7-2208	HARRIS, Becky	7-3415
BEACHAM, Debbie	4-4183	HERNANDEZ, Chris	8-1839
BECKER, Elise	8-3833	HILL, Jean	4-2490
BELL, Michael	8-5920	HORTON, Cora	8-8716
BOHN, Larry	4-6353	JACOBS, Angie	7-8557
BRADLEY, Louise	7-8083	JOHNSON, Bill	7-7965
BRYAN, Cindy	7-4655	JOHNSON, Gary	7-1770

FIGURE 4-3 By formating narrow tables in columns, you can utilize the entire page space

- If your columns use full justification and you manually insert a column break in the middle of a paragraph, the last line before the column break is no longer fully justified. Since this line is in the middle of a paragraph, you might want to justify this line. To do this, place the insertion point at the beginning of the line and choose Format | Justification | All. Then select full justification again at the top of the next column.

CAUTION: *If you forget to reselect full justification at the top of the next column, the last line of each paragraph from that point forward will be fully justified, even though it ends with a hard return.*

- When you add vertical lines to your columns with the "Column Between" border option and then insert a text box in the center of the columns, the line runs through the text box. To avoid this, format the text box with a 100 percent white fill. (For more information on graphics, see Chapter 7.) When you're ready to print the document, choose File | Print; select the Details tab; and choose Print Text as Graphics. Set any other options you want and choose Print.

Footnotes and Endnotes

When you need to insert extraneous information or cite references in your documents, take advantage of the Footnote and Endnote features. Footnotes appear at the bottom of the page they're referenced on and endnotes appear at the end of the document. Take special note of the following tips, tricks, and traps.

Footnote/Endnote Tips

The Footnote and Endnote features have lots of options for formatting the footnote/endnote text—as well as the reference—just the way you need. Here are a few tips to make your footnote/endnote work easier:

- You can change or completely remove the separator line that appears above footnotes at the bottom of the page. Choose Insert | Footnote/Endnote; then from the Options pop-down button, choose Separator. Set the options you want, such as changing the line position or length. To remove the line, click the Line Style pop-up button and select the "X" option.

- If you want to insert endnotes at a location other than the end of the document, such as at the end of each section, use an endnote placement code. Place the insertion point where you want the endnotes to appear and choose Insert | Footnote/Endnote. Select Endnote Number, and choose Endnote Placement. If you want the endnote numbering to start over for the next document section, select Insert Endnotes at Insertion Point and Restart Numbering, choose OK, and then choose Close.

- You can change the formatting used for the footnote/endnote reference within the document text, as well as for the actual footnote/endnote text itself by editing the footnote/endnote styles. Choose Insert | Footnote/Endnote. From the Options pop-down button, choose Advanced. Choose In Text to change the formatting used for the reference in the document text, or choose In Note to change the formatting used for the actual footnote/endnote text. Make the changes you want in the Styles Editor dialog box, and choose OK when you're finished. (For more information on editing styles, see Chapter 5.)

CAUTION: *When you're editing a footnote/endnote style, be careful that you don't delete the [Footnote Num Disp] or [Endnote Num Disp] code in the Contents dialog box (unless you want to completely remove the* *footnote/endnote number). If you do accidentally delete this code, press CTRL-Z to undo the deletion. If you want to use this code in another style, you can copy it to the Clipboard, and then paste it in the new style.*

Footnote/Endnote Tricks

Whether you utilize footnotes and endnotes in your documents twice a week or twice a year, the following tricks should come in handy:

- WordPerfect comes with two macros to convert footnotes to endnotes and vice versa. To use these macros, choose Tools | Macro | Play. If you want to convert all the footnotes in your document to endnotes, select the FOOTEND.WCM macro. To convert endnotes to footnotes, select the ENDFOOT.WCM macro instead. Choose Play, and WP goes to work.

- If you need to refer to a footnote/endnote more than once in a document, you can simply insert a superscripted number in the document text for each additional reference. However, in order to have all the references automatically update if footnotes/endnotes are later added or deleted, you need to use the Cross-Reference feature. See the Power Tip "Referencing Existing Footnotes or Endnotes" for the steps on how to do this.

Power Tip... Referencing Existing Footnotes or Endnotes

If you refer to a footnote or endnote more than once in a document and want each reference to automatically update as footnotes/endnotes are added or deleted, you need to use the Cross-Reference feature. After inserting the first footnote or endnote as you normally would, follow these steps to insert any additional references:

1. Click the insertion point in the footnote or endnote text that you want to reference more than once. If you can't see the footnote or endnote text, choose View | Page.

2. Press HOME to place the insertion point just after the footnote/endnote number.

3. Choose Tools | Reference | Cross-Reference to display the Cross-Reference Property Bar.

4. In the Target text box, type an identifying name for this footnote/endnote, such as **SmithRef**.

5. Choose Mark Target on the Property Bar.

6. Click back in the document text and place the insertion point where you want to insert the second reference number.

7. Choose Format | Font. From the Position drop-down list, choose Superscript and choose OK.

8. From the Reference drop-down list on the Cross-Reference Property Bar, choose Footnote or Endnote, depending on which you're using.

9. From the Target drop-down list, select the target name for the footnote/endnote you want to refer to, such as SmithRef. Choose Mark Reference.

10. A superscripted question mark appears in the document. Press RIGHT ARROW to move outside the superscript code.

11. To generate the cross-reference so the correct footnote/endnote number appears, choose Generate on the Cross-Reference Property Bar, and then choose OK.

Repeat Steps 6–11 to insert additional references to the same footnote/endnote. You can insert multiple references to other footnotes/endnotes by repeating the entire sequence. When you're finished, choose Close on the Cross-Reference Property Bar. If footnotes/endnotes are later added or deleted, generate the document again so the cross-references are updated by choosing Tools | Reference | Generate | OK. For more information on the Cross-Reference feature, see Chapter 9.

Footnote/Endnote Traps

Here are a few troubleshooting suggestions to help you avoid potential problems as you're working with footnotes and endnotes:

- If your footnotes don't use the same font as your document text (and you want them to), choose File | Document | Default Font, and select the new font. You can still change the font within the document text as you normally would.

- If you need to change the left and right margins used by the footnotes/endnotes, choose File | Document | Current Document Style. Set the new margins in the Styles Editor dialog box and choose OK. Your document will also use these left and right margins, unless you insert new margin codes in the document text.

- If you accidentally delete the footnote/endnote number while typing the footnote/endnote text, you can insert it again by clicking the Note Number button on the Footnote/Endnote Property Bar.

Page Numbers

Page numbers are an important part of any document—they help you know where you are, and they also help keep your document in the right order. If you decide to insert them in your documents, you have several choices for how and where they display. As usual, we'll give you a few tips, tricks, and traps for working with page numbers.

Page Number Tips

Knowing a few page number tips can help you format your documents the way you like faster and easier. Here are some tips to get you started:

- Your documents can contain several different types of page numbers, such as Roman numerals for the initial pages and then regular numbers for the remaining pages. You can even "number" your pages with upper or lowercase letters. And don't forget that you can restart the page numbering at any time by inserting a new page number code.

- If you want the page number included in a header or footer, use the Page Numbering button on the Header/Footer Property Bar. There's even an option on this button to insert the total number of pages, so you can create "Page X of Y" numbering in your headers and footers.

- The first page of a document or chapter often requires the page number to appear in the bottom center, while the numbers on the remaining pages are in a different location. To easily do this, select the page number position for the majority of the pages, and then place the insertion point on the page where you want the number to appear in the bottom center. Choose Format | Page | Suppress; select Print Page Number at Bottom Center on Current Page; and choose OK.

- You can insert a code anywhere on a page that displays the current page number within the text by choosing Format | Page | Insert Page Number | Insert, and then Close.

- Page numbers use the default document font, but you can also select a different font by choosing Format | Page | Numbering | Font.

NOTE: *Changing the font in the Page Numbering Font dialog box affects only page numbers inserted with the Page Numbering feature. Any page numbers inserted directly into the document text or in a header or footer won't use this font.*

Page Number Tricks

Don't miss these neat ideas for using page numbers:

- Use the Page Numbering feature to give you a third header or footer. For example, if you're using Header A on odd pages and Header B on even pages, but want certain text to appear on the top of *every* page, you can insert it with the Page Numbering feature. To do this, create a custom format (Format | Page | Numbering | Custom Format), delete the actual page number code, and type the text you want.

NOTE: *Text that's included in a custom page number format can only be formatted with the page number font and font size.*

- If your document contains a page formatted with a landscape paper size, the page number position changes to correspond with the landscape orientation. If you want the page number to stay in the same location as it is on the portrait pages, you can do one of two things. First, you can place the text or table in a rotated graphics box and leave the paper size set to portrait. Or you can place the page number in a rotated graphics box so it appears in the correct location. The On the CD section explains how to use a macro to create rotated page numbers.

On the CD▸▸▸ Rotated Page Numbers

In longer documents and reports, you might find a landscape page or two scattered throughout the document. Often, the page number on these landscape pages should appear in the same location as it does on the portrait pages. But the Page Numbering feature moves the page number to correspond with the landscape orientation. One solution to this problem is to place the page number in a rotated graphics box.

The companion CD contains a macro called ROTATE PAGE NUMBER.WCM that automates the process of creating portrait page numbers on landscape pages. The macro removes the page number from the landscape page and inserts it in a rotated graphics box so it appears in the same location as the portrait pages. To use this macro, make sure page numbering is defined and turned on, place the insertion point on the landscape page, and choose Tools | Macro | Play. Select the ROTATE PAGE NUMBER.WCM macro and choose Play.

Page Number Traps

If your page numbers aren't behaving the way you want them to, check to see if one of these troubleshooting tips will solve your problem.

- If you turn on page numbering in a multiple-page merge form document, make sure you insert a page number one code at the top of the merge form file. Otherwise, when you merge, the page numbering won't start over with each new record. To insert a new page number code, place the insertion point at the top of the merge form document and choose Format | Page | Numbering. Choose Set Value, type **1** in the Set Page Number text box, and choose OK twice.

- Page numbers share the same document space as headers and footers. If your document has a header or footer and you also want the page numbers to display at the top or bottom of each page, insert the page number code and formatting *within* the header or footer instead of with the Page Numbering feature. You can insert page number codes by using the Page Numbering button on the Header/Footer Property Bar.

Document Formatting

One of the foundations of WordPerfect is the ability to format and change the look of your document text. Some of the simplest ways to do this include inserting tab settings, changing the font, and utilizing special characters. In this section, you'll learn some tips for accessing the more powerful aspects of these basic formatting features.

Tabs and Dot Leaders

Tabs could probably be considered one of the original document-formatting tools. Tabs are used to position text at a specific location on a line. They've come a long way from the days of typewriters, as these tips show.

- If you want to insert text at a specific tab stop, you don't need to press the TAB key to get there. WP 8's new Shadow Cursor feature lets you simply click the insertion point on the line where you want to begin typing, and WP automatically inserts the correct number of tabs for you. To use the shadow cursor, move the insertion point over a blank area of the document. The shadow cursor jumps between each tab stop on the line, indicating what type of tab will be used there. When the shadow cursor appears where you want to begin typing, just click the mouse button. Remember that the shadow cursor can be turned on and off by clicking the Shadow Cursor icon on the Application Bar at the bottom of the screen.

- If you want each paragraph in your document to begin with a tab, you don't need to insert the tabs manually. Instead, use the Paragraph Format feature (Format | Paragraph | Format) to have WP automatically indent the first line of each new paragraph.

- Normally, pressing TAB in a table causes WP to move the insertion point to the next table cell. If you want to insert a tab within a table cell, press CTRL-TAB or Indent (F7).

- While WP lets you create dot leader tabs to any location, there's an easier method for inserting dot leaders to the center of the page or to the right margin. To insert dot leaders to the center of the page, just press Center (SHIFT-F7) *twice*. Similarly, press Flush Right (ALT-F7) twice to insert dot leaders to the right margin.

■   You can change the character used for dot leaders. For example, you can select one of the WP symbols to repeat across the page as a dot leader:

✂ ✂ ✂ ✂ ✂ ✂ ✂ ✂ ✂ ✂ ✂ ✂ ✂ ✂

To change the dot leader character, choose Format | Line | Tab Set. In the Dot Leader Character text box, delete the current character. Then type the new character or press CTRL-W, select the WP symbol you want, and choose Insert and Close. Choose OK and the new dot leader character will be used from that point forward in the document.

■   The easiest way to set and manipulate tabs is on the Ruler (View | Ruler). Right-clicking the lower portion of the Ruler provides a menu for selecting the type of tab to set, as well as other options:

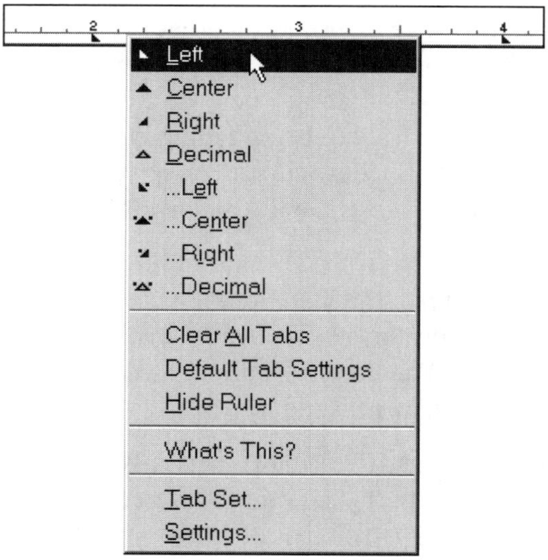

To set a tab on the Ruler, right-click and select the type of tab you want; then click the desired location on the Ruler. You can click and drag tab stops to move them. To move, copy, or delete a group of tabs at the same time, hold down the SHIFT key, and then click and drag over the tab stops. Drag the selected tabs off the Ruler to delete them, and drag them to a new location to move them, or hold down the CTRL key as you drag them to copy them.

■ The Underline Tabs feature is a great way to quickly create horizontal lines in your document, such as "fill-in-the-blank" lines. These lines automatically adjust to new margin settings and move up or down as text is added or deleted (as opposed to remaining in a fixed position on the page). See the Power Tip "Creating Horizontal Lines" for instructions on how to do this.

Power Tip⟩⟩ Creating Horizontal Lines

The Underline Tabs feature gives you a quick and easy method for creating horizontal lines within the text of your document. Here's how it works:

1. Place the insertion point at the top of the document and choose Format | Font.

2. From the Underline drop-down list, choose All, and then choose OK.

3. Now place the insertion point where you want the line to begin. Turn on underline by pressing CTRL-U.

4. If you want the line to extend to the right margin, press Flush Right (ALT-F7). Otherwise, press TAB until the line is the length you want.

5. When the line is the desired length, press CTRL-U again to turn underline off.

Repeat the last three steps to insert additional lines in the document. If you frequently use this feature, you can add the Underline Tabs code to your default document style so it's automatically turned on for each new document, allowing you to skip the first two previous steps. See Chapter 5 for more information on styles.

Fonts and Font Attributes

Another basic formatting tool is the ability to change the font or font attributes of document text. As with tabs, there are lots of font tips and shortcuts for getting maximum results with minimal effort. Here are just a few:

- If you frequently use font attributes such as redline, small caps, and superscript, one of the fastest ways to select them is by adding a Font Attributes button to your Property Bar or toolbar. To add this button, right-click the Property Bar or toolbar and choose Edit. From the Feature Categories drop-down list, select Format. In the Features list box, select Font Attributes and choose Add Button, and then OK. Now, when you want to use a font attribute, just click the font attribute button and select the attribute you want. (For more information on customizing toolbars, see Chapter 13.)

- If you want to change the font, font size, or font attributes of a single word in the document, you don't need to select the word first. Instead, just place the insertion point anywhere within the word and select the new font or font attribute. For example, press CTRL-B and the entire word is bolded, or choose a new font or font size from the Property Bar.

- Changing text that's formatted with one font attribute so it uses another doesn't have to be a huge chore. For example, if you want to change all the underlined text in your document to use italics, you don't have to manually search through the document. The REPLACE ATTRIBUTES.WCM macro included on the companion CD automates this process for you. See the On the CD section for more information.

- There are times when you might want to reduce the amount of space between letter pairs in a word, especially when you're working with larger fonts. You can change the amount of space between pairs of letters with manual kerning (Format | Typesetting | Manual Kerning), or you can change the spacing between all letters in a word with the Word/Letter Spacing feature (Format | Typesetting | Word/Letter Spacing). For example, in Figure 4-4, the top word was typed normally in a 72-point font. The middle word uses manual kerning of –0.1" between the "W" and "o," and –0.05" between the "P" and the "e." In the bottom example, the entire word was formatted with 90 percent of letter spacing.

On the CD... Find and Replace Font Attributes

Searching for text formatted in one font attribute, such as underline, and formatting it with a different attribute instead, such as italics, is easy with the help of the REPLACE ATTRIBUTES.WCM macro on the companion CD. This macro quickly searches through your document and replaces one or more font attributes with other selected font attributes. You're also given the options of starting the search at the location of the insertion point instead of the top of the document, and adding the new font attribute to the text (instead of replacing), so the original attribute also remains in place.

To use this macro, choose Tools | Macro | Play. Select the REPLACE ATTRIBUTES.WCM macro and choose Play. When the Replace Attributes dialog box appears, make the selections you want. Choose OK and the macro makes the changes to the document.

■ If your printer has built-in fonts, you can select which TrueType or ATM fonts are displayed in WordPerfect when that printer font is selected. To do this, choose Format | Font | Font Map, and select the Display tab. From the Printer Font Face drop-down list, select the printer font you want to configure. From the Display Font Face drop-down list, select the desired graphical font. Choose OK twice when you're finished.

Special Characters

One way you can easily enhance your documents is by adding special characters and symbols. WP comes with 15 symbol sets that contain hundreds of different characters you can insert into your documents. These symbols are accessed by pressing CTRL-W or by choosing Insert | Symbol. Here are a few tips for using these symbols, as well as creating new ones of your own.

FIGURE 4-4 The middle word uses manual kerning and the bottom word uses automatic letter to reduce the space between letters

NOTE: *If the symbols appear as hollow squares when you insert them, it indicates that the WP symbol fonts have not been correctly installed. To reinstall the symbol fonts, run the Corel WordPerfect Suite 8 Setup. Follow the prompts to perform a custom installation, and then deselect all of the options. Select Required Components in the list and choose Components; then select Perfect Fit and choose Components. Select Symbol Fonts and choose OK twice. Choose Next to continue with the installation.*

■ WP symbols can be formatted with font size codes. By selecting a large font size, such as 100 points, the symbols can be used as simple graphics images (see Figure 4-5). If you format symbols with very large fonts, it's a good idea to place them in a text box so they can be more easily positioned within the document text.

■ Each time you start WordPerfect, the default symbol set displayed when you press CTRL-W is Iconic Symbols. By assigning a short macro to the CTRL-W keystroke, you can have WP display a different symbol set. See the "How to Change the Default Symbol Set" section for more information.

■ If the symbol sets don't contain the exact symbol you need, you can try creating it yourself with the Overstrike feature. For example, you can use Overstrike to create a zero with a slash through it. Choose Format | Typesetting | Overstrike. In the Overstrike Characters text box, type the two characters you want WP to overlay on each other, such as **0/**. You can select characters from the symbol sets by pressing CTRL-W and selecting the symbol you want. Choose OK when you're finished.

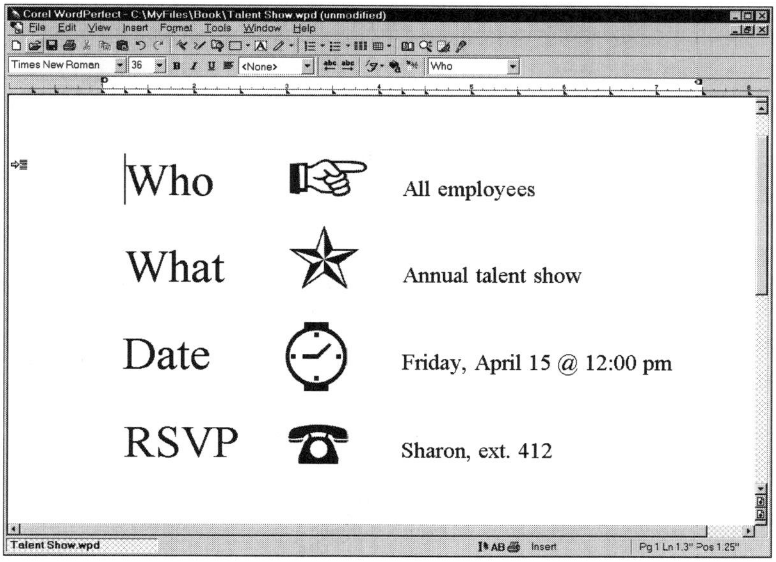

FIGURE 4-5 Symbols can be used as simple graphics when they're formatted with large fonts

TIP: *You can use the drop-down menu to the right of the Overstrike Characters text box to format the characters with font attributes such as bold, very large, and superscript.*

How to... Change the Default Symbol Set

When you press CTRL-W to display the Symbols dialog box, the Iconic Symbols set displays by default, unless you've already selected a different set during the current session of WordPerfect. If you want to change the symbol set that displays by default, you can assign a short macro to the CTRL-W keystroke. Then, each time you press CTRL-W, your favorite symbol set is displayed.

The companion CD contains a macro called SYMBOL SET.WCM that is used in conjunction with the following steps to change the default symbol set. You need to copy the SYMBOL SET.WCM macro from the CD into your default macros directory so you can edit it (usually \Corel\Suite8\Macros\WPWin). Then follow these steps:

1. Choose Tools | Macro | Edit. Select the SYMBOL SET.WCM macro and choose Edit to open the macro. This macro contains three short lines.

2. On the first line of the macro, change the number assigned to the vSetNum variable to match the number of the set you want to use as the default. The following table shows which set the numbers correspond with:

Set Number	Symbol Set
0	ASCII
1	Multinational
2	Phonetic
3	Box Drawing
4	Typographic
5	Iconic
6	Math/Scientific
7	Math/Scientific Extended
8	Greek
9	Hebrew
10	Cyrillic

How to... Change the Default Symbol Set (*continued*)

Set Number	Symbol Set
11	Japanese
12	User-Defined
13	Arabic
14	Arabic Script

For example, if you want the default symbol set to be the Greek characters, change the first line of the macro so it looks like this:

```
vSetNum:=8
```

3. When you've made the change, choose Save & Compile on the Macro toolbar; then choose File | Close.

4. Now you're ready to assign this macro to the CTRL-W keystroke. Choose Tools | Settings; and double-click Customize.

5. Select the Keyboards tab. If you've already created a custom keyboard, select it and choose Edit. Otherwise, choose Create; type a name for your keyboard, such as **custom**; and choose OK.

6. In the list of keystrokes, select W+ CTRL. Choose Remove Assignment to delete the current Insert Symbol assignment.

7. Select the Macros tab, and then choose Assign Macro to Key. Select the SYMBOL SET.WCM macro and choose Select. Choose Yes to save the macro with the full path.

8. Choose OK, and then choose Select. Choose Close twice.

Now, each time you press CTRL-W, the Symbols dialog box appears and automatically displays your favorite symbol set. (For more information on creating custom keyboards, see Chapter 13.)

Document Tools

WordPerfect offers many tools that make creating and editing your documents as effortless as possible. Tools such as the Spell Checker help ensure that your documents are professional and error free. Find and Replace, Reveal Codes, and shortcut keystrokes give you the ability to edit and troubleshoot your documents as quickly as possible. This section will give you some helpful tips for using these powerful tools.

Spell Checker

The Spell Checker used by WordPerfect is actually a separate utility that's also used by the other WP Suite programs. There are many ways you can customize the Spell Checker and push its capabilities to the limits—here are just a few ideas:

- If you accidentally add a misspelled word during a spell check, you can edit your user word list (supplementary dictionary) and delete the incorrect word. To do this, go to a blank document window and choose Tools | Spell Check. Choose No to keep the Spell Checker open. From the Options pop-down button, choose User Word Lists. In the list at the bottom of the dialog box, select the incorrect entry and choose Delete Entry. Choose Yes to confirm the deletion. Repeat this to delete any other incorrect words. When you're finished, choose Close twice.

- You can customize the Spell Checker so it suggests certain replacement alternatives for a specific word during a spell check. For example, whenever your document contains "usa," you can set up the Spell Checker to give you the replacement suggestions of "United States of America," "United States," and "U.S.A." (see Figure 4-6). To set up replacement alternatives, go to a blank document window, choose Tools | Spell Check, and then choose No. From the Options pop-down button, choose User Word Lists. In the Word/Phrase text box, type the word you want the Spell Checker to flag, such as **usa**. In the Replace With text box, type the first replacement suggestion, such as **United States of America**, and choose Add Entry. Repeat this to add another entry with the same original word and the next replacement suggestion. When you're finished, choose Close twice.

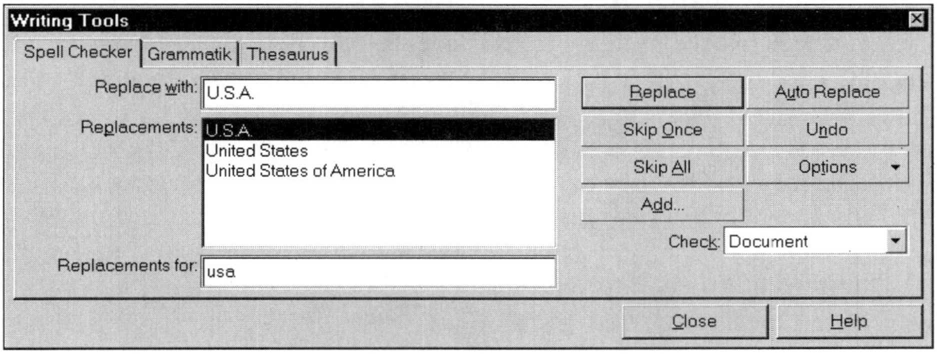

FIGURE 4-6 You can customize the Spell Checker with replacement alternatives for certain words

NOTE: *If you only enter one replacement suggestion for a word, the QuickCorrect feature (which shares the same user word list as the Spell Checker) automatically corrects the word as soon as you type it in a document. If you have QuickCorrect turned off, the Spell Checker will then flag the word during a spell check and offer the replacement suggestion you entered.*

- If a portion of your document contains foreign words or technical words that aren't in the Spell Checker's dictionary, you can have WP completely skip that section during a spell check. This saves you from having to skip over each unrecognized word. To do this, select the text that you want to skip, and choose Tools | Language | Settings. Select Disable Writing Tools, and choose OK.

- If you need to spell check your documents in another language, you can purchase the Corel Language Module, which contains dictionaries for many different languages. Then tell WP to use that dictionary by going to a blank document window and choosing Tools | Spell Check | No. From the Options pop-down button, choose Main Word Lists. Choose Add, select the filename for the new dictionary file (MOR file) and choose Open; then choose Close twice.

Find and Replace

When you need to hunt through your documents for a specific word or code, WP's Find and Replace feature makes short work of what otherwise would be a long, tedious task. Don't miss these great Find and Replace tips:

- Use Find and Replace to quickly delete certain codes or text from a document in one step, such as removing all the graphics boxes from a document. See the Power Tip "Removing All Graphics Boxes" for more information on how to do this.

Power Tip... Removing All Graphics Boxes

WP's powerful Find and Replace feature lets you delete certain codes or text from a document in one easy step. For example, you can remove all the graphics boxes in a document. Follow these steps:

1. Press CTRL-HOME *twice* to place the insertion point at the top of the document before all codes.

2. Choose Edit | Find and Replace.

3. Choose Match | Codes. Select the code you want to remove, such as Box (all) to remove any type of graphics box, and choose Insert and Close. If you want to delete text from the document, type that text in the Find text box.

4. Make sure the Replace With text box is blank (or shows <Nothing>). Choose Replace All to remove the text or codes.

5. WP tells you how many occurrences of the box or code were removed from the document. Choose OK; then choose Close.

■ The Find and Replace feature can quickly locate text that's formatted with a specific font or font size. For example, you can locate the word "WordPerfect" only when it appears in an Arial 14-point italic font. Any other occurrences of "WordPerfect" in the document would be ignored during the Find and Replace. To do this, choose Edit I Find and Replace, and type the text you want to search for. Choose Match I Font; select the font options you want to match; and then choose OK and continue with the find and replace.

TIP: *You can also specify the font, font size, and font attributes that are used for the replacement text by typing the text in the Replace With text box and choosing Replace I Font, and then selecting the replacement font options.*

■ If you want WP to select the text from the location of the insertion point to a specific word or phrase, choose Edit I Find and Replace. In the Find text box, type the word or phrase you want the selection to extend to in the document. Then choose Action I Extend Selection. Choose Find Next to have WP select from the current location up to and including the word you're searching for.

NOTE: *If you have the Begin Find at Top of Document option selected in the Find and Replace dialog box, WP always selects text from the beginning of the document to the first occurrence of the word.*

Reveal Codes

One of WordPerfect's signature power tools is Reveal Codes, which lets you look behind the scenes at your document's formatting. If you're a Reveal Codes user, don't forget these helpful tips:

■ You can change the window size of the Reveal Codes window for the current document by simply dragging the divider line. If you want to change the default window size used by Reveal Codes, turn Reveal Codes on by choosing View I Reveal Codes. Then right-click in the Reveal Codes window and choose Settings. In the Window Size text box, type the percentage of your document screen that you want Reveal Codes to occupy and choose OK.

NOTE: *The Display Settings dialog box also lets you select such things as the Reveal Codes colors, font, and whether or not the codes display in detail all the time.*

- To delete codes from a document, all you need to do is drag them out of the Reveal Codes window.

- You can edit many codes by simply double-clicking the code in the Reveal Codes window. When you do this, the corresponding dialog box appears where you can make any changes. For example, you can double-click margin codes, Advance codes, font codes, and so on. This is often the fastest way to get to a specific dialog box for making changes.

Shortcut Keystrokes

If you like to keep your hands on the keyboard and avoid reaching for the mouse unless absolutely necessary, then WordPerfect's shortcut keystrokes are for you. WP has many keystrokes set up to make navigating through your documents easier. Plus, you can create your own custom keyboards to map those shortcuts and features you use most often. (See Chapter 13 for more information on creating keyboards.)

Here are a few of our favorite shortcut keystrokes for navigating and editing documents:

- To quickly select text with the keyboard, hold down the SHIFT key and use the arrow keys or other positioning keys (such as HOME or END) to select the text you want.

- Press CTRL-BACKSPACE to delete the current word.

- Press CTRL-RIGHT ARROW to move a word to the right, or press CTRL-LEFT ARROW to move a word to the left.

- To move to the top of the next page in the document, press ALT-PAGE DOWN. Similarly, press ALT-PAGE UP to move to the top of the previous page.

- To move down one screen, press PAGE DOWN. To move up one screen, press PAGE UP.

Summary

This chapter was designed to give you some quick power tips for a few features that we weren't able to cover in depth elsewhere in this book, such as headers/footers, columns, and Spell Checker. Along with tips, we pointed out some common pitfalls and included ideas for using the features in unique ways.

If you're not very familiar with one of the features discussed in this chapter, the best thing you can do is practice! Experiment with the different options and settings and see how they affect your document. Utilize WP's excellent online help if you need additional information, or check out the extensive support database information on Corel's Web site (www.corel.com). You might be amazed at the complex tasks you can achieve with these seemingly simple features.

In Chapter 5, we'll delve into the Styles feature. You'll learn how to save and reuse your custom formatting so all your documents have a consistent look and feel.

PART II

Power Tools for Formatting Documents

Chapter 5

Easy Formatting with Styles

When it comes to creating documents, we often spend most of our time formatting—adding font codes, setting the line and paragraph spacing, making sure the headings all look the same, and so on. But formatting a document can also be one of your *least* time-consuming chores. When you take advantage of WP's Styles feature, you can shave minutes—even hours—off the time it takes to format documents.

Styles serve an important role in ensuring that your documents have a consistent look and feel. They allow you to set up your custom formatting only once, and then instantly apply that formatting throughout your documents. In this chapter, you'll learn how to create and use the different types of styles in WordPerfect, such as QuickFormat and QuickStyles, including how to chain styles together. You'll also learn how to edit WP's system styles and save your styles so you can use them in other documents.

Styles Overview

Styles can be a confusing concept, especially if you've never worked with them before. Before we delve into the specifics of creating and editing styles, this section will give you a brief overview of what a style is, what kinds of things you can include in a style, and what types of styles WordPerfect uses.

What Is a Style?

Styles can be considered "giant" formatting codes that contain lots of little individual codes. For example, when you format a paragraph with a drop cap, border, and line spacing, three separate codes are inserted in your document. If you create a style with those same three codes and then format the paragraph with the style, the text appears exactly the same and only one code is inserted in your document.

But reducing the number of codes in a document isn't the main advantage of using styles. Styles are especially helpful when it comes to keeping a document's formatting consistent. For example, suppose you have a 150-page document with dozens of section headings formatted in Garamond 14-point and you need to change all those headings to use Futura 16-point instead. Changing each heading individually could take you all day. If you've formatted your headings with a style, however, you can simply edit the style once and all the headings in your document are automatically updated. And because you've used styles, you can be confident that each heading in your document is formatted exactly the same.

Styles are used to format sections of a document, such as paragraphs or headings, as well as entire documents. You can have multiple styles in a document and they can be copied to other documents and templates. Styles are connected so that changing a style automatically updates any document text that's formatted with that style.

Style Contents

While styles are most commonly used to format headings, they can contain much more than basic formatting codes. This unique capability of WordPerfect gives you tremendous control and flexibility. Here are just a few of the things you can include in a style:

- Text (including multiple paragraphs)
- Graphics elements, including clipart, text boxes, graphics lines, and watermarks
- Tables
- Table of Contents and Index codes
- Headers and Footers
- Column definitions
- Sound clips
- Comments

Styles have the potential to format your documents with nearly anything you need.

Types of Styles

WordPerfect uses three basic style types for formatting text: character styles, paragraph styles, and document styles. Each type serves a different purpose (see Figure 5-1).

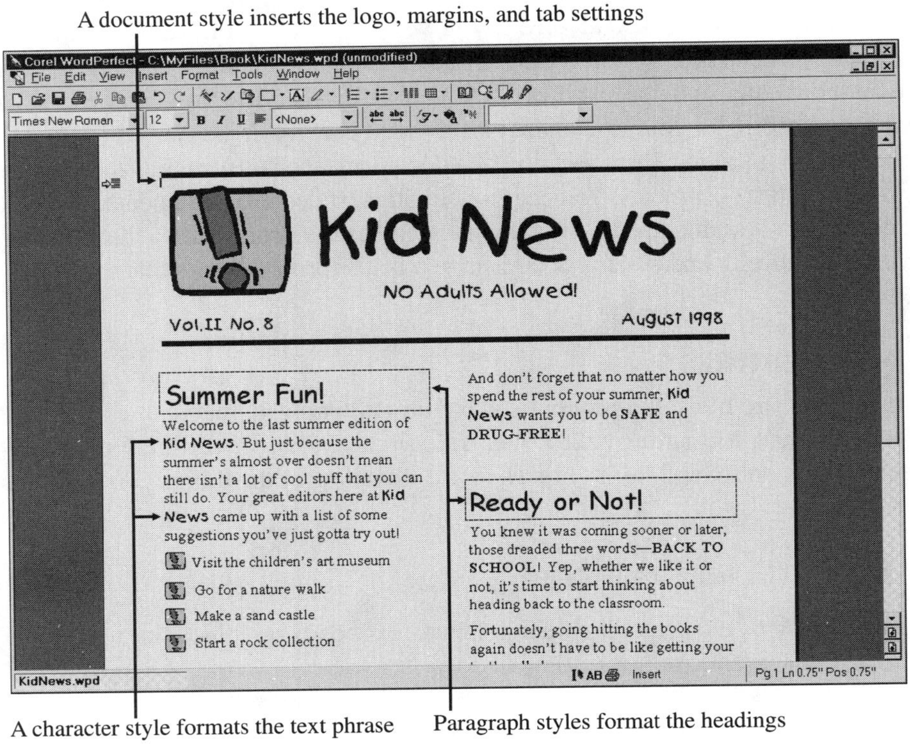

A document style inserts the logo, margins, and tab settings

A character style formats the text phrase   Paragraph styles format the headings

FIGURE 5-1 The three main style types—document, paragraph, and character—each serve a different function

NOTE: *Other types of styles are also used throughout WordPerfect. For example, graphics styles are used to format boxes, borders, lines, and fills. System styles format such things as footnotes, table of contents headings, and more. For more information on graphics styles, see Chapter 7. System styles will be discussed later in this chapter.*

Character Styles

Character styles are used to format any amount of text—from individual characters to multiple paragraphs. Character styles are referred to as "paired" because they have an "on" code and an "off" code. Any text in between the two codes is formatted with the style. Character styles are usually applied by selecting the text you want to format in the document and turning on the style.

Character styles can also be "paired-auto," which means that you can modify the style without having to go through any dialog boxes. For example, when you select text that's formatted with a paired-auto style and make a change right in the document itself, *any* text in the document that's formatted with that same style is automatically updated to use the same formatting.

Paragraph Styles

Like character styles, paragraph styles are paired or paired-auto styles with "on" and "off" codes. One of the main differences from character styles is that paragraph styles automatically format an entire paragraph without requiring it to be selected first. For example, if you place the insertion point anywhere within a paragraph and select a paragraph style, WP automatically places the style codes at the beginning and end of the paragraph.

NOTE: *Paragraphs are any amount of text that ends with a hard return, including single-line headings.*

Document Styles

Document styles are also known as "open" styles. Document styles aren't paired, so only one code gets inserted in your document and the formatting takes effect from that point forward. Document styles are commonly used to insert such settings as margins and page numbering that you want the entire document to use. Document styles can also be used for inserting elements such as text, graphics, and tables.

Creating Styles

Creating a style in WordPerfect 8 is much easier than in earlier versions. The QuickFormat and QuickStyles features automatically create styles for you based on the formatting used in existing text. In addition, you can create custom styles using the Styles Editor dialog box, which gives you more control over what your style contains and how it functions in the document. In this section, you'll learn how to create styles using all three methods—QuickFormat, QuickStyles, and the Styles Editor.

QuickFormat

The QuickFormat feature lets you easily copy the formatting of one section of text to other locations in the same document. QuickFormat creates either a paragraph paired-auto style or a character paired-auto style using the formatting that you've already applied to existing text. For example, if you've formatted a heading in your document a certain way and decide that you want to use that same formatting for the other document headings, you can use QuickFormat to automate the process and link all your headings together.

QuickFormat can copy the font, font size, and font attributes used in existing text, as well as paragraph formatting such as indentation, borders, drop caps, and spacing. Follow these steps to use QuickFormat:

1. If you haven't already, format a paragraph or phrase of text in your document with the formatting you want to copy to other locations.

2. Make sure the text you want to copy the formatting to is already typed in the document.

3. If you want to copy the entire paragraph formatting and create a paragraph style, place the insertion point anywhere within the formatted paragraph. If you want to create a character style and copy only the font, font size, and font attributes, select the formatted text.

4. Choose Format | QuickFormat or click the QuickFormat button.

5. The QuickFormat dialog box appears. Unless the insertion point is in a table, the bottom two options in the dialog box will be unavailable. (For more information on using QuickFormat in tables, see the Power Tip "Using QuickFormat in Tables.")

6. If you selected text first, the Selected Characters option is already selected. Choose OK and the mouse pointer changes to a paintbrush icon. Otherwise, the Headings option is selected to create a paragraph style. Choose OK and the mouse pointer changes to a paint roller icon.

7. If you have a paintbrush icon, click and drag over the new text that you want to copy the formatting to. If you have a paint roller icon, simply click anywhere in the new paragraph and the entire paragraph is updated. Repeat this to format other areas of the document.

8. When you're finished, turn QuickFormat off by choosing Format | QuickFormat or by clicking the QuickFormat icon on the toolbar again.

Power Tip... Using Quick Format in Tables

In addition to copying text formatting, you can use QuickFormat to copy formatting from one table cell to another. QuickFormat copies the cell's border/fill, fonts, font attributes, and other formatting such as justification. You can also copy a table's overall formatting to another table, including the table border/fill and default line style. Follow these steps to use QuickFormat in tables:

1. Format a table cell or entire table with the settings you want to copy. If you're copying an entire table format, the table border and fill must be set by right-clicking the table, choosing Border/Fill, selecting the Table tab, and choosing the options you want.

2. Turn on QuickFormat by right-clicking the table and choosing QuickFormat. You can also click the QuickFormat button on the toolbar or choose Format | QuickFormat. The QuickFormat dialog box displays with all options available.

3. The default selection is Selected Table Cells, which lets you copy the current cell's format to other cells. If you want to copy the entire table format instead, select Table Structure. Choose OK. (The mouse pointer changes to a paint roller icon.)

4. Click in each new table cell that you want to copy the formatting to. To copy the entire table settings, click anywhere in the new table.

5. When you're finished, turn QuickFormat off by right-clicking the table and deselecting QuickFormat, or by clicking the QuickFormat toolbar button again. You can also choose Format | QuickFormat to turn QuickFormat off.

Table cells formatted with QuickFormat are not linked together, so any changes you make to a cell after using QuickFormat are not automatically applied to the other cells.

When you use QuickFormat in document text, a character or paragraph paired-auto style named QuickFormat1 is created around each section of formatted text. If you use QuickFormat again to format other sections of text, the new style is named QuickFormat2, and so on. You can rename the QuickFormat style to use a more descriptive name by choosing Format | Styles, selecting the QuickFormat style, and choosing Edit. Type a new name in the Style Name text box and choose OK, and then Close.

TIP: *If you need to use the same QuickFormat style on a new section of text after turning QuickFormat off, place the insertion point in the new text and select the QuickFormat style from the Styles drop-down list on the Property Bar.*

If you later want to modify the formatting used by QuickFormat, all you have to do is select one of the formatted areas (it doesn't have to be the original section). Make sure you select the entire paragraph or section of formatted text, and then make the changes you want. Each "linked" section in the document is automatically updated to use the new formatting.

If you want to remove the QuickFormat link from any of the formatted sections so the text is no longer updated with the other QuickFormat sections, place the insertion point in that section and choose Format | QuickFormat | Discontinue. Select Current Heading to remove the link from the current section only, or select All Associated Headings to remove the link from every section.

Choose OK. The text is still formatted with a QuickFormat style, but the styles are no longer linked together.

TIP: *If you discontinue the QuickFormat links and later want to update all the formatting, choose Format | Styles, select the QuickFormat style in the list, and choose Edit. Make any changes to the codes in the Styles Editor dialog box, and then choose OK and Close. (For more information on the Styles Editor, see "Using the Styles Editor" later in this chapter.)*

QuickStyles

The QuickStyles feature is very similar to QuickFormat. With QuickStyles, you can have WP automatically create a paired-auto paragraph or character style based on the formatting used in existing text. As with QuickFormat, QuickStyles are linked together so that a change you make in document text formatted with a QuickStyle is automatically applied to the other sections using the same QuickStyle. One difference between QuickStyles and QuickFormat is that you don't need to have the additional text you want to format already typed in your document before creating a QuickStyle.

To create a QuickStyle, follow these steps:

1. Format a section of text in your document with the formatting you want to use in other locations. Just like QuickFormat, QuickStyles will capture the current font, font size, and font attributes, as well as paragraph formatting such as indentation, paragraph borders, drop caps, and spacing.

2. When you're ready to create the style, place the insertion point anywhere within the paragraph. If you want to create a character style and copy only the font, font size, and font attributes, select the text that uses that formatting.

3. If you have the Property Bar displaying, choose QuickStyle from the Styles drop-down list:

Or, choose Format | Styles | QuickStyle. The QuickStyle dialog box appears.

```
QuickStyle                                              [?][X]

Create a style based on the formatting in effect at the insertion
point.

Style name:    [_____]

Description:   [_____]

Style type ─────────────────────────────────────────
    ⦿ Paragraph with automatic update
    ◯ Character with automatic update

           [  OK  ]    [  Cancel  ]    [  Help  ]
```

4. In the Style Name text box, type a name for your style, such as **Main Heading**. In the Description text box, type a description.

5. If you're creating a paragraph style, leave Paragraph With Automatic Update selected. If you selected text in the document and want to create a character style with only the font and font attributes, select Character With Automatic Update.

6. Choose OK. If the Style List dialog box is displaying, choose Apply.

WP creates a new style and applies it to the current paragraph or selected text. Once your style has been created, you can apply it to other sections of your document whenever you need to. To do this, place the insertion point anywhere in the new paragraph if you created a paragraph style, or select the new text if you created a character style. Then, from the Styles drop-down list on the Property Bar, select the style you created. You can also choose Format | Styles, select the style in the list, and choose Apply.

Just like text formatted with the QuickFormat feature, when you modify QuickStyle text in the document by selecting the entire paragraph first (or by selecting the formatted text if it's a character style), each instance of the QuickStyle in the document is automatically updated. You can still modify individual words within the formatted text without affecting the other QuickStyle links by making sure you don't select the entire paragraph or section of text.

If you want to remove the QuickStyle links so text isn't automatically updated, choose Format | Styles. Select your QuickStyle in the list and choose Edit. From the Type drop-down list, select Paragraph (paired) for a paragraph style or Character (paired) for a character style. Choose OK, and Close. The text is still formatted with a style (which can be edited from the Styles Editor), but if you modify text in the document window, the other sections are no longer affected.

NEWSLETTER.WPD: *The companion CD contains a sample document named NEWSLETTER.WPD that uses QuickStyles to format the headings.*

Using the Styles Editor

If you want to have more control over the codes included in your style and how your style behaves in different circumstances, create it with the Styles Editor (see Figure 5-2). The Styles Editor lets you include other elements than just formatting codes in your style; these include as text, graphics, and tables. Plus, you can determine what type of style is used and how the style is turned on and off.

To create a new style with the Styles Editor, choose Format | Styles. From the Style List dialog box, choose Create. In the Style Name text box, type a name for your style, and then type a description in the Description text box. The remaining options in the dialog box are explained in the next sections.

TIP: *Style names are listed alphabetically in the Style List dialog box and on the Styles Property Bar drop-down list. If you want your custom styles to appear at the top of the list, type a space before the style name, or include a character such as an exclamation point or asterisk as the first character, such as !Heading.*

Style Type

The Type drop-down list in the Styles Editor lets you select what type of style you're creating—character, paragraph, or document. Remember that character and paragraph styles format selected text or paragraphs, while document styles insert formatting that affects the document from that point forward. The paragraph and character styles each have two options—paired and paired-auto. Paired styles are the standard style types with "on" and "off" codes. Paired-auto styles are the same ones used by QuickFormat and QuickStyles that allow you to update the styles by simply selecting and changing the text within the document.

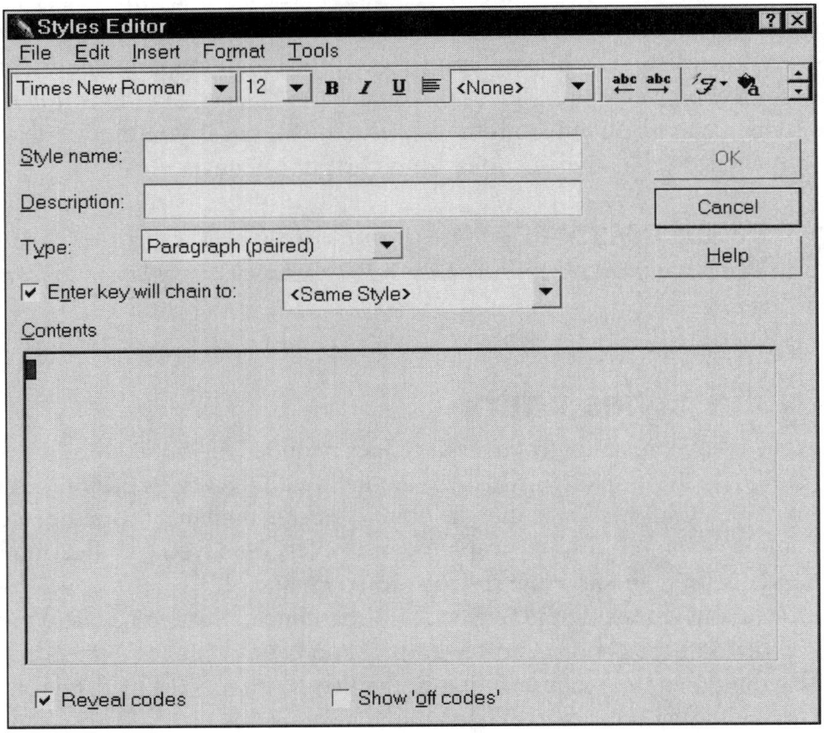

FIGURE 5-2 The Styles Editor dialog box gives you control over your styles

Enter Key Action

If you're creating a paragraph or character style, WP lets you determine how your style will behave when the ENTER key is pressed. (This option isn't available when you're creating a document style.) There are three basic options: the style is simply turned off; the style is turned off and then immediately turned on for the next paragraph; or the style is turned off and a *different* style is turned on for the next paragraph.

The default setting is to have the same style turned on again for the next paragraph. If you want the style to be turned off and not turned on again automatically, select <None> from the Enter Key Will Chain To drop-down list or deselect the Enter Key Will Chain To checkbox. To have a different style turned on when ENTER is pressed, select that style from the Enter Key Will Chain To drop-down list. The second style must already be created before you can select it. (For more information, see the "Chaining Styles" section later in this chapter.)

CAUTION: *If you're creating a character style and select <Same Style> from the Enter Key Will Chain To drop-down list, a hard return will not be inserted into your document when you press ENTER after selecting the style. Instead, pressing ENTER causes the style to be turned off and back on again in the same line of text.*

Contents

The Contents text box of the Styles Editor contains the heart and soul of your style. This is where you insert all the formatting, text, and other codes that you want inserted in the document when the style is turned on. You can insert codes into the Contents text box in several ways:

- Use the pull-down menus at the top of the Styles Editor dialog box to select the formatting you want. For example, choose Format | Paragraph | Border/Fill to select a paragraph border.

- Use the options on the Property Bar displayed in the Styles Editor. For example, select a font from the font drop-down list.

TIP: *The Property Bar is too long to display all at once in the Styles Editor dialog box. To see the rest of the Property Bar, click the down arrow at the right edge of the Property Bar. Click the up arrow to return to the previous display.*

- Press shortcut keystrokes such as CTRL-B to turn on bold or CTRL-SHIFT-D to insert a date code. To insert a tab in the Contents dialog box, press CTRL-TAB or choose Insert | Tab.

- Paste in text or codes that you've copied to the Clipboard from the document screen.

Reveal Codes

The Reveal Codes checkbox at the bottom of the Styles Editor lets you see the codes in your style just as they would appear in Reveal Codes from a document screen. When this checkbox is selected, the codes also behave as they do in Reveal Codes. For example, you can drag a code out of the Contents text box to delete it, you can double-click certain codes to edit them, and if you place the insertion point just before a code, it expands to show you the exact settings it contains.

If you deselect the Reveal Codes checkbox, the Contents text box appears as it would in a regular document, showing you any formatted text or graphics that are included in the style (see Figure 5-3). This makes it easier to format the text, graphics, and tables in the style so they appear correctly when they're later inserted into the document.

NOTE: *Since many styles only contain formatting codes and not text or graphics, deselecting the Reveal Codes checkbox often simply displays a blank screen.*

For example, if your style includes a graphic, you can insert it into the style and then deselect the Reveal Codes checkbox to see the graphics image. From here, you can use your mouse to size or move the image, or you can right-click the image and format it as you would in a regular document. (For more information on formatting graphics, see Chapter 7.)

FIGURE 5-3   Deselecting the Reveal Codes checkbox allows you to see formatted text, tables, and graphics

Off Codes

If you've set up your style to be turned off when the ENTER key is pressed (by selecting <None> from the Enter Key Will Chain To drop-down list), you can also have WP insert specific codes when the style is turned off. To insert these codes, select the Show 'Off Codes' checkbox at the bottom of the Styles Editor. When you select this option, a "comment" code appears in the Contents text box.

Contents

| Font: Arial | Font Size: 14pt | Bold | Right Tab | Answer: | Bold | Hd Left Ind | Font: Times N |

ew Roman | Codes to the left are ON - Codes to the right are OFF |

HRt

☑ Reveal codes   ☑ Show 'off codes'

Comment code separating "on and off" codes

Any codes to the left of the comment code are inserted when the style is turned on. Any codes to the right of the comment are inserted when the style is turned off (at the end of the text formatted with the style). To insert "off" codes, place the insertion point after the comment code in the Contents text box and insert the codes you want. For example, you might press ENTER to insert an extra hard return after the paragraph that's formatted with the style.

NOTE: *Some paired codes, such as bold and italics, won't have their "off" counterpart displayed to the right of the comment code. However, these codes are still turned "off" at the end of the text formatted with the style. Paired codes appear in the Contents text box as a right-pointing arrow, such as the* bold *code.*

Finishing Up

When you're finished setting all the options and codes for your style, choose OK. Your new style should appear in the Style List dialog box. Choose Close to close the Style List dialog box. The "Using Styles" section will show you how to apply your custom style to text in the document.

NOTE: *Custom styles are only saved with the current document in which they were created. If you want to use your style in other documents, be sure to read the "Saving and Retrieving Styles" section later in this chapter.*

Using Styles

Now that you know how to create your own custom styles, you're ready to use them in your documents. Formatting text with a style is a quick and easy process, which is one of the reasons the Styles feature is so useful. In this section, you'll learn the different techniques for turning styles on and off.

When you're ready to turn on a style, you first need to know what type of style you'll be using—character, paragraph, or document—since that determines how you prepare the document. Once you have that information, follow the appropriate preparation steps below:

- *Document Style*   Place the insertion point where you want the formatting changes to begin taking effect, such as at the top of the document.

- *Paragraph Style*   If the paragraph has already been typed in the document, place the insertion point anywhere in the paragraph text. Otherwise, place the insertion point where you want to begin typing the text.

- *Character Style*   If the text has already been typed, select the text you want to format. Otherwise, place the insertion point where you want to begin typing.

Once the insertion point is correctly positioned, you can select the style in one of two ways. First, you can select it from the Styles drop-down list on the Property Bar. This list displays all the available styles in your document, along with an option to create a new QuickStyle.

NOTE: *When the insertion point is in document text that's formatted with a paragraph style, the Styles text box on the Property Bar displays the name of the style currently in use. The current style name also appears in the Application Bar at the bottom of the screen. Only paragraph style names appear—character and document styles do not.*

Second, you can select a style from the Style List dialog box (Figure 5-4) by choosing Format | Styles. This dialog box lists all the available styles in your document, whether or not they're actually being used somewhere in the current document. Select the style you want to use and choose Apply.

TIP: *If you want to see what formatting codes are inserted by a style, turn on Reveal Codes and click the Style code. The code "expands" to show you the formatting codes it contains. If all of the style information doesn't fit in the expanded code, you can double-click the style code to open the style in the Styles Editor dialog box and view its contents.*

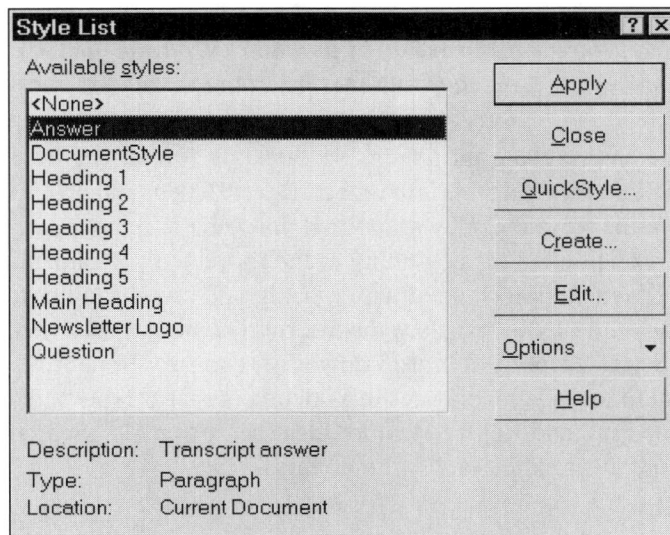

FIGURE 5-4 The Style List dialog box shows the available styles in a document

NOTE: *The DocumentStyle and the five heading styles are part of WordPerfect and automatically appear in every style list. These styles will be discussed further in the "Editing Styles" section.*

Turning Styles Off

If the insertion point is placed in existing text (or if you have text selected) when you select a paragraph or character style, WP automatically formats the text with that style. If the text is not already typed, select the style and begin typing the text you want to format. Press ENTER when you're finished. Depending on how the style was set up, pressing ENTER can have different results. For some styles, pressing ENTER simply inserts a hard return and turns the style off, so you can continue typing text normally. For other styles, however, pressing ENTER turns the style off and then immediately back on again for the next paragraph.

If the style is turned back on after pressing ENTER and you don't want to continue formatting text with that style, from the Styles Property Bar drop-down list, choose <None>. Or you can choose Format | Styles, select <None>, and choose Apply.

TIP: *Some paragraph styles, such as those used with numbered and bulleted lists, can be turned off by pressing ENTER and then BACKSPACE. This deletes the new style code that was inserted for the next paragraph.*

Sometimes you might want to remove the style formatting from a particular section of text. One way to do this is to turn on Reveal Codes and delete the unwanted style code from the Reveal Codes window. If you want to remove a character style, place the insertion point at the beginning of the formatted text and choose Format | Styles | Off. If the text is formatted with a paragraph style, another technique you can use to remove the style is to place the insertion point anywhere in the paragraph and from the Styles Property Bar drop-down list, choose <None>.

If you want to locate all the places in a document that are formatted with a style, you can use the Find and Replace feature. See the Power Tip "Searching for Style Codes" for more information on how to do this.

Power Tip... Searching for Style Codes

WordPerfect makes it easy to locate style codes in a document with the Find and Replace feature. You can search for *any* style code, or you can search for text formatted with a specific style. If you want to search for text formatted in a specific style code and replace it with another style, see the On the CD section "Searching and Replacing Styles." Here's how to search for a style code:

1. Place the insertion point at the top of the document and choose Edit | Find and Replace.

2. If you want WP to locate all style codes in the document, choose Match | Codes. Select Style in the Codes dialog box and choose Insert and Close.

3. If you want to search for only a specific style code, choose Type | Specific Codes. Select Style in the Specific Codes dialog box and choose OK. Then from the Find Style drop-down list, select the name of the style you want to search for.

4. Choose Find Next to have WP find the first style code in the document.

Continue to choose Find Next to locate any other style codes in your document. WP stops on both the style "on" and style "off" code. Since many paragraph styles have two codes that are inserted when the style is turned on, if the insertion point doesn't appear to have moved when you choose Find Next, simply choose it again to move to the next code.

5

On the CD... Searching and Replacing Styles

Styles are easily edited if you need to change the formatting they use. However, if you want to change a style and you already have another style created that contains the new formatting you want to use, it can be faster to replace all occurrences of the current style with the new style. WP's Find and Replace feature only lets you search for specific style codes—you can't replace them with other styles. However, the companion CD contains a bonus macro called REPLACE STYLES.WCM that lets you search for a specific style in a document and replace it with another custom style.

Before you use the REPLACE STYLES.WCM macro, make sure you've created or retrieved the new style you want to use in the document. Then choose Tools | Macro | Play. Select the REPLACE STYLES.WCM macro and choose Play. The Replace Styles dialog box appears.

Select the style you want to replace from the Replace drop-down list, and select its replacement from the With drop-down list. If you want to search only from the location of the insertion point, select that option. Choose OK and WP replaces the styles in the document.

Chaining Styles

One of the more powerful aspects of the Styles feature is the ability to chain two or more styles together. When styles are chained, turning one style off automatically turns a different style on for the next paragraph. You can chain several styles in a row, so a new style is turned on each time ENTER is pressed. Or you can chain two styles in a loop, so pressing ENTER alternates which style is turned on.

To chain styles together, first make sure that each style is created and available in the current document. Then choose Format | Styles. Select the style that you want to chain another style to and choose Edit. From the Enter Key Will Chain To drop-down list, select the name of the new style that you want to have turned on at the end of this style. Choose OK. Repeat this process to chain any other styles. When you're finished, choose Close.

NOTE: *You can only chain from paragraph and character styles. Document (open) styles cannot chain another style, although they can be selected as a style that is turned on when another style is turned off.*

To use a chained style, select the first style from the Styles Property Bar drop-down list. Type the text you want formatted in that style and press ENTER. The chained style is automatically turned on, so any new text you type is formatted with that style.

A common use for chained styles is to set up a question-and-answer format, such as that used in a court transcript (see Figure 5-5). For specific steps on how to set up Q&A chained styles, see the "How to Create a Q&A Format with Chained Styles" section.

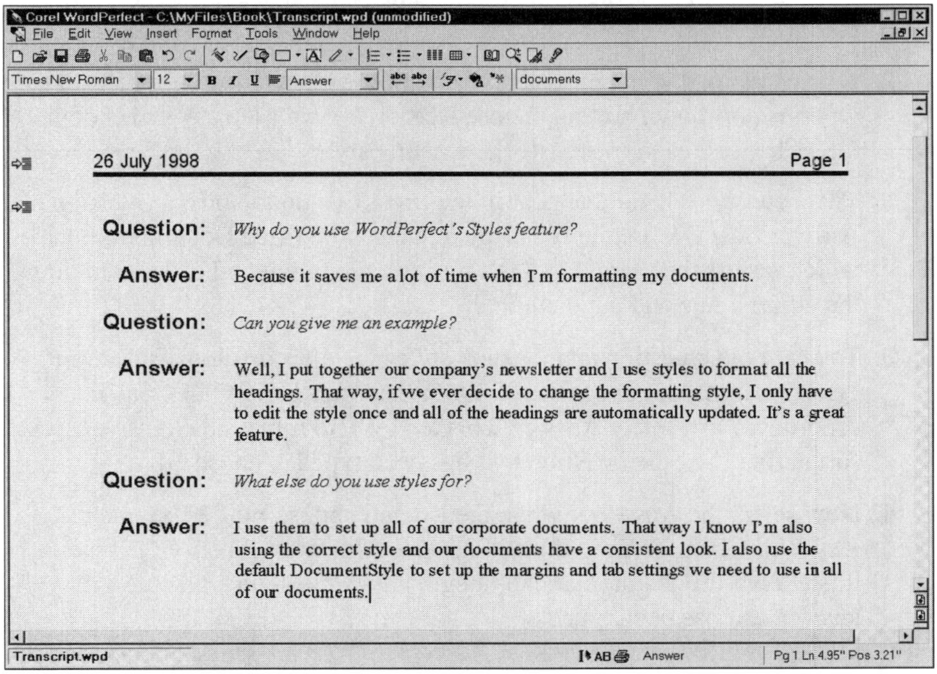

FIGURE 5-5   Chained styles can be used to set up a Q&A format

How to... ▶▶▶ Create a Q&A Format with Chained Styles

In addition to simply turning on one style when another is turned off, chained styles can be used to set up a style "loop," where two styles are alternately turned on each time ENTER is pressed. Chained-style loops are commonly used in transcript documents where a question-and-answer format is needed. The next steps will show you how to set up chained styles to create a Q&A format like the one shown in Figure 5-5.

The companion CD includes a file called Q&A.STY that contains the basic styles used for the question-and-answer format. Following these steps will show you how to set up these styles in a style loop.

1. Copy the Q&A.STY file from the companion CD to your template directory, such as \Corel\Suite8\Template. This is needed so you can edit the styles and save your changes.

2. Go to a blank document window and choose Format | Styles. From the Options pop-down button, choose Retrieve. Type **q&a.sty** and choose OK. Choose Yes to overwrite the existing styles.

   Two new styles should appear in the Style List dialog box—Question and Answer. The Q&A style file also contains a modified DocumentStyle, which inserts the margin and tab settings, along with a header containing the current date and page number.

3. To chain the Question and Answer styles together in a loop, select the Question style and choose Edit. From the Enter Key Will Chain To drop-down list, select Answer. This tells WP to turn on the Answer style formatting after the question text has been typed. Choose OK.

4. Now select the Answer style in the list and choose Edit. From the Enter Key Will Chain To drop-down list, select Question. Choose OK. Doing this allows WP to automatically begin a new question again after the answer text has been typed.

How to...   Create a Q&A Format with Chained Styles (*continued*)

5. To save your changes for future use, choose Options | Save As. Type **q&a.sty** and choose OK. Choose Yes to overwrite the existing file.

6. To begin typing questions, select Question in the list of styles and choose Apply. The style inserts the "Question:" heading followed by an indent code. A Times New Roman italics font is also automatically selected for the question text. All you need to do is type the question and press ENTER.

7. When you press ENTER, the chained style automatically inserts the "Answer:" heading after a blank line, formatted also with an indent code and the proper font codes. Type the answer text and press ENTER.

8. The loop starts over and a new "Question:" heading is automatically inserted. Continue this process to type the questions and answers in the document. Each time you press ENTER, the current style is turned off and the second style is turned on.

When you want to turn the styles off, press ENTER to move to a new line. The "Question:" or "Answer:" heading will be inserted. From the Styles Property Bar drop-down list, choose <None> to turn off the style. You can restart the styles later in the document by selecting Question or Answer from the Styles Property Bar drop-down list.

To use the Q&A format in a different document, choose Format | Styles, and then choose Options | Retrieve. Type **q&a.sty** and choose OK and then Yes. Select the Question style, choose Apply, and you're ready to begin typing the question text.

Editing Styles

One of the foundations of WP's Styles feature is the ability to edit a style's formatting. When you edit a style, any text in the document that's formatted with that style is automatically updated. This not only keeps your document formatting consistent, it saves you countless hours that you'd spend making each change manually. In this section, you'll learn how to edit regular document styles, as well as WP's default system styles—including the heading styles and the DocumentStyle.

If you want to make changes to a style that's being used in the current document, you need to open that style in the Styles Editor dialog box. This can be done in one of two ways. First, you can choose Format | Styles, select the style in the list, and choose Edit. Or you can turn on Reveal Codes and double-click the style code for the style you want to change. This opens that style directly into the Styles Editor dialog box (see Figure 5-6).

Once the Styles Editor dialog box is displaying your style, you can make any changes you want to the codes in the Contents text box, such as adding and deleting codes or text. You can also change the type of style (such as changing a paired-auto paragraph style to a standard paragraph style). When you're finished making changes, choose OK. If the Style List dialog box is displaying, choose Close. The changes you made are instantly applied throughout your document wherever the style is used.

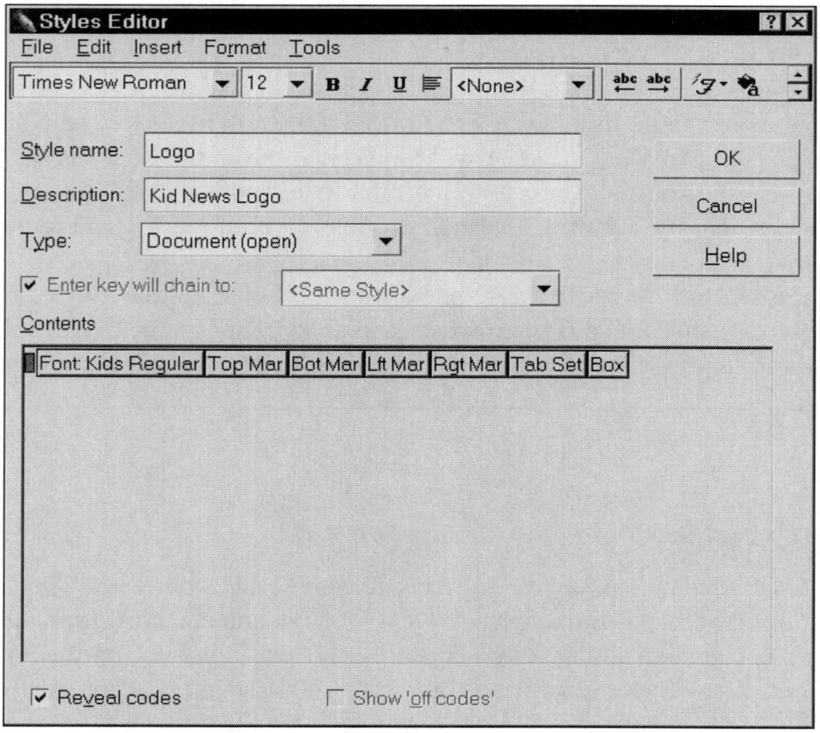

FIGURE 5-6 The Styles Editor dialog box displays the codes used in a style

If text in your document is formatted with QuickFormat, a QuickStyle, or a paired-auto paragraph or character style, you can also change some of the style's formatting directly from the document screen. If you want to change the font, font size, or font attributes, first select an entire formatted paragraph or section of text in the document. If you want to change the paragraph formatting, such as the paragraph border or spacing, place the insertion point anywhere in the paragraph. Make the changes you want and all other sections in your document that use the same style are automatically updated.

NOTE: *If your changes aren't automatically updated in other document locations, make sure that you've selected the entire paragraph or formatted section first and that you haven't discontinued the auto formatting option for that style.*

WP's Default Heading Styles

The list of styles on the Styles Property Bar drop-down list and in the Style List dialog box always include five heading styles—Heading 1, Heading 2, and so on (see Figure 5-4). These heading styles are some of WP's default styles and they're automatically included in every document. Because they're part of WordPerfect's program, they can't be deleted.

The heading styles can be used to format different levels of text headings in your documents (see Figure 5-7). The heading styles use relative size codes, such as Very Large, to format the text size. The first four headings are bolded, and the fifth-level heading is italicized. In addition, each style includes a table of contents code to mark the heading for the appropriate table of contents level. The fourth and fifth headings are indented and are formatted so they're automatically turned on again each time you press ENTER.

You can use the heading styles in your documents as you would any other styles. They can be applied to text that's already typed, or you can select the style first and then type the heading text. If you don't like the default formatting used by the five heading styles, you can edit them as you would other styles. After editing the styles, you can make your changes the new default settings by selecting each heading style you modified in the Style List dialog box and choosing Options | Copy. Select Defalut Template and choose OK.

NOTE: *You can also use the first heading style by choosing Insert |
Outline/Bullets & Numbering, selecting the Text tab, selecting Headings,
and choosing OK.*

The DocumentStyle

In every WordPerfect document, the first code is a DocumentStyle code. If you turn
on Reveal Codes at a blank document screen, you'll see the [Open Style:
DocumentStyle] code. The DocumentStyle is an open style that's part of your
default template. It's listed in the Style List dialog box and, like the heading
styles, can't be deleted. The DocumentStyle contains the initial formatting for a
document, such as the margins, line spacing, justification, and so on. Codes placed
in the DocumentStyle affect all elements of a document, including headers/footers,
comments, and footnotes/endnotes.

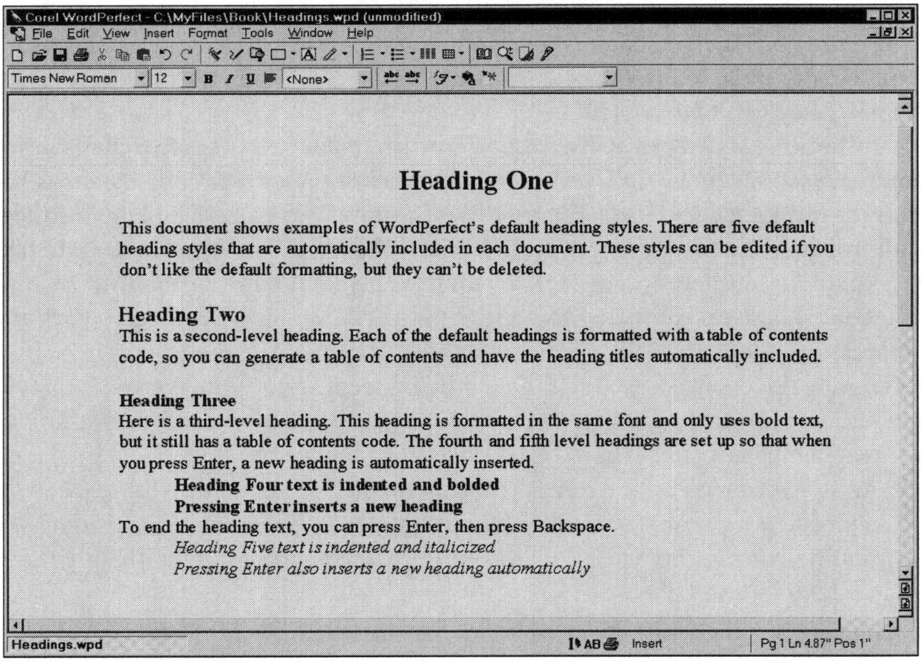

FIGURE 5-7 WP's five default heading styles are available in every
document

When you want to change the overall formatting of your document, you can edit the DocumentStyle and add the codes that you want. This is often better than simply inserting the codes at the top of the document because the DocumentStyle keeps all the codes together in one place and you don't have to worry about them being deleted or moved to another page. In addition, your formatting will be used throughout the entire document, including any headers/footers, footnotes/endnotes, and other elements.

There are three different ways you can edit the DocumentStyle:

- Choose Format | Styles, select DocumentStyle, and choose Edit.

- Choose File | Document | Current Document Style.

- Turn on Reveal Codes and double-click the [Open Style: DocumentStyle] code at the top of the document.

Following any of these steps will open the DocumentStyle in the Styles Editor dialog box. The Styles Editor dialog box looks slightly different when you're editing the DocumentStyle. Several options are unavailable, including the style type, Enter Key Will Chain To drop-down list, and Show 'Off Codes' checkbox. Also, a new Use as Default option appears in the lower-right corner.

Place the insertion point in the Contents text box and use the pull-down menus or Property Bar in the Styles Editor to add the codes you want, such as margin or tab settings. You can include any type of codes or text that you would insert in a regular style.

If you want to have your changes be the default settings in every new document in the future, select the Use as Default checkbox at the bottom of the Styles Editor dialog box. If you only want to change the current document, deselect this checkbox. Choose OK. If you're asked if you want to change all new documents, choose Yes. If the Style List dialog box is displaying, choose Close.

NOTE: *When you add formatting codes within the document text, those codes override any settings in your DocumentStyle.*

System Styles

Special styles called *system styles* are used throughout WordPerfect to format such things as graphics box captions, comments, footnote/endnote numbers, headers/footers, table of contents entries, outline levels, and hyperlinks. WP uses 67 different system styles—not including the DocumentStyle and five heading styles that automatically display in the Style List dialog box.

You can edit the system styles if you want to change the default formatting used for certain features. For example, you can edit the FigureNum style and remove the bold code that formats the "Figure" text and number in a graphics box caption. Or you can edit the Comment style so that the current date is automatically inserted each time you create a comment. You can also determine whether the changes you make will affect only the current document or become the default for all your new documents.

To see a list of the system styles, choose Format | Styles. From the Options pop-down button, choose Setup. Select System under the Display Styles From heading and choose OK. The system styles are added to the list of other styles in the Style List dialog box (see Figure 5-8).

NOTE: *Once you've displayed the system styles, they remain in the Style List dialog box in every document. They are also included on the Styles Property Bar drop-down list, but since there are too many to display at the same time, only the lower portion of the list appears, along with the QuickStyle option.*

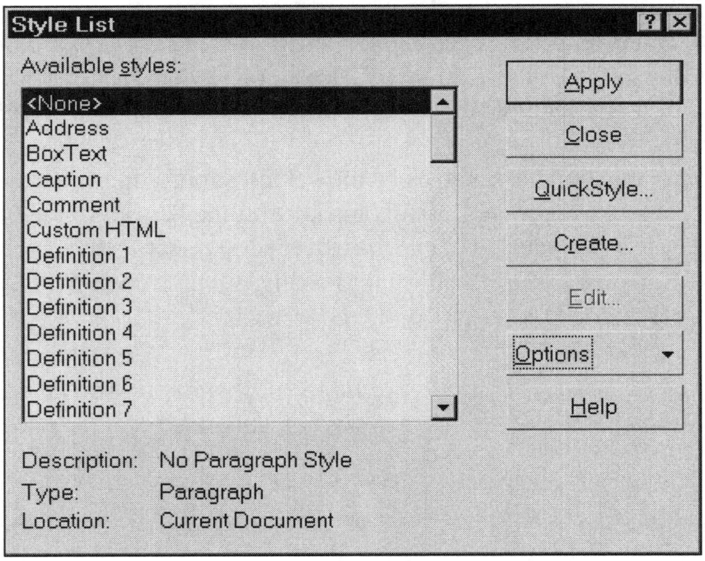

FIGURE 5-8   The system styles can be displayed in the Style List dialog box

To edit a system style, select it in the list and choose Edit. Any codes that are currently used to format the style appear in the Contents text box. Some styles are only formatted with a DocumentStyle code, such as the comment and header/footer styles. This allows that feature to also use any formatting that's been set in the DocumentStyle. You can delete the DocumentStyle from a system style if you don't want the feature to use the DocumentStyle formatting. For example, if you always want your headers to use specific left and right margins—no matter what the document margins are set at—you can edit the Header A style, delete the DocumentStyle code, and insert specific margin codes in its place.

When you're finished making changes to the system style, choose OK. If you want the modified style to be used in all new documents, instead of only in the current document, you need to copy the new style to your default template. To do this, select the style you modified in the list, and from the Options pop-down button, choose Copy. Select Default Template and choose OK.

When you're finished editing the system styles, it's a good idea to remove them again from the list so they don't clutter your style list. From the Options pop-down button, choose Setup, deselect System, and choose OK. Choose Close to close the Style List dialog box.

Saving and Retrieving Styles

When you create or edit a style, your new style is saved as part of the current document and is only available in that document. If you want to use a custom style in other documents, you can either retrieve the style into the new document or copy the style to your default template. When you copy a style to your default template, it's automatically available in all your new documents. If you don't want a style to clutter your default style list, you can retrieve it only into those documents you want to use it in. This section will show you how to use both of these methods to access your styles in other documents.

Copying Styles to the Default Template

If you want to have a custom style available in every new document you create, you can copy it to your default template. Styles that are in your default template are automatically listed in the Style List dialog box on the Styles Property Bar drop-down list. Follow these steps to copy a style that you've already created to your default template:

1. Open the document that contains the custom style.

2. Choose Format | Styles and select the style you want to have available in every new document.

3. From the Options pop-down button, choose Copy.

4. Select Default Template and choose OK.

5. Choose Close to close the Style List dialog box.

Now whenever you create a new document, your custom style is automatically listed on the Styles Property Bar drop-down list, as well as in the Style List dialog box. If you've copied a custom style to your default template and later want to remove it from the default style list, choose Format | Styles. Select the style you want to delete and from the Options pop-down button, choose Delete. Make sure the Including Formatting Codes option is selected. Choose OK, and then Close.

If you edit a style that's been copied to the default template, any existing document that uses that same style is automatically updated with the style changes when you open the document.

TIP: *You can have every new style you create automatically saved in your default template so you don't have to copy each new style individually. To do this, choose Format | Styles. From the Options pop-down button, choose Setup. Select Default Template as the option to save new styles to and choose OK, Close. Now every time you create a new style, it's automatically saved in your default template and is available in new documents.*

NOTE: *WordPerfect only lets you copy styles into your default or additional objects template. However, once a style is copied to your default template, you can copy it into other custom templates by editing the template and using the Copy/Remove Object button on the Template Property Bar. (See Chapter 1 for more information.)*

Saving Style Files

If you don't want your custom styles to clutter your default style list, you can still access them in other documents by saving them and then retrieving them into documents when you need them. Styles can be saved in a separate file, or you can simply save a document that uses a custom style. If you plan to use your custom styles frequently in the future and don't want to risk losing them by deleting the document they're used in, saving them in a separate file is probably the best option.

To save your styles in a separate file, after creating the styles in a document, choose Format | Styles. From the Options pop-down button, choose Save As and the Save Styles To dialog box appears:

```
┌─────────────────────────────────────────────────────────┐
│ Save Styles To...                                 ? X     │
│ ┌───────────────────────────┐                             │
│ Filename:                     ┌─────────────────┐         │
│ ┌──────────────────────────┐  │      OK         │         │
│ │ I                      ┌─┐│  └─────────────────┘         │
│ └──────────────────────┴─┘│  ┌─────────────────┐         │
│                            │  │    Cancel       │         │
│ ┌─ Style type ───────────┐  └─────────────────┘         │
│ │  ⊙ Both                 │  ┌─────────────────┐         │
│ │  ○ User styles          │  │     Help        │         │
│ │  ○ System styles        │  └─────────────────┘         │
│ └────────────────────────┘                                │
└─────────────────────────────────────────────────────────┘
```

WordPerfect classifies styles in two types—user styles and system styles. User styles are those custom styles that you create. System styles are all the styles included by default in WordPerfect (even if you've edited them), including the DocumentStyle. You can have WP save only your custom user styles, only the modified system styles, or both types of styles.

Select the Style Type option you want, and then type a filename for the styles in the File Name text box. You might want to use a file extension that identifies the file as containing styles only, such as STY. Choose OK to save the file, and then choose Close to close the Style List dialog box.

Retrieving Styles

After saving a style file or a document that contains custom styles, you can retrieve those styles into other documents and use them there. To do this, open the document that you want to retrieve the styles into. Choose Format | Styles. From the Options pop-down button, choose Retrieve.

In the File Name text box, you can either type the name of a style file you've previously saved, or you can type the name of a document that contains custom styles. If you specify a document name, WP retrieves any custom styles that have been created and saved in that document. As with saving a style file, WP lets you specify the type of styles you want to retrieve—custom user styles, modified system styles, or both. Select the Style Type option you want and choose OK.

If you see the "Overwrite Current Styles?" message, that indicates that some of the styles being retrieved have the same name as styles that are already in the list. If you choose Yes to overwrite the current styles, WP replaces any styles in the current style list with any new styles you're retrieving that have the same name. If you choose No, styles with the same name are *not* replaced with the styles being retrieved, but any styles with unique names are still added to the new document. The "Overwrite Current Styles?" message is most commonly seen when the style file or document you're retrieving from has a modified DocumentStyle, since every document by default contains a DocumentStyle in the style list. Choose Close to close the Style List dialog box when you're finished.

TIP: *You can use custom styles from WP 6.1 and 7 in WP 8 documents by following these same steps. You can retrieve styles from a style file that was created in 6.1/7 or a 6.1/7 document.*

If you retrieve a style into a document and then edit that style, any other documents that use that style are *not* automatically updated. In order to update the other documents, first resave the modified style in a style file or in the document. Then open the other documents and re-retrieve the edited style from the file or directly from the document, choosing Yes to overwrite the current styles.

Deleting Styles

If you want to remove the formatting inserted by a style throughout a document, there's no need to go through Reveal Codes and delete each style code individually. WordPerfect makes it easy to quickly delete a style from the entire document. When you delete a style, the style name is removed from the Style List dialog box, and any occurrences of the style code throughout the document text are removed.

You can delete the style codes along with any formatting they've inserted in the document, or you can delete only the style and leave the actual formatting codes in the document. For example, if you have a style that contains bold and italic codes, you can have WP delete the style code each time it occurs in the document, and insert in its place the actual bold and italic codes so the overall formatting of the text does not change.

To delete a style from a document, choose Format | Styles. Select the style you want to remove and press DELETE; or from the Options pop-down button, choose Delete. The Delete Styles dialog box appears:

```
┌─────────────────────────────────────────────────┐
│ Delete Styles                          [?][X]     │
├─────────────────────────────────────────────────┤
│  Delete style from document ─────────────────     │
│    ⦿ Including formatting codes                   │
│    ○ Leave formatting codes in document           │
│    ┌──────────┐   ┌──────────┐   ┌──────────┐    │
│    │   OK     │   │  Cancel  │   │  Help    │    │
│    └──────────┘   └──────────┘   └──────────┘    │
└─────────────────────────────────────────────────┘
```

To delete the style and any formatting it inserted in the document, leave the Including Formatting Codes option selected. To have the style code replaced with the individual formatting codes, select Leave Formatting Codes in Document and choose OK. Choose Close.

NOTE: *If you've saved a style in a separate file, deleting it from a document doesn't affect the actual style file. You can still retrieve the style into other documents from the style file, unless you manually delete the style file from your hard drive.*

If a style that's listed in the Style List dialog box is not being used in the current document, you can delete it from the style list without affecting the document at all. If the Style List dialog box has a long list of styles and you're not sure which styles are actually being used in the document, you can quickly remove the unused styles. See the Power Tip "Cleaning Up the Style List" for the steps on how to do this.

Power Tip▸▸▸ Cleaning Up the Style List

The Style List dialog box contains a list of all the styles saved with the current document, whether or not they're actually being used in it. One technique for quickly removing all the styles that *aren't* being used in the current document is to use the Clipboard. Follow these steps:

1. Open the document with the extra styles you want to remove.

2. Choose Edit | Select | All to select the entire text and codes in the document. Press CTRL-C to copy the text to the Clipboard.

3. Leave this document open and switch to a blank document screen. Press CTRL-V to paste in the document text.

4. If your original document contains formatting in the DocumentStyle, that formatting won't be copied over unless it's already part of the default DocumentStyle. If you need to copy this formatting, choose Window and switch back to the screen containing your original document.

5. In the original document, turn on Reveal Codes (View | Reveal Codes) and double-click the [Open Style: DocumentStyle] code at the top of the document. In the Styles Editor dialog box, choose Edit | Select | All. Press CTRL-C to copy this formatting, and then choose Cancel.

6. Choose File | Close | No to close the original document without saving your changes. WP should switch back to the new document screen where you pasted the text. Turn on Reveal Codes and double-click the [Open Style: DocumentStyle] code at the top of this document. Press CTRL-V to paste in the formatting and choose OK.

7. Save and name the new document with the same filename as the original document, or use a different filename if you want to keep the original version. The Style List dialog box now contains only those styles that are actually in use in the document.

Summary

When it comes to formatting documents, styles can be one of WordPerfect's biggest timesaving tools, especially if you learn how to utilize their power and capabilities. Features such as QuickFormat and QuickStyles help you quickly format headings and later update the formatting right from the document screen. If you need greater control and flexibility, you can create your own custom styles with the Styles Editor and even chain them together. If you haven't used styles before, take a few minutes to experiment with them and you'll be surprised at how many hours of formatting time they can save.

In Chapter 6, we'll explore the advanced features of tables and show you how to do everything from formatting a cell to adding complex formulas.

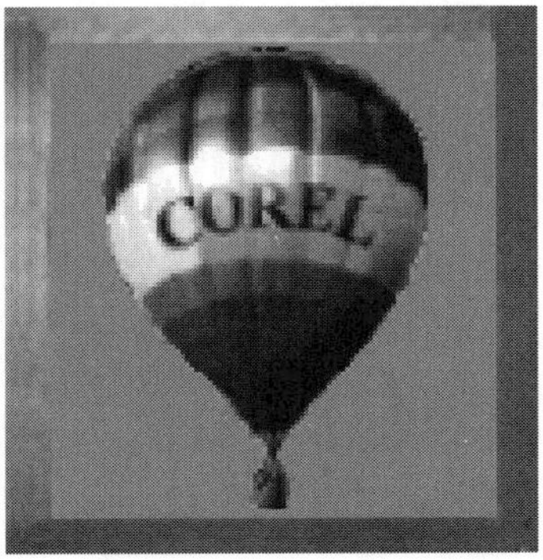
COREL

Chapter
6

Tapping into Table Tools

When WordPerfect first introduced its Tables feature back in version 5.1 for DOS, people were excited about this new way to easily align text and numbers, create different looks with a handful of border styles, and even perform simple math calculations. Tables have certainly come a long way since then. Now you can *really* get excited about creating tables with WP 8's fantastic table tools, including features like QuickJoin and QuickFill, a countless number of border styles, and dozens of powerful formula functions.

In this chapter, we'll explore a variety of WP's power tools for working with tables. We'll start with a brief overview of creating tables, and then show you some shortcuts for quickly formatting tables—and the text in them—to get just the look you need. Along the way, you'll learn a few tricks and tools for getting your table work done in a flash. Finally, we'll cover one of the most powerful aspects of tables—calculating with formulas. You'll learn how to create simple to complex formulas in tables and floating cells, and we'll include a handy reference chart of several common formula functions in WP 8.

Tables Overview

It's probably a safe bet that if you're reading this book, you've created a WordPerfect table before. You should already have a basic knowledge of what cells, columns, and rows are, as well as how to navigate around in a table. With that in mind, we give a brief overview of creating tables and inserting basic cell formatting in this section.

Creating Tables

There are two ways you can create a table in WP 8: the Table QuickCreate button on the toolbar (see the following illustration) or the Create Table dialog box (see Figure 6-1), accessed by choosing Insert | Table. With either method, you specify how many rows and columns you want to begin with. Once the table has been created, you can insert and delete rows or columns, as well as add any formatting you want.

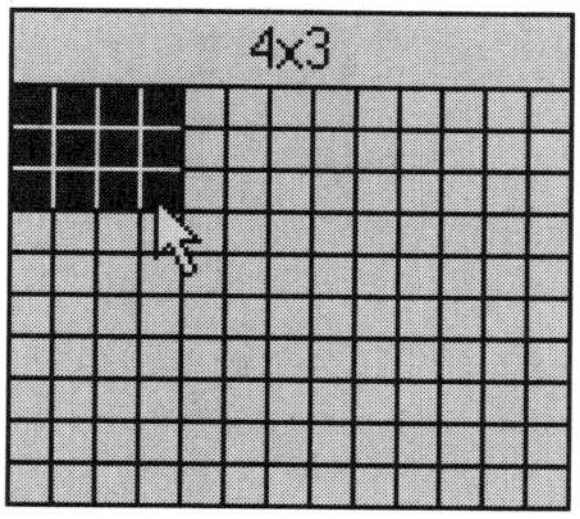

TIP: *If there's text in your document that's typed in tabular or parallel columns, you can quickly convert that text into a table by selecting the text and choosing Insert | Table | OK.*

Tables Property Bar and QuickMenu

The fastest way to format a table is by using the options on the Tables Property Bar and the Tables QuickMenu. The Tables Property Bar automatically appears when the insertion point is in a table, as shown on next page. The Property Bar changes slightly when you select cells, so you always have the table formatting tools you need right at your fingertips.

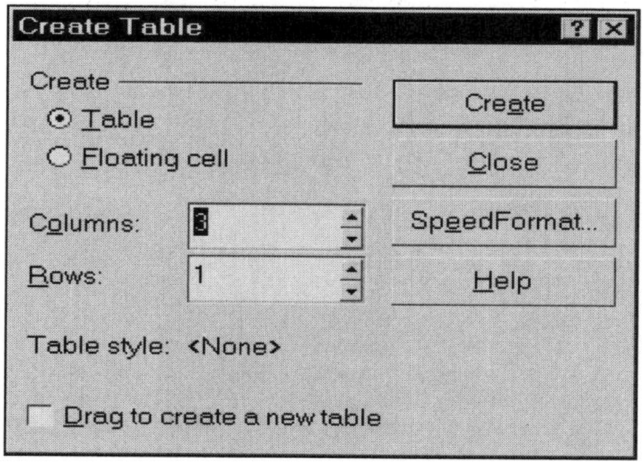

FIGURE 6-1 The Create Table dialog box lets you select the size of the table before creating it

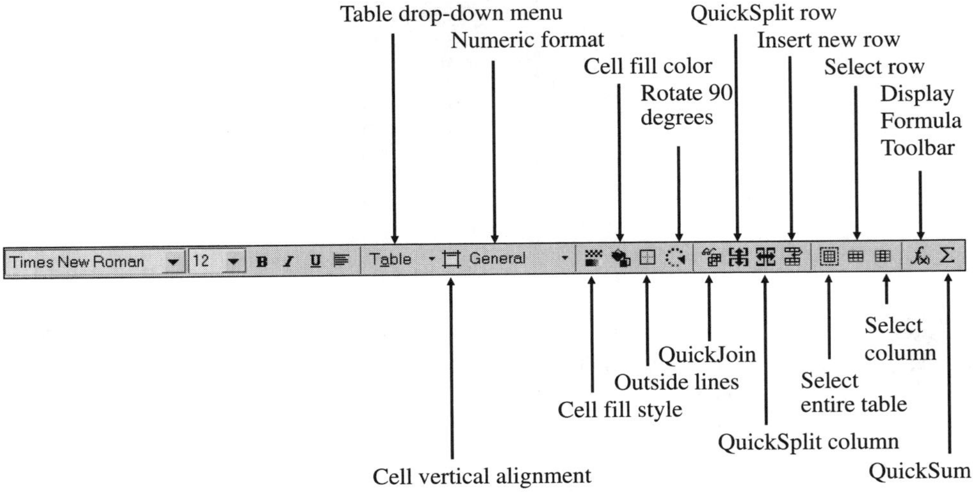
Table drop-down menu
Numeric format
Cell fill color
Rotate 90 degrees
QuickSplit row
Insert new row
Select row
Display Formula Toolbar
Times New Roman
12
Table
General
Cell vertical alignment
Cell fill style
Outside lines
QuickJoin
QuickSplit column
Select entire table
Select column
QuickSum

The Tables QuickMenu appears when you right-click anywhere in a table (see Figure 6-2). The QuickMenu has many of the same options as the Table drop-down menu on the Tables Property Bar and is often a closer reach.

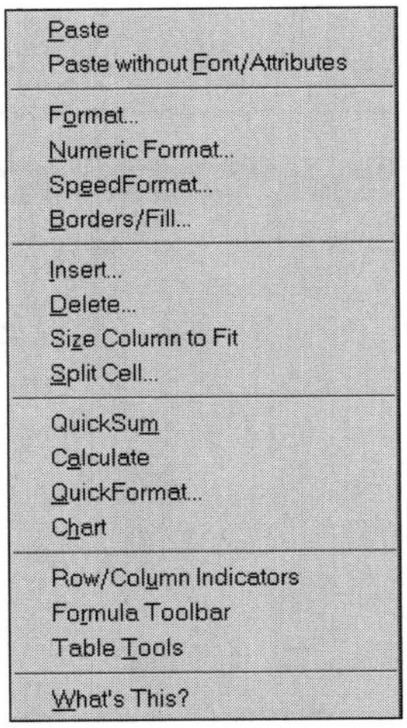
Paste
Paste without Font/Attributes
Format...
Numeric Format...
SpeedFormat...
Borders/Fill...
Insert...
Delete...
Size Column to Fit
Split Cell...
QuickSum
Calculate
QuickFormat...
Chart
Row/Column Indicators
Formula Toolbar
Table Tools
What's This?

FIGURE 6-2 The Tables QuickMenu appears when you right-click in a table

Table Position

When you create a table in WP 8, it fills the entire page width. Even if columns are sized, added, or deleted, the table still takes up the full width. To position the table differently, choose Table | Format on the Property Bar. Select the Table tab; then from the Table Position on Page drop-down list, select the option you want. Choose OK.

NOTE: *Unless you select the From Left Edge option, the table position won't actually change until you resize or delete columns.*

If you want to be able to include document text next to a table (see Figure 6-3), see the steps in the "Placing Text Next to a Table" Power Tip.

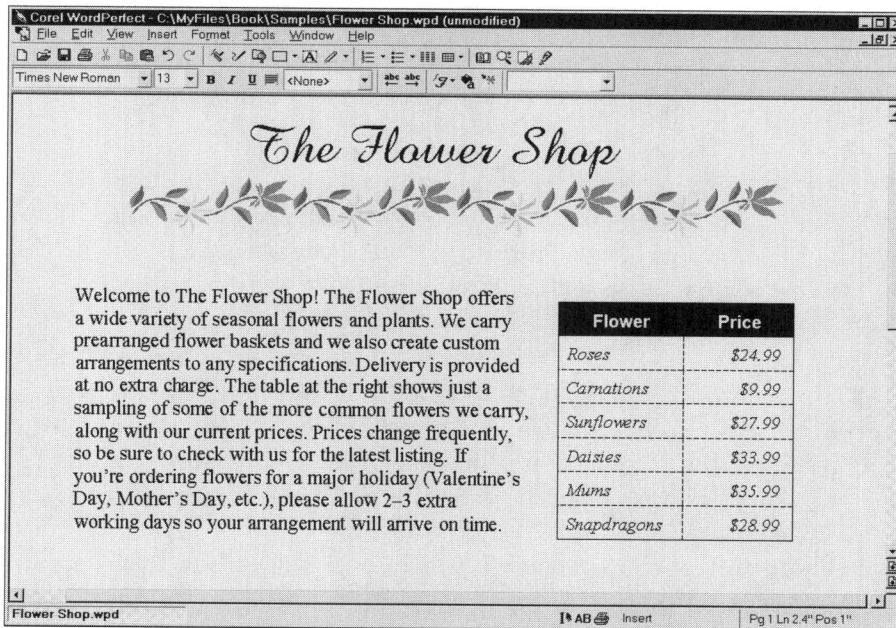

FIGURE 6-3 You can place text next to a table when the table is in a text box

Power Tip ▸▸▸ Placing Text Next to a Table

If you want to be able to include document text next to a table (see Figure 6-3), you need to create the table in a text box. There are two easy ways to do this in WP 8: the Drag to Create Table feature or the shadow cursor.

To use Drag to Create, follow these steps:

1. When you want to create a table, choose Insert | Table. Enter the number of rows and columns you want.

2. Select the Drag to Create a New Table checkbox and choose Create. The mouse pointer icon changes to a hand holding an outlined box.

3. Click and drag a rectangular area the approximate size and location you want for your table. WP creates a text box and inserts a table with the number of rows and columns you specified. You can format this table as you would any regular table.

4. To move the table, click and drag the box outline. To format the text box itself, click outside the table; then right-click the table box and use the graphics options on the QuickMenu, such as Position and Size. (For more information on graphics, see Chapter 7.)

Once you've selected the Drag to Create Table option, it remains in effect for each new table you create, including those created from the Table QuickCreate button on the toolbar. You can turn it back off by choosing Insert | Table and deselecting the Drag to Create a New Table option.

To use the shadow cursor to create a table in a text box, first choose View and make sure shadow cursor is selected. Then simply click and drag a rectangular area in a blank section of the document where you want the table to appear. When you release the mouse button, a QuickMenu appears in the corner. Select Table from the QuickMenu; then enter the number of rows and columns you want in the Create Table dialog box and choose Create.

Basic Cell Formatting

Once you've created a table, you're ready to begin formatting it. Much of this information is set within the Table Format dialog box (see Figure 6-4), which is accessed by choosing Table | Format from the Property Bar, or by right-clicking and choosing Format. From this dialog box, you can set such things as the cell and

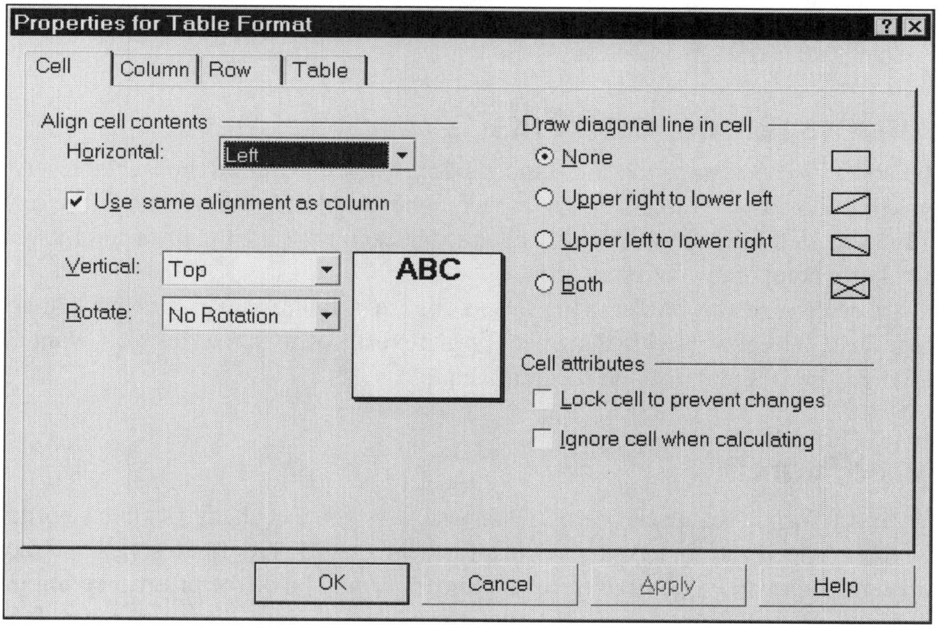

FIGURE 6-4 The Table Format dialog box is where you set much of a table's formatting

column justification, vertical alignment, diagonal cell lines, column width, row height, and table margins.

TIP: *If you want to center decimal-aligned numbers in a table column, select the Column tab in the Table Format dialog box and use Decimal Align as the column justification. Then select From Right Margin and enter an amount to "push" the decimal point over toward the middle of the cell. The amount you use will depend on the width of your column.*

Formatting the Table Structure

Determining the overall look of your table is easier than ever before. Thanks to some great features like SpeedFormat, QuickJoin, and QuickSplit, it only takes a few minutes to create a professional-looking table. In this section, you'll learn how to customize the lines and shading used in a table, including how to apply an "instant" format from a list of predefined table styles. You'll also learn how to place cell boundaries exactly where you want by joining and splitting cells.

Borders, Lines, and Fills

The ability to customize the lines and shading (fill) used throughout a table gives you control over your table's visual impact. For example, Figure 6-5 shows the same table formatted four ways. All that's changed in each table are the lines and fills, but each has a completely different look.

To customize the borders, lines, and fills in a table, you can select either a predefined table style with the SpeedFormat feature or the styles you want for individual cells, columns, and rows in the table.

SpeedFormat

The SpeedFormat feature is one of the fastest ways you can change a table's borders and lines. SpeedFormat lets you select a format from 40 predefined styles and have it instantly applied to your table. To use SpeedFormat, place the insertion point in a table and choose Table | SpeedFormat from the Property Bar. When the Table SpeedFormat dialog box appears (see Figure 6-6), select the style you want for your table. The dialog box shows a preview of the selected style. If you want to remove the current table formatting, select Clear Current Table Format Before Applying at the bottom of the dialog box. Choose Apply to format your table.

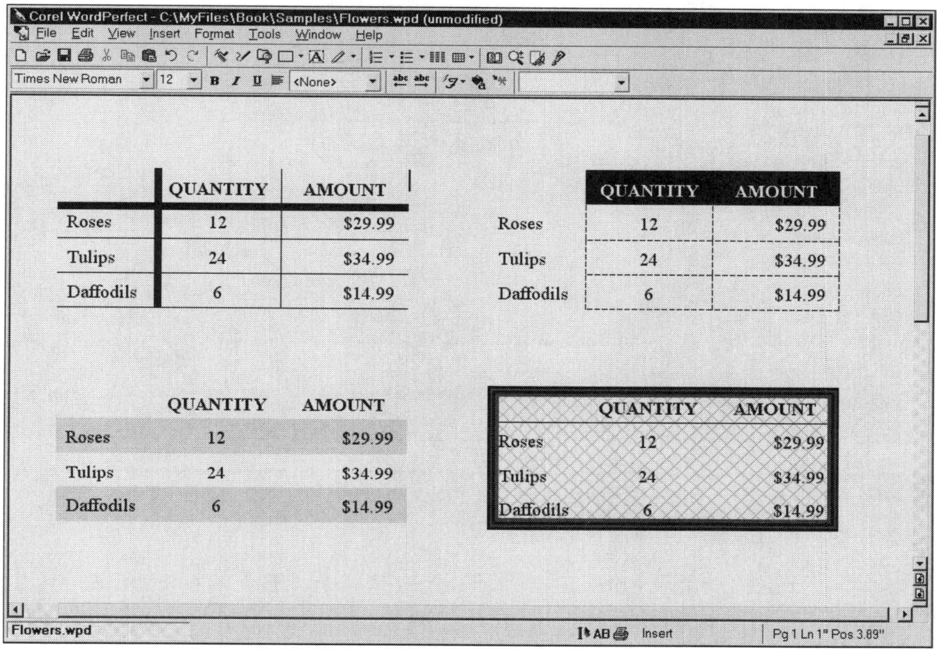

FIGURE 6-5 The only difference between these four tables is the border, lines, and fill selected

NOTE: *After you select a SpeedFormat style, any new tables you create in the current document automatically use the same style.*

If you frequently format your tables with a custom format, you can create your own SpeedFormat style. To do this, first format a table with the desired lines, fill, numeric format, and justification. SpeedFormat only saves the line and fill changes you make to individual cells—it *won't* save the default table border or default line style. When the table is formatted the way you want, choose Table | SpeedFormat from the Property Bar. Choose Create, type a name for your style, choose OK, and then Close.

Custom Lines and Fills

If none of the SpeedFormat styles suit your fancy, you can easily customize the lines and fills used in individual cells. To do this, first select the cell(s) you want to modify.

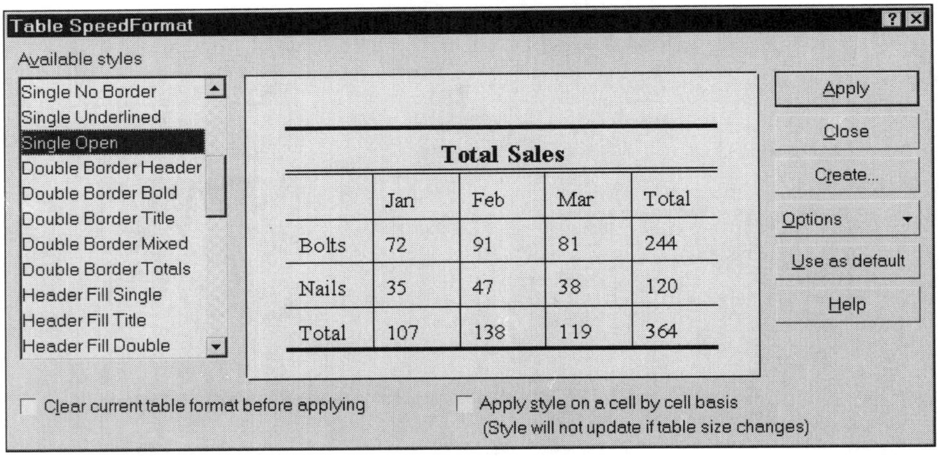

FIGURE 6-6 The SpeedFormat feature has 40 predefined table styles

Then you can use the line buttons on the Tables Property Bar to select the new line style for the side you want to change, such as the left line or the outside lines. Or you can right-click the table and choose Borders/Fill to display the Properties for Table Borders/Fill dialog box (see Figure 6-7). From this dialog box, you can select the line style used for each side of the overall selection, or for each individual cell within the selection.

CAUTION: *When you're changing individual cell lines, make sure that you're consistent in which cell edge you change. For example, changing the top line in one cell and the bottom line of a cell in the next column can result in uneven lines.*

By selecting the Table tab in the Properties for Table Borders/Fill dialog box, you can select a table border, change the default line style used throughout the table, and turn on alternating fill for rows, columns, or both. If you want to make these settings the default for every new table you create, choose Default Settings in the Table Borders/Fill dialog box, and then choose Yes.

TIP: *You can create your own custom line and fill styles if you don't see any you like on the pop-up palettes. To do this, choose Styles from the Table Borders/Fill dialog box. In the Graphics Styles dialog box, you can edit any*

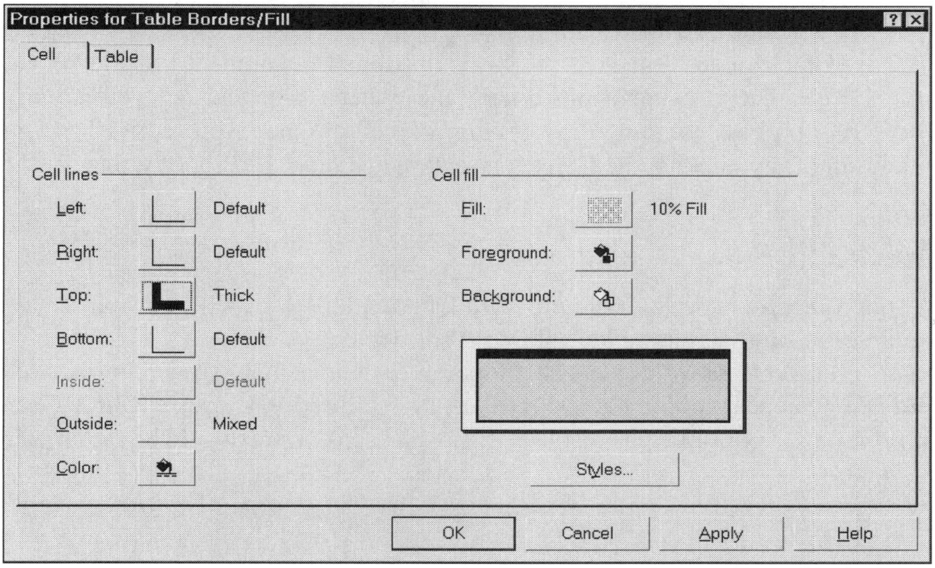

FIGURE 6-7 The Properties for Table Borders/Fill dialog box lets you customize the table lines and shading

of the existing border, line, and fill styles, or create new custom styles. See Chapter 7 for more information on graphics styles.

Joining and Splitting

The ability to join and split table cells is a necessity for creating custom, functional tables. WP 8 has two new features—QuickJoin and QuickSplit—that expedite this process, especially when you're working with large tables. In previous versions of WP, you could join two cells by first selecting the cells, and then right-clicking and choosing Join Cells. You could also split a cell into equal-sized columns or rows by right-clicking, choosing Split Cell, and entering the number of columns or rows you wanted. You can still join and split cells this way in WP 8, but learning to use QuickJoin and QuickSplit can speed up your work immensely.

QuickJoin

To join two or more cells with the QuickJoin feature, you don't need to select the cells first. Instead, just click the QuickJoin button on the Tables Property Bar.

Or you can choose Table | Join | QuickJoin from the Property Bar. The mouse pointer changes to include two horizontal arrows.

Once QuickJoin is turned on, you can simply click and drag the mouse over each group of cells that you want to join. Since QuickJoin remains selected, you can easily repeat this process to join other groups of cells. When you're finished, turn QuickJoin off by clicking the QuickJoin button again on the Property Bar.

QuickSplit

To split a cell into rows or columns with QuickSplit, click the QuickSplit Row or QuickSplit Column button on the Tables Property Bar.

To split a cell, move the mouse pointer over the cell and a dotted horizontal or vertical line appears to indicate where the cell will be split. If you're splitting a cell into columns, a pop-up menu displays the width each column would be at that point.

When the divider line is positioned where you want, click the mouse button to split the cell.

Just like QuickJoin, the QuickSplit feature remains selected, so you can continue to click each place you want to divide a cell. Since you can place the divider wherever you want, you're not forced to split a cell into equal columns or rows. When you're finished, turn QuickSplit off by clicking the Property Bar button again.

TIP: *If you have QuickSplit Column selected and want to split a row, just press and hold the ALT key and WP switches to QuickSplit Row mode, showing you a horizontal guideline. Click to split the row and when you release the ALT key, WP returns to QuickSplit Column mode. You can do the same thing if you're in QuickSplit Row mode and want to split a column.*

NOTE: *If you want to make sure the new columns are the same width after splitting them, select the columns and choose Table | Equal Column Widths from the Tables Property Bar.*

Formatting Table Text

WordPerfect not only simplifies the process of customizing a table structure, it also gives you several useful tools for inserting and formatting the text within a table. In this section, you'll learn about some of these tools, such as the QuickFill feature, which automatically fills in a table with a pattern of text or numbers. You'll also learn how to copy text and formatting from one cell to another, and how to select the numeric format of a cell or column so WP automatically formats numbers and dates for you.

QuickFill

WP's QuickFill feature was designed to help you fill in a table with a pattern of numbers or text. You start the pattern, and then use QuickFill to automatically fill in the remaining cells. For example, if you type "Sunday" in the first cell of a row, select the entire row and then use QuickFill, WP automatically fills in the row with the remaining weekdays, as shown here:

Sunday	Monday	Tuesday	Wednesday	Thursday	Friday	Saturday

QuickFill also works to fill in numbers that increment or decrement by a certain amount. After typing numbers in the first *two* cells to establish the pattern, such as "2" and "4," QuickFill fills in the rest (6, 8, 10, and so on). Only the first entry is needed for QuickFill to fill in Roman numbers, weekdays, month names, and quarters (Quarter 1, Quarter 2, and so on). The first two entries are needed for QuickFill to insert a pattern of numbers.

To use QuickFill, type the first entry in a blank cell. If you're filling in a pattern of numbers, type the second number in an adjacent cell. The pattern of numbers must be based on a value that is added or subtracted. QuickFill won't work with a number pattern that is based on multiplication or division. Then select the cells across the row or down the column that you want to fill in—including the cells that you started the pattern in. Right-click the table and choose QuickFill, or choose Table | QuickFill from the Property Bar.

TIP: *If you want to copy the same text into several cells, just type the text in the first cell and use QuickFill to fill in the remaining cells. Since WP doesn't recognize the text as a pattern, the QuickFill feature simply repeats the same text in each cell.*

NOTE: *QuickFill can't include leading zeros with the table numbers it inserts. However, you can use a macro to quickly number table rows with leading zeros. See the On the CD section for more information.*

On the CD▸▸ Numbering with Leading Zeros

When you use QuickFill to number table rows, the numbers can't include leading zeros, such as 0001, 0002, and so on. The companion CD contains a macro called NUMBER TABLE ROWS.WCM that you can use in place of QuickFill to quickly number table rows.

To use the macro, place the insertion point in the cell where you want the table numbering to begin. Choose Tools | Macro | Play, select the NUMBER TABLE ROWS.WCM macro, and choose Play. A dialog box prompts you for the starting number, the fixed number of digits you want each number to contain, and whether you want to number to the end of the table or a certain number of rows. Enter the amounts and choose OK. The macro begins numbering in the current cell and continues numbering down the column until the number of specified rows or the end of the table is reached.

If you later add or delete rows and need to update the numbers, simply place the insertion point in the first cell and play the macro again. After prompting you for the custom information, the macro replaces the existing numbers with the new numbers.

Copying Cells

Once you've formatted a table cell, there are a couple of easy techniques for copying the text and the formatting to another cell. First, you can drag and drop the text and formatting to the new cell. To do this, select the cell with the text and formatting that you want to copy. Then click and drag the selected cell to the new cell. Before you release the mouse button in the new cell, hold down the CTRL key to copy the text. Otherwise, the text will be moved to the new cell. When you release the mouse button, the original cell's text and formatting—including any fonts, numeric format, justification, shading, and so on—are applied to the new cell. If the new cell previously had any text or formatting, they are replaced with the copied information.

> **NOTE:** *When you move the text to the new cell (by not holding down the CTRL key before releasing the mouse button), the original cell still keeps its formatting.*

A second method you can use to quickly copy a cell's formatting is the QuickFormat feature. This feature copies certain aspects of a cell's formatting to other cells, such as the lines, fill, and justification, but it doesn't copy any of the text. For more information on using QuickFormat, see Chapter 5.

Numeric Format

When you're typing numbers into table cells, they often require special formatting. For example, if the numbers are dollar amounts, they need to have dollar signs, commas, and two decimal places added. Or, if the numbers are fixed percentages, they need a percent sign and a fixed number of decimal places. Rather than type this extra formatting with the numbers, you can use the Numeric Format feature to have WP automatically format the numbers correctly. Setting numeric formats is particularly useful when you're working with formulas, since WP automatically displays the calculated results in the correct format.

To select the numeric format, place the insertion point in the cell or column that you want to format, or select a group of cells. Choose Table | Numeric Format from the Property Bar to display the Properties for Table Numeric Format dialog box (see Figure 6-8). Select the tab at the top of the dialog box to indicate whether you want to format the current cell(s), column, or entire table.

The different numeric formats determine such things as how negative numbers are displayed, whether a currency symbol is used, how many decimal places are displayed, and whether commas are inserted as a thousands separator. When you select a numeric format, the dialog box shows you a preview of how negative numbers are displayed in that format. Not all of the numeric formats are for numbers—the Date/Time format can be used to format dates in a table, and the Text format treats any numbers in the cell as text so they're not included in calculations.

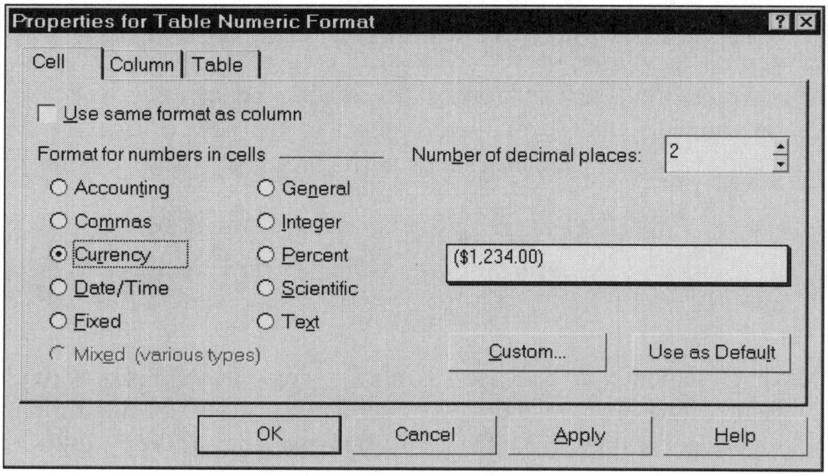

FIGURE 6-8 The Table Numeric Format dialog box helps you format numbers automatically

To customize a particular format, select the format and choose Custom; then set the options you want. If you customize the Date/Time format, select the format you want the date or time to display in when it's inserted in that cell. If you want to select a new format to be used as the default for all your new tables, select the format and choose Use as Default, and then Yes. Choose OK when you're finished.

TIP: *If you don't need to customize the numeric format, you can select it for a cell or group of cells by using the Numeric Format drop-down list on the Tables Property Bar.*

Once you've selected a numeric format, entering numbers in that format is quick and easy, since WP inserts the formatting for you. For example, if you're using the currency format, type a number into the cell without any formatting, such as **1432**. As soon as you move out of the cell, WP adds the formatting to the number, such as "$1,432.00." If you've selected the Date/Time format of "Monday, December 15, 1997," all you need to type in the cell is a date such as **12/21** and WP automatically expands it to "Sunday, December 21, 1997" when you move out of the cell.

NOTE: *If you're typing dates and don't include a year, WP automatically uses the current year. If you type a two-digit year of 00 to 50, WP assumes you mean the year 2000 to 2050. If you type a two-digit year of 51 to 99, WP assumes you mean 1951 to 1999. For other years, you need to specify all four digits.*

Table Tricks and Tools

Corel has gone to great lengths to make your table formatting chores as painless as possible. WP 8 is full of table shortcuts and Property Bars with tools right at your fingertips. Here are some of these useful tricks and tools for working with tables.

- If you want to size the current column so it fits the longest text entry in any cell, choose Table | Size Column to Fit from the Tables Property Bar.

- To have easy access to table formatting features, right-click the table and choose Table Tools to display the Tools palette (see Figure 6-9). From the options on this palette, you can quickly select the lines, fill, numeric format, and other formatting options for selected cells. You can also use it to insert and delete rows, adjust column widths, and join or split cells. The Tools palette remains open until you close it, so you can click and drag it to the edge of your table and place the formatting features within easy reach.

- When Table Guidelines are turned on, WP displays dotted guidelines for any cell lines that have been removed. This helps you see the cell boundaries and is especially useful if you use the mouse to size columns and rows. To turn the Table Guidelines on or off, choose View | Guidelines, select Table, and choose OK.

NOTE: *You can also turn on Table Gridlines (View | Table Gridlines), which hide the current table lines and display dotted lines around every cell in the table. Gridlines don't affect how the table prints, but they allow you to see each cell's boundary without being distracted by table lines.*

- The Row and Column Indicators make it easy to select specific rows and columns in your table. To turn on the row and column indicators, right-click the table and choose Row/Column Indicators. When the

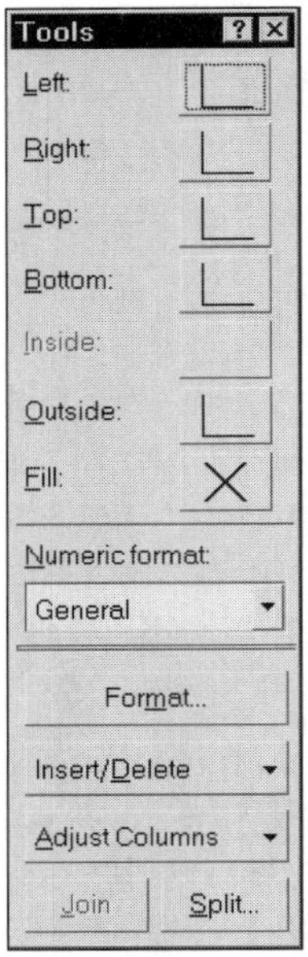

FIGURE 6-9   The Tools palette puts the table formatting features at your fingertips

insertion point is in a table, the indicators appear along the top and left edge of the document window and display the row numbers and column letters (see Figure 6-10). You can click a row or column indicator to instantly select that row or column, or you can select the entire table by clicking the blank indicator in the upper-left corner of the display area.

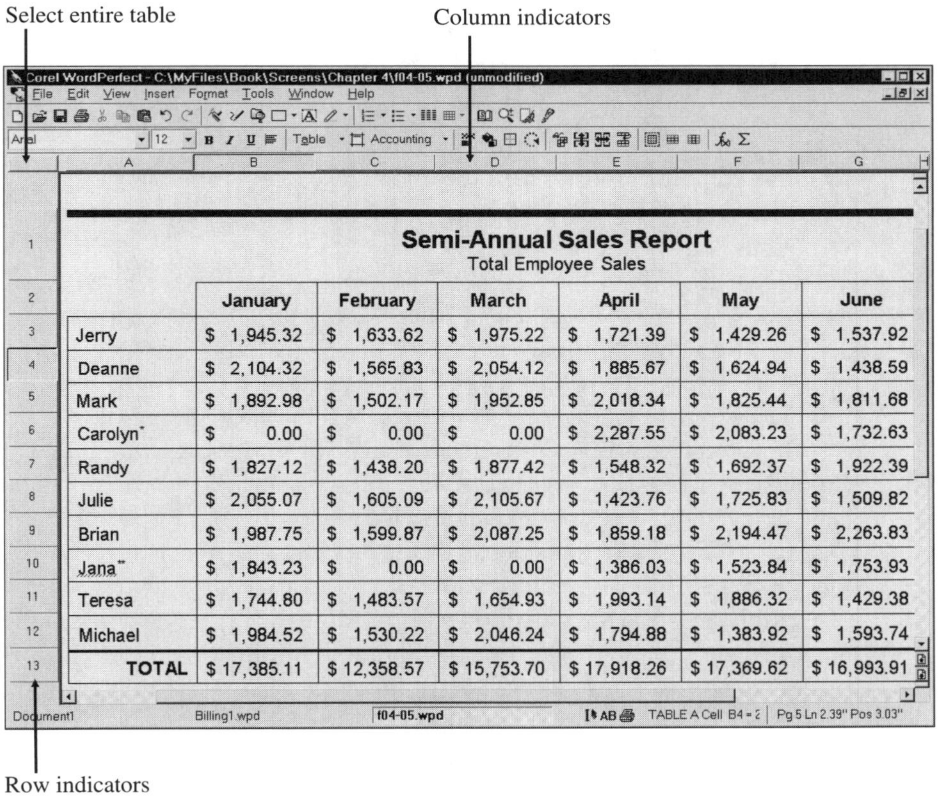

Select entire table   Column indicators

Row indicators

FIGURE 6-10 The Row and Column indicators help you quickly select row and columns

On the CD ▸▸▸ Table Tools Toggle

It can be time-consuming to frequently turn the table guidelines, table gridlines, and row/column indicators on and off because they're all set from different locations. The companion CD contains a bonus macro called TABLE TOOLS.WCM that gives you one central location for turning these table tools on and off.

To use the macro, choose Tools | Macro | Play, select the TABLE TOOLS.WCM macro, and choose Play. When the dialog box appears, select those items that you want to toggle. If the feature is already turned on, selecting it will turn it off, and vice versa. Choose OK. Play this macro each time you want to toggle any of the table viewing tools.

This macro is most useful when it's added as a button to the Tables Property Bar. To add it, right-click the Tables Property Bar and choose Edit. Select the Macros tab and choose Add Macro. Select the TABLE TOOLS.WCM macro and choose Select; then choose Yes to save the macro with the full path. Choose OK to close the dialog box. Now you can simply click the macro button to display the dialog box and select the tools you want to turn on or off. (For more information on adding macros to toolbars, see Chapter 13.)

- If you like to keep your hands on the keyboard, WP has lots of quick keystrokes for working in tables. Try these keystrokes for selecting, sizing, and inserting table rows:

  ALT-INSERT inserts a row above the current row

  ALT-SHIFT-INSERT inserts a row below the current row

  ALT-DELETE deletes the current row

  CTRL-, (comma) decreases the column width

  CTRL-. (period) increases the column width

CTRL-SHIFT-DOWN ARROW selects the current column

CTRL-SHIFT-RIGHT ARROW selects the current row

CTRL-SHIFT-DOWN ARROW-RIGHT ARROW selects the entire table

■ You can quickly create a chart from information in a table (see Figure 6-11). The table and chart are linked together so that any changes you make in the table are updated in the chart. For more information, see the Power Tip "Creating a Chart from a Table."

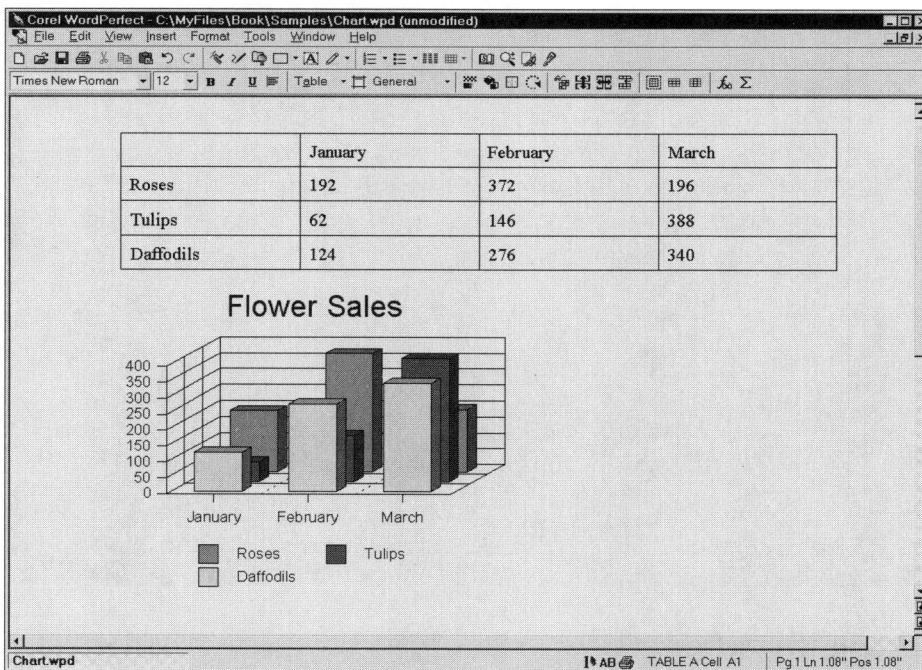

FIGURE 6-11 You can easily create a chart from table data

Power Tip ▸▸▸ Creating a Chart from a Table

WordPerfect makes it easy to create a chart from information in a table (see Figure 6-11). In addition, the chart and table are linked together so you can quickly update your chart when the table data changes. To create a chart, follow these steps:

1. Create a table containing the data you want. Use the first row and column in your table for the data labels.

2. When you're ready to create the chart, place the insertion point in the table and choose Insert | Graphics | Chart. WP creates the chart in a graphics box below the table.

3. Make any changes you want to the chart using the chart-editing tools on the Property Bar and pull-down menus. You can also right-click most elements of the chart to edit them. For example, you can change the title, colors used, grid properties, and so on. (For more information on charts, see Chapter 18.)

4. Click outside the chart when you're finished to return to the document.

5. If you later make changes to the table data, you can update the chart by right-clicking it and choosing Update Chart from Table. To edit the chart elements, right-click it and choose Chart Object | Edit.

■ By locking table cells, the insertion point skips right over them as you're tabbing through the table. Locking cells also prevents others from accidentally changing their text or formulas. To lock a cell, place the insertion point in the cell and choose Table | Format from the Property Bar. Select Lock Cell to Prevent Changes and choose OK. Now, as you press TAB to move through the table, the insertion point moves right over the locked cell.

NOTE: *To unlock a cell so you can edit it, select the cell with the mouse and repeat the previous steps to deselect the Lock Cell option.*

■ WP lets you easily change the left and right margins used in a table column. If you want to change the left and right margins used in an individual cell—without affecting the rest of the column—you can create a style. See the Power Tip "Adjusting Individual Cell Margins" for the steps on how to do this.

Power Tip▸▸▸ Adjusting Individual Cell Margins

You can easily set the left and right margins for an entire column by right-clicking the table, choosing Format, and then selecting the Column tab and entering the amounts you want in the Left and Right text boxes. But if you want to change the left and right margins for an *individual* cell, you need to use a style. Follow these steps:

1. Choose Format | Styles | Create. In the Style Name text box, type **Cell Margins**. In the Description text box, type **Set individual cell margins**.

2. Place the insertion point in the Contents text box, and in the Styles Editor dialog box choose Format | Paragraph | Format.

3. In the Left Margin Adjustment text box, type the amount you want WP to add to or subtract from the current left margin. For example, the default left column margin is 0.083"; so to have a left cell margin of 0.1", enter **0.017"**. If you want to decrease the margin to 0", enter **-0.083"**.

4. If you want to change the right margin, enter the amount of increase or decrease from the current right column margin (the default is also 0.083") in the Right Margin Adjustment text box.

5. Choose OK twice, and then Close.

6. Place the insertion point in the cell you want to format the margins in. Choose Format | Styles, select Cell Margins, and choose Apply. Repeat this in each cell you want to use the new margins in. (For more information on styles, see Chapter 5.)

Creating Formulas

When you're crunching numbers, there's no need to leave WordPerfect for a separate spreadsheet program. The advanced formula functions of WP 8 let you perform calculations from simple addition to complex amortization schedules right from a WP table. In this section, you'll learn how to create formulas in tables, including using QuickSum to instantly add rows or columns of numbers and using the various tools on the Formula Toolbar. In addition, we'll give you a reference guide to several common formula functions with examples of how they're used.

QuickSum

The most common calculation performed in a table is adding a column or row of numbers. With the QuickSum feature, you can instantly total the numbers in a column or row without even typing a formula. Follow these steps to use QuickSum:

1. If you want to total a column of numbers, place the insertion point in an empty cell just below the last number in the column. If you want to add across a row of numbers, place the insertion point in an empty cell just to the right of the numbers. If you want to sum several rows or columns in the table, select the columns and rows. Make sure you include an empty cell at the end of each column or row for the total to be placed in.

CAUTION: *Make sure there aren't any blank cells between the cell where the total will be inserted and the last cell containing a number or the QuickSum feature won't work properly.*

2. Choose Table | QuickSum from the Tables Property Bar. (If you have the Formula Toolbar displaying, you can also choose the QuickSum button there.)

3. WP adds the numbers and places the total in the cell, replacing any existing text. If you later edit the numbers in the table, the total is updated automatically if automatic calculation is turned on. If the total is not updated, you can turn automatic calculation on by choosing Table | Calculate from the Tables Property Bar, selecting Calculate Table, and choosing OK.

TIP: *You can also use QuickSum by placing the insertion point in the cell where you want the total to appear and pressing CTRL-=.*

CAUTION: *The QuickSum feature adds up any numbers it finds in the cells above or to the left of the total cell. If you have a heading cell at the top of the column or row that contains a number, such as a year, that number is included in the total. To avoid this, format the heading cell with the Text numeric format so it isn't included in the calculation.*

Formula Toolbar

When you need to calculate more than a simple sum, you can use WordPerfect's formula functions to get just the right result. Entering formulas in a table or floating cell is easy with the Formula Toolbar.

Cell address where
formula is being inserted   Formula Edit text box

Insert formula into cell

| TABLE A.A1 | X | ✔ | | | | | | | | |
| QuickSum | Functions.. | Names... | View Error... | Calculate | QuickFill | Copy Formula... | | Close | | |

Cancel changes   Turn on Row and
made to the formula   Column indicators

To display the Formula Toolbar, choose Table | Formula Toolbar from the Property Bar. Or right-click the table and choose Formula Toolbar.

To create a formula, first place the insertion point in the cell where you want the formula result to appear. Turn on the Formula Toolbar if you haven't already; then click the insertion point in the Formula Edit text box to turn on Formula Edit mode.

Formulas are made up of a combination of cell references, operators, and formula functions. Table 6-1 gives a brief description of the different types of elements that can be included in a formula.

Formula Element	Example	Description
Cell Reference	B3	Address of an individual cell in the table.
Cell Range	C1:C5 or A1.D4	Rectangular group of cells, where the first cell address is the cell in the upper-left corner and the second cell address is the cell in the lower-right corner.
Cell Intersection	March.Totals	Similar to a cell reference but used when columns and rows have been given names. If Column C is named "March," and Row 4 is named "Totals," the intersection "March.Totals" is Cell C4.
Arithmetic Operators	+, -, *, /	Performs an arithmetic operation, such as addition, subtraction, multiplication, or division. There are nine arithmetic operators.
Logical Operators	=, <, &, !	Compares two or more values and returns a result of 1 if the statement is true, or 0 if the statement is false. There are ten logical operators.
Table Names	Hours, TABLE A.Sales	Cell or group of cells that has been given a unique name. For example, "Hours" might be the name given to Column C, or "TABLE A.Sales" might refer to the cell range D1:D6 in Table A. Table names are described in the next section.
Formula Functions	SUM (A1:A10), MATCH (A1:E9, "August"), PMT (9%/12, 5000, 24, 0, 0)	Any of WP's formula functions that perform a specific calculation. Functions often contain cell addresses, ranges, and names. The functions are described later in this chapter.

TABLE 6-1 Elements That can be Included in Formulas

NOTE: *For more information on the available arithmetic and logical operators, choose Help | Help Topics. Select the Index tab, type* **arithmetic** *in the text box and choose Display twice.*

There are several ways you can insert the formula elements into the Formula Edit text box:

■ Type some or all of the formula directly into the text box.

■ Click the insertion point in other cells of the table, or select a group of cells, to insert the cell reference or range in the text box.

■ Use the Names button on the Formula Toolbar to insert a named cell or region into the text box.

■ Use the Functions button on the Formula Toolbar to select and insert a formula function.

After you've inserted the formula in the Formula Edit text box, click the check-mark button to insert the formula into the cell. The result of the formula calculation displays in the cell. If no values have been entered yet in the cells referenced by the formula, the formula result displays "0." If the formula has any errors, the cell displays two question marks (??) and an error message appears. You can view the error message at a later time by placing the insertion point in the cell with the error and choosing View Error on the Formula Toolbar.

TIP: *If you know the syntax of the formula, you can bypass the Formula Toolbar and type it directly into the table cell. To do this, place the insertion point in the cell and type + or = followed by the formula, such as +SUM(A1:A3). When you move out of the cell, the formula is calculated.*

NOTE: *The Application Bar at the bottom of the screen displays the formula used in the current cell (if there is one). If you want to enlarge this portion of the Application Bar so that more of the formula displays, right-click the Application Bar and choose Settings. Then drag the left edge of the General Status box to enlarge it. Choose OK when you're finished.*

For practice inserting some basic table formulas, you can set up an invoice like the one shown in Figure 6-12. See the "How to Create a Table Invoice" section for more information.

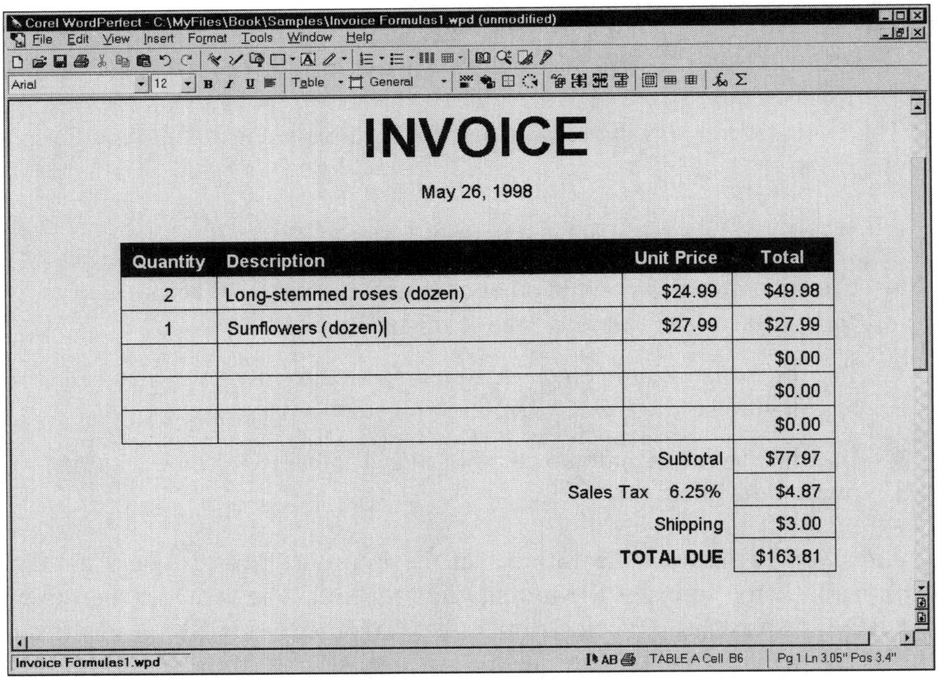

FIGURE 6-12   You can use formulas to automatically calculate an invoice

How to... Create a Table Invoice

Formulas are commonly used in table invoices, such as the one shown in Figure 6-12. The formulas automatically determine the cost of each item (based on the quantity and unit price), the sales tax, and the total amount due. This section will show you how to insert basic table formulas in an invoice.

Follow these steps to set up an invoice with formulas:

1. Open the INVOICE FORMULAS.WPD file from the companion CD.
   This file contains the basic table structure and formatting for the invoice shown in Figure 6-12.

How to...   Create a Table Invoice
(continued)

2. The first formula will calculate the total cost of an item, based on the quantity and unit price. To create this formula, place the insertion point in the first blank cell under the "Total" column heading (Cell E5). Choose Table | Formula Toolbar to display the Formula Toolbar.

3. Click in the Formula Edit text box to turn Formula Edit mode on. The formula should multiply the amount in the quantity cell with the amount in the unit price cell. Click the insertion point in the first cell under the "Quantity" column heading (Cell A5). This inserts the A5 cell reference into the text box.

4. Type * to signal multiplication.

5. Click the insertion point in the first cell under the "Unit Price" column heading (Cell C5). This inserts the C5 reference into the text box.

6. Click the check-mark button to insert the formula. "$0.00" displays because there are currently no numbers in the table. (The Total column has already been formatted with the Currency numeric format, so the dollar signs and decimal places automatically display.)

7. Now copy this formula down to the other rows in the invoice. Choose Copy Formula on the Formula Toolbar. Select Down, type **4** in the text box, and choose OK.

8. Click the insertion point in the cell to the right of "Subtotal" (Cell E10). Since the subtotal is a simple total of all the cells above it, choose QuickSum on the Formula Toolbar.

9. Place the insertion point in the cell to the right of the Sales Tax Rate (Cell E11). The sales tax is calculated by multiplying the sales tax rate by the subtotal. Click in the Formula Edit text box to turn Formula Edit mode on. Then click in the cell that contains the sales tax rate (currently 6.25 percent), and the reference D11 is inserted in the text box.

10. Type * to enter a multiplication symbol, and then click in the cell with the Subtotal amount (Cell E10). Since the sales tax rate in the table uses a percent sign, WP automatically determines the tax correctly. Click the check-mark button to insert the formula.

How to... Create a Table Invoice
(continued)

11. Finally, place the insertion point in the "TOTAL DUE" cell (Cell E13). This formula should be the sum of the subtotal, sales tax, and shipping (if any). Click the insertion point in the Formula Edit text box again.

12. Choose Functions on the Formula Toolbar. Select SUM in the dialog box and choose Insert.

13. With "List" selected in the text box, use the mouse to select the three cells that need to be added—the subtotal, sales tax, and shipping amount. The formula should update to look like this: SUM(E10:E12). Click the check-mark button.

To use the invoice, simply enter the information in the table and the formulas automatically calculate the individual item costs, subtotal, sales tax, and total. If you want to change the sales tax rate, just edit the existing rate in the table (Cell D11), making sure you keep the percent sign. If you add new rows to the middle section of the table, they won't contain the formula in the "Total" column. You'll need to copy the formula from one of the existing rows into the new row.

Table Names

As described in Table 6-1, one of the elements you can include in a formula is a table name. You can name an entire table or floating cell, or any table component, such as a cell, cell range, column, or row. When you're creating formulas, table names are often easier to remember than specific cell references and they can help make troubleshooting formula errors easier. Table names are especially helpful when your formula refers to cells in different tables in the document, since you can use a name like "Rate" instead of a reference like TABLE B.B2.

To name a table or table component, follow these steps:

1. Place the insertion point in the table, floating cell, cell, column, or row you want to name. If you want to name a range of cells, select the group of cells.

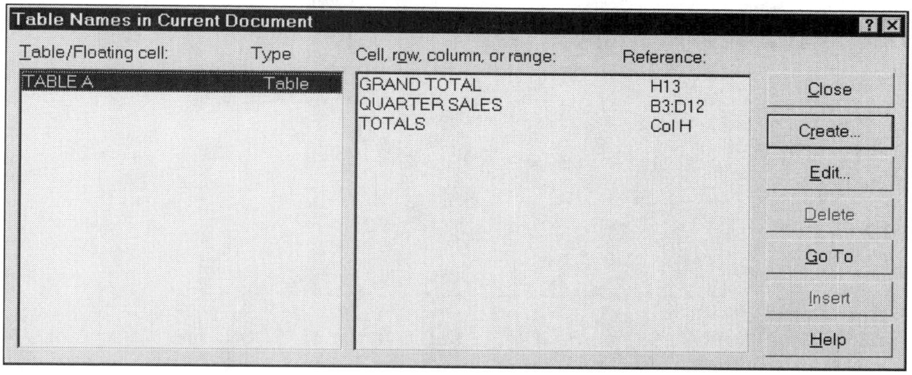

FIGURE 6-13 The Table Names dialog box lets you give unique names to table components

2. Choose Table | Names from the Tables Property Bar or choose Names on the Formula Toolbar. The Table Names dialog box appears, listing any existing tables and table names in the document (see Figure 6-13).

3. If you want to change the name of the entire table or floating cell, select the table or floating cell name in the Table/Floating Cell list and choose Edit. Type the name you want to use for the table or floating cell and choose OK.

NOTE: *By default, tables are named with consecutive letters in the order they appear in the document, such as TABLE A, TABLE B, and so on. Similarly, floating cells are named with consecutive letters.*

4. If you want to name the current cell, cell range, row, or column, choose Create. You can either type a name or have WP use the existing text in the cell for the name. For example, if the insertion point is in a cell with the text "Totals," you can have WP use that name for the entire column.

5. Select the option you want to name, such as Cell/Range, Column, or Row. The Reference: text at the bottom of the dialog box indicates what table component will be named with the currently selected option:

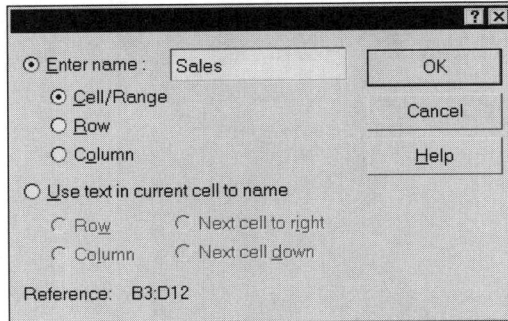

6. If you select Enter Name, type a name in the text box. The name can contain letters, numbers, spaces, and the symbols #, $, ?, @, or _. You can also include WP symbols in your name by pressing CTRL-W and selecting the symbol you want. However, the first character of the name must be a letter or underscore (_).

7. Choose OK when you're finished. The new table name appears in the list box, along with its corresponding reference in the table.

To use a name in a table formula, place the insertion point in the Formula Edit text box where you want the name inserted; then choose Names on the Formula Toolbar. Select the name you want to insert and choose Insert.

You can quickly move to a named area of the table by choosing Table | Names, selecting the named component, and choosing Go To. You can also press CTRL-G to display the Go To dialog box; then select Table and from the Cell/Range drop-down list, select the named area you want to go to.

TIP: *If you have several consecutive columns or rows that contain headings, you can name them all in one step using the corresponding heading text for each name. To do this, select only the cells with the heading information and choose Table | Names | Create. Select Use Text in Current Cell to Name; then select Column or Row and choose OK.*

Formula Functions

WordPerfect 8 comes with nearly 100 functions that you can use in your formulas. These functions range from simple calculations, such as SUM, to complex financial calculations, such as amortization schedules. To use functions in your formulas, you can type them directly in the Formula Edit text box if you know the syntax they require. Or you can insert them from the Table Functions dialog box (see Figure 6-14). To do this, place the insertion point in the Formula Edit text box where you want the function inserted and choose Functions on the Formula Toolbar.

WordPerfect has divided the formulas into different categories, such as mathematical and date. The default list shows all of the functions, but you can see the functions in a specific category by selecting that category from the Type of Functions to List drop-down list. When you select a function in the Functions list, a brief description appears at the bottom of the dialog box.

The text listed in parentheses after a function name indicates the type of information that you need to provide with that function. For example, INT(Number) returns the integer portion of the number included in parentheses. This could be a specific number such as INT(18.25), a cell reference such as INT(A2) to find the integer of the value in Cell A2, or a cell name such as INT(Result) to find the integer of the value in the cell named Result. Other functions ask for a list, which is any combination of items separated with commas, such as cell references, formulas, and

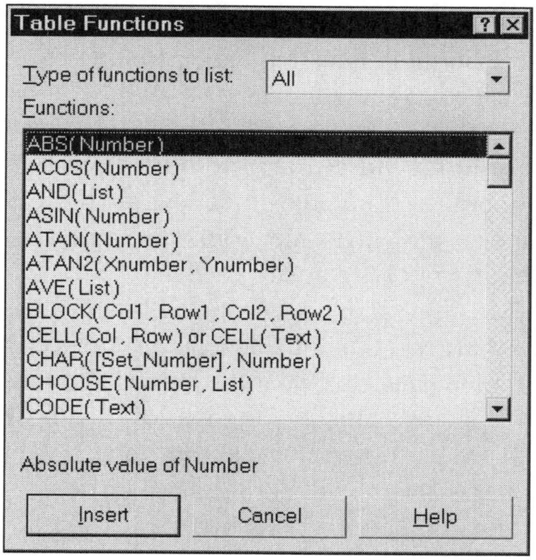

FIGURE 6-14 The Table Functions dialog box lists all the available formula functions

logical statements. Any information listed in square brackets, such as HOUR ([Time_Value]), is optional and doesn't have to be included in the formula.

Function Types

The formula functions in WP 8 are divided into six different categories: mathematical, date, financial, logical, miscellaneous, and string.

MATHEMATICAL The mathematical functions perform arithmetic operations, such as addition and subtraction. They also perform more complex operations, such as logarithms, trig calculations (sine, cosine, and so on), and standard deviations.

DATE The date functions allow you to easily add and subtract dates and times. For example, you can add 60 days to the current day or to a date in another table cell. The date functions work with unique numbers that WordPerfect has assigned to every consecutive date from January 1, 1900 to April 19, 65493. For example, the date value 33962 corresponds to December 25, 1992. Any function that requests the Date, Date_Value, Time, or Time_Value information in parentheses needs to have this unique number. The date and time value for a specific date or time can be determined with other date functions such as MDY, HMS, DATEVALUE, and TIMEVALUE. See the Formula Function Quick Reference section in this chapter for more information on using these functions.

FINANCIAL The financial functions include depreciation, growth, and amortization calculations. These complex functions are useful for determining such things as loan payments and investment growth rates. The financial function arguments are different from the arguments used in other functions and include such items as Cost, Period, Future Value, Payment, and Rate.

One of the most useful aspects of the financial functions is the ability to calculate different elements of a loan, such as what the monthly payments will be based on an initial loan amount, interest rate, and number of months. For example, Figure 6-15 shows a table that uses formulas to calculate any missing element of a loan when the other three items are known. For the steps on how to create this table, see the "How to Create a Loan Calculator" sidebar.

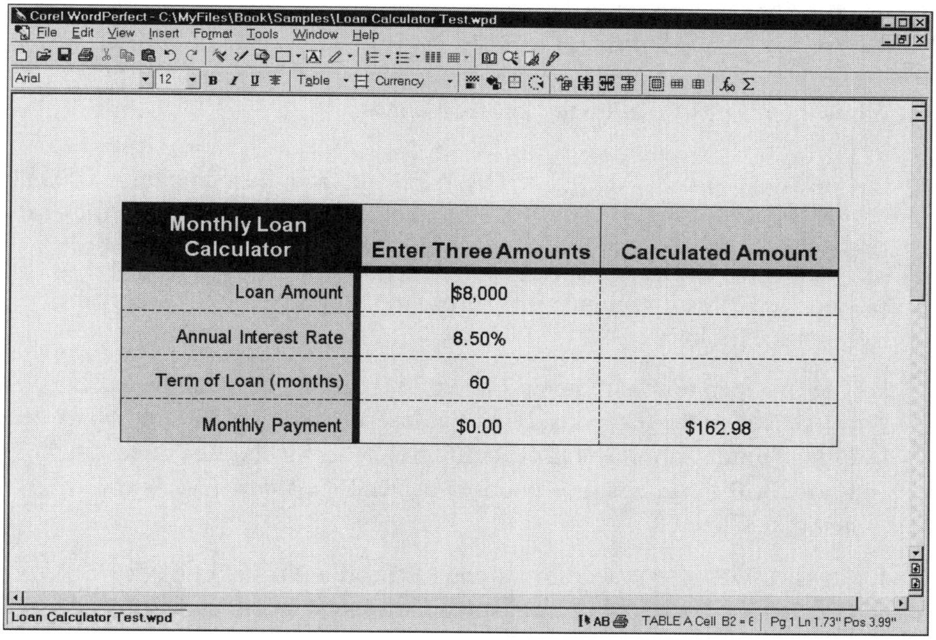

FIGURE 6-15 The financial formula functions can be used to calculate loan elements

How to... Create a Loan Calculator

WP's financial formula functions can be used to easily calculate different elements of a loan, such as the loan amount, interest rate, term of the loan, and the monthly payments. You can set up a table like the one shown in Figure 6-15 so that when any three of the loan elements are entered, the table automatically calculates the missing piece. The steps in this section will show you how to use the financial functions to calculate these values.

Create a Loan Calculator
(continued)

Follow these steps to set up the loan calculator:

1. Copy the LOAN CALCULATOR.WPD file from the companion CD onto your hard drive, and then open it into a document window. This file has the basic table structure and formatting for the loan calculator table.

2. Choose Table | Formula Toolbar from the Property Bar to display the Formula Toolbar.

3. The first step now is to name some of the cells so they can be easily referenced in the formulas. Place the insertion point in the first blank cell of the "Enter Three Amounts" column (Cell B2). Choose Names on the Formula Toolbar, and then choose Create. Type **Loan** and choose OK, and then Close.

4. Press DOWN ARROW to move to the next cell in the column (Cell B3). Choose Names | Create, type **Rate**; choose OK, and then Close.

5. Repeat this to name the next cell **Months** and the final cell in the column **Payment**.

6. So that you don't get error messages as you're creating the formulas, type a **1** in each cell under the "Enter Three Amounts" column. The numbers are automatically formatted based on the numeric format already selected for that cell.

7. Now you're ready to insert the formulas. To speed up this process, the formulas will be given here for you to type in directly, rather than entering the formula functions from the Functions button on the Formula Toolbar. Place the insertion point in the first cell under the "Calculated Amount" column (Cell C2).

8. Click the insertion point in the Formula Edit text box and type this formula:

   IF (Loan=0, PV (Rate/12, -Payment, Months, 0,1) , NA( ))

   Click the check-mark button to insert this formula.

How to... Create a Loan Calculator
(continued)

This formula works by first checking the contents of the cell named "Loan," which is the cell in the "Enter Three Amounts" column where the loan amount would be entered. If this amount equals zero (indicating that it is the missing element and needs to be calculated), the PV (principal value) function is calculated. If the amount in the cell named Loan *doesn't* equal zero, the NA ( ) function leaves the cell in the "Calculated Amount" column blank.

The PV function syntax is PV (Rate%, Payment, Periods, FV, [Type]). The Rate% argument is taken from the value in the cell named Rate and is divided by 12, so it is the monthly rate. The payment is taken from the cell named Payment and is negative to indicate the value of the loan will decrease instead of increase. The periods argument comes from the cell named Months, which contains the number of months for the term of the loan. The Future Value (FV) is set to 0, since you want to pay the loan completely off. And the type of loan is set to 1, indicating that the payments will be made at the end of each month.

9. To insert the next formula, place the insertion point in the next cell down in the "Calculated Amount" column (Cell C3). Click in the Formula Edit text box and enter this formula:

   IF (Rate=0, RATE (Loan, -Payment, Months, 0,1)*12 , NA( ))

   Click the check-mark button to insert this formula. This formula uses the RATE function to determine the interest rate if the cell named Rate is left blank. It uses the other three pieces of information, and is multiplied by 12 to convert the monthly interest rate to an annual rate.

10. Place the insertion point in the next cell in the column (Cell C4) and click in the Formula Edit text box. Enter this formula:

    IF (Months=0, TERM (Rate/12, Loan, -Payment, 0,1) , NA( ))

    Click the check-mark button when you're finished. If the cell named Months is blank, this formula uses the TERM function in conjunction

How to... Create a Loan Calculator (continued)

with the three other pieces of information to determine the number of months for the loan.

11. Finally, place the insertion point in the last cell of the column (Cell C5), click in the Formula Edit text box, and enter this formula:

IF (Payment=0, -PMT (Rate/12, Loan, Months, 0,1), NA( ))

Click the check-mark button to insert it. The PMT function is used to determine the payment amount based on the other pieces of information. The function has a minus sign in front of it to display the result (which is negative because it is paid to the lender) as a positive number in the table.

To use the loan calculator, enter the three pieces of known information and set the fourth cell to zero. The table automatically calculates the missing piece of information and displays it in the "Calculated Amount" column. For example, you can find out the monthly payments for an $8,000 auto loan with an 8.5 percent annual interest rate over five years. To do this, enter **8000** in the Loan Amount cell, enter **8.5** in the Annual Interest Rate cell, enter **60** in the Term of Loan cell, and enter **0** in the Monthly Payment cell. WP calculates the formulas and displays the monthly payment as $162.98. You can change the information in the cells as often as you want to determine different scenarios. The companion CD also contains a document named LOAN CALCULATOR2.WPD, which has a completed table and formulas.

LOGICAL   The logical formula functions can be used to test conditions that have a true or false result, such as whether a cell contains a text value or has any errors. One of the most useful logical functions is IF, which tests a condition and takes one course of action if the value is true (such as calculating a different function or inserting a number), or a different course of action if the value is false. For example, the IF function can be used to calculate a formula only if the cells referenced within the formula contain values. This is useful, for instance, in a checkbook ledger where the running total formula is copied to all of the empty table rows. For example, a formula might look something like this:

IF (ISNA(C3), NA( ), D2-C3)

This formula uses the ISNA function to check if Cell C3 contains a value. If the cell *doesn't* contain a value, the NA function causes the current cell to remain blank. However, when the cell does contain a value, the formula D2-C3 is calculated. Any formula could be used in place of "D2-C3."

CHECKBOOK.WPD: *The companion CD contains a document named CHECKBOOK.WPD that uses table formulas to keep the total hidden. Open this document and add amounts to the table to see the formulas used.*

MISCELLANEOUS The miscellaneous functions deal mostly with the location of information in a table, such as counting the number of items in a cell range or locating cells that match a specific value.

STRING The string functions help you work with text strings, such as converting text to all upper or lowercase, or returning a substring.

NOTE: *When you're inserting a text argument in a formula, the text must be enclosed in quotation marks, unless you're using a cell reference.*

The "Common Formula Functions" reference section contains a list of 25 common WP formula functions, including a brief description and example of how each is used. The sample table shown in Figure 6-16 is referred to in some of the examples.

TABLE FORMULAS.WPD: *The companion CD contias a document named TABLE FORMULAS.WPD that contains a complete, alphabetical listing of all 97 table formula functions. Each function includes a brief description and example.*

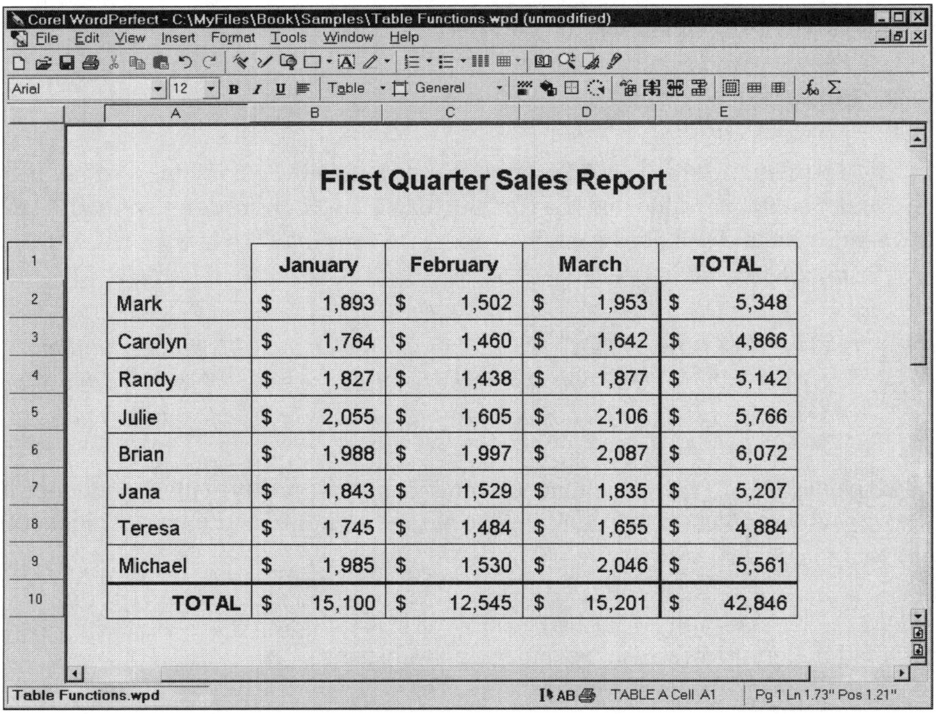

First Quarter Sales Report

	January	February	March	TOTAL
Mark	$ 1,893	$ 1,502	$ 1,953	$ 5,348
Carolyn	$ 1,764	$ 1,460	$ 1,642	$ 4,866
Randy	$ 1,827	$ 1,438	$ 1,877	$ 5,142
Julie	$ 2,055	$ 1,605	$ 2,106	$ 5,766
Brian	$ 1,988	$ 1,997	$ 2,087	$ 6,072
Jana	$ 1,843	$ 1,529	$ 1,835	$ 5,207
Teresa	$ 1,745	$ 1,484	$ 1,655	$ 4,884
Michael	$ 1,985	$ 1,530	$ 2,046	$ 5,561
TOTAL	$ 15,100	$ 12,545	$ 15,201	$ 42,846

FIGURE 6-16 This sample table is used with some of the function examples in the Common Formula Functions Quick Reference section

Quick Reference ▸▸▸ Common Formula Functions

This section contains a list of 25 common WP formula functions. The text in parentheses indicates the function arguments, or information that needs to be provided when the function is used. Any arguments listed in square brackets are optional. Remember that the numbers used in the examples can be replaced with cell references, ranges, or names. Many of the examples include cell references that refer to the sample table shown in Figure 6-16. The companion CD contains a document named TABLE FORMULAS.WPD with a complete, alphabetical listing of all 97 of WP's table formula functions.

Function	Description	Example
AVE(List)	Returns the average (mean) of the numbers in list.	(Refer to Figure 6-16) AVE (8, SUM(2,4,7), 3*5) = 12 AVE (E2:E9) = 5,306
COUNT(List)	Returns a count of the number of items in the given list. Only those cells containing a value are counted.	(Refer to Figure 6-16) COUNT (A1:E1) = 4 COUNT (A7, C2, E10) = 3
DATE( )	Inserts the current date. The format used is the one selected with the Numeric Format feature or the document's current date format.	If the date is 4/8/98 and the DATE ( ) function is used in Cell A3, that cell would contain April 8, 1998 (unless a different date format had been set).
DATETEXT (Date)	Converts a date value into text. The date displays in the format selected in the Numeric Format dialog box or in the document's current date format. See also DATEVALUE.	DATETEXT (33451) = August 2, 1991 DATETEXT (DATEVALUE ("4/26/96")) = April 26, 1996
DATEVALUE (Text)	Returns the date value for the given text string. Each date from January 1, 1900 is assigned a unique consecutive number. The string must be enclosed in quotation marks.	DATEVALUE ("6/24/94") = 34508 DATEVALUE ('1-29') = 35458 if the current year is 1997

Function	Description	Example
FV (Rate%, PV, Payment, Periods, [Type])	Calculates the future value of an investment or loan. The Type argument is 0 if the payment is made at the end of the period, or 1 if it is made at the beginning of the period.	FV (8.5%/12, 90000, -883.20, 10*12, 0) = -43774.39 $43,774.39 is the remaining balance after ten years on a $90,000 loan taken out at 8.5 percent annual interest with a monthly payment of $883.20. The interest rate is divided by 12, so it is a monthly rate, and the number of years is multiplied by 12, so it is also expressed in terms of months.
HMS ([Hour], [Minute], [Second])	Returns the specified time of day as a decimal number (time value). The Hour argument must be from 0 to 24 and the Minute and Second arguments must be from 0 to 59. The resulting decimal is from 0 to 0.9999988, with 0 equal to 12:00 midnight and 0.5 equal to 12:00 noon.	HMS (9,42,38) = 0.404606 (decimal value of (9:42:38 AM) HMS (14:27) = 0.6020833 (decimal value of 2:27 PM) HMS (20) = 0.8333333 (decimal value of 10:00 PM) HMS ( ) = decimal value of current computer time

Function	Description	Example
IF (Condition, Val1, Val2)	Returns Val1 if the condition is true, or returns Val2 if the condition is false. The condition can be any logical statement. Val1 and Val2 can be a number, text string, cell address, or another formula.	(Refer to Figure 6-16) IF (B10<C10, B10*2, B10-C10) = 2554 IF (ISNA (A1), NA ( ), C2-D2) = NA ( )
INDEX (Block, Col, Row)	Returns the number or text in the cell indicated by the column and row number in the given block of cells. Negative column and row numbers count the columns from right to left and rows from bottom up.	(Refer to Figure 6-16) INDEX (B1:C10, 2, -2) = 1,530
INT(Number)	Returns only the integer portion of a number.	INT (15.73) = 15
ISNA(List)	Returns 1 (true) if all the cells in the list are empty. If one or more cells in the list contains a value, 0 (false) is returned.	(Refer to Figure 6-16) ISNA (A1:A9, A10:E10) = 0 (false) ISNA (A1) = 1 (true)

Function	Description	Example
MATCH (Block, Value, [Offset])	Looks up a value in the specified block of cells. If there are more rows than columns in the block, the first column is used as the index. If there are more columns than rows, the first row is used as the index. The Value argument is the exact number or text string you want to find in the index row or column. When the value is found, the number or text in the last cell of the index column or row in the specified block is returned. The offset value can be used to return a cell other than the last cell. A negative offset value counts that number of cells to the left or up from the index cell.	(Refer to Figure 6-16) MATCH (A1:E9, "Carolyn") = 4866 MATCH (E2:E9, MAX (E2:E9), -4) = Brian MATCH (A10:D10, 15201, -9) = March
MAX(List)	Returns the largest number in the given list.	(Refer to Figure 6-16) MAX (E2:E9) = 6072
MDY ([[Month, Day], [Year]])	Returns the date value of the specified month, day, and year. The month should be a number from 1-12, the day from 1-31, and the year must be greater than 1900. Any arguments that aren't included are assumed to be the current month, day, or year. If the cell is formatted with the Date/Time numeric format, the resulting date appears in the specified format, such as 1/29/92 or January 29, 1992.	MDY (1,29,92) = 33631 MDY (1,29) = 35458 if the current year is 1997 MDY ( ) = the date value for the current date

Function	Description	Example
MIN(List)	Returns the smallest number in the given list.	(Refer to Figure 6-16) MIN (E1:E9) = 4866
NA( )	Returns the N/A (not available) value, or an empty cell.	Using NA ( ) in a cell leaves the cell blank.
PMT (Rate%, PV, Periods, FV, [Type])	Returns the payment for a loan or investment. The type argument is 0 if the payment is made at the end of the period, or 1 if the payment is made at the beginning of the period.	PMT (8.5%/12, 12000, 5*12, 0, 1) = -244.47 A monthly payment of $244.47 is needed to completely pay off a $12,000 loan taken at 8.5 percent annual interest and paid over five years. The interest rate is divided by 12, so it is a monthly rate, and the number of years is multiplied by 12, so it is also expressed in terms of months.
PV (Rate%, Payment, Periods, FV, [Type])	Calculates the present value for a loan or investment. The Type is 0 if the payment is made at the end of each period, or 1 if the payment is made at the beginning of each period.	PV (7.5%/12, -900, 15*12, 0, 1) = 97692.87 $97,692.87 is the amount of money that can be borrowed at 7.5 percent annual interest with a 15-year loan and making monthly payments of $900. The payments are negative because they are paid to the lender. The interest rate is divided by 12, so it is a monthly rate, and the number of years is multiplied by 12, so it is also expressed in terms of months.

Function	Description	Example
RATE (PV, Payment, Periods, FV, [Type])	Calculates the periodic interest rate for a loan or investment. The Type is 0 if the payment is made at the end of each period, or 1 if the payment is made at the beginning of each period.	RATE (0, -75, 24, 2000, 0) = 0.00903 A monthly interest rate of 0.903 percent (or an annual interest rate of 10.84 percent) is needed to have an investment of $75 paid at the end of each month for two years reach the value of $2,000. The payment is negative because it is paid into the investment and the future value is positive because it is paid back to you.
ROUND (Number, Precision)	Returns the number rounded to the number of decimal places specified by Precision (up to 15 decimal places). If Precision is negative, the number is rounded to the left of the decimal. For example, a precision of -1 rounds to the nearest 10, -2 rounds to the nearest 100, and so on.	ROUND (42.862, 1) = 42.9 ROUND (56.2, -1) = 60
SUM(List)	Returns the sum of the numbers in the list.	(Refer to Figure 6-16) SUM (B2:D2) = 5348

Function	Description	Example
TERM (Rate%, PV, Payment, FV, [Type])	Calculates the number of periods for a loan or investment. The Type is 0 if the payment is made at the end of each period, or 1 if the payment is made at the beginning of each period.	TERM (9.5%/12, 9000, -250, 0, 0) = 42.5 42.5 months are required to completely pay off a $9,000 loan at 9.5 percent annual interest, with a monthly payment of $250 made at the end of each month. The payments are negative because they are paid to the lender. The interest rate is divided by 12, so it is a monthly rate.
TIME ( )	Returns the current time as a text string. The time is updated each time the table is calculated.	TIME ( ) = 2:32 PM if the current computer time is 2:32 PM
TIMETEXT (Time)	Returns the given time value as a text string.	TIMETEXT (0.404606) = 9:42 AM
TIMEVALUE (Text)	Returns the decimal time value of the time indicated in the text string. The text string must be in quotation marks. The text string can be in the format hour, hour:minute, or hour:minute:second.	TIMEVALUE ("7:30:42") = 0.3129861

Copying Formulas

Tables often contain several rows or columns that use a similar formula, such as the invoice in Figure 6-12. If you create a formula in one cell, you don't need to re-create it in the other cells. Instead, you can copy the formula to other cells in the table. When you copy a formula, any cell addresses in the formula are updated so they're applicable to the new cell's location.

To copy a formula to other cells, place the insertion point in the cell containing the formula. If the Formula Toolbar is displaying, choose Copy Formula on the Formula Toolbar. Otherwise, choose Table | Copy Formula from the Tables Property Bar. The Copy Formula dialog box appears:

If you want to copy the formula to a specific cell in the table, type the cell reference in the To Cell text box. To copy the formula to the cells directly below or to the right of the current cell, select Down or Right and type the number of cells you want to copy the formula into. Choose OK.

NOTE: *If the cells you're copying the formula into already contain text or a formula, that text is replaced with the new formula.*

Relative and Absolute Cell References

When you create a formula using cell references, such as C3-D2, WordPerfect considers those cell addresses to be *relative*. If you copy a formula with relative cell references to other cells, the references in the copied formula are automatically updated so they're in the same relative position to the new cell as those in the original formula were to the original cell. For example, as shown here, the last column contains a formula that multiplies the hourly rate by the number of hours. In this table, the formula in Cell D3 is B3*C3.

Formula B3*C3

BILLING NOTICE

Description	Hours	Hourly Rate	Total
Initial research	3.00	$ 25.00	$ 75.00
Prepare memo	0.50	$ 15.00	$ 7.50
Draft report	4.25	$ 30.00	$ 127.50

Formula B4*C4
Formula B5*C5

Since each row in the table needs a similar formula that multiplies the hourly rate by the number of hours, the formula in Cell D3 can be copied to the cells below it. When this formula is copied to the cell below (Cell D4), the relative addresses in the formula are updated, so the copied formula is now B4*C4. Since the references are updated, the copied formula is able to use the correct values for the current row. Copying formulas with relative cell references is very useful if you want to use the same formula down a column or across a row, yet have the formula update to include the corresponding cells for that row or column.

You can also include *absolute* cell references in a formula. An absolute cell reference is not updated when it is copied, but instead remains the same for all the formulas. To make a cell reference in a formula absolute, enclose the cell reference in square brackets, such as [B3]. For example, as shown next, the hourly rate is included in a cell at the top of the table (Cell B2). Since you want to use this same amount in each formula down the column, you can make it absolute by enclosing the reference in brackets, such as [B2]*C4. Then, when the formula is copied to the cell below, rather than being updated to C3*C5, it is [B2]*C5.

Formula [B2]*C4

BILLING NOTICE

Hourly Rate: $25.00			
Description	Hours		Total
Initial Research	3.00	$	75.00
Prepare Memo	0.50	$	12.50
Draft report	4.25	$	106.25

Formula [B2]*C5
Formula [B2]*C6

NOTE: *You can also create absolute cell references by naming a cell and then using that cell name in the formula. For example, in the previous illustration, Cell B2 could be named "Rate" and then the formula Rate*C3 could be used to calculate the total.*

TIP: *You can create mixed cell addresses with an absolute column letter and relative row number, such as [C]2; or vice versa, such as C[2].*

Calculating Formulas

WordPerfect has a table calculation feature that automatically calculates formulas in a table as soon as you create them or edit the values in any of the referenced cells. In addition, any other tables or floating cells in the document are also calculated each time you edit a formula or cell value. You can turn the automatic formula calculation feature on or off. For example, you can turn it off if you're working in a large table and don't want to wait for all the formulas to update each time you make a change.

To change the calculation mode, choose Table | Calculate from the Tables Property Bar. The Calculate dialog box appears:

To have WP update only the current table when you make a change, select Calculate Table. If you want every table or floating cell in the document updated, select Calculate Tables in Document. To turn off the automatic calculation feature, select Off. Choose OK.

If you've turned off automatic calculation and want to calculate the table manually, you can choose Calculate on the Formula Toolbar if it's displaying, or choose Table | Calculate, and then choose Calc Table to calculate the current table or Calc Document to calculate all the tables in the document.

Removing Formula References

Once you've calculated formulas in a table, you can remove the actual formulas and leave the calculated results as numbers in the cell. This is useful if you want to keep the calculated results without worrying about accidentally changing them as you edit other locations in the table. Or you might copy your table to another document and simply not need the formula references included. WP lets you quickly remove the formula references from the entire table or only selected cells.

To remove all the formulas from a table, place the insertion point anywhere in the table and choose Table | Delete from the Property Bar. In the dialog box, select Formulas Only and choose OK. Any calculated results from the formulas are converted to text or numbers and replace the formula in the corresponding cell.

```
┌─────────────────────────────────────────────┐
│ Delete Structure/Contents            [?][X] │
├─────────────────────────────────────────────┤
│  ┌─ Delete ──────────────┐  ┌─────────────┐ │
│  │ ○ Columns    1    [▲▼] │  │     OK      │ │
│  │                        │  └─────────────┘ │
│  │ ○ Rows       1    [▲▼] │  ┌─────────────┐ │
│  │                        │  │   Cancel    │ │
│  │ ○ Cell contents only   │  └─────────────┘ │
│  │                        │  ┌─────────────┐ │
│  │ ⊙ Formulas only        │  │    Help     │ │
│  └────────────────────────┘  └─────────────┘ │
│  ┌─ Current table size ─────────────┐         │
│  │ Columns:  8                      │         │
│  │ Rows:     13                     │         │
│  └──────────────────────────────────┘         │
└─────────────────────────────────────────────┘
```

If you want to remove the formula reference from a single cell only, place the insertion point in the cell and press SPACEBAR; then press BACKSPACE to delete the space you inserted. Press TAB to move out of the cell, and WP displays a message asking if you want to replace the formula. If you choose Yes, the existing text or numbers in the cell replace the formula. If you choose No, any changes you made to the cell are deleted and the formula remains the same. Choose Yes to remove the formula.

NOTE: *If you replace formulas frequently and don't want to be prompted each time, choose Tools | Settings, and double-click Environment. Select the Prompts tab and deselect the Confirm Deletion of Table Formulas option. Choose OK, and then Close. Now if you make any editing changes in a cell that contains a formula, the formula is automatically replaced with the text or numbers in the cell.*

TIP: *If you want to prevent users from making editing changes in a cell that contains a formula, lock that cell so the insertion point can't be placed in it. To do this, select the cell and choose Table | Format. Select Lock Cell to Prevent Changes and choose OK. You can repeat these steps to unlock the cell if you later need to edit the formula.*

Using Floating Cells

Floating cells are a special kind of table that you can create in your documents. Floating cells are single-celled tables that don't have a border and can be inserted anywhere in a document, such as in the middle of a text line or in a header. You can insert formulas in floating cells and format them with the Numeric Format feature.

Floating cells can be linked to text or numbers in other tables in the document. For example, you can create a floating cell in the body text of a letter that refers to a calculated loan amount from a table in the document (see Figure 6-17). Then, if the information in the table is changed, the floating cell automatically updates to display the correct data.

To create a floating cell, follow these steps:

1. Place the insertion point in the document where you want the floating cell inserted.

2. Choose Insert | Table.

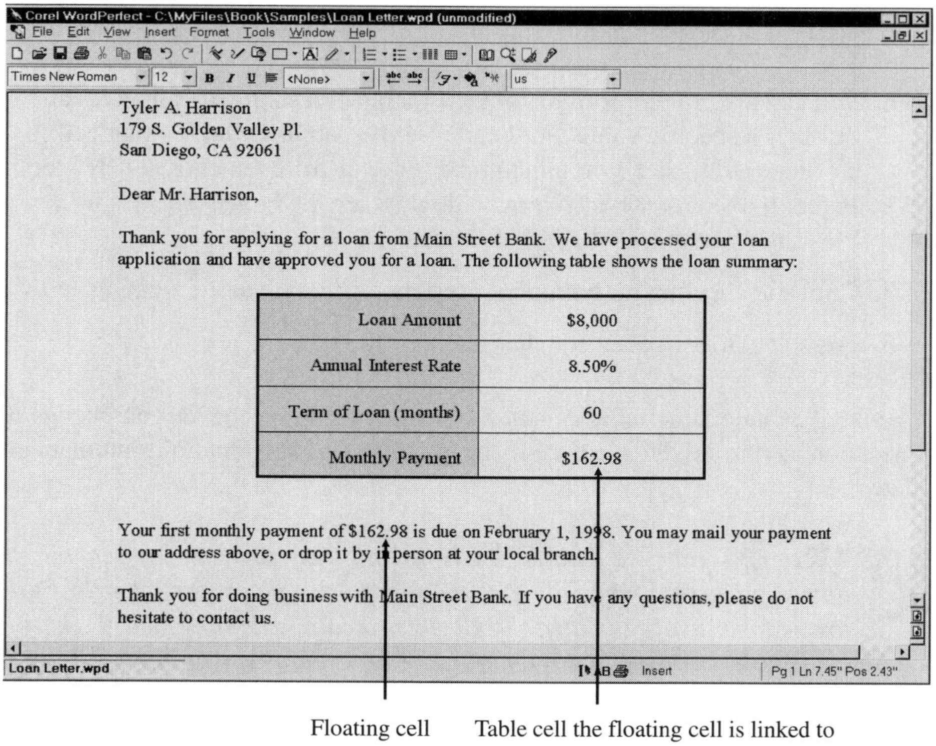

Floating cell   Table cell the floating cell is linked to

FIGURE 6-17 Floating cells can be linked to information in other table cells

3. Select Floating Cell and choose Create. The document doesn't appear any differently, but if you turn on Reveal Codes, you'll see that the insertion point is between two Floating Cell codes. The Formula Toolbar automatically appears when you create a floating cell if it isn't already displaying.

4. If you want the floating cell information to display in a certain numeric format, choose Table | Numeric Format from the Tables Property Bar. Select the format you want, such as Currency, and choose OK.

5. To link the floating cell to a table cell so that it automatically displays the information in that cell, click the insertion point in the Formula Edit text box. If the table cell you want to link to has been named, choose Names on the Formula Toolbar, select the name you want, and choose Insert. Otherwise, click the insertion point in the table cell you want to refer to and the cell reference is automatically inserted in the Formula Edit text box.

6. You can also enter a formula in the floating cell so that it calculates and displays a specific value. For example, you can have the floating cell calculate a due date a certain number of days from the current date (see Figure 6-18). For steps on how to do this, see the Power Tip "Using Floating Cells to Calculate Due Dates."

7. Click the check-mark button to insert the formula into the floating cell.

8. Press END to move outside the floating cell codes.

As long as automatic table calculation is turned on, whenever you change the information in the linked table cell, the floating cell information automatically updates.

TIP: *You can use floating cells to link text together throughout the document so that when the text changes in one place, the other locations are automatically updated. To do this, create a floating cell in the first location and name it with a unique name. Then create additional floating cells where you want the same text referenced and link them to the original floating cell name. Whenever the text in the first floating cell changes, the others are automatically updated.*

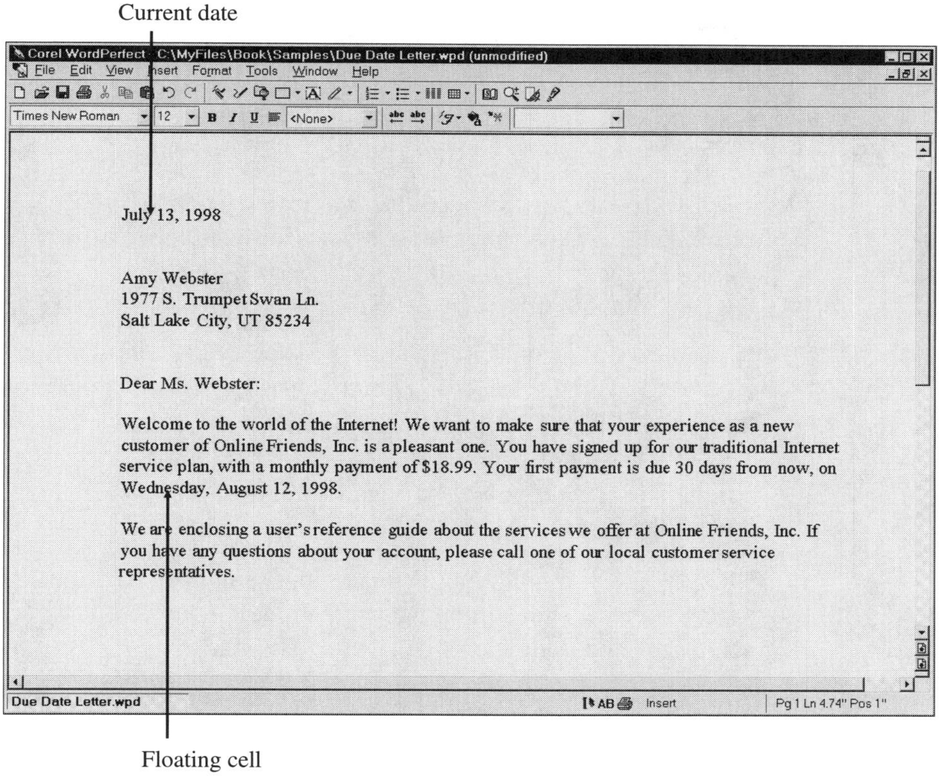

Current date

Floating cell

FIGURE 6-18 Floating cells can contain formulas that calculate due dates

Power Tip... Using Floating Cells to Calculate Due Dates

Floating cells can be used to easily calculate and insert due dates within a document. For example, you can use a floating cell to insert a due date 30 days from the current date within the text of a letter, as shown in Figure 6-18. Follow these steps to create this type of floating cell:

1. Place the insertion point in the document where you want the due date inserted.

2. Choose Insert | Table, select Floating Cell, and choose Create.

3. From the Tables Property Bar, choose Table | Numeric Format.

4. Select Date/Time and choose Custom. From the Date/Time formats, select the format that you want the due date to display in, such as Wednesday, December 17, 1997 or 12/17/97. Choose OK twice.

5. Click the insertion point in the Formula Edit text box. Type **MDY ( ) +30**. If you want to use a due date other than 30 days in the future, substitute that amount in the formula, such as MDY ( ) +60 for a due date 60 days from the current date. You can also use negative numbers to calculate dates in the past.

6. Click the check-mark button to insert the formula. The correct due date should automatically appear in the floating cell. Choose Close to close the Formula Toolbar.

Each time you open this document, the due date changes to reflect the date 30 days from the current date (or whatever future amount you specified). This formula works by taking the date *value* of the current day from the MDY ( ) function and adding 30 to it. The numeric format in the floating cell automatically displays the new date value in the correct date format. If you hadn't selected the numeric format for the cell, the date would appear as the date value number, such as 35700.

Summary

Tables can give you great power and flexibility for displaying both text and numbers in your WordPerfect documents. You can quickly format a table to use the custom border, lines, and fills you want, along with placing cell divisions exactly where you need them. Features such as QuickFill, QuickFormat, and Numeric Format speed up the process of inserting and formatting data in your table. WP has many table shortcuts and tools that make creating tables in your document an easy and enjoyable chore.

Table formulas give you spreadsheet power within WordPerfect. The available formula functions cover everything from simple arithmetic to complex growth and amortization calculations. Formulas are easy to insert and update with the Formula Toolbar, and formulas can quickly be copied to other cells or completely removed from the table. Floating cells are unique, single-celled tables that let you link to information in other tables or contain formulas of their own to display within the text of a document.

In Chapter 7, we'll take a look at the wonderful world of graphics and how you can manipulate them to get just the image you want.

6

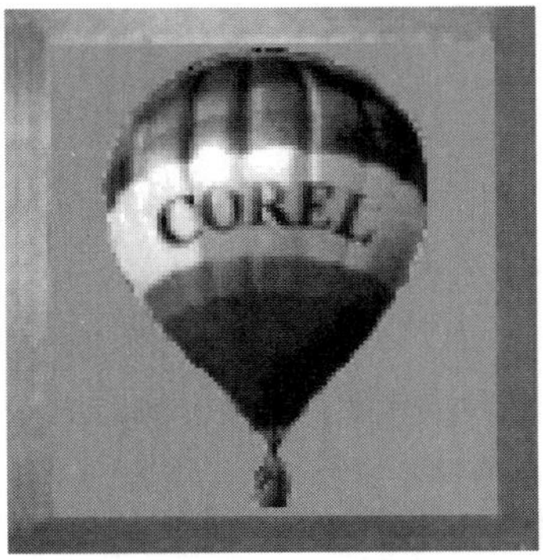
COREL

Chapter 7

Add Impact with Graphics

We're constantly bombarded from all sides with visual images that vie to catch our eye and hold our interest. So how do you succeed in getting your documents noticed? One of the best ways to grab your reader's attention is to include some graphical elements. Graphics not only make documents more eye-catching and interesting to look at, they can also strengthen your document's message. Fortunately, WordPerfect gives you all the tools you need to easily add graphics to your documents and quickly manipulate them into just the image you want.

In this chapter, we'll discuss the many features and power tools available for controlling the images in your documents. You'll learn how to insert and customize clipart images, shapes, and text boxes. We'll show you how to combine text with images, and format graphics boxes with custom graphics styles. In addition, you'll learn how to create unique headings with TextArt and quickly create complex equations with the new Equation Editor in WP 8.

Inserting Images

The hardest part about inserting an image into a WP document is deciding which image to use. For example, you can choose clipart images in an unending variety of formats and styles, photos, and even scanned images. WP 8 makes it easy to insert these different types of images into your documents. The new Scrapbook feature lets you quickly access the thousands of clipart images on the WP Suite 8 CD. Or you can insert individual graphics files from many different formats, such as WPG, BMP, JPG, and so on. If you have a scanner connected to your computer, you can even scan images directly into WP. In this section, we'll give you a brief overview on using these methods to insert images.

Using the Scrapbook

The Scrapbook is a new feature that helps you manage the 10,000+ clipart images included on the WP Suite 8 CD. The Scrapbook organizes the images by category and displays them in miniature format so you can easily browse through them (see Figure 7-1). In addition, the Scrapbook lets you search for images containing a certain keyword.

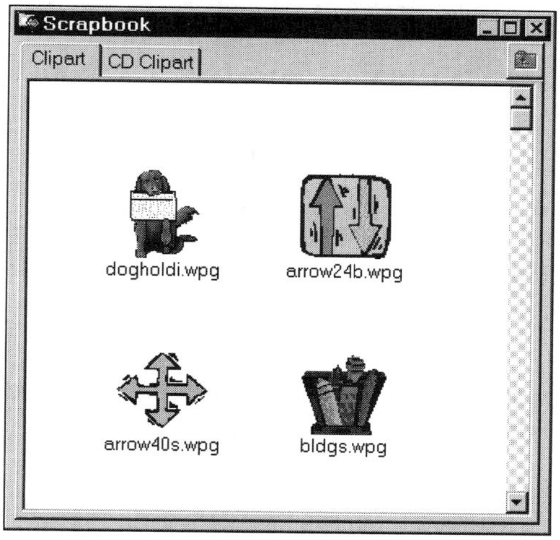

FIGURE 7-1 The Scrapbook helps you manage the many CD clipart images

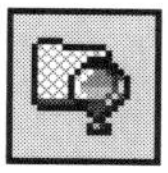

To use the Scrapbook, choose Insert | Graphics | Clipart, or click the Clipart button on the toolbar. When the Scrapbook dialog box appears, scroll through the folders and images until you find an image you want to use. The Scrapbook displays any WPG images that are in its default directory, including those compressed in SCB files. During a typical installation, the COMPACT.SCB file (which contains 62 images) is copied to your default graphics directory and the other SCB files remain on the CD. To view the images on the CD, make sure the WP Suite 8 CD is in the drive; then click the CD Clipart tab and navigate through the available folders.

NOTE: *To have the Scrapbook use a different default directory, right-click a blank area of the Scrapbook and choose Set Default Folder. Type the path to the new directory or choose the Browse button to select it. The Scrapbook displays any WPG files in that directory, along with WPG images compressed in SCB files. If the files aren't compressed in an SCB file, the Scrapbook takes a few seconds to load them each time.*

TIP: *To change how the Scrapbook images display, right-click a blank area of the Scrapbook and choose View; then select the option you want, such as Small Icons. Or deselect Filename to not have the filename display. You can also change the size of the Scrapbook dialog box by clicking and dragging the border.*

If you want to search for images with a particular keyword, switch to the folder that you think will most likely have the image you're looking for. Then right-click a blank area and choose Find. Type the keyword, such as **money,** and choose Find. If an image is found with that keyword, WP highlights it by placing a box around it. To find the next matching image, right-click and choose Find Next, or press F3.

> **NOTE:**   *To see what keywords a particular image uses, right-click the image and choose Properties. You can't change or add the keywords used by an image.*

Once you've found the image you want, all you need to do is click and drag it into the document window. WP places the image in a graphics box, which you can then move, size, or edit using the available tools described later in this chapter.

> **TIP:**   *If you want to save an image from the Scrapbook as a separate WPG file, insert the image into your document and select it with the mouse. Choose File | Save As. Select Selected Image, and then choose OK. Switch to the directory where you want to save the file and type a filename, using a WPG extension.*

Graphics Files

While the Scrapbook lets you easily click and drag images into your documents, it only works with WPG images in a particular directory and compressed SCB files on the WP Suite 8 CD. If you want to insert an image that's in a different directory or a different graphics format, such as BMP or JPG, you need to select that file individually.

To insert a graphics file, choose Insert | Graphics | From File. Switch to the directory containing the file you want, select the file, and choose Insert. WP inserts the image in a graphics box, which you can then move, size, and edit. WP 8 supports a long list of graphics formats. See the "Supported Graphics Formats" box for a list of the image types you can insert into WordPerfect.

> **NOTE:**   *If you want to change the default directory that WP looks in for graphics images, choose Tools | Settings, and double-click Files. Select the Graphic tab, and then type the new directory in the Default Graphics Folder text box (or use the file folder icon to select it). Choose OK and then Close when you're finished.*

Quick Reference ▶▶▶ Supported Graphics Formats

WP 8 supports a wide variety of graphics formats. A typical installation of WP lets you retrieve or save images in any of the formats listed next. You can also install conversions for additional graphics formats (see Chapter 20 for more information).

Bitmap	*.BMP, *.DIB	JPEG Bitmap	*.JPG, *.JPE
CALS Compressed Bitmap	*.CAL	Micrografx Picture Publisher 4	*.PP4
CompuServe GIF	*.GIF	PC Paintbrush Graphic	*.PCX
Corel PHOTO-PAINT 6 & 7	*.CPT	Portable Network Graphic	*.PNG, *.GIF
CorelDRAW 3, 4, 5, 6, 7	*.CDR, *.PAT, *.CDT	TIFF Graphic	*.TIF
CorelDRAW CMX	*.CMX	Windows Metafile	*.WMF
Encapsulated Postscript	*.EPS	WordPerfect Graphics 5, 6/7/8	*.WPG
Enhanced Windows Metafile	*.EMF	WP Works 2.0 Paint	*.WPW

TIP: *If you have the Shadow Cursor turned on (View | Shadow Cursor), you can also quickly insert a clipart image or graphics file by clicking and dragging in a blank area of a document. After dragging the box to the approximate size you want for the graphic, release the mouse button and a pop-up menu appears. Choose the option you want, such as Clipart or Image from File, and then select the image.*

Image on Disk

Inserting a graphics file can greatly increase the file size of a document, especially if the graphics file is large to begin with. To reduce the document's size, you can use the Image on Disk option, which doesn't actually save the graphics file as part of the document. Instead, Image on Disk simply stores the image's path and filename in the document, so that WordPerfect can locate and retrieve the image for viewing and printing in the document.

To use Image on Disk, insert a graphic into the document, right-click it, and choose Content. From the Content Type drop-down list, select Image on Disk. The Save Image As dialog box appears, allowing you to tell WP where to locate the file. Unless you want to save a second copy of the graphics file in a different location, leave the original filename (if it exists) and choose Save. If you're asked if you want to replace the image, choose Yes. Choose OK.

CAUTION: *Documents that contain Image on Disk graphics can't be printed from another computer unless that computer also has the same graphics in the same location on the hard drive.*

TIP: *The WP Suite 8 CD contains several photos in both JPG and BMP format that you can use in your documents. These images are found in the \Photos directory off the root directory of the CD.*

Scanning Images

If your computer has a scanner attached to it, you can scan items such as drawings, photographs, and documents directly into WP 8 as bitmap graphics images.

NOTE: *In order to scan into WP 8, your scanner must have a TWAIN-compatible driver and use 32-bit software.*

To set up your scanner, choose Insert | Graphics | Select Image Source. (This option won't appear unless you have a scanner installed.) Select the image scanner you're using and choose Select. Then, to scan an image, choose Insert | Graphics | Acquire Image. This opens your scanner software, where you can scan and manipulate the image. Once the image has been inserted into your WP document, you can edit it by double-clicking it. This opens the image in either Presentations or your scanning software, where you can make changes to it.

Editing Images

If an image that you've inserted into a document doesn't quite fit your needs, WP gives you lots of powerful tools for manipulating it. For example, you can rotate the image within its box, mirror it, scale it, crop it, change the color brightness, and so on. You can also adjust how images are processed when they're printed. In this section, we'll explain how to use WP's image-editing tools.

On the CD⋯ Adding Graphics to Envelopes

WP's Envelope feature lets you quickly create and print envelopes. But there aren't any options in the Envelope dialog box for adding a graphic to the outside of the envelope. The companion CD includes a macro called ENVELOPE GRAPHICS.WCM that helps you add graphics to an envelope, either next to the return address or in the bottom left corner.

If the address you want to create an envelope for is already typed in the document, select it first. If not, you can type it directly into the Envelope dialog box later. Play the macro by choosing Tools | Macro | Play, selecting the ENVELOPE GRAPHICS.WCM macro, and choosing Play. WP switches to a new document window and displays the Envelope dialog box. Make any changes to the return and mailing addresses (if you didn't select an address earlier, type one in or select it from the Address Book). Set any other options you want for the envelope and choose Append to Doc—*don't* choose Print Envelope.

When the next dialog box appears, select the placement option you want for the graphic and choose OK. Select the graphics image you want to use, and then WP inserts the graphic. After the envelope has been created, you can print it by choosing File | Print | Print.

The \Communication\Mail and \Office\Stamp folders in the CD Clipart section of the Scrapbook contain several useful images that could be placed on the outside of envelopes. To use these images with the Envelope Graphics macro, you need to first save the ones you want as separate WPG files, as explained in the "Using the Scrapbook" section earlier in this chapter.

To change the way an image appears within its box, you need to use the Image Tools dialog box, as shown next. To display this dialog box, right-click the graphic and choose Image Tools. Or you can select the graphic and click the Image Tools button on the Graphics Property Bar. As you're making changes to an image using the tools described in this section, you can return an image to its original settings by choosing Reset Attributes in the Image Tools dialog box.

Image Tools

Rotate Move

Flip Flip

Zoom:

BW threshold:

Contrast:

Brightness:

Fill:

Invert Colors

Edit Contents...

Edit Attributes...

Reset Attributes

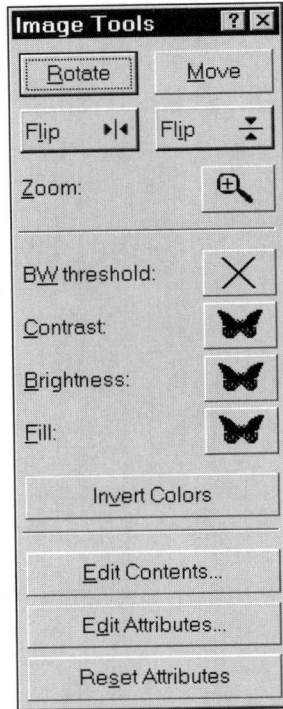

NOTE: *Once the Image Tools dialog box appears, you can click and drag the title bar to move it to a different location if you need to.*

Flipping and Rotating

One of WP's most useful image-editing tools is the ability to flip—or mirror—an image. For example, if you place an image along the right side of text, but the image isn't facing toward the text, you can flip it horizontally (see Figure 7-2). Images can also be flipped vertically.

Flipping an image is the only image-editing technique that can be done from outside the Image Tools editing dialog box. To flip an image, select it and then choose the Flip Left/Right or Flip Top/Bottom button on the Graphics Property Bar. You can also flip an image by displaying the Image Tools dialog box and choosing the Flip Left/Right or Flip Top/Bottom button.

FIGURE 7-2 The image on the right was flipped horizontally to "frame" the text

Rotating

If you don't want to simply flip the image 180 degrees, you can rotate it to any angle you want. For example, the rose image in Figure 7-3 was rotated to 45 degrees in the center and 145 degrees on the right.

To rotate an image, select it and display the Image Tools dialog box; then choose Rotate. WP displays special rotating "handles" in each of the corners. Move the mouse over a rotating handle, and then click and drag to rotate the image to the angle you want. In most cases, rotating an image causes it to be cut off by the edges of the box.

To display the full image after rotating it, you can scale the image down inside the box and then move it back toward the center, as explained in the next section. After scaling and moving the image, you can enlarge the size of the actual graphics box to make the rotated image larger.

FIGURE 7-3 You can rotate images to any angle

NOTE: *If you want to specify an exact rotation angle for an image, choose Edit Attributes in the Image Tools dialog box, and then select Rotate image. Type the angle in the Amount text box and choose OK.*

TIP: *WP also lets you change the center of rotation for an image. After choosing Rotate in the Image Tools dialog box, move the mouse pointer over the center point until it turns into crosshairs. Then click and drag the rotation center to the new location. After positioning the center point, use the rotation handles to rotate the image around that point.*

Moving, Scaling, and Cropping

In addition to rotating an image, you can also change its appearance by moving it within its box, scaling (sizing) it larger or smaller, or cropping out just the section of the image you want.

Moving

You can move an image within its box to control how much of the image is displayed or where the image is centered. Moving an image is often necessary after rotating and scaling it so it appears in the center of the box again. By moving an image inside its box, you can also "cut off" portions of it, as shown in Figure 7-4. In this example, the same image is repeated three times, but the two side images have been moved within their boxes to show only a portion of the image.

To move an image, select it and display the Image Tools dialog box. Choose Move. When you move the mouse pointer over the image, it changes to a four-directional arrow. Simply click and drag the image within the box to position it where you want. When an image is moved beyond the box edge, that portion is no longer displayed. If you want to specify the exact horizontal and vertical amounts to move an image, choose Edit Attributes in the Image Tools dialog box. Make sure

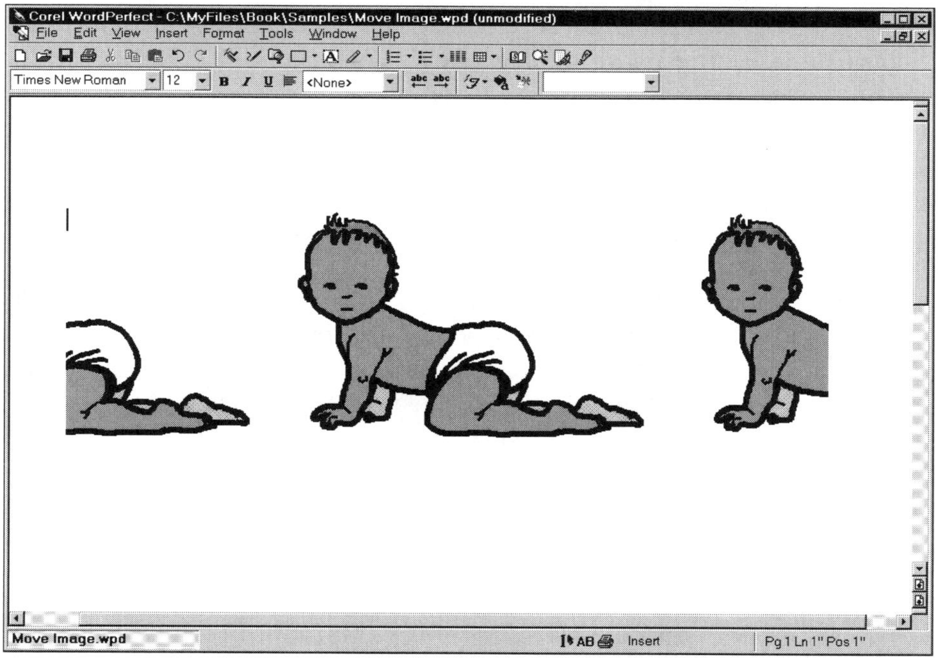

FIGURE 7-4 The left and right images were moved within their boxes to cut off part of the image

that Move Image is selected at the top of the dialog box; then type the horizontal and vertical amounts in the text boxes. The display in the dialog box shows you a preview of how the image will look.

Scaling

As explained in the previous section, when you rotate an image, the box usually cuts off the edges of the image. To solve this problem, you can reduce the size of the image within the box so the entire rotated image displays. You can also use the Scaling feature to enlarge—or zoom in on—a portion of the image.

NOTE: *If you want a rotated image that's been scaled down to appear the same size as the original image, simply enlarge the size of the actual graphics box.*

To scale an image, select it and display the Image Tools dialog box. Click the Zoom button and choose the middle option from the pop-up palette. This displays a vertical scroll bar along the right edge of the image. You can drag the scroll bar up to reduce the size of the image, or drag it down to enlarge it.

After scaling an image, you can use the Move feature to change its position within the box. For example, a rotated and scaled-down image might need to be moved back to the center of the box. When you use the Scaling feature to enlarge an image, the image enlarges from the center. After enlarging, you can move the image to display the portion you want. This is similar to cropping, which will be described in the next section.

Using the vertical scroll bar to scale images automatically scales the width and height of the image equally. You can distort an image by specifying separate scaling amounts for the width and height. To specify exact scaling amounts, select the image and display the Image Tools dialog box. Choose Edit Attributes and select Scale Image. In the Scale X text box, type the amount you want to scale the height. To increase the height, use a number greater than 1. To decrease the height, use a number from 0 to 1. For example, typing **2** will double the original height and typing **0.5** will cut the height in half. In the Scale Y text box, type the amount you want to scale the width. If you want to scale both amounts equally, type that amount in the Both X & Y text box.

Cropping

You can use the Cropping tool to quickly select only that portion of an image that you want to display. Cropping can also be accomplished by enlarging an image and moving it so the desired section displays, as described earlier, but the Cropping tool allows you to do this in a single step. To crop out a portion of an image, select the image and display the Image Tools dialog box. Choose the Zoom pop-up button, and then select the first option.

When you move the mouse pointer over the image, WP displays a magnifying glass and crosshairs. Position the magnifying glass in the upper-left corner of the area you want to zoom in on; then click and drag to select the section of the image. When you release the mouse button, WP changes the box size so only the selection portion displays.

NOTE: *If you want to restore a zoomed image to its original size, choose Reset Attributes in the Image Tools dialog box; then right-click the box and choose Size. Select Maintain Proportions for the Height and choose OK. This also resets any other changes you've made to the image.*

Color, Contrast, and Brightness

WP gives you several options for adjusting the colors of an image. For example, you can convert the image to black-and-white, change the color contrast or brightness, and adjust the way the image is filled in.

Black-and-White

To convert an image to black-and-white, select the image and display the Image Tools dialog box. From the BW Threshold pop-up palette, select the shade that represents the blackness threshold that you want. If you choose a darker threshold, more colors in the image will display as solid black.

To specify an exact blackness threshold amount, choose Edit Attributes from the Image Tools dialog box and select B & W Attributes. Select Black and White if it's not already selected, and then type an amount from 0 to 255 in the Threshold text box. Any color that is darker than the threshold setting will display in solid black.

Since lighter colors have higher values (white is 255), they won't display in black unless the threshold setting is high. Choose OK when you're finished.

Contrast

You can adjust the contrast of an image—or how the different colors blend together. To do this, select the image and display the Image Tools dialog box. From the Contrast pop-up button, select the icon that represents the contrast you want. The lowest contrast setting makes the colors in the image blend together so the image appears completely gray. Higher contrast settings display more distinction between the image colors. To set a specific contrast amount, choose Edit Attributes in the Image Tools dialog box and select Color Attributes. In the Contrast text box, type a number from -1 to 1, with -1 being no contrast (gray) and 1 being high contrast. Choose OK.

Brightness

To change the brightness of the colors in an image, use the Brightness pop-up palette in the Image Tools dialog box. The darkest brightness setting gives you a black silhouette of the image, while the lightest setting makes the image completely white. Lighter brightness settings are used to create watermarks. To set a specific brightness setting, choose Edit Attributes in the Image Tools dialog box, and then select Color Attributes. In the Brightness text box, type an amount from -1 to 1, with -1 being completely black and 1 being completely white. Choose OK.

Fill

You can also convert an image to a transparent outline or an outline filled with white. To do this, select the image and display the Image Tools dialog box. From the Fill pop-up button, choose the center icon to have the image converted to a transparent outline that lets any background detail text in the image show through. To have the image converted to an outline filled with white, choose the third icon. The first icon returns the image to its original colors.

CAUTION: *Some images become completely white when you change the fill options.*

Invert Colors

WP lets you convert the colors in an image to their complementary colors, which often produces a "reverse" effect, as shown here. To invert an image's colors, select the image and display the Image Tools dialog box; then choose Invert Colors.

Printing Options

Depending on your printer, you can make certain adjustments to the way graphics images are printed. Three available dithering methods—Error Diffusion, Ordered Dithering, and Halftoning—determine how the colors or shades of gray in an image are blended together when printed. To change the printing options, select the image and display the Image Tools dialog box. Choose Edit Attributes, and then select Print Parameters to display the Image Print Parameters dialog box (see Figure 7-5). Some of the options in the dialog box may be unavailable, depending on what type of printer you currently have selected.

Select the dither method you want to use for the current image. Each method uses a different technique for combining pixels (dots) to blend colors and shades of gray together. *Error diffusion* uses a random pattern of dots to give you smoother blending and good image detail with bitmapped images. *Ordered dithering* uses an ordered pattern of dots and works well with both bitmapped and vector images.

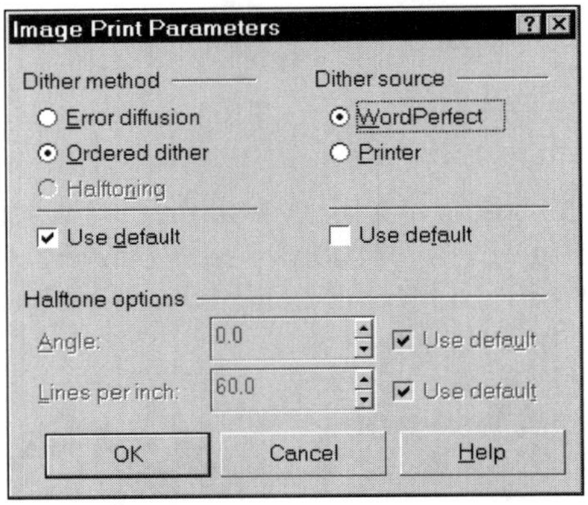

FIGURE 7-5 You can select one of three dithering methods when printing images

Halftoning uses evenly spaced dots of variable diameter, which can give you sharper image detail with bitmapped images (especially useful when making photocopies).

If you select halftoning, you can also specify the number of lines per inch. A lower value increases the number of shades in the image, and a higher value decreases the size of the dots, which improves the image's sharpness. On PostScript printers, you can specify the line angle (0-360) to adjust the pattern orientation.

In the Dither Source group box, you can select whether the image is converted to its final format by WordPerfect or by the printer. Experiment with the various settings to see which results in the best copy on your particular printer. When you're finished setting the options, choose OK twice.

Editing with Presentations

If the Image Tools dialog box doesn't give you the options you need for editing an image, you can use the tools in Corel Presentations. For example, in Presentations you can change the color of a specific section of an image, or delete an item altogether. There are several ways to edit an image in Presentations:

- Double-click the image.

- Right-click the image and choose Edit Image.

■ Select the image, display the Image Tools dialog box, and choose Edit Contents.

When you edit an image, WP displays an editing border around the image and the Presentations menu bars and Property Bars appear. You can click and drag the sizing handles on the editing border to increase the amount of white space around the image inside the box. Then use the tools on the Presentations Property Bars and menu bars to edit the image. (For more information on Presentations, see Chapter 18.)

NOTE: *Many images are grouped as a single unit, so in order to edit a specific element of the image, you might need to first separate the items. See the "Overlapping and Grouping Images" section in this chapter for information on how to do this.*

When you're finished making changes to the image, click outside the image in the WP document screen. Once you've edited an image in Presentations, it becomes an embedded drawing object in the document. Any changes you make to the image do not affect the actual graphics file, but only appear in the current document.

TIP: *If you want to display the image full-screen in Presentations for editing, hold down the ALT key when you double-click the image, or after editing the image once, right-click it and choose Drawing Object | Open.*

Drawing Shapes

Another of WP 8's great new features is the ability to draw shapes such as rectangles, circles, and lines right in your document. WordPerfect lets you select from eight different shapes: rectangles, rounded rectangles, ellipses, circles, polygons, lines, polylines, and arrows (see Figure 7-6). In this section, you'll learn how to insert each of these shapes into your documents.

There are two methods for creating shapes. First, you can choose Insert | Shape, and select the type of shape you want from the menu, such as Polygon or Circle. Or you can use the Draw Object button on the default toolbar.

Click the down arrow on the Draw Object toolbar button to display a pop-up palette of the eight different shapes, shown next. When you select a shape, the icon on the toolbar button changes to show you which shape you've selected. The mouse pointer changes to crosshairs, and you can click and drag to create the shape in the document. If you want to create another shape of the same type, just click the shape

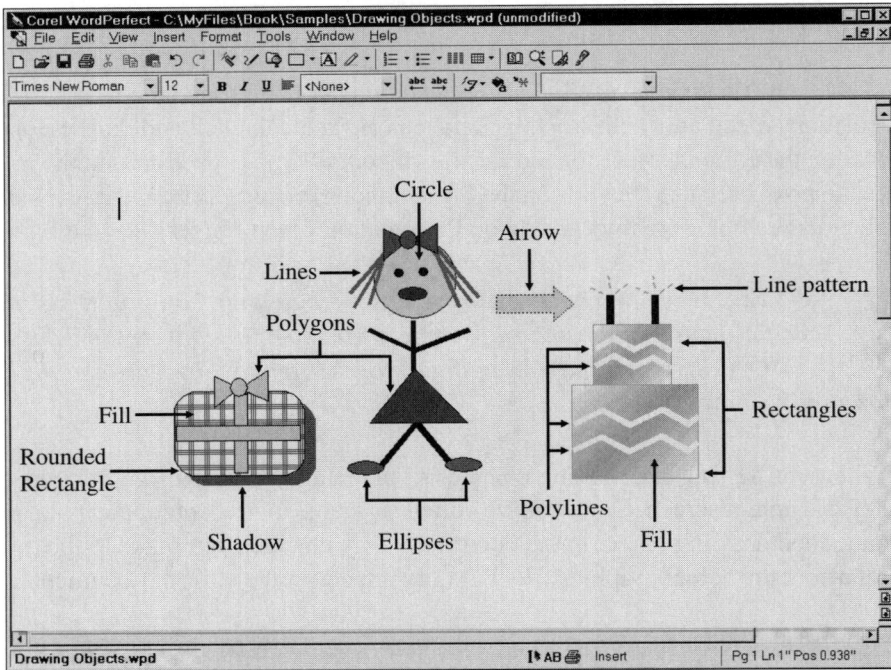

FIGURE 7-6 WordPerfect 8 lets you create shapes right in your documents

icon on the toolbar button (instead of the down arrow) and the mouse pointer changes to crosshairs again so you can draw another shape.

Lines

The ability to insert horizontal and vertical lines in a WordPerfect document is nothing new. WP still lets you insert horizontal and vertical graphics lines in your documents as you could in previous versions. What *is* new, however, is the ability to draw lines at any angle in the document, as well as the ability to draw polylines, or lines with multiple segments.

Drawing Lines

To draw a line in your document, choose Insert | Shape | Draw Line. Or click the Draw Object toolbar button and select the Draw Line icon. When the mouse pointer changes to crosshairs, simply click at the starting point and drag in the direction you want the line to go. When the line is the length you want, release the mouse button. Once you've drawn a line, you can move and size it as you would any graphics box.

TIP: *If you want to draw a horizontal, vertical, or 45-degree angle line, hold down the SHIFT key while you drag the line.*

Polylines

If you want to create a line that has multiple segments and angles, you can use the Polyline feature (see figure 7-6). Choose Insert | Shape | Polyline, or select the Polyline shape from the Draw Object toolbar button. When the mouse pointer changes to crosshairs, click where you want the line to begin. Drag to where the first line angle should be formed and click to insert a point there. Drag the next segment of the line and click to insert another point. Continue this process to add additional segments. When you're finished drawing the line, double-click the mouse button.

TIP: *To create horizontal, vertical, or 45-degree angle line segments, hold down the SHIFT key as you drag that segment.*

If you later want to edit the position or angle of any of the line points, right-click the polyline and choose Edit Points. Move the mouse pointer over the point you want to move and it changes to crosshairs. Then click and drag that point to the new position. Click back in the document text when you're finished.

TIP: *When you draw a line or a polyline, WordPerfect lets you add design elements to the ends of the line, such as arrowheads or dots. To add these end points to a line, select the line and then click the Arrow Start or Arrow End button on the Graphics Property Bar. Select the end point design you want from the pop-up menu. The first three options are the most noticeable with thicker lines; they determine whether the end of the line is rounded and whether it extends past the original end point. To change the design at the other end of the line, select the option you want from the other Property Bar button.*

Horizontal and Vertical Lines

If you want to insert a simple horizontal or vertical graphics line in your document, you can use the Graphics Line feature. To insert a horizontal line from the left margin to the right margin, place the insertion point where you want the line inserted and choose Insert | Shape | Horizontal Line. To insert a vertical line from the top margin to the bottom margin, choose Insert | Shape | Vertical Line.

TIP: *You can also quickly insert full-width horizontal lines and full-length vertical lines by using the Graphics toolbar. To display the Graphics toolbar, right-click the toolbar and choose Graphics. Then click the Horizontal Line or Vertical Line button to insert a line.*

You can customize the line if you don't want it to take the full width or height of the page, or if you want to change the line thickness or style. If the line has already been inserted in the document, double-click the line, or right-click it and choose Edit Horizontal Line or Edit Vertical Line. If you haven't yet inserted the line, choose Insert | Shape | Custom Line, or click the Custom Line button on the Graphics toolbar.

The Create Graphics Line (or Edit Graphics Line) dialog box appears (see Figure 7-7). In this dialog box, you can specify the type of line (horizontal or vertical), the line style, color, thickness, length, and position on the page. You can also specify how much white space is used around the line. If you're creating a horizontal line, a vertical position of Baseline means that the line will be positioned on the line in the document currently containing the insertion point. When you're finished making changes, choose OK.

Rectangles and Polygons

Three similar shapes that WP lets you create in your documents are rectangles, rounded rectangles, and polygons (see Figure 7-6). Rectangles and rounded rectangles always have four sides, with opposite sides being equal in length. Polygons can have any number of sides in multiple lengths, such as triangles or hexagons.

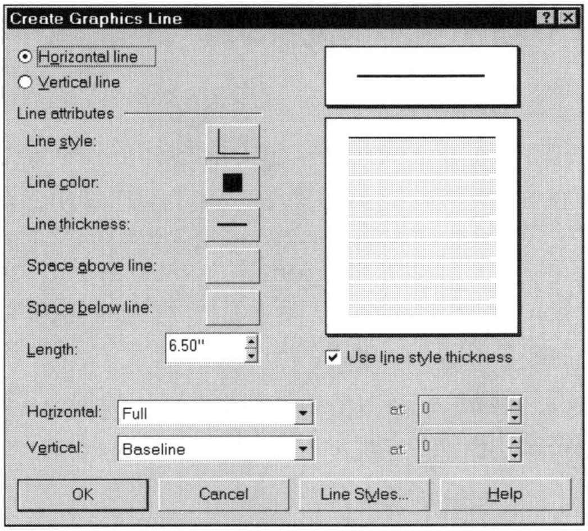

FIGURE 7-7 You can customize the settings for horizontal and vertical lines

To create a rectangle or rounded rectangle, choose Insert | Shape, and select the option you want, such as Rectangle. Or choose the shape you want from the Draw Object toolbar button shown earlier. The mouse pointer changes to crosshairs. Click the insertion point where you want a corner of the rectangle to appear, and then drag until you have the shape you want. When you release the mouse button, the rectangle is completed.

To create a polygon, choose Insert | Shape | Polygon, or select the Polygon icon on the Draw Objects toolbar. Click where you want one corner of the shape to appear; then drag to the next corner and click to insert a point there. Continue dragging and clicking each segment of the shape. When the shape appears as you want, double-click to end the process. If you later want to adjust any of the corners' positions or angles, right-click the polygon and choose Edit Points. Move the mouse pointer over a corner until it turns into crosshairs; then click and drag the corner to the new position. Click outside the polygon when you're finished.

After inserting a rectangle or polygon, you can move or size it in the document as you would any graphics box.

Circles and Ellipses

To create a circle or an ellipse in your document, choose Insert | Shape, and select the option you want, such as Circle. Or choose the shape from the Draw Object toolbar button. Then click the insertion point in the document and drag until the shape is the size you want. Release the mouse pointer when you're done. After inserting the circle or ellipse, you can size or move it as you would other graphics objects.

Arrows

To insert a horizontal arrow into your document, choose Insert | Shape | Arrow. Or choose the arrow shape from the Draw Object toolbar button. Click where you want the point of the arrow to appear and drag to size the arrow as you want. Using the Arrow shape, you can only create horizontal arrows. However, you can rotate an arrow after it's been inserted to a vertical position or to any other angle. See the "Polylines" section earlier in this chapter.

NOTE: *You can also create arrows from lines drawn in the document. See the Polylines section earlier in this chapter for more information.*

Power Tip... Rotating Arrows

The Shape feature of WP 8 only lets you create horizontal arrows in your documents. However, once you've inserted an arrow, you can rotate it to other positions. To rotate an arrow, follow these steps:

1. If you haven't already created the horizontal arrow, create it in your document using the arrow shape tool.

2. Select the arrow and press CTRL-X to cut it to the Clipboard.

3. Choose Edit | Paste Special.

4. Select WPG20 in the Paste Special dialog box and choose OK.

5. This inserts the arrow as a graphics image, so you can manipulate it as you would other images. To rotate the arrow, use the Rotate option in the Image Tools dialog box as explained in the "Flipping and Rotating" section earlier in this chapter. You'll also most likely need to scale the arrow so the complete rotated version displays. (See the "Moving, Scaling, and Cropping" section earlier in this chapter for more information.)

Editing Shapes

Just like clip-art images, shapes can be manipulated and edited once they've been inserted into a document. For example, you can change the colors, set the line width and pattern, or add a shadow. To change the appearance of a shape that's been inserted in a document, click it with the mouse to select it. The Graphics Property Bar changes to display the shape editing tools as shown next. The icons on the Property Bar will be slightly different from those shown here if you have a line or a polyline selected.

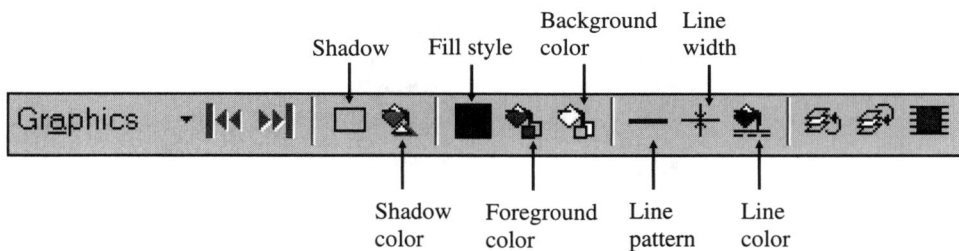

With the object selected, simply choose the Property Bar button for the option you want to modify, such as the Shadow, Fill Style, or Line Width. From the pop-up menu that appears, select the option you want. Once you've formatted an object with the color, fill, and line attributes that you want, you can quickly copy that formatting to other shapes in the document. See the Power Tip "Copying Formatting with QuickFormat" for the steps on how to do this.

NOTE: *When you're editing an enclosed object such as a rectangle or circle, changing the line pattern, line width, or line color affects the border line used around the object.*

Creating Text Boxes

Graphics boxes in WordPerfect don't have to contain clipart images or shapes—they can also contain text. Placing text in a graphics box gives you greater control over where that text is positioned on the page. Here are just a few of the things you can do with text boxes:

- Create a "pull quote" that appears between text columns or in a corner of the page

- Rotate text 90 or 270 degrees so it appears vertically on the page, or rotate it 180 degrees so it's upside-down

- Create headings that span two or more columns
- Combine text with a graphics image or shape

Power Tip... Copying Formatting with QuickFormat

If you want to format several shapes in a document with the same colors, fill style, and line attributes, it can be time-consuming to set the formatting for each individual shape. Instead of formatting each separately, you can use QuickFormat to instantly copy any formatting changes you've made to other shapes. Follow these steps:

1. Select the shape that you've formatted with the settings you want other shapes to use. (The other shapes must already be created in the document.)

2. Right-click the shape and choose QuickFormat. Or click the QuickFormat icon on the toolbar.

3. When the mouse pointer changes to a paint roller icon, simply click each additional shape that you want to use the same formatting. The QuickFormat feature copies any of the settings that you've made from options on the Graphics Property Bar, such as the fill color, fill style, and line width. You can apply the attributes to any shape or line—not just shapes that are the same as the one you originally formatted. If you apply the formatting from a line to an enclosed object, the fill for the object is removed.

4. When you're finished applying the formatting to each additional shape, click the QuickFormat button on the toolbar again, or right-click and choose QuickFormat to turn QuickFormat off.

To create a text box, choose Insert | Text Box or click the Text Box button on the toolbar. WP creates the text box and places the insertion point inside it, ready for you to type the text. Type and format the text as you would in a regular document. You can paste in text that's been copied to the Clipboard, or use any of WP's formatting features. When you're finished, click outside the box. Now you can size the box or change its appearance as you would other graphics boxes.

TIP: *If you want to move a text box with the mouse, click and drag the border of the box. Or you can right-click the box and use the Position option to specify an exact position.*

To edit the text in a text box, simply click inside the box. If you want to rotate the text, right-click the text box and choose Content. Select the rotation option you want, such as 90 Degrees, and choose OK.

NOTE: *If you click inside a box that has rotated text, WP displays the rotated text in a separate editing screen for you to make any changes. Choose the Close button when you're finished to return to the document.*

Overlapping and Grouping Images

When you insert more than one image, shape, or text box into a document, you can overlap the boxes and control which box appears on top of the others. You can also group boxes together so they're easily moved and sized at the same time. This is especially useful if you want to combine text with a graphics image and have them remain together as they're moved or sized on the page. In this section, we'll show you how to change the order of overlapping images, and how to group and separate multiple graphics.

Overlapping Graphics Boxes

Graphics boxes that contain images, shapes, or text can be positioned so they completely or partially overlap each other in a document (see Figure 7-8). This technique is commonly used for combining text and graphics. You can also overlap graphics boxes containing shapes to create different images.

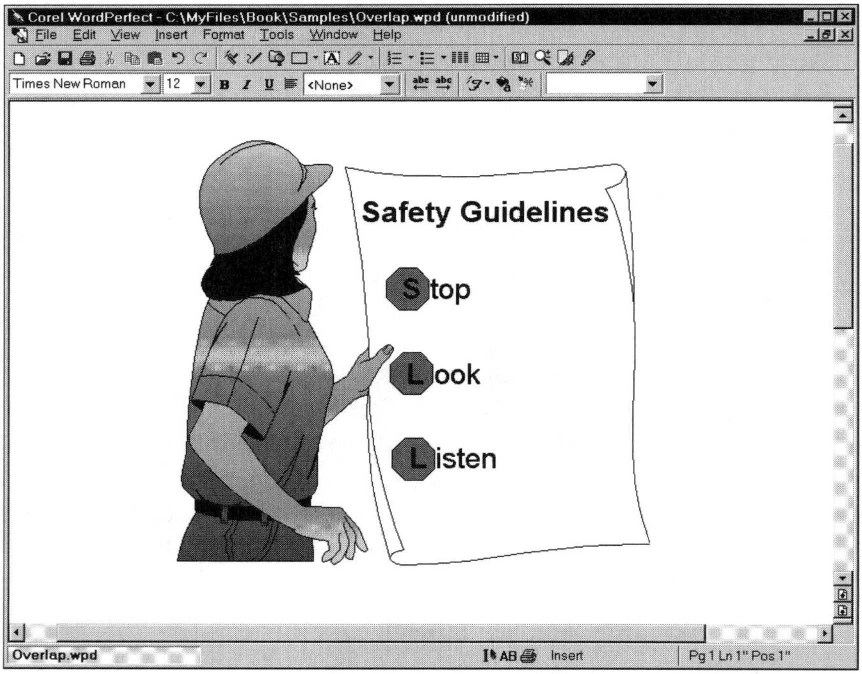

FIGURE 7-8 Graphics boxes containing clipart, text, shapes can be overlapped and ordered

To overlap graphics, simply click and drag them with the mouse until they're placed where you want. Once they're overlapping, you can change the order that they're layered in. To have an image placed on top of all the other images it overlaps with, select the image and choose Graphics | To Front from the Property Bar. Or right-click the image and choose Order | To Front. Similarly, you can move an image *behind* all other overlapping images by choosing Graphics | To Back from the Property Bar, or by right-clicking the image and choosing Order | To Back.

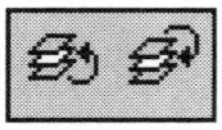

If you have more than two boxes overlapping and want to move an image only one layer forward or backward, select the image and from the Graphics drop-down menu on the Property Bar, choose Forward One or Back One, depending on which direction you want to move the image. You can also select the image and then click the Object Forward One or Object Back One button on the Property Bar.

NOTE: *If you move a graphics image to the front of a stack and text still displays on top of the image, select the image and choose Graphics | In Front of Text from the Property Bar.*

TIP: *If you have several overlapping images and want to select a "buried" image, choose one of the images and select the Previous Box or Next Box button on the Graphics Property Bar until the image you want is selected.*

Grouping and Separating

Once you've positioned multiple graphics boxes where you want them—either overlapping or right next to each other—you can group those boxes together. Grouping allows you to move, size, and edit the images all at the same time. For example, if you position a text box over a graphics image, you can group the two boxes together so that when you click and drag the graphics box to move it, the text box moves with it (and stays in the correct position). Or, if you're drawing an image using several shapes, you can group the shapes together so they're not accidentally deleted or moved out of position.

To group multiple graphics, follow these steps:

1. Select one of the graphics.

2. Hold down the SHIFT key and click just outside the corner of the largest graphic.

3. Click and drag the selection box around the images that you want to group together.

4. Choose Graphics | Group from the Property Bar, or right-click the images and choose Group.

When you use the mouse to move or size grouped images, you'll see the outline of each individual image as you click and drag.

If you need to modify an individual image, you can separate the graphics. To do this, select the grouped image and choose Graphics | Separate from the Property Bar. Or, right-click the image and choose Separate. After making any changes you want, you can group them together again.

Formatting Graphics Boxes

Any time you insert an image or shape into a document, it's placed inside a graphics box. Text boxes are also a special kind of graphics box. You can change the position or size of a graphics box and specify how document text wraps around it. Graphics boxes that contain images or text (but not shapes) can have a border and fill added, as well as a caption. In this section, you'll learn how to format individual graphics boxes.

NOTE: *Graphics boxes can also contain equations, tables, TextArt images, and charts. Equations and TextArt are described later in this chapter. For more information on tables, see Chapter 6. For more information on charts, see Chapter 18.*

Box Position

The easiest way to move a graphics box to a new location in the document is to simply click and drag it with the mouse. If you want to specify an exact position for the graphics box, you can use the Box Position dialog box. To display this dialog box, right-click the graphics box and choose Position. Or select the box and choose Graphics | Position from the Property Bar.

From the Attach Box To drop-down list, select the anchor option you want for the box. Graphics boxes can be anchored within a document in one of three ways:

- *Character* boxes are anchored to a specific location within a line of text, like a character in a word, so they move within that line as text is added or deleted.

- *Paragraph* boxes are anchored to a specific location within a paragraph, so they move with that paragraph as document text is added or deleted. This is the default setting for text boxes.

- *Page* boxes are anchored to a specific location on a page, so they always remain in the same location on the page no matter what text is added or deleted. This is the default setting for clipart images.

Then set the specific position for the box, such as the location from the top of the page or paragraph, or whether a character box appears above or below the text baseline. Choose OK when you're finished.

NOTE: *When you click and drag a paragraph-anchored box, a thumbtack in the margin indicates which paragraph the box will be anchored to. When you click and drag a character-anchored box, you can't move it into a blank area of the page since there's no text there for it to be anchored to.*

Box Size

To change the size of a graphics box, all you need to do is select the box, and then click and drag one of the sizing handles around the edge of the box. If you drag one of the corner handles, the height and width change proportionately. If you drag one of the other sizing handles, the image or shape can become distorted.

TIP: *To avoid image distortion when sizing a graphics box, right-click the box and choose Content. Select Preserve Image Width/Height Ratio and choose OK. Now when you use any of the sizing handles, the image maintains the correct proportions inside the box.*

To specify the exact size for a graphics box, right-click the box and choose Size. Or choose Graphics | Size from the Property Bar. In the Box Size dialog box, type the specific width and height for the box, or select from the other available options. Selecting Full causes the box to take up the full width or height of the page. If you select Maintain Proportions, WP automatically determines the width or height needed to keep the original proportions of the image. For example, if you set a specific amount for the box width, setting the Height to Maintain Proportions ensures that the box will be correctly sized to fit the image without distorting it. Choose OK when you're finished.

Box Border and Fill

Graphics boxes can display an outside border, as well as inside fill pattern or shading (see Figure 7-9). To select a border for a graphics box, select the box and choose the border you want from the Border pop-up palette on the Graphics Property Bar. To select a fill for the inside of the graphics box, select the box and choose the fill pattern you want from the Fill pop-up palette on the Graphics Property Bar.

NOTE: *You can't select a box border or fill for a drawing shape, such as a circle or rectangle.*

You can further customize a border or fill by changing the color, adding a drop shadow, rounding the corners, and so on. To do this, right-click the box and choose Border/Fill. Or, select the box and choose Graphics | Border/Fill from the Property

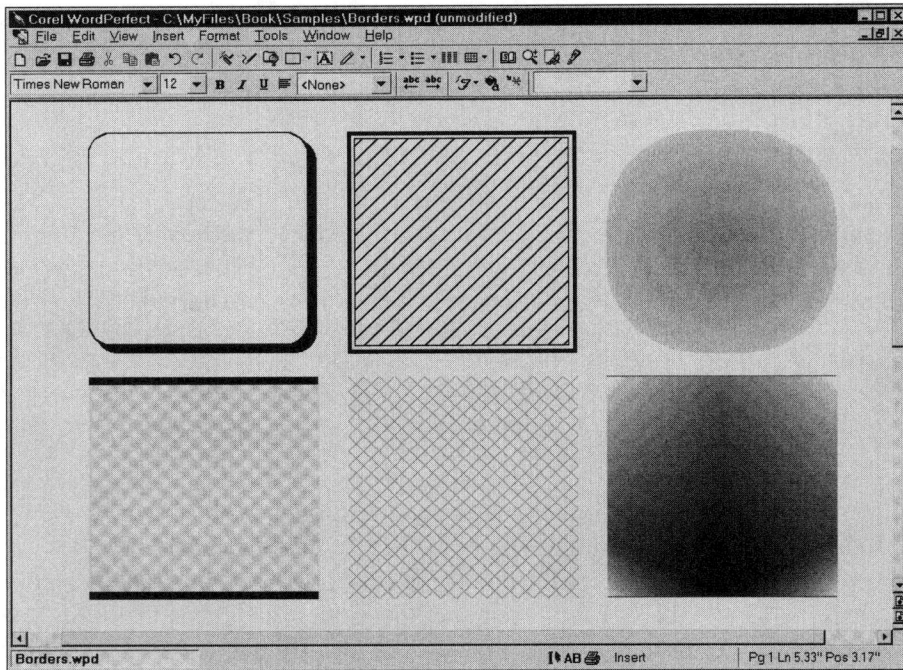

FIGURE 7-9 Graphics boxes can have customized borders and fills

Bar. In the Box Border/Fill dialog box, you can select a border style and then customize it to use a different color, drop shadow, or rounded corners. To customize the fill, select the Fill tab, and then select the fill pattern and colors you want.

If you select the Advanced tab in the dialog box, you can further customize the drop shadow color and width, the radius used for the rounded corners, the spacing inside and outside the border, and the settings for a gradient fill pattern. The preview in the dialog box shows you what the new border and fill will look like. Choose OK when you're finished.

TIP: *If you format one graphics box with a specific border and fill, you can use QuickFormat to quickly copy that border/fill to other boxes. To do this, right-click the box that you've formatted and choose QuickFormat. When the mouse pointer changes to a paint roller icon, simply click each new box that you want to use the same formatting. When you're finished, right-click and choose QuickFormat again to turn QuickFormat off. QuickFormat also copies the wrap option set for that graphics box.*

Wrap Settings

Graphics boxes affect the flow of the document text around them. You can control how the document text behaves by changing the wrap setting of the graphics box. For example, you can have the text squared around the box edges, contoured to the shape of the image, run in front of or behind the box, or not appear on either side of the box (see Figure 7-10). You can also have the text squared or contoured on one side of the box only.

To change the wrap setting of a box, select it in the document. Then choose the Wrap button on the Graphics Property Bar and select the wrap option you want.

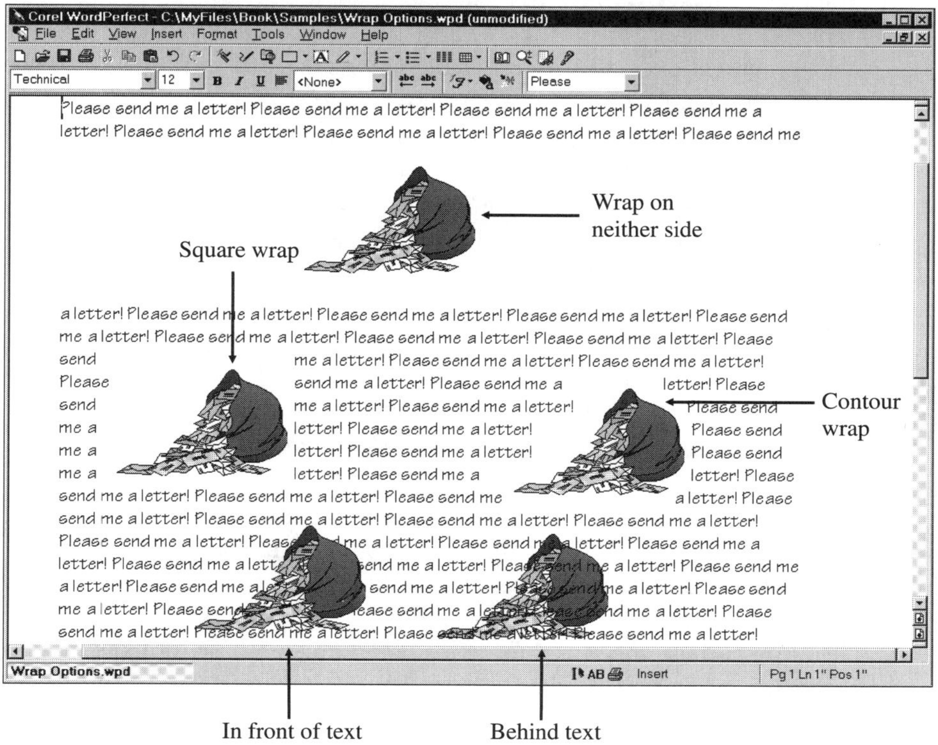

FIGURE 7-10 You can specify how document text wraps around a graphics box

NOTE: *If you select a contour wrap option for a graphics box that has a border or fill, the border and fill are automatically removed to allow text to flow around the image.*

TIP: *If you select the Behind Text wrap option and later need to select that graphics box to move, size, or edit it, right-click the box and choose Select Box from the QuickMenu.*

Box Captions

Captions can be added to any graphics box except those containing shapes. WordPerfect gives you numerous options for controlling where the caption is placed and how it appears. For example, the caption can appear on any side of the box, inside or outside the border, and be rotated to 90, 180, or 270 degrees.

To create a caption for a graphics box, select the box and click the Caption button on the Graphics Property Bar. Or you can right-click the graphics box and choose Create Caption.

For most graphics boxes, WP inserts a label such as "Figure" or "Table," followed by the graphics box number. Some graphics boxes, such as text boxes, just have the box number inserted automatically. Other custom boxes don't insert any formatting (you'll learn more about custom boxes in the next section). If you don't want the box label or number to appear, press BACKSPACE to delete it. Then type the caption text and click outside the box when you're finished. If you later need to edit the caption text, select the box and click the Caption button on the Property Bar again, or right-click the box and choose Edit Caption.

NOTE: *WP automatically renumbers graphics boxes when you add or delete boxes of the same type. For example, if you add a new clipart image, any other image boxes in the document are automatically renumbered.*

If you want to change the caption position or rotate the caption text, right-click the box and choose Caption to display the Box Caption dialog box (see Figure 7-11). Select the position you want for the caption, including the side of the box, whether it appears inside or outside the border, and how it is justified (such as centered or flush right). You can use the Absolute Offset and Percent Offset options to adjust the caption position a certain distance or percentage from the selected location, such as placing it 0.5" from the left edge of the box or 25% from the center. A negative amount moves the caption to the left and a positive amount moves it to the right.

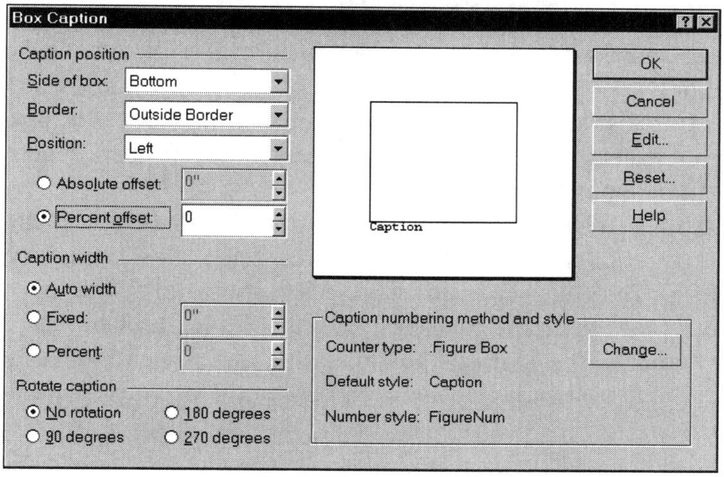

FIGURE 7-11 The Box Caption dialog box lets you customize the caption settings

If you want to change the formatting used for the box number (such as "Figure 1"), you need to edit the style that's formatting the graphics box. In the next section, you'll learn how to edit and create graphics styles. When you're finished making changes, choose OK.

Graphics Box Styles

Every graphics box in a document is formatted with a graphics style. The graphics style determines the initial formatting of the box, including the default border/fill, wrap setting, and caption numbering. While you can modify these elements of individual graphics boxes using the steps in the "Formatting Graphics Boxes" section, if you want to change the default formatting used for all graphics boxes of a certain type, you need to modify the graphics style.

WP 8 has 14 predefined graphics styles to choose from. You can change the style that's used by a particular graphics box in your document, or you can edit a style and modify the formatting it uses for all graphics boxes of that type. In addition, you can create your own graphics styles that contain the custom settings and formatting you frequently use for graphics boxes. In this section, you'll learn how to change the graphics style used by a box, edit the existing styles, and create new styles.

Selecting a Graphics Style

Whenever a graphics box is inserted in your document, it's automatically formatted with one of WP's 14 graphics styles. For example, clipart images use the Image style, which formats the image with no border, a page anchor at the top of the page, 1.5" width, auto height, and caption numbering in the format "Figure 1" on the bottom left (if captions are used).

If you want to change the style of a box that's already been inserted in a document, right-click the box and choose Style. Select the new style from the list and choose OK. The box is updated with the new formatting, with the exception of the actual box position on the page. For example, if you have an image box in the bottom-left corner of the page and you apply the User style to it, the box changes from a page anchor to a paragraph anchor, but it remains in the bottom-left corner of the page.

To create a new graphics box using a specific graphics box style, choose Insert I Graphics I Custom Box. Select the graphics box style you want from the list and choose OK. An empty box is inserted into the document. Double-click the box to edit its contents. If the box is formatted for an image, the Insert Image dialog box automatically displays for you to select the graphics file you want. If the box is formatted for an equation, the old WP 5/6/7 Equation Editor appears. Otherwise, the insertion point is placed inside the box for you to begin typing text.

TIP: *To insert an image in a box that doesn't automatically display the Insert Image dialog box when you double-click it, right-click the box and choose Content. From the Content Type drop-down list, choose Image. If you're prompted to delete the box contents, choose Yes. Then type the path and filename for the image in the File Name text box, or use the file folder icon to select it. Choose OK when you're finished.*

Creating and Editing Graphics Box Styles

If you don't like the default formatting used by a particular graphics box style, you can modify it to suit your needs. In addition, you can create custom styles with the settings you frequently use for graphics boxes. For example, you can change the default caption placement used in table boxes, or you can create a custom style that formats text boxes with a thick border and places them in the lower-right corner of the page.

To create or edit a graphics box style, choose Format | Graphics Styles. You can edit a predefined style, create a new style based on the formatting in an existing style, or create a new style from scratch. Follow one of these steps:

- To edit a predefined style, select the style in the list and choose Edit.

- To create a new style based on an existing style, select the style you want to copy and from the Options pop-down button, choose Copy. Type a name for the new style in the New Name text box and choose OK. Then, with the new style selected, choose Edit.

- To create a new style from scratch, choose Create. Type a name for your style in the Style Name text box.

When the Edit Box Style (or Create Box Style) dialog box appears, choose the button for the element that you want to modify, such as Position or Border/Fill (see Figure 7-12). Make the changes you want, such as selecting a border or caption position. If you set the content type to Image, you can choose Settings and specify default settings for the image itself, such as the image rotation or color brightness.

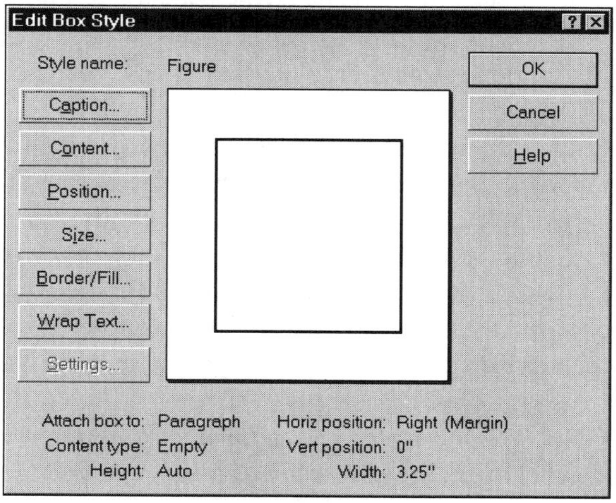

FIGURE 7-12   You can set the formatting options for a graphics box style

If the content type is set to Equation, you can choose Settings and select the default equation font and font size.

When you're finished setting the formatting options, choose OK, and then Close. If you edited an existing style, any boxes formatted with that style are automatically updated. (One common use for graphics styles is to create multilevel caption numbering, such as Figure 1-1. See the On the CD section for more information.

NOTE: *If you later want to delete a custom graphics style that you've created, choose Format | Graphics Styles. Select the style you want to delete and from the Options pop-down button, choose Delete. Choose Yes to confirm the deletion.*

TIP: *You can reset a predefined graphics style to its original formatting by choosing Format | Graphics Styles, selecting the style and from the Options pop-down button, choosing Reset. Choose Yes to reset the style formatting.*

Line, Border, and Fill Styles

WordPerfect also uses styles to format the various line, border, and fill options that are available to features such as graphics boxes, table cells, and page borders. For example, a line style is used to format a dashed line and a border style is used to create a Thick/Thin border. As with graphics box styles, you can edit any existing line, border, or fill style, or you can create your own.

To create or edit a style, choose Format | Graphics Styles, and select the type of style you want to work with at the top of the dialog box, such as Border or Line. To edit a predefined style, select the style in the list and choose Edit. To create a new style based on an existing one, select the style you want to copy from and from the Options pop-down button, choose Copy. Type a name for the new style in the New Name text box, choose OK, and then choose Edit. Or, to create a new style from scratch, choose Create. Type a name for your style in the Style Name text box.

CAUTION: *When you edit a predefined line, border, or fill style, it affects any feature that uses that style, such as table cells and paragraph borders. If you only want to modify one document, create a new style rather than edit a predefined style.*

On the CD ▸▸▸ Multilevel Caption Numbering

When you're working on a document with sections or chapters, you often need to use multilevel caption numbers, such as Figure 2-1 or Table 3.3. The companion CD contains two sets of graphics styles for this type of numbering. Each set contains three graphics styles—one for figures, one for tables, and one for equations. One set separates the numbers with a hyphen (i.e. Figure 1-1) and the other set separates the numbers with a period (i.e. Figure 1.1). The rest of the style formatting is the same as the predefined Image, Table, and Equation graphics styles.

To use these styles, follow these steps:

1. Choose Format | Graphics Styles. From the Options pop-down button, choose Retrieve.

2. Use the file folder icon to the right of the File Name text box to select the MULTILEVEL HYPHEN.STY file or MULTILEVEL PERIOD.STY file from the companion CD. (Make sure you select All Files (*.*) from the File Type drop-down list.)

3. After selecting the filename you want, choose Select and OK. The new styles should appear in the list. Choose Close.

4. To use a style for a new box, choose Insert | Graphics | Custom Box. Select the style, such as Multilevel Figure (1-1), and choose OK. Double-click the box to insert the image, table, or equation. To create the caption, right-click the box and choose Create Caption. The multilevel caption number should be inserted, and you can type the caption text.

5. If the box has already been created in the document, right-click it and choose Style. Select the style from the list, such as Multilevel Figure (1-1), and choose OK.

> **6.** When you start a new document chapter or section and need
> to increase the initial caption number, such as to Figure 2-1,
> place the insertion point before any graphics boxes that
> should use the updated number. Choose Insert | Other |
> Counter. Select Level 1 under the counter name, such as
> Multi Figure or Multi Table, and choose Increase. Repeat
> this each time you want to increase the initial counter
> number.
>
> If you want to set up your own multilevel caption numbering, you
> can find more information by choosing Help | Help Topics, selecting
> the Index tab, typing **Caption,** and selecting the Multilevel Numbering
> topic.

A dialog box appears for you to make the settings for the line, border, or fill. The following sections will explain some of the different options for customizing line, border, and fill styles.

Line Styles

When you're creating or editing a line style, you can customize the line color, pattern, and width, as well as the spacing used below the line. You can also add multiple lines to the style, and each line can have its own custom formatting. For example, you can create a triple-line style where each line has a different color and thickness.

To add another line to the style, choose Add in the Create Line Style dialog box. Use the up and down arrow keys below the preview window to select the line you want to format; then use the pop-up palettes to select the color, pattern, and width for the selected line. To delete a line, select it in the preview window and choose Del.

If you don't see a line pattern you like, you can design your own by choosing Custom from the Pattern pop-up palette, and then selecting the Length and Spacing options for the line segments. To add alternating segments, select the length and spacing for the first segment; then choose Add and select the length and spacing for the alternating segment. You can continue to add alternating segments if you want. Choose OK when you're finished, and then choose Close from the Graphics Styles dialog box.

Border Styles

When you create or edit a border style, you can select the type of line used for each side of the border. You can also change the border color, add rounded corners, select a drop shadow, and adjust the spacing used inside or outside the border.

To change the lines used in the border, first select the sides of the border that you want to modify. You can select or deselect a border side either by clicking the corresponding checkbox, such as Left or Top, or by clicking that side of the border in the preview window. The preview window displays arrows at each end of the border sides that are currently selected.

Use the Line Style pop-up palette to select the line type for the selected border sides. You can remove a line by selecting the "X" option in the palette. If you've created a custom line style and want to use it for the border sides, scroll through the drop-down list at the bottom of the palette and select the custom style. You can also create a new custom line style by choosing Line Styles, and then Create.

If you want to include a vertical border line that's used between columns, or a horizontal separator line that's used between paragraph borders, select the Separator option in the list of sides to modify. Then use the Line Style pop-up palette to select the line type you want for the separator line. While the separator line appears horizontally in the preview window, it is used vertically when applied to columns. When you're finished setting the border options, choose OK, and then choose Close from the Graphics Styles dialog box.

Fill Styles

WP lets you create two types of fill styles: pattern or gradient. Pattern fills consist of a foreground color, a background color, and a predefined pattern, such as solid shading, bricks, or a checkerboard. Gradient fills consist of two colors blended together in a circular, linear, or rectangular pattern.

To create a pattern fill, select the colors and patterns you want to use in the Create Fill Style dialog box. The preview window shows what your fill pattern will look like. To create a gradient fill, select Gradient at the top of the dialog box. From the Gradient drop-down list, select the type of pattern you want to create, such as Circular. Select the foreground and background colors you want. The foreground color is used as the inside color and the background color is the outside color.

The Horizontal and Vertical Offset options let you specify where the center of the pattern is placed. If you're creating a rectangular or linear pattern, you can also specify a rotation angle to rotate the pattern counterclockwise inside the border. The Steps option allows you to specify how smoothly the two colors are blended together. Select Auto Steps to have WP automatically use the maximum number of steps for the selected gradient. When you're finished, choose OK, and then choose Close from the Graphics Styles dialog box.

Using a Custom Style

After you've created or modified a line, border, or fill style, it is automatically available in all your new documents. You can select your custom style for any graphics box, paragraph border, table cell, or other feature in WordPerfect that lets you select a line type, border, or fill pattern. If your custom style doesn't show up in the pop-up palette used for selecting the line, border, or fill, use the drop-down list of style names to select the style.

Using TextArt

TextArt is one of the features in WordPerfect that's the most fun to experiment with. TextArt lets you create unique two-dimensional (2-D) and three-dimensional (3-D) graphics designs from text (see Figure 7-13). These images make great eye-catching logos and banners. Once created, TextArt images can be moved, sized, and positioned just like any other graphics box.

NOTE: *The TextArt 3-D special effects aren't installed during a default installation. To install the 3-D effects (they take less than 1MB of disk space), exit WordPerfect and run the Corel WordPerfect Suite 8 Setup. Follow the prompts to perform a custom installation, and then deselect all of the options. Select Accessories in the list and choose Components; then select TextArt and choose Components. Select 3-D Effects, choose OK, and follow the prompts to continue with the installation.*

To create a TextArt image, choose Insert | Graphics | TextArt. WP creates a full-width graphics box and displays the TextArt dialog box.

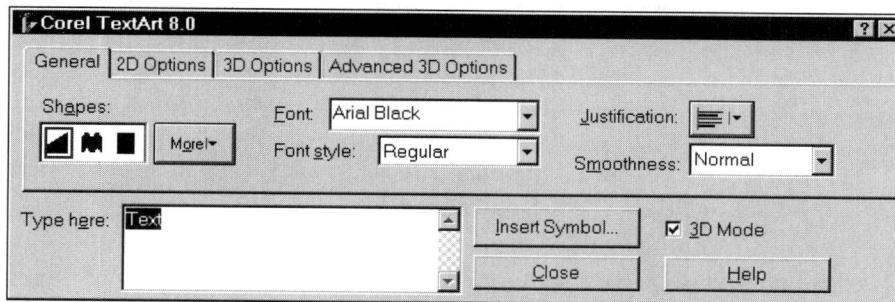

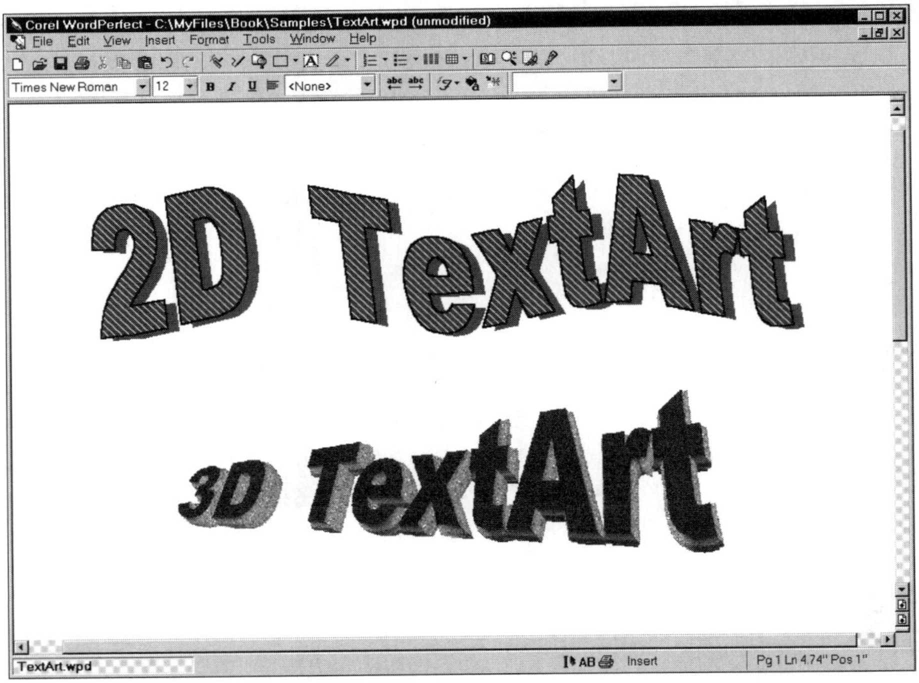

FIGURE 7-13 TextArt images can be 2-D or 3-D

From the Font and Font Style drop-down lists, select the font you want to use. In the Type Here text box, type the text you want to format as TextArt. You can press ENTER to insert new lines if needed. If you want to insert an accented character, fraction symbol, or other non-keyboard character, choose Insert Symbol. The Symbols dialog box displays the available characters for the selected font. Choose the character you want and select Insert and Close.

TIP: *If you have text already typed in your document that you want to format as TextArt, select the text first and then choose Insert | Graphics | TextArt. WP automatically places the selected text (up to 512 characters) in the TextArt dialog box.*

Next, select the shape you want for your TextArt object. The Shapes text box shows the last three shapes you've used with TextArt. To see a list of all the available shapes, click the More pop-down palette and select the shape you want. You can then format your text for 2-D or 3-D TextArt, as explained in the following sections.

2-D TextArt

To format a TextArt object (see Figure 7-13), select the 2-D Options tab in the TextArt dialog box. If you want to select a predefined format, choose an option from the Preset pop-up palette. Otherwise, you can customize your TextArt image with the following options.

- *Pattern*   Select the pattern you want to use inside the text from the Pattern pop-up palette. To fill the text with a solid color, choose None. To remove both the pattern and color (and have outlined text), choose No Fill. You can also specify the text color and pattern color.

- *Shadow*   To change the shadow used with the letters, select the option you want from the Shadow pop-up palette. You can also select the color for the shadow, or remove the shadow completely by selecting the middle option.

- *Outline*   To specify the thickness and color of the text border outline, click the Outline pop-up palette and select the options you want.

- *Rotation*   To rotate the TextArt shape, choose Rotate and then click and drag one of the corner rotation handles. To specify an exact rotation amount, double-click the Rotate button and select the option you want, such as 90 Degrees, or type the rotation angle in the text box and choose OK.

- *Text Color*   Use the Text Color pop-up palette to select the main text color. The text color can also be set from the Pattern, Shadow, and Outline pop-up palettes.

3-D TextArt

3-D TextArt is a new feature in WP 8 (see Figure 7-13). To create 3-D TextArt, first select 3-D Mode in the TextArt dialog box. Then select the 3-D Options tab. If you want to use a predefined format, choose an option from the Preset pop-up palette. Otherwise, you can customize your TextArt image with the following options.

CAUTION: *Using 3-D TextArt can greatly increase the file size of your documents.*

- *Lighting* You can specify the color and direction for two sources of lighting that appear on the edge of the 3-D image. Experiment with different colors and light directions to find the look you like best.

- *Bevel* Use the Bevel pop-up palette to select a beveled edge for your image. When you select a bevel option, the TextArt image appears to have ridges.

- *Depth* To change the height (or thickness) of the image, use the Depth scale.

- *Rotation* To rotate the TextArt image, you can choose a predefined rotation option from the Rotation pop-up palette. Or, to rotate the image with the mouse, click Free Rotate and a circle with crossbars appears over the image. Move the mouse pointer over the horizontal line, vertical line, or circle border and it changes to a hand icon with arrows indicating which way the image will rotate. Click and drag the mouse to rotate the image. When you're finished, click Free Rotate again to remove the rotation guidelines.

- *Texture* To add a texture to the text or bevel, click the Advanced 3-D Options tab at the top of the TextArt dialog box. Use the Face and Bevel pop-up palettes to select the texture you want for each element. Then use the Texture Size and Texture Lighting controls to affect the brightness and size of the texture.

- *Quality* To have the TextArt image print at a higher quality, select the option you want from the Quality drop-down list. Selecting a higher quality will increase the file size of the document.

Finishing Up

When you're finished setting the options you want for your 2-D or 3-D TextArt image, choose Close to insert the TextArt image into the document. If you want to change the size or placement of the TextArt image, size it with the mouse as you would any other graphics box. Or you can right-click the image and use the options on the QuickMenu. If you need to make changes to the TextArt image, double-click it to display the TextArt dialog box again.

NOTE: *Some of the TextArt shapes, such as the semicircle and full circle, are more legible if the height of the TextArt box is increased.*

TIP: *You can save a TextArt image as a WPG file so it can be easily inserted in other documents. To do this, select the TextArt image in the document and choose File | Save As. Choose Selected Image and OK. Type the path and filename where you want to save the image, and then choose Save.*

Creating Equations

When you need to insert equations in your documents, you can use WP's Equation Editor to quickly create and format the equations. The Equation Editor helps you insert all the right symbols and functions for the equation, and then places the equation in a graphics box in the document. WP 8's Equation Editor has been completely revamped from previous versions and now sports an all-graphical interface (see Figure 7-14). Creating simple or complex equations has never been easier.

To create an equation in your document, choose Insert | Equation. This displays the new Equation Editor dialog box with the insertion point in an empty dotted box—called a "slot." The Equation Editor helps you create equations by providing 19 pop-up palettes that contain groups of related equation symbols and functions (see Figure 7-14). The ten palettes on the top row let you insert symbols, characters, spaces, and other markings. The nine palettes on the bottom row contain equation "templates," such as fractions, sums, integrals, matrices and so on. The templates contain empty slots, which you can fill in with the appropriate text or symbols. You can select a template within a template to easily create more complex equations, such as this one:

$$P_M(D_j) = \frac{(M-1)}{M}\, \mathrm{erfc}\left[\sqrt{\frac{q_0^2}{2\sigma_n^2}\left(1 - \frac{M-1}{q_0}\sum_{k\neq 0}|q_k|\right)^2}\right]$$

NOTE: *WP 8 still has the equation editor used in earlier versions. This editor is used whenever you choose Insert | Graphics | Custom Box and select either the Equation style or the Inline Equation style. You can also use it for new equations you create by choosing Tools | Settings, double-clicking Environment, and selecting the Graphics tab. To use the old equation editor as the default each time you create an equation, select WordPerfect 5.1 to 7 Equation Editor. To be prompted for the editor to use, select that option. Choose OK and Close. If you have a document that contains equations created with the old equation editor, it's recommended that you use the old equation editor for editing the equations.*

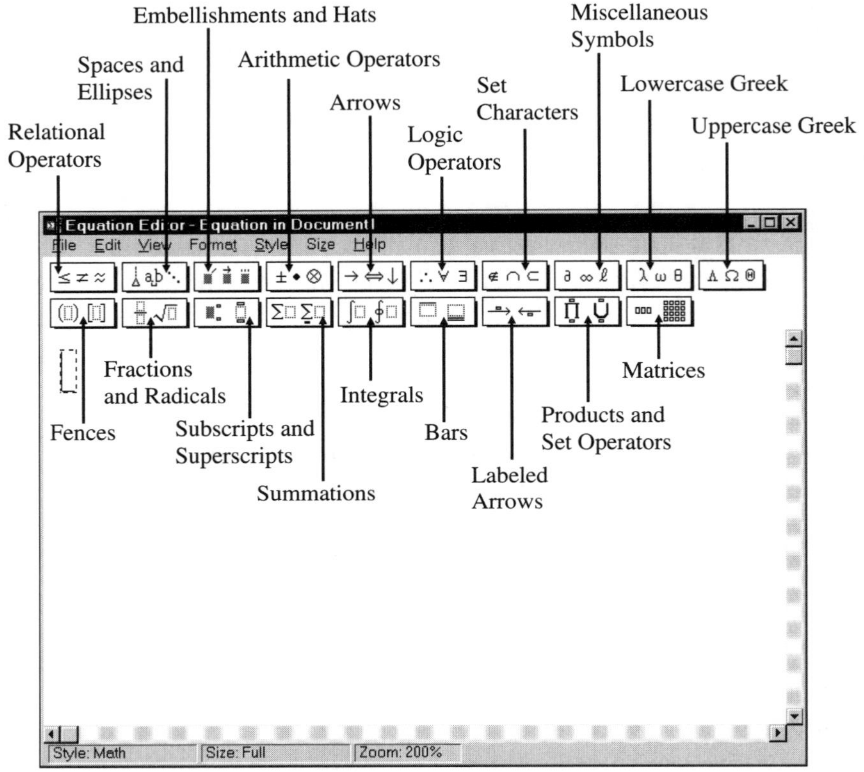

FIGURE 7-14 WP 8 has a brand new graphical Equation Editor

To create an equation, you can select and fill in templates, insert symbols, or type text from the keyboard. The following sections will explain these options in further detail. As you're typing an equation, you can redraw the display by choosing View | Redisplay or by pressing CTRL-D.

Filling in Equation Templates

The template palettes in the Equation Editor dialog box provide frameworks for different equation functions with empty slots for you to fill in. You can use templates to insert parentheses, create fractions, radicals, superscripts, integrals, summations, and so on. To use a template, click the pop-up palette that contains the type of equation element you need (see Figure 7-14). For example, to create a simple fraction, click the Fractions and Radicals pop-up palette and select the first option in the menu. The fraction template is inserted in the Equation Editor:

The areas with dotted lines around them are the empty slots for you to fill in. Type the text for the top portion of the fraction, such as **8**. Then press TAB to move to the next empty slot. Type the text for the lower portion of the fraction, such as **15**. Press TAB again to move out of the template, ready to insert the next equation element.

TIP: *You can press TAB to continuously cycle through each slot in an equation. Pressing SHIFT-TAB moves through the slots in the opposite direction.*

WP automatically formats the spacing in the equation as you create it, so the SPACEBAR is disabled. However, you can adjust the spacing manually, as explained later in this chapter. Elements such as radicals, parentheses, and braces automatically expand to fit their contents. You can insert additional templates within a template to create the equation structure you need. For practice creating a simple equation, see the "How to Create a Simple Equation" section.

TIP: *You can also apply an equation template to text that's already typed. For example, if you type text and then realize you need to place it over another equation element, select the text you've typed and then choose the Fraction template from the Fractions and Radicals pop-up palette. WP inserts the selected text in the first slot of the template, so you can press TAB to create the fraction denominator.*

How to▸▸▸ Create a Simple Equation

Creating equations in WP 8 is easy with the new graphical interface. Follow these steps to practice creating this basic equation:

$$x = \frac{-b \pm \sqrt{b^2 - 4ac}}{2a}$$

1. Choose Insert | Equation to display the Equation Editor.

2. Begin the equation by typing **x=**. There's no need to insert spaces, since WP automatically adds them.

3. To create the fraction element, click the Fractions and Radicals pop-up palette (see Figure 7-14), and select the first fraction symbol.

4. Type **–b**. Then to insert the symbol ±, click the Arithmetic Operators pop-up palette, and select the symbol.

5. To create the radical, click the Fractions and Radicals pop-up palette and select the Radical template.

6. Type **b**. To insert the superscript number, click the Subscripts and Superscripts palette, and then select the first item for a superscript. Type **2** in the superscript slot and press TAB to move outside of it.

7. Type **–4ac**. Press TAB twice to move to the next empty slot—the lower portion of the fraction.

8. Type **2a** and press TAB to move back to the main equation level.

9. Choose File | Exit and Return to Document to insert the equation in your document.

Inserting Symbols

When you need to insert symbols, operators, or special characters into your equations, you can use the symbol palettes on the top row in the Equation Editor (see Figure 7-14). Most of the symbols or characters can be inserted simply by selecting the symbol you want from the pop-up palette. To add a symbol from the Embellishments and Hats pop-up palette, first type the character that you want to use the embellishment, and then select the embellishment or hat from the palette.

> **TIP:** *If you need to insert Greek characters, you don't have to use the Greek character palettes. Instead, you can press CTRL-G and type the letter you want. For example, pressing CTRL-G and then typing **a** will insert the Greek alpha character α.*

Typing Text

WP uses the currently selected style to determine how the text you type in an equation is formatted. By default, the Math style is selected, where WP automatically adds the spacing and evaluates the text you type to determine whether it should be formatted as variable text or as an equation element, such as "sin." The Equation Editor recognizes standard functions such as "sin" and "log" and formats them with the correct typeface and spacing. For example, if you type **sinxyz** in the Equation Editor, WP automatically formats it as this:

$$\sin xyz$$

In addition to the Math style, the Equation Editor has several other styles that you can use for typing and formatting text in special instances. To change the style, choose Style and select the one you want. Any text you type after that point is formatted in that style. Or you can apply a style to text that's already typed in an equation by selecting the text, choosing Style, and selecting the style you want. The available styles are described next:

■ *Math* The Math style differentiates between functions (such as sin or log), variables, numbers, and symbols and formats them accordingly.

Spacing is added automatically, so the SPACEBAR is disabled. You can change the default formatting used for each of these elements, as explained in the "Customizing Settings" section.

■ *Text* The Text style turns off the automatic spacing feature and formats everything as plain text. With the text style selected, you can press SPACEBAR to insert spaces. This style is useful if you need to type text in an equation and don't want it formatted in italics.

■ *Function* The Function style formats text with the same font and spacing used for recognized functions such as "sin" and "log." This is useful if your equation uses a function that's not recognized automatically by WP.

■ *Variable* The Variable style formats all text in italics. This is useful if your equation contains text that's recognized as a function by WP but should be formatted as a variable.

■ *Greek* The Greek style allows you to type Greek characters from the keyboard. When the Greek style is turned on, any letter you type is inserted as its Greek equivalent. You can type both uppercase and lowercase Greek letters.

■ *Matrix-Vector* The Matrix-Vector style formats text in bold, which is the default style used for matrix-vector elements.

TIP: *To format text in a different font than is used in one of the styles, choose Style | Other, and select the font you want to use.*

Controlling Spaces

Unless you have the Text style selected, WordPerfect doesn't let you insert spaces in an equation by pressing the SPACEBAR. The Equation Editor automatically inserts spaces between various equation elements. However, you can manually adjust the spacing in an equation if you need to. To do this, place the insertion point where you want the spacing adjusted and use one of these two methods:

■ Choose the Spaces and Ellipses symbol palette (see Figure 7-14). This palette contains four options for inserting different-sized spaces and one option for removing a space. Select the spacing option you want from the palette.

■ Press the shortcut keystroke for the spacing you want, as shown in this table:

Zero space (remove space)	SHIFT-SPACEBAR
One point space	CTRL-ALT-SPACEBAR
Thin space	CTRL-SPACEBAR
Thick space	CTRL-SHIFT-SPACEBAR

Customizing Settings

You can customize many of the default settings in the Equation Editor, such as the formatting for the different styles, the size of different equation elements, and the spacing used between equation elements.

Style Settings

To change the default font and formatting used for the different elements, such as variables, functions, or plain text, choose Style | Define. Select the font you want to use from the drop-down list for the corresponding style. To use the bold or italic version, select that option. Choose OK when you're finished.

Size Settings

To change the font size used for regular equation text, superscript text, symbols, and other equation elements, choose Size | Define. Type the point size you want for each element and choose OK.

TIP: *You can format text that's typed in an equation with a font size by selecting the text, choosing Size, and choosing the size type you want. To specify an exact point size, choose Size | Other, and type the point size you want.*

Spacing Settings

The Equation Editor lets you control how much space is used between lines in the equation, between text and a superscript, between a fraction numerator and the divider line, and so on. To format the spacing settings, choose Format | Spacing. Click in the text box of the element you want to modify (you might need to scroll down the list) and the preview window shows you where that space is being used. Type the new spacing percentage or amount and choose OK when you're finished.

Shortcut Keystrokes

If you create a lot of equations, you might tire of selecting common equation templates from the palettes. The Equation Editor has lots of shortcut keystrokes set up to help you quickly insert some of the common templates, such as fractions, parentheses, and superscripts. Table 7-1 gives a list of the shortcut keystrokes for some of the more common equation templates. To use these keystrokes, first press CTRL-T so WP recognizes the next keystroke as a template shortcut; then press the shortcut keystroke.

To Insert	Press CTRL-T, then
Parentheses ( )	SHIFT-(or SHIFT-)
Square Brackets []	[or]
Curly Brackets	SHIFT-{ or SHIFT-}
Straight Brackets | |	|
Top/Bottom Fraction	f
Left/Right Fraction	/
Superscript	h
Subscript	l
Superscript and subscript	j
Radical	r
Nth root	n
Summation	s
Product	p
Integral	i
Matrix	m
Underscore character	u

TABLE 7-1 Equation Editor Template Shortcut Keystrokes

Editing Equations

After you've inserted an equation into your document, you can move or size it as you would any graphics box. If you need to edit the equation, double-click the equation to display the equation in the Equation Editor. Make any changes you want and choose File | Exit and Return to Document.

Summary

WordPerfect 8 lets you enhance your documents by adding a variety of graphical elements. You can insert clipart images and edit them within their boxes—for example, rotating them, scaling them, or converting them to black-and-white. The new Draw Object feature lets you quickly insert different shapes into your documents; they can then be customized with shadows, colors, and borders. Multiple graphics boxes can be grouped together so they're easily moved or sized at the same time. Text can be formatted in a graphics box and easily placed at any location in the document. You can control the size, placement, and appearance of graphics boxes, and use Graphics Styles to format the default settings for boxes, borders, lines, and fills. The TextArt and Equation features of WP help you insert unique types of graphical elements into your documents. All in all, WP's many graphics tools help you quickly create documents that are visually appealing and interesting to your readers.

In Chapter 8, we'll take a look at how the Sort feature can help you organize your information in the blink of an eye.

7

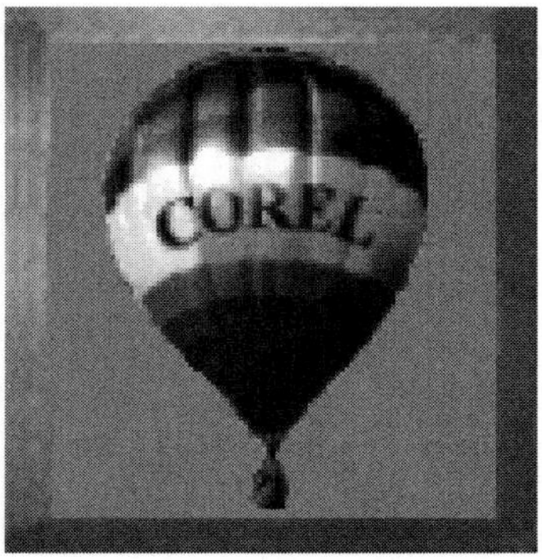
COREL

Chapter 8

Get Organized with Sort

When things are organized, everything tends to run smoother. You can get your work done faster, and you know right where to find something when you need it. However, *getting* organized in the first place is often a frustrating and time-consuming battle. That's where WordPerfect's Sort feature can come to the rescue. The Sort feature can instantly organize the information in your documents in any number of ways. In addition, the Sort feature can pull out just those pieces of information that meet certain criteria, such as those with a specific date or ZIP code.

This chapter will show you how to use the Sort feature to effortlessly organize and order information in your documents. You'll learn how to sort different types of information, such as merge records, table rows, and parallel columns, as well as how to use sort "keys" to define the order the information is sorted in. You'll also learn how to select only those groups of information in a document that match a specific condition. Finally, we'll list some common trouble spots with Sort and show you how to avoid them.

Sort Overview

The Sort feature helps you arrange information alphabetically or numerically, as well as in ascending or descending order. The information you sort can be formatted in a variety of different ways, such as in a list, merge data file, or table, and you can specify which pieces of information are evaluated during the sort. One of the biggest hurdles in effectively using the Sort feature is in understanding the terms it uses. In this section, we'll review the basic terminology used by the Sort feature, as well as the steps for performing a simple sort.

Sort Terminology

In order to use the Sort feature to its full potential, you need to understand the terms it uses. Here's a brief review of some of the sort terminology (see Figure 8-1):

- *Record*   A record is the group of information that WordPerfect keeps together during a sort. A record can consist of a line, paragraph, merge record, table row, or parallel column row. Records can be further divided into fields, columns, lines, and words.

- *Line*   A line ends with a hard return. Each line can be separated into fields and words.

- *Field*   A field is one segment of a line or merge record. In regular text, codes such as tabs and indents separate a line into fields. In a merge record, fields are separated by END FIELD codes.

- *Column*   A column is the equivalent of a field in tables or parallel columns. A column is one of the vertical sections in a parallel column row or table row.

- *Word*   A word is a further subdivision within a field. Words are usually separated by spaces, but can also be separated by forward slashes or hard hyphens.

- *Key*   A key identifies which field, line, and word in a record is examined when the sort is performed. For example, if you want to sort a merge data file alphabetically by last name, you need to set up a key that tells WP where it can find the last name in each record, such as the second word in the first field. You can define up to nine sort keys, which allows you to continue sorting according to a different piece of information when duplicates are found—for example, by first name for those records that have the same last name.

Starting a Sort

To perform a sort, open the document containing the information you want to sort. If you only want to sort a portion of the document or table, select that section first. Then choose Tools | Sort to display the Sort dialog box (see Figure 8-2). This is where WP lists the available sort "definitions," or settings for a sort. A *sort definition* tells WP what type of information to sort (lines, table rows, merge records, and so on), as well as what sort keys to use and what records to extract, if any.

The sort list includes any new sort definitions you've created, as well as the five basic sort definitions that WP includes by default—one for each of the sort types.

Line
Line   Word   Record (highlighted)

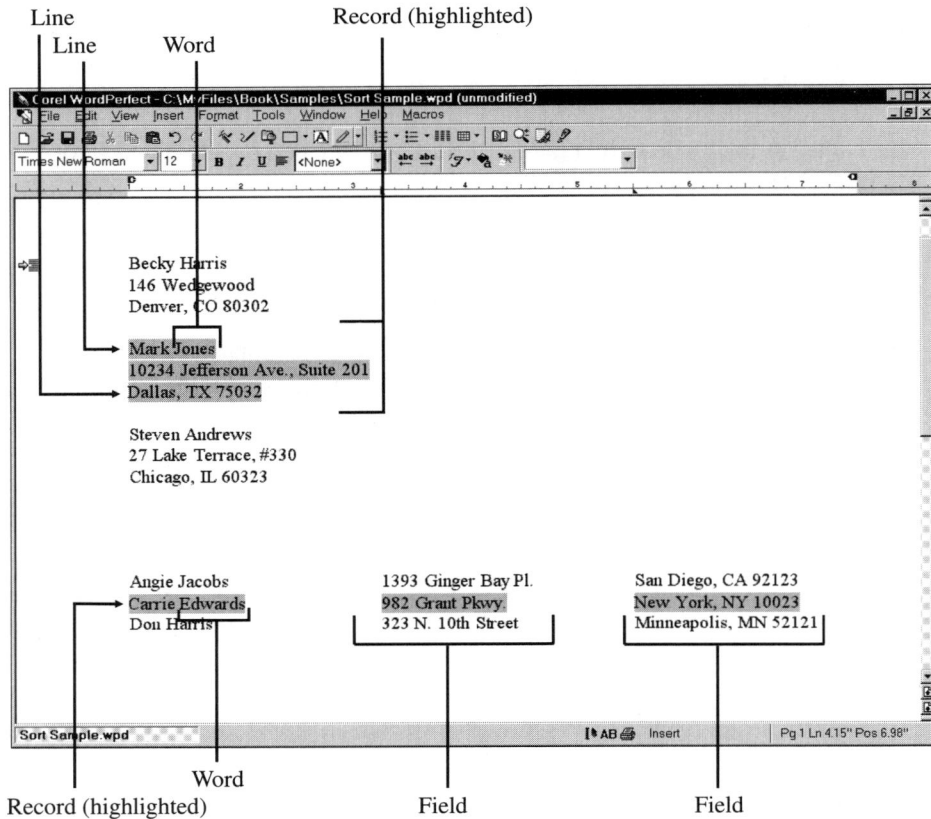

Word
Record (highlighted)   Field   Field

FIGURE 8-1 Components of a paragraph and line sort

The default definitions are set up to sort alphabetically according to the first word in each record type, such as the first word in a line or the first cell in a table row.

NOTE: *The last sort definition you used in a document appears at the top of the list. WP also detects what type of document is currently open and displays the Sort dialog box with the corresponding predefined option selected. However, you can still select a different sort definition or set up a new one if you want.*

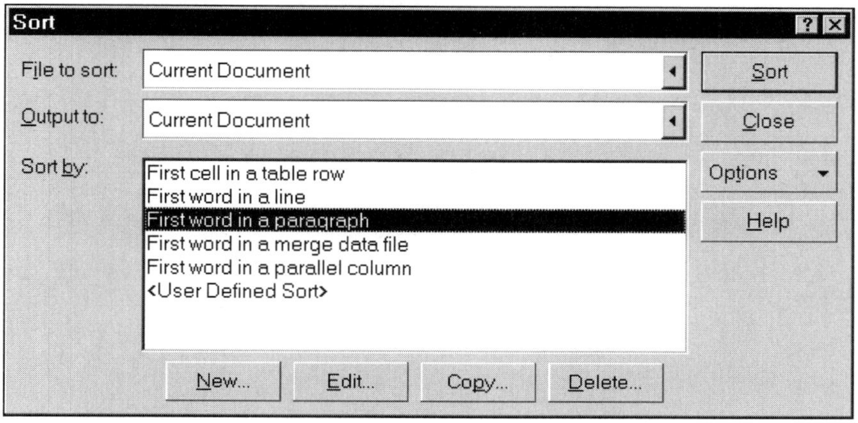

Sort

File to sort:	Current Document ◀	Sort
Output to:	Current Document ◀	Close
Sort by:	First cell in a table row	Options ▾
	First word in a line	
	First word in a paragraph	Help
	First word in a merge data file	
	First word in a parallel column	
	<User Defined Sort>	

New...   Edit...   Copy...   Delete...

FIGURE 8-2 The Sort dialog box lists the available sort definitions

The buttons at the bottom of the dialog box help you manage the available sort definitions.

- *New*   If you want to create a new sort definition, choose New. This displays the New Sort dialog box (see Figure 8-3), where you can specify the settings for the sort. (These options will be described later in this chapter.) If you want to save your sort definition settings, type a description in the Sort Description text box. Choose OK when you're finished. When you create a new definition, it's added to the list of available definitions for all your future documents.

NOTE: *If you don't type a sort description, WP uses the description <User Defined Sort>. The <User Defined Sort> definition appears in the list of available definitions and can be selected in other documents just like other sort definitions. However, the settings in the <User Defined Sort> definition are replaced each time you create a new sort without giving it a unique description.*

- *Edit*   You can view or change the settings for a sort definition by selecting it in the list and choosing Edit. The Edit Sort dialog box has the same options as the New Sort dialog box (see Figure 8-3). Make any changes you want to the sort settings and choose OK when you're finished.

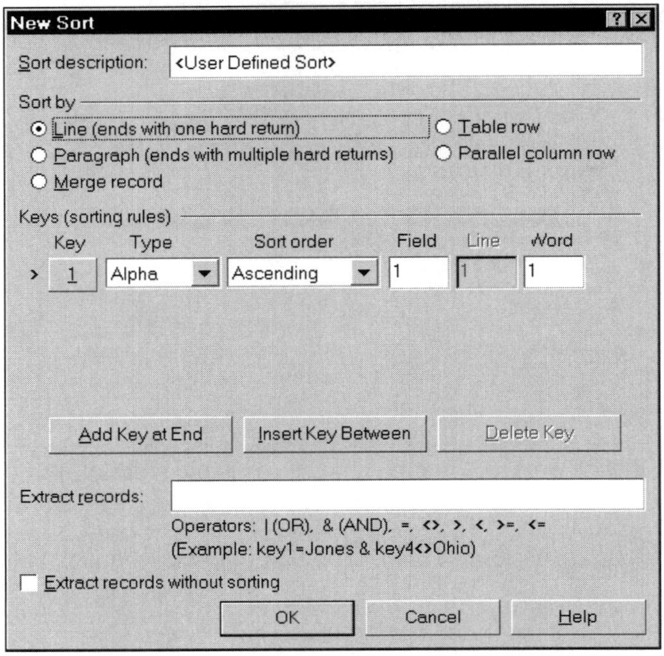

FIGURE 8-3 The New Sort dialog box lets you set up the sort options

- *Copy* You can copy an existing sort definition if you want to modify the settings, but still have the original definition available. To do this, select the definition and choose Copy. Type a new description in the Sort Description text box; then change any settings you want and choose OK.

- *Delete* If you want to remove a definition from the Sort dialog box, select it and choose Delete. Choose Yes to confirm the deletion. You can delete the default sort definitions if you want.

When you're ready to sort, select the definition you want and choose Sort. The sorted text automatically replaces the original text in the document. If you want to keep the "pre-sorted" version of the document, you can save the document with a new filename after sorting, or you can sort directly into a new document window. For the steps on how to do this, see the "Sorting to a New Document" Power Tip.

Power Tip... Sorting to a New Document

Normally, the Sort feature automatically replaces the original document text with the sorted text. However, you can have WP place the sorted text in a new document window so the original file remains unchanged. This method only works when you want to sort the entire document. Follow these steps:

1. Save the document you want to sort. It can either be open in a document window or saved somewhere where you have access to it.

2. Go to a blank document window and choose Tools | Sort. Select the sort definition you want to use (you can create or edit a definition if needed).

3. Click the drop-down arrow to the right of the File to Sort text box and choose File on Disk. When the Select Input File dialog box displays, select the document that you want to sort and choose Select.

4. If you want the sorted document to be automatically saved in a new file, click the drop-down arrow to the right of the Output To text box and choose File on Disk. Switch to the directory where you want the sorted file saved and type a new filename in the File Name text box. Choose OK.

5. Choose Sort to begin the sort. If you didn't specify a filename, the sorted document appears in the blank document window, where you can save it with a new filename. If the insertion point was not in a blank document window, the sorted text is inserted into the current document at the location of the insertion point. Otherwise, the sorted document is saved in the filename you specified. You can open this file to see the results of the sort.

Undoing a Sort

Sometimes the results of a sort don't turn out quite like you expected. When this happens, you can undo the changes made during the sort if you've selected the Undo Sort option. However, this option is *not* turned on by default, so you need to select it the first time you do a sort. To select it, choose Tools | Sort. From the Options pop-down button, select Allow Undo After Sorting. You only need to select this option once and it remains selected for all your future sorts, unless you deselect it again. If you want to sort the current document, continue with the sort as you normally would. Otherwise, choose Close to return to the document.

Once the Undo Sort option is turned on, you can undo the changes made during a sort by simply pressing CTRL-Z or by choosing Edit | Undo. WP returns the document to the condition it was in just prior to the sort.

Sort Types

WordPerfect can sort information that's organized in one of five different ways: lines, paragraphs, merge records, table rows, and parallel column rows. Each of these sort types is broken into records and fields differently. Table 8-1 shows a summary of each sort type.

Sort Type	Record Ends With	Fields Separated By
Line	Hard Return	Tab, Indent, Flush Right, Center, or Margin Release
Paragraph	Two or more Hard Returns, or Hard Page	Tab, Indent, Flush Right, Center, or Margin Release
Merge Record	END RECORD	END FIELD
Table Row	Row	Cell
Parallel Column Row	Last Hard Column in row	Hard Column

TABLE 8-1 Summary of Sort Types

When you're creating or editing a sort definition, select the type of sort in the New Sort dialog box that matches the organization of the document you're sorting (see Figure 8-3). Here are a few things to remember when you're selecting the sort type:

- If you want to sort paragraphs, make sure the document has at least two hard returns between each paragraph.

- You can sort labels with a paragraph sort.

- If you're sorting a table, any rows that have been formatted as header rows won't be included in the sort.

- You can sort tables that have cells joined horizontally in the same row, but not tables that have cells joined vertically in the same column.

- If your merge data file has a FIELDNAMES code at the top of it, it will be ignored during the sort.

Defining Sort Keys

Sort keys make up the heart of the Sort operation. The sort keys tell WordPerfect which pieces of information in a record to examine and which order they should be sorted in. Each sort definition must have at least one key, but you can add up to nine keys to tell WP how to refine a sort when duplicate information exists.

To define the keys for a sort, choose Tools | Sort. Choose New to create a new sort definition, or select an existing sort definition and choose Edit. Make sure the correct type of sort is selected at the top of the dialog box, such as Line or Paragraph. Then follow these three steps:

1. Use the Field, Line, and Word text boxes to tell WP where the information you want to sort by is located within each record. For example, Figure 8-4 shows a list of file numbers, names, and addresses separated by tabs. To sort this list by the last name, you would set up the sort key for Field 2, Word 1. The tabs separate the line into fields (see Table 8-1), so the last name is the first word in the second field. If you're setting up a table or parallel column sort, the Field text box changes to Column.

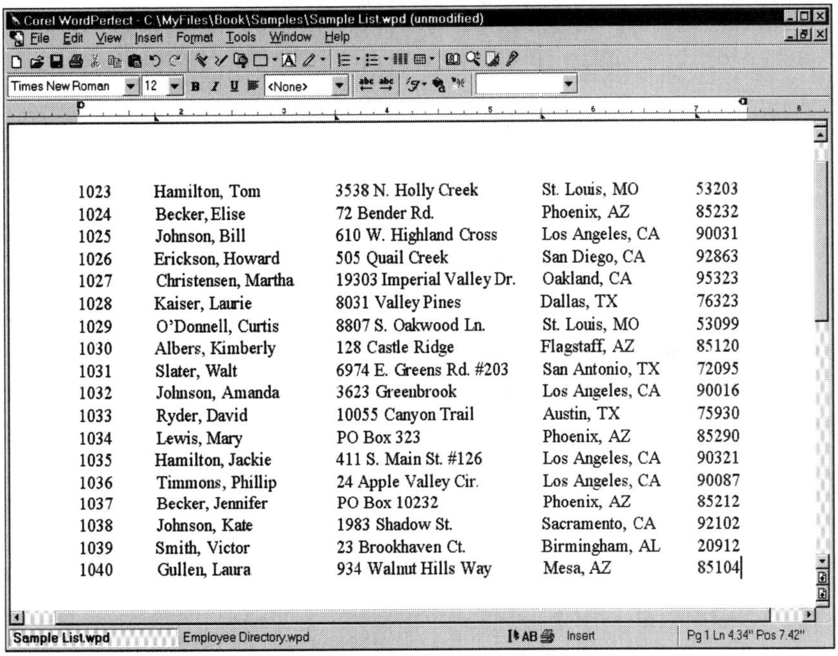

1023	Hamilton, Tom	3538 N. Holly Creek	St. Louis, MO	53203
1024	Becker, Elise	72 Bender Rd.	Phoenix, AZ	85232
1025	Johnson, Bill	610 W. Highland Cross	Los Angeles, CA	90031
1026	Erickson, Howard	505 Quail Creek	San Diego, CA	92863
1027	Christensen, Martha	19303 Imperial Valley Dr.	Oakland, CA	95323
1028	Kaiser, Laurie	8031 Valley Pines	Dallas, TX	76323
1029	O'Donnell, Curtis	8807 S. Oakwood Ln.	St. Louis, MO	53099
1030	Albers, Kimberly	128 Castle Ridge	Flagstaff, AZ	85120
1031	Slater, Walt	6974 E. Greens Rd. #203	San Antonio, TX	72095
1032	Johnson, Amanda	3623 Greenbrook	Los Angeles, CA	90016
1033	Ryder, David	10055 Canyon Trail	Austin, TX	75930
1034	Lewis, Mary	PO Box 323	Phoenix, AZ	85290
1035	Hamilton, Jackie	411 S. Main St. #126	Los Angeles, CA	90321
1036	Timmons, Phillip	24 Apple Valley Cir.	Los Angeles, CA	90087
1037	Becker, Jennifer	PO Box 10232	Phoenix, AZ	85212
1038	Johnson, Kate	1983 Shadow St.	Sacramento, CA	92102
1039	Smith, Victor	23 Brookhaven Ct.	Birmingham, AL	20912
1040	Gullen, Laura	934 Walnut Hills Way	Mesa, AZ	85104

FIGURE 8-4 This document can be sorted with a line sort

2. From the Type drop-down list, select whether the information in the key location should be sorted alphanumerically or numerically. The Alpha option sorts text and numbers alphabetically, and the Numeric option sorts numbers in numeric order. When you use the Alpha option, numbers are sorted before letters according to the individual digits (and not the value of the overall number). For example, in an alphanumeric sort, 86 is sorted *after* 530, since 8 is larger than 5. However, in a numeric sort, 86 is sorted *before* 530, since the number value of 86 is less than 530.

3. From the Sort Order drop-down list, select whether the information in the key location should be sorted in ascending or descending order. Ascending order sorts from A to Z and 0 to 9, while descending order sorts from Z to A and 9 to 0.

Here are a few tips and tricks for defining sort keys:

- If you use a negative number in the Word text box, WordPerfect counts from the end of the field or line. For example, a setting of Field 1, Word –1 points to the last word in the first field—no matter how many words are before it. Similarly, a setting of Field 3, Word –2 points to the second-to-last word in the third field.

- Most keyboard symbols, such as the asterisk, parentheses, and exclamation point, are sorted before letters or numbers. If the word you're sorting uses one of these symbols as the first character, it won't be sorted correctly with the rest of the text. For example, a word in parentheses will be sorted at the top of the list, no matter what the word inside the parentheses begins with.

- You can have uppercase letters sorted before lowercase letters if the information is identical, such as "May" before "may." To do this, after setting up your sort options in the New Sort dialog box, choose OK to return to the Sort dialog box. Then from the Options pop-down button, choose Uppercase Sorts Before Lowercase. This option remains in effect for all your future sorts until you deselect it. If this option is not selected, WP sorts lowercase letters before uppercase letters.

Adding Multiple Keys

You can further control how the information in your document is sorted by defining multiple sort keys. The order of the sort keys in the New Sort dialog box determines the order in which the document information is evaluated. If duplicate information is found in the first sort key location (such as several records in the same state), WP uses the second sort key to further sort those duplicate records (such as by the city name). If duplicates also exist there, a third key can be used to further sort, and so on. For example, Figure 8-5 shows the sort keys that would be needed to sort the information in Figure 8-4 according to the state, then city name, then last name, and finally first name. For another example of sorting with multiple keys, see the "How to Sort Dates" section.

To add a sort key to the end of the key list, choose Add Key at End. To add a sort key *above* another key in the list, first select the existing key by clicking the key number, and then choose Insert Key Between. Next, follow the three previous steps

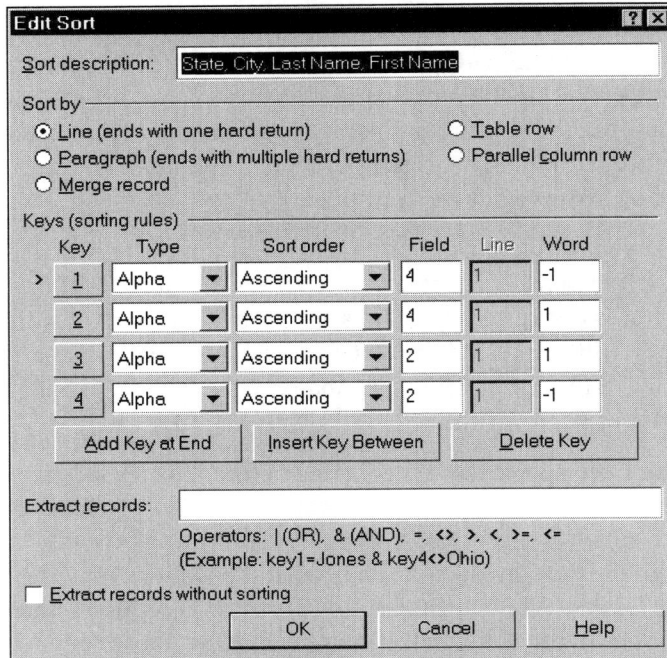

FIGURE 8-5 These keys sort Figure 8-4 by the state, city, last name, and
then first name

to set the location, sort type, and sort order for the new key. Each key should point
to a different location in the record, and each key can have a different sort type and
order.

NOTE: *If you want to remove a sort key from the list, click the key number
to select that key, and then choose Delete Key.*

When you're finished setting up the sort keys, choose OK; then choose Sort to
begin the sort or choose Close to return to the document.

How to... Sort Dates

You can use multiple sort keys to sort information chronologically by dates—either in ascending or descending order. In order to sort dates, they must be in a numeric format separated by spaces, forward slashes, or hard hyphens, such as 1 29 93, 1/29/93, or 1-29-93. Dates in a format such as January 29, 1993 can't be sorted chronologically. (To insert a hard hyphen, press CTRL+-.)

The next steps will show you how to sort a list of dates in chronological order, such as the one shown here:

3/20/96	Submit first copy
12/2/95	Resubmit application
9/8/95	Finalize application
3/13/96	Review initial submission changes
8/14/95	Prepare rough draft of application

1. Open the document that contains the dates you want to sort. If you don't want to sort the entire document, select the portion that should be sorted. If you want to practice with a sample document, open the DATE SORT.WPD file from the companion CD.

2. Choose Tools | Sort | New. In the Sort Description text box, type **MM/DD/YY Dates**.

3. Select Line for the sort type. If the dates are in a table or parallel columns, select Table Row or Parallel Column Row instead.

4. The first sort key needs to sort the dates according to the year. For Key 1, select Numeric from the Type drop-down list. If you want the dates to be sorted in descending order (most recent on top), choose Descending from the Sort Order drop-down list. Then type **3** in the Word text box, since the year is the third word in the date. If the dates aren't located in the first field in your document, type the appropriate field number in the Field (or Column) text box. For example, if the dates are in the second column of a table, type **2** in the Column text box.

How to... **Sort Dates**
(continued)

---

5. The second key should further sort records with duplicate years according to the month. To set up this key, choose Add Key at End and select Numeric from the Type drop-down list. If you set the first key to descending order, choose Descending from the Sort Order drop-down list. Leave the Word text box set at 1, since the month is the first word in the date. If needed, type the appropriate field number in the Field or Column text box.

6. Finally, add a third sort key to sort records in the same month according to the day of the month. Choose Add Key at End and select Numeric from the Type drop-down list. In the Word text box, type **2**. If needed, change the order to descending, and type appropriate field or column number.

7. Choose OK, and then choose Sort to sort the dates.

Extracting Records

In addition to changing the order of information in a document, you can use the Sort feature to find records that match certain criteria. For example, you can select only those records that have a specific ZIP code. Or you can pull out all the records with the same last name. This process is called *extracting* records, and it works hand-in-hand with the sort keys.

To extract records during a sort, choose Tools | Sort. If you want to edit an existing sort definition, select it and choose Edit. Otherwise, create a new definition by choosing New. Type a description in the Sort Description text box and select the type of sort you're performing, such as Merge Record.

Next, set up the keys for your sort, following the guidelines in the "Defining Sort Keys" section earlier. When you're extracting records, you must set up a sort key that points to the location of each piece of information you want to evaluate. For example, if you want to extract records that match a certain ZIP code, you need to set up a sort key that defines the field and word where the ZIP code information is located in each record.

Once you've defined the sort keys for the information you want to evaluate, type the selection criteria in the Extract Records text box for the records you want to pull out. The selection statement is a combination of the key number, a logical operator, and the matching information. For example, Figure 8-6 shows a sample merge data file. In Figure 8-7, the sort keys are defined to sort the records according to the ZIP code (Key 1), then by the last name (Key 2), and finally by the first name (Key 3). The "key1=52109" statement in the Extract Records text box will pull out only those records with a ZIP code of 52109, since Key 1 points to the ZIP code location in each record. When the sort is completed, only those records with a ZIP code of 52109 remain, and those records are further sorted according to last name and first name.

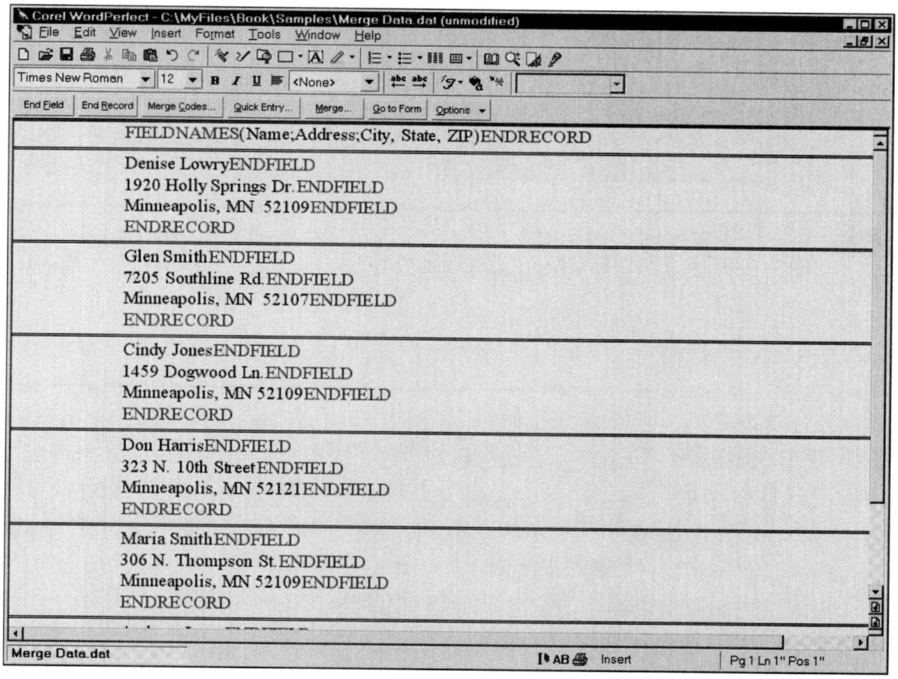

FIGURE 8-6 You can extract records from a merge data file that match certain criteria

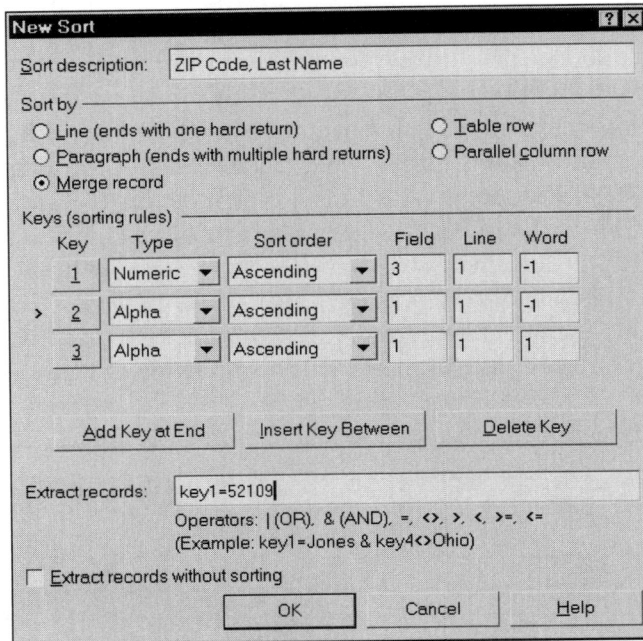

FIGURE 8-7 These sort settings extract only those records from Figure 8-6 with 52109 in the ZIP code field

Operator	Description	Example
=	Equal To Selects records that exactly match the condition	Key2=Smith Selects only those records with a last name of Smith
<>	Not Equal To Selects records that don't match the condition	Key2<>Smith Selects all records except those with a last name of Smith

TABLE 8-2 Operators for Extracting Records

Operator	Description	Example
>	Greater Than Selects records that have information greater than the given condition	Key1>80000 Selects all records with a ZIP code greater than 80000 Key3>M Selects all records with a first name beginning with M-Z
<	Less Than Selects records with information less than the given condition	Key1<40000 Selects all records with a ZIP code less than 40000 Key2<Jones Selects all records that come before Jones alphabetically
>=	Greater Than or Equal To Selects records with information that matches or is greater than the given condition	Key1>=73234 Selects all records that contain the ZIP code 73234 or have a ZIP code greater in value
<=	Less Than or Equal To Selects records with information that matches or is less than the given condition	Key3<=Don Selects all records with a first name of Don, as well as all those with first names that come before Don alphabetically
|	OR Selects records that meet the condition of either key	Key2=Smith | Key3=Robert Selects all records with a last name of Smith, as well as all records with a first name of Robert
&	AND Selects records that meet the condition of both keys	Key2=Jones & Key1<>52109 Selects all those records with a last name of Jones, except for those with the ZIP code of 52109

TABLE 8-2 Operators for Extracting Records (*continued*)

There are eight logical operators that you can use in your selection statements. Table 8-2 gives a description and example of each type of operator. The examples in the table refer to the sample merge file and key definitions shown in Figures 8-6 and 8-7.

NOTE: *Selection statements are not case sensitive, so "key2=smith" finds the same records as "key2=Smith" or "key2=SMITH."*

If you want to extract the records in a document that match the selection statement criteria *without* sorting them according to the key information, select Extract Records Without Sorting. This option allows you to set up the sort keys you need for the extraction without changing the order of the original document.

TIP: *If you want to perform a global search through an entire record and not just a sort key location, you can use keyg or key0. For example, the selection statement "keyg=Harris" will find all records that have "Harris" anywhere in the record—even if it's not a location assigned to a sort key.*

When you're ready to perform the sort and extract the records, choose OK to return to the Sort dialog box, and then choose Sort. Just as during a regular sort, the extracted records automatically replace the original text in the document. If you want to keep the original document, be sure to save the document with a new filename. You can also sort and extract directly into a new document window as explained in the "Sorting to a New Document" Power Tip earlier in the chapter. To undo the results of the sort, press CTRL-Z.

NOTE: *If you're working with a merge data file, you can also use the Merge feature to select records that match a certain criteria when you perform a merge. See Chapter 2 for more information.*

Specifying Multiple Conditions

The AND (&) and OR (|) operators allow you to check for more than one condition when you're extracting records, such as finding those records with a specific last name and in a certain ZIP code. You can also use parentheses to group selection conditions together. The parentheses tell WP in which order to process the information when evaluating records for matching conditions. For example, using the selection statement (key1>90000 & key2=Smith) | key2=Jones

will extract any records with a last name of Smith if they have a ZIP code over 90000, as well as any records with a last name of Jones, no matter what the ZIP code is. On the other hand, using the statement

key1>9000 & (key2=Smith | key2=Jones)

will extract any records in a ZIP code over 90000 (no matter what the last name), as well as any records with a last name of either Smith or Jones.

The ability to group selection conditions together with parentheses gives you a great deal of control and flexibility in determining the final output. For example, you can use selection conditions to extract records from a specific date forward. For the steps on how to set this up, see the "How to Select from a Specific Date Forward" section.

How to... Select from a Specific Date Forward

You can use multiple conditions in a selection statement to extract records with a date after a specific date. For example, the table shown next includes a date in one column. You can set up a selection statement that extracts only those rows with a date on or after 6/15/96. In order to work with dates in a sort, the dates must be in numeric format and be separated by spaces, forward slashes, or hard hyphens (entered by pressing CTRL+-).

Ref. No.	Name	Admission Date	Primary Doctor
43232	BARR, Paul	10/12/95	M. Johnson
46323	BELL, Michael	12/5/94	L. Kirkpatrick
46654	BRADLEY, Louise	8/16/96	S. Johnson
46885	CALDERON, Carlos	6/15/96	D. Peterson
47321	COBB, Helen	1/22/97	S. Thomas
47886	DAILEY, Michelle	4/2/97	M. Johnson
48011	DEWITT, Rick	7/24/95	L. Kirkpatrick
48325	DOMINGUEZ, Oscar	6/1/96	B. Kendall
48378	EDWARDS, Kerri	2/4/96	R. Goodman
48765	ERICKSON, Howard	9/7/96	M. Johnson

How to...   **Select from a Specific Date Forward**
(continued)

Follow these steps:

1. Open the document that contains the records you want to extract from. If you want to practice with a sample table, open the TABLE SORT.WPD file from the companion CD.

2. Choose Tools | Sort | New. In the Sort Description text box, type **After Specific Date**.

3. Select the type of sort for the document you're working with, such as Table Row.

4. When you're sorting or extracting dates, you need to define three sort keys: one for the year (Key 1), one for the month (Key 2), and one for the day (Key 3). To define Key 1, select Numeric from the Type drop-down list. Type **3** in the Word text box (for the year), and then type the column or field where the date is located. For the previous sample table, type **3** in the Column text box.

5. Choose Add Key at End. Select Numeric from the Type drop-down list. Type the appropriate column or field number, such as Column **3** for the sample table. Leave the Word set at 1, since the month is the first word.

6. Choose Add Key at End and select Numeric from the Type drop-down list. Type the same column or field number, such as Column **3**. In the Word text box, type **2**.

7. In the Extract Records text box, type the selection statement using this format:

   (((key2=MM & key3>=DD) | key2>MM) & key1=YY) | key1>YY

   Replace the MM, DD, and YY text in the statement with the date you want to use. For example, to select records on or after the date 6/15/96, the statement would look like this:

   (((key2=6 & key3>=15) | key2>6) & key1=96) | key1>96

   To select records *before* a certain date instead of after, change the three greater than symbols (>) in the selection statement to less than symbols (<).

Select from a Specific Date Forward
(*continued*)

8. Choose OK, and then Sort to begin the sort.

This selection statement works by first extracting those records with a month of June and a date greater than or equal to 15 (key2=6 & key3>=15), resulting in all records from the last half of June for any year. Added to this are any records with a month *after* June (key2>6), giving you any dates from July through December, again in any year. Then this group of records is narrowed by pulling out only those with a year equal to 96 (key1=96). Finally, any additional records with a year greater than 96 (for any month) are added to the overall list (key1>96). The result of the previous table looks like this:

Ref. No.	Name	Admission Date	Primary Doctor
46885	CALDERON, Carlos	6/15/96	D. Peterson
46654	BRADLEY, Louise	8/16/96	S. Johnson
48765	ERICKSON, Howard	9/7/96	M. Johnson
47321	COBB, Helen	1/22/97	S. Thomas
47886	DAILEY, Michelle	4/2/97	M. Johnson

Troubleshooting Sort Problems

As we mentioned earlier, sometimes your sorts don't always turn out the way you anticipated. The Undo Sort option is a great way to restore your document to its original condition, but the next step is determining just where the sort went wrong. In this section, we'll give you a list of some common trouble spots with Sort, and show you how to avoid them.

■ *Name Suffixes* When you're sorting a list of names that use suffixes, such as "Jr.," "Esq.," or "Ph.D.," you might find that WP is sorting according to the suffix instead of the last name, such as sorting "Thomas Harrison, Esq." with the "E's" instead of the "H's." You can avoid this by using a hard space between the last name and the suffix. For example, this list of names contains a mixture of names with and without suffixes:

```
Dr. Cynthia S. Webber, Ph.D.
Roger P. Butler
Charles P. Eaton, Sr.
Daniel Hanson, Jr.
Kathy Callahan
John H. McDaniel, Esq.
Ann Marie Hicks
```

To sort this list correctly according to last name, define a sort key with Field 1, Word –1 (the negative number tells WP to look at the last word on the line). Then make sure that each name that uses a suffix has a hard space between the last name and the suffix. To insert a hard space, press CTRL-SPACEBAR. When you use a hard space, WP doesn't recognize the suffix as a separate word, so the names are sorted correctly according to the last name.

■ *Hanging Indents*   A common mistake made when sorting paragraphs with hanging indents—such as in the sample bibliography here—is not setting the field number correctly for the sort key. Since hanging indents involve two separate codes that are both field separators—an indent code and a margin release code—the text at the beginning of the paragraph is considered to be in field *three*.

```
Baldanza, Frank, Mark Twain, New York, Barnes & Noble,
     Inc., 1961, pp. 112–120.
Day, Martin S., A Handbook of American Literature, new
     York, Crane, Russak & Company, Inc., 1975, pp.
     166–170.
```

■ *Blank Table Rows*   When you sort a table with blank rows, the blank rows are always moved to the top of the table during the sort. To avoid this, select only those rows that contain text before you start the sort. This lets the blank rows remain at the bottom of the table and the other rows are sorted correctly.

■ *Tabbed Lists*   If you're sorting a list separated by tabs and the sort doesn't work correctly, check to see how many tabs you have between each field. Since tabs are field separators, you should only have *one* tab between each text column. If you simply press TAB several times until the text is lined up, the sort won't work correctly because each line has a different number of fields. To solve this problem, insert a tab setting at the top of your document with a tab stop at each location where you want text to line up, and then press TAB once between each tabbed column.

■ *ZIP+4 Codes*   When you're sorting ZIP codes, watch out for ZIP+4 codes, such as 73034-1234. If your document has ZIP+4 codes, make sure you use a hard hyphen between the ZIP code segments, which allows WP to view the ZIP code as two words during the sort. Hard hyphens can be inserted by pressing CTRL+-. Then set up the sort definition with *two* numeric sort keys for the field containing the ZIP code—the first sort key for the first word (the five-digit ZIP code) and the second key for the second word (the four-digit extension).

On the CD ⟩⟩⟩   Sorting Titles with "A," "An," and "The"

When you're sorting a list of titles, you often want to sort those titles that begin with articles such as "A," "An," and "The," according to the *second* word of the title. There's no automatic setting in the Sort feature to ignore initial articles such as "A" and "The" when sorting, but you can use a macro to help get around this problem.

The companion CD contains a macro called SORT TITLES.WCM that can sort text with initial articles in two different ways. First, the macro can use hidden text to temporarily "hide" any of the three common articles ("A," "An," or "The") when they appear at the beginning of a line. Then, after the text is sorted, the hidden text is removed and the initial articles are displayed again. The final result of a sort with this option might look like this:

Oliver Twist
A Tale of Two Cities

Or the macro can move the beginning articles to the end of the title text and insert a comma before them. The result of a sort with this option might look like this instead:

Oliver Twist
Tale of Two Cities, A

This macro only works with a line sort and the titles you're sorting must be in the first field of the line. Make sure the text you're sorting doesn't contain any Hidden Text codes. To use the macro, open the document you want to sort and choose Tools | Macro | Play. Select the SORT TITLES.WCM macro and choose Play. A dialog box appears asking you where you want the initial articles placed. Select the option you want and choose OK.

Summary

The Sort feature is a great boon in helping you get organized and *stay* organized so you can get your work done faster. You can easily sort several different types of records, including paragraphs, table rows, and merge data files. The ability to define up to nine sort keys lets you precisely determine how the information is sorted. In addition, you can use selection statements to extract records that match certain conditions. Common trouble spots can be avoided by knowing a few simple tricks. Once you know how to put the Sort feature to work, you'll be amazed at the instant results!

In Chapter 9, we'll show you how to further organize your documents with features such as Outline, Index, Table of Contents, and Cross Reference.

Chapter
9

The Reference Tools

One of the marks of a good reference is that its information is both accurate and easily accessible. After all, what good is a table of contents if it has incorrect page numbers or an index that can't help you find what you're looking for? Fortunately, WordPerfect has several tools that make it easy to include reference information throughout your documents and keep it up to date at the same time.

In this chapter, we'll show you how to use four of WP's reference tools to organize your documents and help your readers find what they need. You'll learn how to use the Outline feature to insert paragraph numbers, as well as how to use the Table of Contents and Index features to reference the main topics in your document. We'll also show you how to use the Cross-Reference feature to keep references to page numbers, graphics boxes, and other items within a document automatically updated.

Inserting Paragraph Numbers with Outline

WP 8's Outline feature makes it easy to create an outline using a variety of numbering formats and styles. A traditional outline helps you organize the main ideas for a document, but you can also use the Outline feature to number paragraphs (see Figure 9-1). This technique is commonly used in legal documents. As you add, delete, and move paragraphs in the document, the remaining paragraphs are automatically renumbered.

To start numbering paragraphs in a document, place the insertion point where you want the first number to appear and choose Insert | Outlines/Bullets & Numbering. The Bullets and Numbering dialog box appears with the Numbers tab selected (see Figure 9-2).

Select the numbering format you want to use. As you select each format, a description appears at the top of the dialog box. The preview indicates whether that format has multiple levels and whether or not each level is indented. Each multiple-level format has eight different levels available. When you've selected the format you want, choose OK.

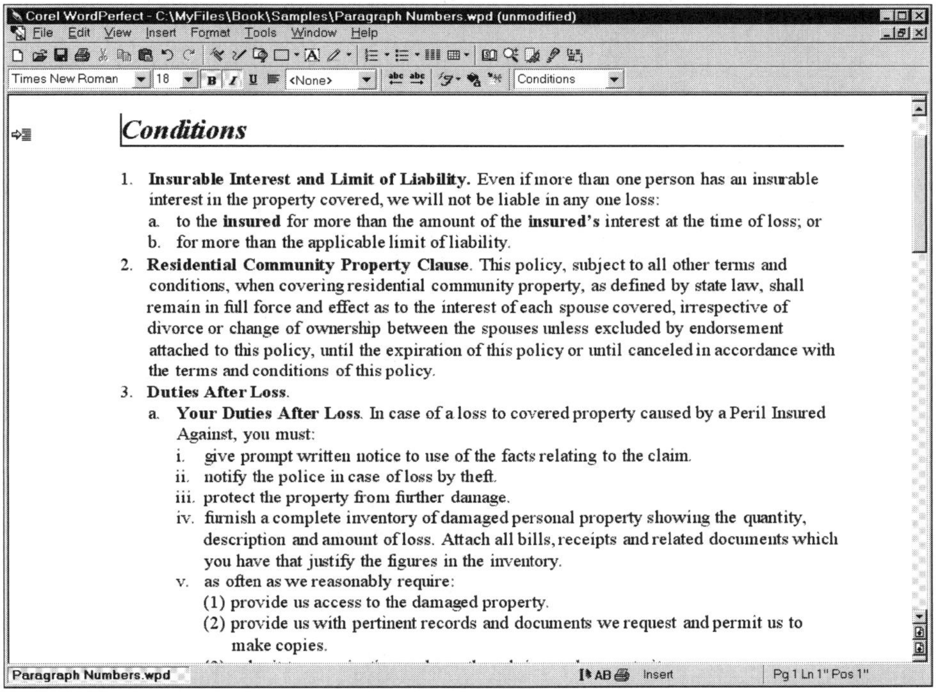

FIGURE 9-1   The Outline feature can be used to number paragraphs

NOTE: *The Paragraph and Numbers formats appear identical in the Bullets and Numbering dialog box. Each format uses multiple indented levels, but the Paragraph format (on the top row) inserts an indent code following the paragraph number, while the Numbers format (on the bottom row) doesn't include any formatting after the paragraph number.*

TIP: *If you want to number paragraphs without multiple levels, you can use the QuickBullets feature instead of going through the Bullets and Numbering dialog box. Simply type the number or letter you want in the document (such as 1., I., or A.) and press TAB. For more information on QuickBullets, see Chapter 3.*

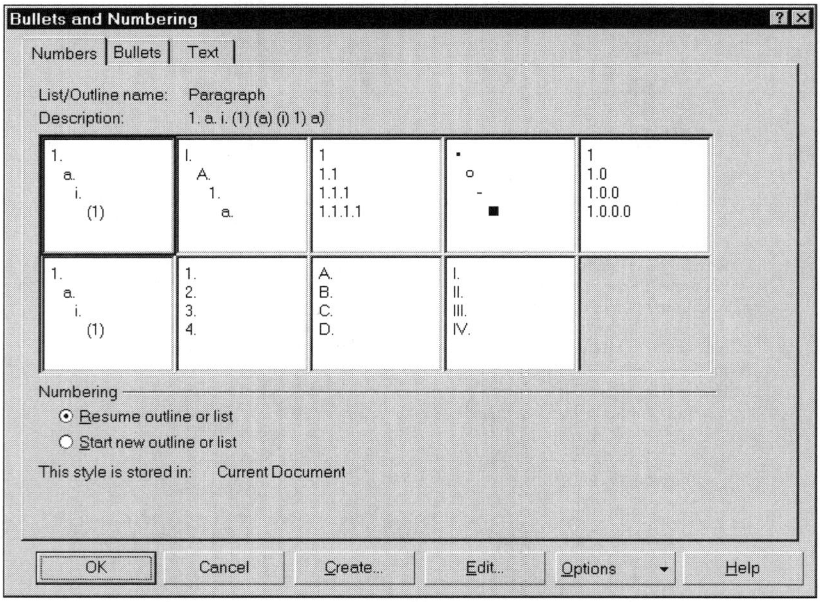

FIGURE 9-2 You can choose from several numbering formats

WP inserts the first paragraph number and displays the Outline Property Bar:

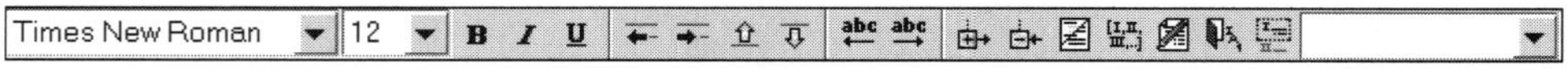

TIP: *Move the mouse pointer over a button on the Outline Property Bar to see a description of that button's function.*

Type the text for the first paragraph and press ENTER. WP automatically inserts the next paragraph number. If you want this paragraph to use a number from the next level, press TAB or click the Demote button on the Outline Property Bar. Depending on the numbering format you selected, the paragraph might also be indented when you move to the next level.

Each time you press ENTER, WP inserts the next paragraph number for the same level as the previous paragraph. You can press TAB to change it to the next level, or if you want to move back to the previous level, press SHIFT-TAB or click the Promote button on the Property Bar.

TIP: *If you want to insert a hard return without having the next paragraph number inserted, press SHIFT-ENTER. If you need to insert a tab without changing to the next level, press CTRL-TAB or press F7 to insert an Indent code.*

Continue this process to create and number the paragraphs in your document. When you've finished, press ENTER to move to a new line, and then press BACKSPACE to delete the paragraph number that was inserted.

TIP: *If you want to add paragraph numbers to existing text in a document, select the text and choose Insert | Outline/Bullets & Numbering. Select the numbering format you want and choose OK.*

When you add paragraph numbers with this method, the numbers always appear to the left of the text. You can also insert numbers manually within a paragraph. For more information on how to do this, see the Power Tip "Manual Paragraph Numbers."

Power Tip... Manual Paragraph Numbers

WP 8 makes it easy to insert paragraph numbers anywhere in a document without any formatting or tabs. For example, you can insert several paragraph numbers within the same paragraph and have those numbers automatically updated as items are added and deleted.

To insert a manual paragraph number, follow these steps:

1. Place the insertion point where you want the number inserted and press CTRL-SHIFT-F5 to display the Insert Paragraph Number dialog box. (You can also add the Insert Paragraph Number button to a toolbar or Property Bar.)

2. From the Number Type drop-down list, select the numbering format you want to use, such as Legal or Paragraph.

3. In the Outline Level text box, type the level number you want inserted.

4. In the Start Value text box, type the starting number.

5. Choose OK to insert the number.

WP formats the number according to the format you selected. For example, if you select the Paragraph number type, type **2** in the Outline Level text box, and type **3** in the Start Value text box, WP inserts "c." into the document.

To insert another number, just press CTRL-SHIFT-F5 again. WP automatically selects the same numbering format and level you've previously selected, and increments the Start Value by one so that the next number will be inserted. Change any of the settings if you want, such as moving to the next or previous level, and then choose OK to insert the number.

If you want to resume paragraph numbering later in a document, place the insertion point where you want to start the numbering and choose Insert | Outline/Bullets & Numbering. The format you were using earlier in the document should already be selected. Make sure Resume Outline or List is selected. If you want to start the numbering over at that point in the document, select the numbering format you want and select Start New Outline or List. Choose OK.

Modifying Paragraph Numbers

Once you've added paragraph numbers to a document, you can easily make changes and have the numbers automatically updated. For example, you can move paragraphs, select a new numbering type, or insert body text. Follow these guidelines to make changes to the paragraph numbers.

PARAGRAPH NUMBERS.WPD: *If you want to practice making changes on a document with paragraph numbers, open the PARAGRAPH NUMBERS.WPD file from the companion CD.*

- If you want to use a different numbering format, place the insertion point at the beginning of the paragraphs and choose Insert | Outline/Bullets & Numbering. Select the new format in the dialog box and choose OK.

NOTE: *If none of the preexisting formats meet your needs, you can edit them or create your own. See the "Customizing a Numbering Format" section later in the chapter for more information.*

- To add new paragraphs within the document, place the insertion point at the end of the paragraph above where you want the new paragraph inserted. Press ENTER to insert a new line, and then use TAB or SHIFT-TAB to change the paragraph number to the level you want.

- To change the level of an existing paragraph, place the insertion point at the beginning of that paragraph and press TAB to change to the next level or press SHIFT-TAB to change to the previous level. You can also use the Promote and Demote buttons on the Outline Property Bar to change the level.

- To move a paragraph, you can simply use cut-and-paste and the paragraph numbers will be updated. However, WP also offers some specific features for easily moving a single paragraph or an entire "family." A *family* is the current paragraph and any subordinate (indented) levels below it, until the next paragraph of the same level is encountered. To move a single paragraph, place the insertion point anywhere in the paragraph and then use the Move Up and Move Down buttons on the Outline Property Bar to position the paragraph where you want.

  To move an entire family, place the insertion point in the first paragraph for the family you want to move. Click the Hide Family button on the Outline Property Bar to temporarily hide all of the subordinate levels under that paragraph. Then use the Move Up and Move Down buttons on the Property Bar to position the paragraph. After you've moved the paragraph, click the Show Family button to redisplay the subordinate paragraphs.

- If you want to insert paragraphs that aren't numbered, place the insertion point at the end of the line just above where you want the body text inserted and press ENTER. Then press BACKSPACE to delete the number that was inserted. You can also press SHIFT-ENTER to insert a hard return without a new number.

TIP: *You can convert a numbered paragraph to body text or vice versa by placing the insertion point anywhere in that paragraph and pressing CTRL-H.*

- To temporarily hide any body text in the document and show just the numbered paragraphs, choose the Show/Hide Body Text button on the Outline Property Bar. Click the button again to redisplay the body text.

- If you want to see only those paragraphs with certain levels, such as the first two levels, click the Show Levels button on the Outline Property bar, and then select the number of levels you want to display, such as Two. To have all of the levels display again, choose Eight from the Show Levels button.

NOTE: *If you choose <None> from the Show Levels button to hide all of the numbered paragraphs, the Outline Property Bar no longer appears. If you want to redisplay the paragraphs, use the Show Levels button on the Outline Tools toolbar (to display this toolbar, right-click any displaying toolbar and select Outline Tools).*

- If you want to start numbering at a specific number or start the numbering over at any point in the document, place the insertion point in the paragraph you want the new numbering to begin with. Click the Set Paragraph Number button on the Outline Property Bar and type the new paragraph number in the text box. If you're changing the number for a subordinate paragraph, you need to type a number for each level and separate the numbers with a comma, space, or period. For example, if you're changing a second-level paragraph, you can type **3.2** or **3 2**.

NOTE: *You must type the new paragraph number with numbers, such as 4.2.3, even if the level format uses letters or Roman numerals. WP automatically converts the numbers to the correct type of numbering for that level.*

TIP: *If you're changing the number of a subordinate paragraph and want the previous levels to update as new paragraphs are added or deleted, type a question mark for all but the last level number. For example, to set a third-level paragraph at number 4, type **? ? 4**.*

Customizing a Numbering Format

If none of WordPerfect's predefined numbering formats meet your needs, you can easily edit them or create your own formats. To edit or create a numbering format, choose Insert | Outline/Bullets & Numbering. To edit one of the existing formats, select the format and choose Edit. To create a new format, choose Create. The Create Format dialog box appears (see Figure 9-3). If you're creating a new format, in the List/Outline Name text box, type a name for your format. In the Description text box, type a description.

TIP: *If you simply want to change the amount of space inserted between the paragraph number and the text, insert a new tab stop. The easiest way to do this is with the Ruler Bar. For more information on setting tabs with the Ruler, see Chapter 4.*

Each level in the format can use text (such as "Article"), a number or bullet, and a style. The style determines the formatting for that particular level, such as how many tabs (if any) are inserted before and after the paragraph number. To set up the formatting for each level, follow these steps:

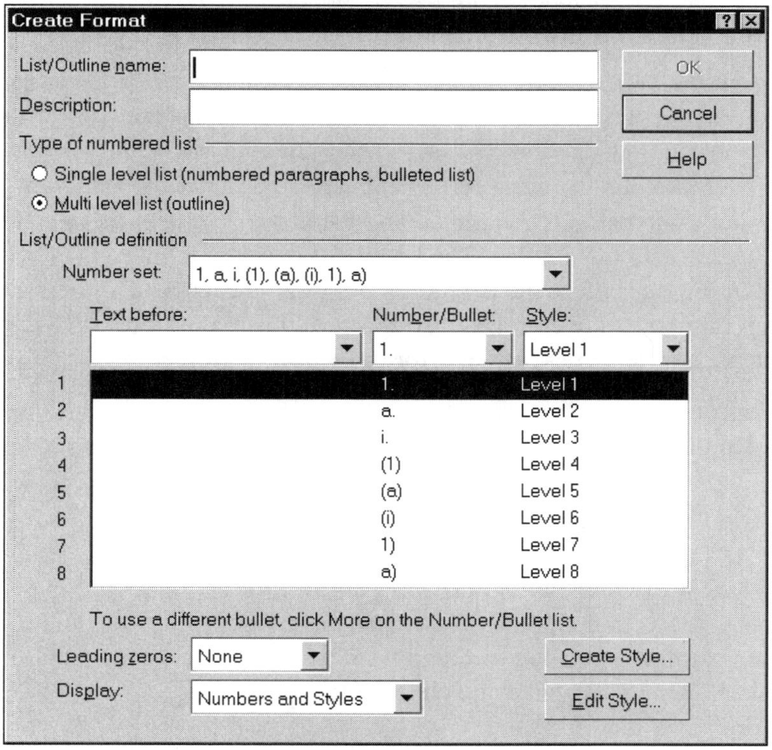

FIGURE 9-3 You can create or edit a numbering format

1. Select the level in the list box that you want to format.

2. If you want any text inserted before the paragraph number, such as "Article" or "Section," select it from the Text Before drop-down list or type it in the Text Before text box.

3. If you want to use one of the standard numbering formats, such as Legal or Paragraph, select the option you want from the Number Set drop-down list. Otherwise, type the number, letter, or bullet you want to use for that level in the Number/Bullet drop-down list. You can also select a number or bullet from the Number/Bullet drop-down list. If you want to select a WP symbol that's not listed, choose More from the drop-down list, select the symbol you want to use, and choose Insert and Close.

4. Type any other text you want inserted with the number in the Number/ Bullet text box, such as a period or parentheses. If you want the level number to include the previous level numbers as well, as in the legal formats, type the combination of numbers, letters, and bullets in the text box, such as **1.1** or **A-1**.

5. From the Style drop-down list, select the style that you want to use to format the current level. The Level 1–Level 8 styles insert a consecutive number of indent codes before the paragraph number, and one indent code following the number. For example, the Level 2 style inserts one indent code before the number, and the Level 3 style inserts two indent codes before the number. The Legal 1–Legal 8 styles don't insert any indent codes before the paragraph number, so each level appears at the left margin. If none of the existing styles meet your needs, you can edit or create a style. (See Chapter 5 for more information on styles.)

6. Repeat these steps to select the text, number, and style for each additional level.

When you're finished setting up your numbering format, choose OK. WP returns to the Bullets and Numbering dialog box with your new format in the upper-left corner. If you want to be able to use your custom format in other documents, you need to copy it to your default template. To do this, select your custom format in the Bullets and Numbering dialog box, and from the Options pop-down button, choose Copy. Select Default Template and choose OK.

TIP: *If you want any custom numbering formats you create in the future to be automatically saved in your default template, from the Options pop-down button, choose Setup. In the Save New Styles To group box, select Default Template and choose OK.*

If you've edited one of the predefined formats and want to restore it to its original settings, select it in the Bullets and Numbering dialog box, and from the Options pop-down button, choose Reset; then choose Yes. If you want to delete a custom format, select it, and from the Options pop-down button choose Delete, and then choose Yes. To start an outline in the current document, select the format you want and choose OK. Otherwise, choose Cancel to return to the document.

Creating a Table of Contents

A table of contents lets your readers see a document's organization at a glance (see Figure 9-4). WordPerfect's Table of Contents feature not only speeds up the process of formatting the section headings and page numbers, it also allows you to instantly update the page numbers when changes are made. Creating a table of contents involves three simple steps: marking the text you want included in the table of contents, defining the table of contents, and generating it.

HANDBOOK.WPD: *If you want to practice creating a table of contents with a sample document, open the HANDBOOK.WPD document from the companion CD. Follow the next steps to mark the section headings in the sample document for a table of contents; then define and generate the table of contents on the first page.*

Marking Text for a Table of Contents

Before you can create a table of contents, you need to tell WP what text you want included in it. You do this by marking the section headings and subheadings throughout the document. When the table of contents is generated, WP automatically displays the marked text with the correct page number.

To mark text, choose Tools | Reference | Table of Contents. This displays the Table of Contents toolbar:

Table of Contents level:	Mark 1	Mark 2	Mark 3	Mark 4	Mark 5	Define...	Generate...	Close

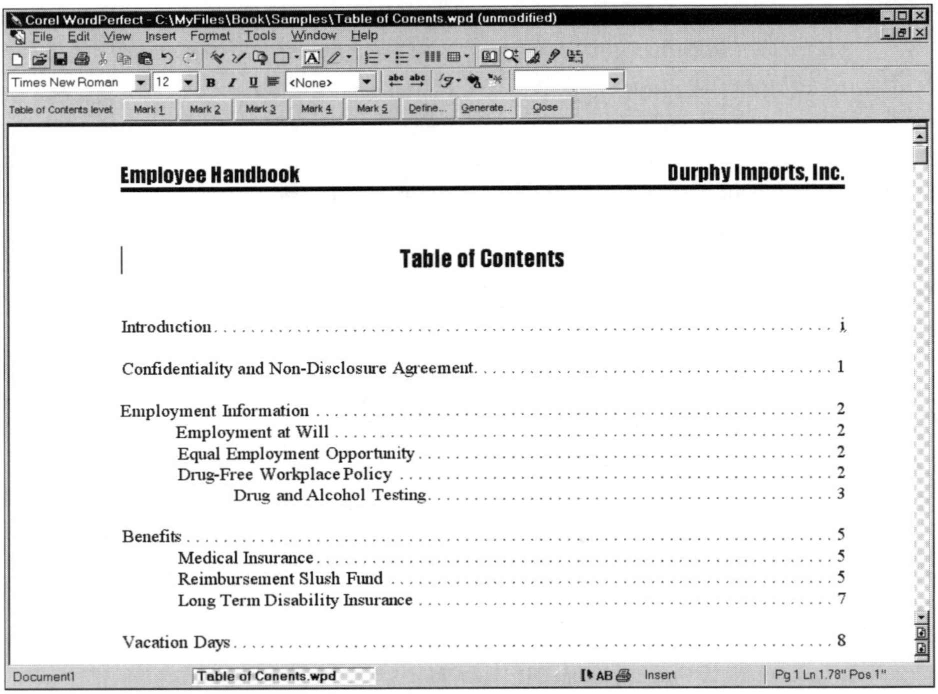

FIGURE 9-4 A table of contents is easily created in WP

Select the text in your document that you want to appear in the table of contents, such as a section heading or subheading. On the Table of Contents toolbar, click the button for the level you want to use for that text, such as Mark 1 for a first-level entry or Mark 2 for a second-level (indented) entry. Continue this process to mark all the text throughout the document.

NOTE: *Be consistent with the levels you use to mark the text. For example, always mark section headings as level one, subheadings as level two, and so on.*

TIP: *If you want text to appear in the table of contents that isn't actually typed in the document itself, you can use the Hidden Text feature. See the Power Tip "Marking with Hidden Text" for more information.*

Power Tip→→ Marking with Hidden Text

At times, you might want text to appear in the table of contents that isn't actually typed in the document. For example, you might have a chapter title that's inserted as a graphics image. In these situations, you can use the Hidden Text feature to type and mark the text for the table of contents. Follow these steps:

1. Place the insertion point on the page you want to reference in the table of contents, such as the page containing the graphics image.

2. Type the text that you want to appear in the table of contents. Don't worry about its location or wrapping, because it will be hidden later.

3. Select the text and mark it for the table of contents level you want using the Table of Contents toolbar.

4. Select the text again and choose Format | Font. Select Hidden and choose OK. If the text is still displaying, you can choose View | Hidden Text to hide it.

When you generate the table of contents as explained in the section "Generating a Table of Contents," you must first display the hidden text in order for it to be included in the table of contents. To do this, choose View and select Hidden Text if it's not already selected. Then generate the table of contents. After this is done, hide the text by choosing View | Hidden Text. Each time you regenerate, you need to turn on hidden text before generating to have the hidden text appear correctly in the table of contents.

If you use styles to format the headings and subheadings in your document, you can have the heading text automatically marked for a table of contents by including the mark codes within the styles. For more information, see the section "How to Mark Text with Styles."

How to➤➤➤ Mark Text with Styles

When you use styles to format the headings and subheadings in your document, you can insert a code in the style that automatically marks the heading text for the table of contents. The default heading styles that come with WordPerfect (Heading 1–Heading 5) already include mark codes for a table of contents. For example, the Heading 1 style includes a Level 1 mark text code, the Heading 2 style includes a Level 2 mark text code, and so on. (For more information on using or editing these heading styles, see Chapter 5.)

Follow these steps to add a table of contents mark code to your existing custom styles.

1. Choose Format | Styles. Select the style you want to edit and choose Edit.

2. Select the Show 'Off Codes' option at the bottom of the dialog box to display the comment code.

3. Click the Comment code in the Contents text box to place the insertion point immediately before it. Press SHIFT-RIGHT ARROW to select just the comment code and not any of the other formatting codes in the style:

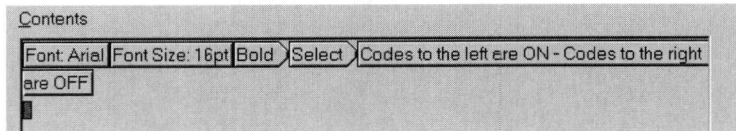

4. In the Styles Editor dialog box, choose Tools | Reference | Table of Contents. The Table of Contents toolbar appears at the bottom of the screen.

5. Choose the toolbar button for the table of contents level you want to use with this style, such as Mark 1 or Mark 2. WP places the [Mrk Txt ToC] codes around the comment code:

6. Choose OK, and then Close.

Defining a Table of Contents

Another important step in creating a table of contents is to "define" the table of contents by telling WP where to create it and how to format it. To do this, place the insertion point where you want the table of contents to appear, such as on a blank page at the top of the document. If the Table of Contents toolbar isn't already displaying, choose Tools | Reference | Table of Contents.

n **NOTE:**   *When you create a new page at the top of the document for a table of contents, the document page numbers are thrown off. To fix this, place the insertion point on the first page of the document text (after the table of contents page) and choose Format | Page | Numbering. Choose Set Value, type **1** in the Set Page Number text box, and choose OK twice.*

Choose Define on the Table of Contents toolbar, and the Define Table of Contents dialog box appears (see Figure 9-5). In the Number of Levels text box, type the number of levels that you want the table of contents to use, such as **3**.

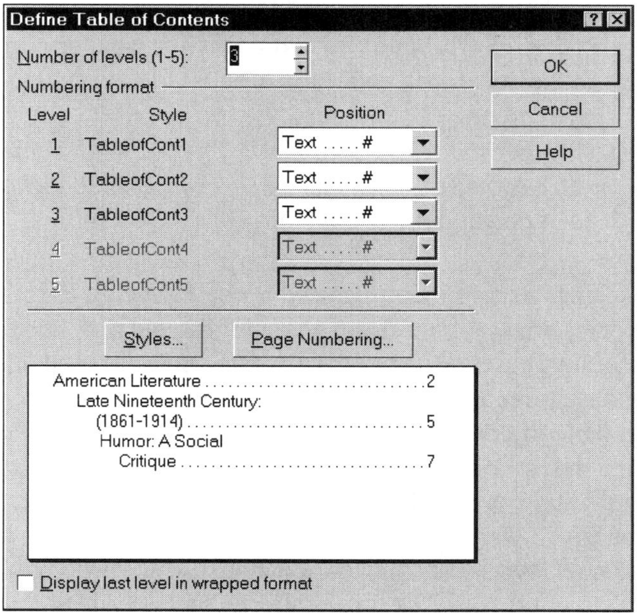

FIGURE 9-5 You can select the formatting used for each level of the table of contents

CAUTION: *Make sure that you define enough levels for the text you've marked in the document. For example, if you used the Mark 4 button to mark text for a fourth-level entry, but only define three levels in the dialog box, the fourth-level text won't be included in the table of contents.*

From the Position drop-down menus, select the page number style you want for each level, such as flush right with no dot leaders or immediately after the text. Each level can use a different page number style. The preview window in the dialog box shows the page number style you've selected for each level.

If you want to change the format of the actual page number, choose Page Numbering. The Page Number Format text box already includes a code for the page number:

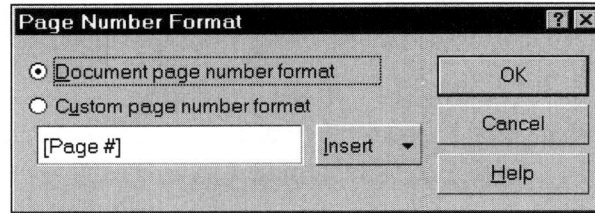

Type any text you want included with the page number, such as **Page**. You can also use the Insert drop-down button to add codes for chapter numbers, the total number of pages in the document, and so on. Choose OK when you're finished.

NOTE: *The preview display in the Define Table of Contents dialog box doesn't show customized page number formats, even though that format will be used in the actual table of contents.*

You can also change the formatting used for each level of the table of contents. For example, you can have all first-level entries displayed in bold or in a larger font. To change the formatting, choose the Styles button. Select a level number in the list to see what style is currently being used to format that level.

The default table of contents styles format each level with initial tab codes, as well as a hanging indent code. You can select a different style to format the selected level, create a new style, or edit the existing style. To edit the style, choose Edit and make any changes you want to the formatting in the Styles Editor dialog box. (For more information on styles, see Chapter 5.) Choose OK when you're finished, and then choose OK to return to the Define Table of Contents dialog box.

When you've set all the options for the table of contents, choose OK. The text "<< Table of Contents will generate here >>" is inserted in the document.

TIP: *If you later want to change any of the settings for your table of contents, place the insertion point at the top of the table of contents and choose Define on the Table of Contents toolbar. Make any changes you want and choose OK.*

Generating a Table of Contents

The final step in creating a table of contents is to generate it. When you generate a table of contents, WP finds all the marked text in the document, adds it to the table of contents with the selected formatting, and includes the page number that the text appears on.

To generate the table of contents, choose Generate on the Table of Contents toolbar. If the toolbar isn't displaying, choose Tools | Reference | Generate. The Generate dialog box appears:

If you plan to use your document in an electronic format, you can select Build Hypertext Links to have WP format the table of contents page numbers as hyperlinks. Then you simply click the page number, and WP automatically jumps to the corresponding section in the document. (For more information on hyperlinks, see Chapter 12.)

NOTE: *The Save Subdocuments option only applies if you're generating a master document and want any subdocuments to be condensed and saved with the generated changes.*

Choose OK to generate the table of contents. If you later edit the document so the page numbers change, simply click the Generate button on the Table of Contents toolbar again and choose OK to regenerate the table of contents and have the page numbers updated.

NOTE: *If some of your table of contents entries contain stray formatting such as bold or italics, it's likely that the mark codes in the document text include those formatting codes. To solve this problem, go to the section in the document where that text is marked and turn on Reveal Codes (View | Reveal Codes). If the [Mrk Txt ToC] code is inserted before formatting codes such as bold or italics, delete the [Mrk Txt ToC] code and remark the text, making sure you select only the text and not any formatting codes.*

CAUTION: *If you make formatting changes to the table of contents itself, that formatting will be lost each time you regenerate the table of contents. You can specify formatting for the table of contents within level styles as explained in the "Defining a Table of Contents" section, or you can add the formatting as a last step only when you're sure you won't need to regenerate the table of contents.*

Creating an Index

An index is another useful reference tool that helps readers find specific information in a document. With WP's Index feature, you can quickly create—and update—an index with the various document topics under headings and subheadings, along with the corresponding page numbers (see Figure 9-6).

Creating an index is very similar to creating a table of contents. First, you need to mark the text in your document that you want included in the index; then you need to define the index so WP knows where to place it and how to format it; and finally you need to generate the index.

Marking Text for an Index

In order to create an index, you need to tell WP what text you want referenced in the index by marking it throughout the document. Each time a specific topic or subject is referred to in your document, you can mark it for the index heading and subheading you want it to appear under. Then the index lists each page number where that topic is referenced.

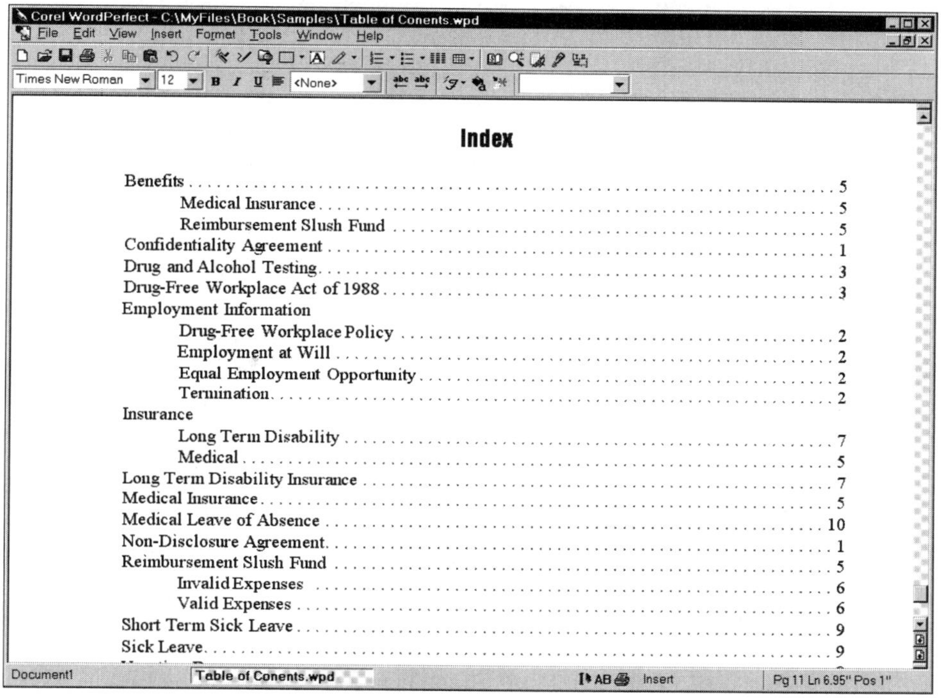

FIGURE 9-6 An index is arranged with headings and subheadings

NOTE: *The heading or subheading text in an index doesn't have to appear in the document itself. For example, you can mark a document section about George Washington under the index heading "Washington, George" even though that exact text doesn't actually appear in the document.*

You can mark text for an index in two different ways: manually or with a concordance file. When you use a concordance file, you create a list of the words and phrases that you want to have indexed. WP then searches through the document and automatically marks each occurrence of those exact words to be included in the index. You can also combine both methods and manually mark some items, while you use a concordance file to mark other text. For more information on concordance files, see the "How to Create a Concordance File" section.

To mark text manually for an index, first choose Tools | Reference | Index to display the Index toolbar:

| Heading: | ▼ | Subheading: | ▼ | Mark | Define... | Generate... | Close |

Place the insertion point in the document section that you want to reference in the index. Then use the Heading and Subheading text boxes on the Index toolbar to indicate what heading and subheading (if any) you want for this information. This can be done in one of three ways:

- If the text you want to use for the heading or subheading is already typed in the document, select it and then click in the Heading or Subheading text box on the Index toolbar. WP inserts the selected text as the heading or subheading.

- If you want to specify a heading or subheading that's not part of the document text, click in the Heading or Subheading text box and type the text as you want it to appear in the index.

- If you've previously marked text in the document with the heading or subheading you want to use, select it from the Heading or Subheading drop-down list on the Index toolbar. This saves you from having to retype the same heading/subheading text each time you want to use it.

If you don't want to use a subheading, make sure the Subheading text box is empty. Once you have the heading and subheading text the way you want, choose Mark on the toolbar to insert the mark code in the document. Repeat this process to mark each location in the document that you want referenced in the index.

NOTE: *The index entries use the capitalization and punctuation you type in the Heading and Subheading text boxes on the Index toolbar. Be consistent in the way that you capitalize entries, such as using initial capitals or all lowercase letters.*

TIP: *If you want to delete or change an index entry, turn on Reveal Codes (View | Reveal Codes) and delete the [Index] code. Then use the Heading and Subheading text boxes on the Index toolbar to mark the entry again if you want. The Heading and Subheading drop-down lists still display entries that have been deleted from the document until you close and open the document again.*

How to▸▸▸ Create a Concordance File

A concordance file is an easy way to automatically index every occurrence of a specific word or phrase in your document. For example, if you want an index to contain the page number each time the word "401(k)" appears in the document, you can add that word to the concordance file. You can include both headings and subheadings in a concordance file. To see a sample concordance file, open the CONCORDANCE.WPD file from the companion CD. This concordance file is created to index the HANDBOOK.WPD sample document, also on the companion CD.

To create a concordance file, go to a blank document window and type each word or phrase that you want included in the index on a separate line. The index will generate faster if the concordance file is in alphabetical order. After typing the entries in the concordance file, you can use the Sort feature to quickly sort them alphabetically. (See Chapter 8 for more information on sorting.) For example, a concordance file for an employee handbook might look like this:

> Benefits
> Confidentiality Agreement
> Drug and Alcohol Testing
> Drug-Free Workplace Policy
> Employment at Will
> Equal Employment Opportunity

Unless you indicate otherwise, each entry in the concordance file is included as a heading in the index. If you want an entry to be a subheading, you need to mark it as a subheading in the concordance file using the Index toolbar. Follow the steps in the "Marking Text for an Index" section to mark the concordance entry with the heading and subheading you want. If you want a word or phrase to be included as both a heading and a subheading, include it twice in the concordance file and mark one of the two entries as a subheading.

The index entries use the capitalization you type in the concordance file. However, WP will locate any text in the document that matches the concordance entries regardless of capitalization. For example, if you type "Medical Plan" in the concordance file, the index entry will appear as "Medical Plan," and WP will reference any occurrences of the text "Medical Plan," "medical plan," or other variations of the capitalization throughout the document.

When you're finished creating the concordance file, close and save it with any filename you want. You'll tell WP which concordance file to use when you define the index, as explained in the "Defining an Index" section.

Defining an Index

To define the location and formatting for the index, place the insertion point in the document where you want the index created, usually at the end of the document. Choose Define on the Index toolbar. The Define Index dialog box appears (see Figure 9-7).

From the Position drop-down list, select the page number style you want, such as flush right without dot leaders or immediately following the text. If you want to customize the page number format, choose Page Numbering and make the selections you want (for more information, see the "Defining a Table of Contents" section earlier in this chapter). If you've created a concordance file to use with your index, type the name in the File Name text box or use the file folder icon to select the file.

TIP: *If you want to change the formatting used for the heading and subheading levels, choose Change. Select the index level you want to change; then choose Edit. Make any changes you want to the style and choose OK (for more information on editing styles, see Chapter 5). Choose OK when you're finished.*

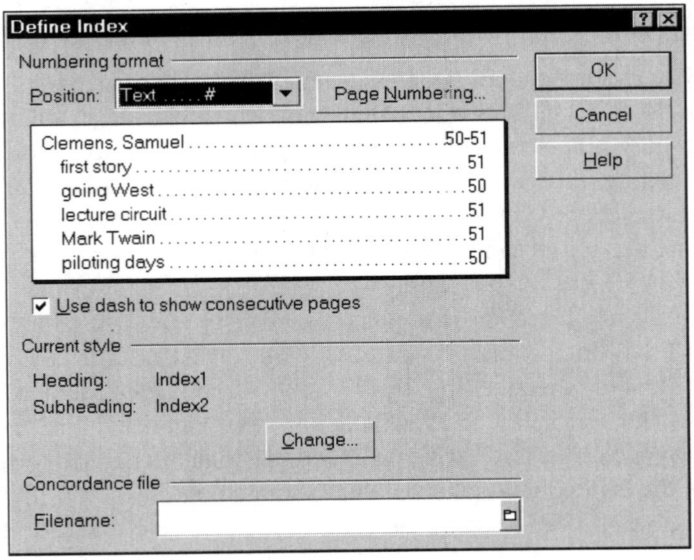

FIGURE 9-7 You can define the format for an index

When you're finished setting the options for your index, choose OK. WP inserts the text "<< Index will generate here >>" in the document.

NOTE: *If you later want to change any of the index settings, place the insertion point at the top of the index and choose Define on the Index toolbar. Make any changes you want and choose OK.*

Generating an Index

Generating an index is exactly the same as generating a table of contents, since the Generate feature automatically generates mark codes for table of contents, indexes, and cross-references at the same time. To generate the index, choose Generate on the Index toolbar or choose Tools | Reference | Generate. Make any selections you want in the Generate text box (for more information, see the "Generating a Table of Contents" section earlier in the chapter). Choose OK to create the index.

On the CD ▸▸▸ Index Alphabet Dividers

A common practice in indexes is to include a large capital letter, such as A, B, and so on at the beginning of each alphabetic section. The companion CD includes a macro called INDEX DIVIDER.WCM that divides an index into sections with the appropriate large capital letter on a line at the beginning of each section.

To use this macro, create and generate the index as explained in the "Creating an Index" section. Make sure that there are no blank lines within the index. If you want the index formatted in columns, play the macro *before* turning columns on. Then place the insertion point on the first line of the index. Choose Tools | Macro | Play, select the INDEX DIVIDER.WCM macro, and choose Play.

If you later regenerate the index, the capital letters inserted by the macro are deleted. However, you can simply play the macro again to add them.

Creating Cross-References

When you need to refer your readers to areas within the same document, such as a specific page number or figure, you can use WP's Cross-Reference feature. For example, you can easily insert and update references such as "see page 27" or "the chart in Figure 3."

A cross-reference is used to link two parts of a document together—the target and the reference. The *target* is the actual page, figure, footnote, or other item that you are referring to from another location in the document. The *reference* is the document text that refers to another item, such as "see page 14." You can create references to page/chapter numbers, paragraph/outline numbers, footnote/endnote numbers, caption numbers, and counter numbers.

To create a cross-reference, you need to mark both the target and the reference with a cross-reference code. Then you can generate the document to update the cross-reference numbers.

Marking a Target

To mark a target that you want to refer to from another location in the document, choose Tools | Reference | Cross-Reference to display the Cross-Reference toolbar:

Reference ▼	Page	Target:	▼	Mark Reference	Mark Target	Generate...	Close

Place the insertion point where the item is that you want to reference. For example, if you want to refer to a page number, place the insertion point somewhere on that page. If you're referencing a footnote or endnote, you can place the insertion point either inside the actual footnote/endnote text or just after the footnote/endnote number in the document. If you're referencing a graphics box number, you can place the insertion point inside the caption (if there is one), or just after the graphics box code in the document. For paragraph/outline numbers, place the insertion point just after the paragraph number.

TIP: *You can turn on Reveal Codes (View | Reveal Codes) to make sure that the insertion point is correctly positioned after the code you're referencing, such as the graphics box code or paragraph number code.*

CAUTION: *If you're referencing a graphics box and don't insert the target code inside the caption, make sure that if you later move the box to a different location, the target code remains immediately after the [Box] code in Reveal Codes.*

In the Target text box on the Cross-Reference toolbar, type a unique name for this target. WP uses the target name to tie the reference and target together. Type a name that will help you remember the contents of the target, such as **Sales Chart** or **Smith Citation**. After typing the target name, choose Mark Target on the toolbar to insert the target code in the document.

Marking a Reference

Once you've inserted a target code, you can refer to that target as many times as you need to throughout the document. Place the insertion point in the document where you want the reference inserted and type any preceding text, such as **See page** or **See figure**.

From the Reference pop-down button on the Cross-Reference toolbar, select the type of item you want to refer to at the location of the target, such as Footnote or Caption Number. If you're referencing a graphics box and select Caption Number, the entire style and formatting of the caption number will be inserted in the reference, such as "**Figure 1**" for an image box. If you want only the number of the box to be included in the reference, such as "1," you can reference the Counter number. For more information, see the Power Tip "Referencing a Graphics Box."

From the Target drop-down list, select the target name that you want to refer to. Then choose Mark Reference on the toolbar. A question mark is inserted in the document, indicating the location of the reference. When you generate the document, WP finds the matching target code and inserts the type of reference you selected, such as the page number or footnote number.

TIP: *If you want to reference two different items at the location of the target, such as "see Figure 1, page 24," insert two reference codes—one for the caption number and one for page number. Use the same target name for each reference.*

Power Tip ››› Referencing a Graphics Box

WP's Cross-Reference feature gives you two options for referring to a graphics box, such as "see Figure 2" or "the data in Table 8." First, you can have the reference automatically include the entire caption number and formatting for the graphics box. Or you can have the reference include only the number of the box without any additional text or formatting.

A caption's formatting is determined by the graphics style for the type of box being used, such as a figure box or a table box. For example, if you create a caption for a box containing clipart, WP inserts "Figure" followed by the box number in a bold font, such as "**Figure 1**." For a text box, however, the caption number is simply a bolded number, such as "**2**." (For more information on graphics styles, see Chapter 7.)

If you want the reference in your document to include the entire formatted box number, select Caption Number from the Reference drop-down list when marking the reference. Remember that if you're referencing an image or figure box, WP includes the text "Figure," so you don't need to type it before inserting the reference code.

If you want the reference to only insert the box number, select Counter from the Reference drop-down list when marking the reference. Then select the counter for the type of box you're using, such as Figure Box or Table Box. Choose OK.

Finish marking the reference by selecting the target name from the Target drop-down list and choosing Mark Reference.

To generate the cross-references and update any question marks, choose Generate on the toolbar; then choose OK. If you later edit the document so the page numbers change, or if you add and delete graphics boxes, footnote/endnotes, or paragraph numbers, you need to regenerate the document to update the cross-references. Choose Generate on the toolbar or choose Tools | Reference | Generate. Then choose OK to generate the document.

NOTE: *If a question mark still appears after generating the cross-references, that indicates that either the reference or the target was not properly marked.*

Summary

WordPerfect has lots of helpful tools for making sure the reference information in your documents is both accurate and easily accessible. The Outline feature lets you add paragraph numbers in a format that suits you best. You can use the Table of Contents and Index features to help readers find specific information in a document. And the Cross-Reference feature makes it easy to create references within a document. With all of these features, WP automatically renumbers and updates the document as changes are made and the document is regenerated.

In Chapter 10, we'll introduce you to the powerful Macros feature and show you how you can automate your common WP tasks.

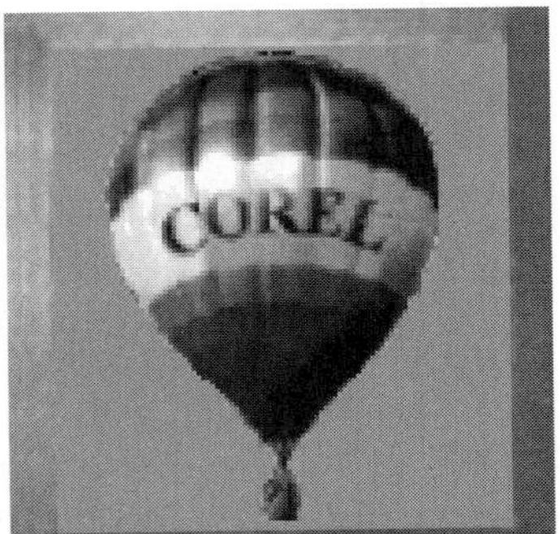
COREL

PART
III

Power Tools for Automating Tasks

Chapter

10

Getting Started with Macros

If you need to add some power to your WordPerfect work, look no further than a little word with a lot of potential—*macro*. WP 8's Macro feature gives you the ultimate control when it comes to automating your work. Macros can range from simple recorded tasks to complex interactions with other Windows programs, but they all share the same underlying purpose—to speed up your work by automatically performing certain tasks for you.

Macros have so much power and potential that we're going to take two chapters to cover them. In this chapter, we'll start with the basics and give you an overview of recording and playing macros. Then we'll show you how you can start writing your own macros, including how to insert commands and troubleshoot errors. You'll also learn some fundamental macro techniques, such as using variables and gathering information. Then in Chapter 11, we'll discuss some of the more advanced macro programming techniques.

Macro Overview

So what exactly *is* a macro? A *macro* is basically a "mini" computer program that works inside WordPerfect. Macros can automate WP tasks, such as setting margins, creating a table, or inserting text into a document. You can also use programming commands to control how a macro works, such as prompting the user for information, making decisions based on certain conditions, or repeating a set of commands several times. Macro commands also give you the power to create your own dialog boxes and interact with other Windows programs.

You can create a new macro by recording a series of actions, by inserting macro commands directly into a macro file, or by using a combination of both techniques. Once a macro has been created, it can be played an unlimited number of times to perform its task practically instantaneously. Macros are usually saved as separate files with a WCM file extension, but they can also be saved as part of a template document. (For more information on templates, see Chapter 1.)

Recording Macros

The easiest way to create a new macro is to *record* it. When you do this, WP simply "records" each action you take within WordPerfect in the macro file. Then, when you later "play" the macro, WordPerfect instantly repeats those same actions. Recorded macros are useful for tasks that you find yourself repeating often, such as setting specific search options or creating comments that contain similar text. Rather than repeat the same steps each time you need to perform the task, you can record those steps into a macro and have WP quickly perform them for you.

To record a macro, choose Tools | Macro | Record. WP displays the default directory for your macros. In the File Name text box, type a name for your macro. If you don't type the WCM file extension, WP automatically adds it for you. Choose Record.

NOTE: *If you want to record a macro that's saved as part of the current template instead of as a separate file, choose Tools | Template Macro | Record. Type a name for the macro in the Name text box and choose Record. Template macros can only be played when using a document created with that template.*

WordPerfect takes you back to the document window and displays the Macro toolbar with the Record button already selected:

At this point, any actions you perform in WP are recorded into the macro. For example, you can type and format text, use the Find and Replace feature, open and close documents, insert graphics, and so on.

As you use the pull-down menus and dialog boxes while the macro is recording, WP records only the end results of your actions. For example, suppose you choose File | Open and select a document to open while the macro is recording. When you later play the macro, that specific document is automatically opened without the Open File dialog box ever appearing.

NOTE: *If you want to have a dialog box appear when the macro is later played so you can select a specific file or graphic, you can edit the macro and add the needed macro commands, such as FileOpenDlg or GraphicCreateBox. See the "Writing and Editing Macros" section later in this chapter for more information on editing macros.*

While you're recording a macro, you can use the mouse to select pull-down menu items or choose toolbar/Property Bar buttons, but you *can't* use it to select text or change the location of the insertion point in the document. If you need to move the insertion point as you're recording, use positioning keys such as the arrow keys, PAGE UP, and HOME. If you need to select text, you can also use the keyboard by holding down SHIFT and then using positioning keys, such as the arrow keys or PAGE UP and PAGE DOWN. Or you can select predefined groups of text, such as a sentence or page, by choosing Edit | Select, and then selecting the option you want, such as Sentence.

When you're finished recording the steps you want included in your macro, click the Stop button on the Macro toolbar. Or you can choose Tools | Macro | Record again to end recording of the macro.

Inserting Pauses

In addition to recording specific actions in a macro, you can also record pauses. Then, each time you play the macro, WP pauses at that point and allows you to type in text from the keyboard or add other formatting before continuing with the rest of the macro. For example, you can have a macro set up the heading of a memo and pause to allow you to type in the name of the person the memo is to and the subject of the memo.

To insert a pause in a macro, begin recording the macro as explained in the "Recording Macros" section earlier. When you get to the point where you want the macro to pause, click the Pause button on the Macro toolbar. If you've switched to a new document window during the macro and the Macro toolbar isn't displaying, choose Tools | Macro | Pause. While the macro is paused, you can type text or insert formatting, but it won't be recorded as part of the macro. To end the pause, click the Pause button on the Macro toolbar again. Or choose Tools | Macro | Pause a second time.

When you later play a macro that includes a pause, WP inserts any text or formatting up to the location of the pause in the macro. While the macro is paused, type the text or insert the formatting you want; then simply press ENTER to end the pause and continue with the rest of the macro. If there are additional pauses, repeat these steps at each one.

TIP: *Pressing ENTER during a pause doesn't actually insert a hard return into the document, but instead ends the pause so the macro continues. If you want to insert a hard return during a pause, press SHIFT-ENTER instead.*

MEMO MACRO.WCM: *To try out a simple macro with pauses, choose Tools | Macro | Play. Select the MEMO MACRO.WCM macro from the companion CD and choose Play. This macro opens a new document window and inserts the heading for a memo. The macro pauses for you to type in each part of the memo heading (such as "To," "From," and "Subject"). After typing each item, press ENTER to continue with the macro.*

QuickMacros

Recording a macro is a great way to avoid repeating the same formatting steps over and over in a document. However, if you're only formatting one document, you might not want to save the recorded macro in a file because you won't likely need it in the future. In situations like this, you can record a QuickMacro. A QuickMacro is a temporary, unnamed macro that is automatically deleted when you exit WordPerfect.

To record a QuickMacro, choose Tools | Template Macro | Record. Leave the Name text box blank and choose Record. Record any steps you want in the QuickMacro, following the guidelines in the "Recording Macros" section earlier. The only difference between recording a QuickMacro and a regular macro is that you can't record a pause in a QuickMacro. When you're finished, choose the Stop button on the Macro toolbar or choose Tools | Template Macro | Record again.

To play a QuickMacro, choose Tools | Template Macro | Play. Leave the Name text box blank and choose Play. The steps you recorded are instantly played back. You can play the QuickMacro macro as many times as you need to. If you record another QuickMacro, it automatically replaces the existing QuickMacro. As soon as you exit WordPerfect, the QuickMacro is deleted.

10

TIP: *If you use QuickMacros frequently, you can add QuickMacro Record and QuickMacro Play buttons to a toolbar. To do this, right-click the toolbar you want to add the buttons to and choose Edit. From the Feature Categories drop-down list, select Tools. In the Features list, select QuickMacro Record and choose Add Button. Then select QuickMacro Play and choose Add Button again. When you're finished, choose OK. Now you can record a new QuickMacro by clicking the QuickMacro Record button. After recording a QuickMacro, you can play it by clicking the QuickMacro Play button. (For more information on customizing toolbars, see Chapter 13.)*

Playing Macros

Once a macro has been created (whether it was recorded or written from scratch), you can play it as many times as you want in any document. To play a macro, choose Tools | Macro | Play. The Play Macro dialog box displays the macros in your default macro directory. Select the macro you want to play, or type the name in the File Name text box. If the macro is in a different directory, you can switch to that directory. When the macro you want is selected, choose Play.

NOTE: *If you want to change the default directory used for your macros, choose Tools | Settings and double-click Files. Select the Merge/Macro tab. In the Default Macro Folder text box, type the path to the directory you want to use for your macros (or use the file folder icon to select it). Choose OK, and then choose Close when you're finished.*

WordPerfect 8 comes with 28 macros already created for a variety of different tasks, such as converting footnotes to endnotes and creating "reversed" (white-on-black) text. Many of these macros are installed in your default macro directory during a typical installation; however, not all of them are automatically installed. See the "WP 8 Shipping Macros" Quick Reference section for more information on these macros.

TIP: *You can access several of the common shipping macros from the Shipping Macros toolbar. To select this toolbar, right-click any displaying toolbar and choose Shipping Macros. A new toolbar displays with buttons for several shipping macros. Move the mouse over a button to see a QuickTip with a description of the macro that button plays. To play a macro, simply click the button.*

Quick Reference ▶▶▶ WP 8 Shipping Macros

WordPerfect 8 comes with 28 "shipping" macros that help you perform a variety of tasks, as described in the list here. Those macros in the list that are marked with an asterisk are *not* automatically installed during a typical installation. If you want to use a macro that hasn't been installed, simply copy it from the

\Corel\Suite8\Macros\WPWin directory on the WP Suite 8 CD to the default macro directory on your hard drive (usually the same directory).

ADRS2MRG.WCM	Creates a merge data file from the information in the Address Book.
*ALLFONTS.WCM	Creates a document with a sample of every font available to the current printer.
CHECKBOX.WCM	Inserts a hyperlink checkbox at the location of the insertion point that adds or removes an "x" in the box each time it's clicked.
CLOSEALL.WCM	Closes all open documents and prompts you to save any that have been modified.
*CTRLM.WCM	Displays the PerfectScript Command Inserter (for more information, see the "Inserting Commands" section later in this chapter).
*CTRLSFTF.WCM	Prompts for FROM and TO values when using the old WordPerfect 5.1–7 Equation Editor.
*CVTDOCS8.WCM	Converts multiple documents from another document type to WP 8 format.
ENDFOOT.WCM	Converts endnotes in a document to footnotes.
*EXPNDALL.WCM	Expands all QuickWords in the document at the same time.
*FILESTMP.WCM	Creates a header or footer containing the path and filename of the current document.
FLIPENV.WCM	Creates an envelope rotated 180 degrees (upside-down) to allow printing a return address 0.25" from the envelope edge on printers with large minimum margins.
*FONTDN.WCM	Decreases the current font size by two points.
*FONTUP.WCM	Increases the current font size by two points.
FOOTEND.WCM	Converts footnotes in a document to endnotes.

10

*GOTODOS.WCM	Opens a DOS window.
*LINENUM.WCM	Places the insertion point at a specified line and character number when troubleshooting macro errors. (See "Troubleshooting Errors" later in this chapter for more information.)
*LONGNAME.WCM	Changes the name of selected documents from a DOS eight-character filename to a Windows long filename based on the document summary description.
PARABRK.WCM	Creates paragraph breaks between document sections using various symbols or small graphics.
PLEADING.WCM	Sets up a pleading document with lines and numbers.
PROMPTS.WCM	Used with the Template feature when building prompts in a new template. (For more information, see Chapter 1.)
REVERSE.WCM	Creates white text on a black background (or uses other color combinations) for selected text or table cells.
SAVEALL.WCM	Prompts you to save all open documents.
*SAVETOA.WCM	Saves the current document and backs up a copy onto a disk in the A: drive.
*TCONVERT.WCM	Converts templates from WordPerfect 6.0 for Windows that use automated prompts. (For more information, see Chapter 1.)
UAWP8EN.WCM	Used by the PerfectExpert. Do *not* delete this macro from the default macro folder.
WATERMRK.WCM	Creates a full-page watermark using text or a graphics image.

| WP_ORG.WCM | Creates an organization chart using an embedded Presentations drawing (see Chapter 18 for more information). |
| WP_PR.WCM | Sends a WordPerfect outline to Presentations for use in a slide show. |

*Indicates those macros that are *not* installed into the macros directory during a typical installation.

Here are some tips and ideas for playing macros:

- WP displays the names of the last nine macros you played on the Tools pull-down menu (with the exception of QuickMacros). To play one of these macros again, choose Tools | Macro and select the name of the macro you want to play.

- Assign your favorite macros to keystrokes, toolbar buttons, or pull-down menus for quick access. For more information, see Chapter 13.

- Create hyperlink text items, buttons, or graphics that play a macro when they're clicked. For more information on creating hyperlinks, see Chapter 12.

- You can have a macro automatically play each time you start WordPerfect by using a startup option. To do this, right-click the WP 8 icon on the Windows desktop and choose Properties. (If you don't have an icon on the desktop, right-click the Start button on the Windows taskbar and choose Open; then navigate through the folders until you see the WordPerfect 8 icon. Right-click the icon and choose Properties.) Select the Shortcut tab and place the insertion point at the end of the path in the Target text box (after any quotation marks). Type **/m-macroname**, replacing "macroname" with the name of the macro you want to play, such as **/m-setup.wcm**. If the macro isn't in your default macro directory, type the path along with the filename. Choose OK.

10

■ Use the Repeat feature to play a macro several times in a row. To do this, choose Edit | Repeat Next Action. Type the number of times you want the macro to play and choose OK. Then play the macro by choosing Tools | Macro | Play, selecting the macro, and choosing Play. You can also select the macro you want to play by clicking a toolbar button or by pressing a keystroke the macro has been assigned to.

■ If you want to have easy access to macros in more than one location, such as on your hard drive and on the network, you can set up the Supplemental Macro Folder. To do this, choose Tools | Settings and double-click Files. Select the Merge/Macro tab. In the Supplemental Macro Folder, type the path to the secondary directory you want to use for your macros, such as a network directory. Make sure the Update Favorites with Changes option is selected; choose OK, and then Close. To play a macro from the secondary directory, choose Tools | Macro | Play, and then choose Favorites | Supplemental Macros to switch to that directory. (If the menu bar isn't turned on, click the Toggle Menu On/Off button.) Select the macro you want and choose Play.

Writing and Editing Macros

While recording macros is a great way to quickly repeat tasks in WP, as well as become familiar with the Macros feature, you're limited in the things you can accomplish. You can add more power and flexibility to your recorded macros by editing them and adding macro commands. In addition, you can create macros from scratch by typing or inserting macro commands.

To create a new macro, go to a blank document window and choose Tools | Macro | Macro Toolbar. To edit an existing macro, choose Tools | Macro | Edit, select the macro you want, and choose Edit. When you're working on a macro, WordPerfect automatically switches to Draft view and displays the Macro toolbar (see Figure 10-1). In addition, line numbers are automatically turned on and QuickCorrect is disabled, since SmartQuotes aren't recognized in macros.

Typically, the first line of every macro is the Application command, which tells WP what application (such as WordPerfect) and language (such as English) to use for the current macro. This command is automatically included as the first line in recorded macros. It's also a good idea to include the Application command in macros

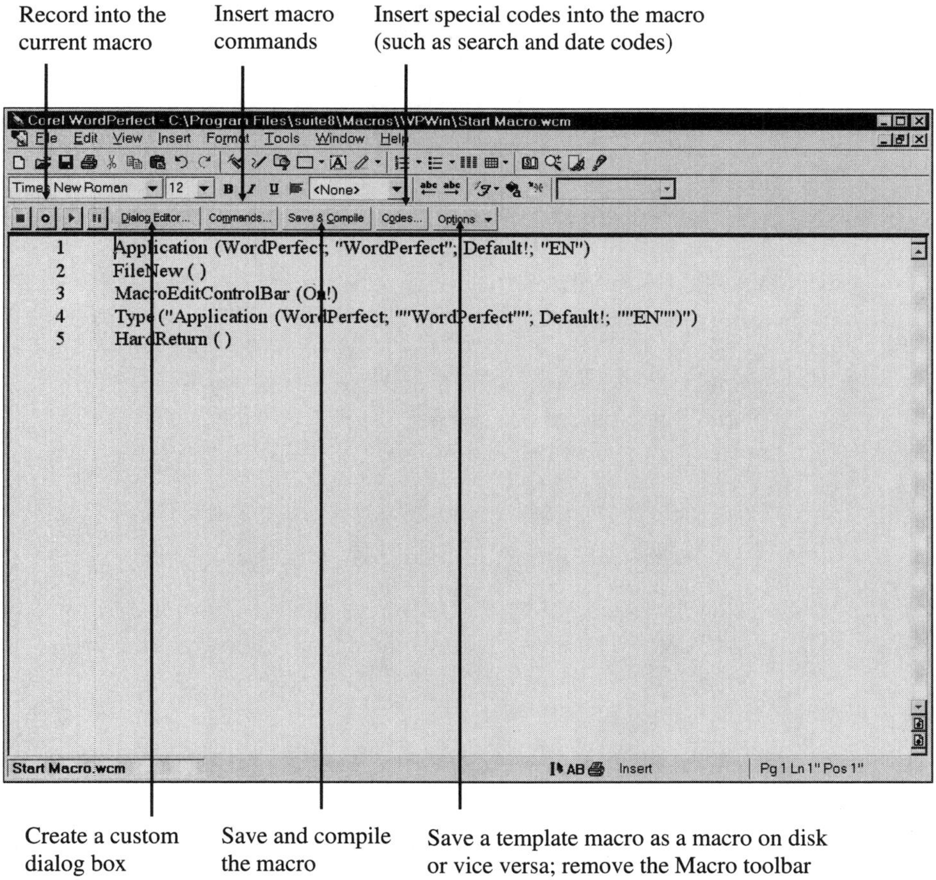

Record into the
current macro

Insert macro
commands

Insert special codes into the macro
(such as search and date codes)

Create a custom
dialog box

Save and compile
the macro

Save a template macro as a macro on disk
or vice versa; remove the Macro toolbar

FIGURE 10-1 WP automatically displays macros with line numbers and the
Macro toolbar

you write from scratch, even though it's not required for the macro to run. If you
frequently create macros, you can use a "setup" macro to automatically open a new
document, select the Macro toolbar, and insert the Application command on the first
line. See the On the CD section "Quickly Starting New Macros" for more
information.

On the CD▶▶▶ Quickly Starting New Macros

Each time you start writing a new macro, you have to switch to a new document, turn on the Macro toolbar, and type the Application command. If you create a lot of macros from scratch, you can save time by having a macro to do this initial setup for you. The companion CD includes a macro called START MACRO.WCM that opens a new document window, turns on the Macro toolbar, and types the WP 8 Application command: Application (WordPerfect; "WordPerfect"; Default!; "EN"). Since WP automatically turns off QuickCorrect and turns on line numbering when the Macro toolbar is displayed, you're all set to start your macro.

To make this macro most useful, you can assign it to a keystroke, such as CTRL-SHIFT-M. Follow these steps:

1. Choose Tools | Settings and double-click Customize.

2. Select the Keyboards tab. Select the keyboard you want to edit, such as <WPWin 8 Keyboard>, and choose Edit. (For more information on creating or editing keyboards, see Chapter 13.)

3. In the list of keystrokes, select the keystroke you want to use for the macro, such as M+CTRL+SHIFT.

4. Select the Macros tab; then choose Assign Macro to Key.

5. Select the START MACRO.WCM macro and choose Select. Choose Yes to save the macro with the full path.

6. Choose OK, and then choose Select to select the keyboard. Choose Close twice.

Now, whenever you want to start creating a new macro, just press the keystroke you used, such as CTRL-SHIFT-M. WP goes to a new document window, turns on the Macro toolbar, and types the Application command on the first line for you.

Inserting Commands

WordPerfect 8 has over 2,000 commands that you can use in your macros. These commands are divided into two categories: product commands and programming commands. *Product* commands are specific to an application such as WordPerfect or Presentations. They perform various functions within that application, such as changing margins, turning features on or off, inserting graphics, and so on.

Programming commands work across applications and control the behavior of the macro. These commands can do such things as make decisions, repeat statements until a condition is met, and jump to a subroutine. Many of the programming commands are also found in other computer programming languages. For example, the commands If/EndIf, For/EndFor, and Call are also common in C and Pascal.

> **NOTE:** *WordPerfect 8 has over 150 new product and programming commands. For a list of these new commands, choose Help | Help Topics, select the Contents tab, and then double-click Macros. (If you haven't installed the Macro Help file, see the "Getting Help" section later in this chapter.) Double-click Macro Programming, double-click Upgrade Help, and then double-click the New Commands: Programming Commands option (for new programming commands) or the What's New in Corel WordPerfect 8 Macros option (for new product commands and system variables).*

Both product and programming commands usually require some information in parentheses after the command, called *parameters*. The parameters provide needed information to the command and can be different kinds of information, such as text, numbers, variable names, or measurements. For example, in the command MarginLeft (2.5"), the parameter in parentheses tells WP what specific setting to use for the left margin. Some parameters indicate different options or styles available only to that particular command. These parameters end in an exclamation point, such as in the command AttributeAppearanceOn (Italics!). If there is more than one parameter, the parameters are separated with semicolons, such as TabSet (Relative!; 2.5"; TabLeft!).

You can insert commands into a macro by typing them, by using the PerfectScript Command Inserter, or by recording them. In this section, you'll learn how to use all three methods. As you insert commands, keep these formatting guidelines in mind:

■ Macro commands are not case sensitive, so WP recognizes "hardreturn," "HardReturn," and "HARDRETURN" as the same command. Similarly, you can use any case for variable names.

- You can format the macro file and not have it affect the actual macro execution. For example, you can change the font, insert tab settings, and so on.

- You can use spaces, hard returns, tabs, and indents within a macro file to make it easier to read. Long macro commands can wrap onto a new line without affecting the macro execution. However, *don't* insert a hard return within a text string enclosed in quotation marks.

TIP: *As you're writing a macro, you can insert comments that help you remember information, such as what a specific command is doing or what a numeric code is for. For more information on commenting your macros, see the "How to Add Comments to a Macro" section.*

How to... ▸▸▸ Add Comments to a Macro

A good habit to get into as you're writing macros is to add comments. Comments are ignored when the macro is played, but they can help you troubleshoot a macro or simply remember what a certain macro command or value is for. Comments are especially useful if someone else will be using or editing your macro. For example, if your macro contains this set of commands, you might later forget what they're checking for:

```
If (?LeftCode = 223)
    DeleteCharPrevious ( )
EndIf
```

By adding a comment, you can easily remember what's happening at that point, as shown here:

```
If (?LeftCode = 223)    //If left code is a graphics box, delete it
    DeleteCharPrevious ( )
EndIf
```

How to... ▸▸▸   **Add Comments to a Macro**
(*continued*)

Comments can be added to a macro in one of two ways. First, you can use the comment macro command, which is two forward slashes (//). This command can be used on a line by itself, or at the end of a line that contains other macro commands, as shown in the previous example. To insert this type of comment, simply type // and then type the comment text. The comment ends with a hard return.

Second, you can use WP's Comment feature to insert a comment. This is especially useful if you want to include longer comments. Since macros are always displayed in draft mode, comments used with this method appear in a shaded box, as shown in this example:

> This sample macro shows how you can have a macro that's set up to play from a hyperlink automatically delete the hyperlink text or button after it has played. For example, if you have a QuickWord that inserts a hyperlink to play a macro, when you click the hyperlink, the macro plays, then removes its hyperlink text or button.
>
> To use this technique, simply use these codes at the beginning of your macro, while the insertion point is still just after the hyperlink in the document. Macro codes included after the hyperlink is deleted will still play normally.

```
1    Application (A1; "WordPerfect"; Default; "EN")
2    RevealCodes (On!)
3    If (?LeftCode = 223) //223 = Box
4            DeleteCharPrevious ()
5    Else
```

To insert a comment with this method, place the insertion point in the macro where you want the comment inserted and choose Insert | Comment | Create. Type the text for the comment and choose the Close button on the Comment Property Bar when you're finished.

If you want to temporarily keep a group of existing macro commands from being compiled or executed as you're troubleshooting a macro, you can place those commands in a comment. To do this, select the commands in the macro and choose Insert | Comment | Create. WP automatically creates a comment containing the selected text. To convert the commands back to regular text, place the insertion point just after the comment and choose Insert | Comment | Convert to Text.

10

Typing Commands

If you know the command name and parameters for a command you want to use in your macro, you can type the command directly into the macro document. For example, you can type **HardReturn** to have the macro insert a hard return at that point when the macro is played. As you're typing commands, pay attention to the spelling, as well as any quotation marks, semicolons, and parentheses. Most macro commands don't have any spaces in the command name, so type a command such as "AddressBookSelectionFormatAddr" as all one word.

> **NOTE:**   *If there are no parameters for a command, you don't have to include the parentheses. For example, typing **HardReturn ( )** or **HardReturn** gets the same result—a hard return inserted in the document.*

If you're not sure of a command's specific name or parameters, you can look it up in WP's Macros Help. See the "Getting Help" section later in this chapter for more information. Or you can use the PerfectScript Command Inserter to insert the command for you, as explained in the following section.

Using the PerfectScript Command Inserter

The PerfectScript Command Inserter helps you insert commands into your macros with the correct spelling and parameters. The Command Inserter displays a list of all the available commands, including what parameters are needed for each command (see Figure 10-2). If a parameter requires specific style options, those are also displayed.

To use the Command Inserter, place the insertion point in the macro where you want to begin inserting commands. Choose Commands on the Macro toolbar. Or, if you've installed the CTRLM.WCM shipping macro, you can press CTRL-M to display the Corel PerfectScript Commands dialog box.

From the Command Type drop-down list, select the type of command you want to insert. For example, to insert a product command that gives you access to a WordPerfect feature, select WordPerfect-EN. (The "EN" indicates the language code—English in this case.) To insert a programming command, such as If, For, or Call, select PerfectScript-EN from the drop-down list. The Commands list box displays a list of the available product or programming commands, depending on the option you selected from the Command Type drop-down list.

FIGURE 10-2 The PerfectScript Command Inserter helps you insert macro commands

NOTE: *When you select WordPerfect-EN from the Command Type drop-down list, the commands at the top of the list that begin with a question mark are system variables. For more information on using system variables, see the "Gathering Information" section later in this chapter.*

When you select a command in the list box, a brief description of that command appears at the bottom of the dialog box. Any parameters for the selected command are listed in the Parameters list box. If the parameter name appears in bold, it is required and must be included with the command. If the parameter name appears in italics, it indicates that the parameter can have multiple settings and should be included in curly brackets, such as "TabSet (Relative!; {2.25"; TabRight!; 2.5"; TabLeft!})." Otherwise, the parameter is optional. If a parameter uses specific style options, those choices are listed in the Enumerations list box when you select the parameter name (see Figure 10-3).

To insert a command into your macro, select the command you want in the Commands list box. To quickly jump to a command, click in the Commands list box and start typing the name of the command. If the command doesn't have any parameters, choose Insert to insert it directly into your macro.

If the command *does* have parameters, choose Edit or double-click the command to place it in the Command Edit text box. Then, to insert a parameter, select the first parameter in the Parameters list box. If the selected parameter has options in the

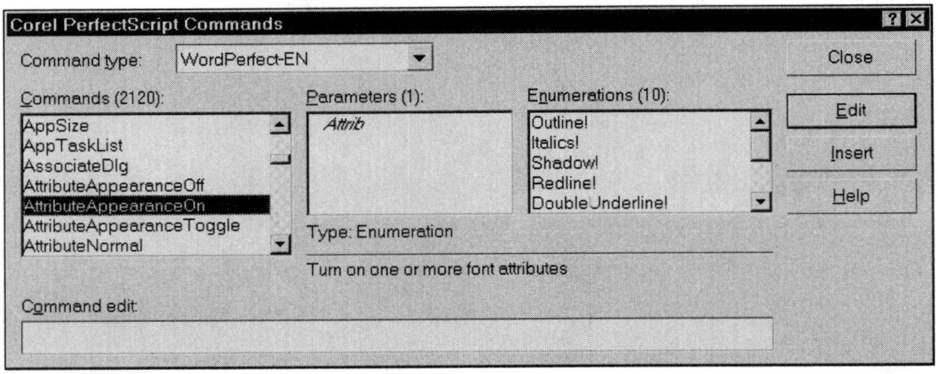

FIGURE 10-3 Specific style options for a parameter are listed in the Enumerations list box

Enumerations list box, double-click the style option you want. Both the parameter name and style are inserted in the Command Edit text box.

If the selected parameter doesn't have any enumeration options, double-click it in the Parameters list box. WP inserts the parameter name in the Command Edit text box, followed by a colon. Click the insertion point in the Command Edit text box after the parameter name and colon and type the parameter information.

Repeat this process to insert any other parameters for the command in the Command Edit text box. Make sure you insert the parameters in the order in which they appear in the Parameters list box. When you've inserted all the parameters, choose Insert to put the command into your macro. WP automatically inserts a hard return in your macro after each inserted command, so you can continue inserting additional commands from the Command Inserter.

NOTE: *When you insert commands with the Command Inserter, WP automatically includes the parameter name and a colon before each parameter value, such as "TableCreate (Columns:4; Rows:3)." The parameter names help identify each piece of information but aren't necessary for the macro to function correctly. In this example, the command "TableCreate (4; 3)" would work just the same.*

You can insert both product and programming commands into your macro by selecting the type of command you want from the Command Type drop-down list. If you need to type text in the macro or make any changes to commands that have been inserted, you can leave the Command Inserter dialog box open and simply click in the document window to make any changes. When you're finished inserting commands, choose Close to close the dialog box.

Recording Commands into a Macro

A final method you can use to insert commands into a macro is to record them. The "Recording Macros" section earlier in this chapter explained how to create a new macro by recording it. In addition to recording the entire macro from start to finish, you can also record commands directly into a macro that you're writing or editing. This technique is especially useful if you want the macro to perform certain formatting steps, since it saves you from having to locate and insert each individual product command. To record commands into a macro, follow these steps:

1. Place the insertion point in the macro where you want the new commands inserted.

2. Click the Record button on the Macro toolbar (see Figure 10-1).

3. WP takes you to a blank document screen. Perform the actions that you want to record, such as selecting a paper size, switching printers, formatting a graphics box, and so on. For more information, see the "Recording Macros" section earlier in the chapter.

4. When you're finished, click the Stop button on the Macro toolbar or choose Tools | Macro | Record.

5. WP returns you to the macro with the new commands inserted. You can edit or delete any of the recorded commands and continue creating the macro as usual.

Getting Help

With over 2,000 macro commands available for your WP macros, it's doubtful you'll remember how each command works or what each of the parameters is used for. The Command Inserter dialog box gives you a brief description of each command and lists the available parameter names, but sometimes you need to know more information about a specific command. Fortunately, WP 8 comes with an extensive Macro Help file that has descriptions of each of the available commands, as well as several examples of using various commands.

The Macro Help file is not automatically installed during a typical installation of WordPerfect 8, so you need to install it if you haven't already done so (it requires about 1.6MB of disk space). Follow these steps to install it:

1. Exit WordPerfect and make sure the Corel WP Suite 8 CD is in your CD drive.

2. Choose Start on the Windows taskbar, and then choose Corel WordPerfect Suite 8 | Setup & Notes | Corel WordPerfect Suite 8 Setup.

3. Follow the installation prompts and select the option for a Custom installation. Make sure the path is correct and choose Next.

4. Choose Selection Options, select Deselect All, and choose OK.

5. Select Corel WordPerfect 8 in the list and choose Components.

6. Select the checkbox next to the WordPerfect Macro Help option and choose OK.

7. Choose Next and continue with the installation.

Once you've installed the Macro Help, you can get help on any macro command by choosing Help | Help Topics. Select the Contents tab, double-click Macros, and then double-click Macro Programming. Now, double-click the List of Commands option and double-click the type of command you want to look up, such as Product Commands or Corel PerfectScript Programming Commands. WP displays a help window with an alphabetical list of commands in that category. Click a letter button to jump to the commands that begin with that letter. To view the specific information about a command, click the button next to the command name.

TIP: *If you're using the Command Inserter, you can get quick help on a particular command by selecting the command name in the Commands list box and then right-clicking the command. WP displays the help topic information for that specific command.*

Saving and Compiling

Once you've typed or inserted all the commands for your macro, you're ready to save and compile the macro. When a macro is compiled, the commands are converted into "machine language" so they can later be executed. Each time you make a change to a macro, it needs to be recompiled. WP uses the PerfectScript utility to compile the macro commands.

NOTE: *When you record a macro, it is automatically compiled for you.*

The compiling process is done each time you save the macro. To do this, choose the Save & Compile button on the Macro toolbar. If you haven't yet saved the macro with a name, the Macro Save As dialog box appears. Type a name for your macro in the File Name text box and choose Save.

TIP: *You don't need to type the WCM extension when you type a name for the macro—WP automatically adds it for you.*

While the macro is being compiled, you might encounter error messages. These messages often indicate misspelled commands, missing parentheses or semicolons, or other syntax errors. For more information on fixing these mistakes, see the following "Troubleshooting Errors" section.

NOTE: *If your macro contains syntax errors, WP still saves the macro even though it hasn't correctly compiled. This means that you can close the macro without losing any of your changes and finish working on it another time.*

TIP: *If you have macros from WP 7, you should recompile them in WP 8 before playing them. Recompiling them will speed up the execution of the macro. To recompile a macro, choose Tools | Macro | Edit, select the WP 7 macro you want to recompile, and choose Edit to open the macro into a document window. Press SPACEBAR to insert a space, and then press BACKSPACE to delete it. (You must make a change to the macro in order for it to recompile.) Choose Save & Compile on the Macro toolbar to recompile the macro for WP 8; then choose File | Close.*

Troubleshooting Errors

As you compile and play macros, you're likely to run into an error or two. Finding and fixing errors—a process called "debugging"—is a natural part of any type of programming. There are three types of errors you can encounter with WP macros: syntax errors, run-time errors, and logic errors. In this section, we'll explain each of these error types and give you some hints to help solve and avoid them.

Syntax Errors

Syntax errors occur as you're compiling a macro. They flag commands that the compiler can't recognize due to problems such as misspelled command names, missing semicolons, and incorrect quotation marks. For example, this command has two syntax errors:

```
FilOpen ("c:\myfiles\test.wpd)
```

The first error is the misspelling of the "FileOpen" command name and the second is the missing double quote mark at the end of the filename. The correct command should look like this: FileOpen ("c:\myfiles\test.wpd"). WP will display an error message like this one when you try to compile a macro with syntax errors:

The error message usually refers you to a line and character number in the macro where WP thinks the problem is. However, this reference is only where WP first notices that there's a problem—the actual mistake could be several lines above or below the given reference. Choose Cancel Compilation to return to the macro and fix the error.

TIP: *If you're working in a long macro, you can use the LINENUM.WCM shipping macro to quickly take you to the specific line and character number indicated by the macro error. This macro isn't installed by default, so you'll need to copy it from your WP Suite 8 CD in order to use it.*

If you're getting syntax errors during a macro compilation, check for these common mistakes:

■   Make sure the command name is spelled correctly and doesn't contain any spaces (except for a few commands like "Case Of" that require a space). Using the Command Inserter can ensure that the commands are spelled correctly (see the "Inserting Commands" section earlier in the chapter).

■   Make sure you've used semicolons (not commas) to separate any parameters and that you've included both opening and closing parentheses around the parameters. If you've omitted an optional parameter, but have included other parameters *after* the optional ones, you still need to include semicolons for the optional parameters, such as in the command "Menu (vChoice; Digit!; ; ;{"Option 1"; "Option 2"})."

■   Make sure you haven't used any SmartQuotes in your macro. SmartQuotes are automatically disabled when you have the Macro toolbar displaying, but they can manually be turned back on.

■   Make sure you haven't inserted a hard return inside a text string that's enclosed in quotation marks. You can insert hard returns between parameters (after semicolons) if you want, but let text inside quotation marks wrap normally to another line.

■   Make sure you have an "EndIf" command for each "If" command, an "EndFor" for each "For," and so on. (For more information on these commands, see Chapter 11.)

Run-Time Errors

Even if you can compile your macro without any syntax errors, you can still receive error messages when the macro is played. These errors are called "run-time" errors because they happen while the macro is running. For example, if the macro tries to open a file that doesn't exist, you'll receive an error message like this one during the macro:

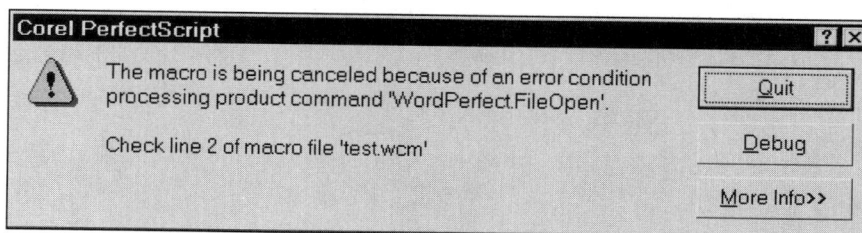

```
┌─────────────────────────────────────────────────────────────┐
│ Corel PerfectScript                                  ? X     │
├─────────────────────────────────────────────────────────────┤
│  ⚠  The macro is being canceled because of an error condition│  ┌──────────┐
│     processing product command 'WordPerfect.FileOpen'.       │  │   Quit   │
│                                                              │  └──────────┘
│     Check line 2 of macro file 'test.wcm'                    │  ┌──────────┐
│                                                              │  │  Debug   │
│                                                              │  └──────────┘
│                                                              │  ┌──────────┐
│                                                              │  │More Info>>│
│                                                              │  └──────────┘
└─────────────────────────────────────────────────────────────┘
```

When a run-time error occurs, the macro execution is stopped at that point. The error message indicates which command the macro couldn't execute completely and refers you to a line number in the macro. To solve a run-time error, choose Quit in the error message dialog box, open the macro, and find the line containing the command causing the error. Then ask yourself these questions:

- Is the macro in a table, header/footer, footnote/endnote, graphics box, or some other "structure" when the command is encountered? If so, make sure the command is appropriate for that structure. For example, you can't change the formatting of a table unless the insertion point is in the table. Or you can't open a document if a graphics box is currently selected.

- Is the macro trying to set a margin? If so, make sure the margin amount is within the minimum margins available for the currently selected printer.

- Is the macro trying to open a document or switch to a blank document screen? If so, make sure the document exists and that there aren't already nine documents open. You can use the FileExists command in your macro to make sure a file exists before the macro tries to open it, as shown in this example:

```
FileExists (vExist; "c:\myfiles\test.wpd")
If (vExist = True)
    FileOpen ("c:\myfiles\test.wpd")
Else
    MessageBox (; "Error"; "The file was not found.")
EndIf
```

- Is the macro performing a search and returning a "Not Found" error? If so, you can use the OnNotFound macro command to tell WP what to do when a "Not Found" condition occurs so the macro execution isn't stopped. For more information on using the OnNotFound command, see the Power Tip "Avoiding 'Not Found' Errors."

Power Tip... Avoiding "Not Found" Errors

A "Not Found" condition occurs in a macro when a search can't find any matches, as well as when the macro tries to open a file that can't be found or select a font that isn't currently installed. Normally, a "Not Found" condition causes the macro to stop and display an error message, but you can avoid an error by using the OnNotFound macro command.

The OnNotFound command tells WP what line in the macro to move to when a "Not Found" condition occurs. For example, in the sample macro next, the macro searches through a document for the text "Chapter" and centers each occurrence. The OnNotFound command tells the macro to move to the label "End@" after the last match has been found, where the macro quits without displaying an error. (For more information on using loops and labels in a macro, see Chapter 11.)

```
OnNotFound (End@)
Label (Search@)
    SearchString ("Chapter")
    SearchNext (Extended!)
    Center ( )
Go (Search@)
Label (End@)
    Quit
```

When you use the OnNotFound command, make sure you insert it *before* the commands where the "Not Found" condition could occur. You can also include multiple OnNotFound commands at different places throughout a macro. When a "Not Found" condition occurs, WP moves to the label name specified in the most recent OnNotFound command.

10

Logic Errors

A third type of error you can encounter while playing a macro is a logic error, where the macro doesn't run the way you expect it to. With a logic error, the macro compiles and plays without WP actually giving you any error messages—as far as WP is concerned, the commands in the macro worked just fine. But the end result isn't quite what you had in mind. For example, suppose you want to have a macro go through an alphabetized list and insert a large capital letter at the beginning of each section ("A," "B," and so on). However, when you play the macro, the large letters are inserted sporadically throughout the first section instead. The macro didn't give you any errors, but there's a problem behind the logic of the macro that needs to be fixed.

NOTE: *If you're playing a macro that seems to get stuck without doing anything (but the macro is still playing), it's likely that the macro commands are repeating in an endless loop. To stop the macro, press ESC.*

Fixing a logic error takes a little more detective work on your part because WP doesn't give you any indication of what macro command is causing the problem. However, there are a few different techniques you can use to help pinpoint the error.

- Turn the display on at the top of the macro with the Display (On!) command so you can watch what the macro is doing in the document. Macros execute pretty fast, so you can also insert a Speed command to slow it down. The Speed command tells WP how many tenths of a second to wait between executing each command. For example, inserting the command **Speed (20)** at the top of the macro tells WP to wait two seconds between each command.

- Insert a Quit command at various places throughout your macro so you can see if it's working correctly up to that point. For example, you might start off by inserting a Quit command toward the beginning of the macro. Once you know the first part is working correctly, move the Quit command a little bit further into the macro to check the next section.

- Use the Step (On!) command to have WP go through your macro one command at a time until a Step (Off!) command is encountered or the end of the macro is reached. When you insert the Step (On!) command in your macro, WP displays the Debugger tool of the PerfectScript utility (see Figure 10-4). For more information on using the Debugger, see the "How to Use the PerfectScript Debugger" section.

NOTE: *You can also use the Debugger when you receive a run-time error by choosing Debug in the error dialog box.*

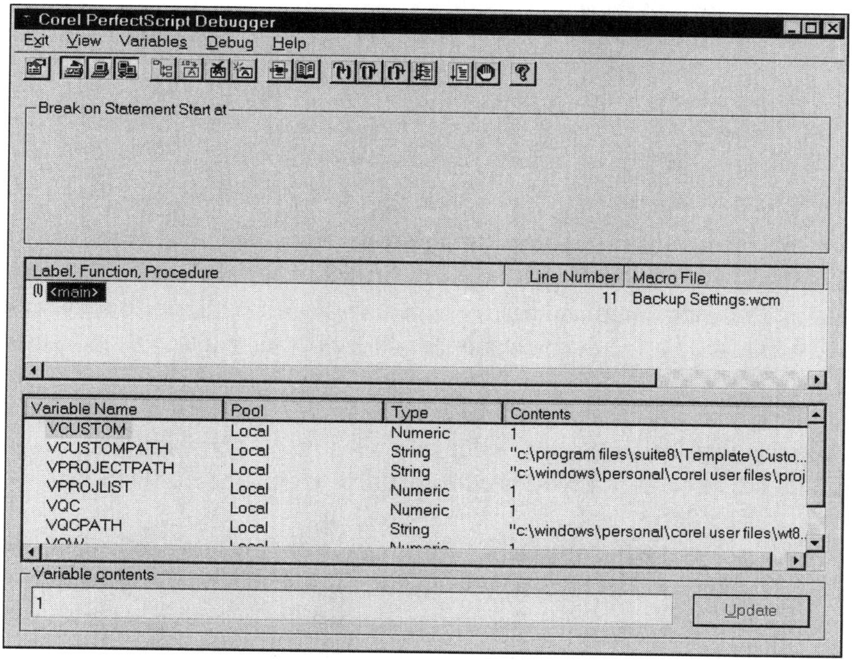

FIGURE 10-4 The PerfectScript Debugger tool helps step through your macros one command at a time

How to... ▸▸▸ Use the PerfectScript Debugger

The PerfectScript Debugger is a useful tool that helps you pinpoint errors in your macros. The Debugger allows you to "step" through your macros one command at a time, so you can watch what the macro is doing and view the values of any variables (see Figure 10-4).

The easiest way to debug a macro with the Debugger is to add a Step command to your macro. If the macro you want to debug isn't already open in a document window, choose Tools | Macro | Edit, select the macro, and choose Edit. Place the insertion point where you want the macro to begin the debugging process and type **Step (On!)**. If you also want to watch what's happening in the document window as the macro plays, type **Display (On!)**. Choose Save & Compile on the Macro toolbar; then choose the Play button to start the macro. (You can also debug a macro directly from the PerfectScript utility by choosing Start on the Windows taskbar, and then choosing Corel WordPerfect Suite 8 | Tools | Corel PerfectScript. From the PerfectScript dialog box, choose File | Debug | Play, select the macro you want to debug, and choose Debug.)

The PerfectScript Debugger dialog box gives you several options for stepping through the macro. You can step through one command at a time, set specific "breakpoints" that the debugger stops at, or "animate" the macro and have the information for each command briefly appear in the PerfectScript Debugger dialog box. Each time the PerfectScript Debugger dialog box displays, it shows you which line number is currently being executed, which function or procedure you're in (if any), and the contents of any variables.

If you want the PerfectScript Debugger dialog box to show the actual command on the line being executed, you need to change one of the PerfectScript settings. From the PerfectScript Debugger dialog box, choose View | Settings. Select the Compile tab, select the Include Debug Information option, and choose OK. In order for this setting to take effect, you need to recompile the macro. Choose Debug | Stop Debugging; then choose Quit. Recompile the macro by pressing SPACEBAR and BACKSPACE in the macro, and then choosing Save & Compile. Then begin the debugging process again.

Follow one of these steps to debug your macro:

- ■ To have the macro execute the current command and stop at the next command, choose Debug | Step Into, or click the Step Into Routine Calls button on the toolbar in the dialog box. If your macro uses functions and

How to... Use the PerfectScript Debugger (*continued*)

procedures, you can use the Step Over Routine Calls and Step to the End of the Current Routine buttons to bypass stepping through the commands in the current function or procedure.

- To have the macro execute the commands in the macro until the next "breakpoint," choose Debug | Continue or choose the Continue to Next Breakpoint button. By default, the macro breakpoints are at the start of the macro, the end of the macro, and any errors that occur during the macro. You can add other breakpoints, such as a specific line number or a call to a label, by choosing Debug | Breakpoints. From the Type drop-down list, select the type of breakpoint, such as Label Call, and then type any requested information, such as the Label name. Choose Add to add the breakpoint; then choose Close.

- To have the debugger "animate" the commands so the dialog box briefly displays for each command before executing the next command, choose Debug | Animate or choose the Animate Macro Execution button on the toolbar. While the macro is playing, you can stop the animation by selecting a variable name in the Debugger dialog box. To change the amount of time that the debugger pauses between each command, choose View | Settings and select the Debug tab. In the Delay text box, type the number of seconds to have the debugger pause and choose OK.

If you want to stop the debugging process before the macro has finished, choose Debug | Stop Debugging; then choose Quit.

Basic Macro Techniques

As you write macros, there are several techniques you can use to make your macros more powerful, more efficient, and in many cases, more compact. Many of the more advanced techniques, such as making decisions, looping, and creating dialog boxes will be discussed in Chapter 11. In this section, you'll learn some basic concepts and techniques you can use when writing macros, such as searching, using variables, and gathering information.

Searching in a Macro

WordPerfect has a robust Find and Replace feature that lets you search through your documents for text and codes, replacing them with other text and codes if you want. In addition, you can set options that search for the whole word only, position the insertion point before or after the word when a match is found, match the case of the text, and so on.

Macros can take advantage of the available Find and Replace options and perform powerful searches in a document. However, as you use search commands in a macro, there are a few areas you need to pay special attention to so the search turns out the way you want. These areas include the initial search settings, searching for codes, and recording a search.

Initial Search Settings

You can customize WP's Find and Replace feature with several settings before performing an actual search. For example, you can tell WP where to place the insertion point when a match is found (before, after, or select the match), whether the search should be case sensitive, and whether the search should begin at the top of the document. These settings are made from the pull-down menus in the Find and Replace dialog box (see Figure 10-5).

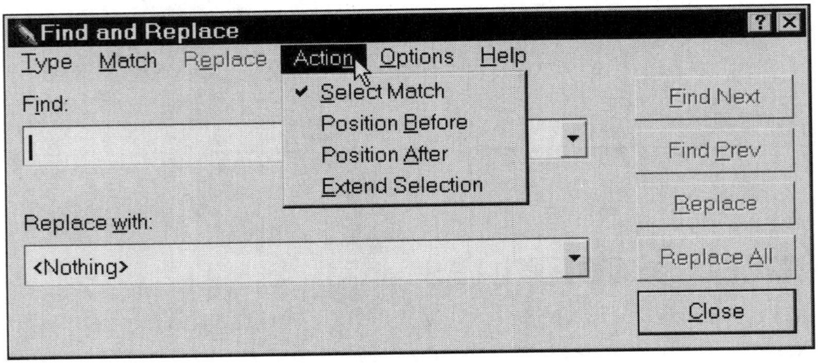

FIGURE 10-5 Settings made from the Find and Replace dialog box can affect a macro search

When these options are changed, they remain in effect for any other searches until you exit WordPerfect. For example, if you select Match | Case in the Find and Replace dialog box to make a search case sensitive, any other searches you perform during the current session of WP are also case sensitive, unless you deselect that option. This is important to remember when writing macros that perform a search, because the Find and Replace settings you have selected when you're testing the macro might not be the same settings someone else has selected when the macro is played later.

To avoid any problems, you can use macro commands to select the settings you need in order for the search the macro is performing to be successful. For example, if you want to make sure that the search the macro performs is *not* case sensitive, have the macro turn that option off before the search is performed.

WP has macro commands that control all of the search settings. Insert these commands into your macro before the actual search or replace command. You can enter each of these commands directly into the macro by typing them or using the Command Inserter. The search setting commands begin either with "Search," such as SearchCaseSensitive and SearchFindWholeWordsOnly, or with "Match," such as MatchPositionBefore and MatchSelection. Or you can record your search and select the options you want from the Find and Replace dialog box. (See the "Recording a Search" section later in this chapter for more information.)

SAMPLE SEARCH MACROS: *If you want to review some sample macros that use initial search settings, take a look at the REPLACE STYLES.WCM, SORT TITLES.WCM, and REPLACE ATTRIBUTES.WCM macros on the companion CD.*

Searching for Codes

The Find and Replace feature lets you search for practically any code and replace it with another code if you want. When you search for codes in a macro, you need to make sure that the codes are inserted in the macro properly. Search codes can't simply be typed into a macro—they must either be recorded or inserted through the Macro Codes dialog box. For example, if you want to search for a bold on code, the macro command would look like this in the document screen:

```
SearchString ("[Bold On]")
```

However, if you turned on Reveal Codes, the command would look like this:

SearchString◇("Macro Func")HRt

If you're inserting the SearchString (or ReplaceString) command directly into the macro by typing it or by using the Command Inserter, when you're ready to insert the code, choose the Codes button on the Macro toolbar. WP displays the Macro Codes dialog box (see Figure 10-6). Select the code you want to search for and choose Insert to insert it into your macro. If you want to search for a merge code, select the Merge tab and select the code you want. When you're finished inserting codes, choose Close.

NOTE: *The other types of codes in the Macro Codes dialog box—Date and Other—are used to insert date formats and page number formats in a macro. These codes must be used in conjunction with the DateFormat and PageNumberFormat commands. You can also record the selection of a date format or page number format into a macro.*

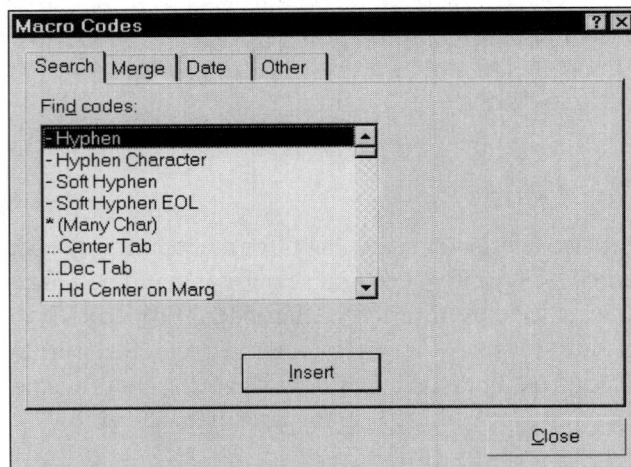

FIGURE 10-6   You can insert codes in your macros to use during a search

Another way to search for codes in a macro is to record the search. For more information on recording for a search, see the following "Recording a Search" section.

SAMPLE SEARCH CODE MACRO: *If you want to look at a sample macro that searches and replaces codes, see the REPLACE ATTRIBUTES.WCM macro on the companion CD.*

Recording a Search

If you're not sure of all the macro commands you need to have the search in your macro work correctly, you can record the search. Recording a search ensures that each command's syntax is correct, and also easily allows you to search and replace codes. Follow these steps to record a search:

1. Open the macro document and place the insertion point where you want the search commands to be inserted.

2. Click the Record button on the Macro toolbar.

3. WP takes you to a blank document screen. Before you can access the Find and Replace feature, the document must contain some text. You can either type a word, such as **test**, in the current document window, or you can open a document that you want to record the search on. If you want to perform several different searches or if you also want to record several formatting steps once text has been found, you might find it easier to open a document that contains the information you'll be searching for.

4. Choose Edit | Find and Replace. Use the pull-down menus in the Find and Replace dialog box to select the various settings for your search. If an option that you want to use is already selected, select it again in order for that setting to be recorded into the macro. For example, if you want WP to place the insertion point at the beginning of any matching text, choose Action | Position Before—even if that option already has a check mark next to it.

5. In the Find text box, type the text that you want to search for. If you want to search for codes, choose Match | Codes, and then insert the codes you want from the Codes dialog box.

6. If you want to replace the text with other text, type that text in the Replace With text box. To include codes in the replacement, choose Replace | Codes and insert the codes you want.

7. Choose the option you want to begin the search or replace. For example, choose Find Next to search forward in the document, choose Find Prev to search backward, choose Replace to find and replace the first occurrence, or choose Replace All to find and replace every occurrence. If WP displays a prompt telling you the text isn't found in the current document, choose No.

8. Repeat these steps to perform any other searches. When you're finished, click the Stop button on the Macro toolbar or choose Tools | Macro | Record.

9. WP returns you to the macro with the new search commands inserted.

At this point, you need to do a little bit of cleanup. If you typed text at the top of the blank document before searching, delete the "Type" command that was inserted at the beginning of the search commands. If you opened a document to record the search with, delete the "FileOpen" command.

If the document you were recording the search with didn't actually contain the text or codes you were searching for, WP doesn't include the SearchNext command as part of the recorded macro commands. For example, if you just typed some text in the blank document window in order to be able to activate the Find and Replace feature and record the search settings, it's likely that the text you were searching for wasn't found in that document. If the SearchNext command *wasn't* recorded with the other search commands, place the insertion point where you want the actual search performed—usually just after the SearchString command—and type **SearchNext (Extended!)**. If you want to search backward in the document, type **SearchPrevious (Extended!)**.

NOTE: *When you search in a macro, make sure you also account for any "Not Found" errors that might occur. See the Power Tip "Avoiding 'Not Found' Errors" earlier in this chapter for more information.*

Using Variables

A common practice in macro programming is the use of variables. *Variables* are indispensable tools that allow you to easily use the same information repeatedly throughout a macro, as well as change and manipulate the value of a piece of information. A variable defines a "holding area" in memory for a piece of information. For example, you can create a variable named "Last Name" that contains the last name of a person. Each time you play the macro, the variable can contain a different last name. Variables can be used throughout a macro, and the information stored in them can change while the macro is playing.

Naming and Assigning Variables

You can create and define custom variables in a macro that contain almost any type of information. You can assign the information to a variable within the macro itself, or you can prompt the user for the information and then assign it to a variable. The name you use for a variable can be practically anything you want. However, it must start with a letter and can't be more than 50 characters long. In addition, you can't use any programming or product command name, such as "Call" or "Cut."

TIP: *To avoid conflicts with macro commands and to help identify variables within your macro, you can use a common programming convention of naming your variables with a lowercase "v" before the variable name. For example, you can name a macro "vCopy," even though "Copy" by itself is an invalid variable name. All of the variable names used in the macros on the companion CD follow this naming convention.*

You can assign information to a variable in a number of different ways, including the following:

- Use the Assign macro command. For example, the macro statement **Assign (vCity; "San Diego")** assigns the text "San Diego" to the variable named "vCity."

- Use the shortcut to the Assign command—a colon followed by the equal sign (:=). For example, the macro statement **vRepeat:=25** assigns the number 25 to the variable named "vRepeat."

- Use a macro command such as GetString that prompts the user for information and automatically assigns that information to a variable. For example, the following macro prompts the user to enter their name with the GetString command and assigns it to the variable "vName." Then that variable is typed into the document in bold text. (For more information on the GetString command, see the "Gathering Information" section later in this chapter.)

```
GetString (vName; "Please enter your name")
AttributeAppearanceOn (Bold!)
Type (vName)
AttributeAppearanceOff (Bold!)
```

You can assign almost anything to a variable, including text, numbers, or measurements. You can also assign expressions to a variable, such as in these examples:

```
vSubTotal:=25+50
vTax:=0.075 * vSubTotal
vCount:=vCount+1
```

In the first example, the variable "vSubTotal" contains 75, or the result of adding 25 and 50. In the second example, the variable "vTax" contains the result of multiplying whatever is in vSubTotal by 0.075. And in the third example, the variable "vCount" contains the previous value of vCount with 1 added to it. For example, if vCount was originally set to 1, the command in the example above would increase the value in vCount to 2. In order for this type of macro statement to work correctly, you must assign an initial setting to the variable (referred to as "initializing"), such as **vCount:=0**.

Array Variables

A more powerful type of variable is called an *array* variable. One array variable can contain several different elements. For example, if you assign the 12 month names to an array variable named "vMonth," the first element of vMonth would equal

"January," the second would equal "February," and so on. Array variables are a useful method for keeping related pieces of information together without having to assign each of them to a separate variable name. In the previous example, you could assign "January" to the variable "vMonth1," "February" to "vMonth2," and so on, but array variables eliminate this need.

Before you can use an array variable, you need to tell WP how many maximum elements it can have. This is done with the Declare command. For example, this command tells WP that the array variable vMonth will have a maximum of 12 elements:

```
Declare vMonth[12]
```

The maximum number of elements is included in square brackets after the variable name. Once you've declared a variable, you can assign the individual elements to the array using any of the methods described earlier in the "Naming and Assigning Variables" section. You need to indicate the element number for the current information in square brackets after the variable name. For example, these commands assign "January," "February," and "March" to the first three elements of the array variable vMonth:

```
vMonth[1]:="January"
vMonth[2]:="February"
vMonth[3]:="March"
```

Since the elements in an array variable are numbered, a useful technique for assigning the individual elements to an array variable is to use a ForEach loop. This saves you from having to use a separate Assign statement for each element and reduces the amount of code in your macro. For more information on doing this, see the Power Tip "Assigning Arrays with the ForEach Command."

Power Tip➤➤➤ Assigning Arrays with the ForEach Command

If you have a list of related items that you want to assign to an array variable, you can use a ForEach loop to cut down on the number of commands in your macro. For example, the following ForEach loop assigns the weekday abbreviations to an array variable named vWeekday:

```
vCount:=1
ForEach (vName; {"Sun"; "Mon"; "Tue"; "Wed"; "Thu"; "Fri"; "Sat"})
    vWeekday[vCount]:=vName
    vCount:=vCount+1
EndFor
```

The ForEach command processes each item listed in curly brackets and assigns it to the variable vName. The commands inside the ForEach loop assign the current vName text to the array variable vWeekday, using the vCount variable to indicate the array element number (the vCount variable is incremented by 1 each time). For example, the first time through the loop, vCount equals 1 and vName equals "Sun," so "Sun" is assigned as the first element of vWeekday (vWeekday[1]). The second time through the loop, "Mon" is assigned as the second element of vWeekday (vWeekday[2]), and so on. For more information on using ForEach loops, see Chapter 11.

After you've assigned the individual elements to an array variable, you can easily access any of the elements by specifying which element you want in square brackets. For example, after assigning the month names to the vMonth array variable, you could use this command to type the seventh element ("July") into the document:

```
Type (vMonth[7])
```

In addition, you can use another variable to specify the array element, as in this example:

```
vNum:=10
Type (vMonth[vNum])
```

These commands would insert the text "October" into the document if the vMonth array had been assigned the month names.

BILLING.WCM: *For a sample macro that uses array variables, take a look at the BILLING.WCM macro on the companion CD. This macro assigns various procedures done at a physical therapy office to an array variable and displays them as checkboxes in a dialog box. The macro then evaluates which options were checked and inserts them into a document.*

Gathering Information

Many times, a macro needs to gather information of some sort—either from the user or from WordPerfect—before it can proceed. For example, you might need to ask the user a yes/no question or prompt him or her to type in specific information. Or you might need to determine information such as whether the insertion point is in a table or what the current page number is.

Fortunately, gathering this sort of information is relatively easy and painless. If you need to get information from the user, you can use macro commands such as GetString or MessageBox. If you want to get information from WordPerfect, you can use system variables. In this section, you'll learn how to use these various techniques.

POSTCARD.WCM: *If you want to look at a sample macro that uses these different techniques for gathering information, open the POSTCARD.WCM macro from the companion CD. This macro creates a designated number of postcards with a message. The macro first determines whether the current document is blank and if not, opens a new document window. Then the macro prompts the user to enter the number of total postcards, the message text, and the margins for each card. Finally, the macro asks if a border should be placed around each postcard.*

GetString, GetNumber, and GetUnits

When you want to prompt the user to type in information during a macro, you can use one of three commands: GetString, GetNumber, or GetUnits. Each of these commands displays a simple prompt with a text box for the user to type in information, as shown next. You can specify the prompt text, as well as the text that appears in the prompt title bar. The information typed into the text box is assigned to a variable.

NOTE: *You can also prompt the user to type in information by creating a custom dialog box. For more information on creating dialog boxes, see Chapter 11.*

The difference between the GetString, GetNumber, and GetUnits commands is the way WP views the information entered into the text box (that's subsequently assigned to a variable). With the GetString command, the information is viewed as text and can contain text or numbers. If you use the GetNumber command, the user must type a number in the text box and the resulting variable can then be used in numeric expressions, such as additions or subtractions. If you use the GetUnits command, WP views the information as a measurement, which can then be used to set margins, advance the insertion point, and so on.

The GetString command uses this format: GetString (Var; Prompt Text; Title; Max Length). The prompt text, title, and max length parameters are all optional. For example, this command displays the prompt shown earlier:

```
GetString (vMessage; "Enter the message text";
"Postcard Macro"; 100)
```

In this example, the information typed into the text box is assigned to the variable "vMessage," and the user can't type more than 100 characters.

The GetNumber and GetUnits commands are almost identical to the GetString command, with the exception that they don't have a Max Length parameter option. If you use the GetUnits command, the user can type a value in any of the available units of measure, as shown in the following table. For example, to enter two inches, you would type either **2"** or **2i** in the text box. Or, to enter two centimeters, you would type **2c**.

Unit of Measure	Abbreviation
Inches	" or i
Centimeters	c
Millimeters	m
Points (72 per inch)	p
WP Units (1200 per inch)	w

NOTE: *If the user doesn't include a measurement abbreviation with the number, such as "c" for centimeters, WP uses the default units of measure for the measurement, which are WordPerfect units (1200ths of an inch). However, you can use the DefaultUnits command in your macro to tell WP what units of measure to use if none is indicated with the measurement value. For example, the command **DefaultUnits (Inches!)** tells WP to view a measurement as inches unless a different measurement abbreviation is used.*

MessageBox

The MessageBox command is a great way to ask the user a "yes/no" question during a macro. When you use the MessageBox command, WP displays a small dialog box with your custom text and title, along with the type of buttons you want, such as OK and Cancel buttons, Yes and No buttons, or Retry and Cancel buttons. In addition, you can specify the type of icon you want included in the message box.

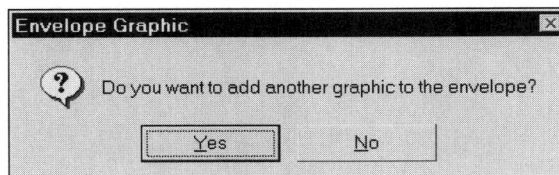

WP assigns a number representing the button the user chooses in the message box to the variable you specified in the command. Then you can evaluate that variable to determine what action to take next. The MessageBox command uses this format: MessageBox (Var; Title; Prompt; Style). For example, this command displays the message box shown earlier:

```
MessageBox (vChoice; "Envelope Graphic"; "Do you want to add
another graphic to the envelope?"; YesNo! | IconQuestion!)
```

In this example, the message box displays "Yes" and "No" buttons, along with the question mark icon. The number for the button the user chooses in the message box is assigned to the variable "vChoice." If "Yes" was chosen, the variable vChoice would contain the value 6, and if "No" was chosen, the variable vChoice would contain 7. Table 10-1 shows a list of the values for each button. The following commands demonstrate how you can check to see which button was pressed and then jump to a label name in the macro accordingly. (See Chapter 11 for more information on the IF command.)

```
If (vChoice = 6)
   Go (Top@)
Else
   Go (End@)
EndIf
```

Button Name	Button Value (returned in variable)
OK	1
Cancel	2
Abort	3
Retry	4
Ignore	5
Yes	6
No	7

TABLE 10-1 Message Box Button Values

The "Message Box Options" quick reference section gives a list of the button combinations you can select for the message box, as well as the available icon styles.

Quick Reference ▶▶▶ Message Box Options

When you use the MessageBox command, you can specify which button combinations display, as well as which icons are used (if any). The MessageBox command uses this format: MessageBox (Var; Title; Prompt; Style).

The following list shows the available style names you can use in the MessageBox command. If you want to use an icon, be sure to separate it from the button style with a vertical bar, such as **YesNo! | IconQuestion!**. If you don't specify a button combination, an "OK" button is used. If you don't specify an icon, none is used.

Button Combinations

AbortRetryIgnore! (Abort, Retry, and Ignore buttons)
OK! (OK button—default if no combination is specified)
OK Cancel! (OK and Cancel buttons)

RetryCancel! (Retry and Cancel buttons)
YesNo! (Yes and No buttons)

YesNoCancel! (Yes, No, and Cancel buttons)

Button Icons

IconNone! (No icon—default if none is specified)

IconAsterisk! (Lowercase blue "i" in a white bubble)
IconExclamation! (Black exclamation point in a yellow triangle)
IconHand! (White "X" in a red circle)

IconInformation! (Lowercase blue "i" in a white bubble)
IconWarning! (Black exclamation point in a yellow triangle)
IconError! (White "X" in a red circle)

IconQuestion! (Blue question mark in a white bubble)
IconStop! (White "X" in a red circle)

System Variables

In addition to getting information from the user with commands such as GetString and MessageBox, you can get information about the status of various conditions in

WordPerfect. For example, you can determine the current document's path and filename, whether or not any text is currently selected, what character or code is to the left or right of the insertion point, or what settings a graphics box uses. This information comes from *system variables.* WP 8 has over 400 different system variables that can tell you all kinds of information about the current conditions while a macro is playing.

NOTE: *To see a list of the available system variables, choose Help | Help Topics. Select the Contents tab; then double-click Macros. Double-click Macro Programming, then List of Commands, and then System Variables. To see information about a specific system variable, click the button to the left of the variable name.*

On the CD... Current System Codes

When you're working with a macro that uses system variables, sometimes it's helpful to know the values of certain system variables, such as ?LeftCode or ?Line. The companion CD contains a macro called SYSTEM CODES.WCM that displays a message box with the current values of several common system variables.

To use this macro, place the insertion point where you want to check the settings of the current left/right characters or codes, or the current line or position value. Choose Tools | Macro | Play, select the SYSTEM CODES.WCM macro and choose Play. A message box appears showing the current system variable values. The "CtoN" values are the numeric equivalents of the characters to the left and right of the insertion point. If there are no characters, "N/A" is listed. When you're finished, choose OK.

System variables begin with a question mark, such as ?LeftChar or ?PathDocument. The values they contain range from "True" or "False," to a number indicating a specific style, to a text string such as the path of the current document. One common use for system variables is to make sure that the current document conditions are correct before the macro proceeds, such as making sure text is selected or the document screen is blank. For example, if a macro is going to make changes to a table, you can use a system variable to make sure the insertion point is in a table first, as shown next. This prevents errors from occurring while the macro plays.

```
If (?InTable = False)
    MessageBox (X; "Place the insertion point in the table and
play the macro again."; "Error"; OK! | IconError!)
    Quit
EndIf
```

TIP: *You can quickly insert system variables from the Command Inserter dialog box. Choose Commands on the Macro toolbar and select WordPerfect-EN from the Command Type drop-down list. The system variables display at the top of the list and begin with a question mark. To find out more information about a specific system variable and the values it contains, select and right-click the variable name in the Commands list box.*

Summary

When you need WordPerfect power, macros are the perfect solution. Macros can automate practically any task and dramatically speed up your work in the process. You can record your WP actions in a macro and have them instantly repeated when you later play the macro. In addition to recording macros, you can write and edit macros by typing macro commands or inserting them with the Command Inserter. There are several ways you can troubleshoot the different types of errors in your macros to get them in working order as soon as possible.

Learning basic macro programming techniques such as searching for text and codes, using variables, and gathering information is the first step in creating powerhouse macros. In Chapter 11, we'll delve into some of the more advanced techniques for writing macros, including making decisions, looping, creating custom dialog boxes, and using functions and procedures.

Chapter

11

Advanced Macro Programming

So you know what a macro is and you've even created a few, but now you're ready for some real power and automation. WordPerfect offers hundreds of commands that you can use to control how a macro behaves. In effect, you're creating a miniature computer program when you create a macro. But don't let the idea of "programming" intimidate you. Creating advanced macros is really not as tough as it sounds. Before you know it, you'll be cranking out macros left and right.

In this chapter, we'll explain some of the macro commands and programming techniques that you can use to create truly powerful macros. You'll learn how to create subroutines with functions and procedures, make decisions within a macro, and repeat commands in a loop. We'll show you how to create custom dialog boxes in practically any shape or form, and also how to update the dialog box automatically while it's displaying. Finally, we'll get you started with some really advanced stuff, like writing to the Windows registry and using OLE and DDE automation. (If you're new to macros, make sure you've read Chapter 10 first.)

Creating Subroutines

Subroutines can make your macros more efficient and easier to troubleshoot. A *subroutine* is a group of commands that is separated in some way from the main section of the macro. You can use subroutines to divide a long macro into smaller sections, making it easier to troubleshoot errors. In addition, subroutines can make a macro shorter and more efficient, since the commands in a subroutine can be processed as many times as you need throughout the macro.

You can create a subroutine with one of three different macro commands: Label, Procedure, or Function. In this section, you'll learn the difference between these commands, as well as how to use them to create subroutines in your macros.

Using Labels

The Label command serves as a marker within a macro and consists simply of a name in parentheses, such as "Label (Top)." You can use the Label command to mark

the beginning of a subroutine, allowing you to instruct the macro to move to that section anytime while the macro is playing. The label name can be practically anything you want, as long as it starts with a letter, is no longer than 30 characters, and isn't a programming or product command.

TIP: *A convention often used with label names is to end them with the @ symbol, such as "Label (Search@)." This helps distinguish labels from functions and procedures in the macro.*

Labels can be inserted anywhere within a macro and are basically ignored when the macro encounters them as it processes the commands. The macro doesn't stop when it reaches a label, but continues with the commands immediately following it. However, you can also tell the macro to move to a label at any time so the commands following it are executed. This can be done with either the Go or Call command.

NOTE: *If you use the Label command in a macro, you must refer to that label name somewhere in the macro, either by calling it or by using it with a command such as OnError or OnNotFound. Otherwise, you'll get a syntax error when you compile the macro.*

The Go Command

When you want a macro to jump to a specific location in the macro and continue from that point forward, you can use the Go command. The Go command contains the label name you want to move to in parentheses. As soon as a macro encounters the Go command, it jumps to the specified label and continues, whether that label occurs before or after the Go command. If there are any commands immediately following the Go command, they won't be executed (unless they also come after a label that is specified at some point).

The following is an example of a macro that uses the Go command to avoid an error:

```
If (?NumberOpenDocuments = 9)
   Go (Error@)
EndIf
FileOpen ("c:\myfiles\test.wpd")
Quit
```

```
Label (Error@)
MessageBox (X; "Error"; "You have nine documents open.")
Quit
```

In this example, the macro checks to see if there are already nine open documents and if so, the Go command causes the macro to jump to the Label (Error@) command. Once there, the macro continues and displays a message box before quitting. If there are less than nine documents open, the macro continues executing the commands after the EndIf command and opens the TEST.WPD file.

NOTE: *If the Quit command was not inserted after the FileOpen command in the preceding example, the macro would continue processing the commands after Label (Error@), causing the error message box to be displayed every time, even when no error occurred.*

The Go command can also be used to create a loop in a macro by continually directing the macro back to a label that occurs prior to the Go command. You can break out of the loop by evaluating a condition during the loop and then using another Go command, or by using a command such as OnNotFound if the loop is performing a search (see Chapter 10 for more information on the OnNotFound command). For example, these macro commands move the insertion point to the right, one character at a time, until an asterisk (*) is encountered:

```
Label (CheckChar@)
If (?RightChar = "*")
   Go (End@)
EndIf
PosCharNext ( )
Go (CheckChar@)

Label (End@)
Quit
```

In this example, the Go (CheckChar@) command causes the macro to continually jump back up to the Label (CheckChar@). As soon as the character to the right of the insertion point is an asterisk, the Go (End@) command breaks the macro out of the loop and moves to the Label (End@).

NOTE: *This type of loop can also be accomplished with the While command. See the "Creating Loops" section later in the chapter for more information.*

SAMPLE GO MACROS: *For additional examples of macros that use the Go command with labels, see the SORT TITLES.WCM and ENVELOPE GRAPHICS.WCM macros on the companion CD.*

The Call Command

The Call command directs a macro to a specific label name in the macro, much like the Go command. However, the Call command also has the macro return to that point after the commands in the label subroutine have been executed. This allows you to easily process the same commands in a subroutine from different locations throughout a macro and have the macro return to the appropriate location each time.

To use the Call command, you need to include the Return command at the end of the subroutine. The Return command marks the end of the subroutine and tells the macro to go back to the command immediately following the original Call command. For example, in these macro commands a subroutine is called three times during the macro:

```
Type ("Here is one line:")
Call (InsertLine@)
Type ("Here are two lines:")
Call (InsertLine@)
Call (InsertLine@)
Quit

Label (InsertLine@)
HardReturn ( )
GraphicsLineCreate (HorizontalLine!)
GraphicsLineEnd (Save!)
HardReturn ( )
Return
```

In this example, the macro first types a line of text and then calls the InsertLine@ subroutine, which inserts a horizontal graphics line. When the Return command is reached, the macro jumps back to the line immediately following the Call command. Here, the macro types a second line of text and then calls the InsertLine@ subroutine twice more before quitting. Using the Call command makes this macro shorter since you don't have to repeat the same group of commands each time you want to insert a graphics line.

CAUTION: *If you use the Return command in a section of the macro that isn't called as a subroutine, it causes the macro to quit (or return to a parent macro if the macro was nested).*

SAMPLE CALL MACROS: *For additional examples of macros that use the Call command to process subroutines multiple times, see the REPLACE ATTRIBUTES.WCM and INDEX DIVIDER.WCM macros on the companion CD.*

The Call command is also useful for breaking up a macro into smaller sections. This programming technique makes your macro more manageable and also makes it easy to see the overall process of the macro at a quick glance, as shown in this example:

```
Call (GetSettings@)
Call (CalcLineHeight@)
Call (InsertWatermark@)
Quit

Label (GetSettings@)
...more macro commands
Return

Label (CalcLineHeight@)
...etc.
```

In this macro, the macro would first jump down to the GetSettings@ label and execute the commands there until it encountered a Return command. After returning to the top part of the macro, the commands in the CalcLineHeight@ subroutine would be processed until a Return command was found. Finally, the InsertWatermark@ subroutine would be processed and the macro would quit. While the macro would work the same without the subroutine divisions, the separations help you quickly see the overall organization of the macro.

NOTE: *For another example of a macro that uses the Call command with subroutine divisions, see the PLEADING.WCM macro that's included with WP 8 (in your default macro directory).*

TIP: *You can also have a macro execute commands that are in a completely separate macro and then return to the main macro. For more information, see the Power Tip "Nesting Macros with the Run Command."*

Power Tip... Nesting Macros with the Run Command

The Call command is a great way to break up a macro into smaller subroutines, making the macro more manageable and easier to troubleshoot. You can also break up a macro into several smaller macros, and then use the Run command to execute each individual macro. By storing subroutines as separate macros, you can easily access the same commands from more than one macro. This technique is similar to using a library file of functions and procedures.

To use the Run command, place the insertion point in the macro where you want a second macro to play and type **Run ("macro.wcm")**. Replace "macro.wcm" with the filename of the macro you want to play. If the macro isn't in your default macro directory, include the path to the macro.

When the Run command is encountered in a macro, WP executes the commands in the specified macro until the end of that macro is reached or until a Return command is encountered. Then the original macro continues with the command immediately following the Run command. If the macro you're nesting includes a Quit command, both macros will end.

11

Using Procedures and Functions

You can also create subroutines in a macro with the Procedure and Function commands. These commands are similar to the Call command in that they jump to a specific subroutine, execute the commands there, and then return to the main section of the macro. But there are also some differences:

- Procedures and functions are not executed by the macro unless they are specifically called. If they occur in the middle of a macro, the macro simply skips over them. If they are placed at the end of the macro, a Quit command is not needed before them.

- Information can be "passed" to a procedure or function through the command parameters.

- Procedures and functions are called from the main macro by simply typing their name and including any parameters in parentheses.

- Variables used inside of a procedure or function are specific to that subroutine. You can use the same variable names as the main section of the macro without affecting the original variables. In addition, you *can't* access variables defined in the main section of the macro unless the information is passed to the procedure or function, or unless those variables are defined as global variables.

- A function can return a value to the main section of the macro.

Creating Procedures

A procedure is a subroutine that begins with the Procedure command and ends with the EndProc command. Procedures allow you to "pass" information to them when you call the procedure, such as text, numbers, measurements, or variables. The Procedure command uses this syntax:

Procedure Name (variable; variable; etc.)

The name of a procedure can be any unique name. The parameters in parentheses are variable names for each piece of information that is passed to the procedure. You can have as many variables as you want (or none).

When you call a procedure, type the name of the procedure followed by the information that you want to pass to it in parentheses. For example, this sample macro passes two pieces of information to the procedure named FormatText:

```
GetString (vName; "Enter your name:"; "Enter Name")
FormatText (24p; vName)

Procedure FormatText (vSize; vPerson)
FontSize (vSize)
Type (vPerson)
EndProc
```

In this example, the macro first prompts the user to enter their name and assigns it to the variable vName. Then the FormatText procedure is called and is passed two pieces of information: a point size measurement and the information in the vName variable. When the Procedure command receives this information, it in turn assigns it to the vSize and vPerson variables. Then the commands in the procedure change the font size and insert the person's name into the document.

CAUTION: *Make sure the order of the information passed to the procedure matches the variable names used in parentheses after the Procedure command.*

NOTE: *If the procedure doesn't use any parameters, you still need to include the parentheses. For example, a procedure might be defined as* **Procedure FormatText ( )** *and would be called with* **FormatText ( ).**

If you pass a variable to a procedure, you don't have to use the same variable name within the procedure. In the preceding example, the variable vName is passed to the procedure, but the procedure reassigns the information in that variable to the variable vPerson. You can also assign the passed information to the same variable name, but if you change the value of the variable within the procedure, the original variable remains the same.

TIP: *If you want to change the value of a variable within a procedure and have the original variable change as well, include an ampersand (&) before the variable name in both the calling statement and the Procedure command, such as* **FormatText (&vName)** *and* **Procedure FormatText (&vPerson).** *The ampersand passes the memory location of the variable, so both variables are changed (the variable names don't have to be the same).*

If you try to access a variable that *hasn't* been passed to the procedure, you'll receive an error message unless that variable has been defined as a global variable. To define a global variable, use the Global command at the beginning of the macro before any of the variables are defined, such as **Global (vName)**. Then you can access the global variable in a procedure without having to pass that information.

SAMPLE PROCEDURE MACRO: *For another example of a macro that uses a procedure, see the BACKUP SETTINGS.WCM macro on the companion CD.*

Creating Functions

Functions are practically identical to procedures. The only difference is that a function can return a value. For example, a function can calculate a number or manipulate a text string and then return the result to a variable in the main macro. When you call a function, you assign it to whatever variable you want to contain the result. Then, within the function, you use the Return command to specify what information to return and assign to that variable. For example, the GetFirstWord function in this sample macro returns the first word of a text string to the variable vWord:

```
vWord:=GetFirstWord ("Corel WordPerfect 8")
MessageBox (X; "Function Result"; "The first word is "+vWord)


Function GetFirstWord (vText)
vList[]:=StrParseList (vText; WhiteSpace!)
```

```
Return (vList[1])
EndFunc
```

The GetFirstWord function is passed the text "Corel WordPerfect 8" and assigns it to the variable vText. Then the StrParseList command is used to assign each word of the phrase to the array variable vList. The Return command returns the first element of the vList array variable, which is the first word in the string ("Corel" in this example). This result is assigned to the variable vWord. The macro then returns to the main section of the macro and continues, where it displays a message box with the results.

TIP: *If you don't want a function to return a value, just use the Return ( ) command without any information in parentheses.*

NOTE: *For another example of a macro that uses functions, see the PLEADING.WCM macro that's included with WP 8 (in your default macro directory).*

If you have several functions and procedures that you use frequently, you can easily access them from any macro without having to re-create them. For example, if you've created a procedure in one macro that displays a "Please Wait" dialog box, you can tell WP to use it from the first macro. This is done with the Use command.

The Use command simply identifies the macro file that contains functions or procedures that you want to access from the current macro. To use this command, place the insertion point at the top of the macro that you want to access the functions or procedures in. Then type this command: **Use ("macroname.wcm")**. Substitute the filename of the macro containing the functions and procedures in place of "macroname.wcm," but make sure you keep the filename in quotation marks. If the macro isn't in your default macro directory, type the path along with the filename.

TIP: *If you find yourself using certain functions and procedures frequently, you can place them all in a single macro that only contains functions and procedures. This type of macro is commonly called a "library" file since it doesn't actually perform a task on its own. The companion CD contains a library file to get you started. For more information, see the "Function and Procedure Library" sidebar.*

On the CD ▶▶▶ Function and Procedure Library

The companion CD contains a library file called LIBRARY.WCM that contains several functions and procedures you can use in your own macros. Some of the functions and procedures include:

- Functions to return the filenames from a specified directory in either an array variable or a delimited string.

- Functions to convert MM-DD-YY dates to the Julian date values, and vice versa.

- Functions to convert decimal values to an Hour:Minute format, and vice versa.

- Functions to read and write information from the registry.

- A procedure to create a "Please Wait" dialog box.

- A procedure to set default Search settings, so you can make sure your searches behave the way you want.

Open the LIBRARY.WCM file to see a description of all the available functions and procedures, as well as specific comments for using each one. To use one in a macro, make sure the LIBRARY.WCM file is in your default macro directory and insert this command at the top of the macro:

Use ("library.wcm")

Then follow the instructions in the LIBRARY.WCM file for the specific function or procedure that you want to use.

Making Decisions

One of the most useful macro programming tools for creating advanced macros is the ability to have a macro make a decision and then perform certain actions based on the result. For example, you can have a macro check to see if the current document is blank and if it isn't, open a new document window. Or you can have the macro display a menu and then take a different action depending on what option was chosen. These actions are possible with the help of the If and Switch commands.

The If Command

The If command is one of the most common ways to make a decision in a macro. The If command evaluates a certain condition and if it is true, performs a set of actions. You can use the If command to evaluate both regular variables and system variables. For example, the following If statement checks to see if a document has been named yet and if not, displays the Save As dialog box:

```
If (?Name = "")
    FileSaveAsDlg ( )
EndIf
```

When you use the If command, you must also include an EndIf command to tell WP where the conditional commands stop. If the condition in the If command is true, WP processes all of the commands until the EndIf command is reached. If the condition is false, WP skips to the command immediately following the EndIf command.

You can also use the Else command to tell WP what actions to perform if the condition is false. When the Else command is used, WP processes any commands between the If and Else commands if the condition is true, or any commands between the Else and EndIf commands if the condition is false. For example, in the following If statement, the macro sets different margins if the insertion point is on the first page of the document:

```
If (?Page = 1)
    MarginTop (2.0")
```

11

```
   MarginLeft (1.5")
Else
   MarginTop (1.0")
   MarginLeft (1.0")
EndIf
```

As you use the If command in your macros, keep in mind these tips:

■ You can use several different operators to evaluate the condition, including equal to (=), not equal to (<>), less than (<), greater than (>), less than or equal to (<=), and greater than or equal to (>=).

■ You can evaluate more than one condition in the same If statement using the AND and OR operators. For example, you can use **If ((vMonth = 12) AND (vDay > 15))** to process the commands only if *both* conditions are met (the variable vMonth equals 12 and the variable vDay is greater than 15). The OR operator will process the set of commands if *either* condition is met.

■ You can nest If statements within each other, as shown in this example:

```
If (?Position = vHeadingPos)
   SelectCharNext ( )
   If (?SelectedText <> vFirstLet)
      vFirstLet:=?SelectedText
      Call (InsertLet@)
   Else
      PosLineDown ( )
   EndIf
EndIf
```

■ You can use other commands in the evaluation portion of the If statement, such as in this example:

```
If (DoesFileExist (StrLeft (vPath; StrLen (vPath)-3)
   + "bak") = True)
```

SAMPLE IF/ENDIF MACROS: *For additional examples of macros that use If statements, see the PROJECT CLEANUP.WCM and TABLE TOOLS.WCM macros on the companion CD.*

The Switch Command

Another helpful macro command for making decisions is the Switch command. Like the If command, the Switch command evaluates a condition and then performs a set of actions based on the result. But while the If command checks for a true or false condition, the Switch command looks at the value of a specific variable and then searches through a series of CaseOf statements until it finds one that exactly matches the contents. When a match is found, the commands associated with that CaseOf statement are executed.

For example, in the following macro commands, the contents of the variable vMonth are evaluated:

```
Switch (vMonth)
   CaseOf "June":
      FileOpen ("c:\myfiles\report\semi.wpd")
   CaseOf "December":
      FileOpen ("c:\myfiles\report\annual.wpd")
   Default:
      FileOpen ("c:\myfiles\report\monthly.wpd")
EndSwitch
```

In this example, the macro looks at the contents of the vMonth variable. If vMonth contains "June," then the SEMI.WPD file is opened. If vMonth contains "December," the ANNUAL.WPD file is opened. If the contents of vMonth don't match any of the CaseOf statements, the commands after the Default command are executed and the MONTHLY.WPD file is opened.

The Switch command must always have an EndSwitch command inserted at the end of the CaseOf statements. WP only performs the commands between the matching CaseOf statement and the next CaseOf statement in the list. After those commands have been processed, WP jumps to the first command after the EndSwitch command to continue with the macro.

11

Here are a few tips for using the Switch command:

■ You can insert more than one macro command after each CaseOf statement. Or you can call a subroutine using the methods described in the "Creating Subroutines" section earlier in the chapter.

■ The matching information for a CaseOf statement can consist of text in quotation marks or numbers. Make sure you include a colon after the CaseOf information and before the associated macro commands.

■ You can have the same CaseOf commands performed for more than one matching condition by separating each condition with a semicolon. If the contents of the variable match any of the listed items, the commands after the CaseOf statement are executed. For example, the following CaseOf statement would be executed if the information in the Switch command matched any of the six conditions:

```
CaseOf "January"; "February"; "March"; 1; 2; 3:
```

■ If you want the macro to continue executing the commands in the next CaseOf statement instead of moving to the EndSwitch command, insert the Continue command at the end of the CaseOf statement.

■ You can evaluate regular variables as well as system variables in the Switch statement.

The Switch command is often used to determine what option was selected in a custom dialog box (see the "Creating Dialog Boxes" section later in the chapter for more information). You can also use the Switch command to evaluate what option was selected in a simple menu created with the Menu command. For more information, see the "How to Create Menus" section.

SAMPLE SWITCH/ENDSWITCH MACROS: *For additional examples of macros that use the Switch command, see the ROTATE PAGE NUMBER.WCM and REPLACE ATTRIBUTES.WCM macros on the companion CD.*

How to▸▸▸ Create Menus

When you want a macro to give the user a list of choices and then take a different action depending on their selection, you can use the Menu command. The Menu command displays a simple menu on the screen, such as the one shown here:

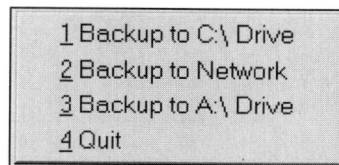

```
1 Backup to C:\ Drive
2 Backup to Network
3 Backup to A:\ Drive
4 Quit
```

The menu options can be numbered (1–9) or lettered (A–Z). You can also have the menu centered in the screen or placed at another location. The following Menu command creates the menu just shown:

```
Menu (vChoice; Digit!; ; ;{"Backup to C:\ Drive";
"Backup to Network";"Backup to A:\ Drive"; "Quit"})
```

The first parameter of the Menu command (vChoice in this example) is the name of the variable that contains the result of the selected option. For example, if the user selects the second option, the vChoice variable contains the value 2.

The second parameter indicates whether the menu should use numbers (Digit!) or letters (Letter!). If you use the letter option for the menu, the selection is still returned as a number to the variable. For example, if option "C" is chosen from the menu, the variable contains the value 3.

The third and fourth parameters indicate the horizontal and vertical position of the menu. If these options are left blank, as they are in this example, the menu is automatically centered in the screen. If you want to specify the position for the menu, type the number of pixels from the left side of the window where you want the menu to start for the third parameter, and the number of pixels from the top of the window for the fourth parameter. For example, this command would display the menu in the top-left corner of the screen:

11

How to... Create Menus
(*continued*)

```
Menu (vChoice; Letter!; 1; 1;{"Option 1"; "Option 2";"Option 3"})
```

The last parameter of the Menu command lists the text that you want to display for each item on the menu. The items need to be enclosed in curly brackets and separated with semicolons. Also, you need to enclose each item in quotation marks unless it is a variable name.

After you've displayed a menu in a macro, you can evaluate the variable that contains the selected option with the Switch command.

Creating Loops

When you need to repeat the same commands in a macro several times in a row, you can use a loop. Like subroutines, *loops* make your macros shorter and more efficient by allowing you to repeat commands without having to retype them each time. Unlike a subroutine, however, the commands in a loop are repeated in succession, rather than being called at any time during the macro. You can create several different types of loops in your macros, including For, While, and Repeat loops.

For–EndFor Loops

A For loop repeats a set of commands a specific number of times. When you create a For loop, you must also include an EndFor command. Any macro commands between the For and EndFor command are executed until the loop has completed. Each loop uses a "control" variable to keep track of how many times the loop has been executed. You specify the starting and ending value of the control variable, as well as how it is incremented each time.

NOTE: *You can end a loop before it has been executed the specified number of times. For more information, see the Power Tip "Breaking Out of a Loop" later in the chapter.*

WP has three different commands you can use to create For loops: For, ForNext, and ForEach. In the following sections, we'll explain how to use each one.

The For Command

The For command uses an evaluation expression to determine when the loop should end. As long as the evaluation expression is true, the loop continues to execute. Each time through the loop, the control variable is incremented according to the expression given in the command. The syntax for the For command is

For (ControlVar; InitialValue; TerminateExpression; IncrementExpression)

For example, this loop types the numbers 1–10 on separate lines in a document:

```
For (vNum; 1; vNum <=10; vNum+1)
    Type (vNum + ".")
    HardReturn ( )
EndFor
```

In this example the first time through the loop, the control variable vNum is set to the initial value of 1. The commands inside the loop insert the current value of vNum (1), followed by a period and a hard return. Then the EndFor command marks the end of the loop, so the macro returns to the For command and the value of vNum is increased by one (from the "vNum+1" expression). If the value of vNum is less than or equal to ten (from the "vNum <= 10" expression), the commands in the For loop are executed again. Since vNum now equals 2, the number "2." is inserted into the document. This process is repeated until the value of vNum is greater than 10. When that happens, the macro continues with the commands following the EndFor command.

The ForNext Command

The ForNext command is very similar to the For command, but the ForNext command doesn't use evaluation expressions. Instead, you specify a control variable, a starting value, an ending value, and an increment value. Each time through the loop, the control variable is increased according to the increment value.

The commands in the loop are executed until the control variable is greater than the given ending value. The syntax of the ForNext command is

ForNext (ControlVar; InitialValue; FinalValue; IncrementValue)

For example, this loop uses the ForNext command to insert the numbers 1–10 in a document on separate lines:

```
ForNext (vNum; 1; 10; 1)
   Type (vNum + ".")
   HardReturn ( )
EndFor
```

Each time through the loop, the value of vNum is increased by one (the increment value). As long as the value of vNum is not greater than ten (the final value), the commands in the loop are executed.

NOTE: *The increment value is an optional parameter and defaults to 1 if you don't include it. For example, you could use the command **ForNext (vNum; 1; 10)** in the preceding example and get the same results.*

TIP: *You can use a negative number for the increment value parameter if you want the value of the control variable to decrease each time through the loop. When you do this, the loop executes until the control variable is less than the final value. For example, if you used this ForNext statement in the preceding example, the numbers would be inserted in the document in descending order (10–1): **ForNext (vNum; 10; 1; -1)**.*

SAMPLE FORNEXT/ENDFOR MACROS: *For additional examples of macros that use the ForNext command, see the NUMBER TABLE ROWS.WCM and REPLACE STYLES.WCM macros on the companion CD.*

The ForEach Command

The ForEach command repeats a set of commands for a group of values. With the ForEach command, the control variable changes to a different value each time through the loop, rather than simply incrementing numerically. The syntax of the ForEach command is

ForEach (ControlVar; {Value1; Value2; etc.})

You can use as many different values as you want. The values should be enclosed in curly brackets and separated with semicolons. If the values are text and not variable names, enclose them in quotation marks. Each time through the loop, the next value in the value list is assigned to the control variable. For example, this ForEach loop inserts the weekday abbreviations in a document, inserting a tab after each one:

```
ForEach (vWeekday; {"Sun"; "Mon"; "Tue"; "Wed"; "Thu"; "Fri";
   "Sat"})
   Type (vWeekday)
   Tab ( )
EndFor
```

The first time through the loop, the variable vWeekday is assigned the value "Sun," which is inserted into the document followed by a tab. Then the loop repeats and the vWeekday variable is assigned the next value in the list ("Mon"). The loop repeats until each item in the value list has been assigned to the control variable.

TIP: *ForEach loops are commonly used to assign values to array variables. For more information, see Chapter 10.*

SAMPLE FOREACH/ENDFOR MACRO: *For another example of a macro that uses the ForEach command, see the BILLING.WCM macro on the companion CD.*

While–EndWhile Loops

If you don't know exactly how many times you want a loop to repeat, you can use a While loop. A While loop executes a set of commands as many times as needed until the specified condition is true. For example, you can have the commands in a

While loop repeat until the insertion point is on a certain page or until a variable contains a specific value.

As with other loops, you must end a While loop with the EndWhile command. When a macro encounters a While command, it evaluates the expression in parentheses. If the condition is true, the commands between the While and EndWhile commands are executed. When the EndWhile command is reached, the macro returns to the While command and evaluates the condition again. This process continues until the condition is false. At that time, the macro moves to the command immediately following the EndWhile command and continues with the rest of the macro.

For example, this While loop moves the insertion point one character to the right until the character is an asterisk:

```
While (?RightChar <> "*")
    PosCharNext ( )
EndWhile
```

In this example, the macro first evaluates the character to the right of the insertion point using the ?RightChar system variable. If it is *not* equal to an asterisk, the command inside the loop is executed, which moves the insertion point one character to the right. Then the macro jumps back to the While command and checks the right character again. If it is still not equal to an asterisk, the command repeats. As soon as the character to the right is an asterisk, the macro moves to the commands following the EndWhile command.

NOTE: *If the evaluation expression is not true the first time the macro encounters the While command, the commands inside the loop will not be executed at all.*

SAMPLE WHILE/ENDWHILE MACROS: *For additional examples of macros that use the While command, see the DELETE HYPER-LINK.WCM and INDEX DIVIDER.WCM macros on the companion CD.*

Repeat–Until Loops

A final type of loop you can create in a macro is a Repeat loop. A Repeat loop is very similar to a While loop in that it repeats until a specified condition is true. However, unlike a While loop, the commands in a Repeat loop are always executed at least once, since the evaluation expression is checked at the *end* of the loop instead of at the beginning.

The Repeat command must be paired with the Until command. WP executes any commands between the Repeat and Until commands until the specified condition is true. For example, this Repeat loop centers the first line of text on each page until the last page is reached:

```
Repeat
    vCurPage:=?Page
    PosPageTop ( )
    PosLineBegin ( )
    Center ( )
    PosPageNext ( )
Until (?Page = vCurPage)
```

The first time through the loop, WP processes the commands normally since the evaluation condition hasn't been encountered yet. The macro assigns the current page number to the variable vCurPage, centers the first line at the top of the page, and then moves to the next page. The Until command evaluates the current page number to see if it equals the value in the vCurPage variable. If it does, that indicates the insertion point is on the last page of the document (since the PosPageNext command would keep the insertion point on the same page) and the macro quits. Otherwise, the macro returns to the Repeat command to repeat the steps.

TIP: *If you want to create a continuous loop that stops only when an OnNotFound or OnError condition is met, you can use **Until (False)** as the evaluation expression. For an example, see the TEMPLATE DATE.WCM macro on the companion CD.*

11

Power Tip··· Breaking Out of a Loop

Sometimes you might want to break out of a loop early before it has repeated the specified number of times or before the evaluation expression is true. For example, you might not want a For loop to repeat ten times if the insertion point gets moved to a new page.

To break out of a loop, first use an If statement to check the condition that determines whether or not the loop should end, such as the current page number. Within the If statement, you can then use either the Break or Go command to break out of the loop. If you use the Go command, you need to specify a label name that you want the macro to move to and start executing the commands at that point. If you use the Break command, the macro ends the loop and moves to the command immediately following the end of the loop, such as the EndFor, EndWhile, or Until command. For example, this loop will end if the insertion point moves to a new page before the character to the right of the insertion point equals an asterisk:

```
vCurPage:=?Page
While (?RightChar <> "*")
    PosCharNext ( )
    If (?Page <> vCurPage)
        Break
    EndIf
EndWhile
```

Creating Dialog Boxes

When you need to interact with the user during a macro, you could use commands such as GetString, MessageBox, and Menu. But these commands are limited to getting only one piece of information at a time. If you need to get several pieces of information, you can create a custom dialog box.

WordPerfect 8 has macro commands to create dialog boxes in practically any size, shape, or form. You can determine the size and position of the dialog box, and add any combination of controls, such as radio buttons, checkboxes, and list boxes. In addition, you can create powerful dialog boxes that update automatically as the user makes selections in the dialog box.

Creating a dialog box involves three basic steps: defining the dialog, adding the controls you want, and then displaying the dialog box. You can define a dialog box and add controls with either macro commands or the PerfectScript Dialog Editor.

Defining the Dialog Box

The first step in creating a custom dialog box is to define the dialog box. When you define a dialog box, you give it a name, set its size and position, and indicate other options, such as the title bar text and whether OK and Cancel buttons should be used.

A dialog box is defined with the DialogDefine macro command. The DialogDefine command uses this syntax:

DialogDefine (DialogName; LeftPos; TopPos; Width; Height; Style; Title)

A dialog definition statement might look like this:

```
DialogDefine ("Dlg1"; 50; 50; 215; 145; OK!|Cancel!|Percent!;
    "Replace Attributes ")
```

The DialogName parameter is a unique name or number that identifies the dialog box within the macro. If you use text for the name, make sure you enclose it in quotation marks. The dialog name is used by the macro commands that add dialog box controls and display the dialog box.

The LeftPos and TopPos parameters tell WP where to place the dialog box on the screen. These numbers are given in dialog units, which are a special unit of measurement that takes into account the screen resolution and the default font used in the dialog box, so the dialog box looks about the same on any screen resolution.

You can enter either a specific number of dialog units to place the dialog box from the left and top of the screen, or you can type a number that WP interprets as a percentage. For example, to center the dialog box in the middle of the screen, type **50** for both the LeftPos and TopPos parameters, and then use the Percent! style (as explained later).

The Width and Height parameters are also numbers given in dialog units that define the width and height of the dialog box. Generally, you should try to avoid creating dialog boxes larger than about 400 dialog units wide and high.

The Style parameter indicates settings for the dialog box, such as what default buttons you want in the dialog box. The options include:

- *OK!*   Adds an OK button.

- *Cancel!*   Adds a Cancel button.

- *Percent!*   Interprets the TopPos and LeftPos parameters as percentages of the screen width and height.

- *Sizeable!*   Allows the dialog box to be sized by the user.

- *NoTitle!*   Removes the title bar from the dialog box.

- *Modeless!*   Allows the user to click outside the dialog box and work in the document screen while the dialog box is still displaying. If you use this option, make sure you include the InhibitInput (Off!) and Display (On!) commands in your macro.

- *Enter2HRtn!*   Allows the user to press ENTER in a multiple-line edit box to insert a hard return.

If you want to use more than one of the style settings, separate them with a pipe symbol (|). For example, a common style combination is to use OK! | Cancel! | Percent!, which adds OK and Cancel buttons and centers the dialog box (if 50 was used for both the LeftPos and TopPos parameters).

Finally, the Title parameter is the text you want to appear in the title bar of the dialog box. If the text isn't a variable, make sure you include it in quotation marks.

TIP: *If you want to change the default font used in a dialog box, you can use the DialogSetProperties command. Insert this command just following the DialogDefine command in the macro. The syntax for this command is DialogSetProperties (DialogName; FontName; FontSize). For example, you can use the command **DialogSetProperties ("Dlg1"; "MS Sans Serif"; 8p)** to format the dialog named "Dlg1" with an 8-point MS Sans Serif font.*

NOTE: *Dialog boxes can also be created with the visual PerfectScript Dialog Editor instead of with specific dialog macro commands. For more information, see the "How to Use the Dialog Editor" section later in the chapter.*

Adding Controls

Once you've defined a dialog box, you can add the controls that you want to it. WP allows you to add 21 different types of controls to your dialog boxes, including radio buttons, checkboxes, icons, and scroll bars. Figures 11-1 and 11-2 show samples of each of the available controls.

Each type of control is added with its own macro command that begins with "DialogAdd," such as DialogAddRadioButton or DialogAddCounter. The command tells WP the position and size of the control within the dialog box, as well as other settings specific to that type of control, such as the options for an edit box or the formatting for static text.

NOTE: *You can also add controls to a dialog box with the visual Dialog Editor. See the "How to Use the Dialog Editor" section later in this chapter for more information.*

A sample DialogAdd command might look like this:

```
DialogAddCheckBox ("Dlg1"; "ChkBx1"; 10; 30; 75; 12;
   "Include Header"; vHeader)
```

Each DialogAdd command has a different number of parameters, depending on what options be set for it. However, the first six parameters for each DialogAdd command are the same: DialogName, ControlName, LeftPos, TopPos, Width, and Height.

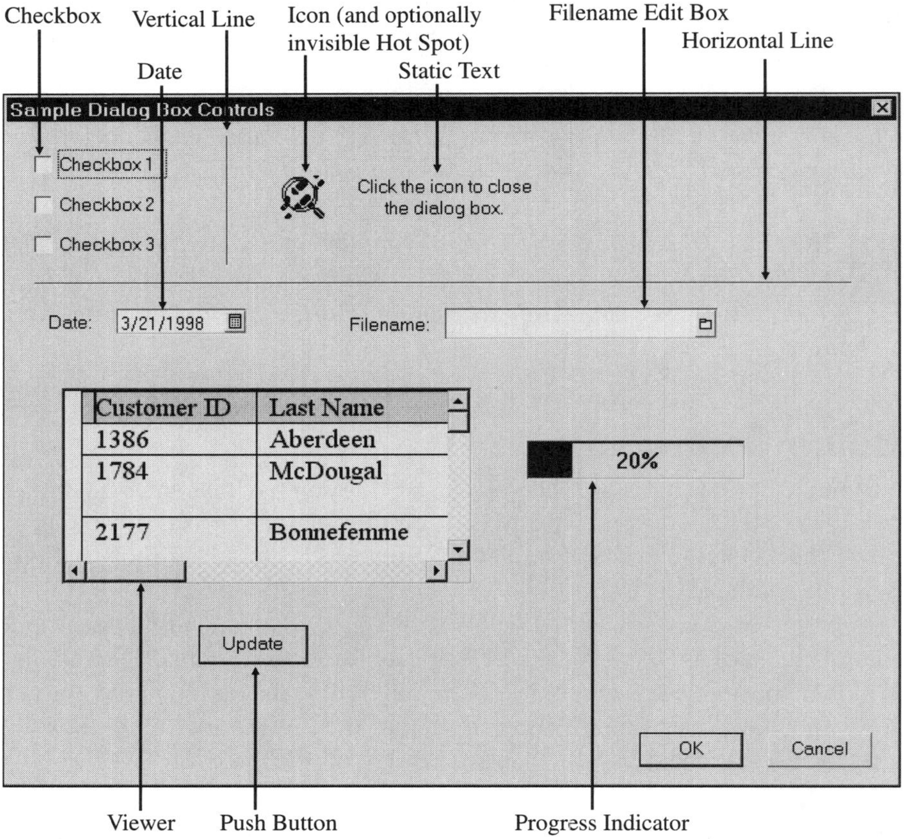

FIGURE 11-1 Some of the available controls you can add to a custom dialog box

- *DialogName* The name of the dialog box that you want to add the control to. This is the same name or number used in the DialogDefine command.

- *ControlName* A name or number that identifies the control. Each control must have its own unique name, such as "Text1" or 1020. If you want to have your dialog box updated automatically as options are selected, you might find it easier to use descriptive names instead of numbers (see the "Using Callbacks" section later in the chapter for more information on updating dialog boxes).

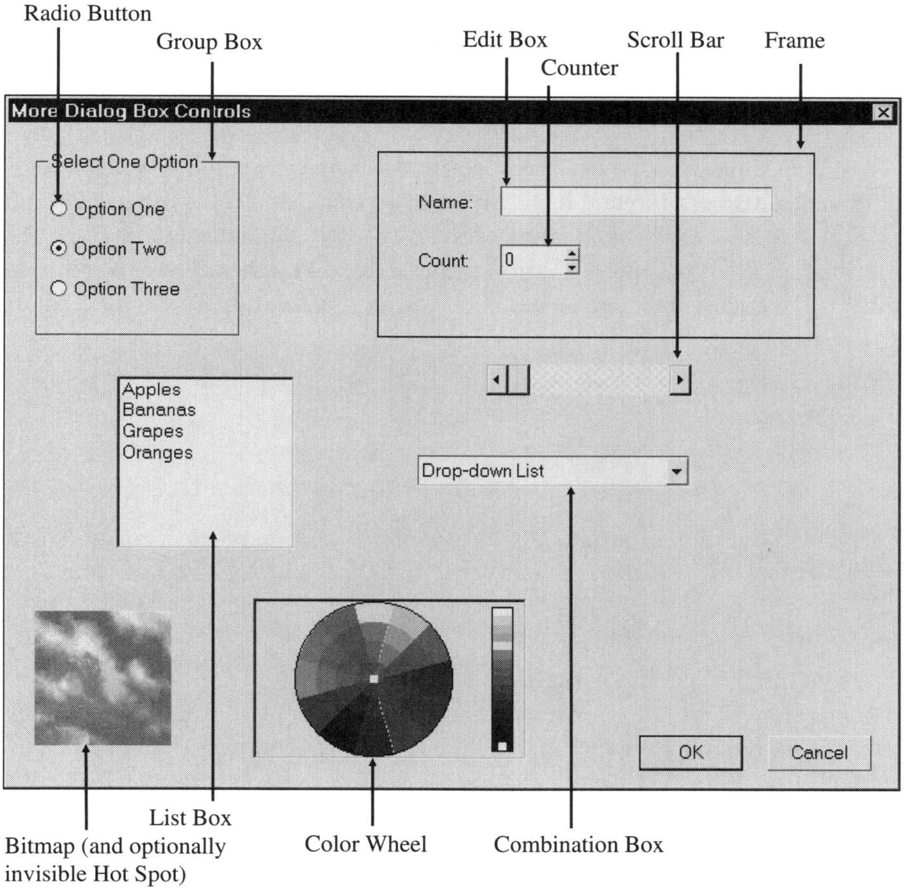

Radio Button

Group Box

Edit Box

Counter

Scroll Bar

Frame

FIGURE 11-2 Additional dialog box controls for custom dialogs

■ *LeftPos*   The number of dialog units from the left side of the dialog box to the left side of the control.

■ *TopPos*   The number of dialog units from the top of the dialog box to the top of the control.

■ *Width*   The width of the control in dialog units.

■ *Height*   The height of the control in dialog units.

NOTE: *The DialogAddHLine and DialogAddVLine macro commands use a Length parameter in place of the Width and Height parameters. The Length parameter contains the length of the horizontal or vertical line in dialog units.*

Any additional parameters are specific to each command. For example, the DialogAddEditBox command has a Style parameter, which sets the formatting for the edit box; a MacroVar parameter, which is the variable name containing the text typed in the edit box; and a LimitText parameter, which defines the maximum number of characters that can be entered. The DialogAddEditBox command might look like this:

```
DialogAddEditBox ("Dlg1"; "Edit1"; 20; 40; 75; 14; Left!;
    vText; 50)
```

NOTE: *Some parameters are optional and don't have to be included, such as the LimitText parameter in the DialogAddEditBox command .*

To find out the specific parameters for each DialogAdd command, you can use the Macro Help files. The easiest way to do this is with the PerfectScript Command Inserter. With the macro open in a document window, choose Commands from the Macro toolbar. From the Command Type drop-down list, select PerfectScript. Then, in the Commands list box, select the command you want to insert, such as DialogAddText. The Parameters list box displays a list of the parameters (see Figure 11-3). For more information about the command or parameters, right-click the command name to open the help file for that command. (For more information on using the Command Inserter, see Chapter 10.)

In the following sections, we'll give you some tips, tricks, and traps for some of the dialog controls. We can't cover all of the available controls, so be sure to use the Macro Help files for more information.

Checkboxes and Radio Buttons

If you want to have a checkbox or radio button already selected when the dialog box is first displayed, assign the variable used in the DialogAddCheckBox or DialogAddRadioButton command to the value of 1 before displaying the dialog box.

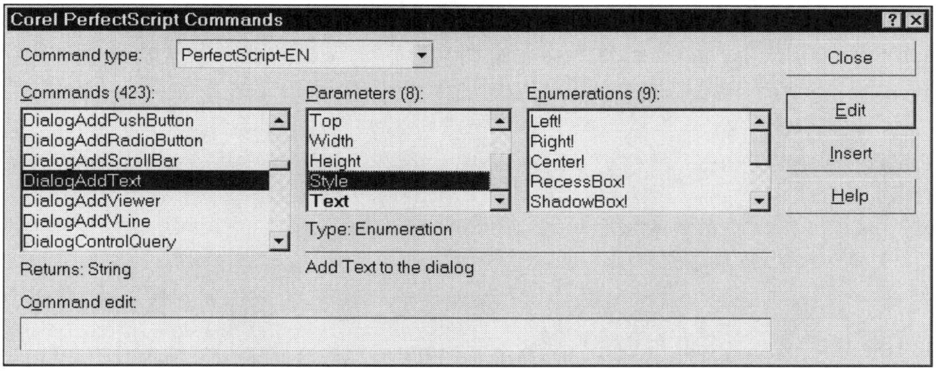

FIGURE 11-3 The Command Inserter displays a list of parameters for the DialogAdd commands. Right-click the command name to open the help file

After the dialog box has been closed, you can use an If statement to determine whether a checkbox or radio button was selected. The variable contains a 1 if it was selected; otherwise it contains a 0.

For example, this portion of a macro displays a dialog box with the checkbox already selected:

```
vHeader:=1
DialogDefine ("Dlg1"; 50; 50; 215; 154; OK!|Cancel!|Percent!;
    "Create Form")
DialogAddCheckBox ("Dlg1"; "ChkBx1"; 10; 30; 75; 12;
    "Include Header"; vHeader)
```

When you add radio buttons to a dialog box, only one radio button can be selected at a time. If you want to have multiple "sets" of radio buttons, add a group box around each set of buttons. Then the user can select one radio button in each group box.

Combination Boxes and List Boxes

You can add items to a combination box or list box with the DialogAddListItem command. This command has three parameters: the dialog box name, the control name of the combination box or list box that you want to add the items to, and the item or list of items that you want to add. If you include more than one item, separate each item with a semicolon and enclose them in curly brackets. For example, these commands add three items to a list box:

```
DialogAddListBox ("Dlg1"; "List1"; 10; 45; 70; 50; Sorted!;
    vFruit)
DialogAddListItem ("Dlg1"; "List1"; {"Apples"; "Oranges";
    "Bananas"})
```

If the items you want to add to the combination or list box are stored in an array variable, you can use a ForNext loop as you're defining the dialog box to add the items. For example, these commands add the values stored in the array variable vMonth to the list box (the vMonth array values must be previously assigned in the macro):

```
DialogAddListBox ("Dlg1"; "List1"; 30; 20; 75; 75;
    Sorted!|NameSearch!; vChoice)
ForNext (X; 1; vMonth[0]; 1)
    DialogAddListItem ("Dlg1"; "List1"; vMonth[X])
EndFor
```

NOTE: *The 0 element of an array contains the total number of items in the array. You can use this value as the final value parameter in a ForNext loop, as shown in the preceding example.*

The combination and list box controls each have several style options available, including having the list items automatically sorted alphabetically and being able to select more than one item in the list.

Dates

When you add a date control to a dialog box, you can set the initial date that's displayed when the dialog box first appears in one of two ways. First, you can assign a specific date to the variable name used in the DialogAddDate command (do this before you display the dialog box). Second, you can use the Year, Month, and Day parameters of the DialogAddDate command to set an initial date. For example, this command adds a date control with the current date automatically displayed:

```
DialogAddDate ("Dlg1"; "Date"; 30; 40; 50; 14; Validate!;
    vDate; ?DateYear;?DateMonth; ?DateDay)
```

In this example, system variables are used to display the current date. If the date is changed by the user, the new date will be stored in the variable vDate when the dialog box is closed.

NOTE: *If you assign an initial value to the date variable and also use the DialogAddDate parameters to set the date, the dialog box will use the value assigned to the variable.*

Edit Boxes

An edit box can be sized so that it accepts one line of text or multiple lines. If you want to use a multiple-line box, use the Multiline! style option. You can add scroll bars to the edit box with the VScroll! and HScroll! style options. In addition, if you want the user to be able to insert a hard return in the edit box, you can either use the WantReturn! style with the DialogAddEditBox command, or include the Enter2HRtn! style with the DialogDefine command.

For example, this command creates a large edit box with a vertical scroll bar that allows hard returns:

```
DialogAddEditBox ("Dlg1"; "Edit2"; 10; 50; 170; 50;
    Left!|Multiline!|WantReturn!|VScroll!; vText; 1000)
```

Some of the other useful style options for the DialogAddEditBox command include:

- *WPChars!* Allows you to insert WP characters by pressing CTRL-W.

- *WordWrap!* Allows the text to automatically wrap to fit the width of the edit box. (Use with the WPChars! style.)

- *Uppercase!* and *Lowercase!* Automatically converts the text typed in the edit box to all uppercase or all lowercase letters.

- *Password!*   Displays text with asterisk characters (*) as it is typed into the edit box. The actual text typed is stored in the macro variable.

- *Attributes!*   Allows you to press CTRL-U to underline text and CTRL-I to italicize text as it's typed into the edit box. (Must be used with the WPChars! style.)

Push Buttons

Push buttons are commonly used to close a dialog box. You can add OK and Cancel buttons to a dialog box with the DialogDefine command (see the "Defining the Dialog Box" section earlier in the chapter). You can also add custom push buttons to a dialog box that contain any text you want. If you want a custom push button to close the dialog box when it's clicked, use the DefaultBttn! style, as shown in this example:

```
DialogAddPushButton ("Dlg1"; "FinishBtn"; 125; 80; 30; 18;
    DefaultBttn!; "Finish")
```

This command creates a button with the text "Finish" on it. If this button is clicked, the dialog box closes. If you want a push button to update information within the dialog box when it's clicked, you can set up a callback routine (see the "Using Callbacks" section later in the chapter for more information).

Static Text

Static text is commonly added to dialog boxes to provide instructions, as well as to label other controls such as edit and filename boxes. When you use the DialogAddText command to label an edit box or other control, you can include an ampersand (&) before a letter to make it a mnemonic. Then the user can access the related control by pressing ALT and the mnemonic letter.

For example, these commands create the text and edit box shown in the illustration:

```
DialogAddText ("Dlg1"; "Text2"; 10; 20; 25; 14; Left!; "&Name:")
DialogAddEditBox ("Dlg1"; "NameBox"; 35; 18; 75; 14; Left!; vName)
```

In this example, pressing ALT-N would place the insertion point in the edit box.

NOTE: *When a mnemonic for static text is pressed with the ALT key, the control added immediately after the DialogAddText command in the macro is given the focus in the dialog box.*

If you want to be able to include an ampersand in static text *without* having it create a mnemonic letter, use the NoPrefix! or WPChars! style in the DialogAddText command.

Hot Spots and Icons

Push buttons are the most common way to close a dialog box, but you can also use a "hot spot." A *hot spot* is an invisible area in the dialog box that closes the dialog box when it's clicked. Hot spots are often used in conjunction with icons or bitmaps in the dialog box, so that clicking the icon activates the hot spot and closes the dialog box.

You can add a bitmap (BMP) file to a dialog box with the DialogAddBitmap command. For example, this command adds the CLOUDS.BMP file included with Windows 95:

```
DialogAddBitmap ("Dlg1"; "Bitmap1"; 10; 10; 50; 50;
    SizeBmptoCtl!; "c:\windows\clouds.bmp")
```

Unlike bitmaps, icons are usually stored within DLL files. If you want to add an icon to a dialog box, you need to know the name or number of the icon in the DLL file. Then you can use the DialogAddIcon command to add the icon to the dialog box. For example, the magnifying glass icon shown in Figure 11-1 is icon number 4098 in the PFICON80.DLL file.

ICON VALUES.WPD: *The companion CD contains a document named ICON VALUES.WPD with the icon numbers and descriptions from the PFICON80.DLL and PFIT80EN.DLL files. Open this document to see a list of available icons and their corresponding numbers.*

NOTE: *In order to determine the icon name or number in a DLL file, you must have a DLL Editor that shows the icons and their respective numbers, such as the Resource Workshop utility included in many C-language packages.*

The parameters for the DialogAddIcon command indicate the name or number of the icon, as well as the "handle" of the DLL file the icon is located in. The icon number must be listed in quotation marks with the # sign just before it. By default, the DialogAddIcon command looks for icons in the PFIT80EN.DLL file. If you want to use an icon from this file, you can use 0 as the dialog handle, as shown in this example:

```
DialogAddIcon ("Dlg1"; "Icon1"; 25; 25; 10; 15; "#582"; 0)
DialogAddHotSpot ("Dlg1"; "HotSpot1"; 25; 25; 10; 15; Click!)
```

These commands add a desert-scene icon to the dialog box along with a hot spot in the same place so that when the icon is clicked, the dialog box closes.

TIP: *You can also use the DblClick! style for the DialogAddHotSpot command so the hot spot must be double-clicked before the dialog box is closed.*

If you want to use an icon from a different DLL file, such as the PFICON80.DLL file, you need to assign the handle of that DLL file to a variable; then use that variable as the last parameter of the DialogAddIcon command. For example, these commands use the magnifying glass icon from the PFICON80.DLL file:

```
vHandle:=DLLLoad ("PFICON80.DLL")
DialogAddIcon ("Dlg1"; "Icon2"; 25; 25; 10; 15; "#4098"; vHandle)
```

TIP: *If you want a different action performed when a hot spot is clicked rather than having the dialog box closed, you can use a callback routine. For more information, see the "Using Callbacks" section later in this chapter.*

How to... Use the Dialog Editor

Creating a dialog box with macro commands can be a time-consuming process to get everything sized and positioned just the way you want. Another option for creating dialog boxes is to the use the visual PerfectScript Dialog Editor. This utility lets you add controls to a dialog box and then size and place them with your mouse.

Dialog boxes created with the Dialog Editor are saved as part of the macro file, but no macro commands are actually inserted into the macro. After creating and saving the dialog box, you can insert the DialogShow command in the macro where you want the dialog box to display.

To use the Dialog Editor, follow these steps:

1. Edit the macro you want to create the dialog box in or start a new macro by going to a blank document window and choosing Tools | Macro | Macro Toolbar.

2. If you're creating a new macro, you first need to save the macro before you can create a dialog box. Choose Save & Compile on the Macro toolbar, type a name for your macro, and choose Save.

3. Choose Dialog Editor on the Macro toolbar. From the Corel PerfectScript Dialogs dialog box, choose File | New. Type a name for your dialog box to replace the "NewDialog" text and press ENTER.

4. Choose File | Open to display a blank dialog box and the Corel PerfectScript Dialog Editor toolbar:

11

How to... Use the Dialog Editor
(*continued*)

5. Now you can add the controls and settings you want for the dialog box. To change the size of the dialog box, simply click and drag the dialog box border. To change the dialog box title or overall dialog box properties, right-click the dialog box and choose Properties; then make the changes you want.

6. To add a control to the dialog box, use the buttons on the Dialog Editor toolbar. The first row of buttons includes options for saving the dialog box, displaying gridlines, and changing the order of the controls. The second row of buttons includes all of the controls that you can add to a dialog box, such as radio buttons, edit boxes, or static text. The third row of buttons contains options for aligning and spacing the controls that you've added. (Move the mouse pointer over a button to see a description.)

How to... Use the Dialog Editor (continued)

7. When you want to add a control, click the button for that control on the Dialog Editor toolbar, or choose Control and select the control you want. Then click the insertion point in the dialog box to insert the control. Once the control has been inserted, you can use the sizing handles to size it, or you can click and drag it to a new location in the dialog box. To change the text or style options for a control, right-click the control and choose Properties; then make the changes you want. You can also change the control name and macro variable used for that control.

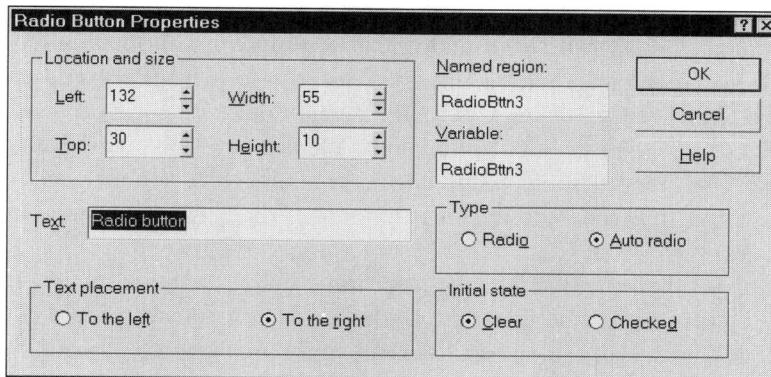

8. You can align controls, such as a group of radio buttons, by clicking and dragging around the controls to select them, and then using the buttons on the third row of the Dialog Editor toolbar to align or space them as you want.

9. When you're finished with your dialog box, choose the Save button on the Dialog Editor toolbar or choose File | Save. Then click the Close button or choose File | Close. Choose File | Close from the Corel PerfectScript Dialogs dialog box to return to the macro.

To use the dialog box in your macro, insert the DialogShow command as described in the "Displaying the Dialog Box" section next. If you need to later edit the dialog box, choose Dialog Editor on the Macro toolbar again, select the dialog box, and choose File | Open.

Displaying the Dialog Box

Once you've defined a dialog box and added the controls you want, you need to tell the macro to display that dialog box. This is done with the DialogShow command. The syntax for the DialogShow command is

DialogShow (DialogName; Parent; Callback Label; Focus)

The DialogName parameter is the name of the dialog box that you want to display. This is the same name that you used in either the DialogDefine command or when naming the dialog with the Dialog Editor. Make sure you include the name in quotation marks unless it is a variable or number.

The Parent and Callback Label parameters are optional and are only needed if you're using a callback with your dialog box so it updates automatically while it's displayed. For more information on using these two parameters and creating a callback routine, see the "Using Callbacks" section next.

The Focus parameter is also optional and identifies which control in the dialog box should contain the initial focus when the dialog box is first displayed. The control name or number from the corresponding DialogAdd command is used to identify the control.

To display a dialog box, place the insertion point in the macro where you want the dialog box to appear and insert the DialogShow command. If you don't need to use a callback with your dialog box, you can simply include the name of the dialog box you want to display, as shown in this example:

```
DialogShow ("Dlg1")
```

When a dialog box is displayed during a macro, the macro pauses until the user closes the dialog box. After the dialog box has been closed, any variables that are associated with the various controls, such as checkboxes and edit boxes, contain the value that was inserted in the dialog box. In addition, a special variable called MacroDialogResult contains the name of the button that was used to close the dialog box.

NOTE: *If you're using a callback with your dialog box, the macro doesn't pause while the dialog box is displayed and the associated variables aren't returned with the inserted values. For more information, see the "Using Callbacks" section next.*

If the user chooses the "OK" button to close the dialog box, the MacroDialogResult variable contains the value of 1. If the user chooses "Cancel," the value of MacroDialogResult is 2. Otherwise, the MacroDialogResult variable contains the control name for the push button or hot spot that closed the dialog box. For example, if you added a default push button to the dialog box with this command:

```
DialogAddPushButton ("Dlg1"; "FinishBtn"; 125; 80; 30; 18;
    DefaultBttn!; "Finish")
```

the MacroDialogResult variable would contain the value "FinishBtn" if that button was chosen to close the dialog box.

After you've displayed the dialog box in the macro, you can remove it from memory by using the DialogDestroy command. This command includes the dialog name that was displayed, as shown in this example:

```
DialogDestroy ("Dlg1")
```

When you remove a dialog box from memory, the MacroDialogResult variable is erased, but any other macro variables still contain the values inserted in the dialog box. You can't display the dialog box again in the macro unless the DialogDefine command is processed a second time.

NOTE: *If you created the dialog box with the Dialog Editor and aren't using a callback, it is automatically removed from memory when the dialog is closed.*

Using Callbacks

Normally, a macro pauses while a dialog box is displayed onscreen. However, you can have the macro continue to execute in the background while the dialog box is displaying by using a callback routine. This allows the macro to "watch" what the user does in the dialog box and react accordingly, without having to close and redisplay the dialog box. For example, if the user selects a certain option in the dialog box, you can have the dialog box automatically add information to a list box or hide an existing control.

Creating a callback involves two parts: defining the callback with the DialogShow command and adding the callback commands in a label or procedure.

Defining the Callback

When you want to use a callback, you need to define it as part of the DialogShow command so WordPerfect knows to treat the dialog box a little differently. This involves specifying the second and third parameters of the DialogShow command. As mentioned earlier in the "Displaying the Dialog Box" section, the syntax for the Dialog Show command is

DialogShow (DialogName; Parent; Callback Label; Focus)

The Parent parameter is the name of the parent window that the dialog box displays in, which is always "WordPerfect" for a WP macro. The Callback Label parameter is the name of a label or procedure that contains the instructions for the macro while the dialog box is displaying. Immediately following the DialogShow command, you need to include the CallbackWait command, which tells the macro to wait until the callback routine has finished and the dialog box has been closed before processing any other commands.

For example, these commands would display a dialog box that uses a callback:

```
DialogShow ("Dlg1"; "WordPerfect"; Update)
CallbackWait
```

In this example, the name of the callback label is "Update." While the dialog box is displayed, certain actions trigger a callback in the macro. For example, if the user clicks a push button or selects a checkbox, the macro jumps to the callback label (Update in this example) and processes any commands there. When the end of the subroutine is reached, the macro continues waiting and watching the dialog box for another trigger action, unless it encountered a command that ended the callback routine and closed the dialog box.

Adding the Callback Commands

When a callback is triggered in a dialog box, the macro moves to the callback label or procedure specified in the DialogShow command. Here, you can check to see which option was selected in the dialog box and take the appropriate action. For example, if a specific button was clicked, you can update the information displayed in a list box.

When you define a callback, the macro creates an array variable with the same name as the callback label. For example, if you use the command DialogShow

("Dlg1"; "WordPerfect"; Update), WP creates an array variable named Update. The third element of this array contains the name of the control that was selected in the dialog box and that triggered the callback.

NOTE: *The fifth element of this array contains a Windows message ID number, which equals 274 if the user pressed ALT-F4 or clicked the Cancel button in the upper-right corner to close the dialog box. This element can be checked to cancel the macro if needed.*

In the callback subroutine, you can use the If and Switch commands to evaluate the contents of the array variable to determine which option was selected in the dialog box. Then you can instruct the macro to perform specific actions. For example, in this simple callback example, WP displays a message box telling you which option you selected in the dialog box:

```
DialogDefine ("Dlg1"; 50; 50; 150; 125; OK!|Cancel!|Percent!;
   "Sample Callback")
DialogAddRadioButton ("Dlg1"; "Radio1"; 10; 10; 50; 12;
   "Radio Button"; vRadio)
DialogAddCheckBox ("Dlg1"; "Check1"; 10; 30; 50; 12;
   "Checkbox"; vCheck)
DialogShow ("Dlg1"; "WordPerfect"; Update)
CallbackWait
DialogDestroy ("Dlg1")
Quit

Label (Update)
If (Update[5] = 274)
   DialogDestroy ("Dlg1")
   Quit
EndIf
Switch (Update[3])
   CaseOf "OKBttn"; "CancelBttn":
      CallbackResume
   CaseOf "Radio1":
      MessageBox (X; "Result"; "You selected a radio button.")
   CaseOf "Check1":
      MessageBox (X; "Result"; "You selected a checkbox.")
EndSwitch
```

In this example, a dialog box is defined with a radio button, a checkbox, and OK and Cancel buttons. The DialogShow command defines the callback subroutine as "Update." Then the CallbackWait command is used to keep the macro from executing the remaining commands until you want the dialog box closed.

As soon as the user selects any option in the dialog box, the callback is triggered and WP moves to the Label (Update) subroutine. Here, the first If statement checks the fifth element of the Update array variable. If it equals 274, indicating that the user pressed ALT-F4 or clicked the Cancel button in the upper-right hand corner, the macro removes the dialog box from memory and quits.

The next statement in the callback subroutine is a Switch command. This command evaluates the contents of the third element of the Update array. This element contains the name of the control in the dialog box that triggered the callback. If the OK button is pressed, the name assigned to this array element is "OKBttn." If the Cancel button is pressed, the name is "CancelBttn." For any other controls in the dialog box, the control name is assigned (from the second parameter of the DialogAdd command), such as "Check1" or "Radio1."

Each CaseOf statement in the Switch command evaluates the contents of the array and tells the macro what action to take when it matches. In this example, if the user selects the checkbox or radio button, a message box is displayed. If the user chooses the OK or Cancel button, the CallbackResume command tells the macro to end the callback, close the dialog box, and continue with the commands following the CallbackWait command. You can have any control close the dialog box and cause the macro to continue by including a CallbackResume command as the last command in that CaseOf statement.

NOTE: *You don't have to include a CaseOf statement for every control in the dialog box—only those controls that you want to trigger the macro to perform certain commands when they're selected.*

CAUTION: *Make sure you include a CaseOf statement for any control that you want to actually close the dialog box, such as the OK or Cancel button. Otherwise, the dialog box will remain displayed when these buttons are chosen.*

Using Region Commands

One of the most useful things you can do with a callback is update the controls in the dialog box, such as adding information to a list box, selecting a new item, or displaying a push button. This is done in the callback subroutine with the region commands. WP has 32 different region commands that can read and set information in a dialog box, as well as change the settings of controls, such as hiding or displaying a control.

Each Region command has slightly different parameters, but they all contain a Named Region parameter. This parameter tells the macro what dialog box and control to use with the command. The Named Region is a combination of the dialog box name (from the DialogDefine command) and the control name (from the specific DialogAdd command), with a period in between. For example, if you want to use the RegionAddListItem command to add an item to a list box named "List1" in a dialog box named "Dlg1," the Named Region parameter would be "Dlg1.List1," such as in this example:

```
RegionAddListItem ("Dlg1.List1"; "New List Item")
```

You can use the region commands to add information to a dialog box, assign information from the dialog box to a variable, select a checkbox, and so on. For example, the following macro displays the dialog box shown in Figure 11-4:

```
DialogDefine ("Dlg1"; 50; 50; 150; 165; OK!|Cancel!|Percent!;
   "Sample Callback")
DialogAddText ("Dlg1"; "Text1"; 10; 10; 110; 12; Left!;
   "Type a list item and choose Add:")
DialogAddEditBox ("Dlg1"; "Edit1"; 10; 25; 75; 12; Left!;
   vText)
DialogAddPushButton ("Dlg1"; "AddBtn"; 95; 25; 30; 12;
   DefaultBttn!; "Add")
DialogAddListBox ("Dlg1"; "List1"; 10; 45; 110; 100; Sorted!;
   vListItem)
DialogShow ("Dlg1"; "WordPerfect"; UpdateList)
CallbackWait
DialogDestroy ("Dlg1")
Quit
```

11

```
Label (UpdateList)
If (UpdateList[5] = 274)
   CallbackResume
EndIf
Switch (UpdateList[3])
   CaseOf "OKBttn"; "CancelBttn":
      CallbackResume
   CaseOf "AddBtn":
      vItem:=RegionGetWindowText ("Dlg1.Edit1")
      RegionAddListItem ("Dlg1.List1"; vItem)
      RegionSetWindowText ("Dlg1.Edit1"; "")
      RegionSetFocus ("Dlg1.Edit1")
EndSwitch
```

In this macro, the callback label UpdateList is defined with the dialog box. If the user types an item in the edit box and chooses the Add button, the UpdateList[3] array element contains the control name "AddBtn," so the commands for that CaseOf statement are executed. First, the macro uses the RegionGetWindowText command

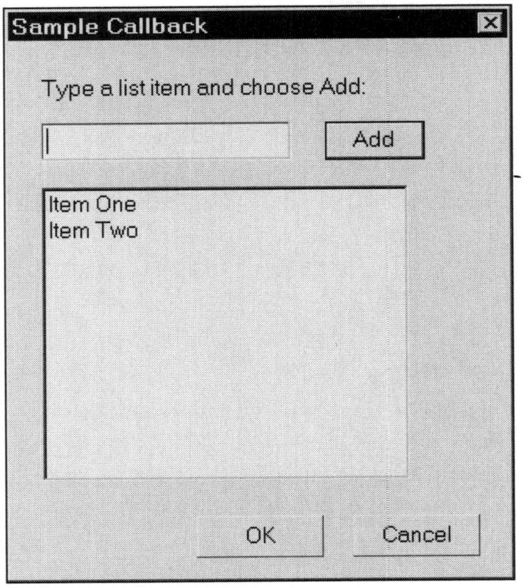

FIGURE 11-4 This dialog box uses Region commands and a callback routine to update the list box

to assign the information that was typed in the edit box to the variable vItem. Then the RegionAddListItem command adds the text in the variable vItem to the list box in the dialog box. The RegionSetWindowText command clears the text in the edit box, and finally the RegionSetFocus command places the focus of the dialog box back in the edit box, so the user can type another list item.

ADD LIST.WCM: *The ADD LIST.WCM macro shown in the previous example is included on the companion CD so you can try it out. In addition, the NUMBER TABLE ROWS.WCM macro on the companion CD includes an example of using callbacks in a macro.*

When you use region commands in a callback, remember that any macro variables associated with the DialogAdd commands won't store the value from that control when you choose the OK button (because of the callback). You'll need to use region commands, such as RegionGetWindowText, RegionGetCheck, and RegionGetListItem, to assign those variables that you want to evaluate later in the macro after closing the dialog box.

The "Common Region Commands" Quick Reference section contains a list of some of the more popular region commands and a description of what they do. For information about the specific region commands and parameters, you can use the Macro Help files or the Command Inserter (see Chapter 10 for more information).

Quick Reference ▶▶▶ Common Region Commands

WordPerfect 8 has 32 region commands that help you read from, write to, and modify dialog boxes while they're displaying. The following is a list of some of the more common commands and a description of what they do. For a complete list, or to see the specific parameters used by each command, use the Macros Help files (see Chapter 10 for more information).

Region Command	Description
RegionAddListItem	Adds a new option to a list box.
RegionEnableWindow	Makes a specified control active or dim (so it can't be used).
RegionGetCheck	Determines whether a checkbox is selected.

11

Region Command	Description
RegionAddListItem	Adds a new option to a list box.
RegionGetListContents	Assigns all the items in a list box to a single variable, separated with semicolons (or another specified character). You can use the StrParseList command to create an array variable from the string, with each list item becoming an element of the array.
RegionGetSelectedText	Assigns selected text in a dialog box to a variable, such as a selected item in a list box or selected text in an edit box.
RegionGetWindowText	Assigns text from an edit box or the dialog box title bar to a variable.
RegionMoveWindow	Moves the dialog box or a control within the dialog box to a new location.
RegionRemoveListItem	Deletes a single item from a list box.
RegionResetList	Removes all the items from a list box.
RegionSelectListItem	Selects a specific item in a list box.
RegionSetCheck	Selects (or deselects) a checkbox.
RegionSetFocus	Makes a control active.
RegionSetWindowText	Inserts text in an edit box or the dialog box title bar.

Working with the Registry

The *registry* is an integral part of Windows that stores specific information about your computer and the programs installed on it. For example, many of WordPerfect's settings are stored in the registry, such as the location of files, environment settings, and last documents opened. You normally don't need to access the registry directly because most of the settings can be changed through the individual programs or through Windows features such as the Control Panel.

Windows does provide a utility for viewing and editing the information in the registry. To use this utility, choose Start on the Windows taskbar; then choose Run. Type **regedit** and choose OK. The Registry Editor dialog box appears. Here, you can navigate through the available folders and subfolders—which are also called "keys"—to view the options stored in the registry. A registry *key* is similar to a directory folder. Each key can contain subkeys. In addition, a key can contain individual items that have both a name and a value associated with them (see Figure 11-5).

CAUTION: *Making incorrect changes to the registry can cause your computer to become nonfunctional. You should avoid making direct changes to the information already stored in the registry unless absolutely necessary.*

WP includes several macro commands for reading information from the registry, as well as writing information to the registry. For example, you can use registry commands to determine certain WP settings that aren't available through system variables. The registry macro commands are also useful for storing custom

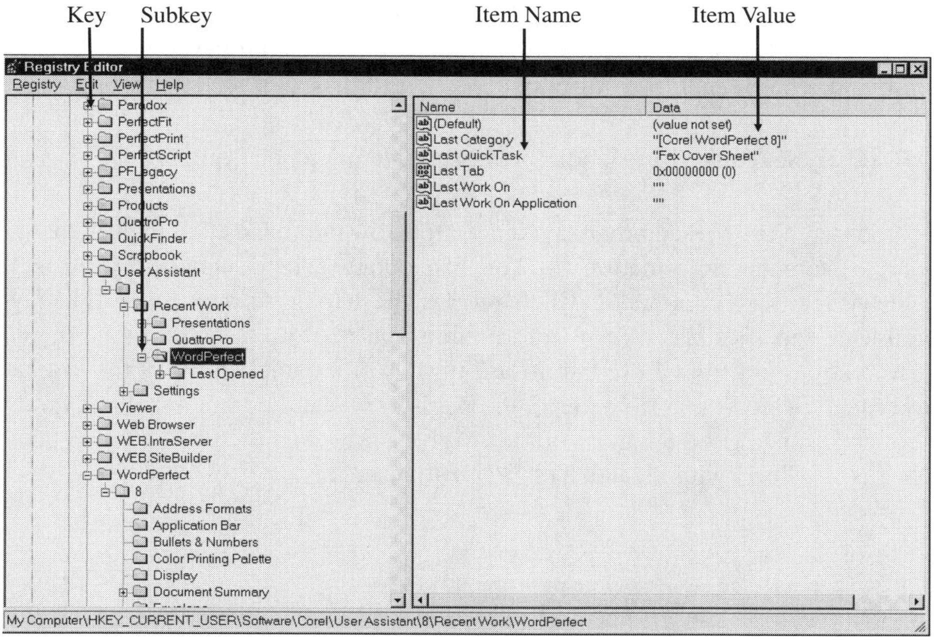

FIGURE 11-5 The Registry Editor is a utility that lets you view and modify the registry

information that you use in your macros. For example, you can create a custom key in the registry that stores a list of items to be displayed in a dialog box. Each time you modify the items in the list box, the updated information is stored in the registry key so it can be accessed the next time you play the macro.

Creating Registry Keys

To create a key in the registry with a macro, you can use the RegistryCreateKey command. This command has two parameters: the "category" you want your key to be created in, such as CurrentUser! for the HKEY_CURRENT_USER key category, and the name you want for the key. For example, the following macro command creates a new key called "MyKey" as a subkey under Software\Corel\WordPerfect\8 in the HKEY_CURRENT_USER category:

```
RegistryCreateKey (CurrentUser!;
  "Software\Corel\WordPerfect\8\MyKey")
```

Once you've created a key, you can add items to it with the RegistrySetValue command. The RegistrySetValue command uses this syntax:

RegistrySetValue (KeyHandle; ItemName; ItemValue; Type)

In order to use this command, you need to know the "handle" of the key that you want to store the information in. You can obtain a key's handle by using the RegistryOpenKey command, which returns the handle to a variable. The Type parameter specifies the type of information you're storing in the key. For most custom keys, you should use the String! type. (For a complete list of the available key types, see the Macro Help file for the RegistrySetValue command.) For example, these commands get the handle of the "MyKey" key, and then add an item named "User Name" to it with the value of "Peter Johnson":

```
hKey:=RegistryOpenKey (CurrentUser!;
  "Software\Corel\WordPerfect\8\MyKey")
RegistrySetValue (hKey; "User Name"; "Peter Johnson"; String!)
```

The new item would be added to that key in the registry:

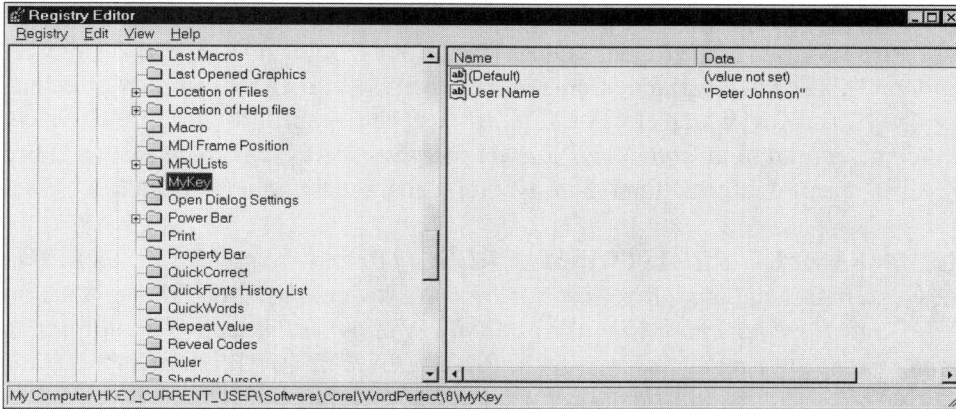

Reading from the Registry

Once you've created a key in the registry and assigned a value to it, you can retrieve that information during a macro. In addition to the custom keys you've created, you can also read information from other existing registry keys. WP has several macro commands that return different types of information from the registry. For example, you can determine the number of subkeys or items under a specific key, as well as the individual item names and values.

If you want to read the value of a key item, you can use the RegistryQueryValue command. Before using this command to read information, you need to use the RegistryOpenKey command to make sure that the key exists and to obtain the handle of the key. If the RegistryOpenKey command returns "0" as the key handle, the key doesn't exist. For example, these commands check to make sure the "MyKey" key has been created and if so, retrieve the value of the "User Name" item and assign it to the variable vName:

```
hKey:=RegistryOpenKey (CurrentUser!;
  "Software\Corel\WordPerfect\8\MyKey")
If (hkey <> 0)
    vName:=RegistryQueryValue (hKey; "User Name")
EndIf
```

If the "User Name" item has not yet been added to the MyKey key, the vName variable will contain 0.

You can use the RegistryQueryKeyCount to assign the number of subkeys under a key to a variable, or the RegistryQueryValueCount command to assign the number of items in a key to a variable. Some of the other useful registry commands include RegistryCloseKey, which closes a key that has been opened; RegistryDeleteValue, which deletes an item from a key, and RegistryDeleteKey, which deletes an entire key. For specific information on these commands, see the Macros Help file.

SAMPLE REGISTRY MACROS: *For an example of a macro that creates and reads from a custom registry key, see the BACKUP.WCM macro on the companion CD. For examples of macros that read WP information from existing keys in the registry, see the BACKUP SETTINGS.WCM and PROJECT CLEANUP.WCM macros on the companion CD.*

Interacting with Other Programs

WordPerfect macros can do a lot of things inside WordPerfect, but they can also interact with other Windows programs. For example, you can have a macro create a drawing in your document using tools from Presentations. Or you can have a macro open Microsoft Excel and retrieve information from a spreadsheet.

WP macros can interact with other programs in several different ways. If the program is part of Corel's WordPerfect Suite, you can include macro commands for that program right within your WP macro. If the program supports OLE automation, such as MS Word or Excel, you can use the new OLE macro commands. If the program doesn't support OLE, you might be able to use Dynamic Data Exchange (DDE) commands to communicate with the program.

Accessing WP Suite Programs

Programs in the WordPerfect Suite, such as Quattro Pro and Presentations, can be easily accessed through WordPerfect macros. For example, you can edit a clipart image with Presentations tools or copy information from a Quattro Pro spreadsheet. This is done by using the specific macro commands for that program.

Each of the three main WP Suite applications—WordPerfect, Quattro Pro, and Presentations—has its own set of macro product commands that control specific features within that application. For example, product commands are used to open a file, change the font, or create a table during a macro. In addition, each application can use the PerfectScript programming commands, such as If and For, to control how the macro behaves.

If you want to use the product commands from another WP Suite program in a WordPerfect macro, you need to use the Application command to tell WP which program the commands belong to. WP macros generally include an Application command at the top of the macro that identifies WordPerfect as the program being used. If you want to use the commands from another program, you need to insert a *second* Application command. For example, if you want to access Presentations commands from a WP macro, you might have these two commands at the top of the macro:

```
Application (WordPerfect; "WordPerfect"; Default!; "EN")
Application (Presentations; "Presentations"; "EN")
```

The first parameter of the Application command tells WP what product prefix will be used for the commands in the macro. The second parameter is the name of the program in quotation marks. The third parameter (which is optional) tells the macro which program will be the default. This parameter should only be used with one Application command. Finally, the last parameter identifies the language of the commands ("EN" is the code for English).

Once you've inserted the Application command for a program, you can include product commands for that program by identifying them with the product prefix (the first parameter). If the product command is from the default program, you don't need to include the product prefix. The product prefix should be typed at the beginning of the command name, followed by a period. For example, these macro commands type text in a WP document, open a spreadsheet in Quattro Pro, copy a block of cells, and then paste that information into the WP document:

```
Application (WordPerfect; "WordPerfect"; Default!; "EN")
Application (QuattroPro; "QuattroPro"; "EN")
Type ("These are the results:")
HardReturn ( )
QuattroPro.FileOpen ("c:\myfiles\accounts.wb3")
QuattroPro.SelectBlock ("A.A2..C5")
QuattroPro.EditCopy ( )
EditPaste ( )
```

Each Quattro Pro macro command begins with the "QuattroPro" product prefix (from the Application command), and is separated from the command with a period.

If the command is a WordPerfect command, no prefix is needed, since WP has been defined as the default program.

NOTE: *You don't need to include product prefixes with programming commands, such as If, For, and Assign, since they aren't specific to a program.*

If you're not sure what product commands are available for another program, you can use the Command Inserter by choosing Commands on the Macro toolbar. From the Command Type drop-down list, select the program that you want, such as Quattro Pro, and then select a command from the list box.

TIP: *You can also record some commands directly into a macro and WP automatically adds the Application command and product prefix. For example, you can begin recording a macro and choose Insert | Graphics | Draw Picture to have WP record the Presentations tools used in creating an embedded drawing.*

If you're going to be inserting several commands from another program, you can temporarily change the default application with the NewDefault command. This saves you from having to type the product prefix in front of each command. For example, if you want to insert a section of Presentations commands in a macro, type this command at the beginning of that section: **NewDefault (Presentations)**.

The information in parentheses is the product prefix used in the Application command. Any commands you type after this point are processed as Presentations commands. If you insert a WordPerfect command after changing the default, make sure you include the "WordPerfect" product prefix and period, such as WordPerfect.HardReturn ( ). You can insert the NewDefault command as many times as you want throughout a macro.

Using OLE Automation

OLE Automation is a standard developed by Microsoft that allows one application to interact with another. Through OLE Automation, a program such as WordPerfect can have access to the "objects" in another program, such as MS Word or Excel. An *object* is part of that program that can be treated as an individual unit, such as an application, document, or cell. The program that contains the objects (such as Word or Excel) is the *OLE Automation Server*. The program that accesses those objects (such as PerfectScript) is the *OLE Automation Controller*.

NOTE: *The program you want to interact with must support OLE Automation. If it doesn't, you might be able to use DDE commands instead to interact with it (see the "Using DDE Commands" section for more information).*

To use OLE Automation commands in a WP macro, follow these general guidelines:

- Insert the Object command at the beginning of the macro to define an object prefix variable and identify the name of the object. Refer to the documentation of the OLE Automation Server program for specific information on the names of available objects.

- Use the CreateObject or GetObject command to assign the "handle" of the object to the object prefix variable. After using one of these commands, the macro is "connected" to the OLE Automation Server.

- After connecting to the OLE Automation Server, you can access the methods and properties of that object. A *method* performs an action on the object, similar to a product command. A *property* contains a value of the object, similar to a system variable. Refer to the program's documentation for information on the specific methods and properties available.

- Each method or property must begin with the object prefix variable and a period. If you want to include several method or property commands for the same object, you can insert them in a With/EndWith statement. Then you only need to include two periods (..) before each method or property name instead of the prefix variable.

For example, these macro commands define an object in Microsoft Word:

```
Application (WordPerfect; "WordPerfect"; Default!; "EN")
Object (DocObj; "Word.Application")
DocObj:=CreateObject ("Word.Application")
DocObj.Visible = True
DocObj.Documents.Add
```

```
With (DocObj)
   ..Selection.TypeText ("This is the first line.")
   ..Selection.TypeParagraph
   ..Selection.TypeText ("This is the second line.")
EndWith
```

The Object command defines the object prefix "DocObj" for the object named "Word.Application." Then the CreateObject command is used to assign the handle of that object to the "DocObj" prefix variable. The DocObj.Visible = True command allows you to see what is happening in the Word document. Notice that the DocObj prefix is used before the Visible command. The With statement identifies the DocObj prefix variable as the default for the statements inside the With and EndWith commands. As a result, only two periods have to be included before each of the commands. The commands in the With statement insert two lines of text separated by a hard return.

For more information on using the OLE Automation commands, refer to WP's Macro Help files, as well as the documentation for the program you want to interact with. In WP, choose Help | Help Topics. Select the Contents tab and double-click Macros; then double-click Macro Programming. Select the Index tab, type **OLE Automation**, and choose Display.

NOTE: *You can also use OLE Automation to control WordPerfect from another program such as Visual Basic or Delphi. For more information, see Chapter 19.*

Using DDE Commands

If the program you want to interact with doesn't support OLE Automation, you might be able to use Dynamic Data Exchange (DDE) commands to communicate with it. DDE allows two programs to exchange data through a DDE "channel." Two applications, such as WordPerfect and Excel, can have a DDE "conversation" by opening a channel, requesting and sending commands or data, and then closing the channel.

NOTE: *The Windows program you want to interact with must be able to accept DDE commands. See the program's documentation for more information.*

To open a DDE channel and begin a DDE conversation, use the DDEInitiate command. This command specifies the program's name and DDE topic. The topic must be recognized by that program (see the program's documentation for more information). The DDEInitiate command returns the "handle" of the DDE conversation. If the conversation was not successfully started, the handle will be 0.

Once the DDE channel has been opened, you can use the DDEExecute, DDEPoke, and DDERequest commands to send commands and data, as well as retrieve information from the other application. For example, this macro uses DDE commands to interact with Excel:

```
Application (WordPerfect; "WordPerfect"; Default!; "EN")
hChan:=DDEInitiate ("Excel"; "System")
If (hChan = 0)
   MessageBox (X; "Error"; "The DDE conversation could not start.")
   Quit
EndIf
DDEExecute (hChan; "[OPEN(""c:\myfiles\test.xls"")]")
DDETerminate (hChan)
hChanDoc:=DDEInitiate ("Excel"; "test.xls")
If (hChanDoc <> 0)
   DDEPoke (hChanDoc; "R1C3"; "This is a test")
   DDETerminate (hChanDoc)
EndIf
```

In this example, the hChan macro is assigned to the handle of the DDE conversation with Excel, using the "System" topic. If this variable is 0, a message box is displayed indicating that the DDE conversation could not be started. Then the DDEExecute command is used to open the TEST.XLS spreadsheet in Excel, using Excel's OPEN command. The DDETerminate command ends this conversation, and a new DDE channel is opened with the TEST.XLS document. If this conversation was successfully started, the DDEPoke command sends information to the spreadsheet and types "This is a test" in Cell C1 (Row 1, Column 3). Finally, the DDETerminate command ends the second DDE conversation.

NOTE: *In order for a DDE conversation to be started successfully, the other program must already be running.*

For more information on using the DDE commands to interact with other programs, see the Macro Help file and the documentation for the program you want to communicate with.

Summary

WordPerfect's robust macro language gives you the power to automate practically any task. You can create efficient macros by organizing commands into subroutines with labels, functions, and procedures. Macros can easily perform tasks such as making decisions and repeating commands in different types of loops. If you want to interact with the user, you can create custom dialog boxes with a variety of controls, such as radio buttons and edit boxes. In addition, you can create a dialog callback routine that automatically updates the dialog box as different options are selected. Advanced macros can perform such tasks as reading information from the Windows registry and controling other programs through OLE Automation and DDE commands.

There's a lot more you can do with macros than we've had room to describe in this chapter. If you want to automate a task and aren't sure how to go about it, take a look through the Macro Help files to see what commands are available. There's a good chance that you'll find a command to do just what you need!

In Chapter 12, we'll show you a different way to automate your documents with the use of hyperlinks.

Chapter

12

Point-and-Click Automation with Hyperlinks

Whenever you "surf" the Internet, you get a lot of practice using your mouse—click one place to move to a new site, click another to start a search, or click somewhere else to start downloading a file. Before long, you find yourself clicking everything in sight just to see what happens. These "hyperlinks," as they're called, can range from colored text to buttons to graphics. But they all have the same purpose—to quickly link you with another location.

Thanks to WordPerfect, you don't need to be on the Internet to take advantage of hyperlinks. WP 8 has its own Hyperlink feature that lets you add hyperlinks right within your documents. These links can move to bookmarks in the same document, open other documents, or take you to an Internet site. They can even play macros. In this chapter, we'll show you how to create and use hyperlinks to add power and automation to your documents.

Hyperlink Overview

A *hyperlink* is an area of your document that performs an action when you click on it with the mouse—for example, moving to a different page or playing a macro. Hyperlinks are usually formatted to appear differently from the regular document text, so they're easily recognized as links. The default WP settings format hyperlinks as either blue, underlined text or as text placed in a button graphics box (see Figure 12-1). You'll learn later in this chapter how to change the appearance of a hyperlink, including how to use a graphics image as a hyperlink.

NOTE: *If a hyperlink appears in black, underlined text and you haven't edited the Hyperlink style, choose Tools | Settings and double-click Display. Deselect the Windows System Colors option, choose OK, and then Close.*

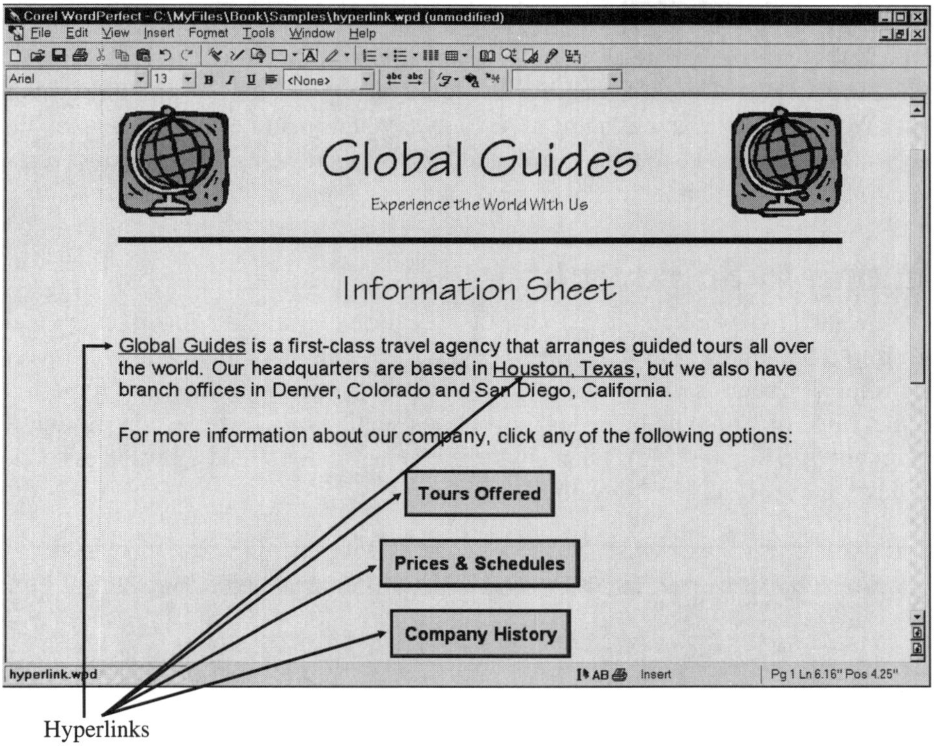

Hyperlinks

FIGURE 12-1 Hyperlinks can appear as blue, underlined text or as button graphics boxes

Hyperlinks can perform any of the following different actions when they're clicked:

- Move the insertion point to a bookmark in the same document

- Open another document and place the insertion point at the top of the document

- Open another document and move to a bookmark located in that document

- Start your Internet browser and display a specific Internet site

- Play a macro

Creating Hyperlinks

Hyperlinks can be created practically anywhere in a WordPerfect document, including headers/footers, footnotes/endnotes, styles, and even in expanded QuickWords. You can have as many hyperlinks as you want in a document, and multiple hyperlinks can be linked to the same location. In this section, you'll learn how to create hyperlinks that link to bookmarks, other documents, Internet sites, and macros.

Linking to Bookmarks

If you want a hyperlink to move to another location in the same document, you can link it to a bookmark. For example, if you have a long document that will be read electronically, such as a company handbook or newsletter, you can create hyperlinks on the Table of Contents page for the various sections and articles throughout the document (see Figure 12-2). Then all the reader has to do to read a particular section is click the hyperlink—no scrolling necessary!

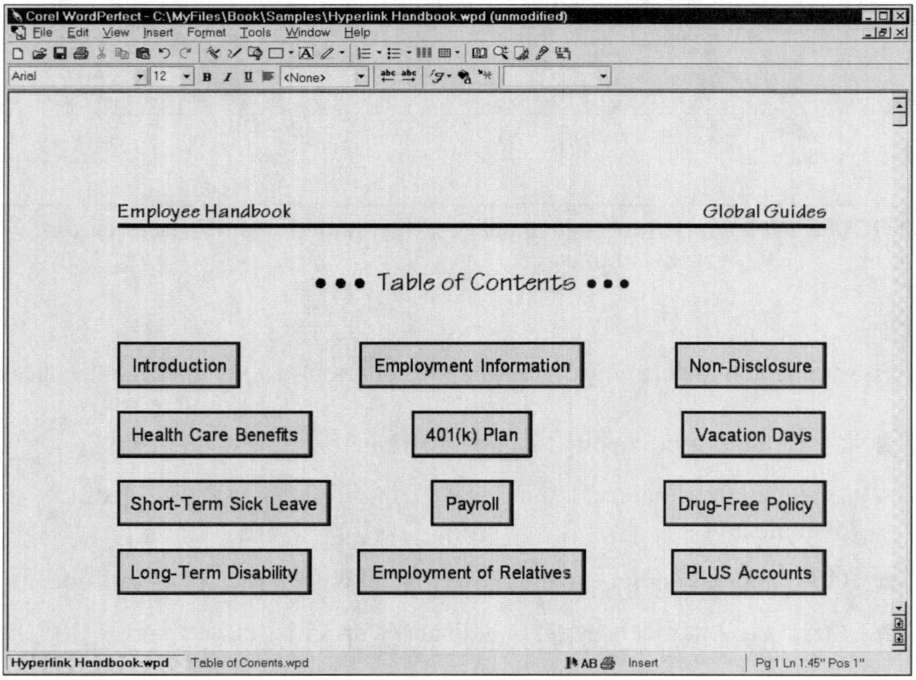

FIGURE 12-2 You can create an interactive table of contents with hyperlinks

HYPERLINK HANDBOOK.WPD: *The companion CD contains a sample document with bookmark hyperlinks called HYPERLINK HANDBOOK.WPD. You can open this document and click the links to see how bookmark hyperlinks work.*

Linking to a bookmark involves two steps. First, you need to create a bookmark at each location throughout the document that you want to link to, such as at the beginning of each section. Then you can create the hyperlinks that jump to the various bookmarks.

TIP: *If you're creating a table of contents, index, or cross-reference, you can have WP automatically create hyperlinks for you as the information is generated. When you select the Build Hypertext Links option in the Generate dialog box, the page numbers or reference numbers are formatted as hyperlinks. For more information on generating hyperlinks automatically, see Chapter 9.*

Creating Bookmarks

To create a bookmark that you can use with a hyperlink, follow these steps:

1. Place the insertion point where you want the bookmark created (and where the hyperlink will move to), such as at the beginning of a document section.

2. If there is a heading or other text already typed in the document that you want to use for the bookmark name, select that text.

3. Choose Tools | Bookmark to display the Bookmark dialog box.

4. Choose Create. WP inserts either the selected text or the text at the location of the insertion point as the bookmark name. If needed, type or edit the bookmark name in the Bookmark Name text box. Use a name that describes the information in the document at that location, so you can easily select the correct bookmark when you're later creating the hyperlink.

5. Choose OK. WP inserts the bookmark code into the document (choose View | Reveal Codes to see the code).

Repeat these steps to create bookmarks at each location in the document that you want to link to. Don't forget to add a bookmark on the table of contents page where the hyperlinks will be located, so you can include a hyperlink at the end of each section to take the reader back to the table of contents page.

NOTE: *If you selected text in the document before creating the bookmark, WP creates a "selected" bookmark. When used with the Hyperlink feature, a selected bookmark behaves the same as a regular bookmark.*

Creating Bookmark Hyperlinks

After you've created bookmarks throughout your document, you can create hyperlinks that link to them. To do this, follow these steps:

1. Place the insertion point where you want the hyperlink to appear.

2. Type the text that you want for the hyperlink and select it.

3. Choose Tools | Hyperlink. The Hyperlink Properties dialog box appears.

4. From the Bookmark drop-down list, select the name of the bookmark that you want to link to (see Figure 12-3).

5. If you want the hyperlink to be formatted as a button (see Figure 12-1), select Make Text Appear as a Button.

6. Choose OK.

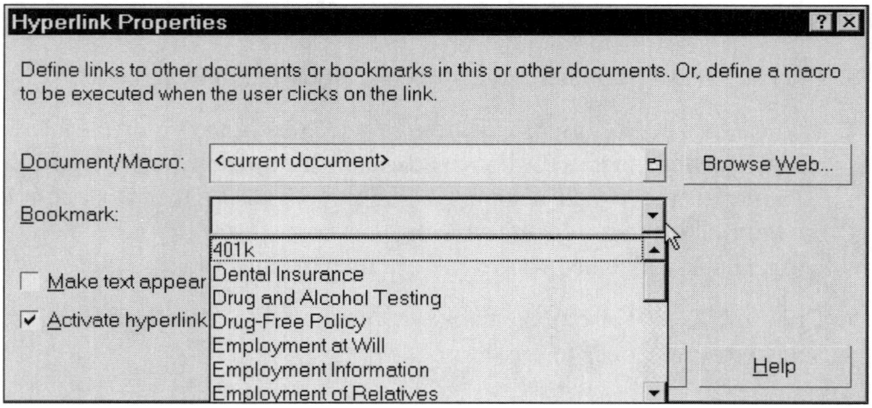

FIGURE 12-3   You can see a list of all the bookmarks that have been created in the document

TIP: *If you're in the process of creating a hyperlink and realize that you haven't yet created the bookmark that you want to link to, you don't need to cancel out of the Hyperlink Properties dialog box. Instead, type a name for the bookmark in the Bookmark text box and choose OK. Then place the insertion point where the bookmark should be created and follow the steps in the preceding "Creating Bookmarks" section to create a bookmark with the exact same name.*

NOTE: *If you're creating a text hyperlink that won't be formatted as a button, you don't have to type and select the text before creating the hyperlink. Instead, you can choose Tools | Hyperlink, set the options you want, choose OK, and then type the hyperlink text. Press END when you're finished to move outside the hyperlink codes.*

Linking to Other Documents

In addition to linking to a location within the same document, you can have a hyperlink open a separate document. For example, if your company newsletter contains a summary of the year-end financial report, you can include a hyperlink that opens the complete report for those who want to read it.

To create a hyperlink to another document, place the insertion point where you want the link to appear and type the text for the link. Then select the text and choose Tools | Hyperlink. In the Document/Macro text box, type the path and filename of the document you want to open. You can also click the file folder icon to the right of the text box, select the document you want, and choose Select.

If the selected document contains any bookmarks, they are listed in the Bookmark drop-down list. To have the hyperlink move to a specific location in the new document when it's opened, select the bookmark from the drop-down list. If you want the insertion point placed at the top of the document, delete any text in the Bookmark text box.

Finally, if you want the link to appear as a button, select Make Text Appear as a Button. Choose OK to create the link and return to the document.

NOTE: *When you use a hyperlink to open another document, the first document containing the hyperlink is automatically closed. If you want to be able to return to the original document, add a hyperlink to the second document that returns to the first.*

Linking to the Internet

If you're able to connect to the Internet from your computer, you can create hyperlinks in your WP documents that jump right to a specific Web site. For example, if you e-mail a weekly status report to your supervisor, you can include links to the home pages of vendors you're working with. Or you can create hyperlinks in your newsletter to Internet sites with investment information related to your company's 401(k) plan (see Figure 12-4).

INTERNET LINKS.WPD: *The companion CD contains a sample document called INTERNET LINKS.WPD with several Internet hyperlinks. You can open this document to experiment with linking to the Internet from WordPerfect.*

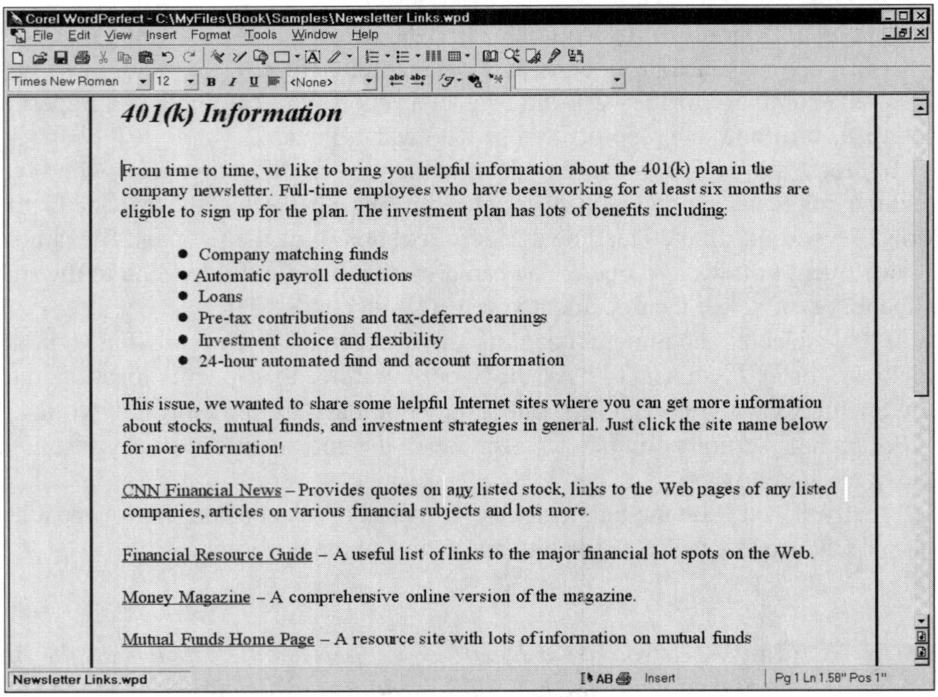

FIGURE 12-4   You can link to the Internet from a WP document

Internet links can be added to your documents with the regular Hyperlink feature or with the QuickLinks feature. The QuickLinks feature lets you type an Internet address in your document, such as **www.corel.com** or **john@corel.com**, and have it automatically converted to a hyperlink. In addition, you can create QuickLinks of your favorite Internet sites, so that when you type an abbreviation, such as **@Corel**, it's automatically expanded into a hyperlink. For more information on creating and using QuickLinks, see Chapter 3.

When you create an Internet link with the regular Hyperlink feature, you can easily use any text for the link, instead of being limited to what you type as a QuickLinks abbreviation. In addition, you don't have to know the exact URL address of the Web site before creating the link. To create an Internet hyperlink, follow these steps:

1. If you aren't currently connected to the Internet, establish a connection by dialing your Internet Service Provider (ISP) with your modem. You can also set up Windows to automatically connect to the Internet as soon as WP loads your browser, so you don't have to remember to do it manually. For more information on how to do this, see the Power Tip "Automatically Connecting to the Internet."

2. Place the insertion point where you want the link inserted in the document.

3. Type the text for the hyperlink; then select it.

4. Choose Tools | Hyperlink.

5. Choose Browse Web. WP opens your Internet browser, such as Netscape. If your browser gives you an error message about being unable to locate the server, that indicates that your computer isn't currently connected to the Internet and you need to establish the connection first.

6. In your browser, switch to the Internet site that you want to create the hyperlink to. You can use search engines to find a site, select a bookmark that you've added in your browser, or simply type in the URL address in the browser's text box.

7. Once you've found the site that you want to link to, if you're using Netscape, minimize or exit Netscape, or press ALT-TAB to return to WordPerfect. The URL address of the last site you were at is added to the Document/Macro text box (see Figure 12-5). For other browsers, you can copy and paste the URL address from your browser to the Document/Macro text box.

12

8. If you want the link to be formatted as a button, select Make Text Appear as a Button.

9. Choose OK to insert the hyperlink in the document.

TIP: *If you know the URL address you want to link to, you can type it directly in the Document/Macro text box (see Figure 12-5) without having to load your browser. If you want to verify the address, choose Browse Web after typing it in the text box. WP loads your Internet browser and tries to go to the site you entered.*

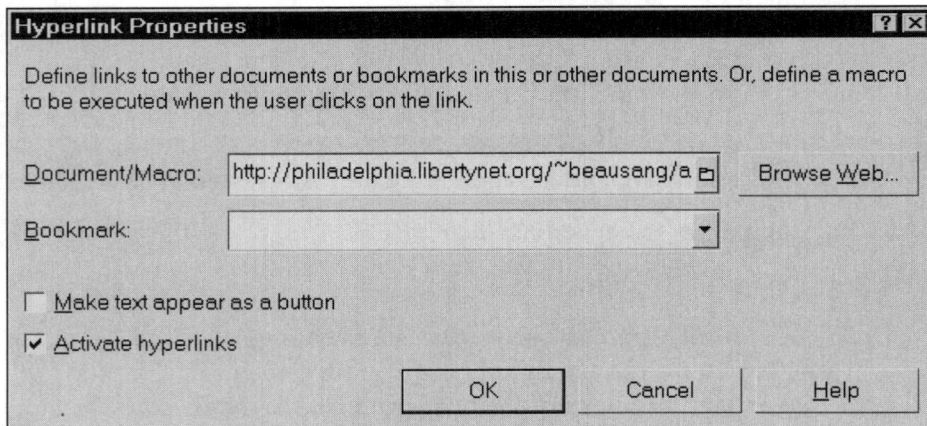

FIGURE 12-5 The last site your Web browser was at is displayed in the Document/Macro text box

Power Tip... Automatically Connecting to the Internet

If you use a modem and an Internet Service Provider (ISP) to connect to the Internet, you can set up Windows so it automatically calls up your ISP whenever you try to link to the Internet from WordPerfect, if you're not already connected. This means you don't have to remember to connect to your ISP before using or creating an Internet hyperlink.

To set this up, follow these steps:

1. Choose Start on the Windows taskbar, and then choose Settings | Control Panel.

2. Double-click the Internet icon; then select the Connection tab.

3. Select the Connect to the Internet as Needed option. From the drop-down list, select the Dial-Up Networking connection for your ISP.

4. Choose OK; then choose File | Close to exit the Control Panel.

Playing Macros

A final option for using hyperlinks to add power and automation to your documents is to have the hyperlink play a macro when it's clicked. For example, you can set up a document with macro hyperlinks to start the merges that your department uses frequently.

12

To create a hyperlink that plays a macro, follow these steps:

1. Place the insertion point where you want the hyperlink inserted.

2. Type the text for the hyperlink and select it.

3. Choose Tools | Hyperlink.

4. In the Document/Macro text box, type the name of the macro that you want to play or use the file folder icon to select it. If you don't include a path, WP looks in the default macro directory for the file. This is useful if several different people will be using the same document to link to macros on their hard drives.

5. If you want the hyperlink to appear as a button, select Make Text Appear as a Button.

6. Choose OK to insert the link.

TIP: *WP 8 comes with a macro called CHECKBOX.WCM that creates macro hyperlink checkboxes in a document. To use the CHECKBOX.WCM macro, place the insertion point where you want a checkbox inserted and choose Tools | Macro | Play. Select the CHECKBOX.WCM macro and choose Play. A macro hyperlink is inserted consisting of an empty checkbox symbol. Each time you click the hyperlink checkbox, a macro is played and toggles the checkbox between unchecked and checked.*

How to▸▸▸ Create Hyperlinks with Graphics

Hyperlinks are usually formatted as either blue, underlined text or as a button. However, you can also turn any graphics image into a hyperlink. Then, when the graphics image is clicked, the hyperlink is performed. Graphics hyperlinks can be used to perform any of the standard hyperlink actions, such as moving to a bookmark, connecting to an Internet site, or playing a macro.

To format a graphics image as a hyperlink, follow these steps:

How to...   **Create Hyperlinks with Graphics (continued)**

1. Insert the graphic into your document, then size and position it where you want it. (For more information on inserting and formatting graphics, see Chapter 7.)

2. Click the graphic once to select it.

3. Choose Tools | Hyperlink.

4. Set the options you want for the hyperlink, such as specifying a bookmark, macro, or Internet site. (For more information on these options, see the preceding sections in this chapter.)

5. Choose OK.

When you're creating a graphics hyperlink, there isn't an option to place the hyperlink on a button. However, you can still format the graphics image to appear on a button, as shown here:

To do this, right-click the graphic and choose Style. Select Button in the list of styles and choose OK.

If you later need to move or change the size of the graphic, right-click the graphic and choose Select Box; then click and drag the image to the new location or use the sizing handles to change its size. You can also right-click the graphic and select any of the QuickMenu options to make changes to the graphic.

Using Hyperlinks

Using a hyperlink is fairly straightforward—just move the mouse pointer over the link and click. Keep in mind these tips as you're using hyperlinks:

- When you move the mouse pointer over a hyperlink, the mouse pointer changes to a hand icon and a QuickTip displays the bookmark, document, Internet address, or macro it's linked to (see illustration). If no QuickTip is displayed, that generally indicates a problem with the hyperlink, such as a link to a bookmark or document that doesn't exist.

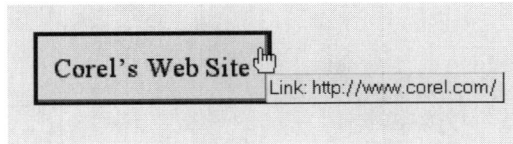

- If you place the insertion point just before a hyperlink or inside of a text hyperlink, the Hyperlink Property Bar displays. This Property Bar contains buttons for moving to the next/previous hyperlink, editing the hyperlink, changing the hyperlink style, and removing the hyperlink. You can also turn on the Hyperlink Tools toolbar, which displays all the time and has a few more buttons (see illustration). To turn this toolbar on, right-click any displaying toolbar and select Hyperlink Tools.

- After clicking a hyperlink that moves to a bookmark in the same document, you can return to the location of the hyperlink by clicking the Hyperlink Return button on the Hyperlink Tools toolbar (see the preceding tip for information on turning this toolbar on). You can also create additional hyperlinks at the end of each section to return to a bookmark at the top of the document.

- If nothing happens when you click a hyperlink, you need to activate hyperlinks in the current document. Choose Tools | Hyperlink, select Activate Hyperlinks, and choose OK. To make sure that hyperlinks are activated by default each time you start WP, choose Tools | Settings and double-click Environment. Select Activate Hyperlinks on Open and choose OK; then choose Close.

- If the hyperlink opens another document, the first document containing the hyperlink is automatically closed. If the first document hasn't been saved, you're prompted to save the changes. You can return to the original document by adding a hyperlink in the second document that returns to the first.

- If your document contains a hyperlink macro, you might want the macro to play only once in the current document. You can nest a macro from the hyperlink macro that deletes the hyperlink text from the document before playing the assigned macro. For more information, see the on the CD section "Deleting a Macro Hyperlink."

On the CD... Deleting a Macro Hyperlink

Hyperlink macros can be useful tools for automating your documents, but they also become part of the document, including being printed with the document. In some instances, you might want to have a hyperlink macro play only once, and then you want the hyperlink removed. This can be accomplished automatically by nesting a macro from the macro assigned to the hyperlink.

The companion CD includes a macro called DELETE HYPERLINK.WCM that you can nest from any macro assigned to a hyperlink. The DELETE HYPERLINK.WCM macro removes either a text hyperlink or a button/graphics hyperlink from the document, while still playing the originally assigned macro.

To use this macro, first copy the DELETE HYPERLINK.WCM macro from the companion CD to your default macro directory (usually \Corel\Suite8\Macros\WPWin). Then open the macro that you want the hyperlink to play when it's clicked. Place the insertion point at the beginning of the macro, after the Application command (if there is one). Insert a new line and type the following command:

```
Nest ("Delete Hyperlink.wcm")
```

Save and close the macro when you're finished. (For more information on creating and editing macros, see Chapter 10.)

12

> Create the hyperlink in your document following the steps in the "Playing Macros" section earlier in this chapter. When you select the macro for the hyperlink, select the actual macro that you want to play—*don't* select the DELETE HYPERLINK.WCM macro. When you click the hyperlink, the hyperlink text or button is deleted from the document and the selected macro is played normally.

Editing Hyperlinks

Once you've added hyperlinks to your document, you can edit them in several different ways without having to re-create them. For example, you can move a hyperlink to a new location, change the action it performs when it's clicked, or modify its appearance. In this section, you'll learn how to edit a hyperlink.

Moving a Hyperlink

With a little preparation, hyperlinks can be easily moved to a different location in your document. Follow these steps to move a hyperlink that's formatted as text:

1. Turn on Reveal Codes by choosing View | Reveal Codes.

2. In the Reveal Codes window, click the [Hypertext] code at the beginning of the hyperlink text. This places the insertion point just before the [Hypertext] code in Reveal Codes.

3. Hold down the SHIFT key and press RIGHT ARROW until the hyperlink text is selected, including the ending [Hypertext] code.

4. Press CTRL-X to cut the hyperlink text to the Clipboard.

5. Place the insertion point where you want the hyperlink moved to and press CTRL-V to paste it in the document.

If you want to move a hyperlink button or graphics image, you can use one of two methods:

■ Right-click the button or graphic and choose Select Box. Move the insertion point over the edge of the button or graphic until it turns into a four-directional arrow; then click and drag the button to the new location on the page.

NOTE: *Hyperlink buttons use a character anchor. As you drag a hyperlink button, the location of the insertion point indicates where the button will be inserted.*

■ Turn on the Hyperlink Tools toolbar by right-clicking any displaying toolbar and choosing Hyperlink Tools. Then click the Hyperlink Toggle button (with the hand icon) to deactivate hyperlinks. Once hyperlinks have been deactivated, you can click and drag hyperlink buttons and graphics to new locations as you normally would. When you're finished moving the hyperlinks, click the Hyperlink Toggle button again to reactivate hyperlinks.

Changing the Hyperlink Action

You can easily change the action performed by a hyperlink, such as changing the bookmark that it moves to, the macro it plays, or the Internet site it opens. You can also modify a hyperlink so it performs a completely different action. For example, you can edit a hyperlink that's been created to play a macro and have it go to a bookmark instead.

To make changes to the action a hyperlink performs, right-click the hyperlink and choose Edit Hyperlink from the QuickMenu. In the Hyperlink Properties dialog box, make any changes you want, such as selecting a new bookmark, macro, or Internet address. (See the "Creating Hyperlinks" section earlier in this chapter for more information.) When you're finished, choose OK to return to the document.

Changing the Hyperlink Appearance

If you want to change the way a hyperlink appears in the document, follow these guidelines:

■ To edit the text used for a text hyperlink, right-click the hyperlink and choose Open Hyperlink. WP places the insertion point inside the hyperlink text. Edit the text as you normally would in a document, using the arrow keys, BACKSPACE, and DELETE to make changes.

TIP: *You can also edit a text hyperlink by using the arrow keys to move into the hyperlink text, and then making the changes you want.*

■ To change the text on a hyperlink button, right-click the button and choose Content from the QuickMenu. Choose Edit, make any changes to the text, and click outside the button when you're finished. The button automatically resizes to fit the new text.

TIP: *To change the font used on all hyperlink buttons, change the default document font by choosing File | Document | Default Font. Select the font you want and choose OK.*

■ To change a text hyperlink to a button, or vice versa, right-click the hyperlink and choose Edit Hyperlink. Select (or deselect) the Make Text Appear as a Button option and choose OK.

■ To change the appearance of a text hyperlink, such as changing the color or removing the underline attribute, you can edit the Hyperlink style. For more information, see the "How to Edit the Hyperlink Style" section.

How to... Edit the Hyperlink Style

You can change the appearance of text hyperlinks in a document by editing the Hyperlink style. If the Hyperlink Tools toolbar isn't already displaying, right-click any displaying toolbar and select Hyperlink Tools. Then click the Hyperlink Style Edit button on the toolbar. This displays the Styles Editor dialog box with the Hypertext system style.

Make any changes you want to the text hyperlink formatting in the Contents text box. For example, to change the color of the hyperlink, double-click the [Color]

How to... Edit the Hyperlink Style
(*continued*)

code, select the new color from the Text Color pop-up palette, and choose OK to return to the Styles Editor dialog box. To delete the underline attribute, click and drag the [Und] code out of the Contents text box. You can also use the pull-down menus in the Styles Editor dialog box to add other formatting, such as a specific font or font size. For more information on editing styles, see Chapter 5.

When you're finished making changes, choose OK. Any hyperlinks in the current document will use the new formatting. Note that the changes you make to the Hypertext style only affect hyperlinks when viewed in WordPerfect. They won't be used when a document is viewed in a Web browser such as Netscape.

Changing the Hypertext style only affects hyperlinks in the current document. If you want your formatting changes to be automatically used in every new document, you need to copy the edited style to your default template. To do this, follow these steps:

1. If you haven't already, follow the guidelines above to edit the Hypertext style to use the formatting you want.

2. From the main document screen, choose Format I Styles.

3. From the Options pop-down button, choose Setup, select System, and choose OK.

4. Select Hypertext in the list of styles.

5. From the Options pop-down button, choose Copy. Select Default Template and choose OK.

6. From the Options pop-down button, choose Setup again, deselect System, and choose OK.

7. Choose Close to close the Style List dialog box.

Now, each time you create a hypertext link, it uses the modified style. You can still change the hyperlink formatting for the current document without affecting any other documents, by editing the style as explained earlier.

12

Removing Hyperlinks

When you're editing a document that contains hyperlinks, sometimes it's helpful to *not* have the hyperlinks perform an action when they're clicked. To temporarily disable hyperlinks in a document, you can click the Hyperlink Toggle button on the Hyperlink Tools toolbar. Or you can choose Tools | Hyperlink, deselect Activate Hyperlinks, and choose OK. This deactivates any hyperlinks in the current document. Repeat these steps to reactive the hyperlinks.

If you want to permanently remove an individual hyperlink from a document, place the insertion point just before the hyperlink in the document so the Hyperlink Property Bar appears. Then click the Hyperlink Remove button on the Property Bar. WP removes the hyperlink formatting, but keeps the hyperlink text in the document (including text on a hyperlink button). If you want to remove both the hyperlink button and the text on the button, right-click the button and choose Delete Box.

> **TIP:**   *You can quickly place the insertion point at the beginning of a hyperlink by turning on Reveal Codes (View | Reveal Codes) and clicking the first [Hypertext] code of a hyperlink.*

Summary

WP's Hyperlink feature can help automate your documents by enabling you to jump to new locations or play macros with just the click of a button. Hyperlinks can be used to move to bookmarks in the same document, open different documents, link to Internet sites, or play macros. You can format a hyperlink as text, a button, or a graphics image, and you can easily change the hyperlink's appearance. Hyperlinks can add a lot of power, flexibility, and ease of use to your documents.

In Chapter 13, you'll learn how to quickly access the features and tools you use most with custom toolbars, menu bars, and keyboards.

Chapter

13

Customizing Toolbars and Keyboards

Think for a minute about the layout of your desk. You've probably arranged it so the items you use most often—the telephone, a stapler, a jar of pens—are within easy reach. If you want to work efficiently, it makes sense to arrange things so you have quick access to them. The same logic applies to WordPerfect—if you put the features and tools you use frequently where you can easily access them, you'll get your work done a whole lot faster.

Fortunately, WordPerfect 8 has lots of ways to set up shortcuts to your favorite features. With the ability to customize any of WP's powerful "bars"—toolbars, Property Bars, menu bars, and Application Bar—as well as create custom keyboards, you can get to the features you want with a simple click of a button or press of a keystroke. In this chapter, you'll learn how to customize WP with shortcuts to your favorite features, macros, and other tools. Along the way, we'll give you lots of quick hints and tips for working with the different bars and keyboards so you can set up WordPerfect just the way you like it.

Toolbars and Property Bars

While toolbars and Property Bars aren't new to WordPerfect, WP 8 gives you even more power and control over them. Toolbars and Property Bars display buttons for use with the mouse and can be customized with shortcuts to frequently used features, macros, and other tools (see Figure 13-1). You can further customize both types of bars by changing the location, font size, and button appearance.

There are also some differences between toolbars and Property Bars. Property Bars can only be displayed one at a time, and WP automatically determines which one is selected based on the current status of the document. For example, if the insertion point is in a table, the Tables Property Bar automatically appears. Or, if you're editing a graphic, the Graphics Property Bar is displayed. WP 8 has 43 different Property Bars that can be displayed at different times. You can edit any of these Property Bars, but you can't create new ones or change which feature they're associated with. On the other hand, you can display up to ten toolbars simultaneously

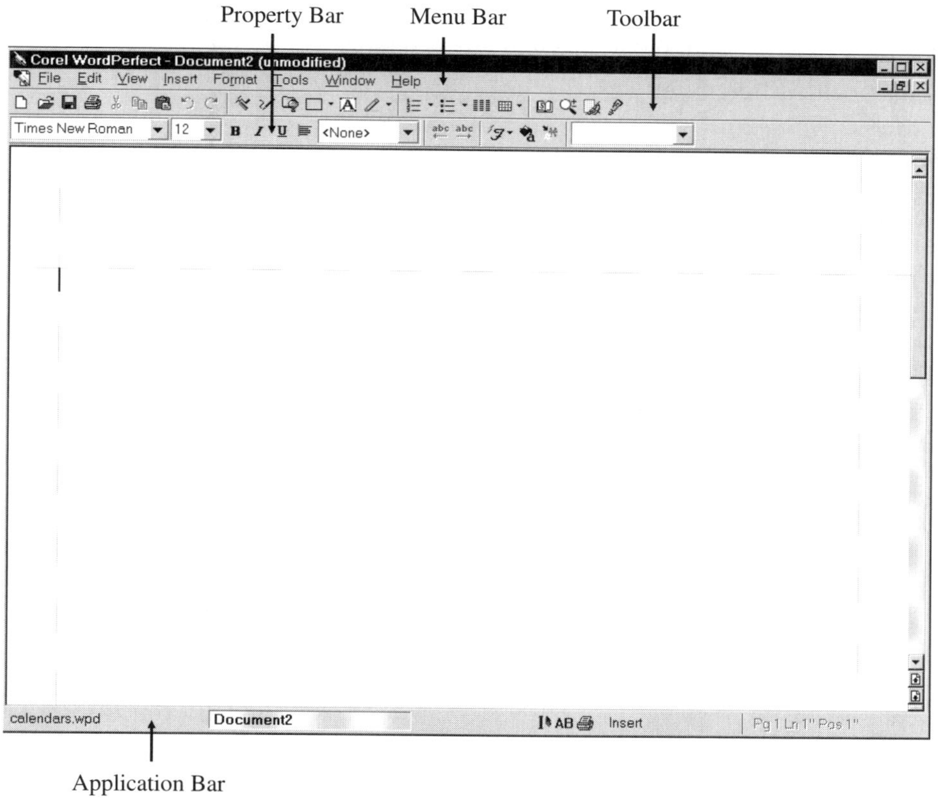

Property Bar   Menu Bar   Toolbar

Application Bar

FIGURE 13-1 WP lets you customize toolbars, Property Bars, menu bars, and the Application Bar

and you can manually turn each one on and off at anytime. WP 8 comes with 14 precreated toolbars and you can create as many custom toolbars as you want.

Toolbar and Property Bar Settings

You can customize the appearance of toolbars and Property Bars by changing such settings as their location on the screen, the button appearance, and the number of rows that display. If you have more than one toolbar displaying, each toolbar can

13

have its own custom settings. For example, one toolbar can be positioned at the bottom of the screen and display text buttons, while another toolbar can be placed along the left side with three rows of picture buttons. Figure 13-2 shows several toolbars with different settings.

NOTE: *Since only one Property Bar can be displayed at a time, each Property Bar uses the same settings.*

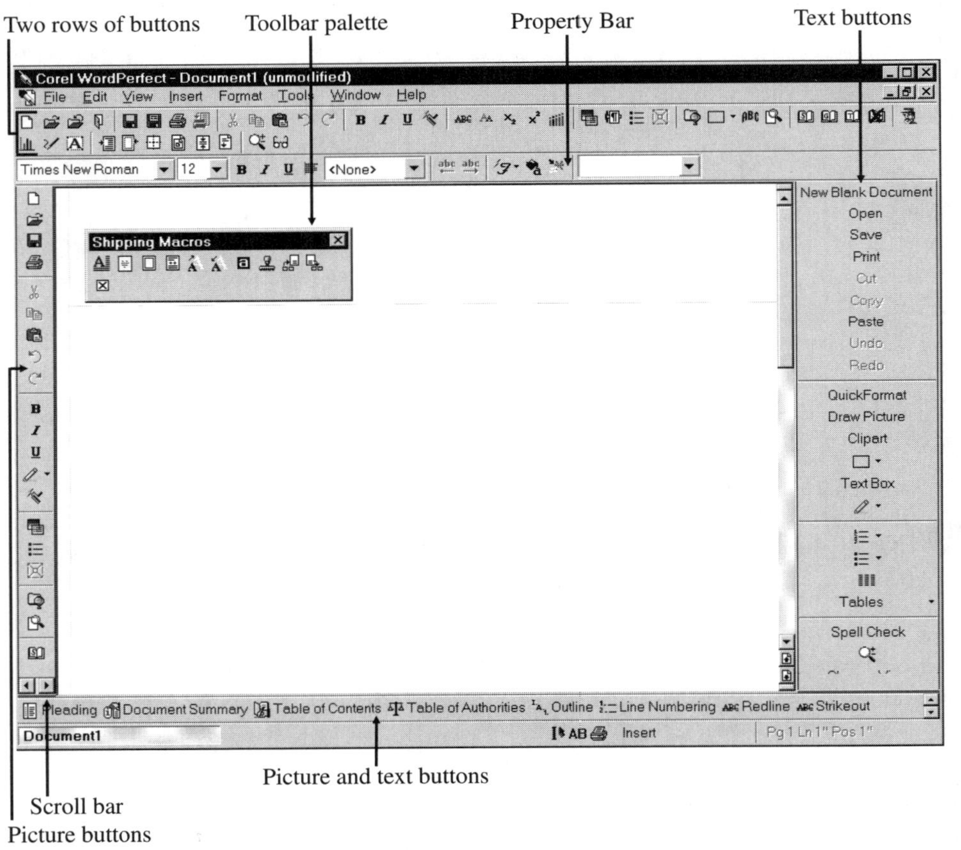

FIGURE 13-2 You can customize the settings for each individual toolbar

To display a new toolbar, right-click a toolbar that's already displaying and select the desired toolbar from the QuickMenu. To turn a toolbar off, right-click any toolbar and deselect the toolbar you want to hide. You can display and hide toolbars by choosing View | Toolbars, selecting or deselecting the desired toolbars, and choosing OK.

TIP: *If you want to turn off the Property Bar, right-click it and choose Hide Property Bar. To display it again, choose View | Toolbars, select Property Bar, and choose OK.*

The fastest way to change the location of a toolbar or the Property Bar is to use your mouse to click and drag it to the new location. Move the mouse pointer over a blank area of the toolbar or Property Bar until it changes into a four-directional arrow. Then click and drag the bar to the edge of the screen you want to move it to, such as the left or bottom edge. As you drag the bar, you'll see an outline of the bar's shape. When it expands to fill the edge of the screen, release the mouse button. If you want the bar to be placed in a floating palette (see Figure 13-2), drag the bar into the middle of the screen, and then click and drag the title bar to move it where you want it.

To manually set the location of the bar, or to change other settings, such as the button appearance, right-click the toolbar or Property Bar and choose Settings. If you're modifying a toolbar, select the toolbar you want to change (remember each toolbar can have its own settings). Choose Options to display the Toolbar Options dialog box (see Figure 13-3).

Select the options you want for the toolbar or Property Bar. As you select the options, the bar updates to show you how it appears with those settings. Changing the font size only affects the bar if it displays text.

NOTE: *WordPerfect bases the bar font size on the Windows 95 menu font size. If the Windows 95 menu font is set to a small font size, the Small option is unavailable in the Toolbar Options dialog box because WP can't reduce the font any smaller. To change the Windows 95 font size, click the Windows 95 Start button, and then choose Settings | Control Panel. Double-click Display and select the Appearance tab. From the Item drop-down list, select Menu. Select the font and size you want from the drop-down menus along the bottom row of the dialog box. When you're finished, choose OK and exit the Control Panel.*

13

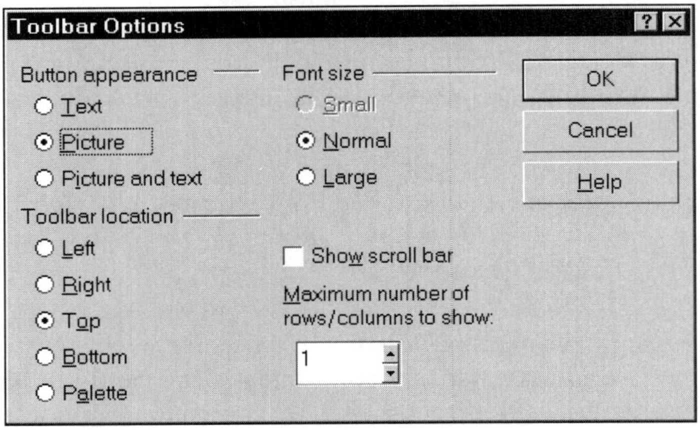

FIGURE 13-3 You can set options for the appearance and location of a toolbar or Property Bar

If you select the Show Scroll Bar option, the scroll bar only appears when the number of buttons exceeds the amount that can display in one row or column. If the bar has more buttons than can be shown in one row or column, you can also choose to have up to three rows or columns display (see Figure 13-2). Type the number you want in the Maximum Number of Rows/Columns to Show text box. When you're finished, choose OK, and then Close.

TIP: *If you have the buttons set to display text, you can see more buttons at the same time by placing the bar along the left or right edge of the screen.*

NOTE: *If you turn a toolbar off and then on again, it returns to the default location at the top of the screen and the default button appearance of picture only.*

Customizing Toolbars and Property Bars

You can customize toolbars and Property Bars to display buttons for your favorite features, macros, and other tools. You can edit any of the existing toolbars or Property

Bars, as well as create new custom toolbars. Follow one of these steps to edit or create a bar:

- To edit a toolbar or Property Bar that's currently displaying, right-click the bar and choose Edit.

- To edit a bar that's *not* currently displaying, right-click an existing toolbar or Property Bar and choose Settings; then select the bar you want to edit in the list and choose Edit.

- To create a new toolbar from scratch, right-click any displaying toolbar and choose Settings. Choose Create, type a name for your new toolbar, and choose OK.

- To create a new toolbar by copying an existing toolbar, right-click any displaying toolbar and choose Settings; then choose Copy. Select the toolbar that you want to make a copy of in the list box and choose Copy. In the Object text box, type a new name for the toolbar and choose OK. Select your new toolbar in the Available Toolbars list box and choose Edit.

TIP: *To copy a toolbar from one computer to another, see the "How to Copy Toolbars Between Templates" section in Chapter 1.*

When the Toolbar/Property Bar Editor dialog box appears (see Figure 13-4), you can add and delete buttons to the bar, as well as move buttons to different positions. Buttons can be created to activate a WordPerfect feature, type keystrokes into the document, execute a program, or play a macro. The following sections will explain these options further.

NOTE: *Each toolbar can hold up to 500 buttons on three viewable rows and up to 12 additional scrollable rows. However, you'll find that smaller bars are easier to work with.*

Adding Features

WordPerfect has hundreds of different features that you can assign to toolbar and Property Bar buttons. In addition to the features already listed on the pull-down menus, you can choose from countless other features, including specific table, graphics, and Web formatting features.

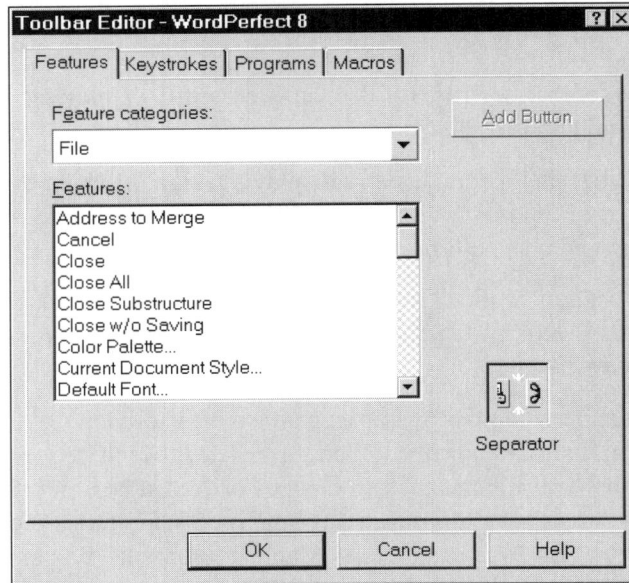

FIGURE 13-4 You can add, delete, and move buttons while the Toolbar Editor dialog box is displaying

To add a button for a feature, select the Features tab in the Toolbar Editor dialog box (see Figure 13-4). From the Feature Categories drop-down list, select the category you want. Most of the categories match the default menu bar headings. Then scroll through the Features list box to find the feature you want. As you select each feature, a brief description of the feature displays in the dialog box, along with a sample of the button icon. For example, to add a Thesaurus button to the toolbar, select Tools from the Feature Categories drop-down categories box, and select Thesaurus in the Features list box.

When you've selected the feature you want, choose Add Button. The new button is added to the far right (or bottom) of the toolbar or Property Bar. You can repeat these steps to add as many other feature buttons as you want to the current bar. Later in this chapter, you'll learn how you can further modify buttons by moving them to a new position, changing the button text, or modifying the image.

TIP: *If the feature you want to add to a button is already on the pull-down menus, you can add a new button by simply selecting the menu options. For example, to add a Thesaurus button while the Toolbar/Property Bar Editor dialog box is displaying, choose Tools | Thesaurus.*

Typing Keystrokes

You can have WordPerfect do some of your typing for you by adding keystrokes to a toolbar or Property Bar button. The Keystrokes option lets you quickly insert text or symbols into your documents. For example, you can add a button that inserts a signature block into a letter or a paragraph break using your favorite symbols.

To use this option, select the Keystrokes tab in the Toolbar Editor dialog box. In the text box, type the text you want to have inserted in your documents, using hard returns if needed (see Figure 13-5). To include a symbol, press CTRL-W to display the Symbols dialog box; then select the symbol you want and choose Insert and Close. If you want to use formatting within the text such as bold or italics, you can use keyboard scripts. For more information on doing this, see the Power Tip "Using Keyboard Scripts."

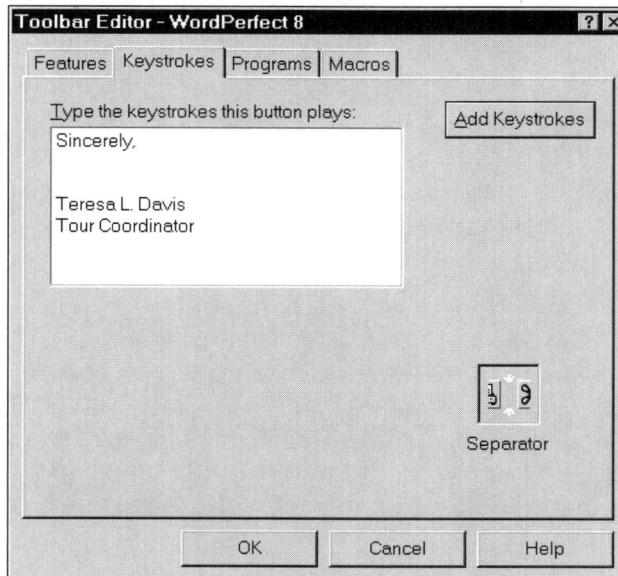

FIGURE 13-5 You can add a toolbar button that types text into the document

TIP: *If the text you want to insert with the button is already typed into a document, you don't have to retype it into the Toolbar/Property Bar Editor dialog box. Before editing the toolbar or Property Bar, select the text you want to use and press CTRL-C to copy it. Then edit the toolbar, place the insertion point in the keystrokes text box, and press CTRL-V to paste it in. Using this method will include any tabs within the text, but not formatting such as bold or italics.*

Power Tip⟩⟩⟩ Using Keyboard Scripts

In addition to inserting text, symbols, hard returns, and tabs in the text box for a keystroke button (see Figure 13-5), you can also use a keyboard script to tell WP to press certain keystroke combinations. For example, you can tell WP to press CTRL-I to turn italics on, press ALT-F to open the File pull-down menu, and then press O to display the Open File dialog box. Follow these steps to use keyboard scripts:

1. If you don't have the Toolbar/Property Bar Editor dialog box displaying, right-click the toolbar or Property Bar you want to add the button to and choose Edit.

2. Select the Keystrokes tab at the top of the dialog box.

3. In the text box, type any text you want WP to insert. You can press ENTER to insert a hard return, or CTRL-W to insert symbols.

4. To have WP perform a keystroke, type the keystroke in curly brackets, using a plus sign to separate the keys, such as **{Tab}** to insert a tab, or **{Ctrl+B}** to turn bold on or off. For example, if you want WP to center the text "Have a *great* day!" on a line, the script would look like this:

    {Shift+F7}Have a {Ctrl+I}great{Ctrl+I} day!

5. If you want to use pull-down menus, use the ALT key and the appropriate mnemonic letter, such as **{Alt+F}** to open the File pull-down menu. Place curly brackets around single letters that activate options on a menu. For example, the following text would simulate choosing File | Open, typing the filename **test.wpd,** and choosing Open.

{Alt+F}{O}test.wpd{Alt+O}

6. When you've inserted the keystrokes you want, choose Add Keystrokes to add the new button.

When you're finished, choose Add Keystrokes to add the new button, which uses a gray sphere icon (you'll learn later in the chapter how to change this). Whenever you click this button, the text you typed is inserted into the document at the location of the insertion point.

TIP: *If you want to edit the text that's inserted with a button, make sure the Toolbar/Property Bar Editor dialog box is displaying and double-click the Keystrokes button. Choose Properties and make any changes you want to the keystrokes. Choose OK twice when you're finished.*

NOTE: *You can also use the QuickWords feature to quickly insert text into a document. For more information on QuickWords, see Chapter 3.*

Executing Programs

A third type of button you can add to your toolbars and Property Bars is one that runs another program. For example, you can add a button that runs the Windows Calculator, opens a DOS window, or starts your communication program. Program buttons can also be used to open specific files. See the Power Tip "Opening Files from a Toolbar Button" for more information.

13

To add a program button, select the Programs tab in the Toolbar/Property Bar Editor dialog box. Choose Add Program and use the Open File dialog box to select the program-executable file you want, such as C:\WINDOWS\CALC.EXE. When you've selected the file, choose Open. The new button uses that program's icon if possible.

TIP: *You can modify the program settings for the new button, such as adding startup options or having the program run minimized. To do this, make sure the Toolbar/Property Bar Editor dialog box is still displaying and double-click the program button. Choose Properties. Make any changes you want, such as typing startup options at the end of the Command Line text box. Choose OK twice when you're finished.*

Power Tip... Opening Files from a Toolbar Button

In addition to adding executable programs to a toolbar or Property Bar button, you can add individual files. Then, when you click the button, WP opens the file in the associated program, based on the file extension. For example, if you add a document with a WPD extension, WP automatically opens it in a document window. Or, if you add a file with a TXT extension, the file is opened in Windows Notepad.

To add a file to a button, follow the steps in the "Executing Programs" section and select the file as the program name. Once the Open File dialog box displays, you'll need to select All Files (*.*) from the File Type drop-down list so you can see all the available files. The icon used for the new button indicates which program WP will load the file in. If the icon is a generic Windows icon, that indicates that the file extension is not associated with a specific program.

If you frequently create documents with a file extension that's not associated with WordPerfect, such as LTR, you can create an association for that extension. To associate a file extension so files are automatically opened in WP, follow these steps:

1. On the Windows taskbar, choose Start | Programs | Windows Explorer.

2. In Explorer, choose View | Options. Select the File Types tab and choose New Type.

3. In the Description of Type text box, type a description such as **WordPerfect Document**.

4. In the Associated Extension text box, type the file extension you want to associate, such as **LTR**.

5. Choose New to define a new action. In the Action text box, type **Open**. Choose Browse and switch to the directory with the WPWIN8.EXE file (usually \Corel\Suite8\Programs). Select the WPWIN8.EXE file and choose Open.

6. Choose OK, then choose Close twice, and finally choose File | Close to exit the Explorer.

Playing Macros

Finally, you can have a toolbar or Property Bar button play a macro when it's clicked. Macros are helpful tools for automating tasks that you frequently perform. (For more information on creating and using macros, see Chapters 10 and 11.)

To add a macro to a button, select the Macros tab in the Toolbar/Property Bar Editor dialog box. If the macro is saved as a file on disk, choose Add Macro. If the macro is saved as part of the current template, choose Add Template Macro. Select the macro you want to use and choose Select. If you're adding a macro from disk, WP asks if you want to save the macro with the full path. If you choose Yes, WP stores the entire path to the macro, which allows you to play a macro that's saved in any folder on your hard drive. If you choose No, WP just stores the filename of the macro. When you later click the button to play the macro, WP looks for the macro in the default macro folder first, followed by the supplemental macro folder if one is specified. If the macro isn't in either location, an error occurs.

WP adds a new button with a tape recorder icon, although you can change the icon if you want as explained later in this chapter.

TIP: *WP comes with a toolbar already set up with several of the common shipping macros on it, such as the watermark, paragraph break, and reverse text macros. To use this toolbar, right-click any toolbar and select Shipping Macros to display the new toolbar.*

On the CD... CD Macros Toolbar

The companion CD is loaded with helpful macros that work hand-in-hand with the various WordPerfect features discussed throughout this book. For example, there are macros for numbering table rows, backing up the files that contain your custom settings, placing graphics on envelopes, and so on. We've also included a special toolbar that contains buttons for many of the macros on the CD.

To use this toolbar, first copy the MACROS TOOLBAR.WPT file from the companion CD to the same directory on your hard drive as your default template (WP8US.WPT), which is usually \Corel\Suite8\Template\Custom WP Templates. Choose File | New. From the project category drop-down list, select Custom WP Templates.

Select "Create a blank document" in the list and from the Options pop-down button, choose Edit WP Template. Choose Copy/Remove Object from the Template Property Bar. From the Templates to Copy From drop-down list, select the MACROS TOOLBAR template. Make sure the Object Type drop-down list is set to Toolbars, then, in the Source list on the left, select the Maximize WP 8 Macros toolbar.

Choose Copy. Choose Close, and then choose the Close button on the Template Property Bar. Choose Yes to save your changes.

To select the new toolbar, right-click a toolbar and select the Maximize WP 8 Macros toolbar. Before you can use the macros from the toolbar, you need to copy them from the companion CD to the default macro directory on your hard drive, which is usually \Corel\Suite8\Macros\WPWin. Then click a button to play the macro.

Manipulating Buttons

When you have the Toolbar/Property Bar Editor dialog box displaying, you can further customize the current bar by moving or deleting buttons, adding separators, or changing the button icons. Use these tips to create just the bar you want.

- To delete a button, click and drag the unwanted button off the bar. When the mouse pointer changes to a garbage can, release the mouse button.

- To move a button to a new location on the bar, click and drag the button to the desired position. If there are more buttons than will display at one time in a row, change the toolbar to a floating palette temporarily while you reorder the buttons. To do this, click and drag the bar into the middle of the document window. After changing the order of the buttons, drag it back to the desired position.

TIP: *You can also move and delete buttons at any time from a document window without having to display the Toolbar/Property Bar dialog box. Just hold down the ALT key as you click and drag the button to a new location or off the bar to delete it.*

- If you have several toolbars displaying, you can copy or move a button from the current toolbar to another toolbar. To move a button, click and drag it to the new toolbar. To copy a button, hold down the CTRL key as you click and drag the button. You can only move or copy buttons off of the current toolbar. If you want to delete or move the button you added to the new toolbar, you need to choose OK, right-click the second toolbar, and choose Edit.

13

■ To add a separator line to the bar to help organize the buttons, move the mouse pointer over the Separator icon in the Toolbar/Property Bar Editor dialog box until it turns into a four-directional arrow. Click and drag the separator icon to the bar and release the mouse pointer where you want the separator inserted. You can move a separator once it's been inserted by clicking and dragging it to the new location.

■ To change the button text or QuickTip (see illustration), double-click the button to display the Customize Button dialog box. Or you can right-click the button and choose Customize. In the Button Text text box, type the text that you want to appear on the button (up to 48 characters). This text only displays when you have the toolbar set to display the buttons with text. In the QuickTip text box, type the text you want to appear on the QuickTip that appears whenever you move the mouse pointer over the button (up to 128 characters). Choose OK.

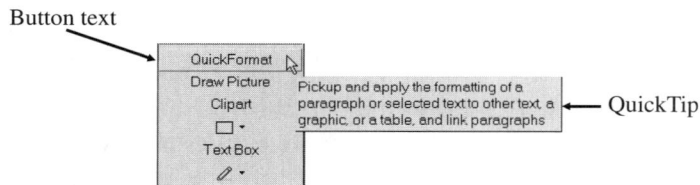

Button text

QuickFormat

Draw Picture
Clipart

Pickup and apply the formatting of a paragraph or selected text to other text, a graphic, or a table, and link paragraphs ◀── QuickTip

Text Box

■ To change the icon used on a button, double-click the button and choose Edit from the Customize Button dialog box. This displays the Image Editor dialog box (see Figure 13-6). The Image Editor is a small 16 x 16 bitmap editor that gives you 15 colors for creating or editing an image. To clear the current image, choose Clear. You can work with two colors at a time by clicking the left and right mouse button on the colors you want to select, and then clicking in the image itself to modify it. Select the Single Pixel or Fill Whole Area option to determine how much of the image is changed with the selected color. The previews show you how the button will appear on the toolbar. You can choose Undo to undo the last five changes you made. Choose OK when you're finished.

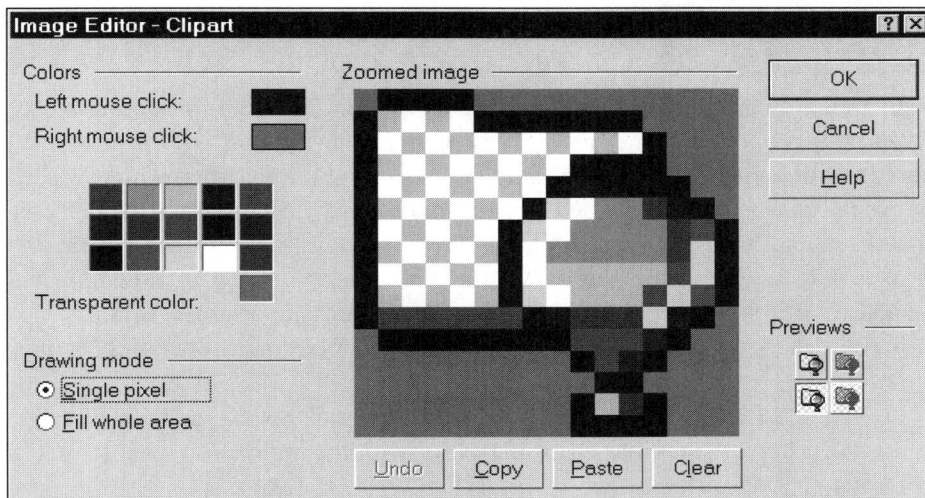

FIGURE 13-6 You can edit the image used on a button in the Image Editor

TIP: *If you're not much of an artist, you can copy the icon from another toolbar button to use on a new button. WP has hundreds of available icons that can be assigned to buttons. For more information on how to do this, see the section "How to Copy Button Icons" next.*

When you're finished making changes to the toolbar or Property Bar, choose OK to close the Toolbar/Property Bar Editor dialog box. If you've created a custom toolbar, you can rename or delete it by choosing Tools | Settings and double-clicking Customize. Select the custom toolbar in the list. To delete the toolbar, choose Delete; then choose Yes. To change the name of a toolbar, choose Rename, type the new name and choose OK. Choose Close twice when you're finished. (You can't delete or rename the precreated toolbars that come with WP.)

TIP: *If you've modified one of the toolbars or Property Bars that come with WordPerfect, you can reset it to its original settings. To do this, choose Tools | Settings and double-click Customize. Select the toolbar or Property Bar that you want to reset and choose Reset. Choose Yes to confirm the changes, and then choose Close twice.*

How to... Copy Button Icons

With the hundreds of icons already available in WordPerfect 8 for toolbar buttons, there's no need to spend time creating your own icon in the Image Editor dialog box. You can easily copy existing icons onto your custom buttons. For example, you can change the tape recorder icon used for a macro button to an icon that better represents what the macro does, such as one of the several printer icons for a macro that prints or faxes a document. Once you copy an icon to a button, you can still edit it in the Image Editor if you want to further distinguish it from the original feature.

To copy an icon to a new toolbar or Property Bar button, follow these steps:

1. If the Toolbar/Property Bar Editor dialog box is not currently displaying, right-click the toolbar or Property Bar with the button you want to modify and choose Edit.

2. First, temporarily add a new feature button with the icon you want to use so you can copy the icon to the Clipboard. To do this, make sure the Features tab is selected in the Toolbar/Property Bar Editor dialog box. From the Feature Categories drop-down list, select the category that would most likely have a feature with the icon you want. Then scroll through the features listed in the list box. As you select each feature, the icon it uses is displayed at the bottom of the dialog box:

   ✉ Create an envelope

3. When you find a feature with an icon you want to use, choose Add Button to add a new button with that icon.

4. Double-click the new button and choose Edit to display the Image Editor. Choose Copy to copy the image to the Clipboard.

5. Choose OK twice; then click and drag the button off the toolbar or Property Bar to delete it.

6. Now, double-click the button that you want to use the new icon on. Choose Edit.

How to... Copy Button Icons (*continued*)

7. In the Image Editor, choose Paste to paste in the copied icon. If you want to make changes to the icon, use the tools in the Image Editor. For example, to change the color of a section, select Fill Whole Area. Then, click the color you want to use from the color palette. Click the section of the icon that you want to change and any adjacent pixels will be formatted with the new color.

8. Choose OK twice when you're finished.

Menu Bars

The menu bar has long been a standard fixture in computer programs. The menu bar displays across the top of the screen and gives you access to a program's various features. WordPerfect 8 puts control of menu bars in your hands by giving you the ability to edit existing menu bars and even create new ones. For example, you can remove menu items that you never use, or you can add entire new menu headings complete with separator lines and submenus:

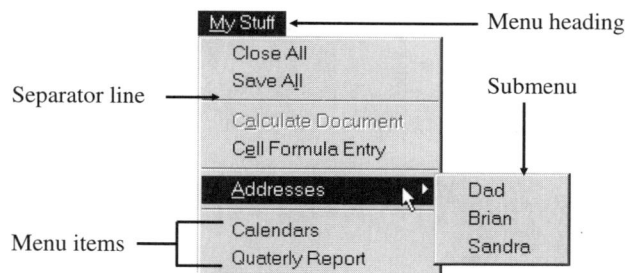

WordPerfect 8 comes with four precreated menu bars: WordPerfect 8, WordPerfect 7, Internet Publisher, and Equation Editor. The WordPerfect 8 menu bar is displayed by default. The Internet Publisher and Equation Editor menu bars are displayed when using those features. The WordPerfect 7 menu bar is included for those users who want to have the menu options in the same location as they were in WP 7. To select a different menu bar, right-click the menu bar and select the one you want to display.

Customizing a Menu Bar

You can customize a menu bar by editing an existing bar or creating a new one. To do this, right-click the menu bar and choose Settings. To edit an existing menu bar, select it and choose Edit. To create a new bar, select a menu bar in the list that you want to base your new bar on and choose Create. Type a name for your menu bar, such as **Custom,** and choose OK.

The Menu Editor dialog box appears (see Figure 13-7), which looks very similar to the Toolbar/Property Bar Editor dialog box. With the Menu Editor dialog box

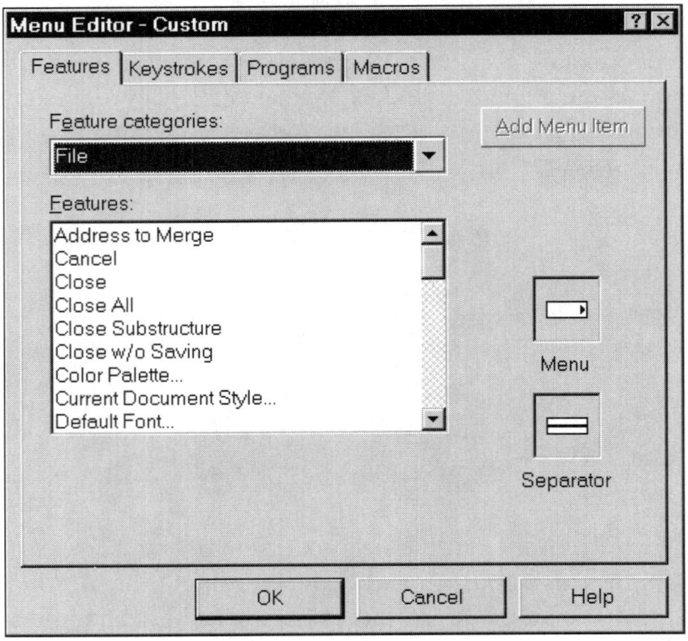

FIGURE 13-7 The Menu Editor lets you customize menu bars

displaying, you can add new menu headings and menu items, move items to new locations, and delete menu items from the bar.

Follow these guidelines to add different types of items to your menu bar:

- *Headings*   To add a new menu heading to a menu bar, move the mouse pointer over the Menu icon in the Menu Editor dialog box until it turns into a four-directional arrow. Then click and drag the icon to the menu bar. Release the mouse pointer where you want the new menu heading inserted (a vertical bar indicates where the new heading will be inserted). The new heading uses the text "Menu." If you move the mouse over the new heading, the menu will be empty, as shown here:

  To change the text of the heading, double-click the new "Menu" item. In the Menu Item text box, type the name you want for the heading. Use an ampersand to indicate a mnemonic letter. For example, typing **&My Stuff** would create a menu labeled My Stuff. In the QuickTip text box, type a description for the menu. Choose OK when you're finished.

- *Items*   To add individual items to a menu bar menu, select the tab in the Menu Editor dialog box for the type of item you want to add. Just as with toolbar and Property Bars, you can add menu items that activate WP features, insert keystrokes, execute a program, or play a macro. For example, to add a menu item that closes the document without saving it, select Close w/o Saving in the Features list box and choose Add Menu Item. See the steps in the "Customizing Toolbars and Property Bars" section earlier in this chapter for more information on adding the four types of items to your menu bar.

  The new item is added on the far right of the menu. To change the text of the item, double-click the item and type the new text in the Menu Item text box. As with menu headings, you can include an ampersand (&) to indicate a mnemonic letter. Choose OK when you're finished. To move the item to an existing menu, simply click and drag it to the menu, releasing the mouse button when it's positioned on the menu where you want.

13

- *Submenus* To add a submenu, click and drag the Menu icon from the Menu Editor dialog box and release it within an existing menu instead of on the main menu bar. Then double-click the "Menu" submenu text to customize the text, using an ampersand (&) for a mnemonic letter. Once you've created a submenu, you can add or move menu items to the submenu.

- *Separators* To add a horizontal separator line to a menu, move the mouse pointer over the Separator icon in the Menu Editor dialog box until it turns into a four-directional arrow. Then click and drag the icon to the menu and release the mouse button when it's positioned within a menu or submenu where you want.

To move menu items or headings to a different location, simply click and drag the item to the new position. You can move individual menu items, entire menus, or submenus. You can also drag a menu heading to an existing menu to convert it into a submenu. As you're dragging an item, a bar indicates where the item will be inserted. To delete an entire menu or individual menu item, click and drag it off the menu bar. When the mouse pointer turns into a garbage can, release the mouse button.

When you're finished making changes to the menu bar, choose Close. If you want to select the new menu bar, choose Select, and then Close.

NOTE: *To delete a custom menu bar, right-click the menu bar and choose Settings. Select the menu bar you want to delete, choose Delete, and then choose Yes. While you can't delete a menu bar that's included with WP, you can reset it to its original settings. Select the toolbar in the Customize Settings dialog box and choose Reset. Choose Yes to confirm the change. Choose Close when you're finished.*

The Application Bar

The Application Bar that appears at the bottom of the screen can be customized to display the information you need, such as the current printer that's selected or the current font being used. It's also a great source of quick shortcuts that can save you

time. For example, you can customize the Application Bar to display the current date, and then click that icon to insert the date text into your document.

To customize the Application Bar, right-click it and choose Settings. (If the Application Bar isn't displaying, choose View | Toolbars, select Application Bar, and choose OK.) This displays the Application Bar Settings dialog box (see Figure 13-8). In this dialog box, select the items you want to add to the Application Bar. To delete an item, deselect it in the dialog box or simply click and drag it off the Application Bar. When you select an item, the dialog box displays a brief description of that item.

Follow the guidelines displayed in the dialog box to customize the items. For example, you can move an item by clicking and dragging it to a new location. Or you can make an item smaller or larger by clicking and dragging the left edge of the

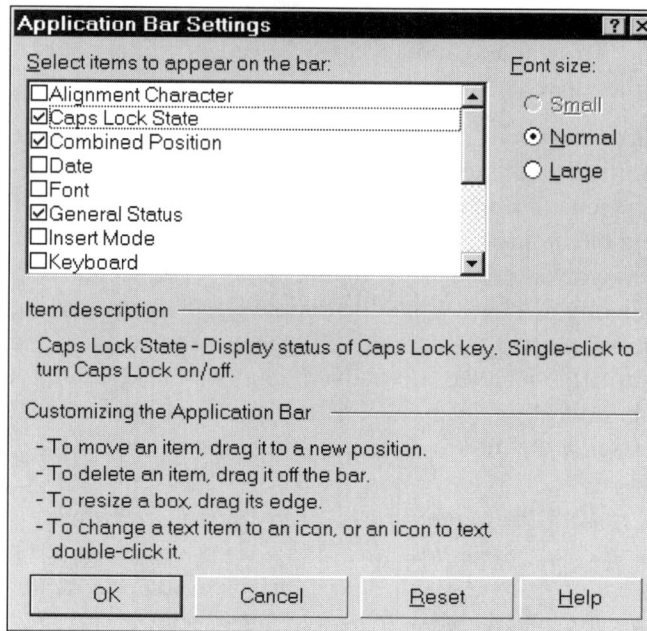

FIGURE 13-8 You can customize options on the Application Bar

item. If you want an item to display as text instead of an icon—or vice versa—double-click the item. The following illustration shows a sample customized Application Bar:

| Document1 | 🔟 🕐 Times New Roman Regular | Insert | | Pg 1 Ln 1" Pos 1.04" | I▸ AB | HP LaserJet 4P |

When you're finished making changes, choose OK.

Application Bar Tips

The Application Bar provides lots of great shortcuts for accessing features quickly, switching between documents, and even copying text between documents. Here are a few tips to try:

■   Each open document displays a tab on the Application Bar with its filename. To switch to another open document, simply click the document tab for that document.

■   You can quickly move and copy text between open documents using the document tabs on the Application Bar. Select the text you want to move or copy; then click and drag the selection to the Application Bar. Without releasing the mouse button, move the mouse pointer over the document tab where you want to paste the information. The second document automatically displays. Continue to hold down the mouse button as you drag the mouse to the location in the second document where you want the information inserted. If you want to move the selection, release the mouse button. If you want to copy the selection, hold down the CTRL key as you release the mouse button.

TIP: *If you want to have the choice of moving or copying the text with or without the font attributes, click and drag the selected text using the right mouse button instead of the left button. When you release the mouse button in the new document, a QuickMenu appears giving you options to move or copy the text with or without the font attributes.*

■   To insert the current date as text into your document, click the date icon on the Application Bar (you have to customize the Application Bar to include this button). Similarly, you can click the time icon to insert the current time at the location of the insertion point.

- If the insertion point is in a table, column, merge data file, or text formatted with a paragraph style, the General Status button on the Application Bar displays information about the current position, such as the table cell or style name. If you click the General Status button, a dialog box appears based on the current position. For example, if the insertion point is in a table, clicking the General status buttons displays the Table Format dialog box. If you're in a merge data file, it displays the Insert Merge Codes dialog box, and so on.

- Many Application Bar buttons display their corresponding dialog box when they're clicked. For example, clicking the Print button displays the Print dialog box, and clicking the Font button displays the Font dialog box. Other buttons that display dialog boxes include Alignment Character (the Tab Set dialog box), Combined Position (the Go To dialog box), Keyboard (the Customize Settings dialog box), and Zoom (the Zoom dialog box).

- Some Application Bar buttons toggle a feature on and off when they're clicked. For example, you can turn Caps Lock on and off by clicking the Caps Lock button on the Application Bar. Other toggle buttons include Insert Mode (toggles between Insert and Typeover mode), Num Lock, Scroll Lock, Select On/Off, and shadow cursor.

Keyboards

If you prefer to keep your hands on the keyboard instead of reaching for the mouse to click toolbar buttons or menu bars, WordPerfect hasn't forgotten about you. WP lets you assign the same features, keystrokes, programs, and macros that you can assign to toolbars or menu bars to shortcut keystrokes instead.

WordPerfect comes with several predefined keyboards with shortcut keystrokes already defined. For example, the default WPWin 8 Keyboard has the common assignments of CTRL-B to turn bold on and off, CTRL-S to save the document, and so on. If you're a former WordPerfect for DOS user, you can select the WPDOS 6.1 Keyboard that has the WP DOS keystroke assignments, such as SHIFT-F7 for Print and F5 for the Open File dialog box. You can edit the keystroke assignments on one of these existing keyboards, or you can create your own custom keyboards.

Customizing a Keyboard

To create or edit a keyboard, choose Tools | Settings and double-click Customize. Select the Keyboards tab. A list of the currently available keyboards is displayed.

TIP: *If you've added the Keyboard button to the Application Bar, you can quickly create or edit a keyboard by clicking the Application Bar keyboard button.*

In WP 8, you can edit any of the predefined keyboards, as well as create new ones. To edit an existing keyboard, select it in the list and choose Edit. To create a new keyboard definition, choose Create. Type a name for your keyboard and choose OK. The Keyboard Shortcuts dialog box appears (see Figure 13-9).

As with the other bars discussed in this chapter, you can set up shortcut keystrokes to activate features, type text, execute programs, or play macros. The list of shortcut keys on the left shows which keystrokes currently have items assigned to them. WP lets you assign items to practically any keystroke combination, including function keys, number pad keys, positioning keys such as HOME and PAGE DOWN, as well as the standard letter keys.

To set up a keystroke shortcut, select the keystroke you want to use in the list on the left of the dialog box. If you want to change the assignment of a character key, such as A, *, or -, select Allow Assignment of Character Keys. If the keystroke has

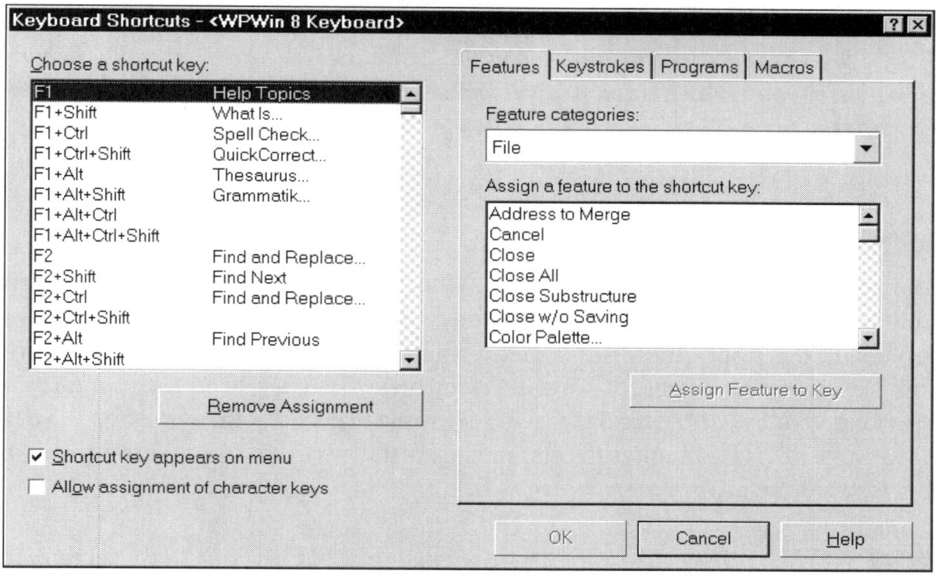

FIGURE 13-9 You can set up shortcut keystrokes for features, macros, and other tools

already been assigned to a shortcut item, that shortcut displays next to it in the list. If you want to change the assignment of the keystroke, choose Remove Assignment.

NOTE: *Changing the keystroke assignments only affects the keys when pressed within WordPerfect.*

Now, use the tabs on the right side of the Keyboard Shortcuts dialog box to assign the feature, keystrokes, program, or macro you want to the selected keystroke. For example, to assign a feature to a key, use the Feature Categories drop-down list to select the category containing the feature you want to add; then select the feature in the list and choose Assign Feature to Key. For more information on adding these four types of items, see the "Customizing Toolbars and Property Bars" section earlier in this chapter.

When you're finished making changes to the keyboard, choose OK. Make sure the keyboard you want to use is selected in the list and choose Select. Choose Close twice to return to the document.

NOTE: *If you've edited one of the default keyboards and want to restore it to its original settings, choose Tools | Settings and double-click Customize. Select the Keyboards tab, select the keyboard you want to reset and choose Reset; then choose Yes. To delete a custom keyboard, select the keyboard in the list and choose Delete; then choose Yes. Choose Close twice when you're finished.*

Summary

No matter *how* you like to do your work, WordPerfect's there to make sure you can get it done quickly and easily. With the ability to customize toolbars, Property Bars, menu bars, the Application Bar, and keyboards, you can have all of your favorite tools right at your fingertips. WordPerfect makes it easy to create buttons and keystroke shortcuts for features, keystrokes, macros, and other programs. So go ahead and take a few minutes to set things up just the way you like them—you'll be surprised at how much time you can save!

NOTE: *Your custom toolbars, menu bars, and keyboards are saved in the default template, which is usually WP8US.WPT. For more information on templates and on backing up your custom files, see Chapter 1.*

PART IV

Power Tools for Working with Other People and Programs

Chapter

14

Publishing on the Internet

The Internet is one of the fastest growing and most publicized aspects of the computer revolution, and for good reason: it extends the power of network computing to the entire world. If you have a computer, a modem, and a phone line, you can do business, learn, communicate with others, and much more. The World Wide Web is probably the most popular method of using the Internet because it provides a graphical interface and takes advantage of the multimedia capabilities of computers. Not so long ago, you had to be a techno guru in order to establish your own presence on the Web, but those days are past. Now you can create Web pages with ease using WordPerfect.

In this chapter, we'll explain how to use WordPerfect 8's wide range of Internet tools. First, we'll show you how to create links to the Internet in any WordPerfect document. Then you'll learn how to use the Internet Publisher to create and design your own Web pages. We'll show you how to include basic elements such as headings, lists, and hyperlinks, as well as more advanced features such as tables, form controls, and Java applets. You'll also learn some tips for troubleshooting problems as you publish your documents to the Internet.

Adding Internet Links to Documents

It's not uncommon anymore to refer to Web sites and e-mail addresses right in your regular WordPerfect documents, in addition to documents that you publish on the Web. By creating these references as hyperlinks, they become "hotspots" that automatically jump to the specified Web page in your browser (or begin a new e-mail message) as soon as you click them. You can add hyperlinks to your documents with the QuickLinks feature, which automatically formats Internet addresses as you type them, or with the Hyperlink feature, which lets you create links from any text in your document.

QuickLinks

The simplest way to create an Internet link in a document is to type any text that begins with "www," "ftp," "http," or "mailto." For example, if you type **www.corel.com** in a document, the Quick Links feature automatically converts it to a hyperlink that appears in blue, underlined text as soon as you press SPACEBAR or ENTER. When you click on this link, your Web browser opens and automatically takes you to Corel's Web site. If you type an e-mail address, such as **mailto:john@corel.com**, a hyperlink is created that begins a new e-mail message to that address when you click on it (if you have a supported e-mail program).

TIP: *You can type e-mail addresses without the "mailto" prefix and WP still formats them correctly as hyperlinks. For example, if you type* **president@whitehouse.gov,** *it's automatically formatted as an e-mail hyperlink.*

NOTE: *If you want to type Internet addresses in your document without having them automatically formatted as hyperlinks, you can turn off the QuickLinks feature. Choose Tools | QuickCorrect, select the QuickLinks tab, and then deselect the Format Words as Hyperlinks When you Type Them option. Choose OK.*

You can also set up the QuickLinks feature to automatically convert abbreviated text to a hyperlink as you type it in a document, such as @Corel. To do this, choose Tools | QuickCorrect and select the QuickLinks tab. In the Link Word text box, type the link text as you want it to appear in the document, such as **Corel**. In the Location to Link to text box, type the Internet site or e-mail address that the text should be linked to, such as **www.corel.com**.

TIP: *If you're not sure of the exact Internet address, you can click the file folder button to the right of the Location to Link to text box and use Corel's Internet browser in the Open File dialog box to find the site. See the "Browse the Internet from WordPerfect" Power Tip for more information.*

Power Tip... **Browse the Internet from WordPerfect**

WordPerfect 8 has a great new feature that turns the Open File dialog box into a small Web browser. This helps you locate a Web site when you're not sure of the specific address. If you need to enter an Internet address in a dialog box, such as the Location to Link to text box when setting up a Quick Link, click the File Folder button to the right of the text box.

When the Open File dialog box appears, click the Goto/From Corel Internet button on the toolbar. The regular file list is replaced with Corel's Web site home page. You can switch to a different Web site by typing a URL in the File Name text box, as well as by clicking links in the Web documents themselves. Once you've located the Web site you want, choose Select and the correct URL address is automatically inserted in the text box. (For more information on using the Open File dialog box as a Web browser, see Chapter 16.)

Once you've specified the QuickLink text and destination, choose Add Entry to add the QuickLink to the list. Notice that an @ symbol is placed in front of the link text you typed. WordPerfect uses this symbol to identify QuickLinks as you type them in a document. When you type the link text in a document (starting with the @ symbol), such as **@Corel**, WP automatically formats it as a hyperlink and removes the @ symbol. If you move the mouse pointer over the hyperlink, it changes to a hand icon and the hyperlink destination appears in a pop-up bubble:

Corel Link: Http://www.corel.com

Click the link to open the Web site in your browser or begin a new e-mail message. For more information on creating and using QuickLinks, see Chapter 3.

Hyperlinks

QuickLinks aren't the only way to create Internet links in your documents. You can also use the Hyperlink feature to convert any document text into an Internet link. To do this, type the link text in the document, select it, and then choose Tools | Hyperlink.

If you already know the Web site address that you want to link to, type it in the Document/Macro text box. If not, you can click the file folder icon to the right of the text box and use the Corel Internet feature (see the "Browse the Internet from WordPerfect" Power Tip for more information). Or you can choose Browse Web to open your browser and switch to the site you want. If you're using Netscape, when you close the browser or minimize it to return to WordPerfect, the URL address of the last site you were at is added to the Document/Macro text box.

NOTE: *If you're using a browser other than Netscape, you can copy and paste the URL address from your browser to the Document/Macro text box.*

TIP: *You can also use the mailto: command when you're creating a hyperlink. Instead of typing an URL in the Document/Macro text box, type* **mailto:** *followed by an e-mail address, such as* **mailto:john@corel.com**. *When the hyperlink is clicked, a new e-mail message is started to the specified address.*

If you want the hyperlink to appear in a graphics button instead of as blue, underlined text, select the Make Text Appear as a Button option. Choose OK to create the hyperlink. When you click the hyperlink, your browser is automatically opened to the specified Web site.

TIP: *You can also use a graphics image for a hyperlink. For more information on creating hyperlinks from graphics in regular WordPerfect documents, see Chapter 12. For the steps on creating graphics hyperlinks in a Web page, see the "Inserting Lines and Graphics" section later in this chapter.*

If you want to edit a hyperlink after it's been created, right-click the hyperlink and choose Edit Hyperlink. Make any changes you want in the Hyperlink Properties dialog box and choose OK. You can also modify the hyperlink appearance in regular documents by editing the hyperlink style. For more information on creating and editing hyperlinks, see Chapter 12.

Creating a Basic Web Page

Documents published on the Internet are text files formatted with a language called Hypertext Markup Language (HTML). But you don't have to know this special language in order to create Web Pages. Instead, WordPerfect's Internet Publisher can help you easily create HTML documents using the WordPerfect formatting features you're already familiar with. The Internet Publisher isn't a separate program, but rather a mode of WordPerfect that displays a document as it will appear in a Web browser and only gives you access to the WordPerfect features that are supported in HTML. After you've created a Web page, you can use the Internet Publisher to create an HTML version of the document with the correct HTML codes.

NOTE: *You can also create Web pages with Corel Barista, which displays your document as a Java application, so you can use any of WordPerfect's formatting features in your Web documents. For more information, see Chapter 20.*

Getting Started

You can use the Internet Publisher to create a Web document from scratch or to convert an existing WordPerfect document to HTML format. There are several different ways you can access the Internet Publisher. Follow one of these steps to create a new Web document:

- Choose File | Internet Publisher. In the Internet Publisher dialog box, choose New Web Document. Select Create a Blank Web Document in the list box and choose Select.

- Go to a blank document window and click the Change View button on the toolbar.

- Choose File | New. From the Project Category drop-down list, select either [WordPerfect 8] or Web Publishing. Then select [WordPerfect Web Document] in the list and choose Create. This displays the Internet Publisher PerfectExpert panel on the left side of the document window (see Figure 14-1).

TIP: *You can also create a new Web document by using one of the PerfectExpert projects. WordPerfect 8 comes with projects already set up to help you create résumés, alphabetical listings, personal pages, job postings, company handbooks, and more. To use one of these projects, choose File | New and from the Project Category drop-down list, select Web Publishing. Select the project you want and choose Create. Replace the sample text in the document with your own text and add any other formatting you want before publishing the document to HTML. (For more information on projects, see Chapter 1.)*

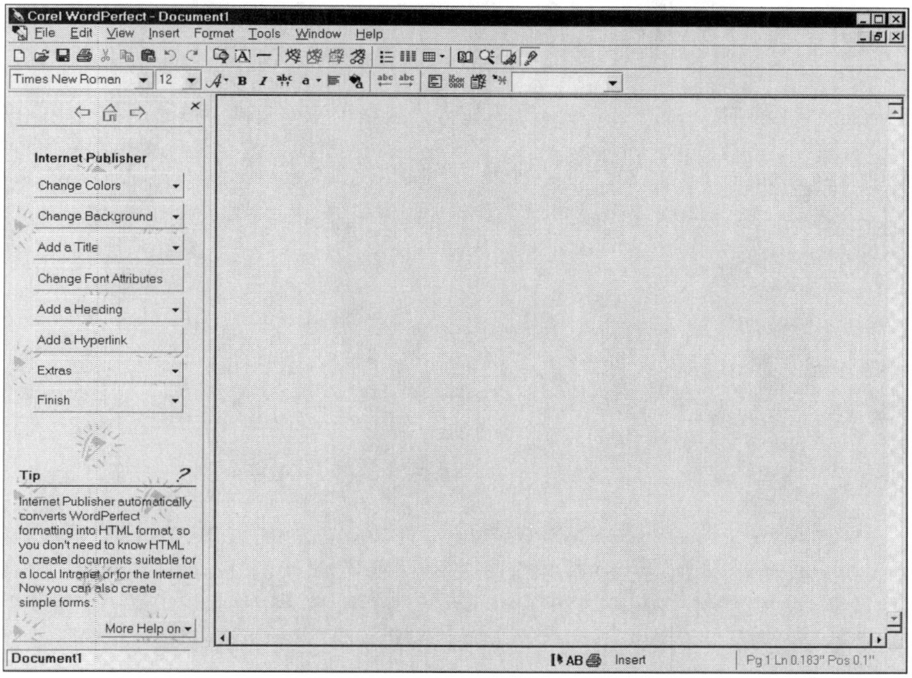

FIGURE 14-1 The Internet Publisher screen with the PerfectExpert panel

If you want to convert an existing document to HTML format so you can publish it on the Web, open that document in WordPerfect. Click the Change View button on the toolbar, or choose File | Internet Publisher and then choose Format as Web Document. Unless you've already disabled it, you'll see a warning message telling you that you may lose some formatting. If your document contains any formatting that's not supported in HTML, such as drop caps or watermarks, it will be removed from the document. See the "Features Not Supported in HTML" Quick Reference section for a list of WordPerfect features that don't have HTML formatting equivalents.

NOTE: *If you don't want this warning message to appear each time you format a document with the Internet Publisher, select the Do Not Show Me This Message Next Time I Choose Web View option in the dialog box.*

TIP: *If you want to be able to use some of the non-supported features in your Web documents, you can publish your document with Corel Barista (see Chapter 20 for more information).*

14

Quick Reference ▶▶▶ Features Not Supported in HTML

When you use the Internet Publisher, only those features in WordPerfect that are supported in HTML are available on the pull-down menus. If you format an existing document with the Internet Publisher, codes and features that don't have an HTML equivalent are deleted from the document. The features that aren't supported in HTML include the following:

- Drop Caps
- Fills (shading)
- Headers and Footers
- Margins

- Page Numbering
- Tabs and Indents
- Vertical Lines
- Watermarks

In addition, footnotes are converted to endnotes, and some features, such as Bullets and Fonts, have modified options. If you want to be able to use some of the non-supported features in your Web documents, you can publish your document with Corel Barista (see Chapter 20 for more information).

Choose OK to clear the message. If you want to keep a copy of the original document, choose File | Save As and type a new filename for the Web version of the document, so you don't accidentally save the Web formatting changes over the original version.

The Internet Publisher looks a little different from the regular document screen (see Figure 14-1). For example, the background color of the editing window changes to gray, which is the default background color for Web pages (you can easily change this color, as explained in the "Changing the Colors and Background" section). In addition, the toolbar and Property Bar change to reflect the new set of features compatible with HTML. And the margin guides are removed, since Web documents are automatically formatted to fit the browser's screen when they're displayed, so margins aren't needed.

If the PerfectExpert panel is displaying (see Figure 14-1), you have easy access to all of the Web formatting features, including changing the colors and fonts, adding headings or hyperlinks, and publishing the document to HTML format. If you want to display the PerfectExpert panel, click the PerfectExpert button on the toolbar or choose Help | PerfectExpert. If the PerfectExpert panel doesn't show the Internet Publisher features, click the Change View button on the toolbar twice.

NOTE: *To close the PerfectExpert panel, click the Cancel button in the upper-right corner of the panel or choose Help | PerfectExpert.*

Setting the Title

One of the first things you should do when you're creating a Web page is specify the title. The title of the page appears in the title bar of the browser and is also used when someone bookmarks your page. To specify the title, choose File | Properties. Select Custom Title and type the title in the text box. Choose OK.

If you don't specify a title in the HTML Document Properties dialog box, the browser uses the highest-level heading found in the document as the title. (For more information on creating and formatting headings, see the "Formatting Text" section.)

NOTE: *If the PerfectExpert panel is displaying, you can also specify the document title by choosing Add a Title | For the Title Bar and then typing the title text.*

Changing the Colors and Background

If you don't like the default colors WordPerfect uses for Web pages, they're easy to change. You can change the colors used for the page background, document text, and hyperlinks. In addition, you can select a graphics image to be repeated as a background "wallpaper" design. To change the colors or background, choose Format | Text/Background Colors. The HTML Document Properties dialog box appears, with the Text/Background Colors tab selected (see Figure 14-2).

NOTE: *You can also change the text and background colors by choosing File | Properties and selecting the Text/Background Colors tab.*

WordPerfect lets you select the colors used for regular text as well as and the different types of hyperlinks in your Web page. To change a color, select the new

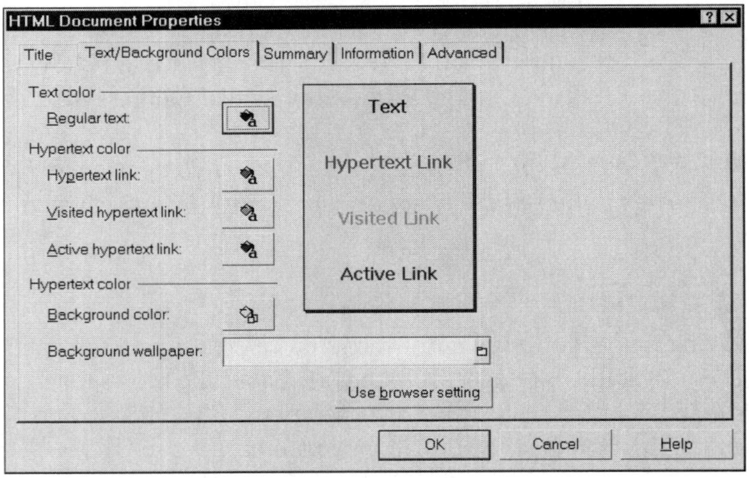

FIGURE 14-2 You can specify the Web page colors and background wallpaper image

color from the pop-up palette to the right of the option you want to change. The following list is a brief description of each option.

- *Regular Text* Text typed in the document (including headings) that's not formatted as a hyperlink.

- *Hypertext Link* Text that's formatted as a hyperlink to jump to another Web page or location in the current Web document. This color is used for hyperlinks that have not yet been clicked by the user.

- *Visited Hypertext Link* A hyperlink that's already been selected by the user. The user's browser determines the length of time that a hyperlink remains marked as visited.

- *Active Hypertext Link* A hyperlink that's currently selected. The specified color displays briefly when the hyperlink is clicked.

You can use either a solid color for your page background or a repeated bitmapped graphics image—called "wallpaper." To use a solid color, select the color you want from the Background Color pop-up palette (some colors may not be supported if you're running in a 256-color screen resolution). To select a wallpaper image, click the file folder icon next to the Background Wallpaper text box and select the graphic you want to use. WordPerfect comes with a large number of background textures to choose from (found in the \Corel\Suite8\Graphics\Textures directory), or you can use another bitmap image. The image you select is repeated in a tile pattern across the background of the page.

NOTE: *You can't use WPG files for wallpaper images; you must select a bitmap image. Common bitmap formats includeBMP, DIB, GIF, and JPG.*

As you select the color and background options in the HTML Document Properties dialog box, a preview shows a sample of your settings. Be careful to choose text colors that show up well on the selected background. This is particularly important when using a wallpaper image, which may use a number of different colors. You don't want your text to get lost in your splendid background.

TIP: *You can also choose from a variety of predefined color schemes and wallpaper images. For more information, see the "Quick Color and Background Settings" Power Tip.*

Formatting Text

While the Internet Publisher doesn't have as many text-formatting features as WordPerfect normally does, you still have several options for formatting the text in your Web pages. For example, you can change the font and font size, use several different paragraph and heading styles, and specify the justification.

NOTE: *Remember to save your Web document frequently as you format it (it's saved as a regular WordPerfect document). When you publish your Web document to HTML format, a copy of the document is created with the HTML codes. (For more information on publishing to HTML format, see the "Previewing and Publishing Web pages" section later in the chapter.)*

14

Power Tip... Quick Color and Background Settings

The PerfectExpert can help you quickly format the colors and background of your Web pages. You can select from several predefined sets of colors that work well together, or choose a wallpaper image from a visual pop-up palette. If the PerfectExpert panel isn't currently displaying, choose Help | PerfectExpert; then click the Change View button on the toolbar *twice* to display the Internet Publisher options on the PerfectExpert panel.

To change the text and background colors, select the color scheme you want from the Change Colors drop-down list on the PerfectExpert panel, such as Cyan or Mauve. These settings affect the text and hyperlink colors, as well as the solid background color. If you're using a wallpaper image, you can select the Wallpaper Dark or Wallpaper Light color scheme to make the text legible on a dark or light background.

To select a background wallpaper texture, use the Change Background pop-down palette on the PerfectExpert panel. This displays 20 common background textures that come with WordPerfect. These textures are saved as GIF files in the \Corel\Suite8\Template\Custom WP Templates directory. If you choose Custom from the pop-up palette, the HTML Document Properties dialog box appears and you can select a specific bitmap image for the wallpaper. (The \Corel\Suite8\Graphics\Textures directory contains over 80 other different background textures in ten different categories.)

Selecting a Font

To change the font or font size in a Web page, you can use the Font Face and Font Size drop-down lists on the Property Bar, just as you would in any WordPerfect document. You can also change the font and font size by choosing Format | Font or by choosing Change Font Attributes on the PerfectExpert panel. This displays the

Font dialog box, which has different options than it does in a regular WordPerfect document (see Figure 14-3), due to the differences in HTML formatting options. For example, there are only seven font sizes to choose from (ranging from 8 points to 36 points).

Be aware that the fonts you use in your Web documents only appear in the user's browser if they already have the exact same font installed on their system. If not, the browser uses its default font—usually a serif font such as Times New Roman—for the text. As a general rule, try to avoid fancy or unusual fonts, since most people won't be able to view them anyway.

TIP: *One way you can include unusual fonts in your Web documents is to place the text in a graphics text box. See the "Inserting Lines and Graphics" section later in the chapter for more information.*

The Internet Publisher also supports several standard font and font size attributes, such as bold, italics, and very large. In addition, two new font attributes are available for Web documents—monospaced and blink. The monospaced attribute formats text in a font similar to Courier, where every character and spaces take up the same amount of space. The blink attribute creates blinking text when the document is displayed in Netscape (in WordPerfect, blinking text appears in the shadow font attribute).

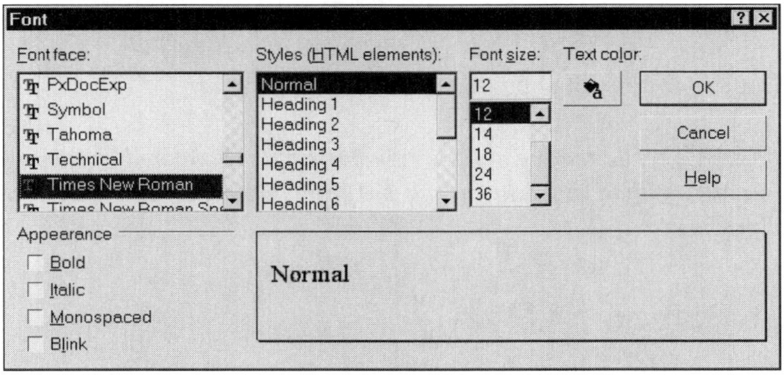

FIGURE 14-3 The Font dialog box in the Internet Publisher has different options

CAUTION: *The blink attribute is only supported in Netscape Navigator. Use the blink attribute judiciously (if at all), because many Web users find it particularly annoying.*

To use a font attribute, select it from the Font Attributes drop-down list on the Power Bar:

☑ Normal
☐ Bold
☐ Italic
☐ Underline
☐ Strikeout
☐ Redline
☐ Blink
☐ Subscript
☐ Superscript
☐ Fine
☐ Small
☐ Large
☐ Very Large
☐ Extra Large
☐ Hidden

You can also select the bold, italic, and monospaced attributes from the Font dialog box or from their individual buttons on the Power Bar.

NOTE: *The redline and strikeout attributes are listed on the Power Bar's Font Attribute drop-down list, but they might not be supported in every browser.*

Using a Paragraph Style

You can also format your Web document text with paragraph styles. The Internet Publisher supports four HTML paragraph styles: normal, address, indented quotation, and preformatted text. Figure 14-4 shows a Web page that uses the different styles and Table 14-1 contains a brief description of each style.

To use a paragraph style, place the insertion point where you want the style to begin or select existing text in the document. You can choose a style from the Styles

Normal style   Indented Quotation style

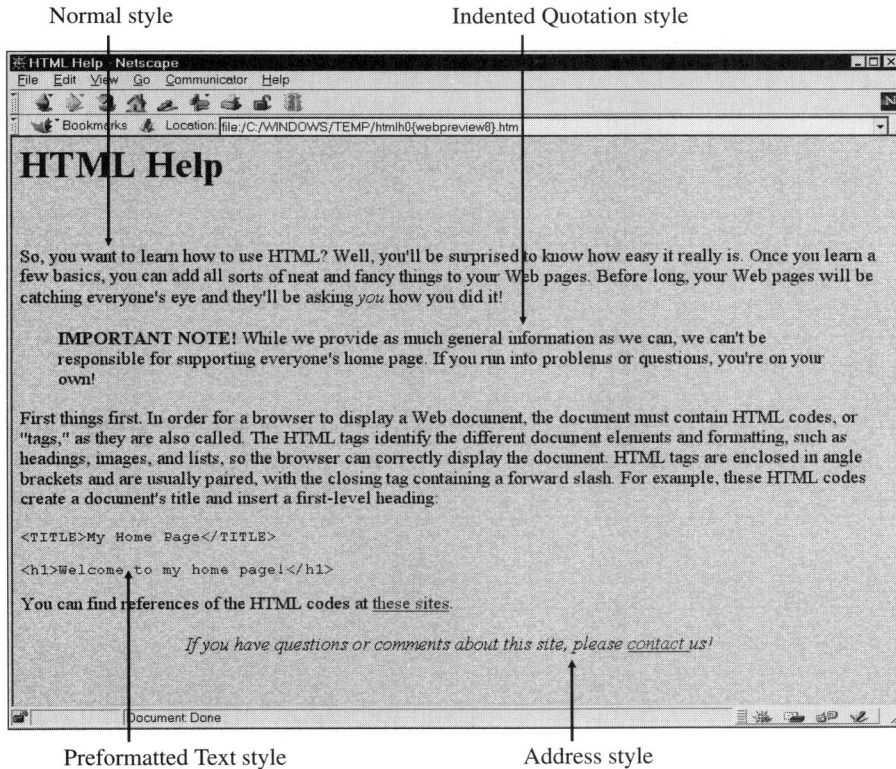

FIGURE 14-4 The Internet Publisher supports four HTML paragraph styles

Preformatted Text style   Address style

Style	Description
Normal	Regular body text.
Address	Italics, commonly used to display information about the page author.
Indented Quotation	Normal text, indented on the left and right sides for block quotations.
Preformatted Text	Text in a monospaced font, preserving spaces and line breaks exactly as shown in the original document. Soft returns in the WordPerfect document are formatted as hard returns in the browser.

TABLE 14-1 HTML Paragraph Styles in the Internet Publisher

14

list box in the Font dialog box (see Figure 14-3), or from the Font/Size drop-down list on the Property Bar:

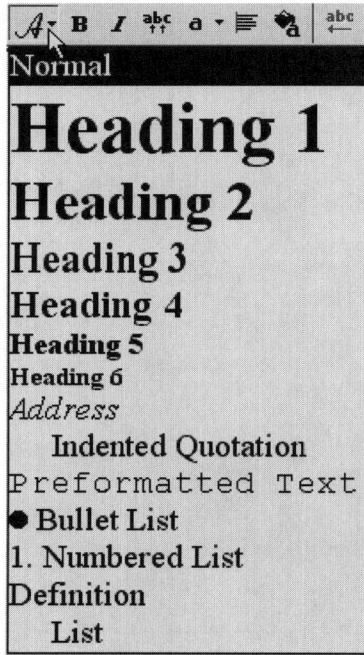

NOTE: *In addition to listing the paragraph styles, both style list locations include the available heading styles and list options (see the "Typing Headings" and "Creating Lists" sections for more information).*

After selecting a paragraph style, type the text you want formatted in that style (if you didn't already have text selected), and press ENTER. The style is automatically turned on again for the next paragraph. If you're finished formatting with the style, select the Normal style from the Font dialog box or the Font/Size drop-down list on the Property Bar.

NOTE: *Pressing ENTER in a Web document automatically inserts an extra blank line, unless you're using a style that formats text differently. For more information on line and paragraph breaks in Web documents, see the Power Tip "Tabs, Line Breaks, and Paragraph Breaks."*

> ## Power Tip▸▸▸ Tabs, Line Breaks, and Paragraph Breaks
>
> As surprising as it sounds, HTML doesn't support tabs or indents. If you try to press TAB while in the Internet Publisher, nothing happens, unless you're creating a definition list, where you *can* press TAB to indent text after an initial heading (see the "Creating Lists" section for more information). If you want to indent text in a Web page, you need to insert hard spaces by pressing CTRL-SPACEBAR (if you insert regular spaces, the extra spaces are automatically removed when the page is displayed in a browser).
>
> Instead of indenting paragraphs, HTML automatically separates paragraphs with a blank line. Each time you press ENTER in the Internet Publisher, a blank line is inserted to give you an accurate representation of how the document will appear when it's displayed in a browser. If you want to insert a hard return *without* the extra blank line, you can insert a line break by choosing Insert | Line Break or by pressing CTRL-SHIFT-L.
>
> In some instances the display of blank lines in WP isn't quite accurate, such as when you select the Address or Preformatted Text style, or when you begin a bulleted, numbered, or definition list. When you select any of these styles, WordPerfect removes the blank line just above the formatted text. However, this blank line will still appear when the document is displayed in a browser. In addition, pressing ENTER while one of these styles is selected doesn't automatically insert an extra blank line.

Typing Headings

The Internet Publisher lets you easily create headings in six different levels (each level is formatted with a different size). To use the different headings, place the insertion point where you want to type the heading, or click anywhere in a line of existing text. You can select a heading in one of three ways:

- Choose Format | Font and select the heading from the Styles list box.
- Select the heading from the Font/Size drop-down list on the Power Bar.

14

■   Select the heading from the Add a Heading drop-down list on the PerfectExpert panel.

After selecting a heading style, type the heading text if needed. All of the heading styles (except for Heading 6) already include codes to mark the heading text for different levels in a table of contents.

> **NOTE:**   *If you don't specify a title for your Web document, the highest-level heading in the document is displayed in the title bar of the browser. (See the "Setting the Title" section earlier in the chapter for more information.)*

Changing the Justification

HTML supports three alignment options: left, center, and right. To change the justification, place the insertion point where you want the new alignment to begin. Choose Format | Justification and select the option you want, such as Center. You can also change the alignment by using the Justification button on the Power Bar.

> **NOTE:**   *If you didn't have text selected in the document when you changed the justification, the new alignment affects the document from the insertion point forward, until you change it again.*

Creating Lists

In addition to formatting your Web documents with paragraph styles and headings, you can easily create three different types of lists: bulleted, numbered, and definition (see Figure 14-5). Bulleted lists begin each line with a bullet, numbered lists are numbered automatically, and definition lists allow you to indent paragraphs underneath a list heading.

To create a list, place the insertion point where you want the list to begin. (If you've already typed the list items, select them in the document.) Choose Insert | Outline/Bullets & Numbering. Select the type of list you want to create and choose OK. If you're creating a new list, type the list item text and press ENTER to insert the next item. Unlike regular paragraphs in a Web document, pressing ENTER in a list does not cause a blank line to be inserted.

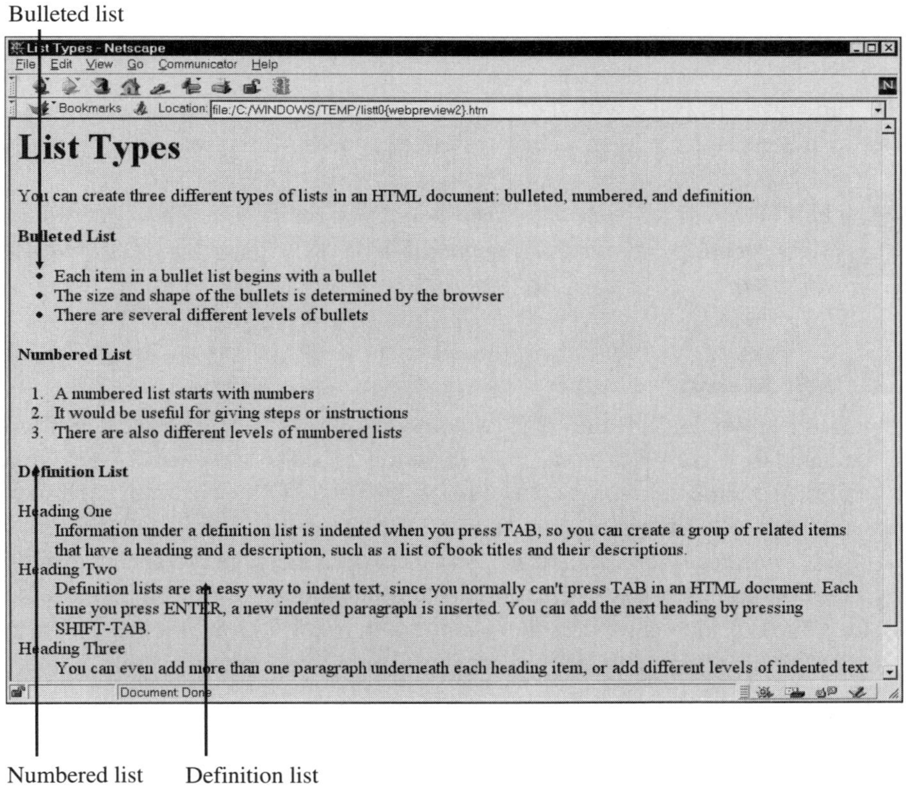

Bulleted list

Numbered list   Definition list

FIGURE 14-5 You can create three types of lists in a Web document

TIP: *You can also start a bulleted list by clicking the Insert Bullet button on the toolbar or by pressing CTRL-SHIFT-B.*

After pressing ENTER in a list, you can press TAB to insert an indented level on the next line. If you're creating a bulleted list, the indented level uses a different bullet. In a numbered list, the numbering starts over for the indented levels. In a definition list, the paragraph text is indented. Each time you press ENTER, a new item for the same level is inserted. To move back to the previous level, press SHIFT-TAB.

14

NOTE: *The Web browser determines the size and shape of the bullets in a bulleted list, so the bullets may appear differently when you view the Web document in different browsers.*

When you're finished with the list, press ENTER to move to a new line and then press BACKSPACE. This deletes the last item and turns off the feature.

NOTE: *A bulleted list is used when you create a table of contents in a Web document. Each level in the table of contents is indented and uses a different bullet.*

Adding Links

Web pages just wouldn't be the same without lots of links to other places on the Web. You can add hyperlinks to your Web documents just as you can in any regular WordPerfect document. You can create links to bookmarks on the current page, to other pages on your site (including bookmarks on those pages), or to other Web sites altogether. You can also create links that start an e-mail message to a specified address.

One of the easiest ways to create links to other Web sites or e-mail addresses is with the QuickLinks feature. See the "Adding Internet Links to Documents" section at the beginning of the chapter for more information on creating QuickLinks in a document.

If you want to create a link to a bookmark on the same Web page, you first need to create the bookmark. In the Internet Publisher, place the insertion point where you want the bookmark inserted, such as at the beginning of a heading, and choose Tools | Bookmark. Choose Create. If you want to change the name of the bookmark, type the text in the Bookmark Name text box and choose OK. Repeat this process to create other bookmarks in the Web page if needed.

TIP: *Remember to create a bookmark at the beginning of your document (or at the location of the table of contents), and then include links for your readers to return back to the top from other locations in the document.*

Follow these steps to create a link to a bookmark on the same page, another Web page on your site, or a completely different Web site with the Hyperlink feature:

1. Place the insertion point in the Web document where you want the link inserted, type the link text, and then select it.

2. If the PerfectExpert panel is displaying, choose Add a Hyperlink. Otherwise, choose Tools | Hyperlink. The Hyperlink Properties dialog box appears.

3. If you want to link to a bookmark in the current page, select the bookmark name from the Bookmark drop-down list. If you haven't yet created the bookmark, type a bookmark name, and when you're finished creating the hyperlink, create a bookmark with that same name (bookmarks are case sensitive).

4. If you want to link to another page on your own Web site, simply type the filename of that page, such as **info.htm**. If the page is stored in a subdirectory on your Web server (relative to the location of the main HTM file), type the subdirectory name before the filename, such as **pages/info.htm**. If you want to link to a bookmark on the specified page, type the bookmark name in the Bookmark text box (you won't be able to select it from the drop-down list).

5. If you want to link to another Web site and you know the URL address, type the complete address in the Document text box, including the "http://" prefix, such as **http://www.corel.com**. If you're not sure of the address, choose Browse Web to open your browser, and then switch to the site you want. When you find the site, return to WP and the URL is inserted in the text box.

6. Choose OK to create the hyperlink.

If you need to edit a hyperlink after you've created it, right-click the link and choose Edit Hyperlink. For more information on the Hyperlink feature, see Chapter 12.

TIP: *You can also add links to graphics images in your Web document. For more information, see the "Inserting Lines and Graphics" section.*

NOTE: *If you have multiple pages on your Web site, make sure you include a link on each page that returns to your main home page.*

Advanced Web Page Features

Web pages don't have to be limited to simple text and hyperlinks. You can add a lot of variety to your Web documents by using some of the more advanced HTML features. For example, you can insert graphics images in your Web documents and have them formatted as hyperlinks or image maps. You can also easily add tables and columns, create forms that users fill out and return to you, or add Java applets. In addition, if the Internet Publisher doesn't support an HTML feature that you want to use, such as frames or JavaScript, you can insert custom HTML codes right into your WordPerfect document.

Inserting Lines and Graphics

Graphical elements, such as horizontal lines and images, can add a lot of visual appeal to your Web pages. The Internet Publisher makes it easy to include many different kinds of graphical elements, including clip art, scanned images, drawings, TextArt images, charts, and even equations. You can also include text boxes and horizontal lines (see Figure 14-6).

Adding a Horizontal Line

Graphics lines in Web pages have a 3-D recessed appearance and take on the color or pattern of the page background (see Figure 14-6). To add a horizontal line to a Web document, place the insertion point where you want the graphics line inserted (it will be inserted above the current text line). Choose Insert | Horizontal Line or click the Horizontal Line button on the toolbar. If the PerfectExpert panel is displaying, you can also choose Extras | Add a Horizontal Line.

NOTE: *You can't create vertical graphics lines in a Web document since HTML doesn't support them.*

By default, graphics lines take up the full width of the page, but you can change the line length and thickness if you want. To do this, move the mouse pointer over the line until it turns into a selection arrow. Then click once to select the line and use the sizing handles to change the length and thickness. Or double-click the line to display the Edit Graphics Line dialog box and specify the exact length and thickness you want.

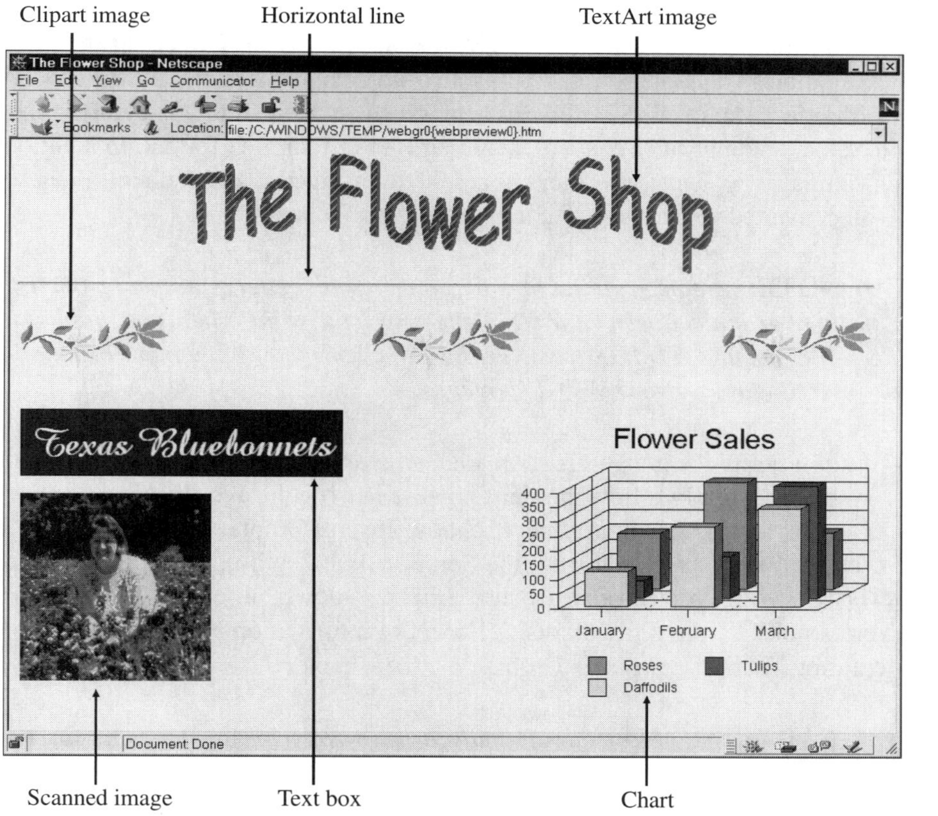

Clipart image   Horizontal line   TextArt image

Scanned image   Text box   Chart

FIGURE 14-6 Web pages can contain a variety of graphical elements

If the graphics line isn't taking the full width of the page, it can be aligned at the left or right margin, or centered between margins. To change the line position, display the Edit Graphics Line dialog box by double-clicking the line (if it's not already displaying) and select the option you want from the Horizontal drop-down list. Choose OK when you're finished.

NOTE: *Graphics lines can't be placed in a blank area of a Web page. They must always appear immediately above or below a line of text.*

14

Adding a Graphics Image

Even though most Web browsers only support images in GIF or JPG format, the Internet Publisher allows you to insert images in your Web documents in any format supported by WordPerfect, such as WPG or BMP. Then, when you publish the document to HTML, WordPerfect automatically converts the images to GIF or JPG format. In addition to graphics images, you can insert text boxes, TextArt images, and equations, and have them all converted so they appear correctly on your Web page.

NOTE: *Some graphics formats convert with better quality than others do. If a graphic doesn't turn out the way you want when you publish the document to HTML, try converting it to a 256-color bitmap in Presentations before inserting it into your Web document.*

To add a graphics image, TextArt image, chart, or other graphical element to your Web page, simply follow the steps you use in a regular WordPerfect document. For example, to insert a clipart image, choose Insert | Graphics | Clipart, then click and drag the image you want from the Scrapbook dialog box. If the PerfectExpert panel is displaying, you can also use the Extras pop-down button to add images from the Scrapbook or from a file on disk. (For more information on inserting graphics, and creating TextArt images and equations, see Chapter 7.)

CAUTION: *Most clipart images have copyright restrictions for using them in electronic formats, such as a Web page. Make sure you're not violating any copyright laws with the images that you insert. For specific information about Corel's clipart usage policy, see the first page in the printed clip-art manual.*

TIP: *Text boxes are a great way to include specialty fonts in your Web pages. Since a text box is converted to GIF format when you publish the document to HTML format, the font appears correctly in any browser. To create a text box in a Web document, choose Insert | Text Box. WordPerfect takes you to a separate screen, where you can type and format the text for the text box, using the font, font size, and font color that you want. When you're finished, choose the Close button.*

After you've inserted an image in your Web document, you can select it, resize it, and position it where you want, as you would in a regular document. By default, graphics in a Web document use a character anchor, so they move to the right or left within a line as text is added or deleted. If you want to have the image appear on the side or center of a paragraph, change it to a paragraph anchor. To do this, right-click the graphic and choose Position. From the Attach Box To drop-down list, select Paragraph. Then, from the Horizontal drop-down list, select the alignment option you want, such as Left Margin. Choose OK.

NOTE: *Graphics images can only be aligned on the left margin, right margin, or center of the paragraph. If you move a graphic by clicking and dragging it, it's automatically aligned at one of these locations.*

TIP: *Animated GIF files are a fun and easy way to add some action and movement to your Web pages. You can find lots of animated GIF files just by searching on the Internet. To use an animated GIF file in your own Web page, insert the GIF file as a normal graphic by choosing Insert | Graphics | From File and then selecting the GIF file. The first frame of hte animated graphic appears in the WordPerfect document. To see the animation, view the document in your browser by choosing the View in Web Browser toolbar button. (Not all browsers support animated GIFs.)*

Web document images also have several special settings that affect how they're handled when the document is converted to HTML. To change these image settings, right-click the graphic and choose HTML Properties. The HTML Properties dialog box appears (see Figure 14-7). You can also change the settings by selecting the graphic and choosing Properties from the PerfectExpert panel.

From this dialog box, you can specify the following settings for the image:

- In the Alternate Text text box, you can type the text that you want to appear in place of the image when the document is displayed in a browser that has the graphics display turned off. The alternate text also appears while the image is loading and in some browsers, appears in a bubble if the user places the mouse pointer over the graphic.

- Large graphics images can take a while to load, especially if the user has a slower connection. In the Low Resolution Graphic text box, you can specify the filename of a lower-resolution graphic (such as a black-and-white version) that displays first until the larger graphic loads on top of it. (The lower-resolution graphic must already be in GIF or JPG

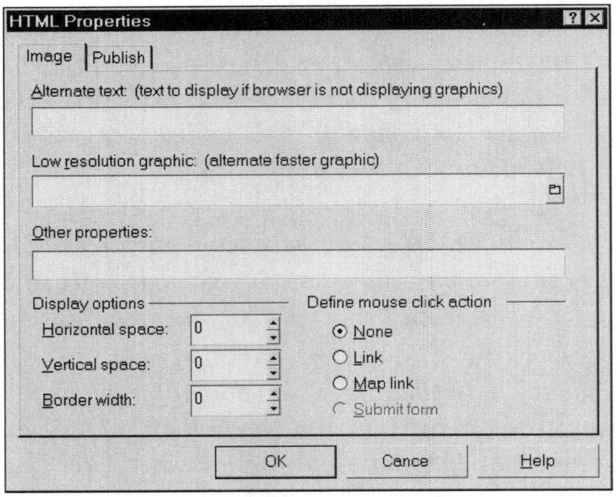

FIGURE 14-7 You can specify special settings for images in your Web document

format.) You can convert an image to a lower resolution by using Corel Presentations.

■ You can change the amount of space used on the left and right sides of the image by typing the number of pixels in the Horizontal text box. To change the amount of space used above and below the image, type the number of pixels in the Vertical text box. In addition, you can specify the border width (in pixels) in the Border Width text box. The spacing and border options you set here won't appear in the WordPerfect document, but they will show up when you view the page in a browser. (You can also select a custom border with WP's Graphics Border feature.)

■ If you want the image to link to another Web page or Web site, select Link in the dialog box, and then select the Link tab that appears. The options here are similar to the Hypertext link options. In the Document/URL text box, type the Web address that you want the image to link to, or type the filename of another page on your Web server. You can also specify a bookmark on the current page, or a target frame if the page uses frames. (See the "Hyperlinks" section earlier in the chapter for more information.)

■ You can use the Map Link option to specify an image map for the graphic, which allows the user to click on different sections of the graphic and have different hyperlinks performed. For more information, see the "How to Create an Image Map" section.

■ If you inserted a graphics image that wasn't originally in GIF or JPG format, you can tell WordPerfect what format to convert it to when you publish the document to HTML. Select the Publish tab in the dialog box, and then select the output format you want (GIF or JPG).

■ If you select GIF as the output format (from the Publish tab at the top of the dialog box), you can also decide how the image will load in the browser. Select Interlaced to have a rough image of the graphic load first and then gradually fill in the details, rather than having the image load from top to bottom in the browser.

■ By default, the Internet Publisher formats GIF files with a "transparent" background, so any white space around the image automatically matches the page background. To deselect this option, select the Publish tab and deselect Transparency.

■ If the image will be stored in a different directory on your Web server than the document HTM file, you can specify that location by selecting the Publish tab and typing the directory name in the Location of Graphic on Web Server text box. This is a relative directory to the location of the HTM or HTML file, so you don't need to type the full path. For example, if your Web pages are stored on the server in a directory called "public_html," which has a subdirectory for graphics called "images," type **images/** in the text box.

NOTE: *You can also specify the directory used for all the images associated with a Web document without having to set each location individually. For more information, see the "Previewing and Publishing Web Pages" section later in the chapter.*

How to... Create an Image Map

Image maps are popular navigation tools for Web pages. An *image map* is an image that's been divided into multiple "regions." Each region is set up as a hyperlink to another destination (such as a different page on the Web server or a different Web site). For example, you could create an image map out of the following graphics image, where each of the four arrows is linked to a different Web site:

If the user clicked on an arrow, the browser would jump to the associated link, whether it was a different page on the server, a bookmark in the same page, or a new Web site.

While image maps are powerful tools, they also require a little more work and knowledge to set up than simple text or image hyperlinks. There are two types of image maps that you can create: server-side image maps and client-side image maps. With a *server-side* image map, the list of coordinates and link references for the image is stored in a separate file (usually ending with a MAP extension), and a program on the Web server makes the link associations. In a *client-side* image map, the coordinates and link references are stored as codes in the HTML file itself, allowing the browser to read the map information. Client-side image maps are generally faster and more efficient, but not all browsers support them.

One of the easiest ways to create an image map is to use a program designed specifically for Web document creation, such as Corel's WebMaster Suite or Corel's WEB.SiteBuilder (see the "Corel's WebMaster Suite" On the CD section later in the chapter for more information). Another option for creating image maps is to use Corel Presentations, which comes with a macro for creating client-side image maps for any graphics image.

How to... Create an Image Map
(*continued*)

Follow these steps to create an image map with Corel Presentations' IMGEMAP.WCM shipping macro:

1. First, create and format the Web page with WordPerfect's Internet Publisher. Insert the graphics image that you want to use for the image map and position and size it in the document where you want.

2. Before you can create an image map in Presentations, you need to have a GIF or JPG version of the graphics image. The easiest way to do this is to publish the document to HTML format. Choose File | Internet Publisher; then choose Publish to HTML. In the Publish To text box, type the filename for the HTML document, using an HTM extension. In the Save New Images and Sound Clips In text box, type the directory where you want the converted GIF image saved. Choose OK. (For more information about publishing to HTML, see the "Previewing and Publishing Web Pages" section later in the chapter.)

3. Start Corel Presentations (keep your Web document open in WordPerfect). In Presentations, choose Tools | Macro | Play. Make sure the WordPerfect Suite 8 CD is in your CD-ROM drive and double-click the Additional Macros shortcut in the file list. (If there isn't a shortcut listed, switch to the \Corel\Suite8\Macros\PRWin directory on the WP Suite 8 CD.) Select the IMGEMAP.WCM macro and choose Play.

4. In the Enter Bitmap text box, type the path and filename of the GIF or JPG image being used in your Web page, or use the file folder icon to select it (it should be in the directory you specified earlier when publishing the document to HTML). If you used a clipart image from the Scrapbook in your Web document, the GIF filename is the first part of the WordPerfect document filename, followed by "{Image0}," where the "0" indicates the graphics number in the document. For example, if you named your WP document MYPAGE.WPD, a clipart image might be saved with the filename MYPAG0{IMAGE0}.GIF.

How to...   **Create an Image Map**
(continued)

5. In the Save File(s) To text box, specify the directory where you want the image map files placed; then choose OK.

6. Choose OK again to clear the message box and the Image Map dialog box appears in the upper-right corner of the screen. The mouse pointer also changes to a hand holding a box outline. Click and drag the first region of the image that you want to have linked to a specific location.

7. Choose Set Map in the Image Map dialog box. In the URL Location text box, type the Web site address that you want to link to, or type an HTM filename if you want to link to a different page on your Web server. If you want to link to a bookmark on the same page, type the page filename, followed by a number sign (#) and the bookmark name, such as **mypage.htm#heading**. Choose OK.

8. Repeat the previous two steps to define each region of the image that you want to map to a different location. When you're finished defining each region, choose Done in the Image Map text box.

9. A message box appears telling you the location and filename of the file containing the image map information, such as BITMAP.HTM. Choose OK and then choose File | Exit to close Presentations.

10. Return to your Web document in WordPerfect. The next step is to tell WP where to find the image map information. Right-click the graphics image in the Web document and choose HTML Properties. Select Map Link and then select the Map Link tab that appears at the top of the dialog box. Type the filename of the HTM file created by the Presentations macro in the File text box. *Don't* include the path to the file on your hard drive; just type the filename, such as **bitmap.htm**. (If you were creating a server-side image map, you would type the name of the map file in the CGI Script text box. These files typically end with a MAP extension.)

11. In the Name text box, type the same name as the HTM filename, but without the file extension, such as **bitmap**. This is the name of the map within the HTML file (Presentations automatically uses the same name for the map and the HTM file). The information should look similar to this:

Image	Publish	Map Link

Server side map information ———————————————

CGI script: [   ]

Client side map information ———————————————

File: [bitmap.htm   ] 📁

Name: [bitmap   ] ▼

12. Choose OK to close the HTML Properties dialog box. Click outside the graphics box to deselect it and make any other changes you want to the Web document. It's a good idea to also include text hyperlinks that correspond to the links in your image map for those users who have the graphics display turned off in their browsers.

13. Republish the document to HTML format by choosing File | Internet Publisher | Publish to HTML. Choose OK.

14. The final step is to upload both HTM files to the same directory on your Web server (the Web document HTM file and the BITMAP.HTM file created by the Presentations macro). If you're using a server-side image map, upload both the HTM document file and the MAP file. See the "Previewing and Publishing Web Pages" section later in the chapter for more information on uploading files.

How to... Create an Image Map *(continued)*

If the image map doesn't work correctly in your browser (we found some problems in Netscape 4.01a), or if you don't want to upload the separate BITMAP.HTM file, you can insert the image map codes directly in your Web document. To do this, in WordPerfect choose File | Open, select the BITMAP.HTM file created by the Presentations macro, and choose Open. When the Convert File Format dialog box appears, make sure that ASCII DOS Text is selected from the drop-down list and choose OK. You'll see the HTML map codes, which look something like this:

```
<MAP NAME="bitmap">
<AREA SHAPE="RECT" COORDS="52,1,135,47" HREF=north.html>
<AREA SHAPE="RECT" COORDS="127,36,180,115" HREF=east.html>
<AREA SHAPE="RECT" COORDS="46,106,132,155" HREF=south.html>
<AREA SHAPE="RECT" COORDS="1,35,54,116" HREF=west.html>
<AREA SHAPE="RECT" COORDS="60,54,127,105" HREF=http://www.corel.com>
</MAP>
<IMG SRC="image0{image0}.gif" USEMAP="#bitmap">
```

Select all of the codes except for the last line, which begins with the "<IMG SRC" code. Choose Edit | Copy to copy the text to the Clipboard, and then choose File | Close to close the file. Now, open your Web document if it's not already open. Place the insertion point at the bottom of the document and choose Format | Custom HTML. This lets WordPerfect know that you're going to be inserting specific HTML codes. Choose Edit | Paste. The map codes are inserted in red, double-underlined text.

Right-click the image map graphic in the document and choose HTML Properties. Select the Map Link tab and delete the filename in the File text box. Leave the map name in the Name text box (such as "bitmap") and choose OK. Then republish the document to HTML format by choosing File | Internet Publisher | Publish to HTML. Upload the HTM file to your Web server again and the image map should work correctly in your browser.

Using Tables and Columns

WordPerfect 8 makes it easy to add tables and newspaper columns to your Web documents. Formatting tables and columns in a Web document is similar to using them in a regular WordPerfect document, but there are a few differences. One of the main differences is the appearance of the borders. In Web documents, table borders have a raised, 3-D appearance (see Figure 14-8).

To create a table, click the Table button on the toolbar and then click and drag the size of the table you want. You can format a Web document table much like a

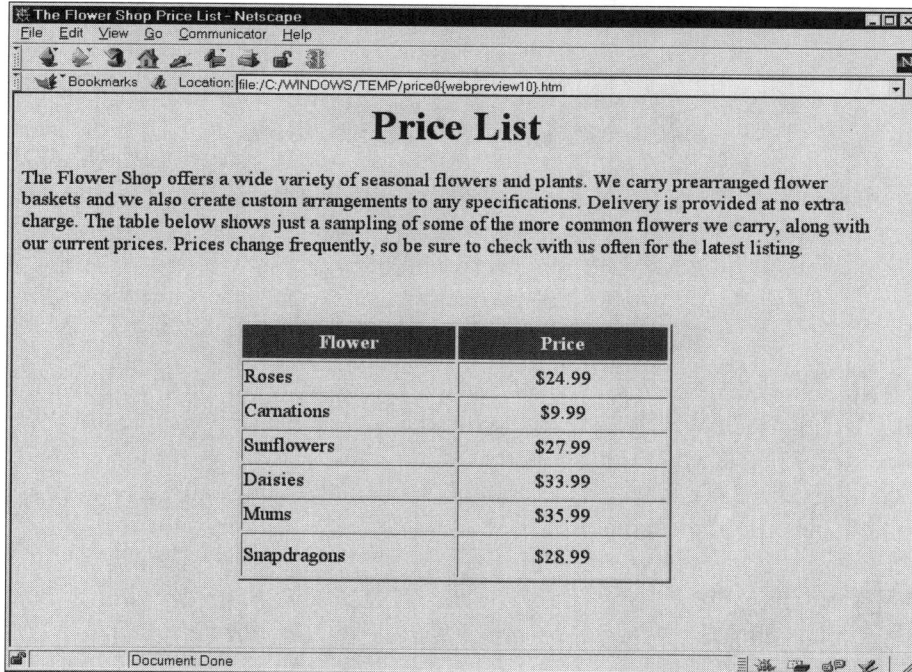

FIGURE 14-8 Table borders in a Web document have a raised appearance

regular table. For example, you can click and drag column borders to change the column widths, join and split cells, add and delete rows, or insert formulas. You can also insert graphics or hyperlinks in a table cell.

NOTE: *While the raised table borders appear gray in WordPerfect, when displayed in the Web browser, the borders use the color of the background or wallpaper.*

If you want to modify the border, table size, or shading of a table, you need to display the PerfectExpert panel. If the PerfectExpert isn't already displaying, choose Help | Perfect Expert. Place the insertion point anywhere in the table and the PerfectExpert changes to display the HTML Table options:

HTML Tables

Change Properties

Turn Border On/Off ▼

Add a Hyperlink

Change Font Attributes

To turn the table borders on or off, use the Turn Border On/Off drop-down menu and select the option you want. To modify the other table settings, choose Change Properties. The HTML Table Properties dialog box appears (see Figure 14-9). In this dialog box, you can modify the border appearance, add shading, or change the position and size of the table.

NOTE: *You can also display the HTML Table Properties dialog box by choosing the Table drop-down button on the Property Bar and then choosing Format.*

Follow these guidelines:

■   To change the thickness of the outside table border, type the number of pixels for the border width in the Table Borders text box. To change the thickness of the inside table lines, type the number of pixels in the Cell Spacing text box. The preview in the dialog box shows a sample of your settings.

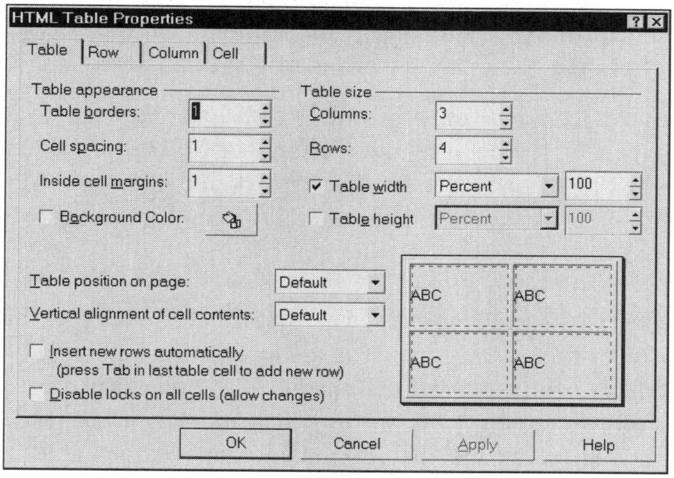

FIGURE 14-9 You can modify the borders and shading in a Web document table

- To change the margins used inside each cell, type the number of pixels in the Inside Cell Margins text box.

- To change the position of the table on the page, select the option you want from the Table Position on Page drop-down list, such as Center.

- You can specify the table width and height based on a number of pixels or a percentage of the screen display. For example, if you set the table height to 100%, it automatically fills the height of the browser window. Select the option you want to change, such as Table Height, and use the drop-down list to select whether you want to specify a number of pixels or a percentage of the screen display. Type the number or percentage in the text box.

NOTE: *The table won't display the width and height settings in WordPerfect, but you can see the changes by viewing the document in a browser.*

- To change the shading used in the table, select the Row, Column, or Cell tab at the top of the HTML Table Properties dialog box (depending on which option you want to change). Then use the Background Color pop-up palette to select the new color. If needed, close the HTML Table Properties dialog box, select a new cell, column, or row, and repeat these steps to change the shading. (If you try to change the shading with the Background Color option from the Table tab, the changes won't take effect.)

■ If you want to change the horizontal or vertical alignment of the text within the table, select the Row, Column, or Cell tab at the top of the dialog box and then select the alignment option you want. (As with the background color, you can't change this option for the entire table from the Table tab.)

When you're finished making changes in the HTML Table Properties dialog box, choose OK. Many of the settings, such as the table width and height, won't appear in the WordPerfect document. Also, cell shading only appears in the browser if there is text in the cell (even though the shading appears in WordPerfect). To view the table in a browser, place the insertion point outside the table and from the PerfectExpert panel, choose Finish | View in Browser. Or click the View in Web Browser button on the toolbar.

Using Columns

To create columns in a Web document, place the insertion point where you want the columns to begin and click the Columns button on the toolbar; then select the number of columns you want. If the text isn't already typed in the document, begin typing the text that you want to appear in columns.

Like tables, columns in Web documents work a little differently from columns in regular WordPerfect documents. The columns are newspaper-style, but instead of going clear to the end of the page before wrapping up to the next column, a new column is started as soon as a line is filled. Once all three columns are filled, a new line is added. In this way, all three columns are kept at the same length, and adjust as needed when new text is added:

When you type newspaper columns in a Web document, WordPerfect	automatically keeps the columns balanced, rather than filling up the entire	page before moving to the next column.

To change the spacing used between each column, place the insertion point where the columns begin and choose Format | Columns | Format. In the Spacing Between Columns text box, type the number of pixels you want inserted between each column. (The Total Width option doesn't remain in effect when the document is viewed in a Web browser.) Choose OK.

NOTE: *WordPerfect uses the Netscape-specific HTML code to create multiple columns. If a document with columns is viewed in a browser other than Netscape, such as Internet Explorer, the columns will be ignored. If you want columns to appear in any browser, you can use a borderless table to get the appearance of vertical columns, or you can use Corel Barista to publish the document (see Chapter 20 for more information).*

Creating Web Forms

Forms are a great way to gather information or feedback from the people who access your Web site. For example, you can conduct a survey or let people sign up for a mailing list. You can add a variety of different controls to your Web forms, such as checkboxes and radio buttons (see Figure 14-10). These controls are very similar to the ones you find in WordPerfect's dialog boxes.

The hardest part about using a Web form is getting the information returned to you correctly from your Web server. Creating the form itself with WordPerfect 8 is fairly easy. To create a form, place the insertion point in the Web document where you want the form to begin and choose Insert | Create Form. You can also start a form by choosing Extras | Add a Form from the PerfectExpert panel, or by clicking the New Form button on the Property Bar.

The insertion point is placed between two yellow tags that mark the beginning and end of the form. In addition, the Property Bar and PerfectExpert panel change to give you quick access to the form fields:

With the insertion point between the two form tags, you can insert the form fields you want, as well as type any label text to identify the fields. To insert a form field, click the field button on the Property Bar for the type of field you want to insert, or use the Add a Form Field drop-down list on the PerfectExpert panel. If you click the Submit Image button on the Property Bar, select the graphics image you want to use.

14

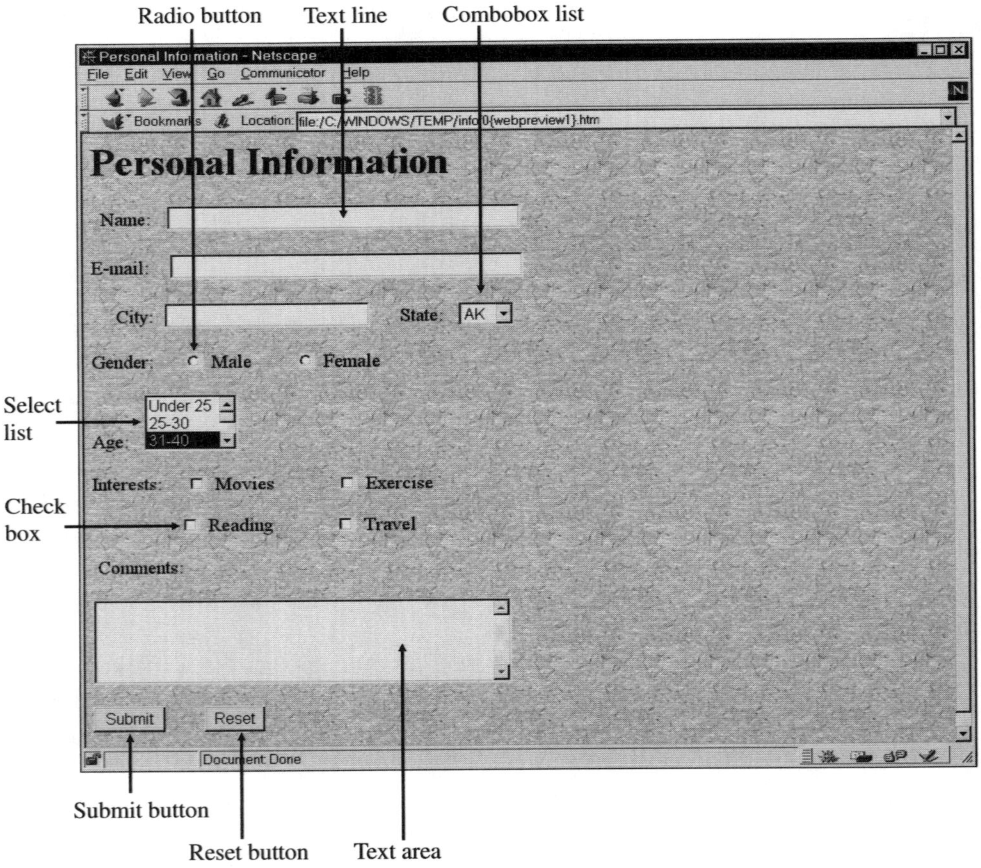

FIGURE 14-10   Web forms help you get information from people who access your Web page

TIP: *Remember that if you want to align text and form fields in your document, you can't use tabs. Instead, you need to insert hard spaces by pressing CTRL-SPACEBAR.*

Once you've inserted a form field, you can modify its properties. For example, you can change the control size, set an initial value, or add items to a selection list.

To edit the properties of a field, you can double-click it (except for a Submit Image control), right-click it and choose Properties, or choose Change Field Properties from the PerfectExpert panel. A dialog box appears with the options you can set for that particular field. The field properties are slightly different based on the type of field you're editing:

- *Radio Buttons and Checkboxes*   For these two fields, you can specify whether or not they're initially selected, the default name assigned to them, and the value they return if they're selected. The field name is used to identify the information when it's returned to you, so type a descriptive name that identifies the contents of that field. For example, you might name a checkbox **New Member** and type a return value of **Yes**. When the information is returned to you, you'll see something like "New Member = Yes." Otherwise, the returned information will look something like "CheckBox1 = on."

- *Submit and Reset Buttons*   Type the text that you want to appear on the button in the Label text box.

- *Submit Image*   Right-click the image and choose HTML Properties; then select the Submit Form tab at the top of the dialog box. Type a name for the field in the Field Name text box.

- *Selection List and Combobox*   When you edit a selection list or combobox, the Listbox/Combobox Properties dialog box lets you add values to the list, change the list height, and determine whether multiple items can be selected (see Figure 14-11). To add items to the list, choose Add and type the list item text in the Option text box. In the Value text box, type the text that you want returned to you if that item is selected (if it's different from the option text). For example, if you want a list box to display state abbreviations, but you want the full state name of the selected option returned to you, type the abbreviation in the Option text box, such as **CA**, and type the full name in the Value text box, such as **California**. If you want this item to be selected when the form is first displayed, select Initially Selected. Choose OK.

  After adding several list items, you can use the Move Up and Move Down buttons to change the list order. The Height text box determines the

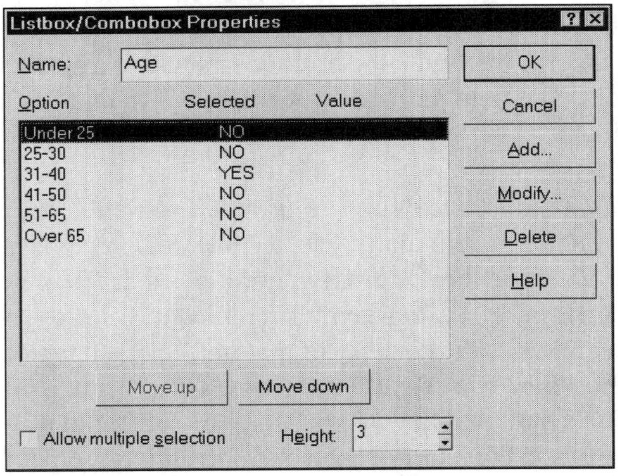

FIGURE 14-11   The Listbox/Combobox Properties dialog box lets you add items to a selection list or combobox

number of lines displayed at any one time in the list. If you want the user to be able to select more than one item, select Allow Multiple Selection.

■ *Text Lines and Passwords*   If you want a text line to contain text when the form is first displayed, type that text in the Initial text box. Type the number of pixels you want for the width in the Width text box, and the maximum number of characters for the text in the Max Char text box.

■ *Text Areas*   If you want a text area to contain initial text, type it in the Initial text box. You can specify the text area width in the Columns text box and the height in the Rows text box. As with text lines, you can specify the maximum number of characters in the Max Char text box. Additionally, you can specify whether the text should automatically wrap to fit the width of the text box.

TIP: *If you select the Wrap and Send option for a text area, the text is returned to you with hard returns inserted wherever the text wrapped in the window. If you have the Wrap at Window option selected, the returned text is not wrapped.*

- *Hidden Fields*   Hidden fields are used to provide information to the browser or the program that processes the form (see the "Processing a Form" section for more information). They require both a name and a value, as specified by the program or browser documentation. Hidden fields display in WordPerfect as this symbol shown at left.

Processing a Form

Once you've created a form and put it on your Web server, where does all the information go once a user fills it out? That depends on how you set up the behind-the-scenes form processing. For example, you can have the form data sent to you in an e-mail message, or you can have it stored in a database. In most cases, you'll need to have access to a special program, such as a CGI or PERL script, that can process the form data for you and return it in an easy-to-read format.

To set up the form processing options, place the insertion point just to the right of the first yellow form tag in your Web document and click the Form Properties button on the Property Bar, or choose Change Field Properties on the PerfectExpert panel. The Form Properties dialog box appears:

First, you need to specify which submission method you want to use—Get or Post. The most common method is Post, which returns the form data as a block to the specified URL address (where the CGI script is located) or to an e-mail address. The Get method places the form data in a long string and appends it to the specified URL address (this is commonly seen with search engines that place a query string in the URL text box of your browser).

In the Action URL text box, type the URL address and filename of the program that will process the form data. This is usually a CGI or PERL script located on a

Web server, such as **http://www.myisp.net/cgi-bin/formmail.cgi**. The script program processes the data in a specific way, such as sending it to you in an e-mail message, inserting it into a database, or creating a customized Web page on the fly. If you simply want the unformatted data sent back to you in an e-mail message, you can use the "mailto" command in the Action URL text box. See the Power Tip "Having Form Data E-Mailed to You" for more information.

NOTE: *Corel WordPerfect Suite 8 does not come with a CGI script for processing form data. However, many Internet Service Providers already have CGI scripts on their servers that will send form data back to you in an e-mail message. Check with your ISP to see if they have one available, or search the Internet for other sites that give you access to a form-processing CGI script.*

Adding Java Applets

Java is a fairly new programming language that's especially popular in Web documents because it's platform-independent, so the same code will work well on any machine. Java is often used to create small programs called "applets" that run in Web documents. A Java applet can be as simple as a scrolling text message or as complex as a small application. The Internet Publisher lets you easily add Java applets to your Web documents, and even lets you view them right in WordPerfect.

NOTE: *JavaScript is another new technology that's becoming popular for running applications in Web documents. Unlike Java applets, which are stored as separate files on the Web server, JavaScript is stored as codes within the HTML document. If you want to use JavaScript in your Web document, you can insert the codes as custom HTML codes. See the "Inserting Custom HTML Codes" section later in the chapter for more information.*

If you want to be able to view Java applets from within WordPerfect, you first need to install the WordPerfect Java support (which isn't installed during a typical installation). To install these files, make sure the WordPerfect Suite 8 CD is in your CD-ROM drive and choose Start | Corel WordPerfect Suite 8 | Setup & Notes | Corel WordPerfect Suite 8 Setup. Follow the prompts until you see the Installation Type dialog box; then select Custom and choose Next twice. Choose Selection Options, select Deselect All, and choose OK. Select Corel WordPerfect 8 in the list (don't select the checkbox next to it) and choose Components. Select Java Applet Support and choose OK; then continue with the installation.

Power Tip→→→ Having Form Data E-Mailed to You

One of the simplest methods for processing a Web form is to have the data sent back to you in an e-mail message. There are two ways you can accomplish this: with the "mailto" command or with a CGI or PERL script on a Web server.

To have a form e-mailed to you with the "mailto" command, edit the form properties as described in the "Processing a Form" section. Select Post as the submission method and in the Action URL text box, type **mailto:** followed by the e-mail address where you want the form data sent, such as **mailto:jdoe@company.com**. When a user fills out your form and chooses the Submit button, an e-mail message is sent to you with an attached text file containing the form data. However, the form data is concatenated in one long text string, so you'll need to do some work to get the data in a usable format. In addition, not all browsers support "mailto" as an Action URL.

A better option is to use one of the many available form mail CGI scripts. These scripts usually return the data to you as the text of an e-mail message, with each field name displayed before the value entered by the user. Most CGI scripts require at least one hidden field in your Web form that specifies the e-mail address where the information should be sent. Additional hidden fields are also commonly used to specify other options, such as the e-mail subject line and how the data should be sorted. Check the documentation for the CGI script you're using to find out which hidden field names and values you need to insert in your form.

You don't have to know how to program in Java to be able to use Java applets in your Web documents. Just by searching a little on the Internet, you can find lots of freeware and shareware Java applets that you can download to use in your own Web pages. In order to use a Java applet in a Web document, you need to know some information about it, such as the class name and the names and values of any parameters. You can generally get this information from either the documentation that came with the applet or from the developer who created it.

14

JAVA APPLETS: *The companion CD contains two shareware Java applets that you can use in your Web pages. All of the needed class files—along with a WordPerfect file containing the parameter information—are stored in a ZIP file. The CLOCK.ZIP contains a Java applet that adds a digital clock to your Web page and the TICKER.ZIP contains a Java applet for a scrolling ticker tape message.*

To insert a Java applet in your Web document, choose Insert | Java | Create Applet, or click the Create Applet button on the Property Bar. The Create Java Applet dialog box appears (see Figure 14-12). In the Class text box, type the name of the main class file for the Java applet (it ends with a CLASS extension). If the Java class file (and any other associated Java files) won't be in the same directory as the HTML document file on your Web server, type the relative path in the Code Base text box. For example, if the Java files will be in a subdirectory called java on your Web Server, type **java/** in the Code Base text box.

CAUTION: *Don't include a path to the class file in the Class text box or that information will be encoded in the HTML document. As a result, the browser will try to look for the Java files on the user's hard drive instead of on your Web server.*

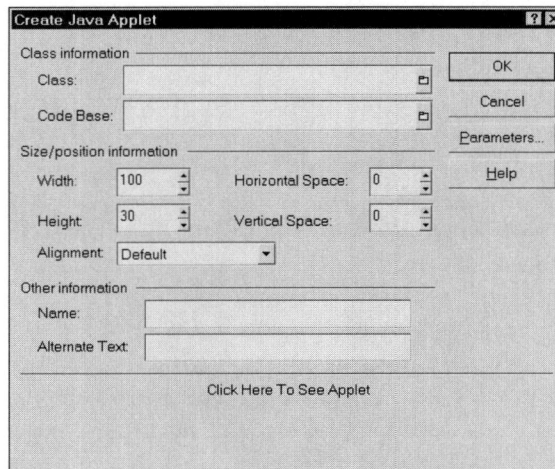

FIGURE 14-12 You can add Java applets to your Web documents

In the Create Java Applet dialog box, you can also specify the width, height, and spacing for the box containing the applet. From the Alignment drop-down list, select the location for the applet on the Web page. In the Alternate Text text box, type the text that you want to appear in browsers that don't support Java applets.

Most Java applets require at least one parameter. The parameters provide information to customize the applet, such as specifying the colors used, the text displayed, and so on. To add the parameter names and values, choose Parameters. Choose Add, type the parameter name and value, and then choose OK. Continue this process to add other parameters (see illustration). If you need to change a parameter name or value, select it in the list and choose Modify. Choose OK when you're finished.

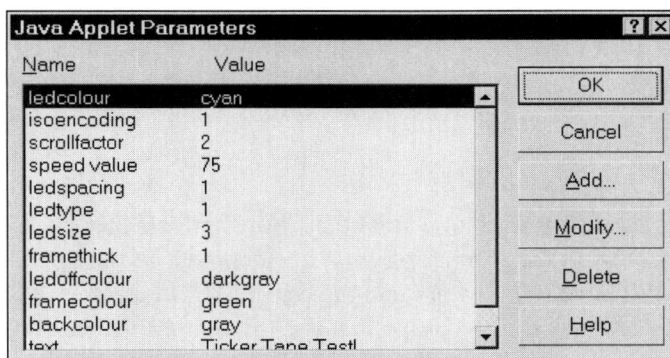

Name	Value	
ledcolour	cyan	
isoencoding	1	
scrollfactor	2	
speed value	75	
ledspacing	1	
ledtype	1	
ledsize	3	
framethick	1	
ledoffcolour	darkgray	
framecolour	green	
backcolour	gray	
text	Ticker Tape Test!	

NOTE: *Each Java applet has its own unique parameter names and values. You'll need to get this information from the documentation that came with the applet or from the developer who created it.*

After specifying the applet settings and parameters, you can see a preview of the Java applet by clicking the "Click Here to See Applet" text at the bottom of the Create Java Applet dialog box. The Java applet displays in the bottom section of the dialog box. To close the display, click outside the applet.

NOTE: *The Java applet will only display in the dialog box if the Java class files are in the same directory as the Web document you're working on. Also, if you've specified a code base location for the Java files on your Web server, the Java applet won't display in the dialog box.*

14

After creating the Java applet, you'll need to remember to upload all the associated Java files to your Web server, along with the published HTML document. See the "Previewing and Publishing Web Pages" section.

Inserting Custom HTML Codes

In order for a browser to display a Web document, the document must contain HTML codes, or "tags," as they are also called. The HTML tags identify the different document elements and formatting, such as headings, images, and lists, so the browser can correctly display the document. HTML tags are enclosed in angle brackets and are usually paired, with the closing tag containing a forward slash. For example, these HTML codes create a document's title and insert a first-level heading:

```
<TITLE>My Home Page</TITLE>
<h1>Welcome to my home page!</h1>
```

When you publish a Web document in WordPerfect, the Internet Publisher automatically converts the formatting in your document to the applicable HTML tags, so you don't have to know anything about HTML to create a Web document. However, there are many HTML tags that the Internet Publisher doesn't support, such as tags that create frames or include JavaScript commands. If you're familiar with HTML programming and want to include other HTML tags in your document, you can insert the tags as custom HTML codes.

NOTE: *WordPerfect's Internet Publisher supports HTML 2.0 and 3.2, as well as some Netscape-specific codes such as blinking text and multiple columns.*

To insert HTML tags in a Web document, place the insertion point where you want the codes inserted and choose Format I Custom HTML. Then type the HTML tag information. The codes are formatted as red, double-underlined text, so you can easily identify them as HTML tags. When you're finished, choose Format I Custom HTML again.

NOTE: *If you type HTML tags in a Web document without using the Custom HTML style, they will simply be displayed as regular body text in the published Web document.*

TIP: *You can usually view the HTML codes for any document you come across on the Web by choosing View | Source in the browser.*

On the CD ▸▸▸ Corel's WebMaster Suite

WordPerfect can handle a lot of HTML formatting, but if you need to create and maintain a complex Web site, you might want to look into using a program specifically designed for Web sites. Corel's WebMaster Suite is one such program. The WebMaster suite includes applications for HTML design (Corel WEB.DESIGNER), database publishing (WEB.DATA), and Web site management (WEB.SiteManager). The companion CD includes the 30-day trial version of the WebMaster Suite. To install the trial version, run the SETUP.EXE file from the Corel WebMaster Suite – Trial Version directory on the CD.

In addition, if you have the Professional Edition of WordPerfect Suite 8, you also have Corel's WEB.SiteBuilder, which is similar to the WebMaster Suite. You can use these programs to easily add advanced HTML formatting such as frames and image maps to your Web documents.

Previewing and Publishing Web Pages

As you're creating a Web page, it's a good idea to occasionally view the document in a Web browser. The Internet Publisher gives a fair approximation within WordPerfect of how your documents will appear in a browser, but nothing can substitute for the real thing. To see a temporary preview, choose Finish | View in

Browser from the PerfectExpert panel, or click the View in Web Browser button on the toolbar.

When you choose this option, WordPerfect creates a temporary HTML version of your Web document (usually in the \Windows\Temp directory) and displays it in your default browser. If you've already published the document to HTML format once and you've specified directories on your Web server for any graphics images or Java applets, those elements might not display correctly in the browser preview. However, they will display when accessed normally through your browser, as long as you've uploaded the files to the correct locations.

Publishing to HTML Format

When you're ready to convert your Web document to HTML format, choose File | Internet Publisher, and then choose Publish to HTML. You can also choose Finish | Publish to HTML from the PerfectExpert panel, or click the Publish to HTML button on the toolbar.

The Publish to HTML dialog box appears (see Figure 14-13). The Publish To text box automatically contains the current path and filename of the WordPerfect document, changed to use an HTM file extension. If you want to save the HTML version in a different location (or with a different filename), type the path and name in the text box, making sure you use an HTM file extension.

TIP: *If you want the current document to be the default home page that automatically displays when someone accesses your Web site, name it* ***INDEX.HTM***.

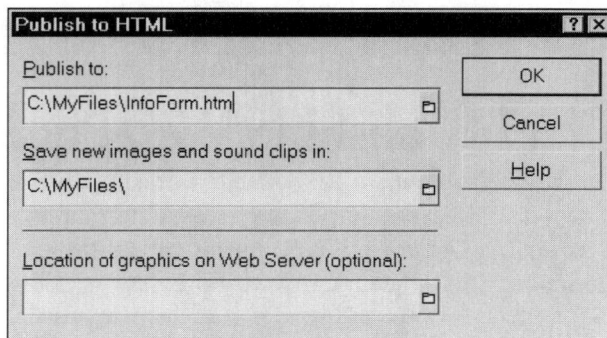

FIGURE 14-13   Use the Publish to HTML dialog box to convert a document to HTML format

In the Save New Images and Sound Clips In text box, type the path where you want any converted graphics files stored. If you included any graphics images in the Web document that weren't already in GIF or JPG format, WordPerfect automatically converts those files when you publish the document to HTML format. (You'll need to remember to later upload the converted files to your Web server.)

The Location of Graphics on Web Server text box lets you specify a relative subdirectory name on your Web server where all the graphics images used for this document will be stored. The directory needs to be *relative* to (a subdirectory of) the location of the actual HTM document file. You only need to type the subdirectory name (not the entire path), such as **images**.

> **CAUTION:** *Don't confuse paths on your hard drive with paths on your Web server. While they may be the same (if you set it up that way), they aren't necessarily the same.*

> **NOTE:** *You can also specify the location of an individual image in your Web document by using the HTML Properties dialog box for that image. See the "Inserting Lines and Graphics" section earlier in the chapter for more information.*

Once you've specified all the settings, choose OK to create the HTML version of the document (with an HTM extension). WordPerfect keeps your regular WP document open in the document window and simply creates a copy of the document (in HTML format) with the filename you specified. After you've created the HTM file, you can upload it to your Web server, along with any associated graphics or Java files (see the "Uploading Your Files" section for more information). Remember that each time you make a change to the Web document in WordPerfect, you need to publish it to HTML format again so the HTM version is also updated.

Uploading Your Files

Before anyone else can see your Web pages on the Internet, the files must be placed on a Web server. This is typically done by uploading the files to your Web server with a File Transfer Protocol (FTP) program. When you upload the files, make sure that you place them in the appropriate directories on the server. For example, you might have several subdirectories for storing graphics and Java files. Check with your Internet Service Provider for specific information on what you need to do to upload files, including which directory you should place your main HTM files in so other users can access them (you might also need to change the directory access permissions).

Depending on how you've formatted your Web document, you might have quite a few files that you need to copy to the Web server. For example, any one Web document can use an HTML file, multiple graphics images (including image map files), a form processing application (and related files), and Java applet classes (and related files). Make sure you copy all the converted GIF files that were created when you published the document to HTML format, as well as any GIF files from other directories on your hard drive (including the background image if you selected one).

NOTE: *The GIF files for the background images on the PerfectExpert's Change Background pop-down palette should be in your \Corel\Suite8\Template\Custom WP Templates directory.*

After you've uploaded all of the files, use your Web browser to go to your Web site and see how your pages look. It's also a good idea to check your Web site from another computer (or have someone else take a look at it), to make sure that your Web page isn't pointing to files on your hard drive. If your pages are missing graphics or don't look quite right, see the "Troubleshooting Tips" section.

TIP: *You should always thoroughly test your pages to make sure that they don't have any broken links and that users can easily get back and forth between the various pages. In addition, you may want to try opening your pages in several different browsers if possible, since not all browsers support the same features.*

Troubleshooting Tips

If you've uploaded all the files to your Web server but your pages still don't view correctly, there are several common problems you can check for:

- Make sure you've uploaded *all* the files you need, including the background image, files for an image map, and files used with any Java applets. It's often a good idea to make a list of relevant files as you're creating Web documents so you don't forget any when it's time to move them to the Web server.

TIP: *You can set up a directory structure on your hard drive that matches the directory structure on your Web server. This lets you test the files locally and then quickly copy all of the files in the directory structure at the same time to your Web server.*

■ If you specified a relative directory for the graphics (see Figure 14-13) or Java applets (see Figure 14-12) in your Web page, make sure that you copy all the images and Java files into the correct subdirectories (which should be under the directory containing the HTM document file). If you didn't specify a relative directory, place all the graphics and Java files in the same directory as the HTM file.

■ If you specified a directory for an individual graphics image using the HTML Properties dialog box, make sure that image is in the correct directory (which might be different from the directory where the rest of your graphics are stored).

■ Your Web document might be pointing to a file stored on your hard drive rather than on the Web server. To check for this problem, display the HTM file in your browser and choose View | Source. Look through the HTML codes for any references to paths on your hard drive. If you find one, edit the HTM document as explained in the "Editing HTML Documents" section and delete the hard drive path (but keep the actual filename).

■ The paths and filenames on a Web server are usually case sensitive, so a filename referenced in the HTM document must exactly match the actual filename. For example, if your Web document refers to a file named "water.gif," but the file on your Web server is named "Water.gif," the browser won't be able to find the file. To view the HTML codes in your Web page and see how the filenames are referenced, display the page in your browser and choose View | Source. If you find a discrepancy, you can either rename the file on your Web server or edit the HTM file so the case matches.

■ In addition to being case sensitive, filenames on most Web servers can't contain spaces or other characters such as ampersands. If an image isn't displaying correctly but uses the same case as the reference in the HTM file and is in the correct directory, check to see if there are any spaces or other unusual characters in the filename. (Many of the background texture files on the WordPerfect Suite 8 CD have spaces in their filenames.) To fix this problem, rename the actual file so it doesn't use spaces or other unusual characters (you can use the underscore character in place of spaces), and then update the reference in the HTM file as well (see "Editing HTML Documents" for more information).

14

Remember that if you move the main HTML file to a different directory on your Web server, you also need to move any associated graphics and Java files—including subdirectories containing those files. If you want to be able to move an HTML file without having to move the associated subdirectories as well, you can specify a base URL for the HTML file. See the Power Tip "Specifying a Base URL" for more information.

Power Tip... Specifying a Base URL

When you specify a relative path for graphics or Java files in a Web document (see Figures 14-12 and 14-13), your browser looks for the files in a subdirectory located under the directory containing the HTML file. For example, if you place an HTML file in a directory called http://www.myisp.net/~jdoe on your Web server and specify a relative graphics directory name of "images," the browser will look for any graphics in the Web document in the http://www.myisp.net/~jdoe/images directory. If you later move the HTML file to a different directory, you must also move the images subdirectory.

If you want to be able to move an HTML file without having to move all of the associated subdirectories, you can specify a base URL. The base URL tells the browser where to look for graphics, sound clips, and Java applets used in that HTML file. To set up a base URL, open the Web document in WordPerfect and choose File | Properties. Select the Advanced tab. In the Base URL text box, type the path on your Web server where the additional files and/or relative subdirectories for the document are located. For example, if you type **http://www.myisp.net/~jdoe/extras** as the base URL, the browser will look in that directory for any graphics or Java files—including subdirectories specified by relative paths. You can then move the actual HTML file to any location and the browser will still be able to find the correct files.

Editing HTML Documents

Even after you've created a Web page and uploaded it to your server, you can still use WordPerfect's Internet Publisher to make changes to the document and keep it updated. All you need to do is open the WordPerfect document (not the HTM file), make your changes, and then republish it to HTML format. (Don't forget to upload the new version back to your Web server.)

If you want to edit an HTML document that didn't start out as a WordPerfect document, you can open the HTM or HTML file as you would any other document. When the Convert File Format dialog box appears, select HTML from the drop-down list (if it's not already selected) and choose OK. After making the changes to the file, choose File | Save, select HTML, and choose Save.

You can also open an HTML document in WordPerfect as a text file so you can see the actual HTML tags, rather than have the Internet Publisher translate them into their corresponding formatting (see Figure 14-14). To do this, choose File | Open, select the HTM or HTML file you want to open and choose Open. When the Convert File Format dialog box appears, select ASCII DOS Text from the drop-down list; then choose OK. WordPerfect opens the document with the HTML source code and tags.

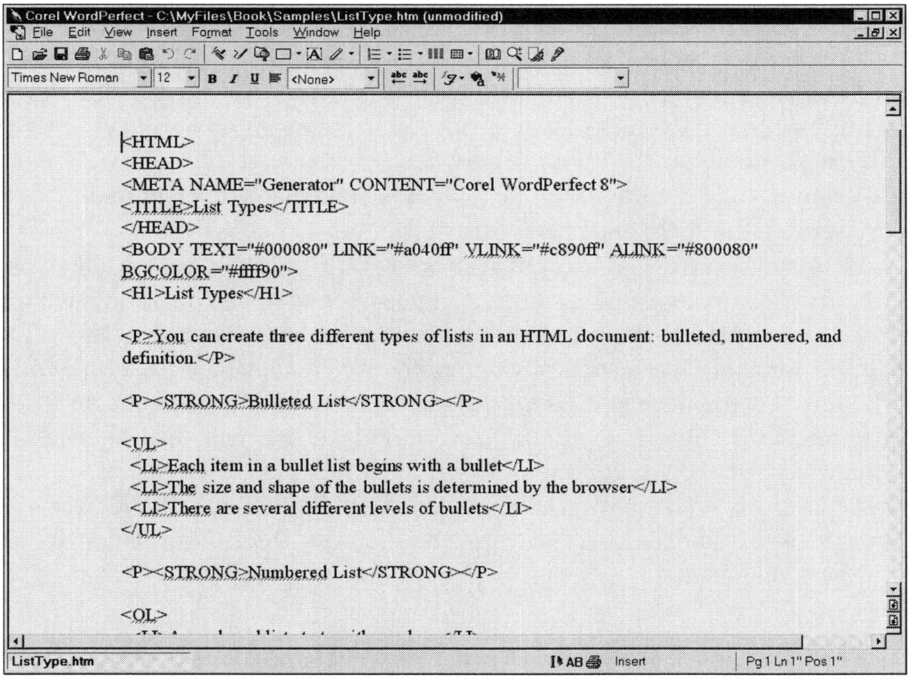

FIGURE 14-14 By opening an HTML document as ASCII text, you can see the HTML tags

After opening an HTML document as ASCII text, you can edit the actual HTML tags. For example, you can remove incorrect paths or filenames or type new HTML codes that aren't directly supported by the Internet Publisher. When you're finished making changes, choose File | Save. Select ASCII DOS Text as the format and choose OK.

CAUTION: *Don't add any formatting to the HTML text file using WordPerfect's formatting features, because it will be lost when the document is resaved in ASCII format.*

NOTE: *If you accidentally save the document in WordPerfect 6/7/8 format, just choose File | Save As, select ASCII DOS Text from the File Type drop-down list, and choose Save.*

Summary

If you want to get connected to the Internet and make your presence known on the Web, WordPerfect can help. WordPerfect 8 is loaded with helpful tools for linking to the Internet and creating your own Web pages. You can use QuickLinks and hyperlinks to jump to Internet sites or create e-mail messages right from your regular WordPerfect documents. When you want to create your own Web pages, WordPerfect's Internet Publisher helps you quickly add backgrounds, format headings, insert graphics, and create lists.

Adding more advanced elements to your Web pages is also a cinch with WordPerfect. For example, you can create tables, set up image maps, include form controls, and add Java applets. The Internet Publisher takes care of the HTML formatting for you, automatically converting your document to use the correct HTML tags. All you have to do is upload the document and related images to your Web server, make sure everything is in working order, and then sit back and communicate with the world!

In Chapter 15, we'll show you how to configure WordPerfect's Address Book to keep track of your contacts and use the Address Book information in your WordPerfect documents.

Chapter 15

Staying in Touch with the Address Book

Most of us don't work in a vacuum, although there are probably times when we wish we did. Instead, we're constantly dealing with coworkers, clients, vendors, and scores of other people and companies. So how can you keep track of all these contacts without losing precious time—or your sanity—in the process? One solution lies in WordPerfect 8's Address Book. This helpful tool organizes information about the people you contact frequently, such as mailing addresses, phone numbers, and e-mail addresses.

In this chapter, you'll learn how to set up the Address Book so it fits the type of work you do. We'll show you how to add entries to it, set up custom fields to contain any type of information, and insert address information into your documents. You'll also learn how to create new Address Books to group similar contacts, import information from database or merge files, customize the way addresses are displayed, and use filters to help you search for an address.

Address Book Entries

To use the Address Book in WordPerfect, choose Tools | Address Book. This will display the Address Book dialog box (see Figure 15-1). The tabs at the top of the dialog box indicate which Address Books are currently open and available. WP comes with two Address Books by default—My Addresses and Frequent Contacts. Later in this chapter, you'll learn how you can create additional books for grouping similar addresses together. For now, select the My Addresses tab if it isn't already selected.

TIP: *You can also access the Address Book outside of WordPerfect by clicking the Windows Start button, and then choosing Corel WordPerfect Suite 8 | Accessories | Corel Address Book 8. The Address Book is also part of CorelCENTRAL (for more information, see Chapter 18).*

Search text boxes

Available Address Books

Column headings

Organization icon

Address group icon

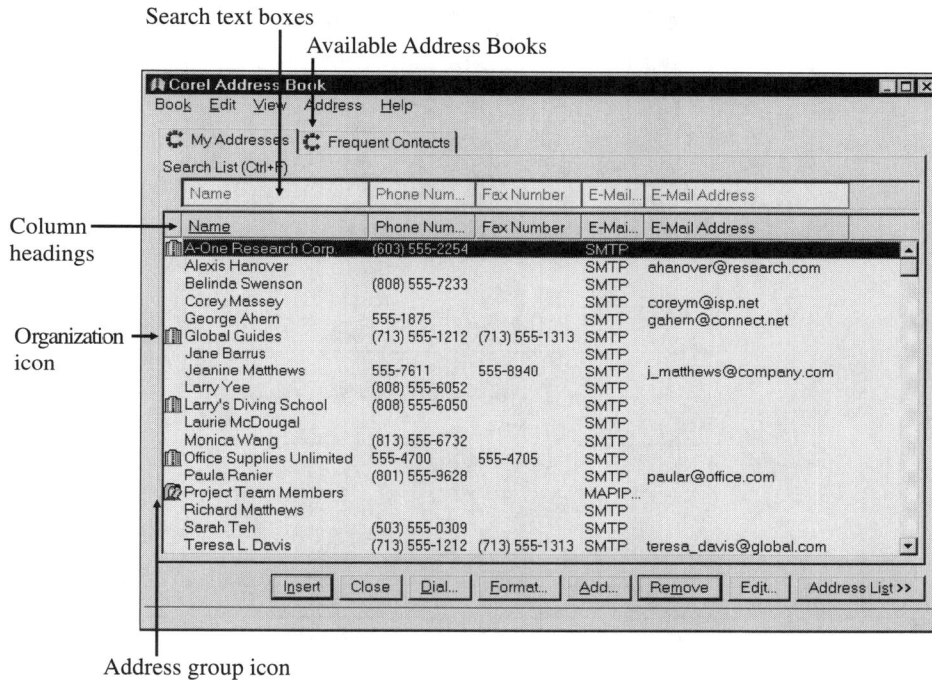

FIGURE 15-1 The Address Book organizes your contact information

Adding a New Entry

To add a new entry to the Address Book, choose Add. The New Entry dialog box appears, asking whether you want to create a new entry for a person or an organization. If you add a person, you can include such information as the street address, e-mail address, work and home phone numbers, company name, and title. Organization entries let you include the name, street address, and phone/fax numbers.

Select the type of entry you want to create and choose OK. In the next dialog box, enter the information for the new entry (see Figure 15-2). The available options

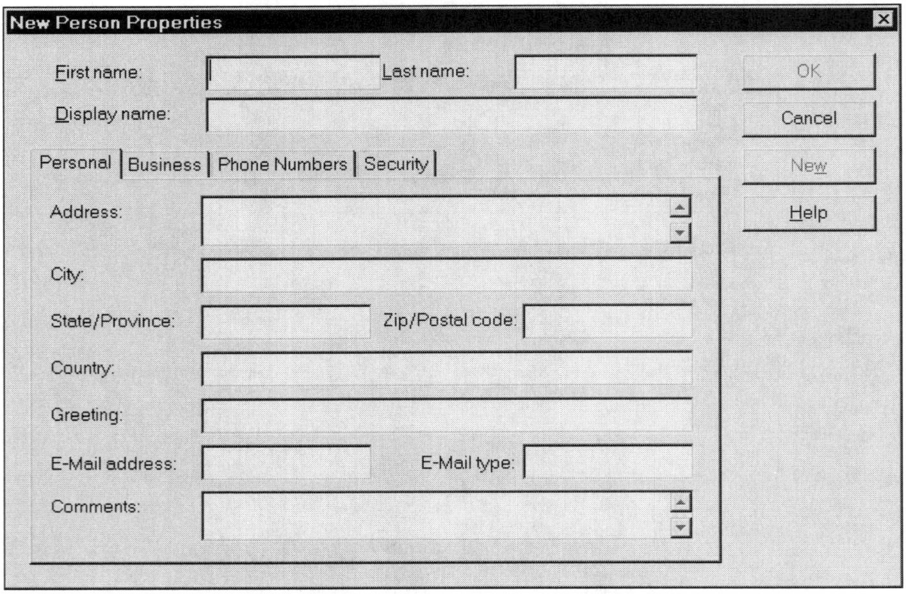

FIGURE 15-2 Creating a new entry for the Address Book

in the dialog box depend on the type of entry you selected. Keep these guidelines in mind as you enter the information:

- Use the dialog box tabs to switch to the different areas for entering information, such as the phone numbers.

- You can insert hard returns in text boxes that have up and down arrow buttons along the right side, such as the Address and Comments text boxes.

- The Display Name text box automatically contains the first and last name you enter for a person, but you can change this text if you want. The display name is the text used for the "Name" field when entries are displayed in the Address Book dialog box and when they're inserted into a document.

- If you type the full state or province name in the State/Province text box, after you choose OK to save the entry, WP automatically converts it to the two-letter postal abbreviation—for example, changing "New York" to "NY." Similarly, if you type a two-letter country abbreviation in the Country text box, WP converts it to the full country name after you choose OK—thus "UK" becomes "United Kingdom."

- You're limited to 35 characters for the First Name, Last Name, and Organization fields, even though WP lets you initially type up to 255 characters in the text box. Once you choose OK to save the entry, the text in those fields is truncated to the first 35 characters.

- When you're creating an entry for a person and type a name in the Organization text box, WP checks to see if an organization entry with that name already exists. If it does, WP displays the entire organization name in the text box as soon as you've typed enough characters for it to be recognized. If the organization doesn't already exist as a separate Address Book entry, a new organization entry is created. After creating the current entry, you need to edit the organization entry and enter the address and phone number information.

When you're finished entering the information, choose OK. If you later want to view or edit any of the settings for an entry, select the entry in the Address Book dialog box and choose Edit.

Creating Custom Fields

While the Address Book provides several fields for entering different types of information, you can also create custom fields—for the person's pager, birthday, or spouse name, for example. Any custom fields you create are automatically available in each Address Book entry.

To create a custom field, display the Address Book (Tools | Address Book) and choose Edit | Custom Fields. The Custom Fields dialog box shows a list of any custom fields you've already created. To add a new custom field, choose New. Type a name for the field, such as **Birthday**, and choose OK.

NOTE: *Certain field names are reserved for future use in the Address Book and can't be used for custom fields. The reserved names include MI (for middle initial), Prefix, Suffix, Email1, Email2, URL, Spouse, and Children. If you try to create a custom field with one of these reserved names, you'll receive an error message. If you want to use one of these fields, create a field with a variation of the name, such as Spouse Name or Sufx.*

You can create as many custom fields as you want. If you want to delete a custom field, select it and choose Delete. To change the name of a custom field, select it and choose Rename; then type the new name and choose OK. Choose OK when you're finished.

To enter information into a custom field, select an entry in the Address Book and choose Edit. Or choose Add to create a new entry. Then, click the Custom tab in the dialog box. A multiple-line text box is included for each of your custom fields (see Figure 15-3). Type the information in the custom fields and choose OK when you're finished.

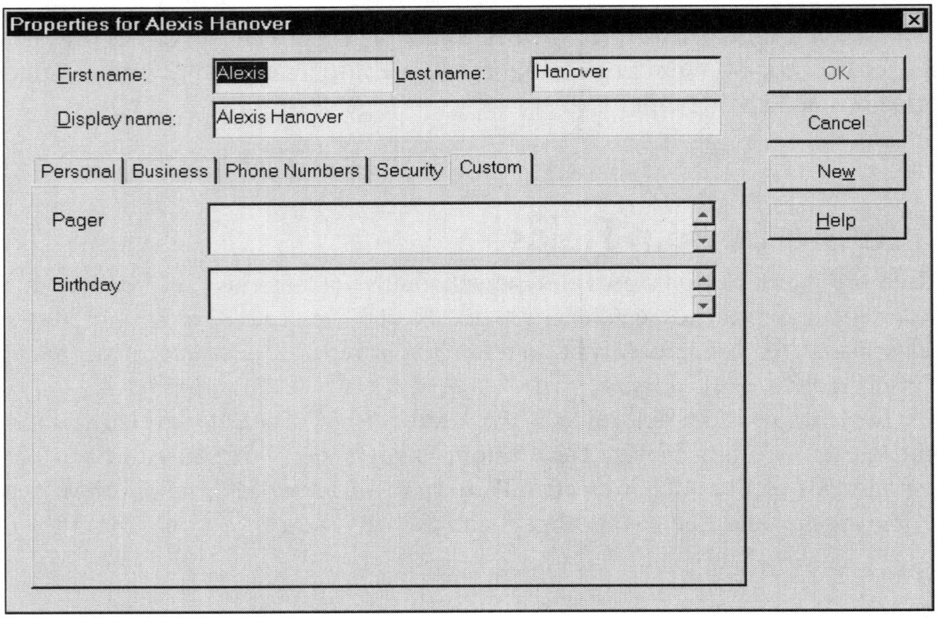

FIGURE 15-3 Custom fields are accessed through the Custom tab

Using Addresses in Documents

The Address Book is designed not only to keep your address information organized, but also to give you easy access to that information when you need to use it in your documents. The Address Book is integrated with many of WordPerfect's features to allow you to quickly select addresses for documents and envelopes. There are three main features in WordPerfect that work with the Address Book: Templates, Envelopes, and Merge.

- The Template feature helps you quickly create documents such as letters and fax cover sheets. Many of the templates let you select an entry from the Address Book to use with the document you're creating. For more information on templates, see Chapter 1.

- The Envelope feature (Format | Envelope) lets you select entries from the Address Book to use for both the return address and the mailing address. To select an Address Book entry, just click the Address Book icon in the Envelope dialog box.

- The Merge feature lets you select an Address Book as the data source for a merge form document. For example, you can set up a form document to create labels, and then merge selected addresses from the Address Book onto the labels. For more information on the Merge feature, see Chapter 2.

Power Tip▸▸▸ Dialing from the Address Book

If you have a modem in your computer that goes through a telephone, you can use the Address Book to dial phone numbers for you. The Address Book uses the Windows 95 Phone Dialer utility to dial the numbers.

To do this, choose Tools | Address Book and select the entry for the person you want to call. Then choose Dial. If you have more than one phone number stored for that person, such as a business and home number, WP displays a dialog box asking which number you want to call. Select the number and choose OK. The Phone Dialer utility dials the number and displays a dialog box telling you to lift the receiver and choose Talk to begin the conversation.

Inserting Formatted Addresses

In addition to using the Address Book with other WP features, you can insert addresses from the Address Book directly into a document. To do this, place the insertion point where you want the address inserted, choose Tools | Address Book, and select the entry you want to insert. To select a format for the address, choose Format. The Format Address dialog box shows a list of the currently available formats, as shown here:

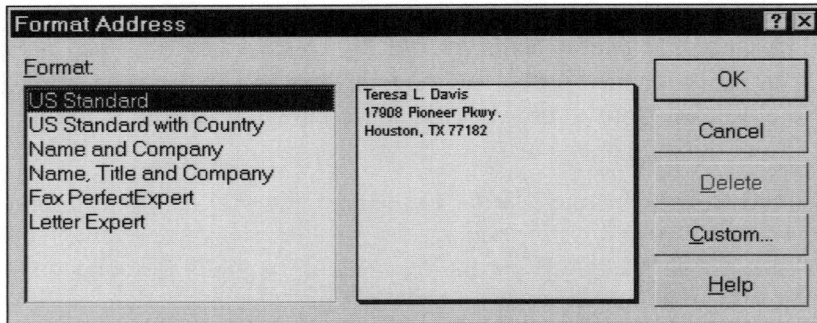

```
Format Address                                         ? X
Format:
┌──────────────────────────┐  ┌──────────────────────┐  ┌──────────────┐
│ US Standard              │  │ Teresa L. Davis       │  │      OK      │
│ US Standard with Country │  │ 17908 Pioneer Pkwy.   │  └──────────────┘
│ Name and Company         │  │ Houston, TX 77182     │  ┌──────────────┐
│ Name, Title and Company  │  │                       │  │    Cancel    │
│ Fax PerfectExpert        │  │                       │  └──────────────┘
│ Letter Expert            │  │                       │  ┌──────────────┐
│                          │  │                       │  │    Delete    │
│                          │  │                       │  └──────────────┘
│                          │  │                       │  ┌──────────────┐
│                          │  │                       │  │   Custom...  │
│                          │  │                       │  └──────────────┘
│                          │  │                       │  ┌──────────────┐
│                          │  │                       │  │     Help     │
└──────────────────────────┘  └──────────────────────┘  └──────────────┘
```

As you select each format in the dialog box, the preview box shows how the currently selected address appears in that format. Select the format you want and choose OK. Then choose Insert or press ENTER to insert the address into the document.

> **NOTE:**   *If an address is inserted with blank lines, choose Tools | Address Book, select the entry you inserted, and choose Edit. Then remove any extra hard returns from the end of the information in the Address text box. Choose OK when you're finished.*

If none of the current address formats meet your needs, you can create your own custom formats. For example, you can set up an address format to insert only the name and e-mail address. To create a new address format, choose Tools | Address Book and select the address you want to insert. Choose Format and select an existing format that's similar to the format you want to create, such as US Standard; then choose Custom.

The Format text box shows the fields and formatting being used for the current format (see Figure 15-4). To delete a field, click in the Format text box and delete the unwanted field. To add a new field, place the insertion point in the Format text box where you want the field inserted, select the field in the list of available fields

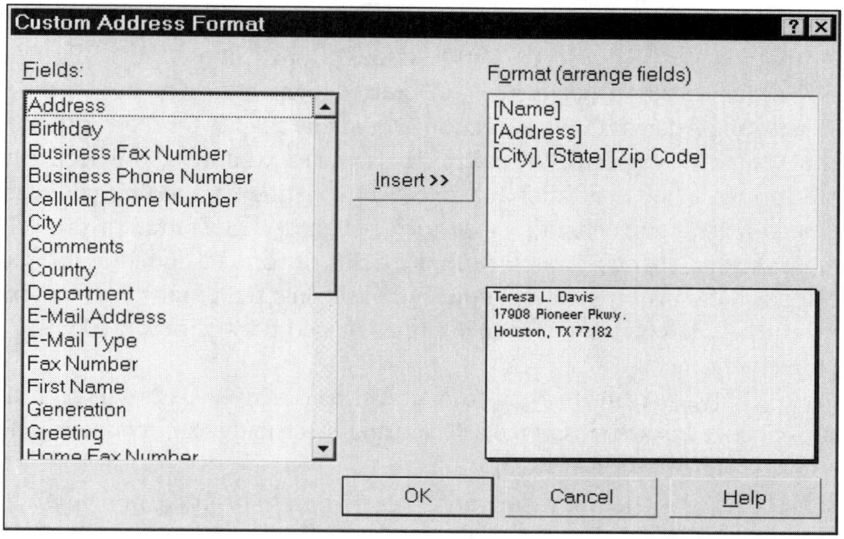

Custom Address Format   ? ✕

Fields:

Address
Birthday
Business Fax Number
Business Phone Number
Cellular Phone Number
City
Comments
Country
Department
E-Mail Address
E-Mail Type
Fax Number
First Name
Generation
Greeting
Home Fax Number

Insert >>

Format (arrange fields)

[Name]
[Address]
[City], [State] [Zip Code]

Teresa L. Davis
17908 Pioneer Pkwy.
Houston, TX 77182

OK   Cancel   Help

FIGURE 15-4 You can create a custom format using any of the available fields

and choose Insert. You can add hard returns, spaces, punctuation, and even text to the Format text box. The preview dialog box shows you how the currently selected address appears in the new format.

When you're finished setting up the new format, choose OK. Type a name for your format and choose OK. The new format now appears in the list of available formats. To insert the currently selected address in that format, choose OK, and then choose Insert.

NOTE: *If you want to delete a custom address format, choose Format in the Address Book dialog box, select the format you want to delete and choose Delete. The formats that are automatically included in the default Address Book, such as US Standard, can't be deleted.*

Inserting Multiple Addresses

WP also lets you easily insert more than one formatted address at the same time into a document. You can use this technique to print out an Address Book (or selected entries from the Address Book) in the format you want. To do this, choose Tools | Address Book, and then hold down the CTRL key as you select each individual entry that you want to insert. To select the entire Address Book, choose Edit | Select All. Or you can select an address group that you've created to insert each address in the group (see the "Creating Address Groups" section later in this chapter for more information).

If you want to have a blank line inserted between each address, you need to create a custom format. Choose Format and select the existing format that you want the addresses to appear in (or that's close to it), such as US Standard; then choose Custom. Make any changes you want to the fields or formatting in the Format text box; then place the insertion point at the end of the last field in the Format text box and press ENTER. If you want two blank lines placed between each address, press ENTER a second time.

Choose OK, type a name for your format, such as **Multiple Addresses**, and choose OK again. Choose Insert to insert the selected addresses in the current document.

NOTE: *You can also use the Merge feature to print the information from an Address Book. For more information on how to do this, see the "Printing the Address Book" On the CD section.*

On the CD ▸▸▸ Printing the Address Book

If you want to print out a list of entries from an Address Book, you can use the Merge feature to merge a form document with the Address Book as the data source. The companion CD includes a merge form document that's already set up to create a list of information from entries in the Address Book.

To use this form document to print out the entries in the Address Book, follow these steps:

1. Go to a blank document screen and choose Tools | Merge. Select Perform Merge.

2. Click the file folder button to the right of the Form Document text box, select the ADDRESS BOOK.FRM file from the companion CD, and choose Select.

3. From the Data Source drop-down list, choose Address Book.

4. From the drop-down list of address books, select the Address Book you want to use, such as My Addresses.

5. If you want to print only selected addresses from the Address Book, choose Select Records. Select each entry you want to include and choose Select Address or double-click it.

6. When you've selected all the entries you want, choose OK; then choose Merge.

WP creates a list of the information from the Address Book. The printed list includes the name, organization, address, phone number, fax number, and e-mail address. If any of these fields are blank, they are not included. (For more information on Merge, see Chapter 2.)

Working with Multiple Address Books

WordPerfect comes with two Address Books by default—My Addresses and Frequent Contacts—but you can create as many other books as you want. For example, you might have separate Address Books for vendor contacts and personal contacts. You can select which Address Books are currently displayed in the Address Book dialog box, as well as which fields each individual book displays. In addition, you can have the same entry located in more than one Address Book, so it's automatically updated in each Address Book whenever you make changes to it. In this section, you'll learn how to create new Address Books, copy and move entries between Address Books, group entries within an Address Book, and share Address Books over a network.

Creating an Address Book

To create a new Address Book, in the Address Book dialog box (Tools | Address Book), choose Book | New. Type the name for your Address Book in the Name text box, such as **Vendors** or **Personal**, and then choose OK. A blank Address Book is added to the Address Book dialog box. Once you've created an Address Book, you can add new entries to it as explained in the "Adding a New Entry" section earlier in this chapter. In addition, you can copy or move addresses from another Address Book, or import addresses from a database or merge data file. These methods will be explained later in this chapter.

You can create as many different Address Books as you want. A tab for each open Address Book displays in the Address Book dialog box (see Figure 15-5). You can switch to a different Address Book by selecting the tab with the Address Book name. WP remembers which Address Book you had selected most recently and automatically displays it each time you display the Address Book dialog box. To change the name of an Address Book, select the Address Book tab and choose Book | Properties. Type the new name in the Name text box and choose OK.

NOTE: *You can't change the name of the My Addresses or Frequent Contacts books.*

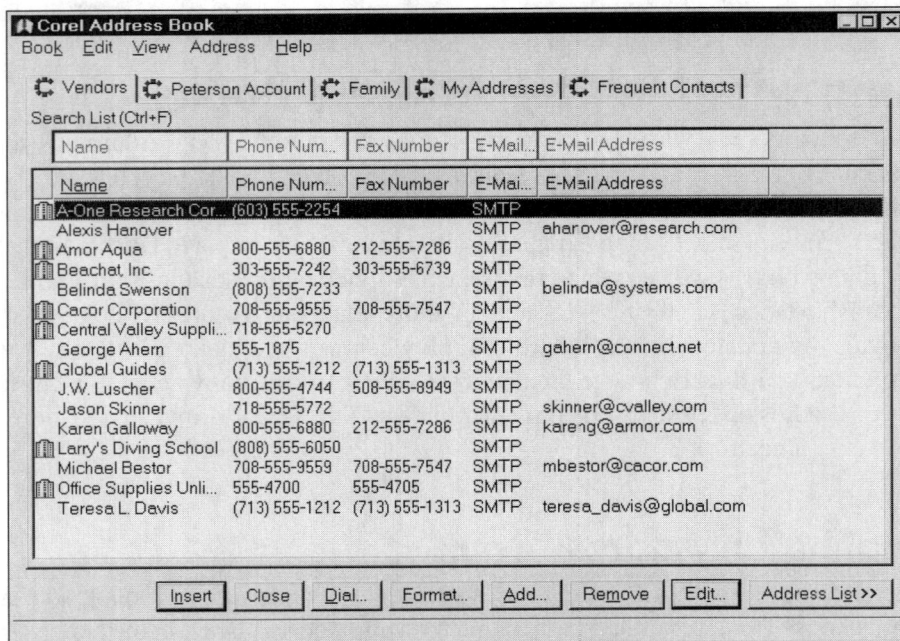

FIGURE 15-5 Each open Address Book has a tab in the dialog box

You can close any of the Address Books so they're not displayed in the Address Book dialog box. To close a book, select the Address Book tab and choose Book | Close. Closing an Address Book doesn't actually delete the Address Book file or any of the addresses in it. To open the Address Book again, choose Book | Open, select the name of the Address Book, and choose OK.

If you want to delete an entire Address Book, choose Book | Delete. Select the Address Book you want to delete and choose OK. Choose Yes to confirm the deletion. When you delete an Address Book, any entries in that book are also deleted. However, if an entry was also included in other Address Books, it is *not* deleted from the other locations.

Copying and Moving Addresses

When you create multiple address books, you can copy and move entries between them. To copy an entry from one Address Book to another, choose Tools | Address Book and make sure both Address Books are open. Then select the entry you want to copy. If you want to copy more than one entry, hold down the CTRL key as you select each entry. If you want to copy all the entries in one book to another, choose Edit | Select All or press CTRL-A. Once the entries are selected, choose Edit | Copy Names. Select the Address Book you want to copy the entries to and choose OK.

TIP: *You can also copy entries by selecting the entries you want, and then clicking and dragging one of the selected entries to the Address Book tab where you want them copied. When the mouse pointer is positioned over the tab name, it changes to show one or two people depending on whether you're copying multiple entries. Release the mouse button to copy the entries.*

When you copy entries between address books by choosing Edit | Copy Names, or by clicking and dragging to the Address Book tabs, the entries remain linked together. This means that if you edit an entry in any of the Address Books, it's automatically updated in *all* Address Books that it has been copied into.

If you want to copy entries to another Address Book and *not* have them linked, select the entries you want to copy in the Address Book dialog box and choose Edit | Copy or press CTRL-C. Switch to the new Address Book by selecting the tab name, and then choose Edit | Paste or press CTRL-V. This method lets you change an entry in one Address Book and not have it automatically changed in the other books.

To move entries between Address Books, select the entries you want to move and choose Edit | Cut, or press CTRL-X. Switch to the Address Book you want to move the entries to, and then choose Edit | Paste or press CTRL-V. If you want to delete an entry from an Address Book, select the entry and choose Remove; then choose Yes to confirm the deletion. The entry is only deleted from the current Address Book, so if it has been copied into other Address Books, those entries still remain. You can also delete entries by clicking and dragging them outside the main list of addresses until the mouse pointer changes to a trash can.

NOTE: *The Frequent Contacts Address Book automatically contains entries that you've used from other Address Books. Each time you insert an address from an Address Book, it's automatically copied into the Frequent Contacts Address Book. The Frequent Contacts book displays the last access date and time of the entry, as well as the number of times it has been used.*

Creating Address Groups

In addition to creating separate Address Books, you can also group addresses together within an Address Book. For example, you can create a group of vendors that deal with a specific product category. Address groups are most helpful when you use the Address Book with the Merge feature, because you can quickly merge a form document with each person in the group by selecting the single address group instead of each individual entry. To create a group, follow these steps:

1. Choose Tools | Address Book and select the tab for the Address Book where you want the group created.

2. Choose Address List. This expands the Address Book dialog box to include a list box along the right side (see Figure 15-6).

3. To add an entry to the group, select it and choose Select Address. You can also add an entry by double-clicking it or by clicking and dragging it into the list box.

NOTE: *When you add an entry to an address group, the original entry still remains in the regular Address Book.*

4. Continue adding the entries you want to the group. You can add entries from another Address Book by switching to it and selecting the entries you want.

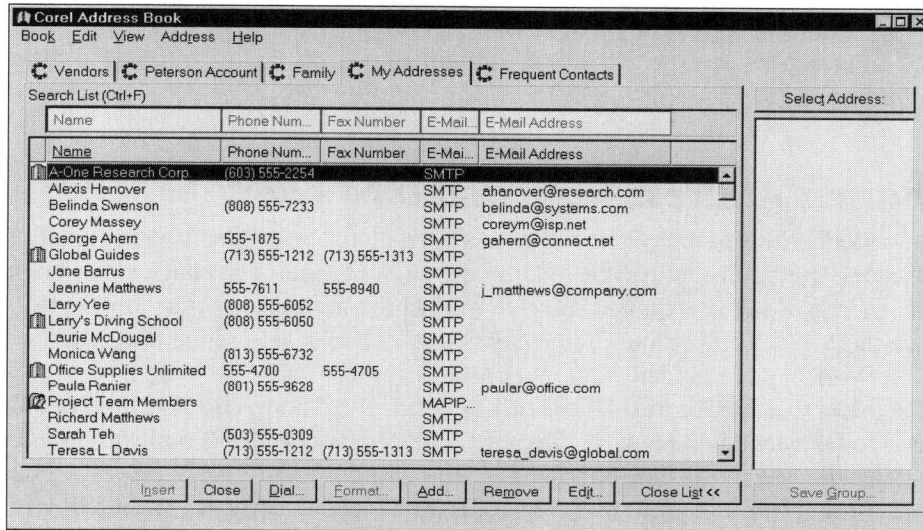

FIGURE 15-6 By choosing the Address List button, the Address Book dialog box expands

5. When you've added all the entries to the group, choose Save Group. Type a name for your group in the Name text box and choose OK. The group is created in the Address Book that was selected when you first added an entry to the group.

6. Choose Close to close the Address Book dialog box.

If you later want to edit the group, choose Tools | Address Book. Select the group name in the Address Book dialog box and choose Edit, then choose Edit Group. To add a new entry, follow the previous steps. To delete an address from the group, select it in the list and press DELETE, or click and drag it out of the list box. When you're finished making changes, choose Save Group. If you want to keep the same group name, choose OK. To save the group with a different name, type the new name in the text box and choose OK.

n **NOTE:** *The Close List button in the Address Book dialog box is only available when the address book list on the right is empty. If you want to return the Address Book to its original appearance after creating or editing a group, close the Address Book dialog box and redisplay it.*

Sharing Address Books on a Network

If you work on a network, you can share Address Books with other users so everyone can access common address information, yet still keep their personal address books. The Address Book you want to share on a network must be a custom Address Book, since the My Addresses and Frequency Contacts books are unique to each user on the network and are hidden from other users.

In order to share Address Books on a network, the Address Book database folder needs to be placed in a network directory. The database folder is typically found in \Corel\Suite8\Shared\Address\Database. You might need to have a network system administrator move the files to a network location where everyone can access them.

n **NOTE:** *If you don't want users to be able to change the entries in the shared Address Book, have the system administrator mark the database files as read-only.*

After the database folder is on the network, each user who wants to access the shared Address Books must specify the network location. To change the location of the Address Book files, follow these steps:

c **CAUTION:** *When you change the location of the Address Book files, the addresses currently in the My Addresses book, as well as any custom Address Books that have been created, will no longer be available. If you want to retain access to these entries, you can export the addresses before changing the location, and then import them into the new books. Follow the steps under "Exporting Addresses" in the next section to export any existing Address Books.*

1. Choose Tools | Address Book; then choose Edit | Settings.

2. Select the Services tab, select Corel Address Book 8 in the list, and choose Properties. Choose Browse, select the network directory that contains the Address Book database folder, and choose OK (see Figure 15-7).

3. Choose OK; then choose Close twice.

4. Choose Tools | Address Book again. Any custom Address Books in the network folder should now be available. If the database files were marked as read-only, each user can only access the Address Book information and not modify it.

Each user will also have access to a personal My Addresses and Frequent Contacts Address Book, which remains hidden from other users. If you exported your Address Book information before changing the database location, create any needed Address Books and import the entries, as explained in the "Importing Addresses" section. If you create a new Address Book and don't want other people to have access to it, you can mark it as Hidden. To do this, after creating the new Address Book, choose Book | Properties. Select the Security tab, select Hidden, and choose OK.

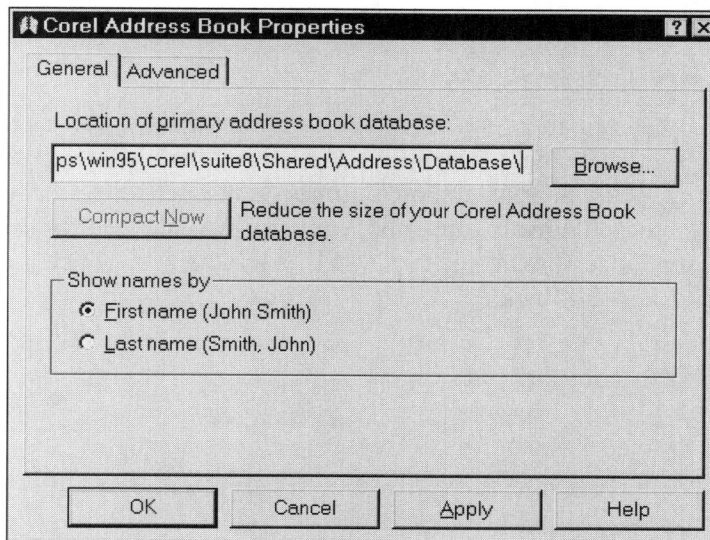

FIGURE 15-7   The Address Book Properties dialog box lets you select a network Address Book

CAUTION: *If you're using the Microsoft driver for NetWare, there is a bug that can cause incomplete information to be written to the Address Book database. If users have the ability to write to the database files on the network, you need to disable the write-behind cache option in Windows 95 to avoid this problem. To do this, click the Windows 95 Start button and choose Settings | Control Panel. Double-click the System icon, and select the Performance tab. Choose File System, select the Troubleshooting tab, and select the Disable Write-Behind Caching for All Drives option. Choose OK, and then Close. You'll need to restart your computer for the changes to take effect.*

Importing and Exporting Addresses

WordPerfect makes it easy to transfer information to and from the Address Book. For example, you can import addresses that you've already entered in a database program or a WP merge data file. Or you can save Address Book entries in a file so you can transfer them between computers, such as copying your Address Book at work to your computer at home. In this section, you'll learn how to import and export addresses.

Importing Addresses

You can import information into WP's Address Book from a variety of different database programs and other types of files. For a list of the formats you can use, see the "Supported Address Book Import Formats" quick reference section. If your database program isn't directly supported, you can use the database program to save the file in a supported format, such as ASCII delimited text, which you can then import into the Address Book.

Quick Reference ▶▶▶ Supported Address Book Import Formats

15

WordPerfect 8 supports the following formats for importing information into the Address Book.

- Address Book Export format (*.ABX)
- ANSI Delimited text
- ASCII Delimited text
- Clipper
- dBASE
- FoxPro
- Merge data/Notebook*
- ODBC (Open Database Connectivity database programs, such as MS Access)
- Paradox

* Merge data files must have field names and can't be in a table format. Also, if the data file is from WP 6.1 or an earlier version, open it first in WP 8 and resave it before importing.

To import addresses, choose Tools | Address Book. Select the Address Book tab where you want the new addresses inserted or create a new Address Book by following the steps in the "Creating an Address Book" section earlier in this chapter. Then choose Book | Import. When the Import Expert dialog box appears, select the option for the type of file you're importing, such as Merge data/Notebook file.

Choose Next. WP prompts you for the filename (or the ODBC data source and table). Choose Browse and select the file you want to import. If you're importing an Address Book ABX file, choose Finish. Otherwise, choose Next.

NOTE: *If you're importing an Address Book (*.ABX) file that uses custom fields, those same fields must already be created in the Address Book or the information in them won't be included. See "Creating Custom Fields" earlier in this chapter for more information.*

TIP: *WP automatically imports every record in the selected data file. If you don't want to import every record, use the Sort feature before importing the addresses to create a new data file with only those records that you want. For more information on selecting records with the Sort feature, see Chapter 8.*

If you're importing an ASCII or ANSI delimited file, the Import Expert dialog box displays a preview of the first several records in the file (see Figure 15-8). If the first line of the file contains the field names, select Yes at the top of the dialog box; otherwise select No. Choose Next. Change the field separator and encapsulation character if needed, and choose Next again.

CAUTION: *If the first line of the delimited file in the preview window is blank, that indicates an extra hard return at the top of the file. Cancel the import process, open the delimited file as ASCII DOS text, delete the hard return at the top of the file, and resave it in ASCII DOS format. Then start the import process again.*

If you're importing a file in a format other than the Address Book (*.ABX) format, the Import Expert next displays a list of the fields in the file being imported, along with a list of the available Address Book fields (see Figure 15-9). This allows you to tell WP which fields in the Address Book to use for the information in your data file. WP automatically matches any of the fields in your data file that have the same name as fields in the Address Book.

If a field in your data file *doesn't* have a matching counterpart in the Address Book, you need to tell WP which Address Book field to use. Those fields that WP can't automatically match display "IGNORE FIELD" next to them. To match a field, select the data field in the list on the left, and select the corresponding Address Book field in

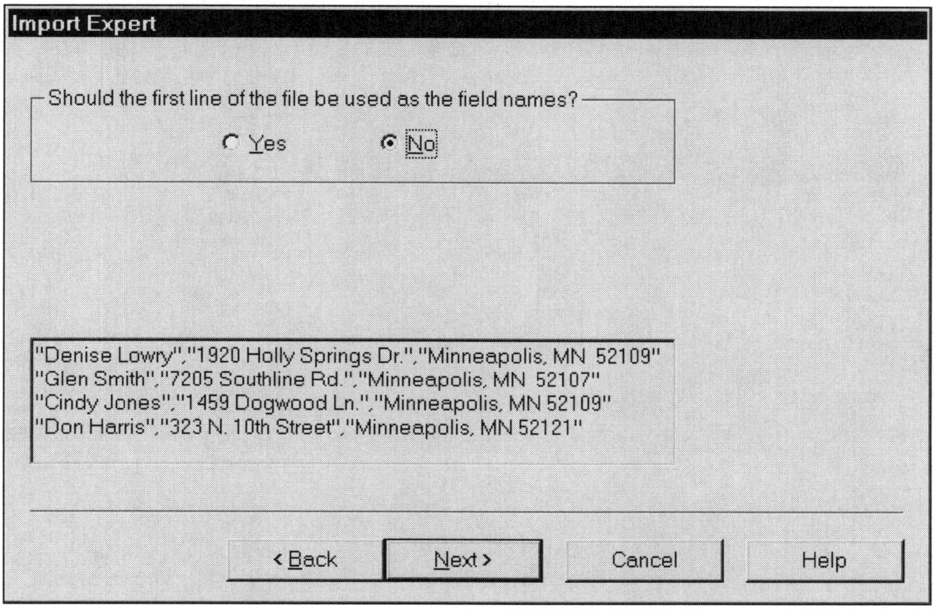

Import Expert

Should the first line of the file be used as the field names?

○ Yes   ● No

"Denise Lowry","1920 Holly Springs Dr.","Minneapolis, MN 52109"
"Glen Smith","7205 Southline Rd.","Minneapolis, MN 52107"
"Cindy Jones","1459 Dogwood Ln.","Minneapolis, MN 52109"
"Don Harris","323 N. 10th Street","Minneapolis, MN 52121"

[< Back] [Next >] [Cancel] [Help]

FIGURE 15-8 Importing an ASCII delimited file to the Address Book

the list on the right. For example, if your data file has a field named "Company," select it in the list, then select Organization in the Address Book Fields list box. If you don't want to include a field from your data file when the information is imported, select it and choose IGNORE FIELD in the Address Book Fields list box.

NOTE: *If you want to import information into a custom Address Book field, you must have the custom field already created before importing the file. If you want to create a custom field, cancel the import process, create the custom fields you need following the steps in the "Creating Custom Fields" section earlier in this chapter, and re-import the file.*

CAUTION: *The Pager Number and Generation Address Book fields can't be edited once the information has been imported into the Address Book. If you want to include a pager number field, cancel the import process, and create a custom field with a slightly different name, such as **Pager**; then re-import the file and select the custom field.*

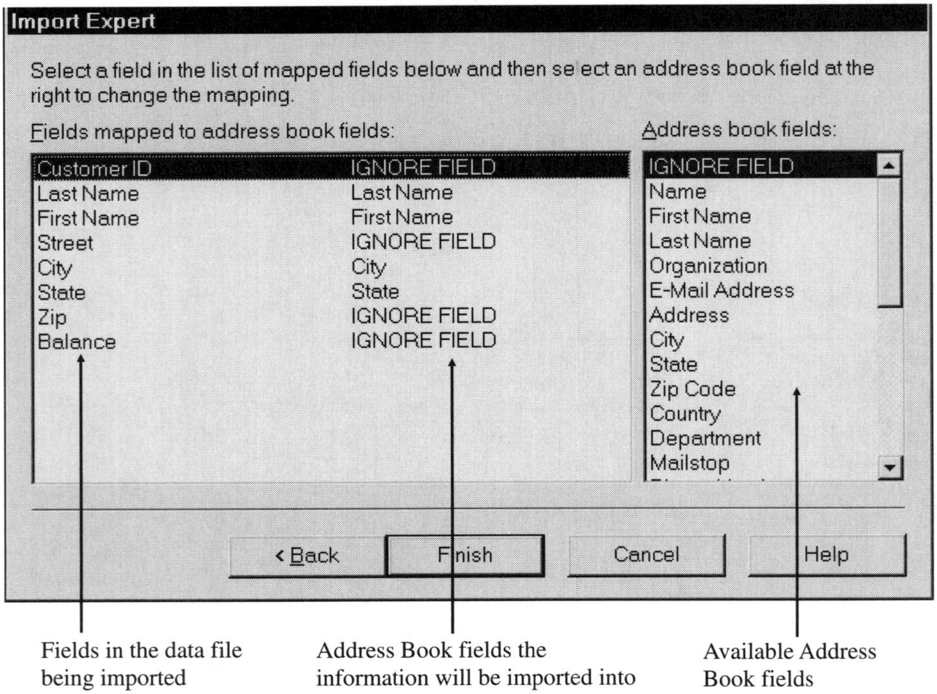

Import Expert		

Select a field in the list of mapped fields below and then select an address book field at the right to change the mapping.

Fields mapped to address book fields:

		Address book fields:
Customer ID	IGNORE FIELD	IGNORE FIELD
Last Name	Last Name	Name
First Name	First Name	First Name
Street	IGNORE FIELD	Last Name
City	City	Organization
State	State	E-Mail Address
Zip	IGNORE FIELD	Address
Balance	IGNORE FIELD	City
		State
		Zip Code
		Country
		Department
		Mailstop

< Back   Finish   Cancel   Help

Fields in the data file being imported

Address Book fields the information will be imported into

Available Address Book fields

FIGURE 15-9   You can select which fields in the Address Book to use for the file you're importing

When you've matched the Address Book fields for each field in your data file that you want to import, choose Finish. WP imports the file and adds each record in the current Address Book as a separate entry. Once the records have been imported, you can view or edit the information for an entry by selecting the entry and choosing Edit.

Exporting Addresses

Entries in an Address Book can also be *exported*, or saved in a file. WordPerfect exports Address Books in *.ABX format, which is an ANSI delimited text file with a special Address Book header. An ABX file can then be imported into another computer's Address Book, giving you an easy method for transferring Address Books between computers.

NOTE: *This method can also be used to transfer Address Book information from WordPerfect 7 to WordPerfect 8.*

To export an Address Book, choose Tools | Address Book and select the tab for the Address Book you want to export. If you don't want to export the entire Address Book, hold down the CTRL key and select each entry that you want to export. Choose Book | Export. If you're exporting selected entries, choose Selected Items. To export the entire book, choose Entire Address Book. Type a name for the exported file in the File Name text box, using an ABX extension, such as **MyAddress.ABX**, then choose OK. Now you can import the ABX file into another computer's Address Book by following the steps in the "Importing Addresses" section.

If you want to save the Address Book information in a format that can be imported into other database programs, you can use the ADRS2MRG.WCM shipping macro to convert the Address Book to a merge data file, and then save that file in ASCII delimited format. For more information, see the "How to Export the Address Book to a Database" section. You can also use CorelCentral to export the Address Book in a variety of formats. See Chapter 20 for more information.

How to ▸▸▸ Export the Address Book to a Database

When you use the Book | Export option in the Address Book dialog box, WordPerfect saves the information in its Address Book format (*.ABX). However, you can also save the Address Book in ASCII delimited format, which many database programs can then import. To do this, follow these steps:

1. Go to a blank document window in WordPerfect and choose Tools | Macro | Play.

2. Select the ADRS2MRG.WCM macro, which is included with WP 8. Choose Play.

3. The Address Book to Merge dialog box appears. In the Select Records list box, select the Address Book that you want to export.

4. If you only want to export selected addresses instead of the entire Address Book, choose Selected Records, and then choose Select Records. Select each entry you want to include and choose Select Address. You can also double-click entries to select them, or click and drag them into the list box on the right side of the dialog box. When you've selected all the records you want, choose OK.

How to... **Export the Address Book to a Database**
(*continued*)

5. Choose OK to start the conversion process. WP creates a merge data file with the information from the Address Book.

6. If you want to change the delimiter options for the ASCII file, such as the field separator and encapsulation character, choose Tools | Settings and double-click Convert. Select the delimiters and characters you want to use by typing them in the text box or selecting a code from the drop-down arrow. Choose OK, and then Close when you're finished.

7. Choose File | Save As. Switch to the directory where you want the file saved and type a name in the File Name text box, using a TXT extension.

8. From the File Type drop-down list, select ASCII (DOS) Delimited Text or ANSI (Windows) Delimited Text. Choose Save.

9. Choose File | Close to close the data file.

Now you can import the delimited TXT file into a database program that recognizes the ASCII delimited format.

Address Book Display

The Address Book dialog box can be customized to display the field information you want, in the order you want. For example, you can have the Address Book display only the name and phone number for each entry. Or you can display information in custom fields that you've created. The display settings are saved within an Address Book, so each book can have different settings. In this section, you'll learn how to customize the Address Book display, as well as sort the entries by different criteria.

Customizing the Display

There are several ways you can customize the display of an Address Book. For example, you can select which fields are displayed, what order they appear in, and how much room each takes up (see Figure 15-10). To change the display of an Address Book, choose Tools | Address Book, and select the tab for the Address Book you want to modify. Then follow these guidelines:

- *Displayed Columns*   To select which fields are displayed in the Address Book, choose Edit | Columns; then select a field you want to add as a column heading, or deselect a field you want to remove. You can also add fields by right-clicking the column heading area and selecting the field you want to add, and you can remove fields by dragging the column heading off the heading area. If the field you want to add as a column heading isn't included on the default list, choose Edit | Columns | More Columns. Select the field you want to add from the Available Columns list box and choose Add. Choose OK when you're finished. New field columns are added to the far right side of the dialog box (you might need to use the horizontal scroll bar to see them).

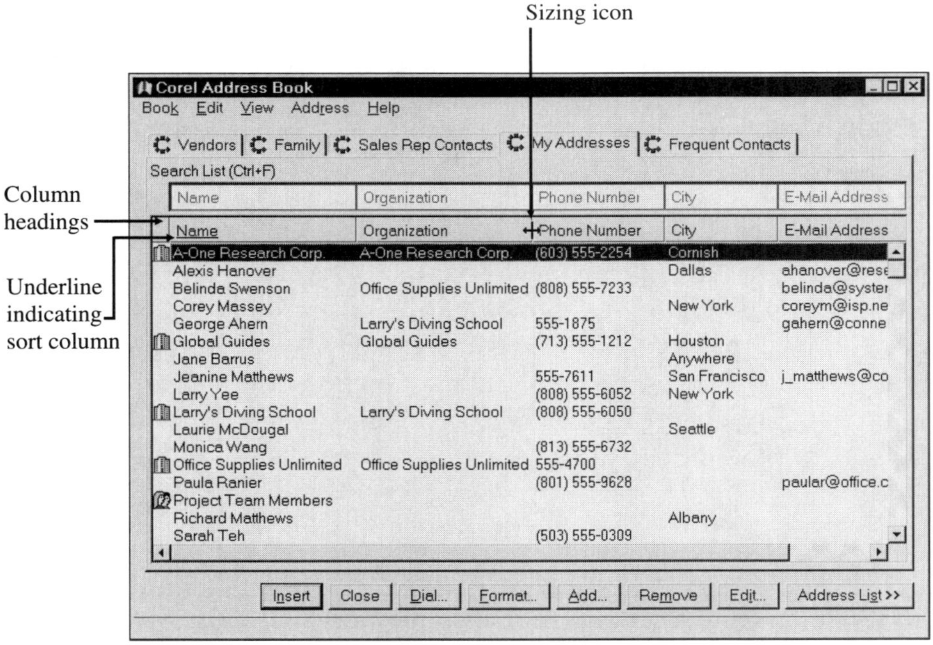

FIGURE 15-10 You can customize the column display in the Address Book

> **TIP:** *If you want the information in the Name field to be displayed last name first, choose View | Name Format | Last First. However, when you make this change, the addresses are also inserted into your documents with the last name first.*

- *Column Order* To change the order of the field columns in the dialog box, you can simply click and drag a column heading to a new position in the row of headings. Or you can choose Edit | Columns | More Columns, select the column heading you want to move in the Selected Columns list box on the right, and then choose Move to the Left (Up) or Move to the Right (Down) until the headings are in the order you want (see Figure 15-11). Choose OK when you're finished.

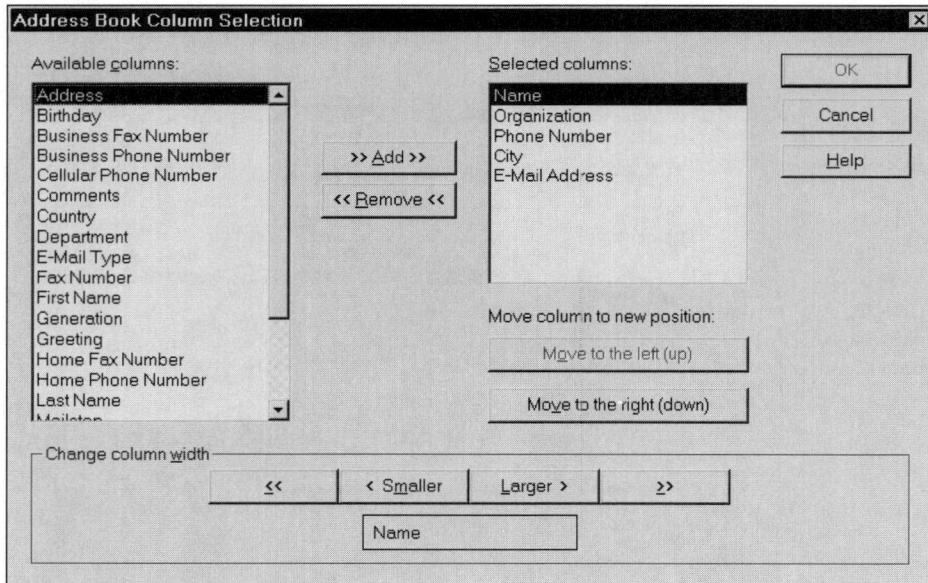

FIGURE 15-11 You can manually adjust the order and size of column headings

- *Column Size*   To change the size of a column, move the mouse pointer over the right edge of the column heading until it turns into a sizing icon (see Figure 15-10). Then click and drag until the column is the size you want. You can also change column sizes by choosing Edit | Columns | More Columns and selecting the column you want to change in the Selected Column list box. The preview at the bottom of the dialog box shows the current size of the heading (see Figure 15-11). Use the Smaller, <<, Larger, and >> buttons to increase or decrease the size of the heading. When you're finished, choose OK.

Sorting Addresses

By default, entries in the Address Book are sorted in ascending order according to the field in the far-left column, which is usually the Name field. You can have the information sorted by a different field if you want, and also choose whether it's sorted in ascending or descending order. You can quickly tell which field is being used to sort the Address Book by looking at the column headings—the underlined heading indicates the field determining the sort order (see Figure 15-10).

When you move a column heading to the far left position, it automatically becomes the field according to which the entries are sorted. To sort the entries by the information in another field, choose Edit | Columns | Sort. Select the column you want to sort by; then select whether you want the information sorted in ascending or descending order and choose OK. To simply change the order from ascending to descending, you can choose Edit | Columns, and then select Sort All Ascending or Sort All Descending.

TIP: *You can also change the sort order of entries by right-clicking the column heading for the field you want to sort by and selecting Sort On 'Field Name' first, where "Field Name" is the name of the current column. To change from ascending to descending order, right-click any column heading and select the option you want, such as Sort All Descending.*

NOTE: *In the Frequent Contacts Address Book, you can sort the entries according to the last time they were inserted in a document or the number of times they have been accessed. By default, the last reference date and time is displayed in the far left column.*

Searching for Addresses

If you have a long list of entries in an Address Book, you can quickly search for an entry that contains text in a specific field. For example, you can search for a last name, city name, or telephone number. In addition, you can set up filters to display only those entries that match a certain criteria, such as those in a specific state or ZIP code.

To search for an address, display the Address Book by choosing Tools | Address Book. Then click in the search text box above the column with the field information you want to search through (see Figure 15-1). For example, to search for a company name, click in the search text box above the Organization column. You can also press CTRL-F and choose OK to place the insertion point in the search text box of the leftmost available column.

With the insertion point in the search text box, begin typing the text that you want to search for. As you type, WP selects the entry that most closely matches the text. When the entry you want is selected, click the entry to end the search.

Using Filters

WordPerfect also lets you use filters to narrow down which entries are currently displayed in an Address Book. For example, you can set up a filter that displays only those entries that have a last name starting with L–N. Or you can display only those entries in a specific city or ZIP code. When you have a filter selected, you can still search for individual addresses within the filtered entries.

To set up a filter, choose Tools | Address Book and select the tab for the Address Book you want to filter. Choose View | Define Filter to display the Building a Filter dialog box, as shown next.

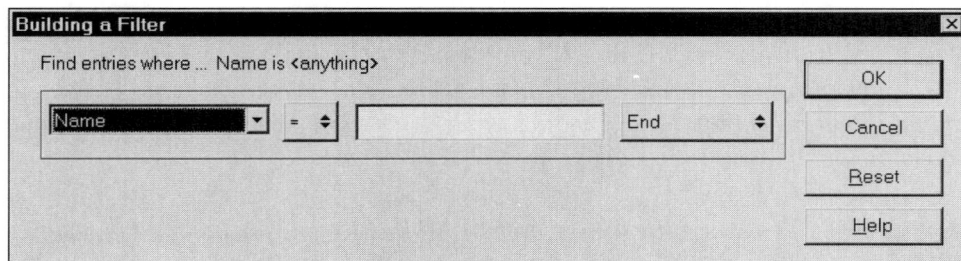

From the first drop-down list, select the field that you want to evaluate, such as Last Name or ZIP Code. From the Operator pop-up button, choose the operator that you want to use, such as = Equal To. Then, in the text box, type the matching condition, such as **Smith**.

TIP: *You can use Less Than and Greater Than to find entries before or after a certain letter of the alphabet. For example, "Last Name > M" finds all entries with a last name that starts with M-Z.*

To add further conditions to your filter, you can use the "And" and "Or" operators from the final pop-up button. Use the And operator to narrow the filter and display those entries that match two or more conditions, or use the Or operator to broaden the filter and display those entries that match just one of several conditions. For example, to find all those entries that have a last name of Matthews *and* that live in New York, the filter would look like this:

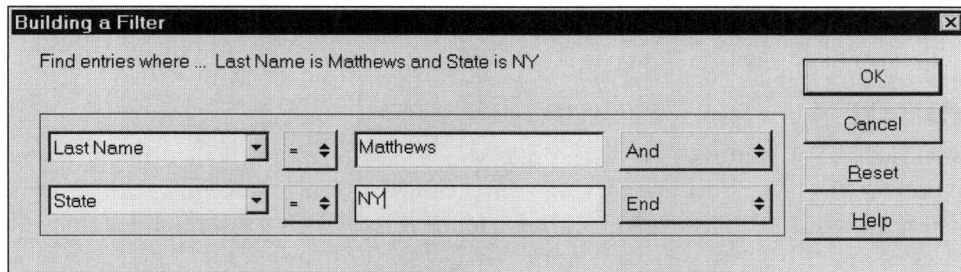

On the other hand, if you set the filter to use Or instead of And, the result would be all those living in New York, as well as all those with a last name of Matthews.

To use the And and Or operators, choose the last pop-up button (which displays "End") and choose the operator you want, such as And. A new row is inserted, where you can select the additional field you want to evaluate, the operator, and the matching condition. You can continue to add more rows if you want. Each row must be connected with the same operator (And or Or). To insert a new row in-between existing ones, choose Insert Row from the pop-up button in the row just above where you want the new row inserted. To delete a row, choose Delete Row from that row's pop-up button.

You can also create groups of conditions, so you can have one group using the And operator and another group using the Or operator. This is similar to grouping mathematical equations with parentheses. To add a new group, choose New Group from the pop-up button of the last condition row. Use the center pop-up button to select whether the entire second group should be evaluated with And or Or, and then set the new conditions in the second group. Each group can have multiple condition rows. For example, Figure 15-12 shows the filters that would display all those records with a last name starting with A–L (the Last Name < M filter doesn't include any names beginning with M). In addition to those entries, any entries that are either in California or that contain the word "Box" in the address are also included in the list.

When you're finished setting up the filter, choose OK to return to the Address Book and view the filtered results. When a filter is active, WP displays a filter icon just above the search list. To change the filter, choose View | Define Filter and make any changes you want. To turn off the filter temporarily, choose View | Filtering Enabled. You can turn the filter back off by choosing View | Filtering Enabled again. You can also right-click the filter icon and use the QuickMenu to edit the filter or turn the filter on or off. To delete the filter, choose View | Define Filter; then choose Reset and OK.

Summary

WordPerfect's Address Book is a great way to organize all the addresses, phone numbers, and other information about the people that you contact on a regular basis. The Address Book helps you quickly get to the information you need by letting you

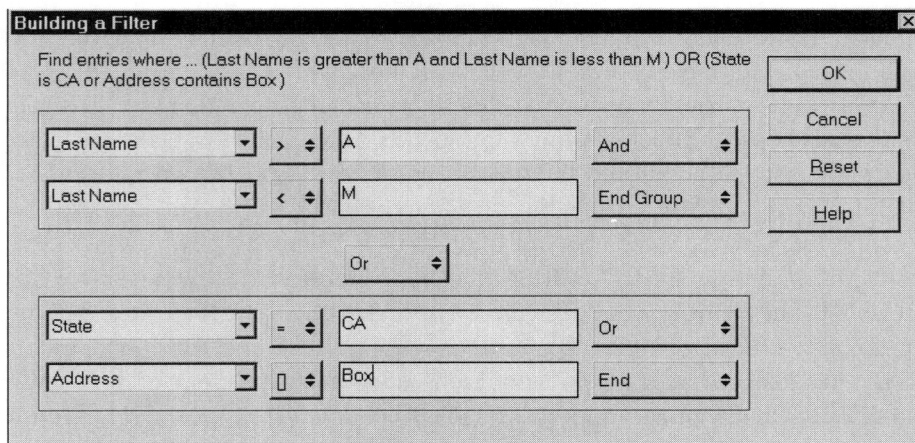

FIGURE 15-12 Using multiple condition groups for a filter

create custom fields, group addresses in separate Address Books, display the information in the format you want, and use filters to narrow down long lists. Once you've found the information, you can easily use it in your documents through features such as Templates, Envelopes, and Merge, or by simply inserting the address at the location of the insertion point.

In Chapter 16, we'll show you how to manage your documents efficiently and share them with others using features such as Versions and Document Review.

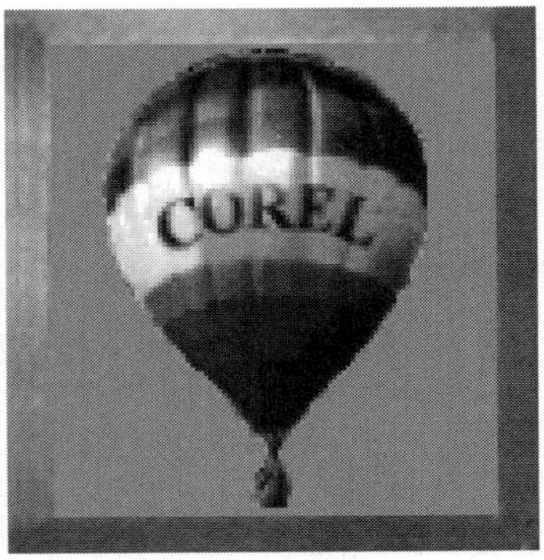
COREL

Chapter
16

Managing and Sharing Files

ow many different documents do you work on in any given day? Five? Fifteen? Fifty? Whatever the amount, it can be frustrating—and time-consuming—to keep track of them all. Maybe you need to find a specific document you created last year, compare a document with the version from two weeks ago, or incorporate the comments of several people into a single document. Without the right tools, tasks like these could take hours.

Fortunately, WordPerfect 8 can greatly reduce the amount of time you have to spend managing and tracking your files. In this chapter, you'll learn how to put WP's file management tools to use. We'll give you some tips for customizing the Open File dialog box and show you how to find files in a flash with QuickFinder. You'll also learn how to create a summary of important document information and keep track of different document versions with the Corel Versions and Document Compare features. Finally, we'll show you how to easily incorporate comments from others with the Document Review feature.

The Open File Dialog Box

The Open File dialog box is no doubt a familiar sight to WordPerfect users. After all, this is where you select the documents you want to open and work on (see Figure 16-1). But even though the Open File dialog box has a fairly simple purpose, there are lots of built-in tools that make it faster and easier to manage your files. In this section, we'll give you several shortcuts and hints for getting the most out of the Open File dialog box.

NOTE: *The Open File dialog box is practically identical to other WordPerfect file management dialog boxes, such as the Save File, Play Macro, and Insert Image dialog boxes. The shortcuts and tips in this section apply to these dialogs as well.*

Customizing the Display

The Open File dialog box can be displayed by choosing File | Open or by pressing CTRL-O. Follow these tips to customize the display of the dialog box to meet your needs:

- By default, the menu bar in the Open File dialog box is turned off. This menu gives you quick access to the Favorites menu, as well as other file management tools. To display the menu bar, click the Toggle Menu On/Off button (see Figure 16-2).

- To turn on the Status Bar, choose View | Status Bar. The Status Bar displays the file size and descriptive name (if any) of the currently selected file (see Figure 16-2). If you select multiple files, the Status Bar displays the total number of files selected, as well as the combined file size. If no files are selected, you can see the total number of files in the directory and the total amount of used disk space.

NOTE: *Descriptive names can be added to a file with the Document Summary feature. For more information, see the "Creating a Document Summary" section later in this chapter.*

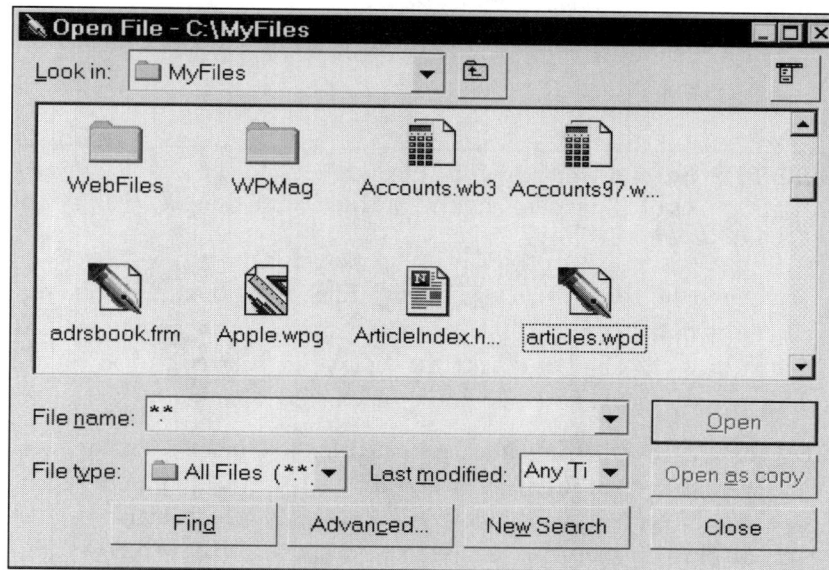

FIGURE 16-1 The default Open File dialog box can be customized in several ways

Column headings   Menu bar   Toggle Menu On/Off

Toolbar →

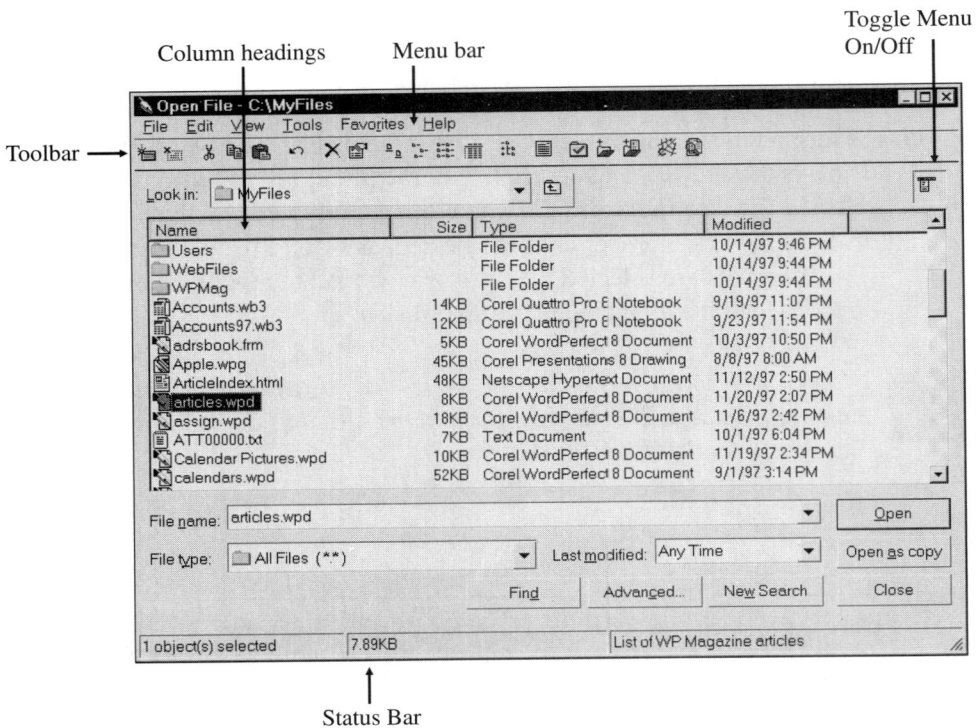

Status Bar

FIGURE 16-2 Several features of the Open File dialog box can be turned on or off. You can quickly sort files by clicking a column heading

- To change the overall size of the Open File dialog box, move the mouse pointer over the corner of the dialog box until it changes into a diagonal arrow; then click and drag until the dialog box is sized as you want. The dialog box uses the new size until you change it again.

- By default, only the filenames are listed in the Open File dialog box. If you want to see the full information for each file, including the file size, date/time, and type, choose View I Details. You can also have the files displayed as large or small icons, similar to other Windows file management windows, by choosing View and selecting the option you want.

TIP: *The display type can also be changed by right-clicking any blank area of the file window, choosing View from the QuickMenu, and then selecting the option you want. Or you can click the appropriate toolbar button to change the display.*

- If you have the file detail information displayed, you can quickly sort the files in ascending or descending order according to the filename, type, size, or date. To sort the files, simply click the heading above the column you want to sort by (see Figure 16-2). For example, to sort according to the date, click the Modified heading. Each time you click a heading, the sort order changes between ascending and descending order.

TIP: *You can change the size of the columns by moving the mouse pointer over the division between two headings until it turns into a double-arrow, and then clicking and dragging until the column is sized as you want.*

NOTE: *When you change the sort order, the setting remains only until you exit WordPerfect. The next time you start WP, the files will be sorted alphabetically according to filename.*

Selecting and Opening Files

When you select a file in the Open File dialog box, you can open, copy, move, or delete it. Here are some tips for selecting files, as well as a few different techniques for opening documents.

- You can select more than one file at a time to open, copy, move, delete, or print. To select multiple files, hold down the CTRL key as you select each file in the list. If the files are listed consecutively, select the first file, hold down the SHIFT key, and then select the last file—all the files in between are automatically selected.

TIP: *You can also select consecutive files by clicking just outside a filename in a blank area of the Open File dialog box, and then clicking and dragging to select the files you want.*

- If you want to view only those files with a specific extension, such as WPD or FRM, select the option from the File Type drop-down list. If the extension isn't listed, type it in the File Name text box, such as ***.LTR**. You can also use wildcards to display files that match a specific pattern, such as **R*.W??**, to display any filenames beginning with "R" that also have a three-letter extension beginning with "W," such as REPORT.WPD and RABBIT.WPG.

TIP: *You can use a macro to display the Open File dialog box and automatically list only those files with a WPD extension. For more information, see the On the CD section "Displaying WPD Files Automatically."*

- If you want to keep the original version of a document intact, open a copy of the document, or make the document read-only. To open a copy of a document, select it in the Open File dialog box and choose Open as Copy. To make a document read-only, select the document, right-click it, and choose Properties. Select Read-Only and choose OK.

- You can open one of the last nine documents you were working on without using the Open File dialog box at all. Just choose File from a WP document screen and select the document you want to open from the bottom of the pull-down menu. Or you can choose File | New to display the New dialog box; then select the Work On tab and select the document you want. Choose Open to open the document.

NOTE: *A list of the last nine opened documents also appears on the File Name drop-down list in the Open File dialog box.*

- Each time you display the Open File dialog box during a WP session, the last directory you were using is displayed. If you always want WP to display your default document directory, choose Edit in the Open File dialog box and deselect Change Default Folder.

TIP: *To change the default document folder, from a WP document screen, choose Tools | Settings and double-click Files. Type the new directory in the Default Document Folder text box or use the file folder icon to select it. Choose OK; then choose Close.*

On the CD ▸▸▸ Displaying WPD Files Automatically

Each time you display the Open File dialog box, WP lists all the files (*.*) in the current directory. If you want to see only those files with a WPD file extension, you have to select WP Documents (*.wpd) from the File Type drop-down list. The companion CD includes a macro called OPENWPD.WCM that you can use to automatically display the Open File dialog box with the WPD file type option already selected.

To use this macro, choose Tools | Macro | Play, select the OPENWPD.WCM macro, and choose Play. The macro displays the Open File dialog box and selects the WP Documents (*.wpd) option from the File Type drop-down list. You can assign this macro to a keystroke such as CTRL-O or CTRL-SHIFT-O to make it easier to use. Or you can assign it to a toolbar button. For more information, see Chapter 13.

The OPENWPD.WCM macro uses the SendKeys command to simulate pressing keystrokes in the dialog box. If the macro doesn't work on your system, you need to edit the macro and increase the amount of time that the macro pauses between each keystroke.

To edit the macro, choose Tools | Macro | Edit, select the OPENWPD.WCM macro, and choose Edit. Increase the value assigned to the vWAIT variable on the second line of the macro (the value is set to 0 initially). For example, you might try changing the value to 5. This value represents tenths of a second, so a value of 5 would pause the macro a half-second between each keystroke. Choose File | Close when you're finished, and choose Yes to save the changes.

■ If you switch to a particular directory often for opening or copying files, you can add it to your Favorites list. To do this, switch to the directory in the Open File dialog box and choose Favorites | Add | Add Favorite Folder. Choose Yes to save the current filter. To edit the name of the Favorites item, choose Favorites | Go To/From Favorites. Select the item in the list, right-click it, and choose Rename. Type the new name and press ENTER. Then you can quickly switch to that directory by choosing Favorites and selecting the item from the list.

■ If you can connect to the Internet from your computer, the Open File dialog box can also serve as a basic Web browser and let you open a file from the Internet (see Figure 16-3). To use this feature, from the Open File dialog box, choose the Goto/From Corel Internet button on the toolbar (the second from the right). WP connects to the Internet (if you're not already connected) and goes to Corel's Web site. You can type an URL in the File Name text box to go to a different site, as well as use the Back, Forward, Refresh, and Stop buttons on the toolbar. To open the currently displayed HTML file into WordPerfect, choose Open and follow the prompts to open the file.

TIP: *If you want to change the default home page that displays in the Open File dialog box, click the Goto/From Corel Internet button and switch to the Web page you want to make the new default. Then choose Internet | Set Home Page.*

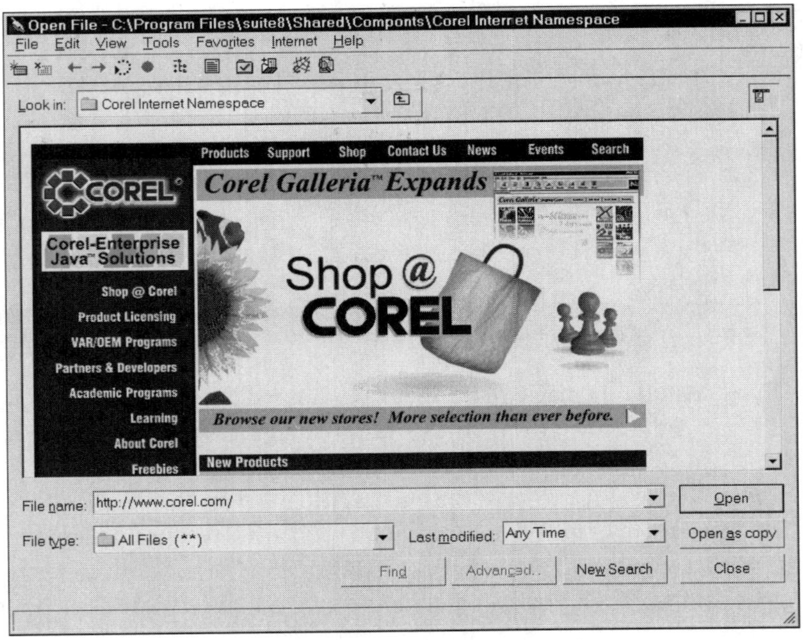

FIGURE 16-3 The Open File dialog box can also serve as a mini Web browser

Viewing and Printing Files

The Open File dialog box also lets you view and print files without having to open them first. Here are a few hints for doing this:

- When you want to preview a file, select the file and click the Toggle Preview On/Off button on the toolbar. By default, the preview displays on the right side of the Open File dialog box (see Figure 16-4). If you want the preview to appear in a separate window, which you can size or move where you want, right-click the viewer window and select Use Separate Window.

NOTE: *The WordPerfect Suite 8 CD includes additional viewers for the Open File dialog box that aren't installed during a typical installation. You can also preview files with the Quick View Plus utility included on the WordPerfect Suite 8 CD. For more information on installing and using these options, see Chapter 20.*

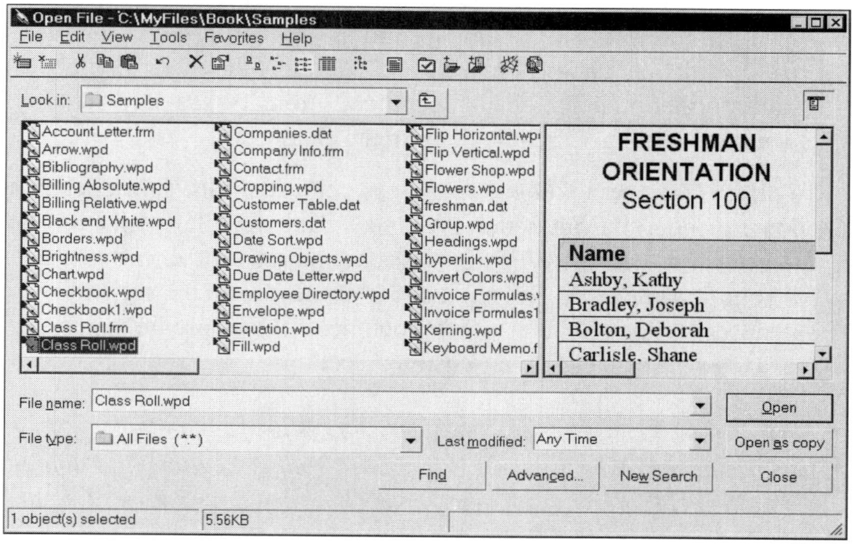

FIGURE 16-4 WP lets you preview a file before opening it. You can also have the preview appear in a separate window

- You can preview a document using WordPerfect's viewer in Content or Page view. To switch the view, right-click the viewer window and select the option you want. Content view displays the document with the text wrapped to fit the size of the viewer window (see Figure 16-4). Page view displays the full page layout (which is generally too small to read).

- If you're using the Content view option, the preview shows the specific fonts selected in the document. You can display the entire document in the same font by right-clicking the viewer window and choosing Draft. To change the font used in Draft view, right-click the viewer again and choose Font; then select the font and font size you want. The font you select is also used to display any documents that don't have a specific font selected in them.

NOTE: *When you use Draft view, any graphics in the document are not displayed.*

- You can copy text to the Clipboard from an unopened document. With the file displayed in the viewer window, select the text you want to copy with the mouse and press CTRL-C, or right-click the viewer and choose Copy. You can then paste the copied text into a WP document.

- If you want to view the document summary for a file, select the file, right-click it, and choose Properties. Then select the Summary tab. (For more information in creating a document summary, see the "Creating a Document Summary" section later in the chapter.)

- To print a document without opening it, select the file, right-click it, and choose Print. The Print option is only available for files with a recognized file extension, such as WPD. If you commonly use other file extensions for your documents, you can add those extensions to the registry so Windows recognizes them as WP documents. For more information, see the "How to Register File Extensions" section.

TIP: *If you want to have the WPD extension automatically added to all new documents you save, in WP choose Tools | Settings and double-click Files. Select Use Default Extension on Open and Save, choose OK, and then Close.*

■ If you want to print a list of files in a directory, switch to the directory and choose File | Print File List. To print the list, make sure Send to Printer is selected and choose OK. If you want to format the list first, select either Display in WordPad or Copy to Clipboard; then choose OK. If you copied the list to the Clipboard, go to a WP document and press CTRL-V to paste in the list, and then make any changes you want.

How to▸▸▸ Register File Extensions

Windows automatically recognizes files with certain extensions as WordPerfect documents, such as WPD, DAT, FRM, and WCM. Files with a recognized extension have the Print option available when you right-click them in the Open File dialog box. If you use another file extension frequently, such as LTR, you can register that extension with Windows so the files are recognized as WP documents.

To register a file extension, follow these steps:

1. From the Windows taskbar, choose Start | Run. Type **regedit** and choose OK.

2. In the Registry Editor, double-click the HKEY_CLASSES_ROOT folder. A list of registered file extensions appears, arranged in alphabetical order:

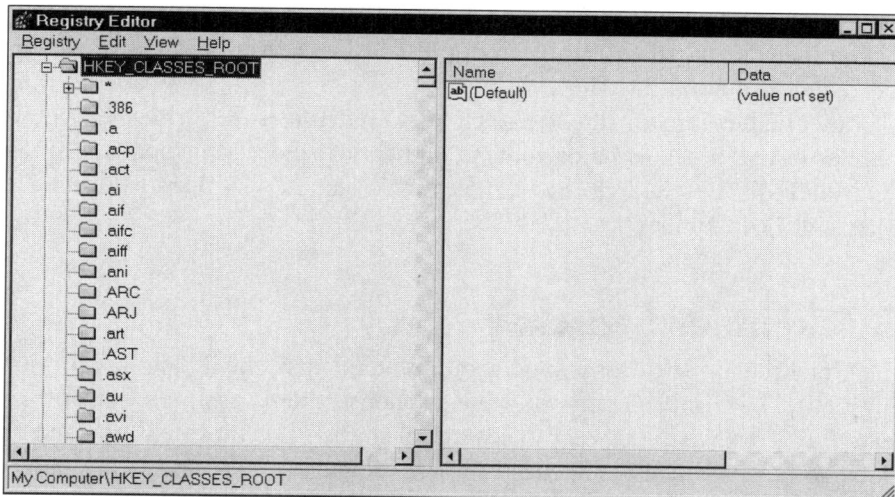

| |
How to...   **Register File Extensions**
(continued)

3. If the extension you want to register is already listed, select it. Otherwise, select HKEY_CLASSES_ROOT and choose Edit | New | Key. Type the extension you want to use—including the period—such as **.LTR,** and press ENTER (it should automatically replace the "New Key #1" text).

4. With the extension selected, double-click the (Default) item on the right side of the dialog box. In the Value Data text box, type **WP8Doc**. Choose OK.

5. Repeat these steps to register any other extensions you want to use. When you're finished, choose Registry | Exit.

Now when you select a document with that extension in the Open File dialog box, the Print option is available when you right-click the file.

Finding Files with QuickFinder

When you're looking for a specific file, don't waste time scrolling through file lists or previewing dozens of different files. Instead, use WP's QuickFinder feature to find the file you want in a matter of seconds. While QuickFinder isn't new to WP 8, it has been changed quite a bit from previous versions to bring you even greater speed and ease in finding files.

QuickFinder consists of two parts: QuickFinder Searcher, which lets you search for files based on filename or content, and QuickFinder Manager, which lets you create and edit "Fast Search" index files. In this section, you'll learn how to use both aspects of QuickFinder.

QuickFinder Searcher

The QuickFinder Searcher is built right into the Open File dialog box. If the Open File dialog box isn't already displaying, choose File | Open. To perform a basic search, type the text you want to search for in the File Name text box and choose Find. WP automatically searches for both filenames *and* document content that matches the text. For example, if you type **Johnson** in the File Name text box and choose Find, QuickFinder searches for files with "Johnson" somewhere in the actual filename, as well as files with "Johnson" anywhere in the document text.

> **TIP:** *If you want to search for a specific phrase, type the text in quotation marks, such as* ***"Peter Johnson."***

You can narrow the search by including only files with a specific extension or files that were last saved within a specific time frame. To search through files with a specific extension, select the option you want from the File Type drop-down list, such as WP Documents (*.wpd). To search through files last saved within a certain time frame, such as the current week, month, or year, select the option you want from the Last Modified drop-down list.

When you choose Find, QuickFinder automatically searches through the files in the current directory, as well as any subdirectories. A new Open File dialog box displays with a list of any matching files.

> **NOTE:** *Depending on how many files and subdirectories are in the current directory, the search might take a few minutes. You can speed up the search time by creating a Fast Search. For more information, see the "QuickFinder Manager" section later in the chapter.*

> **TIP:** *You can also access the QuickFinder Searcher outside of WordPerfect and the Open File dialog box. From the Windows taskbar, choose Start | Corel WordPerfect Suite 8 | Tools | QuickFinder Searcher.*

Performing Advanced Searches

In addition to performing a basic search, you can also set up advanced search options. For example, you can search for files that contain two words on the same page, or files that contain a specific phrase but *not* another phrase. To perform an advanced search, choose File | Open, and then choose Advanced. The Advanced Find dialog box appears (see Figure 16-5).

> **TIP:** *Before choosing Advanced, you can specify basic search options in the Open File dialog box—for example, typing text to match the filename or content in the File Name text box, specifying a file type, or selecting a time frame. Then, when you choose Advanced, the Advanced Find dialog box already contains those settings.*

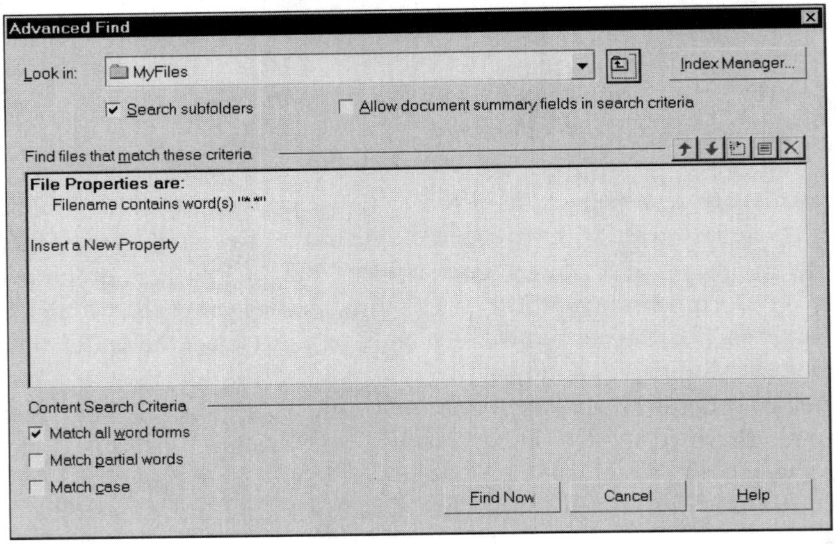

FIGURE 16-5 You can set up advanced search options

In the Advanced Find dialog box, you can specify matching criteria for the filename or content—called search *properties*—as well as other options such as whether the search is case sensitive or includes subdirectories. To add a search property, double-click the Insert a New Property item in the text box. A series of drop-down lists appears:

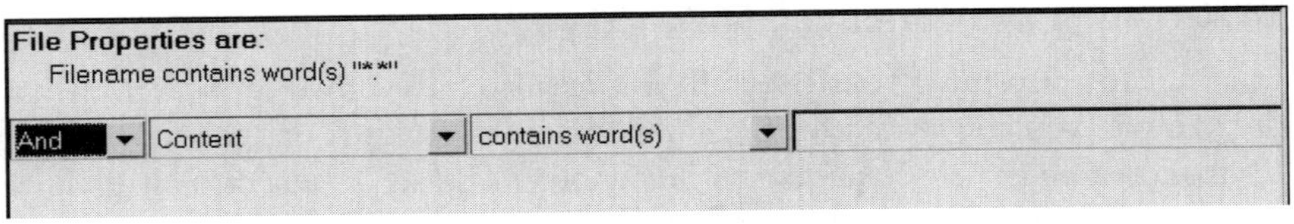

NOTE: *You can also add a search property by clicking the Insert a New Item button above the right corner of the text box (the middle button).*

The first drop-down list is used when you're adding multiple search properties (more on that in a minute). From the second drop-down list, select whether you want to search for files that match a time frame, filename, file content, or either filename or content. Then, from the third drop-down list, select the option you want. The available options depend on which item was selected from the second drop-down list. In the final text area, type the text that applies to the option you selected from the third drop-down list. If you selected an option such as "contains word(s) in same paragraph," type both words with a space separating them.

TIP: *If you want to search for a specific phrase, you can either select "contains phrase" from the third drop-down list or select "contains word(s)" and type the text in quotation marks.*

After you've set all the items for the new property, press TAB or ENTER. The new item is added to the text box under the appropriate heading. For example, if you specified information for a filename or date, the property appears under the "File Properties are" heading. Or, if you specified content, the item appears under the "Content Properties are" heading.

NOTE: *If you need to edit a search property, double-click the item in the text box to display the drop-down lists, and then make any changes you want. If you want to delete a search property, select it and click the Delete Current Item From List button above the right corner of the text box.*

If you want to further narrow your search, you can add multiple search properties. For example, you can search for documents that contain the phrase "Peter Johnson" but *not* "Cheryl Andrews." To specify additional search properties, double-click the Insert New Property item again and select the settings you want. From the first drop-down list, select "And" if you want to find documents that match *both* conditions. If you select "Or," QuickFinder will find those documents that match *either* of the conditions. For example, Figure 16-6 shows the settings that would search for documents created in the last year with a WPD extension that contain "Johnson" and "affidavit" in the same sentence but not "California."

TIP: *You can use the buttons above the right corner of the text box to change the order of the search properties in the list.*

When you've added all the properties, set any other options for the search in the Advanced Find dialog box. For example, the Match All Word Forms option finds

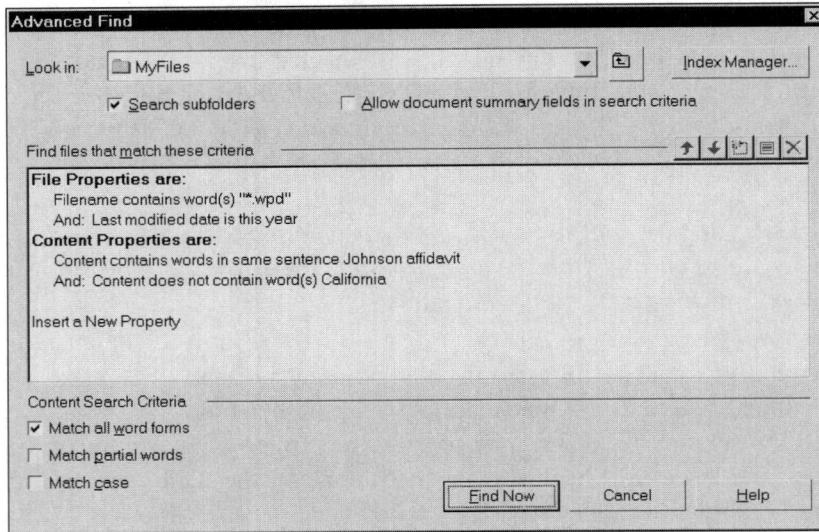

FIGURE 16-6 The Advanced Find dialog box with multiple search properties

any form of the specified text, such as "signs," "signing," and "signed" for the text "sign." The Match Partial Words option finds the specified text even if it is part of a longer word (such as "signature" for the text "sign.")

Choose Find Now to begin the search. The search results appear in a new Open File dialog box. The advanced search settings remain in effect until you close the Open File dialog box or choose New Search.

QuickFinder Manager

If you frequently search through directories that have lots of files and subdirectories, you can greatly speed up the process by using a Fast Search. When you set up a Fast Search, WP creates a highly compressed index file of every word in the selected directories and subdirectories. Then, when you search in that directory, QuickFinder only has to search through one compressed index file instead of multiple files and directories.

You can set up a Fast Search with the QuickFinder Manager. To run QuickFinder Manager, from the Windows taskbar choose Start | Corel WordPerfect

Suite 8 | Tools | QuickFinder Manager 8. The QuickFinder Manager dialog box appears (see Figure 16-7).

> **NOTE:**   *You can also access QuickFinder Manager by choosing Index Manager in the Advanced Find dialog box (see Figure 16-5).*

In QuickFinder Manager, you can set up either a standard Fast Search or a custom Fast Search. A *standard* Fast Search is an index for the files in a single directory, as well as any subdirectories underneath it. A *custom* Fast Search is an index for as many separate directories and subdirectories as you want.

Standard Fast Searches

To create a standard Fast Search, make sure the Standard Fast Search Setup tab is selected and choose Create. In the Folder to Search text box, type the directory you want to search through, or choose Browse to select it. Then select the update option you want. You can have QuickFinder automatically update the index file with new

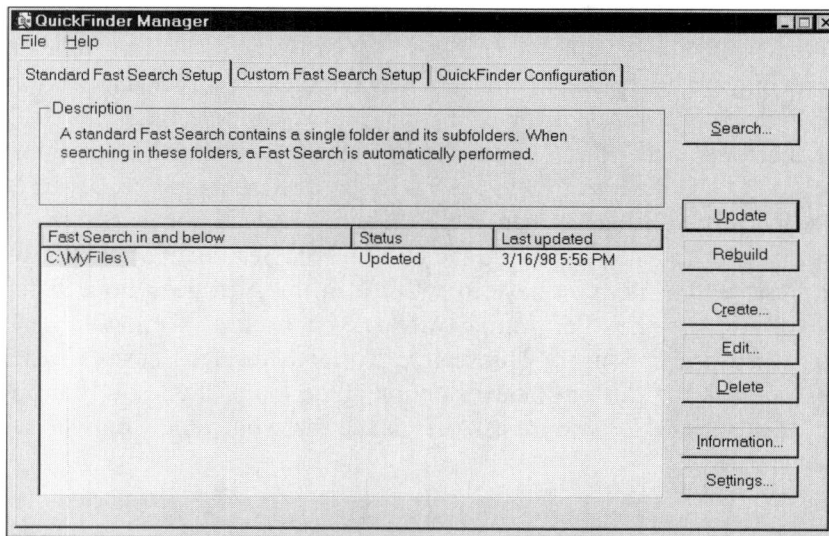

FIGURE 16-7 You can set up Fast Searches in the QuickFinder Manager

files at specified time intervals, or you can manually update the file. If you want to set further options for the Fast Search, such as whether only the document summary should be indexed or whether numbers should be included, choose Options, make the selections you want, and choose OK.

Choose OK to create the Fast Search index file. The new file is listed in the QuickFinder Manager dialog box. To search with a standard Fast Search file, all you need to do is perform a regular QuickFinder search using the steps explained in the "QuickFinder Searcher" section earlier in the chapter. If a Fast Search index file exists in the directory you're searching through, WP automatically uses it.

NOTE: *Standard Fast Search files use an IDX file extension and are saved in the same directory as the directory you're indexing.*

Custom Fast Searches

To create a custom Fast Search, select the Custom Fast Search Setup tab in the QuickFinder Manager dialog box and choose Create. In the Fast Search Name text box, type a descriptive name for the Fast Search, such as **Correspondence**. Select the update option you want. If you want to change the options for the Fast Search, choose Options, make the selections you want, and choose OK.

Now, you can add the directories and subdirectories that you want to have in the same Fast Search. For example, you can have the Fast Search include several different directories on your hard drive, as well as a network directory. To add a directory, type the path in the Folder to Add text box or choose Browse to select it. If you don't want any subdirectories under that directory to be included, deselect Include Subfolders. Choose Add to add the directory to the Folders to Search list box (see Figure 16-8). Continue this process to add as many other directories as you want.

When you're finished setting up the custom Fast Search, choose OK. To use a custom Fast Search file, you have to select it in the Advanced Find dialog box. Follow the steps in the "Performing Advanced Searches" section earlier in the chapter to set up the options for your search. To search through a custom Fast Search file, double-click the Custom Indexes option at the top of the Look In drop-down list, and then select the custom Fast Search file that you want. Continue with the search as normal.

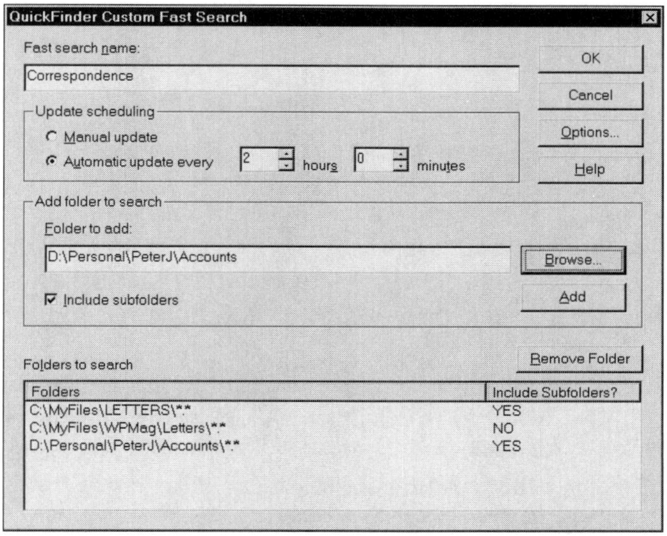

FIGURE 16-8 You can create a custom Fast Search to search through as many different directories as you want

Managing Fast Searches

The QuickFinder Manager dialog box lists each available Fast Search file, along with information about when it was last updated (see Figure 16-7). To manually update a Fast Search file and index any new files in the selected directories, select the Fast Search file in the list and choose Update. If you've deleted several files from the directories in a Fast Search, you can rebuild the Fast Search file by selecting the file and choosing Rebuild. To see the specific settings for a Fast Search file, such as the index file size, select it in the list and choose Information; then choose OK.

The QuickFinder Manager dialog box also gives you several options for determining how you can access QuickFinder settings. For more information, see the Power Tip "Accessing QuickFinder." When you're finished with QuickFinder Manager, choose File | Exit.

Power Tip ➤➤➤ Accessing QuickFinder

In addition to accessing QuickFinder from WP's Open File dialog box or from the Start menu on the Windows taskbar, you can also set up QuickFinder so it's available in several other ways. To set these options, display the QuickFinder Manager dialog box by choosing Start on the Windows taskbar, and then choosing Corel WordPerfect Suite 8 | Tools | QuickFinder Manager 8. Select the QuickFinder Configuration tab and then select from these options:

- To have a QuickFinder icon appear in the right corner of the Windows taskbar, select the QuickFinder Scheduler Icon on Task Bar option. Then you can double-click this icon to display the QuickFinder Manager dialog box.

- Select the On Context Menus option to have a "Find using QuickFinder" option appear when you right-click a file folder in any Windows file management dialog box, including Explorer and WP's Open File dialog box. Then you can right-click a file folder, select Find using QuickFinder, and the QuickFinder Searcher dialog box displays for that folder.

- To have a QuickFinder tab appear in the Properties dialog box for a drive or folder icon, select the Show for Drives and/or Show for Folders options. Then you can right-click a folder or drive icon from any Windows file management dialog box, select Properties, and select the QuickFinder tab. From here, you can display the QuickFinder Manager dialog box, create a Fast Search index file for that folder, as well as update the Fast Search index file.

When you're finished setting the QuickFinder options, choose OK; then choose File | Exit.

Creating a Document Summary

The Document Summary feature is a great way to keep important information about a document all in one place. For example, the document summary can contain the author's name, creation date, and keywords describing the content. To create a summary for a document, choose File | Properties and then type the information in the text boxes (see Figure 16-9). When you're finished, choose OK.

NOTE: *The document summary is saved as part of the document, but doesn't print with the document.*

Here are a few tips for using document summaries:

■   You can customize which information fields are included in the summary. Choose File | Properties, and then choose Setup. Select those fields you want to include from the list on the left (or deselect a field to remove it).

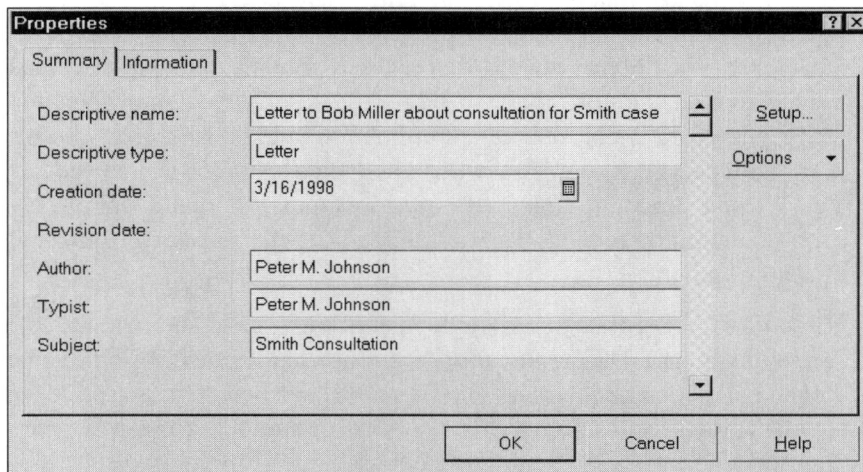

FIGURE 16-9   The Document Summary feature keeps track of important document information

To change the order of the fields, click and drag a field in the list on the right to the new position. If you want these custom fields to be automatically used for new summaries you create in documents, choose Use as Default. Choose OK when you're finished; then enter the summary information.

- To have WP prompt you to create a document summary each time you save a file that doesn't already have a summary, choose Tools | Settings and double-click Summary. Select Create Summary on Save/Exit and choose OK; then choose Close.

- You can easily print, delete, or save a summary. Open the document and choose File | Properties. From the Options pop-down button, choose the option you want, such as Print Summary.

- To specify the default author and typist name used in the summary, choose Tools | Settings and double-click Environment. Type the author name in the Name text box, and choose OK; then choose Close.

- WP can automatically create parts of the summary for you. To specify the default descriptive type, choose Tools | Settings, double-click Summary, and type the information in the Default Descriptive Type text box. If the subject in a document is usually prefaced by text other than "RE:", type that text in the Subject Search Text text box. Finally, to have the filename of the document automatically used for the descriptive name when you save a new document, select the third option in the dialog box. Choose OK; then choose Close. Now when you create a summary, you need to tell WP to extract the subject from the document. From the Options pop-down button in the Properties dialog box, choose Extract Information from Document.

- If you have older files that have document summaries and still use an eight-character DOS filename (with a three-character extension), you can rename the document with a long filename based on the descriptive name from the document summary. To do this for individual files as they're opened, choose Tools | Settings and double-click Summary. Select the On Open, Use the Descriptive Name for the New Filename option and choose OK, and then choose Close. To rename all the documents in a directory at once, play the LONGNAME.WCM macro that comes with WordPerfect.

NOTE: *The LONGNAME.WCM macro isn't installed during a typical installation of WP. For more information on installing it, see Chapter 10.*

Using Corel Versions

16

When you make changes to a document, it can be useful to keep the previous version on hand in case you need to later look back and see the original text. However, once you've made several different revisions to a document, it can be confusing—as well as space consuming—to try and keep track of all the versions. WordPerfect 8 has a brand new feature called Corel Versions that makes the version-tracking process simple and easy.

Corel Versions isn't installed during a typical installation, so follow these steps to install it:

1. Make sure your WordPerfect Suite 8 CD is in the CD-ROM drive and then from the Windows taskbar, choose Start | Corel WordPerfect Suite 8 | Setup & Notes | Corel WordPerfect Suite 8 Setup.

2. Follow the installation prompts until you see the "Installation Type" dialog box. Select Custom and choose Next.

3. Choose Selection Options, select Deselect All, and choose OK.

4. Scroll down the list of components and select Accessories (but don't select the checkbox); then choose Components.

5. Select the checkbox next to Corel Versions. When you select this option, other needed files are automatically selected. Choose OK.

6. Choose Next and continue with the installation.

Once you've installed Corel Versions, you need to enable it. The settings for Corel Versions are controlled through an icon in the Control Panel. From the Windows taskbar, choose Start | Settings | Control Panel. Double-click the Corel Versions icon to display the Corel Versions dialog box.

Select Enable Version Control to be able to use Corel Versions with your WP documents. Corel Versions stores each version of a document in a single, compressed archive file. To change the directory where the archive files are stored, type the path in the Path text box, or choose Browse to select it. You can also have the archive files stored in the same directory as the original files by deselecting the Default Versioning at Single Location option. Choose OK when you're finished.

Archiving a Document

Once you've enabled Corel Versions, you can archive any WP document. Archiving is not an automatic process—you decide which file versions should be archived and when. You can archive as many different document versions as you want.

To archive the current document, first make sure that you've saved the document and then choose File | Version Control | Save Current. The first time you archive a document, you see the New Version dialog box:

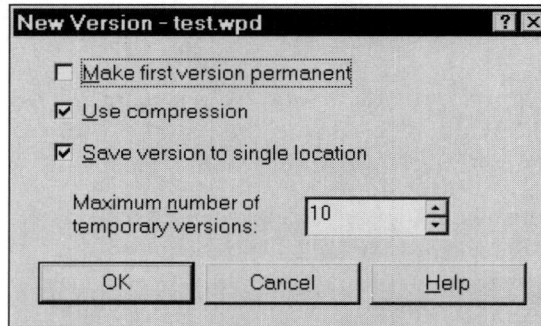

```
New Version - test.wpd                    [?][X]

    ☐ Make first version permanent
    ☑ Use compression
    ☑ Save version to single location

    Maximum number of      [10    ][▲][▼]
    temporary versions:

    [   OK   ]   [  Cancel  ]   [  Help  ]
```

Here, you can set the specific settings for this document's archive file. Each time you archive a document version, you can decide whether to make that version permanent or temporary. A *permanent* archive version is kept until you specifically delete it from the archive file. A *temporary* archive version is kept until the maximum number of temporary versions has been reached, and then it is automatically deleted the next time a temporary version is archived. The default number of temporary versions is 10. You can change this number for each archive file if you want.

TIP: *To change the default number of temporary versions, run Corel Versions from the Control Panel as explained earlier in the chapter and specify the new number.*

If you want to make the first version permanent, select that option. To have the archive file for the current document saved in the path specified in the Corel Versions dialog box, keep the Save Version to Single Location option selected. If you'd rather have the archive file for this particular document stored in the same directory as the file, deselect this option.

NOTE: *If you're working on a network and want others to be able to make revisions to the document, deselect this option so the archive file is stored on the network with the original file.*

Choose OK to archive the file. Corel Versions creates an archive file with a CV extension in the specified directory. The archive filename is the same as the document's path and filename, with a dollar sign used in place of colons and backslashes. For example, if you archive a document named C:\MYFILES\ TEST.WPD, the archive file would be named C$$MYFILES$TEST$WPD.CV.

TIP: *You can also archive an existing document by choosing File | Open and selecting the document you want to archive. Right-click the file and choose Corel Versions | Save. Then set the options for the archive and choose OK.*

Archiving Additional Versions

Once you've created the archive file for a document, you can archive the current version of that document as many times as you need to. Each time you archive the document, you can decide whether that version should be temporary or permanent, and you can also add comments to further identify the version, such as "Version sent to Legal Department."

To archive the current version of the document, save the document and then choose File | Version Control | Save Current. Select Permanent if you want to make this version permanent. Type any comments in the Comment text box and choose OK. Repeat this process each time you want to archive a different version of the document.

Managing Archived Versions

After you've archived different versions of a document, you can view, retrieve, or delete any single version in the archive file; save a version out as a separate file; or compare two versions side by side. In this section, you'll learn how to manage the versions in an archive file.

Viewing and Comparing Archived Versions

To see a list of the versions in an archive file, choose File | Open and switch to the directory containing the original file (the latest version of the document). Right-click the file and choose Corel Versions | History. The Version History dialog box appears (see Figure 16-10).

This dialog box lists each version in the archive file, along with the version number, date and time it was created, user name of the person who saved that revision, and any comments added when the version was saved (use the horizontal scroll bar to view the comments). In addition, you can see which versions were archived as permanent versions.

TIP: *You can change the size of the columns by moving the mouse pointer over the division between two column headings until it turns into a two-directional arrow, and then clicking and dragging to size the column.*

To view an individual version, select it in the list and choose View. The document opens in a separate viewer window. Choose File | Exit when you're finished. If you

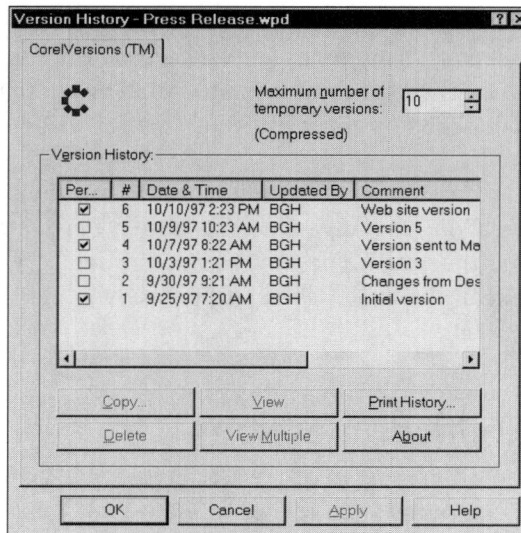

FIGURE 16-10   The Version History dialog box shows a list of each archived version

want to compare two versions side by side, hold down the CTRL key as you select each version, and then choose View Multiple.

TIP: *If you want to compare two versions so you can see exactly what differences they have, save the versions as separate files as explained in the "Retrieving an Archived Version" section, and then use the Document Compare feature to compare them. (For more information, see the "Comparing Two Documents" section.)*

NOTE: *You can print the history list by choosing Print History. The list prints in columns in the default printer font.*

Deleting an Archived Version

Temporary archive versions are automatically deleted as soon as the maximum number of versions is reached. If you want to delete a permanent version from the archive file, or manually delete a temporary version, select the version in the Version History dialog box (if this dialog box is not displaying, follow the steps in the "Viewing and Comparing Archived Versions" section), and then choose Delete. Choose Yes to confirm the deletion.

NOTE: *If you want to delete the original document, as well as the archived file with all the versions, choose File | Open and select the original file. Right-click the file and choose Corel Versions | File | Delete. Choose Yes to confirm the deletion.*

Retrieving an Archived Version

At times, you might decide that you want to replace the current version of a document with a previous archived version. To do this, if the document is already open, choose File | Version Control | Retrieve Current. Otherwise, choose File | Version Control | Retrieve Document, select the original document, and choose Retrieve. The Retrieve Version dialog box appears with a list of all the archived versions. Select the version you want to use and choose Retrieve. If you want to replace the latest version of the document with the selected version, choose Yes. To save the selected version as a separate document, choose No and WP opens that version into a document window and displays a prompt indicating the filename.

> ## Power Tip→→→ Moving and Copying a File with its Archives
>
> If you want to move a file that has archived versions, you can't simply move the original file to a new location, or the archived file will no longer be associated with it. To move a file and keep the archived file associated with it, choose File | Open and select the original file. Right-click the file and choose Corel Versions | File | Move. Select the new directory. If you want to change the filename, type the name in the text box. Choose Save to move the file.
>
> If you want to copy a file to a new location and not bring the archive file with it, simply copy it as you normally would. To copy a file *and* the associated archive file, select the file in the Open File dialog box, right-click it and choose Corel Versions | File | Copy. Select the new directory and/or type a new name in the File Name text box and choose Save.

You can also save an archived version as a separate file by choosing File | Open, selecting the original document, right-clicking it, and choosing Corel Versions | History. From the Version History dialog box, select the version you want to save and choose Copy. Change the path and filename for the document if you want and choose OK.

TIP: *You can also manage the versions in an archive file by right-clicking the file from any Windows file management dialog box, choosing Properties, and selecting the Corel Versions tab. The list of versions in the archive file is displayed, and you have the same options available as the Version History dialog box.*

Comparing Two Documents

When you have two different versions of a document, it can be helpful to see exactly what the differences are between them. This is easily done with WordPerfect's Document Compare feature. The Document Compare feature compares the current document with another version—whether it's the last saved version of the current document or a version saved as a separate file—and marks the text that is different.

Adding Compare Markings

To compare the current document with the last saved version or with another document, choose File | Document | Add Compare Markings. The Add Compare Markings dialog box appears:

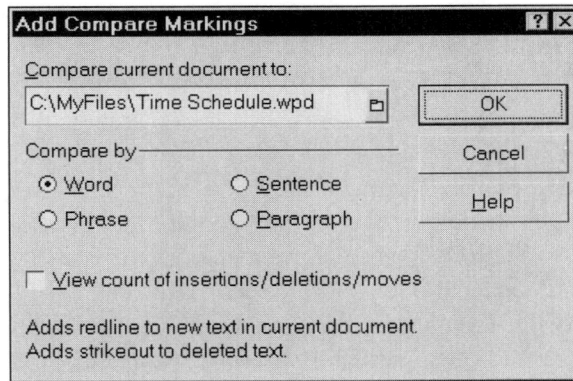

```
┌──────────────────────────────────────────────────────────┐
│ Add Compare Markings                            [?][X]     │
├──────────────────────────────────────────────────────────┤
│  Compare current document to:                             │
│  ┌────────────────────────────────┐  ┌────────────────┐   │
│  │ C:\MyFiles\Time Schedule.wpd  🗁 │  │      OK         │   │
│  └────────────────────────────────┘  └────────────────┘   │
│  ┌ Compare by ─────────────────────┐  ┌────────────────┐   │
│  │  ◉ Word        ○ Sentence       │  │     Cancel      │   │
│  │  ○ Phrase      ○ Paragraph      │  ┌────────────────┐   │
│  └─────────────────────────────────┘  │      Help       │   │
│                                        └────────────────┘   │
│  ☐ View count of insertions/deletions/moves                │
│                                                            │
│  Adds redline to new text in current document.             │
│  Adds strikeout to deleted text.                           │
└──────────────────────────────────────────────────────────┘
```

The Compare Current Document To text box shows the path and filename of the current document. If you want to compare the current document with its last saved version, leave the document filename the same. If you want to compare it to a version that's saved as a separate file, type the path and filename of the other document (or use the file folder icon to select it).

Then select the option that you want to compare the documents by—every word, sentence, phrase, or paragraph. For example, if you want WP to compare the documents sentence by sentence, select Sentence. Then, if any sentences in the two files are different in any way, the entire sentence is marked.

NOTE: *If you compare a document phrase by phrase, WP examines every section of text that is separated with a period, comma, colon, semi-colon, question mark, exclamation point, hard return, or hard page break.*

If you want to see the number of changes made between the two documents, select View Count of Insertions/Deletions/Moves. Choose OK. WP compares the document with the specified file. Any text in the current document that does not exist in the other document (text that has been added or moved) is formatted with the redline attribute. Any text in the *other* document that no longer exists in the current document (text that has been deleted) is displayed in strikeout text. Redline text appears in red on the document screen, but prints on most printers as shaded text. If you want to change the way redlined text is printed, see the Power Tip "Changing the Redline Method."

Power Tip▸▸▸ Changing the Redline Method

The Document Compare feature uses the redline font attribute to mark text that has been added or moved in the current document (when compared to another document). Redline text appears in red on-screen but prints as shaded text. You can change the way redlined text is printed. For example, you can have a vertical bar printed in the left or right margin on each line where redline text occurs.

To change the redline method, choose File | Document | Redline Method. The Printer Default Format option prints redlined text as shaded text on most printers. To have a character appear in the left or right margin on each line where redlined text occurs, select the margin option you want. If you want the character to appear in the left margin on even-numbered pages and in the right margin on odd-numbered pages, select Alternating Margins.

To use a character other than the vertical bar (|), type the character in the Redline Character text box. You can select a symbol by pressing CTRL-W, selecting the symbol you want, and choosing Insert and Close.

If you want to have the new redline method used for all new documents, choose Use as Default. Choose OK to return to the document.

Removing Compare Markings

After you've added compare markings to a document, you can quickly remove them. To do this, choose File | Document | Remove Compare Markings. You can choose to remove the redline markings from the text (keeping the actual redlined text) and delete any strikeout text, or you can choose to delete only strikeout text. Select the option you want and choose OK.

NOTE: *If you chose to delete only strikeout text, any redlined text remains with the redline attribute.*

Document Review

It's not uncommon to incorporate the changes and suggestions from several other people into one final document. For example, you might need to send a proposal around to members of your team and have them add their comments and suggestions. While you could pass out printed copies of the document and then later manually add the comments written by each team member, a better way is to use WordPerfect's Document Review feature.

The Document Review feature lets each person edit the document normally in WordPerfect. However, as text is added in the document, it is automatically displayed in a color assigned to the person reviewing the document. And, as text is deleted, it is formatted in strikeout, again using the reviewer's color. This allows the original author to easily view, accept, and reject the changes suggested by others.

When you want other people to review a document, simply give them a copy on disk or send it by e-mail. You don't need to do anything special to your document before giving it to someone else to review.

TIP: *If several people will be reviewing a document and you want each person's comments included in the same document, give the document to the first person along with a list of the others to pass it along to when they're finished. Some e-mail programs also have an option for automatically forwarding a message to a list of people in succession.*

Reviewing a Document

If you're reviewing a document, open it into a document window. Before making any changes, choose File | Document | Review. Choose Reviewer. If you haven't already specified your name and initials in the Environment Settings, type your name and initials at the prompt and choose OK.

> **TIP:**   *If you want to change the user name and initials, choose Tools | Settings and double-click Environment. Make the changes you want and choose OK; then choose Close.*

The Reviewer Bar appears at the top of the document window. If other people have already reviewed the document, the Reviewer Bar displays their names and associated colors, so you can easily see which changes were made by each person:

Set color:	🖊	Other user colors:	▮ Sarah Barker		⬍
🔲				Close	Help

The Reviewer Bar also displays the color that will be used for the changes you make. To select a new color, choose the Set Color pop-up palette and select the color you want.

> **TIP:**   *To see the document without any colored or strikeout text, click the button in the bottom-left corner of the Reviewer Bar.*

Now you can make any changes to the document using the normal WP editing tools. If you delete text, the text isn't actually deleted from the document, but appears instead in strikeout in your selected color. You can't undelete text that has been previously deleted by another reviewer, although you can make changes to text that has been added.

> **NOTE:**   *If the text you type doesn't appear in color, choose Tools | Settings and double-click Display. Deselect the Windows System Colors option and choose OK; then choose Close.*

In addition to adding and deleting text, you can add comments to the document. Comments allow you to make suggestions or ask questions without actually adding text to the document or altering its formatting. Comments aren't printed with the document and are displayed as icons in the left margin (when the document is displayed in Page mode). The comment icon contains your user initials, so the original author can easily see who inserted each comment.

To create a comment, place the insertion point where you want the comment inserted and choose Insert | Comment | Create. Type the text for the comment. You can use the buttons on the Comment Property Bar (which appears just above the Reviewer Bar) to automatically insert such items as your name, initials, or the current date and time. When you're finished typing the comment, choose the Close file folder button on the Comment Property Bar—not the "Close" button on the Reviewer Bar.

When you're finished making changes to the document, save and close it, and then return it to the author or pass it along to the next reviewer.

Viewing the Revisions

When you receive back a document that has been reviewed with the Document Review feature, you can easily view any changes that were made and decide whether you want to accept or reject those changes. To do this, open the document and choose File | Document | Review; then choose Author. The Reviewer Bar appears showing the user names and colors for each person who reviewed the document, along with several other buttons for reviewing the changes (see Figure 16-11).

The first change in the document is automatically highlighted when you display the Reviewer Bar. To accept this change and make it part of the document, click the Insert Current Annotation button on the Reviewer Bar. To reject the change and return the text to the original format, click the Delete Current Annotation button. When you accept or reject a change, the next change in the document is automatically highlighted. If you want to skip a change, click the arrow buttons on the Reviewer Bar to move to the previous or next change in the document.

TIP: *To accept or reject all the changes at the same time, click the Accept All Annotations or Delete All Annotations button on the Reviewer Bar.*

If you want to view a document without any of the color markings, choose the Display Annotations in Normal Text Color button on the far left of the Reviewer Bar. Each time you click this button, the display toggles between showing the normal text and showing the colored markings.

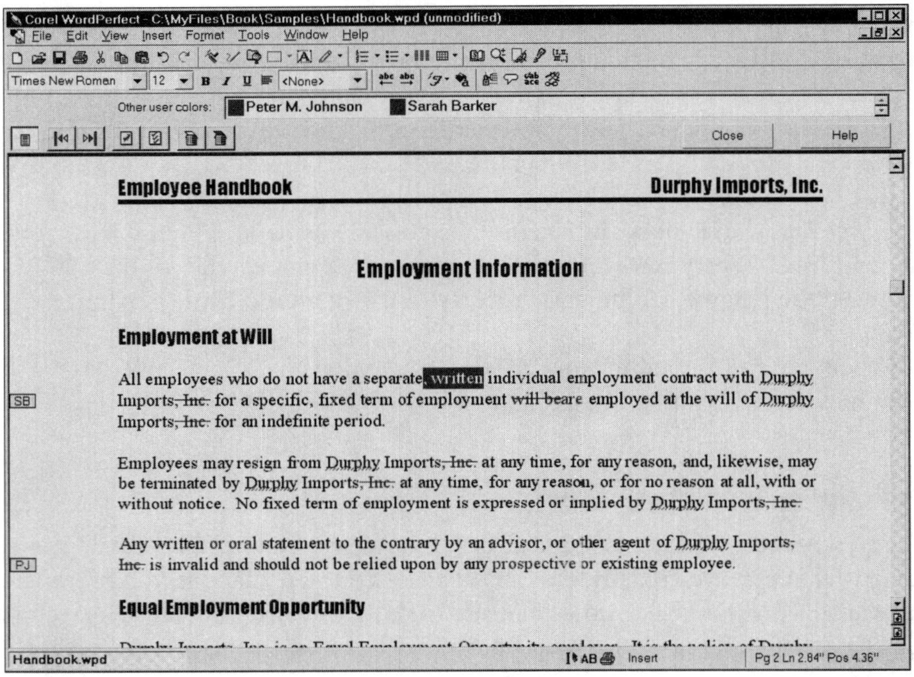

FIGURE 16-11 When you review the document as an author, you can use the Reviewer Bar to accept or reject changes

To view any comments inserted in the document, click the comment icon in the left margin. The comment text appears in a "bubble." If you want to convert the comment to text so it becomes part of the document, choose Insert | Comment | Convert to Text. To delete a comment, turn on Reveal Codes (View | Reveal Codes) and click and drag the [Comment] code out of the Reveal Codes window. To quickly convert all the comments in a document to text or delete all the comments at once, you can use a macro. See the On the CD section "Converting Comments" for more information.

TIP: *To review information about the author of the comment, including the comment creation date and the user name and initials, click the comment icon to display the comment text. Then right-click the comment text and choose Information.*

When you're finished reviewing the changes to the document, choose Close on the Reviewer Bar. Then close and save the document normally.

On the CD... Converting Comments

When you're working on a long document with several comments, it can be tedious to convert each comment to text or delete each comment individually. The companion CD contains a macro called CONVERT COMMENTS.WCM that gives you three options for managing multiple comments. You can convert all the comments in the document to text, move all the comments to a new document window with a reference indicating their page and line number, or simply delete all the comments from the document.

To use the macro, open the document containing the comments and choose Tools | Macro | Play. Select the CONVERT COMMENTS.WCM macro and choose Play. When the dialog box appears, select the option you want and choose OK. The macro searches through the entire document for any comments and either converts them to text, moves them to a new document window, or deletes them. If the comments are moved to a new document window, the macro also includes the page and line number reference where the comment was created and displays a message box telling you which document the comments can be found in.

Summary

Whether you deal with a handful of documents or dozens of files, WordPerfect's file management tools make your work easier and more efficient. The Open File dialog box has lots of helpful options for managing your documents, including the QuickFinder feature, which helps you quickly locate files based on the filename or text within the document. The new Corel Versions feature helps you archive and keep track of earlier versions of a document. You can quickly see the differences between two documents with the Document Compare feature. And when you need to share your documents with others, the Document Review feature makes it easy to view and incorporate changes.

In Chapter 17, you'll learn how to embed and link information from other programs right in your WP documents.

Chapter

17

Linking and Embedding Information

Y ou know that WordPerfect's features and tools make it easy to create documents that contain much more than plain text, such as clipart, tables, and equations. But did you know that you can just as easily insert information that was created in another program? WordPerfect lets you insert everything from drawings and charts to spreadsheets to sound and video clips in your documents. The information retains its original formatting and can even be linked to the source file so it's automatically updated as changes are made.

In this chapter, we'll explain the different options available for inserting information from other programs into your WP documents. You'll learn the various techniques for embedding and linking all sorts of information with OLE. In addition, we'll show you the special WP features for importing spreadsheet/database information and inserting sound files.

Linking versus Embedding

When you want to insert information from another program into a WP document, you have two basic choices. You can *embed* a separate copy of the information, or you can create a *link* to the original source file. Whichever option you choose, the information you're inserting is referred to as an *object*. An object can be practically anything—text, graphics, spreadsheet cells, sound files, scanned images, and so on.

NOTE: *The process of linking and embedding objects is referred to as OLE (Object Linking & Embedding). There are also other methods of inserting information into documents, such as DDE (Dynamic Data Exchange) and the Spreadsheet/Database Import feature.*

Embedding an object is very similar to copying and pasting information with the Clipboard. When you embed an object, a copy of it is inserted into WP and becomes part of the current document. Since the object is no longer connected to the source file, you can make changes to it in WordPerfect without affecting the original information. The main difference between embedding and pasting is that embedding allows you to edit the object using the original program's tools and features. For example, if you embed part of a Quattro Pro spreadsheet, you can still use Quattro Pro whenever you need to make changes to the information.

NOTE: *The file size of a document tends to be larger when you embed an object because the object is stored as part of the document.*

On the other hand, when you link an object in WordPerfect, both the original program and the WP document continue to use the same file. As a result, if you make any changes to the object in one program, the changes are automatically used in the other, and vice versa. For example, if you link a Quattro Pro spreadsheet file in a WP document and then edit the spreadsheet in Quattro Pro, WordPerfect automatically uses the updated information.

As this chapter will show, there are several different ways you can embed and link objects in your documents, including using the Clipboard and the Insert Object feature. In addition, if you're working with sound, spreadsheet, or database files, you have even more options for inserting the information into WordPerfect.

Embedding Objects

As we mentioned earlier, embedding an object is basically the same as copying and pasting information through the Windows Clipboard. The object is inserted into your WP document and you can modify it without affecting the original file. What differentiates embedding from pasting is that you can edit the object using the original program's tools and features.

NOTE: *In order to embed an object, the source program must support OLE. Most Windows programs are OLE compatible.*

You can find examples of embedded objects right within some of WP 8's features. For example, when you create a TextArt image or equation, those items are actually embedded objects. If you edit them, a separate program (TextArt or the Equation Editor) is loaded to allow you to make changes. As another example, if you insert a clipart image into a document and then double-click it to edit it, the image becomes an embedded Presentations drawing object and you can have access to all of Presentations' editing tools. The changes you make only affect the image in the current document—the original image remains unchanged. (For more information on inserting TextArt, equations, and clipart images, see Chapter 7.)

Inserting an Object

When you want to embed an object into a WordPerfect document, you have several choices. You can drag and drop selected information with the mouse, use the Windows Clipboard, or use the Insert Object feature. Embedded objects are inserted in graphics boxes, so they keep their original formatting and appearance. This also lets you easily position the embedded object within the document (see Figure 17-1).

NOTE: *If you want to insert information from a spreadsheet or database without having that information placed in an embedded graphics box, you can use the Import Spreadsheet/Database feature. For more information, see the "Importing Spreadsheets and Databases" section later in this chapter.*

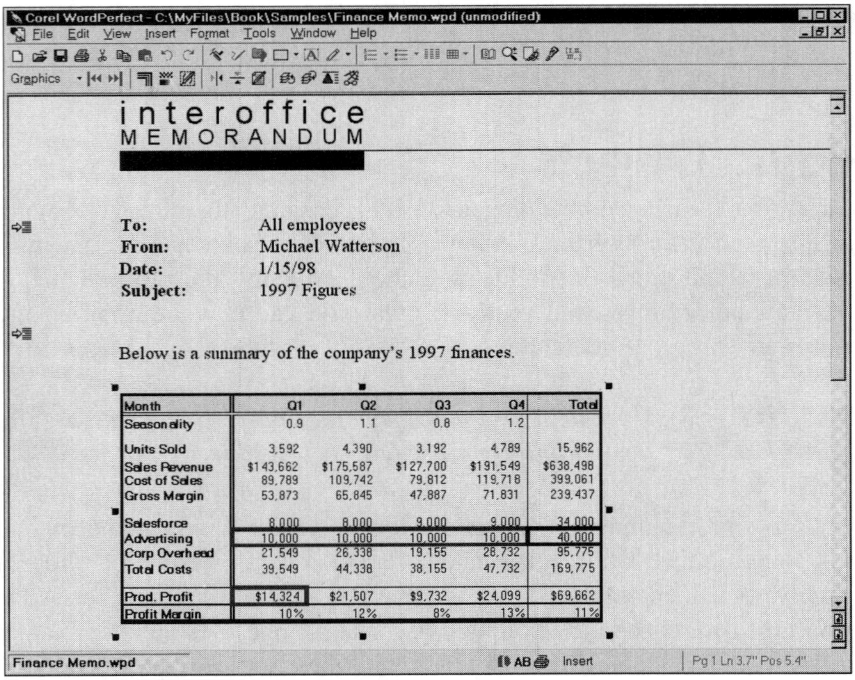

FIGURE 17-1   Embedded objects, such as this spreadsheet, are inserted in a graphics box

TIP: *If you want to insert a sound clip, you can embed it as an object or use WP's Sound feature. For more information, see the "Inserting Sound and Video Clips" section later in the chapter.*

Drag and Drop

One of the easiest ways to embed an object is to simply drag it from the original program to WordPerfect with your mouse. For example, you can drag an image from Presentations or selected cells from a Quattro Pro spreadsheet into your WP document. To do this, open both programs (such as WP and Presentations), and size each in a window so you can see them both at the same time.

TIP: *To place a full-screen program in a window (or vice versa), double-click the title bar or click the Maximize/Restore button on the right edge of the title bar (the middle button). To size the window, click and drag the window border.*

NOTE: *You only need to see a small portion of the WordPerfect document window, since you can easily move the embedded object once it's inserted.*

Once you can see both programs, select the information you want to copy, hold down the CTRL key, and drag it into the WP document. When you release the mouse button, a graphics box containing the embedded object is inserted. You can move or size the graphics box to place it where you want.

TIP: *If you're copying information from a spreadsheet program, such as Quattro Pro or Excel, after selecting the cells, click and drag the border of the selection as you hold down the CTRL key. (If you click the insertion point in the middle of selected cells and begin dragging, you'll simply redefine the selected region.)*

In addition to embedding selected text or objects by dragging them from a program into WordPerfect, you can embed an entire file by dragging the file icon from the desktop or any file management folder. For example, if you want to embed a sound file, you can double-click the My Computer icon on the desktop, and then navigate through the folders until you see the icon for the sound file you want. Then click and drag the file icon into a WordPerfect document window to create an embedded sound object.

If you don't want to embed the entire file, you can create OLE file "scraps" from selected text or objects, which you can then easily drag and drop from the desktop into WordPerfect. For more information, see the Power Tip "Drag and Drop OLE File Scraps."

Power Tip... Drag and Drop OLE File Scraps

If you need to embed the same information in several different documents, you can create an OLE file "scrap." These files are called "scraps" because they only contain a selected portion of another file. Once you've created an OLE file scrap, you can easily drag and drop it into WordPerfect or any other OLE-compatible Windows program.

To create an OLE scrap, select the text or object that you want included in the file scrap, such as a range of spreadsheet cells. Size the source program in a window so you can see at least a portion of the Windows desktop. Then click and drag the selected information to a blank area on the desktop. When you release the mouse button, Windows creates an icon for the OLE file with "scrap" in the filename.

To rename the scrap file, right-click the icon and choose Rename; then type the new filename and press ENTER. You can either leave the scrap icon on the desktop or move it into a folder. When you want to insert the scrap into WordPerfect, make sure you can see both the scrap icon (whether it's on the desktop or in a folder) and a WP document window. Then hold down the CTRL key as you click and drag the scrap icon into WordPerfect. The information in the scrap file is embedded in the document as an OLE object. If you make any changes to it, the original scrap file is not affected.

If you want to edit the original scrap file, just double-click the scrap icon to open the information in the source program and make any changes you want.

Using the Clipboard

If you'd rather work with programs in full-size windows, you can use the Clipboard to copy an object from a program and embed it in WordPerfect. This method is just as easy to use as dragging and dropping, and doesn't require you to have both programs open and visible at the same time. Follow these three steps:

1. Open the source program and create or open a file with the information you want to copy into WordPerfect.

2. Select the text or object you want to copy, such as a group of spreadsheet cells or a drawing image, and then choose Edit I Copy. In some programs, you can also press CTRL-C to copy the selected information to the Clipboard.

3. Switch to WordPerfect and choose Edit I Paste Special to display the Paste Special dialog box (see Figure 17-2). Make sure the object type selected in the list box is correct, for example, Corel Quattro Pro 8 Notebook. The bottom of the dialog box should display the "embed" icon (see Figure 17-2), indicating that the information will be inserted as an embedded object. Choose OK to insert the object.

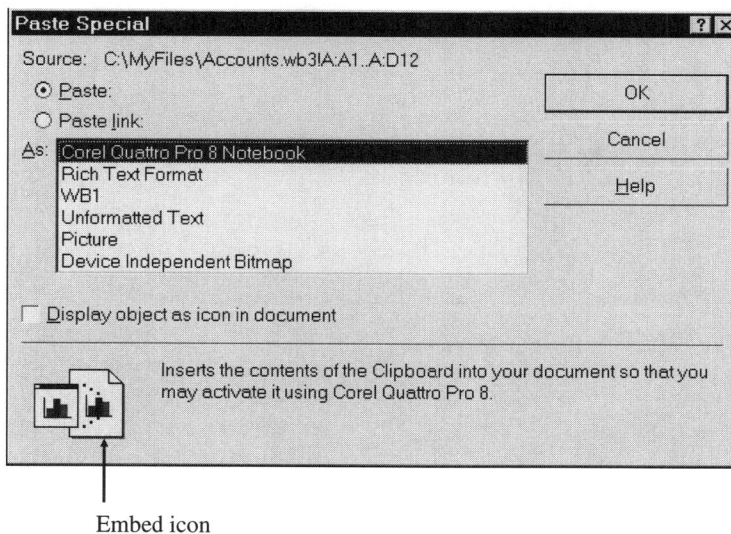

Embed icon

FIGURE 17-2 The Paste Special dialog box lets you embed or link information from the Clipboard

TIP: *You can also insert the object as an icon that expands to display the full object information when it's double-clicked. For more information, see the "How to Use Icons for Embedded Objects" section.*

The Insert Object Feature

A final method for embedding an object in WordPerfect is to use Insert Object. This feature lets you embed objects from existing files, as well as create new objects right in your document using the tools from another program.

To use this feature, place the insertion point in your WP document where you want the object inserted. Choose Insert | Object and the Insert Object dialog box appears (see Figure 17-3). The Object Type list box lists all of the available programs installed on your computer that are registered with Windows to work with OLE.

To create a new embedded object, select the type of object you want to create in the list box, such as Corel Quattro Pro 8 Notebook or Paintbrush Picture. If you want to embed an existing file instead, select Create From File, and then type the path and filename of the file in the File text box, or use the file folder icon to select it.

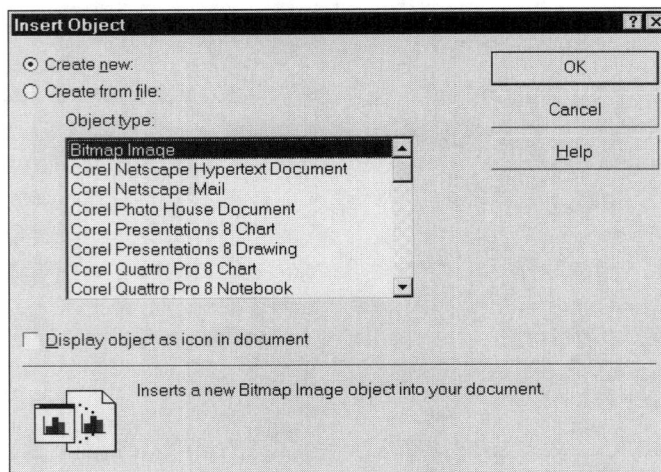

FIGURE 17-3 You can create new embedded objects or select existing files with the Insert Object feature

NOTE: *When you use the Create From File option, the entire file is embedded. If you only want to embed a portion of a file, follow the steps under the "Drag and Drop" or "Using the Clipboard" section earlier in the chapter to select and copy the information you want.*

You can also choose to have the embedded object appear as an icon in the document. For example, you can embed a spreadsheet icon that only displays the spreadsheet information when the icon is double-clicked, giving you more room in your document. Or you can insert a video clip as an icon so it doesn't appear until it's played. For more information, see the "How to Use Icons for Embedded Objects" section below.

Choose OK to insert the object or begin creating a new one. If you're creating a new object, a "frame" appears in the document window and the source program's menu bars and toolbars are displayed. For some object types, the source program is opened in a separate window. Create the object using the available tools. When you're finished, click outside the frame in the document window or, if the program was loaded separately, choose File | Exit & Return to Document.

TIP: *You can click and drag the frame border to increase the workspace inside the frame.*

How to▸▸▸ Use Icons for Embedded Objects

Normally, when you embed an object in a document, the graphics box displays the entire object information (see Figure 17-1). However, you can also insert the object as an icon so the full information only appears when the icon is double-clicked. For example, you can insert an icon for an embedded spreadsheet, and when the icon is double-clicked, the full spreadsheet information displays in Quattro Pro.

If you want to use an icon for an embedded object, you must insert the object with the Insert Object feature. Follow the steps in the "The Insert Object Feature" section to create a new object or insert an object from an existing file. Before choosing OK to close the Insert Object dialog box, select the Display Object as Icon in Document option.

How to...   Use Icons for Embedded Objects *(continued)*

The icon and label that will be used for the object is displayed on the right side of the dialog box. If you want to change the icon or the label text, choose Change Icon. To select a new icon, select From File and then type the path and filename of the file containing the new icon (or use the file folder icon to select it). You can select an ICO file, which contains a single icon, or an EXE or DLL file that might contain several icons. For example, the MORICONS.DLL and PROGMAN.EXE files in the Windows folder each contain several icons. After selecting the file, press TAB to move out of the From File text box and see the available icons in that file:

```
┌─ Change Icon ──────────────────────────── ? ✕ ┐
│                                                │
│  Select icon to represent object        ┌──────────┐
│   ○ Current:   [icon]                   │    OK    │
│                                         └──────────┘
│                                         ┌──────────┐
│   ○ Default:   [icon]                   │  Cancel  │
│                                         └──────────┘
│                                         ┌──────────┐
│   ◉ From file:  C:\WINDOWS\PROGMAN.EXE  │   Help   │
│                                         └──────────┘
│   [icons row]                             [icon]
│                                          Notebook
│   Label:  Notebook                             │
└────────────────────────────────────────────────┘
```

Select the icon you want to use. If the new icon doesn't appear on the right side of the dialog box, select From File again. If you want to change the label text that appears underneath the icon, type the text in the Label text box. Choose OK twice to return to the document. Continue creating the object if needed.

Once you've specified an icon or label text for an embedded object icon, there's no way to change it. Similarly, you can't convert an existing embedded object to an icon or vice versa. If you want to make any changes, you need to embed the object again and select the options you want.

Editing an Object

After you've inserted an embedded object in a document, you can easily make changes to it. To edit most object types, simply double-click the object. If the object is a sound or movie clip, double-clicking the object plays the file. To edit these object types, right-click the object and choose Object | Edit from the top of the QuickMenu. You can also edit any object by selecting it in the document and choosing Edit | Object | Edit.

17

> **NOTE:**   *The QuickMenu or Edit pull-down menu displays the specific type of object, such as "Notebook Object" or "MIDI Sequence Object."*

When you edit an object, a "frame" appears around the object and the source program's menu bar and toolbars appear (see Figure 17-4). For some objects, the source program opens in a separate window with the object loaded. You can make any changes you want to the object. When you're finished, click outside the frame or choose File | Exit & Return to Document. The changes you make only affect the object in the current document.

> **NOTE:**   *You can also open an object into the source program by selecting it and choosing Edit | Object | Open. Or right-click the object and choose Object | Open from the QuickMenu.*

Linking Objects

When you insert an object in a WordPerfect document, you can also choose to link that object to the original file. Then both the WP document and the source program share the same information. If you make changes to the file in the original source program, the object in the WordPerfect document is also updated. Similarly, if you edit the object in WordPerfect, the original file reflects those changes. Linking helps ensure that your documents always have the most recent information.

> **NOTE:**   *If you want to link spreadsheet/database information and have it inserted in a table or merge data file rather than in a graphics box, see the "Linking Spreadsheets and Databases" section later in this chapter.*

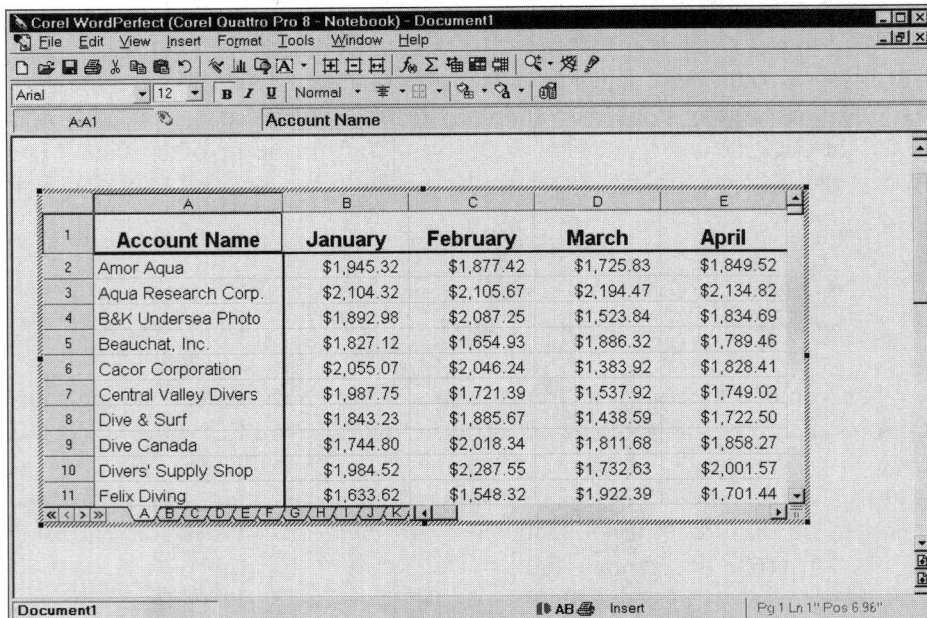

FIGURE 17-4 When you edit embedded objects, the source program's menu bar and toolbars appear

Creating a Link

The techniques for inserting an object into a document and linking it to the source file are almost identical to those described earlier in the chapter for embedding objects. However, unlike embedding objects, you can't use the drag and drop method if you want to create a link. Instead, you need to use either the Clipboard or the Insert Object feature.

To use the Clipboard, open the source program and create or open a file with the information you want to link in WordPerfect. In order to link the information, the file must be saved with a valid filename, so save the file if needed. Select the text or object you want to copy and choose Edit | Copy. Then switch to WordPerfect and choose Edit | Paste Special. In the Paste Special dialog box, select Paste Link (see Figure 17-2). Make sure that the selected object type is correct and choose OK to insert the object.

NOTE: *If the Display Object as Icon in Document option in the Paste Special dialog box is dimmed, the selected object type will create a DDE link instead of an OLE link. For example, if you're pasting information from Quattro Pro, the "Corel Quattro Pro 8 Notebook" object type creates an OLE link, while the "WB1" object type creates a DDE link. DDE links are not inserted in a graphics box, but can still be used to link and update information.*

The Insert Object feature can be used if you want to create a link to an entire file, rather than just a selected portion of a file. To use this feature to create a link, choose Insert | Object. In the Insert Object dialog box, select Create From File, and then type the path and filename of the file in the File text box (or use the file folder icon to select it). Select Link and then choose OK to insert the object.

NOTE: *When linking objects with either method, you can choose to have the linked object appear as an icon in the document. For more information, see the "How to Use Icons for Embedded Objects" section earlier in the chapter.*

Editing a Linked Object

As with embedded objects, you can edit the information in most linked OLE objects by simply double-clicking the object. To edit a linked sound or movie clip, right-click the link and choose Object | Edit from the QuickMenu. When you edit a linked OLE object, the source program opens with the object loaded. You can make any changes you want to the object. When you're finished, save your changes and choose File | Exit to exit the program.

NOTE: *You can also edit linked objects by selecting the object in the document and choosing Edit | Object | Edit.*

In addition, you can make changes to the object information by opening the original file directly in the source program, such as Quattro Pro or Presentations, making your changes, and saving the file. Then you can update the link in the WordPerfect document (see the "Updating a Link" section for more information).

CAUTION: *If you move or rename the original file, you need to edit the link so WP knows where to find the file. For more information, see the Power Tip "Editing the Source File Location."*

If the object was inserted as a DDE link instead of an OLE link (and is not in a graphics box), you can edit the information by opening the file in the source program, making any changes, and then saving the file. If you make changes within the WordPerfect document text, they will be lost the next time you update the DDE link.

Updating a Link

One of the main benefits to linking an object is that you can update the link so your document always has the latest information from the source program. By default, OLE links are set to update automatically, but you can also choose to update them manually. (DDE links must be updated manually.) With the automatic setting, each time you open a document containing a link, you're asked if you want to update the links. Choose Yes to have WP update any linked objects with the most current information from the original file. Once you've opened a document containing an automatic link, the information in the document stays updated as changes are made in the source program.

Power Tip... **Editing the Source File Location**

When you insert a linked object, both the WordPerfect document and the original source program share the same file. If the original file is ever moved or renamed, you need to edit the link in WordPerfect so WP can find the right file. To edit the location of the source file, follow these steps:

1. Open the document in WordPerfect that contains the linked object and choose Edit | Links. (Make sure the object is not selected or the Links option will be dimmed.)

2. Select the link you want to edit in the list box and choose Change Source.

3. Select a new filename or make any changes to the path and filename displayed in the text box. (The options are slightly different if you're editing a DDE link.)

4. Choose OK; then choose Close.

CAUTION: *If the original file is already loaded in the source program when you open a WordPerfect document containing an OLE link to it, the information is not updated even if you choose Yes to update the links. You'll need to update the link manually to get the latest information.*

If you want to have more control over when the object information is updated, you can change the link to a manual one. To do this, open the document containing the linked object and choose Edit | Links (make sure the object is not selected). This displays the Links dialog box (see Figure 17-5). Select the link in the list box and select Manual; then choose Close.

Once you've set a link to update manually, you can update it whenever you want by choosing Edit | Links, selecting the link, and choosing Update Now. Choose Close when you're finished. Use this same process to update any DDE links in your documents.

CAUTION: *If you're updating a DDE link, the original file must be loaded and running in the source program in order for the link to be updated. Also, when you update a DDE link, any changes made to the text or formatting in the WordPerfect document are lost.*

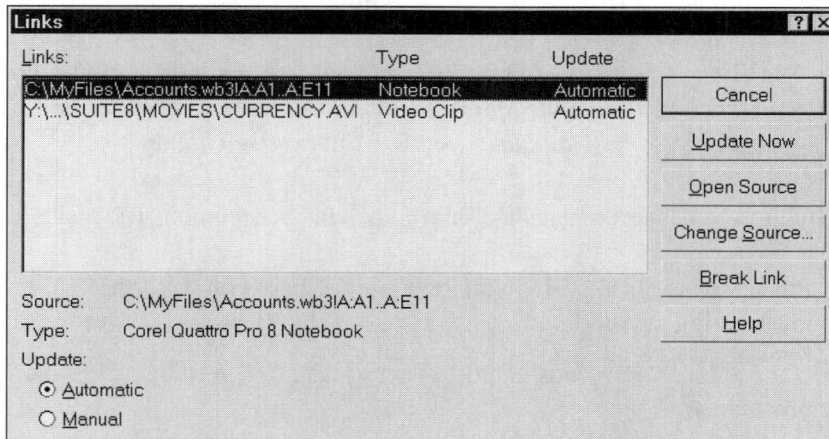

FIGURE 17-5 The Links dialog box lists all the current links in the document

Breaking a Link

If you want to remove the link from an object but still keep the information in the document, open the document and choose Edit | Links. Select the link you want to remove in the list and choose Break Link. Choose Close to return to the document. The information remains in the document but can no longer be updated.

TIP: *You can also break a DDE link by deleting one of the [DDE Link] codes in the Reveal Codes window (View | Reveal Codes).*

NOTE: *If you want to completely delete OLE-linked information from a document, select the graphics box object and press DELETE to remove it. To remove a DDE link, delete the information from the document, including the [DDE Link] codes from Reveal Codes.*

Importing Spreadsheets and Databases

When you're working with spreadsheets and databases, WordPerfect gives you an additional option for inserting the information into your documents—the Spreadsheet/Database Import feature. While embedding an object places the information in a graphics box, *importing* the information places it in a document as regular text. The information can even be imported into a table or as a merge data file. Any formulas from your spreadsheet remain intact, and you can easily select which fields or records from your database you want to include.

NOTE: *If you want to create a link between the information inserted in your document and the spreadsheet/database program, see the "Linking Spreadsheets and Databases" section later in the chapter.*

To import spreadsheet or database information into a document, follow these steps:

1. Place the insertion point in the document where you want the information inserted.

2. Choose Insert | Spreadsheet/Database | Import. The Import Data dialog box appears.

NOTE: *This same dialog box appears if you open a spreadsheet or database file directly from the Open File dialog box.*

3. From the Data Type drop-down list, select the type of information you want to import, such as Spreadsheet or Paradox.

4. From the Import As drop-down list, select the format you want the information inserted as: a table, text, or a merge data file. If you select the text option, the information is separated with tabs and hard returns. (For more information on merge data files, see Chapter 2.)

5. In the File Name text box, type the path and filename of the file you want to import, or use the file folder icon to select it. Then press TAB to move out of the File Name text box.

6. If you're importing a spreadsheet, the Named Ranges list box displays a list of each page in the spreadsheet, as well as any named groups of cells (see Figure 17-6). This lets you import just a portion of the spreadsheet. Each page in the spreadsheet is labeled with a letter, such as <Spreadsheet A> for the first page. If you want to import all the pages in the spreadsheet, select the <Spreadsheet> option. For more information on selecting a range of cells to import, see the Power Tip "Identifying Cell Ranges."

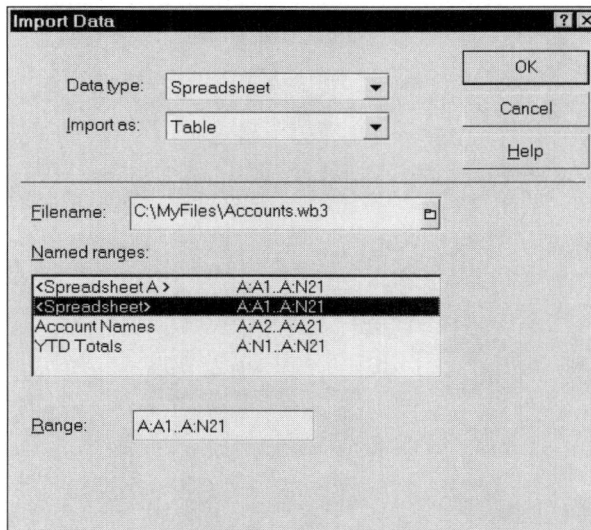

FIGURE 17-6 The Named Ranges list box displays the pages and named areas of a spreadsheet

7. If you're importing a database, the Fields list box displays a list of all the available fields in the database file (see Figure 17-7). If you don't want certain fields to be included in the imported information, deselect them in the list. If you're importing an ASCII delimited file, you can change the field and character delimiters if needed. In addition, you can select which records from the data file that you want to import. For more information, see the "How to Select Database Records" section.

8. After you've selected all the options you want, choose OK to import the information. Once the information has been inserted into the document, you can make any changes you want. If your spreadsheet contains formulas and you imported into a table, the formulas are included.

CAUTION: *If you're importing a spreadsheet that has a lot of columns, the information might run off the right side of the page. To avoid this, you can select a landscape paper size and a smaller font, as well as size the table columns to fit the information.*

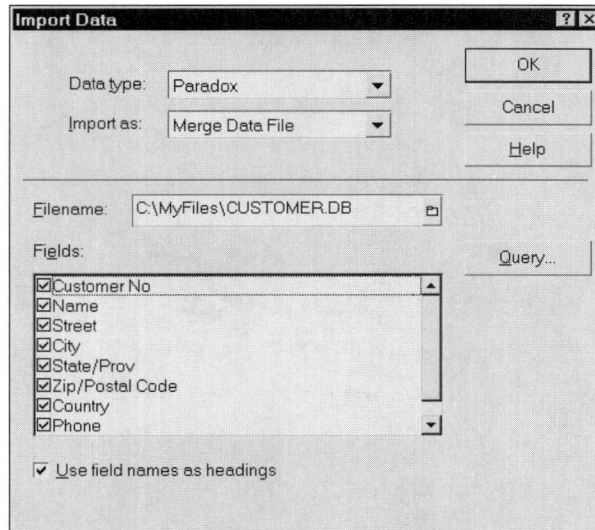

FIGURE 17-7   When you're importing a database, a list of the available fields is displayed

Power Tip... Identifying Cell Ranges

If the specific group of spreadsheet cells you want to import isn't listed in the Named Ranges list box (see Figure 17-6), you can specify the range in the Range text box. The cell range consists of two cell addresses separated by two periods. The first address is the cell in the upper-left corner of the block and the second address is the cell in the lower-right corner. In addition, each cell address is prefaced with a letter indicating the page the cells are located on and a period. This allows you to select cells over multiple pages in the spreadsheet.

For example, to select the block from Cell C1 to Cell E6 on the first page of a spreadsheet (page A), type this range in the Range text box:

A.C1..A.E6

Or, if you want to select the block from Cell A1 on the first page to Cell D5 on the second page, the range would look like this:

A.A1..B.D5

If you're using Quattro Pro and want to name a range of cells to make the importing process easier, select the cells in Quattro Pro, right-click the selection, and choose Name Cells. Type a name in the Name text box and choose Add; then choose Close and save your changes.

How to... Select Database Records

When you're importing a database, such as a Paradox file, you can not only select which *fields* you want to include for each record (see Figure 17-7), but you can also define conditions for which *records* should be imported. For example, you might want to include only those records in a specific state or product category.

How to... Select Database Records
(continued)

To set up the selection conditions, select your database file in the Import Data dialog box, and then ch
oose Query. This displays the Define Selection Conditions dialog box:

This dialog box is very similar to the Select Records dialog box you can use when performing a merge (see Chapter 2 for more information). From the first Field drop-down list, select the field in the database that you want to evaluate, such as the State or Category field. Then, in the Condition 1 text box, type the value or list of values that the matching records should contain. To include a list of matching values, separate each possible match with a semicolon.

For example, to include those records that are in California or Texas, select the State field from the Field drop-down list, and type **CA;TX** in the Condition 1 text box. If you want to further narrow the selection, use the second column to specify another condition. For more information on specifying conditions, choose the Example button.

When you're finished specifying the conditions for the records you want to include, choose OK to return to the Import Data dialog box.

Linking Spreadsheets and Databases

When you import spreadsheet or database information with the Spreadsheet/Database Import feature, the data is simply inserted into your document as regular text. If you want to be able to keep that information updated as changes are made to the original spreadsheet or database file, you can create a link.

Linking spreadsheet and database information is very similar to importing it. First, place the insertion point where you want the data inserted and choose Insert | Spreadsheet/Database | Create Link. When the Create Link dialog box appears, select the filename and other options you want. For more information about the options in the Create Link dialog box, see the "Importing Spreadsheets and Databases" section earlier in the chapter.

When you choose OK to insert the information, WordPerfect places link markers in the left margin at the beginning and end of the linked text, as shown here:

Account Name	January
Amor Aqua	$1,945.32
Aqua Research Corp.	$2,104.32
B&K Undersea Photo	$1,892.98
Beauchat, Inc.	$1,827.12
Cacor Corporation	$2,055.07
Central Valley Divers	$1,987.75
Dive & Surf	$1,843.23

In addition, [Link] codes are placed around the information in Reveal Codes (View | Reveal Codes). If you don't want the link icons to display in the margin, choose Insert | Spreadsheet/Database | Options, deselect Show Link Options, and choose OK.

TIP: *If you click on one of the link icons, a comment box appears with the name of the file that is linked to that information.*

After importing and linking information, you can change the way the information appears in the document, such as changing from a table to a merge data file. In addition, you can select a different range of cells or database fields to be included. To do this, place the insertion point somewhere between the link codes and choose Insert | Spreadsheet/Database | Edit Link. Make any changes to the link, such as selecting a different import type or range of cells, and then choose OK.

CAUTION: *Even though the linked information is inserted as regular text, be careful that you don't make too many formatting changes in the document itself, including changes to the table format. Each time you update the link, any formatting you've done is lost.*

NOTE: *If you want to remove a link from a document, turn on Reveal Codes (View | Reveal Codes) and delete the [Link] code at the beginning or end of the linked text.*

Updating a Spreadsheet/Database Link

When you want to update the information in a spreadsheet/database link, make sure the original spreadsheet or database file has been saved and open the WordPerfect document containing the link. Choose Insert | Spreadsheet/Database | Update; then choose Yes to update the links. The information in the document is replaced with the latest version from the original file. Any formatting changes you've made to the linked information are lost.

TIP: *If you want the linked information to use certain formatting, add that formatting within your spreadsheet or database program so it is always included when the link is updated.*

In addition to updating the link manually, you can also have the link automatically updated each time the WordPerfect document is opened. To do this, open the document with the link and choose Insert | Spreadsheet/Database | Options. Select Update When Document Opens and choose OK.

Inserting Sound and Video Clips

WordPerfect 8 makes it easy to create multimedia documents. You can add variety to your documents with sound files, inserting such things as sound effects, music, or recorded instructions. You can also insert video clips to add animation to your documents. WordPerfect can play video clips in AVI format and sound files in WAV or MIDI (*.MID, *.RMI) format.

NOTE: *In order to play sound, your computer must have a sound card installed. Most sound cards that work with Windows will play both WAV and MIDI files. However, you'll get better-quality sound for MIDI files if your sound card uses wave-table synthesis. Refer to your sound card documentation for more information.*

You have several different options for determining how a sound or video clip appears in a document, as well as how it is played. For example, video clips can be inserted as icons or in a graphics box with the first frame showing (see Figure 17-8). With either method, double-clicking the icon or object plays the video. For more

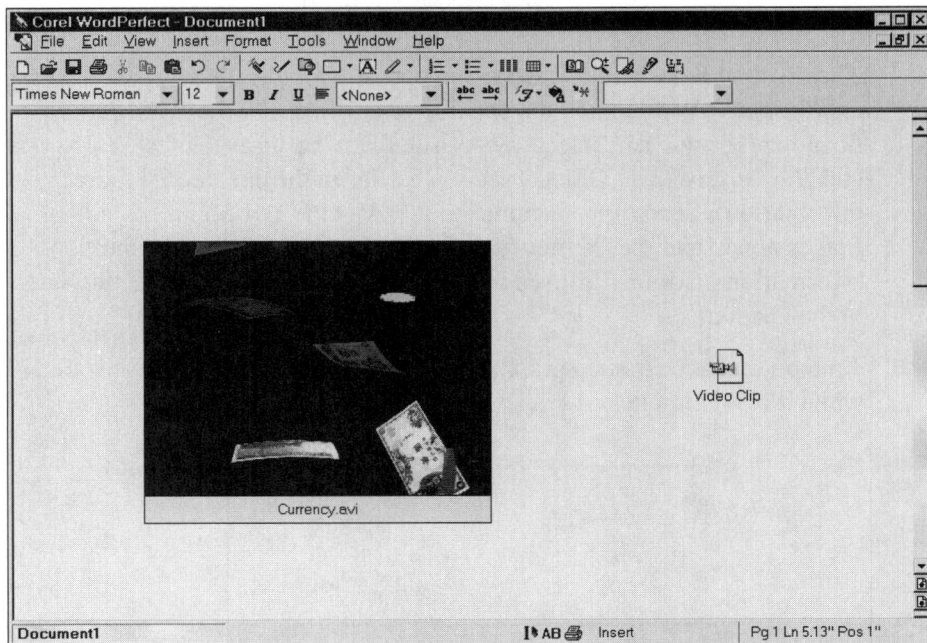

FIGURE 17-8   Video clips can be inserted as icons or in a graphics box with the first frame displaying

information on inserting video clips, see the "Using the Media Player" section later in the chapter.

Sound files can be inserted into your documents in any of the following formats:

- An icon in the left margin that plays the sound file when it is clicked once. These sounds can be from existing .WAV or MIDI files, or they can be recorded right into the document. For more information, see the "Using the Sound Feature" section.

- An icon that appears in a graphics box and plays the sound when it is double-clicked. Since the icon is in a graphics box, it can be placed anywhere in the document.

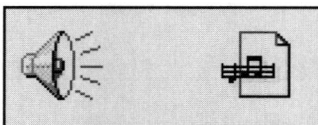

These sound icons can be inserted in one of two ways. First, you can drag and drop a WAV file from the desktop or a folder into the WordPerfect document, or you can select a WAV file from the Insert Object dialog box (see the "Inserting an Object" section earlier in the chapter for more information). Second, you can insert a WAV or MIDI file as a Media Player object and then remove the control bar and border. For more information on doing this, see the "Using the Media Player" section later in the chapter.

- An icon that appears in a graphics box with a label and plays the sound when it's double-clicked.

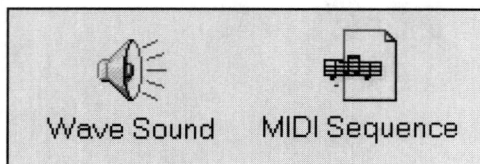

These sound icons can be inserted by using the Insert Object dialog box to create a new Wave Sound object or MIDI Sequence object, and selecting the Display Object as Icon in Document option. For more

information, see the "How to Use Icons for Embedded Objects" section earlier in the chapter.

■ An icon that appears in a graphics box with a border and shaded text label.

Camera.wav	Bach's Brandenburg Concerto No. 3.rmi

These icons play the sound file when double-clicked and also display a control bar in the shaded area that lets you stop or pause the playback. For more information, see the "Using the Media Player" section later in the chapter.

MULTIMEDIA.WPD: *The companion CD contains a sample document called MULTIMEDIA.WPD that has examples of the different ways you can include sound and video clips in your documents. In order to hear the sounds in the document, your computer must have a sound card.*

Using the Sound Feature

WordPerfect's Sound feature provides an easy way to insert sound clips in your documents without having to worry about using any additional sound utilities. Unlike sound files that are embedded as objects, sounds inserted with the Sound feature can be played with a single click of the mouse. The sound icon appears in the left margin.

In addition, the Sound feature lets you record sound files directly into a document, as well as play them back with a toolbar that has options for starting, stopping, rewinding, and fast-forwarding. To insert a sound with the Sound feature, follow these steps:

1. Place the insertion point on the line where you want the sound inserted. (The sound icon will be automatically placed in the left margin.)

2. Choose Insert | Sound. The Sound Clips dialog box appears. This dialog box lists any sound clips currently inserted in the document (see Figure 17-9).

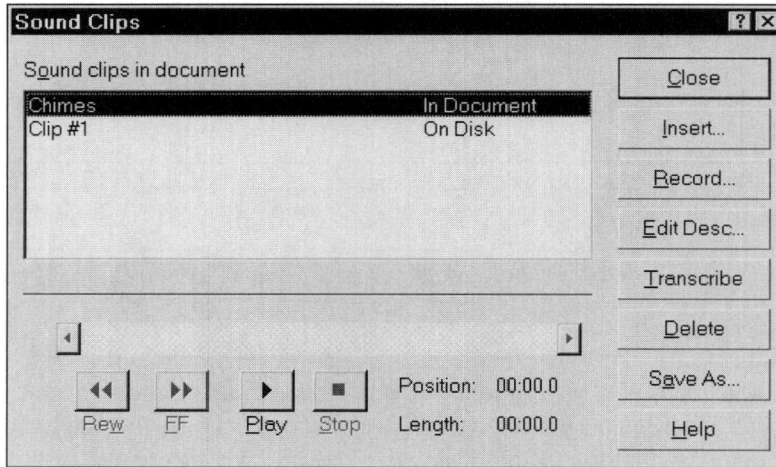

FIGURE 17-9 The Sound Clips dialog box lets you record or insert sound files

3. If you want to insert an existing WAV or MIDI file, choose Insert. In the Name text box, change the description of the sound file if you want. In the File text box, type the path and filename of the sound file, or use the file folder icon to select it. If you want to create a link to the sound file, keep the Link to File on Disk option selected. If you want to actually embed the sound file in the document, select Store in Document. Embedding the sound file in the document makes the document's file size larger, but allows you to give the document to someone else with the sound file included. Choose OK to insert the sound.

4. If you want to record a new sound in the document, choose Record. The Windows Sound Recorder appears. In order to record a sound, you must have a microphone or other input device attached to your sound card. Click the Record button to begin recording; then click the Stop button when you're finished. Choose File | Save, type a filename for the recorded sound, and choose Save. Choose File | Exit to close the Sound Recorder. Then insert the sound using the previous step.

5. Choose Close to close the Sound Clips dialog box.

Playing a Sound

When you want to play a sound inserted with the Sound feature, all you have to do is click the icon in the left margin once. You can also play sounds by choosing Insert | Sound, selecting the sound in the list, and choosing Play. The Sound Clips dialog box also has options for stopping, rewinding, and fast-forwarding a sound (see Figure 17-9).

NOTE: *If you want to change the description for a sound in the Sound Clips dialog box, select the sound and choose Edit Desc; then type a description in the Name text box and choose OK.*

You can also display a toolbar at the top of the document window with options for playing a sound file:

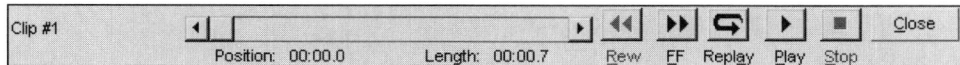

To display this toolbar, right-click a sound icon in the margin and choose Transcribe. Or you can choose Insert | Sound, select a sound file in the list, and choose Transcribe. When you're finished, choose Close on the toolbar.

Using the Media Player

When you insert a video clip or MIDI file in a WordPerfect document, it's played with the Windows Media Player. The Media Player displays a control bar as the sound or video is played, letting you easily stop the playback if you want:

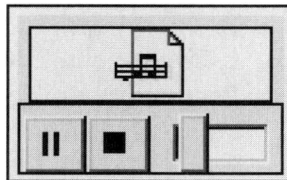

NOTE: *When you insert a WAV file by dragging and dropping it or by selecting it through the Insert Object feature, it is played with the Windows Sound Recorder and doesn't have options for stopping the playback. However, you can play a WAV file with the Media Player if you want.*

To insert a MIDI sound or video clip, choose Insert | Object. Select Create From File and then, in the File text box, type the path and filename to the video clip (*.AVI) or sound clip (*.MID, *.RMI) that you want to insert. You can also use the file folder icon to select the file. If you want to link to the file so the actual file isn't stored in the document, select Link. Choose OK to insert the object.

NOTE: *If you want to play a WAV file with the Media Player, choose Insert | Object, select Create New, select Media Clip in the Object Type list box and choose OK. From the Media Clip menu bar at the top of the screen, choose Insert Clip | Sound, select the WAV file you want to use, and choose Open. Click outside the sound clip in the document to deselect it.*

TIP: *The Corel WordPerfect 8 CD contains three AVI video clips in the \COREL\SUITE8\MOVIES directory. In addition, several WAV and MIDI files are on the CD in the \COREL\SUITE8\SOUNDS directory.*

To play a Media Player object, double-click it. A control bar appears across the bottom of the file with buttons for stopping and pausing the playback. If you click outside the object to deselect it, the playback is paused. The next time you double-click the object, it picks up at the point it left off at.

NOTE: *If you created a link to the Media Player object, the control bar appears in a separate window rather than across the bottom of the file.*

You can remove the control bar from the Media Player object if you want, as well as change the label text or remove the border. For more information, see the Power Tip "Changing the Media Player Options."

Power Tip... Changing the Media Player Options

By default, sound and video clips that are played with the Media Player are displayed with a shaded label that turns into a control bar when the object is double-clicked. You can customize the object and change some of these options. Follow these steps:

1. Right-click the object in the document and choose Media Clip Object | Edit. (For MIDI files, choose MIDI Sequence Object | Edit.)

2. The Media Player menu bar appears at the top of the screen. Choose Edit | Options.

3. If you want to remove the control bar, deselect Control Bar on Playback. To change the text in the shaded label, type the text you want in the Caption text box. If you want to have the control bar appear during playback, you *must* have some text in the Caption text box. When you remove the control bar from an object, you can stop the playback by simply clicking outside the object to deselect it.

4. If you want to remove the border from the object, deselect Border Around Object.

5. If you want the video or sound clip to repeat continuously until the user stops it, select Auto Repeat.

6. Choose OK when you're finished, and then click outside the object frame in the WP document window to return to WordPerfect.

Summary

Incorporating information from other programs into your WordPerfect documents has never been easier. WordPerfect 8 gives you lots of tools and options to get just the results you want. You can embed and link objects from other programs using OLE, so you can quickly edit and update the information. If you're working with a spreadsheet or database, you can also use the Spreadsheet/Database Import feature to import the data as regular WordPerfect text, as well as link it to the original file. Finally, you can create multimedia documents by inserting sound and video clips with a variety of different methods.

In Chapter 18, we'll show you how to integrate your documents even more with the other programs in Corel's WordPerfect Suite 8.

Chapter

18

Integrating WordPerfect with the Suite

O ne of the greatest things about buying a copy of WordPerfect 8 is that you don't get *just* WordPerfect. Instead, you get a whole suite of useful applications, such as Quattro Pro 8, Presentations 8, and CorelCENTRAL 8. And it gets even better— all of the programs in WordPerfect Suite 8 are designed to work and integrate together seamlessly. In addition, the toolbars, menu bars, and features in each program have a similar look and feel, so it's easy to find your way around.

In this chapter, we'll show you how WordPerfect can tap into the powerful features of some of the other applications in the suite. You learn how to share data with Quattro Pro, create charts and drawings with Presentations, and keep track of contacts with CorelCENTRAL. In addition, we'll show you how to customize the Desktop Application Director (DAD) so you can have quick access to all of your favorite programs.

> **NOTE:** *For more information about some of the smaller programs included in Corel WordPerfect Suite 8, see Chapter 20.*

Working with Quattro Pro

Quattro Pro 8 is a powerful spreadsheet program that helps you crunch numbers, analyze complex data, and create all sorts of financial reports. In addition, you can quickly create charts and graphs from the spreadsheet data. While WordPerfect can calculate formulas as part of its Tables feature, sometimes you need the powerful functions of Quattro Pro for complex analyses. Fortunately, it's easy to share information between Quattro Pro and WordPerfect.

> **TIP:** *Quattro Pro comes with several PerfectExpert projects already set up for dozens of different financial reports, such as budgets, cost analyses, retirement planning, and more. You can access these projects from WordPerfect by choosing File | New and then selecting [Corel Quattro Pro 8] from the Project Category drop-down list. Select the project you want in the list and choose Create to start Quattro Pro and set up the report.*

Using Quattro Pro Data in WordPerfect

There are several different ways you can use Quattro Pro data in a WordPerfect document. For example, you can access spreadsheet information during a merge or simply insert a section of a spreadsheet in a document you're creating. When you import Quattro Pro data into WordPerfect, you can insert it as regular text—allowing you to use some of WP's features to format it—or you can insert it as an embedded graphics box that remains linked to the original file.

Merging with Quattro Pro

Spreadsheet programs such as Quattro Pro are often used to store records in a table format, similar to a database (see Figure 18-1). This information can then be easily

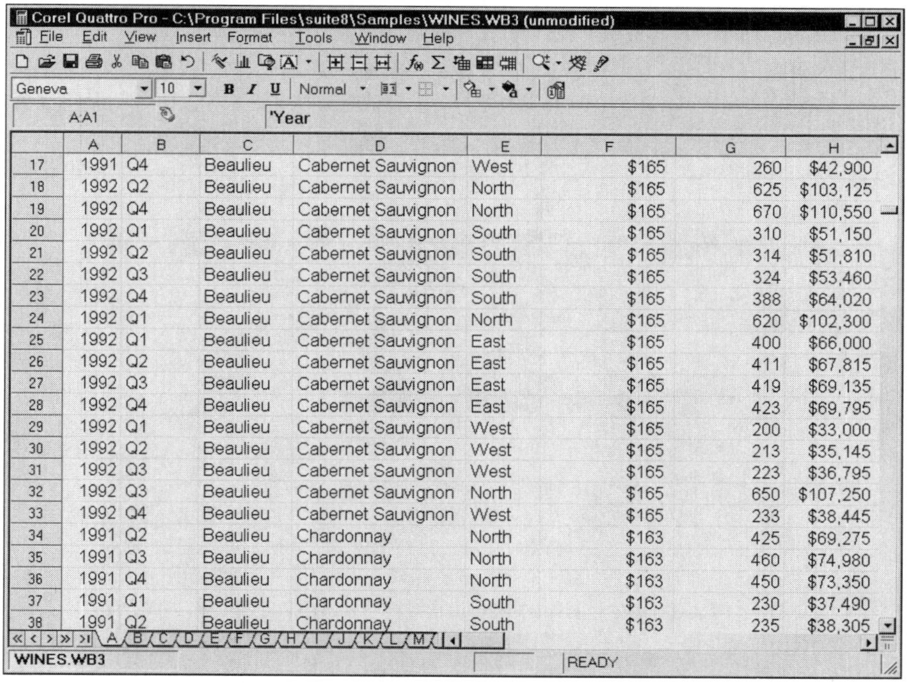

	A	B	C	D	E	F	G	H
17	1991	Q4	Beaulieu	Cabernet Sauvignon	West	$165	260	$42,900
18	1992	Q2	Beaulieu	Cabernet Sauvignon	North	$165	625	$103,125
19	1992	Q4	Beaulieu	Cabernet Sauvignon	North	$165	670	$110,550
20	1992	Q1	Beaulieu	Cabernet Sauvignon	South	$165	310	$51,150
21	1992	Q2	Beaulieu	Cabernet Sauvignon	South	$165	314	$51,810
22	1992	Q3	Beaulieu	Cabernet Sauvignon	South	$165	324	$53,460
23	1992	Q4	Beaulieu	Cabernet Sauvignon	South	$165	388	$64,020
24	1992	Q1	Beaulieu	Cabernet Sauvignon	North	$165	620	$102,300
25	1992	Q1	Beaulieu	Cabernet Sauvignon	East	$165	400	$66,000
26	1992	Q2	Beaulieu	Cabernet Sauvignon	East	$165	411	$67,815
27	1992	Q3	Beaulieu	Cabernet Sauvignon	East	$165	419	$69,135
28	1992	Q4	Beaulieu	Cabernet Sauvignon	East	$165	423	$69,795
29	1992	Q1	Beaulieu	Cabernet Sauvignon	West	$165	200	$33,000
30	1992	Q2	Beaulieu	Cabernet Sauvignon	West	$165	213	$35,145
31	1992	Q3	Beaulieu	Cabernet Sauvignon	West	$165	223	$36,795
32	1992	Q3	Beaulieu	Cabernet Sauvignon	North	$165	650	$107,250
33	1992	Q4	Beaulieu	Cabernet Sauvignon	West	$165	233	$38,445
34	1991	Q2	Beaulieu	Chardonnay	North	$163	425	$69,275
35	1991	Q3	Beaulieu	Chardonnay	North	$163	460	$74,980
36	1991	Q4	Beaulieu	Chardonnay	North	$163	450	$73,350
37	1991	Q1	Beaulieu	Chardonnay	South	$163	230	$37,490
38	1991	Q2	Beaulieu	Chardonnay	South	$163	235	$38,305

FIGURE 18-1 Data stored in a Quattro Pro file can be used in a WP merge

analyzed with the different features of Quattro Pro. If you have data in a Quattro Pro file and want to use it during a WordPerfect merge, there's no need to reenter the information in WordPerfect. Instead, you can directly select the Quattro Pro file as your data source for the merge. In addition, you can also import the Quattro Pro file as a WP merge data file, which you can then edit and save separately.

If you want to merge directly with a Quattro Pro file, you first need to set up a merge form document in WordPerfect. Follow these general guidelines:

1. Go to a blank document window in WP and choose Tools | Merge; then choose Create Document.

2. Select Associate a Data File and type the path and filename of the Quattro Pro spreadsheet file in the text box. If you click the file folder icon, first select All Files (*.*) from the File Type drop-down list, select the Quattro Pro file, and choose Select.

3. Choose OK to begin creating the form document. At this point, you can add any text, formatting, or merge codes that you want for the document.

4. To insert a field from the Quattro Pro file, choose Insert Field on the Merge toolbar. The Insert Field Name or Number dialog box lists a number for each field (column) in the spreadsheet file, along with the data inserted in the first row of the file:

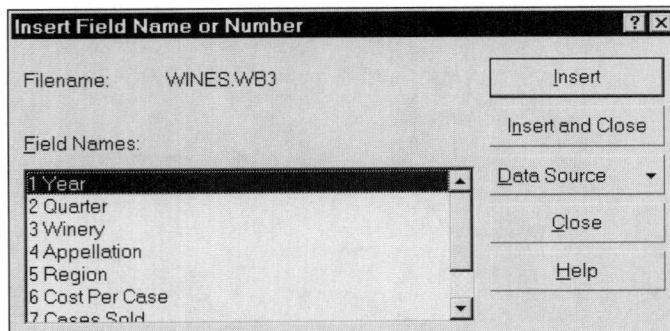

Select the field you want to use and choose Insert and Close. A FIELD code is inserted into the form document with a field number instead of a field name, such as FIELD(1), since WordPerfect doesn't recognize field names in a spreadsheet file.

5. Continue inserting the fields, merge codes, and formatting you want. When you're finished, save the form document; then perform the merge normally with the spreadsheet file selected as the data source. For more information on creating form documents and performing merges, see Chapter 2.

If you'd rather import a Quattro Pro file as a separate merge data file, go to a blank document window in WordPerfect and choose Insert | Spreadsheet/Database | Import. From the Data Type drop-down list, select Spreadsheet, and from the Import As drop-down list, select Merge Data File. In the File Name text box, type the path and filename of the Quattro Pro file (or use the file folder icon to select it). Select any other options, such as specifying a cell range to import (see Chapter 17 for more information). Choose OK to create the data file. You can then use this data file normally for any merge in WordPerfect.

NOTE: *WordPerfect doesn't create field names when you import a spreadsheet file as a merge data file. However, you can manually add field names to the data file. See Chapter 2 for more information.*

Importing Quattro Pro Files

Quattro Pro is the perfect choice when you need to analyze and calculate complex data, but it might not have all the features you want for formatting or printing that data. For example, you can't print in newspaper columns or add a watermark to a spreadsheet in Quattro Pro. For cases like these, you can import the spreadsheet into WordPerfect and then use WP's formatting features to get the result you want.

ACCOUNTS.WB3: *The companion CD contains a sample Quattro Pro spreadsheet named ACCOUNTS.WB3 that you can use to practice importing and embedding data in WordPerfect.*

WordPerfect's Import Spreadsheet/Database feature (Insert | Spreadsheet/ Database | Import) lets you format Quattro Pro information as a table, tabbed text, or a merge data file. You can specify which cells are imported if you don't want to include the entire spreadsheet. If you import the spreadsheet as a table, the formatting and formulas from Quattro Pro remain intact. For more information on using this feature, see Chapter 17.

Another quick way to place Quattro Pro information in WordPerfect is to use the Windows Clipboard. This method is useful if you don't need any formulas but simply want to format some of the data. To do this, select the information in Quattro Pro that you want to copy and choose Edit | Copy. Then, in WordPerfect, place the insertion point where you want the data inserted. If you want to insert the information in a table, simply choose Edit | Paste. If you want to insert the data as regular text (with tabs used between columns), choose Edit | Paste Special. Select Unformatted Text and choose OK.

Once you've inserted the data, you can format and print it using any of WordPerfect's features. For example, you can turn on columns if you inserted the data as regular text (Format | Columns), or you can insert a watermark (Insert | Watermark) behind the imported table.

Embedding Quattro Pro Files

A final method for inserting Quattro Pro information in a WordPerfect document is to embed it as an OLE object. With this method, the spreadsheet information is inserted in a graphics box (see Figure 18-2). You can position the graphics box anywhere in the document and double-click it to edit the information using Quattro Pro's tools. You can even link the object to Quattro Pro so that any changes to the original spreadsheet are automatically used in the WordPerfect document. For more information on embedding and linking Quattro Pro data in WordPerfect, see Chapter 17.

Using WordPerfect Files in Quattro Pro

In addition to inserting Quattro Pro information in a WordPerfect document, you can go the other way and insert information from a WP document into Quattro Pro. For example, you can import a merge data file or a WordPerfect table into a Quattro Pro notebook.

Importing a Merge Data File

If you have information in a WP merge data file that you want to use in Quattro Pro, you can easily import it into a Quattro Pro notebook. Each record in the data file is inserted in a single row, with each field in a separate column (see Figure 18-1). This is done by saving the data file in ASCII delimited format, and then using the

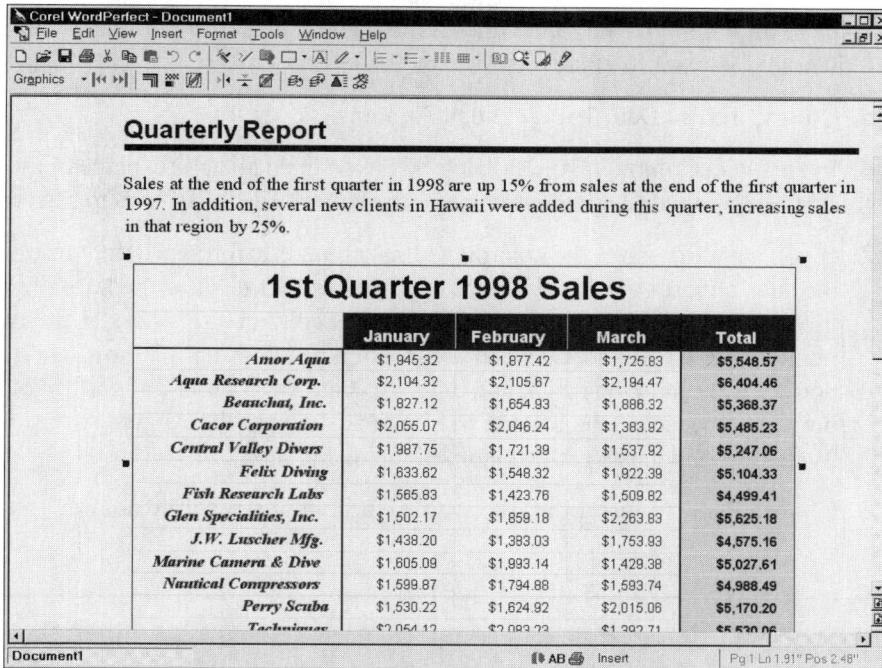

FIGURE 18-2 You can embed Quattro Pro information as an OLE object

QuickColumns feature in Quattro Pro to parse the fields into separate columns. Follow these steps:

1. Open the merge data file in WordPerfect.

2. Choose File | Save As. From the File Type drop-down list, select ASCII (DOS) Delimited Text. The File Name text box should show the original data file's name with a TXT extension. If you want to change the filename, type the new name in the File Name text box (keeping the TXT extension). Choose Save to save the file.

3. Choose File | Close.

4. Start Quattro Pro. If you want to insert the data file information into an existing notebook file, open that file. Place the insertion point in the cell where you want the first record to begin.

5. Choose Tools | Data Tools | QuickColumns.

6. In the QuickColumns Expert dialog box, type the path and filename of the ASCII delimited file you just created, or click the file folder icon to select it.

7. If you want to change the column widths or numeric formats before inserting the data, choose Advanced. The dialog box expands to show the information in the data file (see Figure 18-3). To change a column size, place the mouse pointer over the divider between two column headings until it turns into a double arrow, and then click and drag. To change a column's alignment or numeric type, select the column heading and then use the Alignment and Type drop-down lists at the bottom of the dialog box.

8. Choose Parse to insert the file, with each field in a separate column.

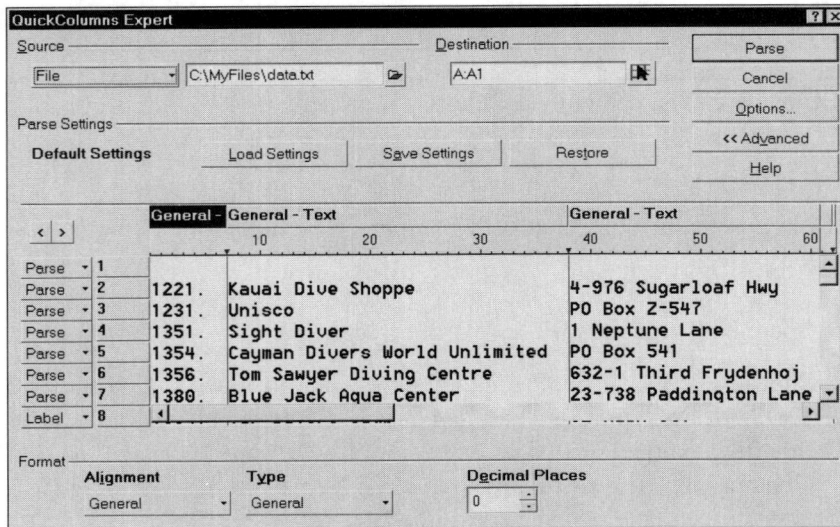

FIGURE 18-3 The Advanced button expands the dialog box to show information from the data file

NOTE: *If you don't want to import the entire data file, you can select which records are included. For more information, see the Power Tip "Selecting Records to Import."*

Power Tip→→→ Selecting Records to Import

If you don't want to import an entire merge data file into Quattro Pro, you have two options for selecting the records that should be included. First, you can use the Sort feature to extract the records you want, before saving the data file in ASCII delimited format. This method allows you to quickly select all the records that match a certain condition, such as all the records in a specific state or ZIP code. For more information on using the Sort feature to extract records, see Chapter 8.

Second, you can use the QuickColumns Expert dialog box to mark individual records in the data file that you want to have skipped as the file is imported. To use this method, follow the steps in the "Importing a Merge Data File" section to save the data file in ASCII delimited format and select it in the QuickColumns Expert dialog box. Choose Advanced in the dialog box to expand it and see a list of the records in the data file (see Figure 18-3). For those records you *don't* want to import, select Skip from the drop-down menu to the left of the row number. Use the vertical scroll bar to see all of the records in the file.

When you're finished, choose Parse to import those records with "Parse" selected from the drop-down menu. If a record has "Label" selected in the drop-down menu, all of the fields in that record will be placed in a single cell, with the delimiters (quotation marks and commas) still in place.

Importing a WordPerfect Table

If you've created a table in WordPerfect and decide that you want to take advantage of some of Quattro Pro's advanced formula functions and other tools for the table data, you don't have to reenter the information in Quattro Pro. Instead, you can easily import the table into a notebook. You can import the table with the original WP formatting, as shown in this example:

	A	B	C	D
1	**Date**	**Description**	**Amount**	**Balance**
2		Initial Balance		$1,500.00
3	11/13/97	Rent Payment	$600.00	$900.00
4	11/14/97	Groceries	$65.24	$834.76
5	11/14/97	Gas	$14.50	$820.26
6	11/15/97	Deposit - paycheck	($800.00)	$1,620.26

Or you can import the table data with the default Quattro Pro notebook formatting, as shown here:

	A	B	C	D
1	Date	Descriptio	Amount	Balance
2		Initial Balance		$1,500.00
3	11/13/97	Rent Payn	600	900
4	11/14/97	Groceries	65.24	834.76
5	11/14/97	Gas	14.5	820.26
6	11/15/97	Deposit -	-800	1620.26

CAUTION: *With either method, any formulas in the WordPerfect table are not included. You'll need to reenter the formulas using Quattro Pro's formula functions.*

To import a table in Quattro Pro and keep a majority of the table formatting done in WordPerfect—including the column widths—follow these steps:

1. In WordPerfect, open the document containing the table or tables you want to import.

2. Choose File | Save As. From the File Type drop-down list, select Quattro Pro 6.0 for Windows. The File Name text box automatically changes the current filename to use a WB2 file extension. Change the filename if you want (keeping the WB2 extension) and choose Save.

3. Choose File | Close to close the document.

4. Start Quattro Pro and choose File | Open. Select the WB2 file you just saved and choose Open. The table is opened in a new notebook, keeping much of the original WP formatting. If the WP document contained more than one table, each table is placed on a separate page of the notebook. (The notebook pages are named "Table A," "Table B," and so on.) Any text in the original WP document that was not part of a table is not imported into Quattro Pro.

NOTE: *If the WP table contained gray-shaded cells, the shading used in Quattro Pro might be too dark to see the text. To change the shading, select the shaded cells in Quattro Pro, right-click the selection, and choose Cell Properties. Select the Border/Fill tab; then from the Fill Color pop-down palette, select the new shading color. Choose OK.*

If you *don't* need any of the formatting from the WordPerfect table, you can simply import the table data as generic Quattro Pro text. This can be done in Quattro Pro 8 by simply opening the WordPerfect document that contains the table. In Quattro Pro, choose File | Open. From the File Type drop-down list, select WP Documents (*.wpd) if the file has a WPD extension, or select All Files (*.*) if it uses a different extension. Select the document and choose Open.

NOTE: *If the WordPerfect document you open contains text that is not in a table, each paragraph is placed in an individual cell. If there is no text in the cell immediately to the right, Quattro Pro displays the entire paragraph in the adjacent cells; otherwise, the text is cut off by the column boundary.*

If you only want to copy the information from an individual WP table, open the document in WordPerfect that contains the table, and then select the rows and columns you want to copy into Quattro Pro. Choose Edit | Copy, choose Selection, and then OK. Switch to Quattro Pro and place the insertion point where you want the table to begin. Choose Edit | Paste to paste in the table information.

After inserting the table data in Quattro Pro, you can use the features and tools in Quattro Pro to format the cells, add formulas, or create charts and graphs. For example, if you have a WP table that includes data grouped by geographical regions, such as states or countries, you can import that data into Quattro Pro and use the Mapping feature to create a map chart of the data (see Figure 18-4). For more information on how to do this, see the "How to Create a Map Chart" section.

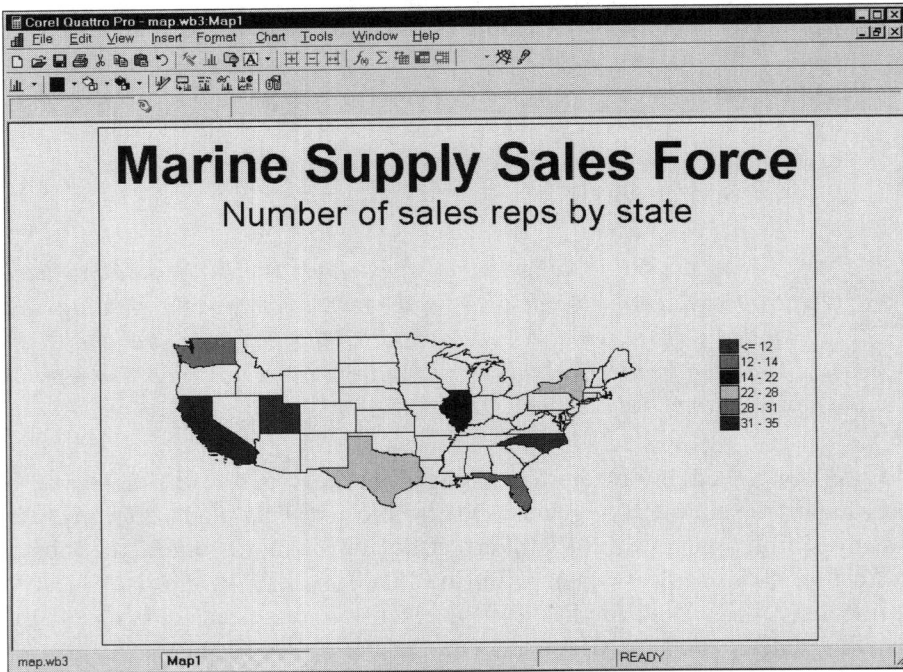

FIGURE 18-4   You can use Quattro Pro's Mapping feature to create a map chart

NOTE: *You can create data charts right in WordPerfect from information in a table by using the Chart feature. This feature uses Presentations' charting tools to create an embedded chart object. For more information, see the "Creating a Data Chart" section later in this chapter.*

How to... Create a Map Chart

One of the unique tools in Quattro Pro is the Mapping feature. This feature can create a map chart based on information grouped according to geographical regions (see Figure 18-4). For example, you might have a table containing the quarterly sales results for each state or country serviced by your company.

How to...   Create a Map Chart
(continued)

The Mapping feature is not installed during a typical installation, so you need to install it first. To do this, make sure the WordPerfect Suite 8 CD is in the drive, and from the Windows taskbar, choose Start | Corel WordPerfect Suite 8 | Setup & Notes | Corel WordPerfect Suite 8 Setup. Follow the prompts until you see the "Installation Type" dialog box; then select Custom, and choose Next twice. Choose Selection Options, select Deselect All, and choose OK. Select Corel Quattro Pro 8 in the list and choose Components. Select Mapping and choose OK. Choose Next and continue with the installation.

To use the Mapping feature, first enter the data in a WordPerfect table or Quattro Pro notebook. The first column should include the geographical regions, such as state or country names. For example, the table might look something like this:

Sales Reps by State	
California	35
Florida	31
Illinois	22
New York	24
North Carolina	12
Texas	28
Utah	10
Washington	14

If you created the table in WordPerfect, import it into Quattro Pro following the steps in the "Importing a WordPerfect Table" section earlier in the chapter. Then, to create the map chart, follow these steps:

1. In Quattro Pro, select the cells containing the information you want to use in the map.

2. Choose Insert | Graphics | Map.

How to...   **Create a Map Chart**
(*continued*)

3. When the Map Expert dialog box appears, select the map that you want for your data, such as USA by State or World by Country. Choose Next.

4. You can chart two sets of data on the map—one set represented by different colors and the other set represented by different patterns. If needed, change the group of cells that will be used for the region names, color data, and pattern data. Choose Next.

5. If any of the state or country names aren't recognized by Quattro Pro, you're prompted to select the correct choice. For example, if your data contained "England," select "Britain" from the list and choose Replace.

6. Select the color scheme you want to use and choose Next.

7. If you want to include an overlay map, such as the major U.S. Highways, select it in the list. You can also choose Mark Points on Your Map to have dots included for major cities or capitols (the Quattro Pro notebook must include the city names you want to highlight on the map). Choose Next.

8. Enter the title, subtitle, and legend title for the map. If you want the map inserted in a separate window, select Map Window. Choose Finish.

9. If you're not inserting the map in a separate window, click and drag the area for the map in the current notebook.

The map chart is created using the selected data. For more information on creating or editing maps in Quattro Pro, refer to Quattro Pro's online help.

Working with Presentations

Presentations 8 is another major component of Corel's WordPerfect Suite 8. Presentations gives you the tools you need to create and edit dazzling slide show presentations, drawings, charts, and clipart images. WordPerfect 8 automatically accesses the tools in Presentations whenever you create a data chart or edit a clipart image. In addition, you can use Presentations to create drawings and organization charts right in your WordPerfect documents.

TIP: *Just like Quattro Pro, Presentations comes with several PerfectExpert projects already set up to create a variety of slide shows, banners, and flyers. To use these projects, in WordPerfect choose File | New and select [Corel Presentations 8] from the Project Category drop-down list. Select the project you want and choose Create. Presentations is automatically loaded with the selected project.*

Creating a Data Chart

When you want to present numbers in an eye-catching format, you can use a chart (see Figure 18-5). Charts can easily be created right within your WordPerfect documents with the help of Presentations. WP's Chart feature creates an embedded Presentations object that lets you access Presentations' powerful charting tools.

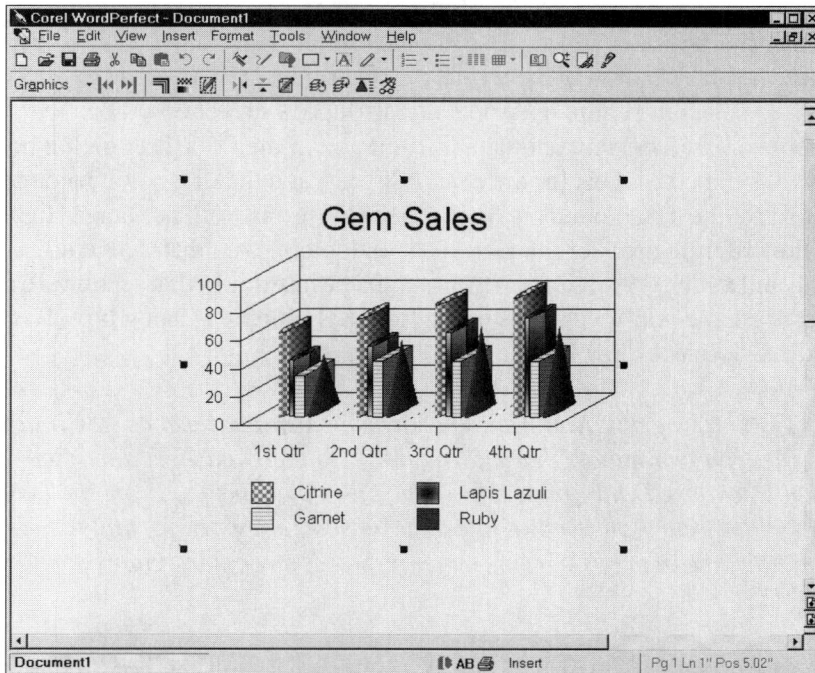

FIGURE 18-5 Charts can be created in WordPerfect with the help of Presentations

Presentations lets you select from nine different types of charts, including bar, line, and pie charts. You can create a chart from data already in a table, or you can create a new chart from scratch.

TIP: *If you create a chart from a table, the chart and table are automatically linked together, allowing you to quickly update the chart if information in the table is changed.*

If you've already inserted the data you want to chart in a table, make sure that the first row and column of the table contain the labels for the information you're charting. Then place the insertion point somewhere in the table and choose Insert I Graphics I Chart. A new chart is created in an embedded Presentations graphics box below the table.

If you don't already have the data in a table, you can create a new chart from scratch. Place the insertion point where you want the chart inserted and choose Insert I Graphics I Chart. An embedded Presentations chart object is created with some sample data (see Figure 18-6). In addition to the chart, the Datasheet and Range Highlighter dialog boxes appear. To clear the sample data from the Datasheet dialog box, click the blank button in the top-left corner of the Datasheet dialog box (above "Labels") to select the entire datasheet. Press DELETE and choose OK.

Type the chart label text and data information in the Datasheet dialog box. The first row contains the labels for the chart's X-axis, and the first column contains the legend text for the data plotted on the chart (see Figure 18-6). The Range Highlighter shades the different areas of the Datasheet dialog box with different colors, so you can easily tell which type of information should be inserted in that section. To change the colors, use the pop-up palettes in the Range Highlighter dialog box. To remove the shading, deselect View Highlighted Ranges.

TIP: *If the data you want to chart is in a spreadsheet or ASCII delimited file, you can import that information into the Datasheet dialog box. To do this, choose Data I Import from the pull-down menus. From the Data Type drop-down list, select the type of information you're importing, and then type the path and filename in the File Name text box. Select any other options you want and choose OK.*

Once you've created the basic chart, you can use Presentations' chart-editing tools to customize it. For example, here are a few ways you can modify the chart:

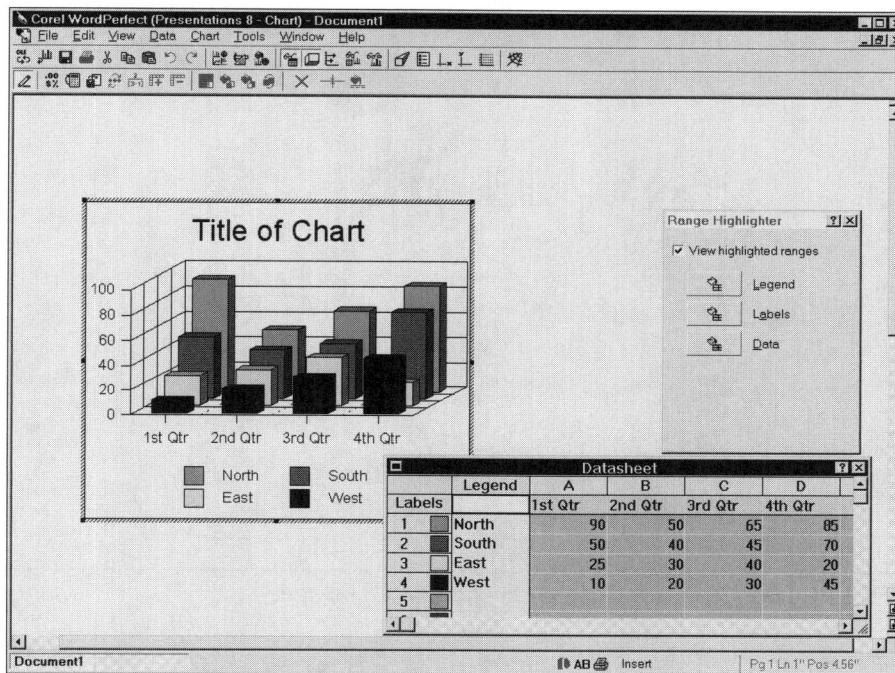

FIGURE 18-6 The sample chart data when creating a new chart

- To change the type of chart, choose Chart | Layout/Type. From the Chart Type drop-down list, select the type of chart you want, such as Pie or Line. Then select the chart style and other options from the Layout/Type Properties dialog box (see Figure 18-7). To preview your chart with the selected settings, choose Preview. If you don't need to make any further settings, choose OK. Otherwise, choose Back, make the changes you want, and choose OK when you're finished.

- To change the chart title, choose Chart | Title. Type the title in the Display Chart Title text box and change the font and font size if you want. Choose OK. To add a subtitle, choose Chart | Subtitle. Select Display Chart Subtitle, type the subtitle text, and select any other options you want. Choose OK.

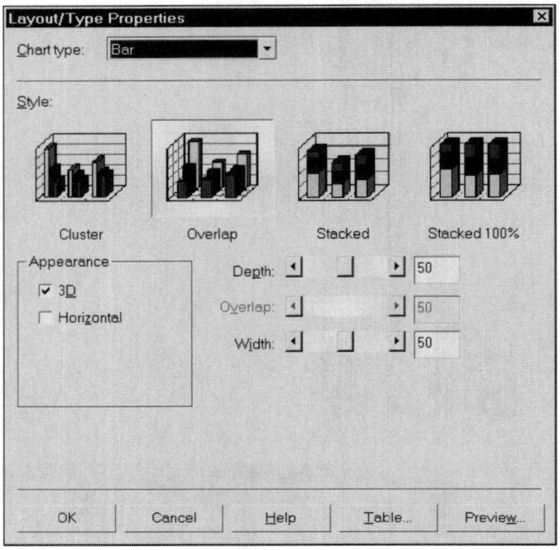

FIGURE 18-7 You can change the chart type and style

- To change the shapes, colors, or patterns used for the chart data, choose Chart I Series. If you're creating a bar graph, select the bar shape for the first series of data. Select the Fill tab and choose the pattern and color you want for that data. To change the settings for the next series of data, click the right arrow at the top of the dialog box and select the options you want. Choose OK when you're finished.

- To change the way the grid looks, choose Chart I Grids. Select the options you want and choose OK.

- You can transpose the chart data so the current X-axis labels become the legend items and vice versa. For more information, see the Power Tip "Transposing Chart Data."

TIP: *You can also change any aspect of a chart by right-clicking that area and selecting from the QuickMenu options. For example, to change the title, right-click the title and choose Title Properties. Or, to change the color of a data series, right-click the legend color of the data in the chart and choose Series Properties.*

Power Tip▸▸▸ Transposing Chart Data

Presentations 8 makes it a snap to transpose your chart data. When you transpose a chart, the current X-axis labels become the data represented by the legend, and vice versa.

To transpose a chart that's not using information from an existing table, right-click the chart and choose Chart Object | Edit if the Datasheet dialog box isn't already displaying. Click the blank box just above "Labels" in the Datasheet dialog box to select all of the data, and then choose Edit | Cut. Choose Edit | Paste Transposed to transpose the information back in the Datasheet dialog box.

If the chart is using data from a table in the document, you can create a new chart with the transposed information. Select the table and choose Edit | Copy. Choose Selection and then OK. Place the insertion point outside the table and choose Insert | Graphics | Chart. When the Datasheet dialog box appears, click the blank box just above "Labels" in the Datasheet dialog box to select all of the data. Press DELETE and choose OK. Choose Edit | Paste Transposed to insert the transposed information for the new chart.

When you're finished making changes to the chart, click outside the chart to return to the document. If you later need to make changes to the chart, right-click it and choose Chart Object | Edit. If your chart is using information from a table in the document and you make changes to the table data, you can update the chart by right-clicking it and choosing Update Chart from Table.

TIP: *If you want the chart to update automatically as you change information in the table, place the insertion point in the table and choose Table | Calculate from the Tables Property Bar. Select Calculate Tables in Document and select Update Associated Charts. Choose OK.*

Creating an Organization Chart

If you want to insert an organization chart in a WordPerfect document, you could try to create and position various text boxes and graphics lines. But a much easier solution is to use Presentations' Organization Chart feature. This feature lets you easily create an organization chart as an embedded graphics object in your WP document (see Figure 18-8).

The easiest way to create an organization chart is with the WP_ORG.WCM macro that's included with WordPerfect 8. To use this macro, place the insertion point where you want the chart created and choose Tools | Macro | Play. Select the WP_ORG.WCM macro and choose Play. The macro creates an embedded Presentations object and begins a new chart (see Figure 18-9).

> **NOTE:** *You can also create an organization chart by placing the insertion point where you want the chart inserted and choosing Insert | Graphics | Draw Picture. Then choose Insert | Organization Chart. Click and drag within the frame to define the size of the chart. Select the layout style you want and choose OK.*

> **TIP:** *You can click and drag the outer frame of the embedded object to increase the size of the organization chart.*

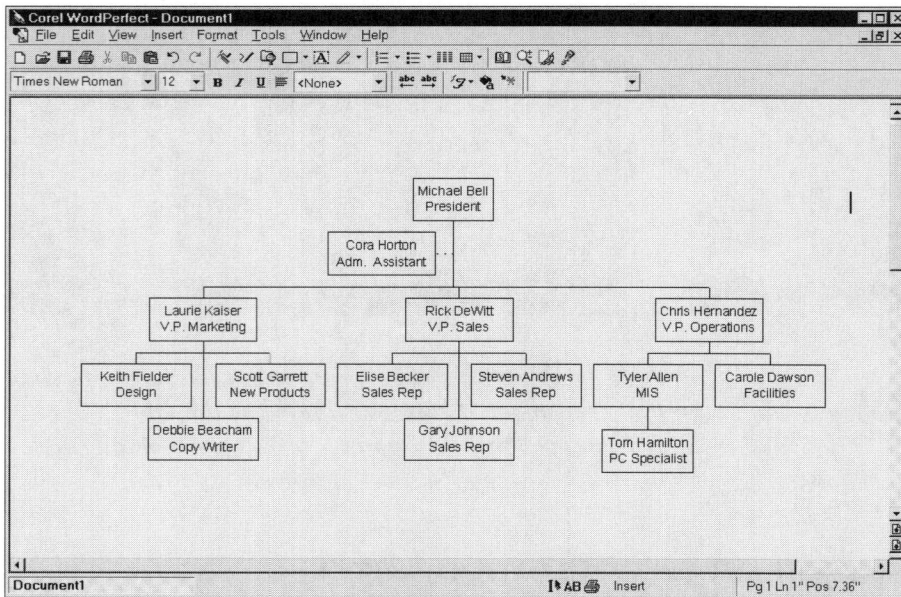

FIGURE 18-8 You can create an embedded Presentations organization chart in a WP document

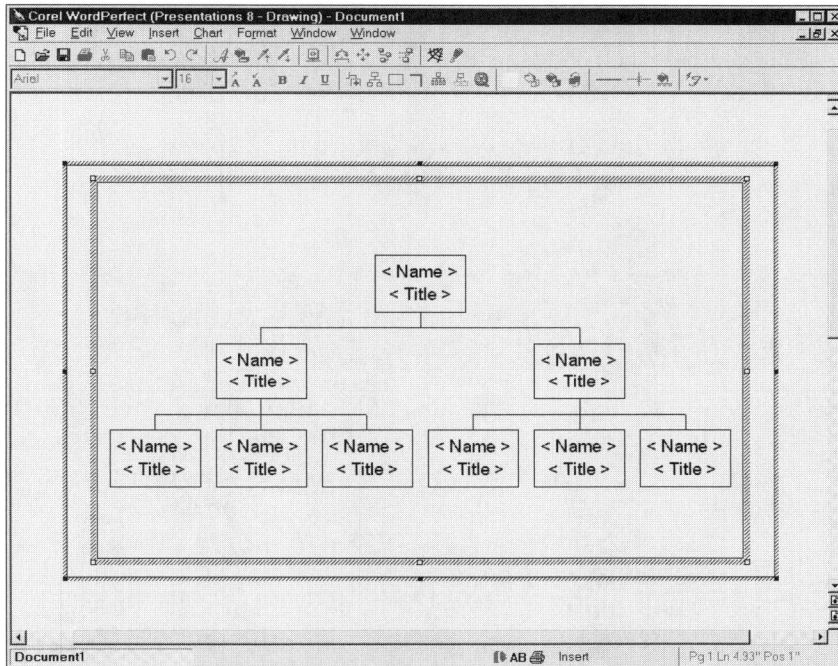

FIGURE 18-9 The WP_ORG.WCM macro inserts a basic chart structure

To change the information in a box, double-click the placeholder, such as <Name>, type the new information, and click outside the box. You can also import information into an organization chart from a WordPerfect outline. For more information, see the Power Tip "Importing an Organization Chart Outline."

Use these tips to customize your organization chart:

- To change the layout or style of the chart, right-click a blank area of the chart and choose Select All. Then choose Format I Branch Structure and select the structure and orientation you want. Choose Close.

- To remove the title field or add a different field of information, hold down the CTRL key and select each box you want to modify. To select all the boxes, right-click a blank area of the chart and choose Select All. Choose Format I Box Fields, add or delete any fields you want, and choose OK.

■ To add a new box, select the existing box that you want the new box placed under and choose Insert | Subordinates. Select the number and other options; then choose OK. You can also insert boxes on the same level as the selected box by choosing Insert | Coworkers.

■ To change the line or box styles, select the boxes you want to modify and choose Format | Box Properties. Make any changes you want and choose OK.

Power Tip... Importing an Organization Chart Outline

A quick way to create an organization chart is to import the information from a WordPerfect outline document. Then the chart automatically conforms to the levels in your outline and you don't have to double-click each individual box to enter the information.

First, create an outline in a blank WP document by choosing Insert | Outline/Bullets & Numbering, and then choosing OK. Type the name of the first person in the chart. If you want to include other information with the name, such as the title or department, press SHIFT-ENTER to insert a hard return without a new outline number. Type the information and press ENTER to insert the next outline number.

Press TAB to move to the next outline level and type the information for the subordinate position. Continue creating the outline, using TAB and SHIFT-TAB to indicate the responsibility level for each person. (If you insert additional lines by pressing SHIFT-ENTER, it doesn't matter if the text is tabbed over to match the indentation of the level.) For more information on creating outlines, see Chapter 9.

When you're finished, save and close the outline document. Then create a new organization chart (if you haven't already) by following the steps in the "Creating an Organization Chart" section. Click outside the chart in the document to deselect it; then right-click the chart and choose Drawing Object | Open. In Presentations, right-click the chart and choose Edit Chart. Choose Chart | Import Outline, select the outline document you created, and choose Insert. Make any other changes to the chart and click outside the chart in the Presentations window when you're finished. Choose File | Exit & Return to Document.

When you're finished with the chart, click outside it to return to the WordPerfect document. If you later need to edit the chart, right-click it and choose Drawing Object | Edit. Then right-click the chart and choose Edit Chart.

Creating and Editing Graphics

WordPerfect 8 has several graphics tools for such things as inserting shapes, rotating clipart images, and changing the color brightness. However, if you need more power and control for editing and even creating images and logos, you can use the tools in Presentations. For example, with Presentations you can change the color of an individual element in a clipart image, insert arches and curves, or contour text around a shape.

You can use Presentations to make changes to a clipart image that you've already inserted into a WordPerfect document, or you can create a new graphics drawing within your document. To make changes to an existing clipart image, you can either double-click the image or right-click it and choose Edit Image. (For more information on inserting clipart images, see Chapter 7.) To create a new drawing, place the insertion point where you want the drawing inserted and choose Insert | Graphics | Draw Picture.

TIP: *If you want to display a clipart image full-screen in Presentations for editing, hold down the ALT key while you double-click the image.*

NOTE: *When you edit a clipart image, the changes only affect the image in the current document and not the original clipart file.*

The clipart image or drawing area becomes an embedded Presentations object. WordPerfect displays an editing frame around the area and the Presentations menu bars and toolbars appear (see Figure 18-10). You can click and drag the sizing handles on the editing frame to increase the drawing space (or the amount of white space around the image).

Now you can use the tools in Presentations to create or edit the image. If you want to modify a specific part of an image, such as changing its color or deleting it completely, you probably need to separate the objects used to create the image first. To do this, select the image, right-click it, and choose Separate Objects. Then select the individual item you want to change and select a new color, change its size, or delete it. (In some cases, you might need to further separate the objects before you can select the specific element you want to change.)

FIGURE 18-10 When you double-click a clipart image in WordPerfect, an editing frame appears along with the Presentations toolbars

You can also insert shapes, text, or additional clipart images into the drawing area, using the options on the Presentations pull-down menus, toolbars, and Property Bars. For example, you can create text that's contoured around a shape. For more information, see the "How to Contour Text" section.

When you're finished making changes to the image, click outside the image to return to WordPerfect. If you're editing the image full-screen in Presentations, choose File | Exit & Return to Document.

How to ▸▸ Contour Text

Presentations makes it easy to contour text around any shape. This technique is great for creating eye-catching logos or headlines, such as this example:

How to... **Contour Text**
(*continued*)

To contour text, follow these steps:

1. Create a new drawing in a WordPerfect document or edit an existing image by following the steps in the "Creating and Editing Graphics" section.

2. In Presentations, choose Insert | Text Line. Click the insertion point where you want the line of text to begin. (Don't worry about exact positioning, because you can easily move it later.)

3. Choose Format | Font. Select the font and font size you want and choose OK.

4. Type the text you want to contour. If you want to insert any symbols, press CTRL-W, select the symbol you want, and choose Insert and Close. Click outside the line of text when you're finished.

5. Now insert the shape that you want the text contoured to, using any of the available shapes in Presentations. For example, choose Insert | Shape | Circle, and then click and drag in the drawing window to insert a circle. The shape will be hidden after you contour the text, so don't worry about the shape's formatting or whether it covers other objects in the drawing.

How to...   **Contour Text**
(continued)

6. Once the shape has been inserted, click it once to select it (if it's not already selected). Then hold down the CTRL key and select the text line so both items are selected:

7. Choose Tools | Contour Text. From the Position Text drop-down list, select the option you want, such as Top Center. Leave the Display Text Only option selected so the shape will be hidden. Choose OK.

Once you've contoured the text, you can move it to a new location in the drawing by clicking and dragging it. You can also change its size by selecting the text, and then clicking and dragging the sizing handles. If you want to change the font size so the text extends to a different length, right-click the image and choose Edit Text. Select the new font size and click outside the image. When you're finished, click outside the drawing area to return to WordPerfect.

Working with CorelCENTRAL

A new addition to the WordPerfect Suite 8 is CorelCENTRAL, a program that helps you organize and keep track of your time, tasks, and personal information. CorelCENTRAL includes an Address Book, calendar, task manager, and card file, as well as a special version of Netscape Communicator 4.01a to handle e-mail, conferencing, and discussion groups.

NOTE: *CorelCENTRAL was not included with the original release of WordPerfect Suite 8. If you purchased this version, you received a voucher in the package with instructions for obtaining CorelCENTRAL when it became available.*

Using the Address Book

CorelCENTRAL and WordPerfect 8 share the same Address Book information. In Chapter 15, you learned how to use the Address Book from within WordPerfect, including how to add and edit entries, create additional books, and import and export addresses. You can also make changes to the Address Book information from CorelCENTRAL. When you use CorelCENTRAL, you have a few more standard fields available for each entry, and you can easily export information in several different file formats. (The Address Book in WordPerfect only exports addresses in WP's ABX format.)

To use the Address Book in CorelCENTRAL, start CorelCENTRAL from the Windows taskbar by choosing Start | Corel WordPerfect Suite 8 | CorelCENTRAL. If this is the first time you've used CorelCENTRAL, you're asked to enter some information about yourself to create a user profile. When CorelCENTRAL appears, switch to the Address Book by choosing View | Main View | Address Book or by clicking the Address Book icon.

The Address Book displays a list of the Address Book entries on the left, and the complete information for the selected entry on the right (see Figure 18-11). If you've created more than one Address Book, you can switch between them by clicking the Address Book tabs at the bottom of the dialog box.

TIP: *You can quickly view only the individuals, organizations, or resources in an Address Book by selecting the option you want from the Groups drop-down list.*

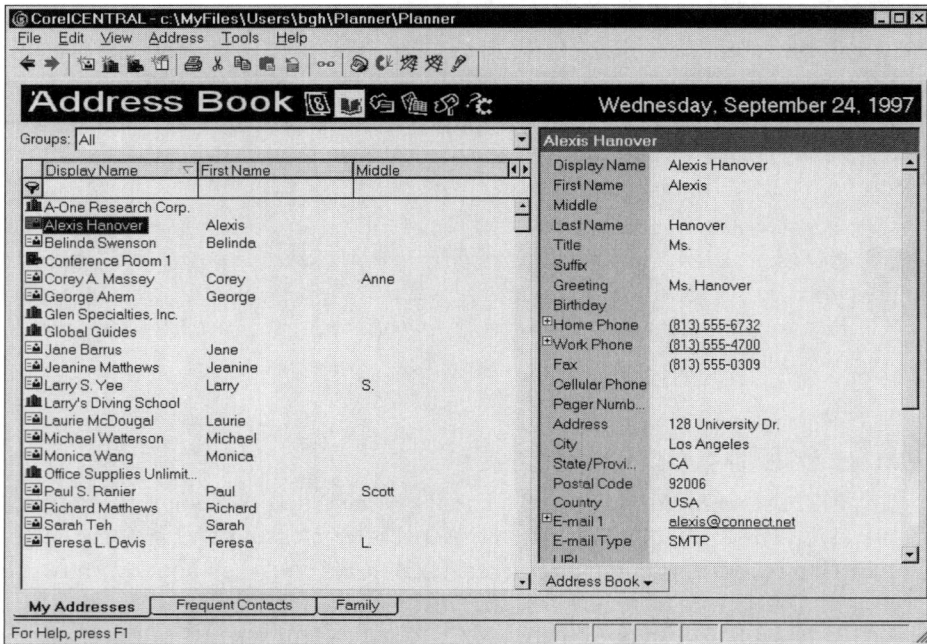

FIGURE 18-11 CorelCENTRAL shares the Address Book information with WordPerfect 8

NOTE: *You can customize which fields display on the left side of the dialog box by clicking the left and right arrows to the right of the field headings. To remove a field from the display, right-click a field heading and deselect it from the list.*

To add a new entry to the Address Book, choose Address | New Person Card, or click the New Person Card button on the toolbar. Type the information in the fields on the right side of the dialog box, pressing TAB after each one. The Address Book in CorelCENTRAL contains four additional standard fields than the WordPerfect 8 Address Book: Middle Name, Title (different from Job Title), Suffix, and Birthday. If you enter information in these fields, you will be able to see and edit it from CorelCENTRAL, but not when you access the Address Book in WordPerfect.

To edit an Address Book entry, select it in the list, and then simply click in the field you want to modify on the right and make changes to the information. If you want to create a custom field, select the field name that you want the new field inserted after, right-click the field name, and choose New Field. Then type a name for the new field. Click in the field area to the right of the field name and type the information for the field.

> **TIP:** *You can send an e-mail message to a person using Netscape by clicking the e-mail address link on the right side of the Address Book. Or you can click a phone number link to use CorelCENTRAL's Phone Dialer and dial the number on your telephone.*

Exporting Address Book Information

When you use the Address Book in WordPerfect 8, you can import information from a variety of different formats, but you can only export it in WordPerfect's ABX format. You can use CorelCENTRAL to export the Address Book information in other formats, such as a merge data file, ASCII text, or vCard (an "electronic business card" format used by applications such as Netscape and Internet Explorer).

> **NOTE:** *You can also use the ADRS2MRG.WCM shipping macro to convert the Address Book information in WordPerfect 8 to a merge data file.*

To export the information in an Address Book, first select the type of entries you want to export from the Groups drop-down list, such as Person. (Because each group type uses different fields, you can only export one type at a time.) Then choose File | Export and choose the format you want, such as WP Merge. Switch to the directory where you want the file created and type a filename in the File Name text box, making sure to keep the file extension (such as DAT or VCF). Choose Save to save the file.

Using the Desktop Application Director

When you install the WordPerfect Suite 8, the Desktop Application Director (DAD) is also installed to give you quick access to all of the suite programs. DAD appears in the notification area on the far right side of the Windows taskbar and includes icons for all of the major programs in the suite:

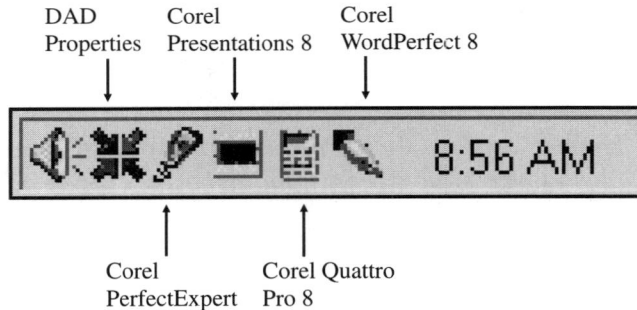

> **NOTE:**   *If you have the Professional edition of Corel WordPerfect Suite 8, DAD also includes icons for CorelCENTRAL, Netscape Communicator, Corel Paradox 8, and Corel WEB.SiteBuilder.*

When you want to use one of the programs in the suite, all you have to do is click the DAD icon once and the program is loaded. DAD is automatically added to your Windows startup group when you install Corel WordPerfect Suite 8, so it's always available when you start your computer. If you want to exit DAD, right-click it and choose Exit DAD. To start DAD again during the same session, from the Windows taskbar choose Start | Corel WordPerfect Suite 8 | Accessories | Corel Desktop Application Director 8.

> **TIP:**   *If you want to remove DAD from your Windows startup group, click the DAD Properties icon. Deselect the Include DAD in Startup Folder icon and choose OK. Or right-click DAD and deselect Display DAD on Startup.*

Adding Programs to DAD

You can easily add other programs that you use frequently to DAD, so you have quick, one-click access to them. To add a new program, click the DAD Properties button on DAD. If the program already has an icon on the Windows desktop, simply click and drag the icon into the DAD Properties dialog box (see Figure 18-12).

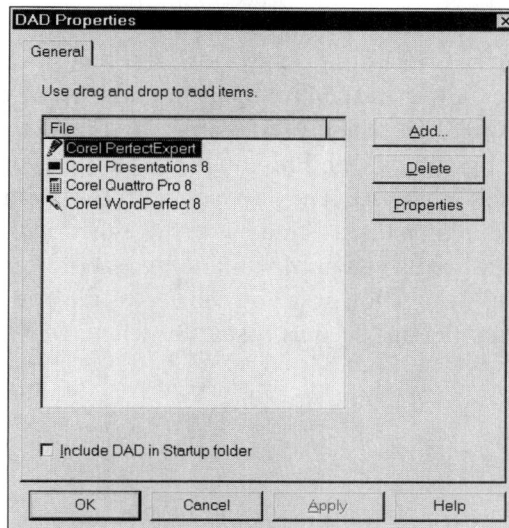

FIGURE 18-12 You can add or remove programs from DAD

Otherwise, choose Add, select the executable file for the program you want to add, and choose Open.

NOTE: *When you add a program to DAD, it's automatically added to the bottom of the list. The only way to change the order of the programs in DAD is to remove them and then add them again in the order you want.*

If you want to remove a program from DAD, select it in the DAD Properties dialog box and choose Delete. If you want to change the properties for a program, such as adding a startup option, select the program in the DAD Properties dialog box and choose Properties. Select the Shortcut tab and make any changes you want, such as adding a startup option to the end of the Target text box. Choose OK when you're finished.

Choose OK to close the DAD Properties dialog box. To run any of the programs, simply click the DAD icon.

Summary

It's no secret that WordPerfect 8 has many powerful features in and of itself. But you can get even *more* power and control by integrating WordPerfect with the other programs in Corel WordPerfect Suite 8. You can share spreadsheet data with Quattro Pro, create charts and graphics with Presentations, manage your contacts with the Address Book in CorelCENTRAL, and have shortcuts to all your favorite programs with DAD. By working hand in hand with the other members of the suite, WordPerfect puts all the tools you need within easy reach.

In Chapter 19, we'll show you how you can access the power of WordPerfect's macro language from programs such as Visual Basic and Delphi.

Chapter

19

Programming with OLE Automation and PerfectScript

WordPerfect's robust macro language is one of its most powerful features—and it's one of the things that sets WordPerfect apart from the competition. Another thing that makes WP 8 high-octane is OLE automation. Through OLE, you can control WordPerfect 8 (as well as Corel's Quattro Pro 8 and Presentations 8) from development environments such as 32-bit Visual Basic and Delphi. And with Corel's OLE Code Inserter (OLECI), you can easily insert any WordPerfect product command in Visual Basic or Delphi to manipulate your WP documents.

For example, say you were writing a Visual Basic (VB) application that needed to get information from a WP 8 document and write it to a database. Through OLECI you could insert the commands to open the WordPerfect document, find the information you need, and then return the information to you—right in your VB code window.

In this chapter we'll show you how to install and use OLECI in your Visual Basic and Delphi code. You'll learn how to insert commands to open, print, save, and close WordPerfect documents, to control the position of the insertion point, and to select document text. You'll even learn how to search for text and WordPerfect codes in your documents. Using the OLE Code Inserter, you can access most of WordPerfect's macro functionality right from your Visual Basic or Delphi program.

What Can OLECI Do for Me?

The OLE Code Inserter helps you insert WP 8 macro commands directly into your Visual Basic or Delphi code. You could use DDE to control WordPerfect through macro commands, but DDE is more cumbersome and sometimes not as stable. You don't actually need the OLE Code Inserter to use WordPerfect macro commands in your VB or Delphi code. You could simply type the commands into your code and they would work (assuming the syntax is correct). However, the advantage of OLECI is that it's fast and easy and you're assured that the syntax of the command is correct.

There are some instances where the macro commands you need to use in VB or Delphi are different than the corresponding command in WordPerfect. For example,

since VB already has its own Print command, you can't use the same command in VB to cause WordPerfect to print. Instead, you need to use the WPPrint command in VB. The Code Inserter automatically inserts the correct name for each command, saving you the time it would take to find the substitute name of the command.

Another benefit to using the OLE Code Inserter is that it inserts the correct values for the macro command parameters. OLE macro commands that require parameters can use only a numeric value for the parameter. For example, if you want to turn off Reveal Codes from your VB or Delphi program, you would need to use "RevealCodes 0" rather than "RevealCodes Off!". OLECI automatically inserts commands with the correct numeric values for each of the command parameters so you don't have to spend time finding them.

It's important to note that although OLECI makes inserting commands easy, it's limited to product commands and system variables. However, since most PerfectScript programming commands (like loops and conditionals) have equivalent commands in VB and Delphi, you shouldn't have any problems. If you ever encounter something that *has* to be done in a macro rather than from your VB or Delphi code, you can simply play a WordPerfect macro from inside your code—easy!

Installing OLECI

The OLE Code Inserter is not installed in the default (or even the custom) WordPerfect Suite 8 installation. However, it is included on the WordPerfect Suite 8 CD as part of the Software Developer's Kit (SDK). To install the SDK, run WP8SDK.EXE from the SDK directory on your WordPerfect Suite 8 CD. By default, the SDK is installed in the \Corel\SDKs\Suite8 directory, but you can specify another directory if you choose.

When you install the SDK, you can select which parts of the SDK you want to include (see Figure 19-1). For controlling WordPerfect from VB or Delphi, it's best to install all of the applications except the Quattro Pro SDK. The OLE Code Inserter is included in the Tools and Utilities option.

Using OLECI

You can use OLECI to insert macro commands in Corel Quattro Pro, Corel Paradox, Borland Delphi 2, Microsoft Excel, and Microsoft Visual Basic (versions 4 and 5). Since most of the concepts related to using OLECI are common to all of these

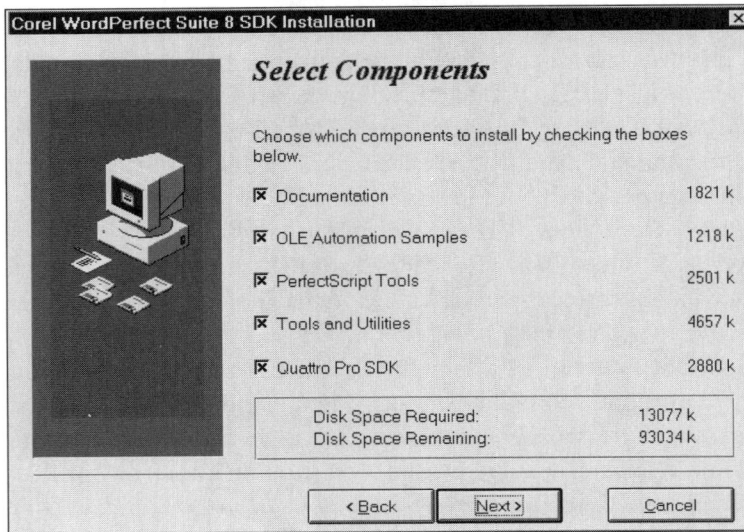

FIGURE 19-1   To use OLECI, you need to install the WP Suite 8 SDK

programs, for simplicity we'll use Visual Basic in this discussion. For specific information on using OLECI in Delphi, see the "Using WP OLE and Persistent Variables in Delphi" section later in this chapter.

Running OLECI

Before starting OLECI, make sure you have a code window open in the program you want to use it with (e.g., Visual Basic or Delphi). OLECI tries to detect which program you're going to use it with and displays an error message if it can't locate a code window for a program it supports.

NOTE: *If OLECI detects that more than one valid code window is open, it displays a prompt asking you which program you want to use. Simply select the option for the program you want and choose OK.*

To start OLECI, choose the Windows Start button, and then choose Programs | Corel SDKs | WP Suite 8 SDK | OLE Automation Command Inserter. When you start OLECI, the OLE Code Inserter dialog box appears. The OLECI dialog box is

very similar to the macro command inserter used in WordPerfect 8 (see Chapter 10 for more information). If you're familiar with WordPerfect's macro command inserter, using OLECI will be a breeze.

By default, the OLECI dialog box displays commands for Corel Presentations. To use OLECI to insert WordPerfect commands, select WordPerfect-EN from the Command Type drop-down list. When you select WordPerfect-EN, the Commands list box displays the available WordPerfect system variables and product commands (see Figure 19-2).

Initializing a WP Object

Before you use OLECI to insert WP macro commands into a function or procedure, you should initialize a WordPerfect object in your program code. You could actually perform this step later, but if you add macro commands and then forget to initialize a WP object, your code won't compile and you'll receive an error message telling you that an object is required.

OLECI makes declaring and initializing an object simple. Just choose the Initialize OLE button in the OLE Code Inserter dialog box.

CAUTION: *Remember that you need to be in a valid code window when you insert commands or initialize a WordPerfect object. If you're not in a code window, an error message appears telling you that you can't use OLECI since you're not in a code window.*

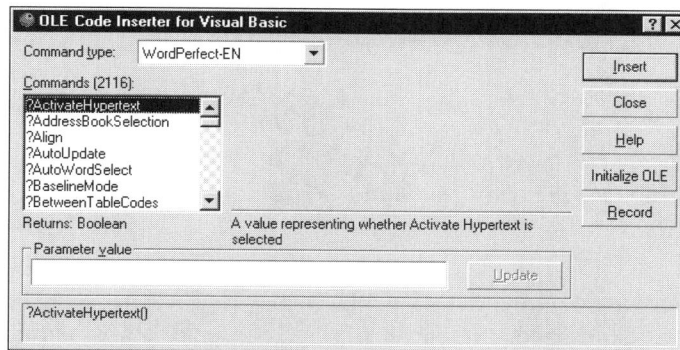

FIGURE 19-2 The OLE Code Inserter dialog box inserts WordPerfect macro commands directly into your VB or Delphi code

When you choose the Initialize OLE button, the Initialize OLE Variables dialog box appears and lets you select the type of variables you want to initialize—Corel WordPerfect, Corel Presentations, or Corel Quattro Pro. Select Corel WordPerfect and choose OK. A message box tells you to place the insertion point where you want your OLE Automation variables declared. It's important to declare the variables before using them in your code, so it's a good idea to declare them at the beginning of the function or procedure where you're going to use the WP OLE commands. Move the insertion point where you want to insert the variables and choose OK. A line is inserted that declares "objWP" as a variant type variable.

TIP: *In Visual Basic you can change the object type from "Variant" to "Object." Where possible, you can keep your code cleaner by avoiding variant type variables, since variant types can accept any data type and therefore require more overhead than declaring a specific type.*

Next, you're prompted to place the insertion point where you want the OLE automation variables initialized. Again, this needs to happen prior to using the automation variables in your code. Usually you can leave the insertion point where it is (right after the line that declares the automation variables) and choose OK. A line of code that initializes your WP variables is inserted.

Inserting WordPerfect Commands

To insert any of the commands included in the OLECI dialog box, select the command you want to insert, and then choose Insert. For example, to insert a command that moves the insertion point to the beginning of the line in the current WordPerfect document, select the PosLineBeg command from the Commands list box and choose Insert.

TIP: *If you know the name (and spelling) of the command you want to insert, you can move to it faster by simply clicking in the Commands list box and then typing the command. OLECI automatically highlights the command as you type.*

The PosLineBeg command is particularly easy to insert because it doesn't have any parameters. Commands that have parameters require a few additional steps to insert. For example, the SwitchDoc command has one parameter—the document you want to switch to. To insert the SwitchDoc command, select it in the Commands

list box. A Parameters list box appears to the right of the Commands list box (see Figure 19-3).

The Parameters list box shows all of the available parameters for the command currently selected in the Commands list box. Insert values for each of the parameters by selecting the parameter, typing a value for it in the Parameter Value text box (such as **1**), and choosing Update. An example of the command as it will be inserted into your code is shown in the lower-left corner of the OLE Code Inserter dialog box. Choose Insert to add the command to your code.

NOTE: *If you're confident that you know all of the parameters for a command, you can insert the command into your code without the parameters and then add them manually. But be careful—if you don't type the commands in the right order, you might be in for a surprise when you run your program.*

Some command parameters require a value defined by WordPerfect, such as the Format parameter of the FileOpen command. When you use the FileOpen command in a WordPerfect macro, you can use "WordPerfect_60!" as the Format parameter, or you can use the predefined numeric equivalent—4. However, OLE only recognizes the numeric values, so in this example, you must use "4" rather than "WordPerfect_60!". Fortunately, OLECI automatically inserts the numeric equivalent for the predefined value.

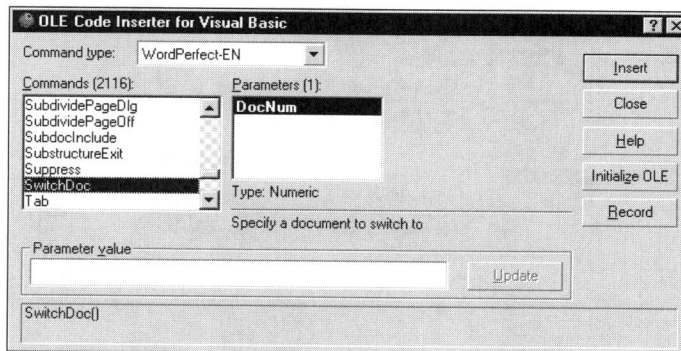

FIGURE 19-3 The Parameters list box shows the available parameters for the selected command

NOTE: *Since the numeric values of predefined parameters aren't documented in WordPerfect's macro help, the best way to ensure you're using the correct values is to use OLECI when inserting macro commands in your code.*

For example, to use the FileOpen command, select FileOpen in the Commands list box, and then select the Filename parameter. Type the filename of the document you want to open in the Parameter Value text box and choose Update. Then select Format in the Parameters list box and double-click the format you want from the Enumerations list box, such as WordPerfect_60! (see Figure 19-4). OLECI automatically inserts the numeric value in the Parameter Value text box. Choose Update to add the parameter, then choose Insert.

CAUTION: *Remember to choose Update after typing each parameter for a command. If you modify a parameter and forget to choose Update, the change you made will be lost when you add the next parameter or choose Insert to insert the command into your code.*

TIP: *After typing a parameter (and before choosing Insert), you can modify that parameter by selecting the parameter in the Parameters list box, changing the value of the parameter in the Parameter Value text box, and then choosing Update. Also, OLECI automatically adds delimiters for each of a command's parameters, so you can skip over any parameters that aren't necessary.*

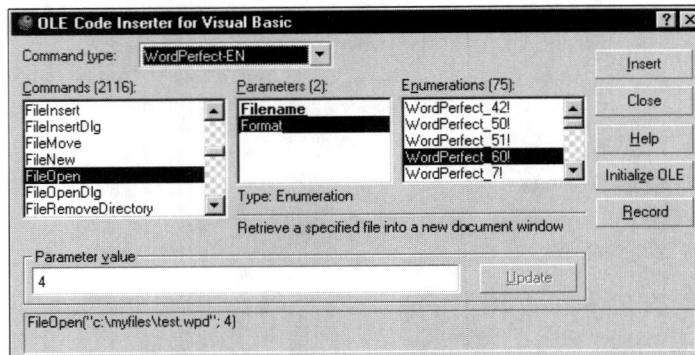

FIGURE 19-4   When you select a predefined parameter value, OLECI automatically converts it to the numeric equivalent

Recording Macro Commands

Another great tool that OLECI offers is the ability to record macro commands and insert them into your code. This can save a considerable amount of time and mouse clicks. In some cases, recording commands is not only helpful, it's necessary (such as when searching for codes in WordPerfect documents).

To record commands into your code, place the insertion point where you want the commands inserted and choose Record in the OLE Code Inserter dialog box.

NOTE: *When you click in the code window, the OLE Code Inserter dialog box may be hidden behind the code window. You can get back to it by clicking the OLE Code Inserter button on the Windows taskbar or by pressing ALT-TAB until the OLE Code Inserter dialog box appears.*

When you choose Record, a small dialog with Pause, Stop, and Cancel buttons appears at the top left corner of your screen. If you're not already in a WordPerfect document window, go to WordPerfect.

NOTE: *After choosing Record, you might not be able to access the Windows taskbar. To enable the Windows taskbar, simply click in the code window to reestablish the focus, move the mouse pointer to the taskbar area, and the taskbar appears.*

Until you choose Pause or Stop, the tokens for any actions you perform in WordPerfect are recorded for insertion into your program code. When you're finished, choose Stop to quit recording. The focus returns to your code window and the commands for the recorded actions are automatically inserted at the insertion point.

If you made any mistakes while recording, you can correct the errors by deleting the commands that were accidentally recorded.

Finishing Your Commands

When you run WordPerfect macro commands through OLE automation, WordPerfect treats the commands as if an actual WordPerfect macro were playing.

To let WordPerfect know that you're finished sending macro commands, you need to include an objWP.Quit command at the end of the commands. (If the variable you declared at the top of the function or procedure is something other than objWP, replace objWP with the name of your variable.)

CAUTION: *Failing to finish your commands with the objWP.Quit command will leave WordPerfect in Macro Play mode with no easy way (short of ending your WordPerfect task) of getting out. Always end your commands with objWP.Quit.*

NOTE: *After inserting the objWP.Quit command, you can still insert other macro commands later in your function or procedure without having to redeclare and reinitialize the automation variables. However, be sure to include another objWP.Quit command at the end of any additional macro commands.*

Determining the Success of the OLE Command

Once you've inserted WordPerfect commands in your code, it's a good idea to add a little more programming to determine if the commands were successful. For example, if the user has a document open and your application sends a FileNew command, you can have your application verify that the FileNew command worked before sending additional commands to WordPerfect. Otherwise, you could end up accidentally modifying the user's document.

The best way to determine the success of a WordPerfect command is to call the command as a function so that it returns a value. To do this, declare a variant-type variable at the top of the function or procedure where you're using the WP commands. Then, after using OLECI to insert a WordPerfect command, go to the beginning of the WP command and insert **ReturnVal =** (where ReturnVal is your variable name). Also, when calling the WP command as a function, the parameter portion of the command must be in parentheses. For example, if you use OLECI to insert a FileOpen command, a command such as the following is inserted:

```
objWP.FileOpen "c:\myfiles\test.wpd", 4
```

After adding the commands to return the success or failure of the WP macro command, the code would look like this:

```
Dim ReturnVal
ReturnVal = objWP.FileOpen("c:\myfiles\test.wpd", 4)
```

A return value of True indicates that the command was successful, while a return value of False indicates that the command failed.

> **TIP:** *When you interact with WordPerfect through OLE, you don't need to worry about whether WordPerfect is currently running. If a current session of WP isn't detected, WordPerfect is automatically started when your program encounters an OLE macro command.*

> **NOTE:** *For additional information on using OLECI, see the SDK documentation. You can find it by choosing Start on the Windows taskbar, and then choosing Programs | Corel SDKs | WP Suite 8 SDK | SDK Documentation.*

Getting System Variables

WordPerfect's system variables give you information about the current state of WordPerfect, such as the current font, document number, or printer port. You can see a list of the 433 available system variables in the Commands list box of the OLE Code Inserter dialog box (the system variables are the commands at the top of the list that start with a question mark).

Getting the value of a system variable is similar to getting the return value of other commands, as explained in the "Determining the Success of the OLE Command" section earlier. First, declare a string or integer type variable, depending on the type of information returned by the system variable.

> **TIP:** *If you're not sure what type of information will be returned in the system variable, declare it as a string type. If it turns out that a numeric value was returned, you can evaluate it as a string or convert it back to a numeric value.*

Next, set the variable equal to the system variable command. For example, you could use the following commands to find out which page the insertion point is on in the current WordPerfect document:

```
Dim iSysVar As Integer
iSysVar = objWP.EnvPage
```

After executing these commands, you can check the value of iSysVar to find the current page number.

Troubleshooting WP OLE Command Errors

Corel programmed WordPerfect's OLE automation to make it as error-proof as possible. That doesn't mean that a command *can't* fail; after all, if you mistype a command or exclude a necessary parameter, you can make any command fail. What it does mean is that if a syntactically correct command executes and fails, it doesn't stop the application that executed it. In fact, unless you specifically check the return value of each WordPerfect command, your program can't tell whether a command was successful and it will continue regardless of the success or failure of the command.

There are two main types of errors you can encounter when using WP OLE automation: run-time errors and logic errors. Run-time errors result from incorrect syntax, such as when your program encounters a command that it doesn't recognize. For example, to close the current document window without saving changes, you'd use the "objWP.CloseNoSave 0" command. If you were to accidentally type "objWP.CloseNoSav 0" (notice that the "e" is missing in "save"), your program would return an error message telling you that it doesn't recognize the command.

Logic errors result from failure to account for unexpected conditions. For example, if you use the "objWP.SubstructureExit" command, the command would fail if the insertion point isn't currently in a substructure (such as a header or footer).

Run-time Errors

As previously mentioned, run-time errors result from incorrect syntax. The best way to avoid these errors is to use OLECI to insert or record your WP OLE commands. OLECI automatically inserts the correct spelling and parameters, so you don't need to worry about the syntax. When you encounter run-time errors, you can do one of two things: delete the command that's causing the error and reinsert it using OLECI,

or check the command for errors and fix the problem manually. Here are some things to consider when checking the syntax of your commands:

- Is the command spelled correctly? Verify that there are no spelling errors anywhere on the command line. With the exception of text within quotes, WP OLE commands are not case sensitive, so don't worry about capitalization when checking the spelling.

- Are the command's parameters correct? Remember that WP OLE command parameters are comma delimited (as opposed to macro commands in WordPerfect, which are semicolon delimited). If the WP OLE command requires parameters, make sure that you're using the numeric values for the parameters and that you've included values for all required parameters.

- Are you calling the command as a function? If so, then be sure that the command's parameters are enclosed in parentheses. For example, to open a document named "test.wpd" in WordPerfect, the command is **objWP.FileOpen "c:\myfiles\test.wpd"**. If you want to return the success of the command to a variable, the same command would look like this: **RetVal = objWP.FileOpen("c:\myfiles\test.wpd")**. Notice that in the second instance, the parameter is in parentheses.

NOTE: *Commands that don't have any parameters don't need parentheses—even when being called as a function.*

- Did you include the WordPerfect object? Without the WordPerfect object portion of the command (usually "objWP"), the command can't perform an action. Leaving out the WordPerfect object won't generate an error message, but it will keep your command from executing properly.

Logic Errors

Logic errors are mistakes that cause an incorrect result or that keep your program from running the way you expect. For example, a mistake that gives an incorrect result is using the objWP.FileOpen command to open a file that doesn't exist. Unless you call the objWP.FileOpen command as a function and evaluate the return value, your program can't tell whether the command was successful—and simply continues to run. Mistakenly assuming that the command was successful often leads to the second type of logic error, where your program doesn't run as you expect it to. If the objWP.FileOpen command fails and you don't catch it, you could end up making changes to a blank screen, or worse, you could make changes to a document the user happened to have open.

When dealing with WordPerfect OLE automation, an ounce of prevention is worth a pound of cure. The best way to solve a logic problem is to avoid the problem altogether. You should account for as many potential problems as possible when writing your code. For example, after assigning the currently selected text to a variable, check the variable to be sure it isn't empty. If no text is selected in WordPerfect, an empty string is returned when you use the objWP.EnvSelectedText command. Here are some ways to avoid logic errors:

- Use return values to determine whether the command succeeds. Calling a command as a function returns the success or failure of the command. By calling each command as a function and evaluating the return value, you can determine whether the command was successful and account for instances where the command fails. See the section "Determining the Success of the OLE Command" earlier in the chapter for more information.

- Use system variables to ascertain WordPerfect conditions. By referring to system variables, you can make sure that conditions are correct in a WordPerfect document before executing a WP OLE command in your program. For example, it's probably a good idea to verify that the insertion point is in a table before trying to change the row height. For more information, see the section "Getting System Variables" earlier in the chapter.

If your WP OLE commands don't produce the results you expect even after accounting for potential problems, the best way to determine the cause of the problem is to step through your code and check the state of WordPerfect after each WP OLE command. To check the state of WordPerfect, you need to turn the display on in your program (objWP.Display 1), or quit the macro after each WP OLE command (objWP.Quit).

Tips on Using Common Commands

For the most part, using WP OLE commands in your program is as easy as writing a regular WP macro. You just need to remember a few new rules, like using return values and comma delimiting. However, there are a few commands that require a little more explanation. The following are some hints and things to watch out for.

Selecting a Printer

When selecting a printer through WP OLE commands, you must be sure that the printer name you specify exactly matches the name as it appears in the Current Printer list in the Print dialog box. In this case, capitalization and spaces *do* matter. If the printer name you specify isn't found in the list, the default Windows printer is selected instead.

> **NOTE:**   *It's probably a good idea to use the ?CurrentPrinterPort system variable after changing the printer to verify that the correct printer was chosen.*

Editing a Substructure

Attempting to edit a substructure (such as a header or footer) that doesn't exist can throw off your code. It's always a good idea to check for the existence of a substructure before trying to edit it. The following code shows an example of how to check for a substructure and account for the possibility that it doesn't exist. In this example, if Header A doesn't exist, then it is created.

```
If objWP.EnvHeaderAOccur = 0 Then
    RetVal = objWP.HeaderA(1) '1 = Create
Else
    RetVal = objWP.HeaderA(2) '2 = Edit
End If
```

Searching for Text

If you know how to perform a search in a WP macro, then searching a WP document with WP OLE commands should be no problem. The problem you need to watch out for is providing too little information for the search.

When you perform a search in WP, you can specify several parameters. These include specifying the text to search for, where to position the insertion point when a match is found, whether the search is case sensitive, whether to find whole words only, whether to search in selected text only, and whether to search forward or backward from the insertion point. If you leave any of these commands out of your search routine, WordPerfect uses the settings that were selected the last time a search was performed.

Unless you're sure that the settings used in the last search are the same as the ones you want to use in a current search, it's a good idea to set each of the parameters for every new search. This means that every search routine should include the following commands: objWP.SearchString, objWP.SearchCaseSensitive, objWP.SearchFindWholeWordsOnly, and a command that tells WP where to place the insertion point when a match is found (objWP.MatchPositionBefore, objWP. MatchPositionAfter, objWP.MatchSelection, or objWP.MatchExtendSelection). Also, if you want the search to begin at the top of the document rather than at the location of the insertion point, you need to include the objWP.PosDocVeryTop command in your code (prior to the objWP.SearchNext command).

NOTE: *The objWP.MatchExtendSelection command lets you select text and codes between the insertion point and the item you're searching for. However, you can't use this command to select text and codes from the insertion point to a specific bookmark. To get around this, see the Power Tip "Selecting with Bookmarks."*

The following code shows the commands used for searching the word "Right." Note that the search is case sensitive and it positions the insertion point immediately after the word that is found.

```
objWP.SearchString "Right"
objWP.SearchCaseSensitive 1   '1 = case sensitive
objWP.SearchFindWholeWordsOnly 1   'Find "Right", not "Alright"
objWP.MatchPositionAfter
objWP.SearchNext 1   '1 = extended search
objWP.Quit
```

Probably the quickest way to insert WP OLE search commands into your code is to record the search. For specific steps on how to record a search, see the "How to Record a Search" section.

If you need to determine whether the search was successful, you can call the objWP.SearchNext or objWP.SearchPrevious command as a function. If the return value is True, the item you searched for was found. If the return value is False, the item wasn't found.

Power Tip... Selecting with Bookmarks

By using the MatchExtendSelection () command with WordPerfect's Find feature, it's easy to select text and codes between the insertion point and the item you're searching for. WordPerfect's Find feature lets you search for Bookmark codes, but it doesn't let you search your document for a *specific* bookmark. So you can't use the Find feature to select text and codes from the insertion point to a bookmark.

The solution to this problem is actually even easier than using the Find feature. Just turn Select on in your code (**objWP.SelectOn 1**), and then use the BookmarkFind command to find your bookmark. As long as the bookmark you specify exists, the text and codes between the insertion point and the bookmark are selected.

CAUTION: *If you turn display on in your code prior to performing a search, and the macro performs a search that fails, a message box appears notifying the user that the search failed. When this happens, the macro stops until the user chooses OK. If you don't want the macro to stop and wait for user input when a search fails, be sure to turn display off (objWP.Display 0) before performing a search. Display is off by default, so if you haven't turned display on, you don't need to worry about turning display off.*

How to... Record a Search

Before recording a search, prepare by making sure that WordPerfect is open and that it has some text in the current document window. After preparing for the search, place your insertion point where you want the search commands inserted in your program code, and then display the OLE Code Inserter dialog box. Follow these steps to record the search:

1. Choose Record in the OLECI dialog box.

2. Change to the WordPerfect document window. (Remember that you might need to click in the code window to access the Windows taskbar.)

How to...   **Record a Search**
(continued)

3. In WordPerfect, choose Edit | Find and Replace to display the Find and Replace dialog box. You might need to move the OLE Code Inserter dialog box to the right side of the screen if it's blocking the Edit pull-down menu.

4. Set any search parameters that you want to record.

5. Choose Find. If the Not Found message appears, choose OK.

6. Choose Stop in the OLE Code Inserter dialog box. When you do this, focus returns to your code window and the search commands are inserted at the insertion point.

7. Make sure the insertion point is on the line following the recorded search commands. The command to actually perform the search isn't included in the recorded commands, so you need to insert it. To perform an extended search from the insertion point to the end of the document, type **objWP.SearchNext 1** (replace the "1" with "0" if you want to perform a regular instead of an extended search). To search backward from the insertion point to the beginning of the document, type **objWP.SearchPrevious 1** instead.

8. If you aren't going to use any other WP OLE commands in the current function or procedure, type **objWP.Quit** to end the OLE commands.

If the text you want to search for is contained in a variable, you can replace the text you recorded (including the quotes) with the variable name.

Searching for Codes

The process of searching for codes is the same as searching for text. The only difference is that when specifying the search string, you need to use the numeric value of the code you want to search for. For example, the numeric value of the Bold On code is 368. Therefore, the following command is used to search for the Bold On code:

```
objWP.SearchString "~~368~~~"
```

When searching for codes, you need to include the numeric value and the tildes (~) within quotes. Also, note that the numeric value is preceded by two tildes and followed by three tildes. The two tildes before the numeric value are the same for any code, but the number of tildes following the numeric value reflects the number of digits in the numeric value. For example, if the numeric value consists of one digit, you should include only one tilde after it. In the preceding example, the numeric value for Bold On (368) consists of three digits and therefore requires three tildes following the numeric value.

Finding the Numeric Value

The easiest way to find the numeric value for a code you want to search for is to use Appendix A of this book. Appendix A lists all of WordPerfect's searchable codes in alphabetical order with their corresponding numeric values. When using a value from Appendix A with the objWP.SearchString command, remember that you need to precede the value with a double quote and two tildes and then follow the value with one, two, or three tildes (depending on the number of digits in the value) and another double quote.

Another way to find the numeric value of a code is to record a WordPerfect search for that code. (For information on how to record a search, see the "How to Record a Search" section earlier in this chapter.) After recording the search, you'll likely need to edit the obj.SearchString command that was inserted. First, make sure that the number of tildes inserted is correct. By default, two tildes are inserted following the value, so if the numeric value of the code is one or three digits long, you'll need to delete or add a tilde.

Next, make sure that the numeric value inserted for the code is correct. If the number that was recorded is less than 256, then it's fine. If the number is greater than 255, you need to subtract 2 from the number. For example, if you record a search for a Bold On code, 370 is inserted as the numeric value. However, to get the correct numeric value for Bold On, you need to subtract 2 from 370 and replace the value with 368. If you have a question about the return value for a certain code, refer to Appendix A at the end of this book.

Passing Information to and from WP

When you're developing applications that interact with WordPerfect, you will often need to pass information to WordPerfect or gather information from WordPerfect. In this section, you'll learn some different ways you can pass information between WP and your application.

Using the Windows Clipboard

Probably the easiest way to pass information between WP and your program is to use the Windows Clipboard. The Clipboard is relatively fast and the objWP.EditCut, objWP.EditCopy, and objWP.EditPaste commands make it easy to get information in WP to and from the Clipboard. Also, Visual Basic and Delphi include commands that make it easy to access the Clipboard.

The biggest drawback to using the Clipboard to pass information is the fact that it is used so frequently. When you write to the Clipboard, you risk overwriting something that the user needs stored. If you're sure that the user doesn't need the Clipboard contents, this tool provides an easy way to pass information. If there's a possibility that the user could be storing something that will be needed later, you should avoid passing information through the Clipboard.

Using the Registry

Writing to the Windows registry is another way to pass information between your program and WordPerfect. WP 8 includes several macro commands that make it easy to write to the registry (see Chapter 11 for information on using macro commands to write to the Windows registry). Writing to the registry is useful if you want to hide information from the user. Although it's possible for users to see the registry if they know how to edit it, it's unlikely that they'll see the information you're storing. Also, it's unlikely that a user will accidentally delete the registry, so you can depend on the information being available in future sessions of your application.

As with the Windows Clipboard, there are some things to look out for when writing to the registry. First, Microsoft recommends that you don't write more than 2,048 bytes to a single registry entry. If the text you need to pass between programs is larger than 2,048 bytes (approximately half of an 8.5" x 11" page with a 12 point font), or if you don't know how much text is going to be passed, it's probably best to avoid writing to the registry.

Also, to avoid cluttering up the registry, it's best to set a single key that you write to rather than creating a different one each time you need to pass information. If possible, make sure your applications clean up after themselves by deleting values from the registry when they're no longer needed. Many Windows applications use the registry, so the smaller the registry is, the faster Windows can access it.

CAUTION: *Writing to the registry is not for the faint of heart. The registry is somewhat fragile in that accidentally changing the wrong item can cause Windows programs to fail or to work incorrectly. The authors of this book accept no responsibility for systems that crash after modifying the registry.*

Using Text Files

Another way of passing information from WordPerfect to your application is to save the information in a text file. This method is especially useful if you need to pass large blocks of information. The only limitation on the size of the file is the space available on your hard disk. However, because text files are not well structured and are accessed from the hard disk rather than from memory, creating text files is not as fast as writing to the Clipboard or the registry.

Using INI Files

Like text files, passing information through an INI file requires your program to access files on the hard disk. But because INI files are structured, your program can locate and gather the information it needs faster and easier. Delphi includes commands that take advantage of the structure used to read and write INI files, so using INI files is especially easy in Delphi. In Visual Basic you can use the WritePrivateProfileString and GetPrivateProfileString Windows API commands to communicate through an INI file.

Using Persistent Variables

With persistent variables, you can assign information to a WordPerfect variable that you can later access in your VB or Delphi program. The amount of information a persistent variable can hold depends on the amount of available memory. Unfortunately, you can't create or access persistent variables through WP OLE automation. Instead, you need to use PerfectFit commands.

Preparing PerfectFit

To use PerfectFit commands to create or access persistent variables, you first need to assign an object reference to a variable. To do this, at the beginning of the function or procedure where you want to reference the persistent variable, type the following command: **Set PSObj = CreateObject("PerfectFit.PerfectScript")**.

NOTE: *For instructions on creating persistent variables in Delphi, see the "Using WP OLE and Persistent Variables in Delphi" section later in this chapter.*

After assigning the object, you can create, access, edit, or delete a persistent variable anywhere in the current function or procedure.

TIP: *If you need to create or access system variables in multiple functions or procedures, you can assign the object reference in the general declarations area of your form. Once the object is declared in the general declarations area, it's available to all functions and procedures in that form.*

Creating a Persistent Variable

To create a persistent variable, use the PSObj.VariableName command to specify the variable name. Then set the value of the variable using the PSObj. SetPerfectScriptVariable command. The following example shows how to assign the text "This is sample text" to a persistent variable named "vTest":

```
PSObj.VariableName = "vTest"
PSObj.SetPerfectScriptVariable "This is sample text"
```

TIP: *You can assign only 512 characters to a PerfectFit variable when you assign the variable to a literal string of text (such as "This is sample text"). However, if you select text in your WordPerfect document and then assign the selected text to the persistent variable, you can assign much more than 512 characters.*

Getting the Value of a Persistent Variable

To find the value of a persistent variable, you must first specify the name of the variable using the PSObj.VariableName command. Then use the PSObj.

GetPerfectScriptVariable command to access the value of the persistent variable. The following example assigns the value of a persistent variable named "vTest" to a VB edit box named txtVarValue:

```
PSObj.VariableName = "vTest"
txtVarValue.Text = PSObj.GetPerfectScriptVariable
```

NOTE: *When you use PerfectFit to access persistent variables, you don't need to end your PerfectFit commands with a Quit command like you do in WP OLE.*

Checking the Existence of a Persistent Variable

Before you can find out whether a persistent variable exists, you must specify the name of the variable by using the PSObj.VariableName command. Then use the PSObj.PerfectScriptVariableExists command to determine the existence of the variable. The following example checks to see if variable vTest exists and then displays a message box that displays the value of vTest or tells the user that vTest doesn't exist:

```
PSObj.VariableName = "vTest"
If PSObj.PerfectScriptVariableExists Then
    MsgBox "vTest = " & PSObj.GetPerfectScriptVariable
Else
    MsgBox "vTest doesn't exist."
EndIf
```

Discarding Persistent Variables

Persistent variables remain in memory until they're discarded or until the PerfectFit Macro Facility closes (which is often when the computer is shut down). Leaving a persistent variable in memory can cause a conflict if you try to create a variable with the same name later. Also, if you don't need the persistent variable any longer and you leave it in memory, it ties up memory that could be used elsewhere.

To discard a persistent variable, specify the variable that you want to discard (using the PSObj.VariableName command), and then use the PSObj.

DiscardPerfectScriptVariable command. The following example checks to see whether a persistent variable named vTest exists, and discards it if it does:

```
PSObj.VariableName = "vTest"
If PSObj.PerfectScriptVariableExists Then
   PSObj.DiscardPerfectScriptVariable
EndIf
```

NOTE: *Once you specify the name of a persistent variable, all of the PerfectFit commands in the current function or procedure refer to that persistent variable until a different name is specified using the PSObj. VariableName command.*

TIP: *The WordPerfect 8 SDK includes the code for a sample Visual Basic program that shows how to use persistent variables. The program is named PFAUTO.VBP and is located in the Corel\SDK\Suite8\OLEAuto\Vb\ PFAuto directory. You must install the SDK as explained earlier in this chapter to use this file.*

Using WP OLE and Persistent Variables in Delphi

Using OLECI in Delphi 2 is similar to using it in Visual Basic, so most of the instructions given in this chapter apply. However, there are a few differences that you'll need to be aware of in order to use WP OLE commands in Delphi.

Initializing OLE Automation Variables

In Delphi you can use the OLE Code Inserter to insert the commands that initialize the WP OLE automation. The first command that's inserted when you choose the Initialize OLE button in the OLECI dialog box declares the "objWP" object. The scope of the object depends on where this command is inserted. If you need to use WP OLE commands in more than one procedure or function in the current unit, it should be declared with the unit information (usually after the Uses clause). If you're going to use WP OLE commands in only one function or procedure, you can insert the declaration before the procedure's "begin" command.

The second command that's inserted assigns the WP OLE object to "objWP." This command needs to be inserted after the "begin" command in the function or procedure and before any WP OLE commands.

Last, you're reminded to add OLEAUTO to your Uses statement for the current project. If you don't do this, you'll get an Undeclared Identifier error message when you compile your code.

The following example shows Delphi code for a procedure that assigns the name of the current document to a variable named "sName":

```
procedure TForm1.bttnGetNameClick(Sender: TObject);
Var
sName : String;
objWP : Variant;
begin
     objWP := CreateOleObject( 'WordPerfect.PerfectScript');
     sName := objWP.EnvName;
     objWP.Quit;
end;
```

CAUTION: *As with Visual Basic, you must finish your WP OLE commands with the objWP.Quit command. If you forget to quit the WP OLE automation, WordPerfect will think that a macro is still playing—even after your application has finished.*

Creating and Accessing Persistent Variables

The commands used for creating and accessing persistent variables in Delphi are similar to the commands used in VB, but again there are a few differences. First, you need to include OLEAUTO in the Uses clause of the unit where you're referencing the persistent variables. Next, you need to declare a variable to reference the PerfectFit object by typing **PSObj : Variant;** in the Var section of the unit. Also, you need to assign the variable you declared to the PerfectFit object by typing **PSObj := CreateOLEObject('PerfectFit.PerfectScript');** in the FormCreate procedure in your unit. (You could declare and assign the variable to the PerfectFit object in the function or procedure where you're referencing the persistent variable, but the scope would be limited to that function or procedure.)

The VariableName, SetPerfectScriptVariable, GetPerfectScriptVariable, PerfectScriptVariableExists, and DiscardPerfectScriptVariable commands all work the same in Delphi as they do in Visual Basic (see the "Using Persistent Variables" section for more information on using these commands). Note that when using the SetPerfectScriptVariable command in Delphi, the value you're setting the variable to needs to be in parentheses after the command. For example, the code to assign the text "This is sample text" to a persistent variable named vTest looks like this:

```
PSObj.VariableName := 'vTest';
PSObj.SetPerfectScriptVariable('This is sample text');
```

On the CD ▸▸▸ Persistent Variables in Delphi

The WordPerfect 8 SDK includes a sample VB program that shows how to use persistent variables in Visual Basic. This book's companion CD includes a similar application that shows how to use persistent variables in Delphi. Both the executable file and the code are included. The executable is named PERSISTVARS.EXE. The program file for the code is named PERSISTVARS.DPR.

To use PERSISTVARS.EXE, from the Windows taskbar choose Start | Run and run PERSISTVARS.EXE. The Persistent Variables Sample Application dialog box appears with names and values already included in the Names and Values edit boxes. The Names edit boxes show the names of persistent variables that will be created when you choose Set Variables; the Values edit boxes show the values that will be assigned to the variables in the Names edit boxes. Notice that there are three types of variables that will be assigned: String, Integer, and Double.

When you choose the Set Variables button, the values of each persistent variable is shown in the Results edit boxes. After setting the persistent variables, choose Exists? to verify that the persistent variables exist. The checkboxes beneath the Exists? button show which variables exist.

To discard the persistent variables, choose the Discard Vars button. To show that the variables have been discarded, the Discard checkbox associated with each persistent variable is selected. Now if you choose Exists?, the checkboxes should be deselected.

Choose Exit to exit the program.

Summary

Through OLE automation, you can take advantage of much of WordPerfect's macro functionality right from inside your Visual Basic or Delphi program. The OLE Command Inserter helps you insert WordPerfect commands in your VB or Delphi code and ensures that the syntax and parameter values for each command are correct. In addition, you can pass information between WordPerfect and VB or Delphi using a variety of different techniques, including persistent variables, which utilize PerfectScript programming.

In Chapter 20, you'll learn about some of the tools included with WordPerfect Suite 8 that aren't installed by default, but can help you create and publish WordPerfect documents even faster and easier than before.

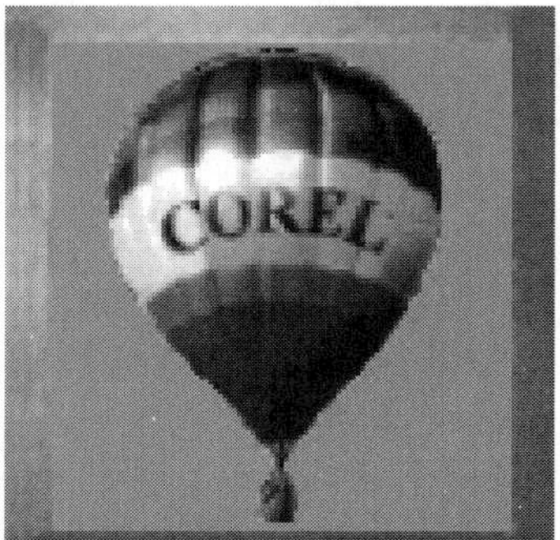
COREL

19

Chapter
20

Bonus Tools in WordPerfect Suite 8

Want to know a secret? There's a whole lot more to Corel's WordPerfect Suite 8 than WordPerfect, Quattro Pro, and Presentations. Corel loaded up the CD with lots of bonus tools and utilities that can help you get your work done faster and easier. But since these tools aren't installed during a typical installation, many people don't even know they're available.

In this chapter, we'll highlight some of the useful tools on the WordPerfect Suite 8 CD. You'll learn about utilities for working with fonts and graphics, such as Bitstream Font Navigator, and Corel Photo House. We'll show you how tools such as Quick View Plus and Envoy can help you view different types of files. You'll learn how to get more out of the Internet with Corel Barista and Netscape Conference. And finally, we'll point out some of the other helpful utilities on the CD, such as the Spell Utility and the additional text conversions.

NOTE: *Unfortunately, we don't have the space here to cover each of these applications in depth. Instead, we'll give you an overview of each utility so you can decide which tools would best meet your needs.*

Installing the Bonus Tools

Most of the bonus tools can be installed through a custom installation of the WordPerfect Suite 8 CD. The two exceptions are the Quick View Plus utility and the Software Developer's Kit (SDK), which each have a separate installation. For a list of all the tools and features that *aren't* installed during a typical installation of WordPerfect Suite 8, see the "Tools and Utilities Not Installed by Default" Quick Reference section.

TIP: *Some of the bonus applications, such as CorelMEMO and the Envoy Viewer, can be used directly from the CD without installing them to your hard drive. In addition, the extra macros, graphics, sounds, movies, fonts, and PerfectExpert projects can also be accessed directly from the CD, saving space on your hard drive.*

Follow these basic steps to perform a custom installation of WordPerfect Suite 8:

1. Place the WordPerfect Suite 8 CD in your CD-ROM drive (if it isn't already there). If the initial menu appears, choose Corel WordPerfect Suite Setup. Otherwise, from the Windows taskbar, choose Start | Corel WordPerfect Suite 8 | Setup & Notes | Corel WordPerfect Suite 8 Setup.

2. Follow the prompts until you see the Installation Type dialog box. Select Custom and choose Next.

3. Make sure the installation path is correct and choose Next.

4. To quickly clear all the selection options, choose Selection Options, select Deselect All, and choose OK.

5. Select the checkbox next to the tool or feature you want to install, such as Bitstream Font Navigator 2.0. To install many of the bonus tools and features, you need to select the main option or category in the list, such as WordPerfect 8 or Accessories (*don't* select the checkbox next to it), and then choose Components until you find the item you want. Once you've located the individual option you want to install, select the checkbox next to it. The sections later in this chapter will give specific instructions for locating each tool mentioned.

6. When you've selected all the options you want, choose Next and continue with the installation.

Tools for Fonts and Graphics

Using different fonts and graphics in your documents is already a snap with the features in WordPerfect 8, but the process gets even easier with the tools on the WP Suite 8 CD. For example, you can manage your fonts more efficiently with Bitstream Font Navigator, and edit bitmapped images and scanned photos with Corel Photo House.

TIP: *The Corel WordPerfect Suite 8 CD contains over 10,000 graphics images. Many of the images can be accessed through the Scrapbook feature, and other images can be found in the \Corel\Suite8\Graphics directory on the CD. In addition, you'll find over 200 photos in the \Photos directory on the CD. See Chapter 7 for more information on inserting and using graphics in your documents.*

Quick Reference ▶▶▶ Tools and Utilities Not Installed by Default

During a typical installation of Corel's WordPerfect Suite 8, several tools and utilities are not installed. These additional options can be installed by performing a custom installation as explained in the "Installing the Bonus Tools" section. In addition, some of the extra files, such as the macros, graphics, sounds, movies, fonts, and PerfectExpert projects, can be used directly from the CD, saving space on your hard drive. The following is a list of all the features not installed during a typical installation.

WordPerfect 8

WordPerfect Macro Help	Information on creating and using WordPerfect macros (see Chapter 10)
Some of the WordPerfect Macros	Precreated macros to automate tasks (see Chapter 10)
Java Applet Support	Files to insert and run Java applets in Web documents (see Chapter 14)
Some of the PerfectExpert Projects	Precreated document formats (see Chapter 1)

Quattro Pro 8

Database Desktop	Files to view, edit, query, and link to external databases from Quattro Pro
Help files for Database Desktop and Data Modeling Desktop	Information for using external databases
Mapping	Files to create chart maps (see Chapter 18)
Some of the PerfectExpert Projects	Precreated spreadsheet formats
Quick Template Builder	Files that let you create custom Quattro Pro templates

Presentations 8

Some of the Presentations Macros	Precreated macros to automate tasks
Some of the Slide Show Masters	Predefined slide show master files

Presentations 8

Presentations Macro Help	Information for creating Presentations macros
PerfectExpert Projects	Precreated slide show formats
Movie Clips	AVI video clips (see Chapter 17)
Some of the Import File Filters	Files to read formats such as Harvard Graphics
Sound Files	WAV and MIDI music and sound effects (see Chapter 17)
Graphicsland Program	Lets you send Presentations slide shows to Graphicsland Slide Service and create 35mm slides
CorelMEMO	Creates an electronic bitmapped notepad
Scanner Driver	Scanner drivers for TWAIN support

CorelCENTRAL

Some of the Card Files	Predefined card files to keep track of various categories
Netscape Conference	Files to let you hold "real-time" conferences online (see "Netscape Conference" in this chapter

Envoy 7

Envoy 7 Viewer	Files to view any Envoy document (see "Envoy 7 Viewer" in this chapter)
Envoy Help*	Information for using Envoy
Envoy Samples*	Sample Envoy documents
Viewer Extensions*	Files to let you use Web links, Help Online, and right-click mouse support
Envoy 7 Driver**	Files to create (publish) Envoy files

20

Other Programs & Utilities

Corel Photo House*	Program to create and edit bitmapped images (see "Corel Photo House" in this chapter)
Corel Time Line**	Project management program
Bitstream Font Navigator 2.0	Font manager program (see "Bitstream Font Navigator" in this chapter)
Corel WordPerfect SGML	Files to create SGML-coded documents
Some of the TrueType fonts	Font files
Reference Center User Guides	Help files in Envoy format for the WordPerfect Suite 8 products (see "Envoy 7 Viewer" in this chapter)
Some of the Text Conversions	Files to convert document formats (see "File Format Conversions" in this chapter)
Some of the Graphics Conversions	Files to convert graphics formats (see "Tools for Fonts and Graphics" in this chapter)
Additional Inso Corporation Viewers	Files to preview different document formats in the Open File dialog box (see "Tools for Viewing Files" in this chapter)
Corel Barista	Files for publishing Web documents as a Java applet (see "Corel Barista" in this chapter)
Corel 3-D TextArt Components	Files to create 3-D TextArt images (see Chapter 7)
Corel Versions	Files to create and manage different file versions (see Chapter 16)
French Writing Tools	Files for using the French writing tools (Spell-As-You-Go, QuickCorrect, and so on)
Some of the Clipart and Graphics	WPG graphics images (see Chapter 7)

Other Programs & Utilities

ODBC Core and System Files	Files for accessing databases
ODBC Drivers	Files for using specific databases
Additional Thesaurus Definitions	Expanded Thesaurus definitions
Spell Utility	Program for adding words to the Speller dictionary (see "The Spell Utility" in this chapter)

* Available only in the Standard Edition of Corel WordPerfect Suite 8

** Available only in the Professional Edition of Corel WordPerfect Suite 8

Bitstream Font Navigator

When you want to select a new font for a document, there's no shortage of choices. Corel's WordPerfect Suite 8 CD comes with over 1,000 TrueType fonts, and you probably already have several fonts installed from your other Windows programs. Having a large number of fonts installed at the same time can bog down your system, so keeping track of what fonts you have available—without actually installing them all—can be tricky. That's where Bitstream's Font Navigator 2.0 utility comes in handy.

Font Navigator is a program that lets you easily manage your font files. Font Navigator displays a list of all the font files found in the directories you specify, whether or not they're currently installed (see Figure 20-1). In addition, you can see a list of installed fonts, create groups of related fonts, quickly install or uninstall fonts from your system, and easily view and print font samples.

To install Font Navigator, follow the steps in the "Installing the Bonus Tools" section earlier in the chapter. Bitstream Font Navigator 2.0 is a main option in the Custom Installation dialog box. To run Font Navigator after installing it, from the Windows taskbar, choose Start | Programs | Bitstream Font Navigator | Font Navigator 2.0.

The first time you run Font Navigator, a Wizard asks you to select the drives and directories it should search through for font files. You can include directories on your hard drive, CD-ROM drive, and network drive. For example, if you want to be able to view the available fonts on the WordPerfect Suite 8 CD, make sure the CD is in the drive and select your CD-ROM drive from the list.

NOTE: *You can also see a printed list of the available fonts on the WordPerfect Suite 8 CD in the front part of the printed Clipart manual.*

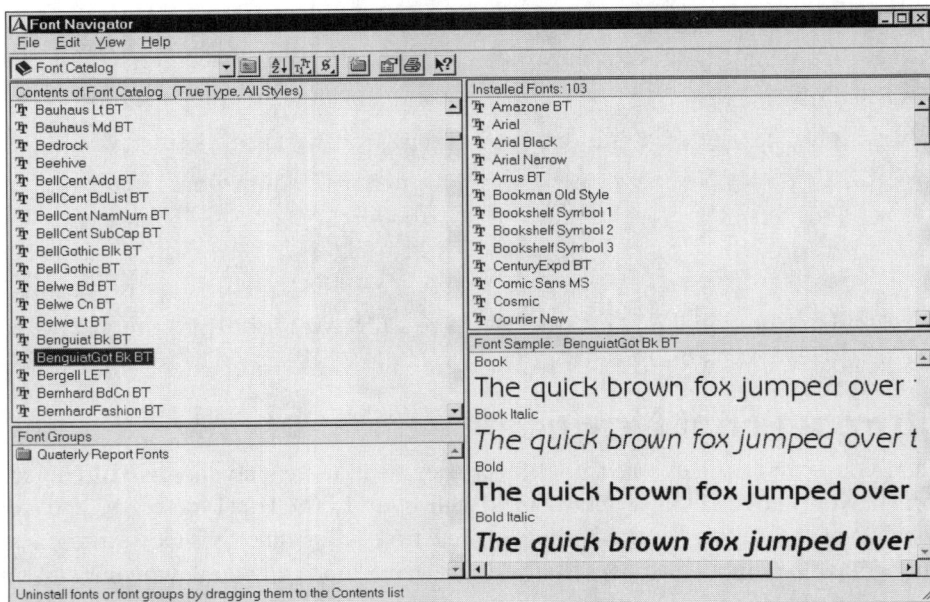

FIGURE 20-1 Bitstream's Font Navigator 2.0 helps you manage your font files

In the Font Navigator dialog box, the Font Catalog on the left lists all of the available font files in the selected directories. When you select a font in the list, a sample appears in the lower corner (see Figure 20-1). Those fonts with a checkmark next to them are currently installed in Windows (and are also listed on the right side of the dialog box). To install a new font, simply click and drag it from the Font Catalog list to the Installed Fonts list. To uninstall a font, select the font in the Installed Fonts list on the right and press DELETE (the actual font file is not deleted).

CAUTION: *If you uninstall a font, make sure that you reformat any documents using that font, or reinstall the font before opening or printing the document.*

NOTE: *You can also install fonts using Windows Control Panel. For more information, see the Power Tip "Installing Fonts from Windows."*

Power Tip▸▸▸ Installing Fonts from Windows

Bitstream's Font Navigator 2.0 is a great utility for managing, installing, and uninstalling fonts. However, if you don't want to install Font Navigator, you can also add and remove fonts using the Windows Control Panel. Close Font Navigator if it's open, then follow these steps:

1. From the Windows taskbar, choose Start | Settings | Control Panel.

2. Double-click the Fonts icon.

3. To add fonts, choose File | Install New Font.

4. Use the Drives drop-down list and the Folders list box to select the directory containing the font files. The fonts on the Corel WordPerfect Suite 8 CD are found in the \Corel\Appman\Wkswpi8\Fonts\Corel directory (or the \Corel\Suite 8\Appman\Wkswpi8\Fonts\Corel directory on the Professional Edition CD).

5. Any font files in the selected directory are displayed in the List of Fonts list box. Select the font you want to install. To select more than one font, hold down the CTRL key as you select each font.

6. Choose OK to install the selected fonts.

7. Exit the Control Panel by choosing File | Close twice.

20

Here are a few of the things you can do with Font Navigator 2.0:

■ Create font groups of related fonts. For example, if you have a set of fonts that you only use when creating a monthly report, you can place those fonts in a font group and then quickly install the entire group when you're working on a report (and uninstall them when you're finished).

- List fonts according to format (TrueType or PostScript Type 1) or style (Decorative, Monospaced, Sans Serif, Script, Serif, or Symbol).

- Print different samples of a selected font, including a sample with all the letters, numbers, and common symbols; a sample with a sentence in various point sizes and a paragraph of text; or a chart showing every character in the font. (The font doesn't have to be installed to print a sample.)

- Change the sample text displayed in the dialog box or printed with a font sample.

- Add and remove fonts from the Font Catalog list, including deleting the actual font file from your hard drive.

Corel Photo House

WordPerfect 8 and Presentations 8 have several tools for editing and creating graphics images, but if you do a lot of work with bitmapped images and scanned photos, you might want to take a look at Corel Photo House. Corel Photo House is a program that makes it easy to touch up photographs, add special effects, and create your own bitmapped images (see Figure 20-2).

NOTE: *Corel Photo House is only included with the standard edition of Corel WordPerfect Suite 8. It is not included with the Professional edition.*

To install Corel Photo House, follow the steps in the "Installing the Bonus Tools" section earlier in the chapter. The Corel Photo House program is one of the main options you can select in the Custom Installation dialog box. Corel Photo House requires about 15MB of disk space. After installing Corel Photo House, you can run it from the Windows taskbar by choosing Start | Corel WordPerfect Suite 8 | Corel Photo House.

Corel Photo House supports a large number of file formats, including Photo CD files and images from video capture cards. You can drag and drop images from other applications into the Photo House dialog box to make changes. If you open a vector image, such as a WPG file, Photo House creates a duplicate bitmap file, leaving your original file intact.

FIGURE 20-2 Corel Photo House helps you touch up scanned photographs and create bitmapped images

Once the image is in Photo House, you can use the many photo-editing and painting tools to manipulate and make changes to the image. For example, you can use the "Remove Red Eyes" tool to touch up a photograph, or add designs with a specialty paintbrush. You can also create a new bitmap image from scratch. When you're finished, you can save the image in a variety of bitmap formats, including BMP, PCX, TIF, and GIF.

TIP: *WordPerfect 8 can import images in a variety of different bitmap and vector formats (see Chapter 7 for more information). The WordPerfect Suite 8 CD also contains additional conversions for graphics files that aren't installed during a typical installation. For more information, see the Power Tip "WP's Additional Graphics Conversions."*

> ## Power Tip▸▸▸ WP's Additional Graphics Conversions
>
> If you work with images in a format that's not extremely common, such as TGA or Photo CD, you might be able to use those images in WordPerfect 8 by installing the additional graphics conversions. These additional conversions support the following bitmap and vector formats. (See Chapter 7 for a list of the standard graphics formats supported by WordPerfect 8.)
>
> | | | |
> |---|---|---|
> | AutoCAD | Lotus PIC | PSD |
> | CGM Import | MAC Paint | Scitex CT |
> | GEM | Photo CD | TGA |
> | HPGL | PICT | Wavelet |
>
> To install conversions for any of these additional formats, follow the steps in the "Installing the Bonus Tools" section earlier in the chapter. In the Custom Installation dialog box, select Accessories and choose Components; then select Conversions, Viewers, Tools, and choose Components again. If you want to install all of the available graphics conversions, select the checkbox next to Graphics Conversions. If you want to select which conversions should be installed, select the Graphics Conversions option and choose Components; then select the type of format, such as Bitmap Graphic Conversions, and choose Components again. Select the conversion formats you want to install and continue with the installation.

Tools for Viewing Files

When you're looking through a list of filenames, it's often helpful to be able to view the contents of a file before you open, move, copy, or delete it. In Chapter 16, you learned how to look at the contents of a file in WordPerfect's Open File dialog box with the Preview option. In addition to the viewer in the Open File dialog box, WordPerfect Suite 8 comes with a couple of other file-viewing utilities. Both the Quick View Plus program and the Envoy 7 Viewer let you view and print files that originated in other programs.

TIP: *You can also install additional conversions for viewing files with the Preview option in WordPerfect's Open File dialog box. To do this, follow the steps in the "Installing the Bonus Tools" section earlier in the chapter. In the Custom Installation dialog box, use the Components button to see the options in Accessories, then Conversions, Viewers, Tools, and then Viewers. Select the Additional Inso Corporation Viewers option and continue with the installation.*

Quick View Plus

Quick View Plus is a file-viewing utility that integrates seamlessly into Windows 95 or Windows NT. It allows you to not only view files created in over 200 different programs, but also print them, use copy and paste, or search for text in the files. In addition, you can use Quick View Plus to see the individual files stored in a compressed file (such as a ZIP file), and decompress a selected file without affecting the original compressed file. Quick View Plus also integrates with Web browsers such as Netscape and Internet Explorer, so you can view files within the browser.

Quick View Plus uses a separate installation from the rest of the WordPerfect Suite 8. To install Quick View Plus, place the WordPerfect Suite 8 CD in your CD-ROM drive. If the initial screen appears, choose Quick View Plus. Otherwise, from the Windows taskbar, choose Start | Run. Type the path to your CD-ROM drive, followed by **autorun**, such as **e:\autorun**. Then choose Quick View Plus from the initial screen. Follow the prompts to install the program.

After you've installed Quick View Plus, all you have to do to view a file is right-click the file in any file management dialog box and choose Quick View Plus. For example, you can right-click a file in WordPerfect's Open File dialog box, in the Windows Explorer, or as you're browsing through folders from the My Computer icon on the desktop. The Quick View Plus dialog box opens with the file displayed (see Figure 20-3).

In Quick View Plus, you can change the view type (Document | View), search for text, copy and paste information using the Clipboard, or print the file. You can also resize and move the Quick View Plus dialog box. When you're finished, choose File | Exit Quick View Plus.

TIP: *If you exit by choosing File | Close this View or by clicking the Cancel button in the upper-right corner of the dialog box, Quick View Plus remains loaded and appears as an icon in the navigation area of the Windows taskbar. You can double-click the icon to display the Quick View Plus dialog box, browse through folders, and select a file to view.*

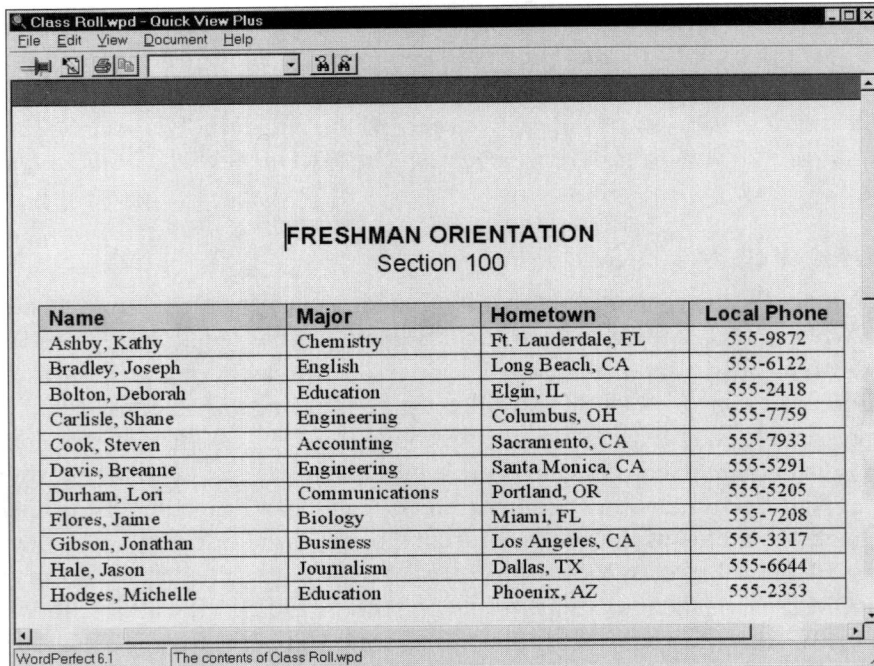

FIGURE 20-3 Quick View Plus allows you to view files in over 200 different formats

Envoy 7 Viewer

Envoy 7 is an electronic publishing tool that allows you to distribute formatted documents across programs and platforms. You can use practically any program to create a document and then publish it to Envoy format (*.EVY). Then you can distribute the Envoy document to others, who can use the Envoy Viewer to view the file with its original formatting intact, and even add notes and annotations to it.

The Envoy 7 Viewer is included as part of Corel's WordPerfect Suite 8. With this tool, you can view files in Envoy format that you've received from others. Envoy files are smaller in size than the original document and can even be viewed across platforms (Macintosh or UNIX, for example).

> **NOTE:** *The Standard Edition of WordPerfect Suite 8 only includes the Envoy 7 Viewer. If you have the Professional Edition of the suite, you also have the Envoy 7 driver, which allows you to publish documents in Envoy format. Publishing a document to Envoy format is as easy as printing. You can install the Envoy 7 driver by performing a custom installation.*

You can either run the Envoy 7 Viewer directly from the WordPerfect Suite 8 CD, or you can install it to your hard drive. To run the viewer from the CD, choose Start | Run from the Windows taskbar. Choose Browse, switch to the \Corel\Suite8\Envoy directory on the CD, and select the ENVOY7.EXE file. Choose OK. Once in Envoy, choose File | Open and open the EVY file you want to view (see Figure 20-4).

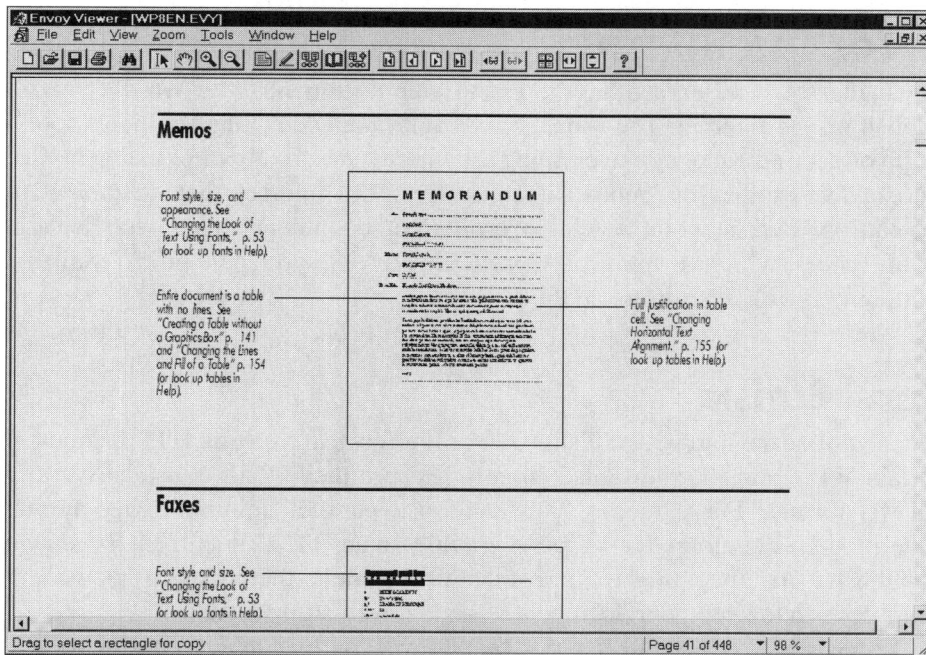

FIGURE 20-4 The Envoy 7 Viewer lets you view files with their original formatting

To install the Envoy 7 Viewer to your hard drive, follow the steps in the "Installing the Bonus Tools" section earlier in the chapter. In the Custom Installation dialog box, select Envoy 7 and choose Components; then select Envoy 7 Viewer (and any other options you want to install). Choose OK and continue with the installation. After installing the Envoy Viewer, you can run it from the Windows taskbar by choosing Start | Corel WordPerfect Suite 8 | Tools | Envoy 7 Viewer.

TIP: *The WordPerfect Suite 8 CD includes several reference manuals for each of the major applications in Envoy format. To use the reference manuals, make sure the WordPerfect Suite 8 CD is in the drive, and from the Windows taskbar choose Start | Corel WordPerfect Suite 8 | Setup & Notes | Reference Center. When the Corel Reference Center appears, click the manual you want to view, and it is opened in the Envoy Viewer.*

Tools for the Internet

In Chapter 14, you learned how to create Web documents with WordPerfect 8 to publish on the Internet. The WordPerfect Suite 8 CD contains additional tools to help you take advantage of everything the Internet has to offer. For example, Corel Barista lets you easily publish documents to the Internet that contain all the formatting used in your regular WordPerfect documents. And with Netscape Conference (which is part of CorelCENTRAL), you can hold "real-time" conferences with other users on the Internet.

Corel Barista

When you use the Internet Publisher in WordPerfect 8 to create an HTML document, certain WP features are disabled, simply because they won't transfer over to the HTML format. For example, you can't use parallel columns, page borders, watermarks, or contoured text around graphics in an HTML document. If you want to publish a document on the Internet that uses some of these features, you can use Corel Barista to keep your document's original formatting intact.

Corel Barista 2.0 is a technology that allows you to display a document on the Internet as a Java application. (Java is a programming language used by Web browsers such as Netscape and Internet Explorer.) When someone accesses your Web site, their browser displays your document in a Java applet area, allowing Barista—not HTML—to handle its formatting. Any formatting you can use in

WordPerfect can be included in a Barista document and then displayed on the Internet (see Figure 20-5).

To install the Barista files, follow the steps in the "Installing the Bonus Tools" section earlier in the chapter. From the Custom Installation dialog box, select Accessories and choose Components. Select Corel Barista and choose OK; then continue with the installation. The Barista files are placed in the \Corel\Suite8\Shared\Barista directory on your hard drive.

In order to use Barista to publish a document on the Internet, you first need to copy the Barista files to your Web server. Copy all the files in the Barista folder, along with all the subfolders, to your Web server directory. This is the same directory that any Barista documents you create will need to be placed in. Otherwise, users won't be able to view your Barista document correctly.

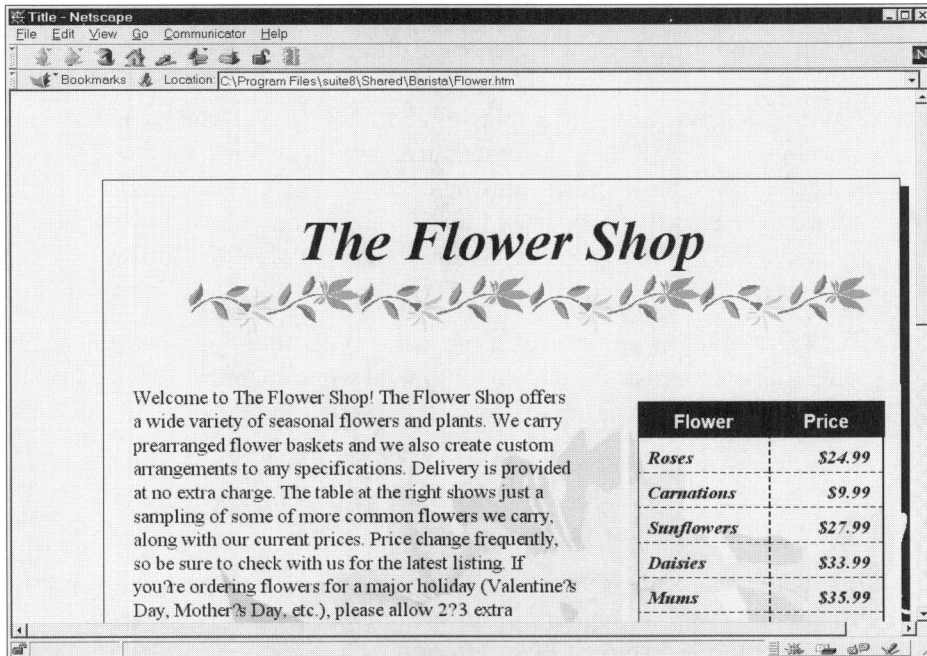

FIGURE 20-5 Corel Barista allows you to use any WP formatting for your Web documents

To create a Barista document, first create the document normally in WordPerfect, using any formatting features that you want. When you're finished, choose File | Send To | Corel Barista. Type a filename for the document. If you want to see the document in your browser before uploading it to your Web server, make sure you save the document in the same directory as the Barista files on your hard drive. If you don't want your file to display in your browser, deselect Launch Browser. Choose Send to create the Barista document. After creating the Barista document, upload it to your Web server and place it in the same directory as the Barista files.

TIP: *You can also create a Barista document by using the Corel Barista printer driver. This method gives you some additional options, such as creating a "slide show" of your document. To use this method, create the document and choose File | Print. Select Corel Barista from the Current Printer drop-down list and choose Print. When the Corel Barista Driver Properties dialog box appears, select the options you want.*

A few things to remember about Barista documents:

- Java applications can only display three fonts: Times New Roman, Arial, and Courier New. If your document uses any other fonts, they will be replaced with the closest match when you publish it to Barista. In addition, because the supported fonts don't contain bullets, any bullets or other symbols in your document won't be included in the Barista document.

- The more graphics and complex formatting you use in your document, the longer it will take for the document to load when someone accesses your Web site.

- Those who view a Barista document from your Web site won't be able to print it or copy information from it to the Clipboard. (Java does not currently support these features.)

- In order for someone to view your document on the Internet, they must be using a browser that supports Java, such as Netscape Navigator 3.0 or later, or Internet Explorer 3.0 or later.

Netscape Conference

WordPerfect Suite 8 includes a special version of Netscape Communicator 4.01a that was designed to integrate seamlessly with CorelCENTRAL 8. One part of Netscape Communicator is Netscape Conference, which lets you hold "real-time" conferences with other Internet users. Netscape Conference includes tools that let you interact with other users through your Internet connection in the following ways:

- Chat in an audio or written conversation

- Collaborate and sketch ideas on a virtual whiteboard

- Browse a Web site together

- Exchange files

NOTE: *CorelCENTRAL and Netscape Communicator 4.01a were not included in the original release of WordPerfect Suite 8. If you purchased this version, you received a voucher in the package with instructions for obtaining CorelCENTRAL when it became available.*

To install Netscape Conference, follow the steps in the "Installing the Bonus Tools" section earlier in the chapter. In the Custom Installation dialog box, select CorelCENTRAL 8 and choose Components. Select Netscape Communicator, choose Components, and then select Netscape Conference and choose OK to continue with the installation.

To use Netscape Conference, start CorelCENTRAL and choose Tools | Conference or click the Conference button on the toolbar. The first time you use Netscape Conference, you need to enter some information about yourself. When the Netscape Conference dialog box appears, you can "call" another user and begin your conference session (see Figure 20-6).

Other Helpful Tools

Some tasks that you might think can't be done in WordPerfect 8 *can* actually be accomplished with the help of some of the tools that aren't installed by default. For

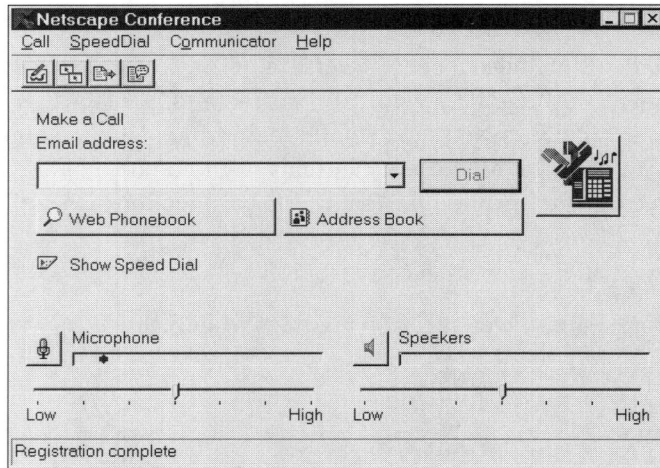

FIGURE 20-6   Netscape Conference lets you collaborate with other Internet users in a real-time conversation

example, WordPerfect 8 doesn't let you add words to the main Spell Checker dictionary, but you can add words with the bonus Spell Utility. In addition, you can't import or save files in certain formats, such as Multimate or WordStar, from the default installation of WordPerfect 8, but you can use these files by installing the additional text conversions.

The Spell Utility

The Spell Utility allows you to create and edit main word lists (dictionaries) used by the Spell Checker. For example, you can create a separate medical or law dictionary, or simply add words to the default main word list. In addition, you can use the Spell Utility to merge word lists together and convert dictionaries from previous versions of WordPerfect.

To install the Spell Utility, follow the steps in the "Installing the Bonus Tools" section earlier in the chapter. If you have the standard edition of WordPerfect 8, select Accessories in the Custom Installation dialog box and choose Components. If you have the Professional Edition, select Required Components and choose Components. Then, in either version, use the Components button to view the options

under Corel Writing Tools, then English Writing Tools, and then Optional Files. Select Spell Utility, and continue with the installation.

To use the Spell Utility, from the Windows taskbar choose Start | Run. Choose Browse and switch to the \Corel\Suite8\Programs directory. Select the WTSPTLEN.EXE file and choose Open; then choose OK. When the Spell Utility dialog box appears, you can select the tab for the option you want to perform (see Figure 20-7).

NOTE: *The default main word list for WordPerfect 8 is named WT80EN.MOR and is stored in the \Corel\Suite8\Programs directory.*

TIP: *If you use the Spell Utility frequently, create a shortcut for it on the Windows desktop or Start menu.*

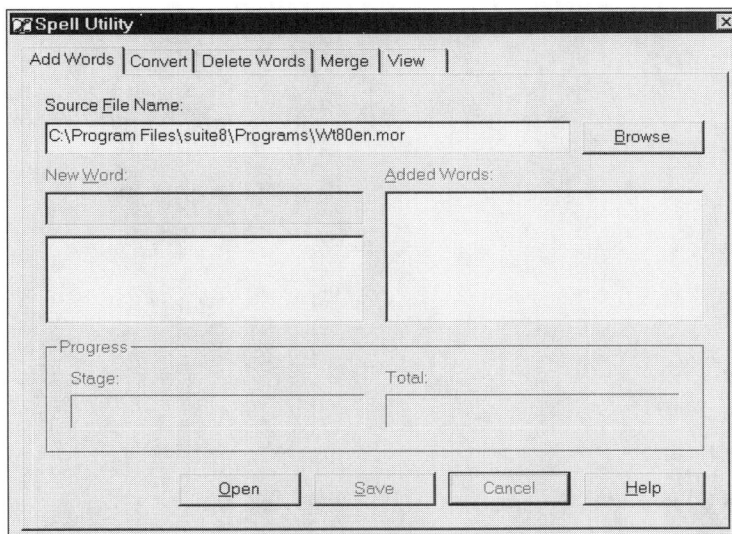

20

FIGURE 20-7 The Spell Utility lets you add and edit the main word lists used by the Spell Checker

File Format Conversions

WordPerfect 8 automatically includes several options for converting files to and from different file formats. If you need to open or save a file in a format that isn't automatically supported, you can check to see if that format is part of the additional text conversions. The "Additional Text Conversions" Quick Reference section lists the conversion formats that can be installed, but aren't installed by default.

To install the additional text conversions, follow the steps in the "Installing the Bonus Tools" section earlier in the chapter. In the Custom Installation text box, select Accessories and choose Components. Then use the Components button to see the options under Conversions, Viewers, Tools, and then Text Conversions. Select Conversion Set 3 (the other two sets are installed during a typical installation), choose OK, and continue with the installation.

Quick Reference ▶▶▶ Additional Text Conversions

WordPerfect 8 can convert files to and from the following formats if you install the additional text conversions.

- Borland Sprint
- Display Write
- IBM DCA RFT
- IBM DCA FFT
- Kermit (7-Bit Transfer)
- MS Word 4.0–5.5
- Multimate
- Navy Dif

- Office Writer
- PlanPerfect
- Professional Write
- Volkswriter
- WordPerfect 2.x Macintosh
- WordStar 2000 1.0–3.0
- WordStar 3.3–7
- WP Works 2.0 Document

Summary

From the powerhouse programs of WordPerfect, Quattro Pro, and Presentations, to the smaller utilities and programs on the CD, Corel's WordPerfect Suite 8 has the tools you need to get your work done faster and easier than ever before. Bonus programs such as Bitstream Font Navigator, Corel Photo House, and Quick View Plus add functionality and efficiency to your Windows work. In addition, tools such as Corel Barista and the Spell Utility help you accomplish more from within WordPerfect.

The information we've given in this book is just the start of what you can accomplish with WordPerfect 8 and the other programs in the suite. We hope we've inspired you to take those extra few minutes to learn a new feature or tool in WordPerfect 8. It will open a whole new world of possibilities!

PART V

Appendixes

Appendix

A

Code Values for Searching in WP OLE

This Appendix contains an Alphabetical listing of WordPerfect's searchable codes with their corresponding numeric values. These values can be used when searching with OLE Automation commands. For more information on using these values, see Chapter 19.

334	...Center Tab		307	Box: Char Anc.
336	...Dec Tab		212	Box Num Dec
328	...Hd Center on Marg		194	Box Num Disp
329	...Hd Center Tab		203	Box Num Inc
332	...Hd Dec Tab		184	Box Num Meth
330	...Hd Flush Right		174	Box Num Set
327	...Hd Left Tab		308	Box: Para Anc.
331	...Hd Right Tab		309	Box: Pg Anc.
333	...Left Tab		17	Calc Col
335	...Right Tab		11	Cancel Hyph
70	? (One Char)		28	Cell
0	? (One Char)		338	Center on Marg (all)
1	* (Many Chars)		324	Center Tab
390	All Merge Codes		339	Center Tab (all)
396	Asian Wrap		146	Change BOL Char
399	Attached Text		145	Change EOL Char
398	Attached Text On		215	Chap Num Dec
400	Attached Text Opt		197	Chap Num Disp
6	Auto Hyphen EOL		206	Chap Num Inc
140	Bar Code		187	Chap Num Meth
62	Binding Width		177	Chap Num Set
134	Block Pro Off		397	Char Count
133	Block Pro On		121	Char Shade Change
384	Bold Off		221	Char Style Off
368	Bold On		220	Char Style On
132	Bookmark		51	Cntr Cur Pg
48	Bot Mar		52	Cntr Pgs
391	Box (all)		78	Col Border

77	Col Def		219	Endnote Num Dec
120	Color		201	Endnote Num Disp
125	Comment		210	Endnote Num Inc
127	Condl EOP		191	Endnote Num Meth
211	Count Dec		181	Endnote Num Set
193	Count Disp		99	Endnote Placement
202	Count Inc		55	Endnote Space
183	Count Meth		372	Ext Large Off
173	Count Set		356	Ext Large On
128	Date		405	Fancy Border
129	Date Fmt		139	Filename
383	Dbl Und Off		376	Fine Off
367	Dbl Und On		360	Fine On
344	DDE Link Begin		90	First Ln Ind
345	DDE Link End		154	Flt Cell Begin
101	Dec/Align Char		155	Flt Cell End
326	Dec Tab		122	Font
342	Dec Tab (all)		123	Font Size
100	Def Mark		167	Footer A
68	Delay		168	Footer B
69	Delay Codes		74	Footer Sep
409	Deletion Off		171	Footnote
408	Deletion On		59	Footnote Count Msg
16	Do Grand Tot		56	Footnote Min
12	Do Subtot		218	Footnote Num Dec
14	Do Total		200	Footnote Num Disp
8	Dorm HRt		58	Footnote Num Each Pg
126	Dot Lead Char		209	Footnote Num Inc
350	Dropcap Definition		190	Footnote Num Meth
9	End Cntr/Align		180	Footnote Num Set
172	Endnote		61	Footnote Sep Ln
57	Endnote Min		54	Footnote Space

60	Footnote Txt Pos		34	HRow-HPg
98	Force		22	HRt
151	Formatted Pg Num		23	HRt-SCol
87	Gen Txt Begin		24	HRt-SPg
88	Gen Txt End		2	HSpace
310	Graph Line		143	Hypertext Begin
105	HAdv		144	Hypertext End
25	HCol		85	Hyph
26	HCol-SPg		7	Hyph SRt
311	Hd Back Tab		5	- Hyphen
316	Hd Center on Marg		107	Index
317	Hd Center on Pos		407	Insertion Off
318	Hd Center Tab		406	Insertion On
322	Hd Dec Tab		380	Italc Off
319	Hd Flush Right		364	Italc On
340	Hd Flush Right (all)		84	Just
314	Hd Left Ind		131	Just Lim
315	Hd Left/Right Ind		119	Kern
313	Hd Left Tab		65	Labels Form
320	Hd Right Tab		124	Lang
312	Hd Tbl Tab		374	Large Off
165	Header A		358	Large On
166	Header B		86	Leading Adj
73	Header Sep		323	Left Tab
153	Hidden Off		337	Left Tab (all)
152	Hidden On		81	Lft HZone
117	Hidden Txt		75	Lft Mar
404	Highlight Off		91	Lft Mar Adj
403	Highlight On		394	Line Count
27	HPg		147	Link
32	HRow-HCol		148	Link End
33	HRow-HCol-SPg		351	Linked Object

410	Ln Brk		269	MRG: EMBEDMACRO
79	Ln Height		236	MRG: ENDFIELD
97	Ln Num		237	MRG: ENDFOR
192	Ln Num Meth		238	MRG: ENDIF
182	Ln Num Set		239	MRG: ENDRECORD
80	Ln Spacing		235	MRG: ENDSWITCH
150	Macro Func		240	MRG: ENDWHILE
96	Math		270	MRG: FIELD
95	Math Def		271	MRG: FIELDNAMES
18	Math Neg		272	MRG: FIRSTCAP
256	MRG: ASSIGN		274	MRG: FOREACH
284	MRG: ASSIGNLOCAL		273	MRG: FORNEXT
226	MRG: BEEP		275	MRG: GETSTRING
227	MRG: BREAK		276	MRG: GO
257	MRG: CALL		277	MRG: IF
228	MRG: CANCELOFF		278	MRG: IFBLANK
229	MRG: CANCELON		279	MRG: IFEXISTS
258	MRG: CAPS		280	MRG: IFNOTBLANK
260	MRG: CASEOF		281	MRG: INSERT
262	MRG: CHAINDATA		282	MRG: KEYBOARD
263	MRG: CHAINFORM		283	MRG: LABEL
261	MRG: CHAINMACRO		285	MRG: LOOK
264	MRG: CHAR		286	MRG: MRGCMND
265	MRG: CODES		287	MRG: NESTDATA
266	MRG: COMMENT		288	MRG: NESTFORM
230	MRG: CONTINUE		289	MRG: NESTMACRO
267	MRG: CTON		241	MRG: NEXT
231	MRG: DATE		242	MRG: NEXTRECORD
232	MRG: DEFAULT		290	MRG: NTOC
233	MRG: DISPLAYSTOP		291	MRG: ONCANCEL
268	MRG: DOCUMENT		292	MRG: ONERROR
234	MRG: ELSE			

243	MRG: PAGEOFF
244	MRG: PAGEON
306	MRG: POSTNET
245	MRG: PRINT
255	MRG: PROCESSOFF
247	MRG: PROCESSON
293	MRG: PROMPT
246	MRG: QUIT
252	MRG: REPEATROW
248	MRG: RETURN
249	MRG: RETURNCANCEL
250	MRG: RETURNERROR
251	MRG: REWRITE
294	MRG: STATUSPROMPT
252	MRG: STEPOFF
253	MRG: STEPON
254	MRG: STOP
295	MRG: STRLEN
296	MRG: STRPOS
297	MRG: SUBSTDATA
298	MRG: SUBSTFORM
299	MRG: SUBSTR
259	MRG: SWITCH
300	MRG: SYSTEM
301	MRG: TOLOWER
302	MRG: TOUPPER
303	MRG: VARIABLE
304	MRG: WAIT
305	MRG: WHILE
113	Mrk Txt List Begin

114	Mrk Txt List End
111	Mrk Txt ToC Begin
112	Mrk Txt ToC End
225	Open Style
93	Outline
379	Outln Off
363	Outln On
136	Ovrstk
395	Page Flow
64	Paper Sz/Typ
94	Para Border
388	Para End (all)
142	Para Num
217	Para Num Dec
199	Para Num Disp
208	Para Num Inc
189	Para Num Meth
179	Para Num Set
89	Para Spacing
222	Para Style
224	Para Style End
223	Para Style Txt
135	Pause Ptr
63	Pg Border
213	Pg Num Dec
195	Pg Num Disp
71	Pg Num Fmt
204	Pg Num Inc
185	Pg Num Meth
50	Pg Num Pos
175	Pg Num Set
118	Ptr Cmnd

347	Publish Data End		381	Shadw Off
346	Publish Data Start		365	Shadw On
382	Redln Off		387	Sm Cap Off
366	Redln On		371	Sm Cap On
157	Ref Box		375	Small Off
160	Ref Chap		359	Small On
156	Ref Count		3	- Soft Hyphen
164	Ref Endnote		4	- Soft Hyphen EOL
163	Ref Footnote		141	Sound
162	Ref Para		19	SRt
158	Ref Pg		20	SRt-SCol
159	Ref Sec Pg		21	SRt-SPg
161	Ref Vol		385	StkOut Off
82	Rgt HZone		369	StkOut On
76	Rgt Mar		839	Style
82	Rgt Mar Adj		67	Subdivided Pg
325	Right Tab		110	Subdoc
341	Right Tab (all)		115	Subdoc Begin
29	Row		116	Subdoc End
30	Row-SCol		378	Subscpt Off
31	Row-SPg		362	Subscpt On
214	Sec Pg Num Dec		349	Subscribe Data End
196	Sec Pg Num Disp		348	Subscribe Data Start
205	Sec Pg Num Inc		13	Subtot Entry
186	Sec Pg Num Meth		49	Suppress
176	Sec Pg Num Set		377	Suprscpt Off
353	SGML Char Ref		361	Suprscpt On
354	SGML Entity Ref		343	Tab (all)
392	SGML Ignore Off		83	Tab Set
393	SGML Ignore On		109	Target
149	SGML Tag (End)		321	Tbl Dec Tab
10	SGML Tag (Start)		137	Tbl Def

35	Tbl Off		66	Two-Sided Print
36	Tbl Off-SCol		72	Txt Dir
37	Tbl Off-SPg		386	Und Off
44	THCol		370	Und On
45	THCol-SPg		103	Undrln Spc
355	Third Party		104	Undrln Tab
102	Thousands Sep		106	VAdv
46	THPg		373	Very Large Off
41	THRt		357	Very Large On
42	THRt-SCol		216	Vol Num Dec
43	THRt-SPg		198	Vol Num Disp
108	ToA		207	Vol Num Inc
47	Top Mar		188	Vol Num Meth
402	Tot Pgs Disp		178	Vol Num Set
401	Tot Pgs Meth		169	Watermark A
15	Total Entry		170	Watermark B
38	TSRt		53	Wid/Orph
39	TSRt-SCol		130	Wrd/Ltr Spacing
40	TSRt-SPg		138	Writing Tools

Appendix
B

What's On the Companion CD

To help you get the most out of this book, we've included sample projects and files from each of the chapters on the accompanying CD. The companion CD also includes a wealth of macros, experts, templates, and other valuable utilities from Corel and third party providers that will help you maximize your productivity in Corel WordPerfect 8, as well as Windows 95 or Windows NT.

This appendix lists the files on the CD, along with a brief description. But first, here are a few guidelines for using the files on the CD:

- To use the sample files from the book, refer to the indicated chapter for more information.

- Files that end with a ZIP extension are compressed files that need to be extracted with a ZIP utility. If you don't already have one, you can use the WinZip utility included on the companion CD. Run the WINZIP95.EXE file to install this utility.

- Files that end with an EXE extension can be run from Windows to install the associated program or decompress the associated files.

- WordPerfect macros that end with a WCM extension can be copied into your default macro directory and played from within WordPerfect (see Chapter 10 for more information).

- Before playing macros from the CD, copy them to your hard disk and verify that they aren't marked as read-only. You can check the read-only status of a file in WordPerfect by choosing File | Open, selecting the file, right-clicking it, and selecting Properties. In the Properties dialog box, verify that Read Only is not selected, then choose OK. Removing the read-only attribute allows WordPerfect to recompile the macros so they can play correcty on your system.

CAUTION: *Several of the utilities and programs included on the CD are shareware, which means that you are responsible for registering those programs if you continue to use them. Make sure you read the documentation that is included with the utility for specific information on the free trial period and the cost of registering the program.*

The following sections list each of the items on the CD and tell what these files can do for you.

Trial Versions

The CD includes trial versions of three different programs that you can install and use: Client Manager 3.2, Corel WebMaster Suite, and Corel WordPerfect Suite 8. The files for each program are stored in a separate directory on the CD.

Client Manager 3.2

Client Manager 3.2 from Software Studios is a full-featured address book that takes advantage of WordPerfect's merge and macro functionality. Through Client Manager, you can maintain information about clients and groups of clients and easily merge your information with WordPerfect forms.

To install Client Manager, run SETUP.EXE from the CD's Client Manager directory. Then follow the instructions to finish installation. This is the complete Client Manager product, but prior to being registered it is limited to 30 names. For registration information, see Client Manager's online help. Go to www.studio2.com on the Internet for more information about Client Manager and other Software Studios products.

Corel WebMaster Suite

If you're looking for an easy way of designing, creating, and maintaining your Web pages, then the Corel WebMaster Suite may be just what you need. This 30-day trial version of the suite includes products such as Corel WEB.DESIGNER for web page authoring, Corel WEB.PhotoPaint for bitmap image and photograph editing, Corel WEB.SiteManager creating and managing web sites, and Corel WEB.DATA for publishing database info to HTML.

To install the Corel WebMaster Suite trial version, run SETUP.EXE from the Corel WebMaster Suite – Trial Version directory on the CD. For more information about the Corel WebMaster Suite, go to Corel's home page on the Internet at www.corel.com.

Corel WordPerfect Suite 8 with Product Showcase

You've probably already purchased WordPerfect Suite 8, but you may have friends or co-workers who want to see what WordPerfect 8 and the other suite products have to offer before buying it. This 30-day trial version of Corel WordPerfect Suite 8 is the perfect solution. It gives you the functionality of the suite products without the up-front price tag.

In addition to the WordPerfect Suite 8 trial version, the CD also includes a showcase presentation of Corel WordPerfect Suite 8. In the showcase presentation, Corel uses video, sound and animation to bring WordPerfect's rich feature set to life.

To install the Corel WordPerfect Suite 8 trial version or watch the showcase presentation, run SETUP.EXE from the root directory on the CD. Then just follow the instructions to complete the installation or see the presentation.

WordPerfect Macros

The companion CD contains over 35 WordPerfect 8 macros from two third-party vendors: IVY International Communications and Software Studios. To use these macros, first copy them into your default macro directory (usually \Corel\ Suite8\Macros\WPWin). Then, make sure the macro files aren't marked as read-only as explained earlier in this appendix. See Chapter 10 for more information on playing and using macros.

IVY Macros

The IVY Macro directory on the CD contains a selection of useful WordPerfect 8 macros from IVY International Communications' **80 Macros for Corel WordPerfect 8** product. These macros automate tasks such as creating envelope borders, graphics catalogs, and index tabs. There's even a macro for testing your typing speed. Here is a brief description of each macro:

■ 8DIRSEARCH.WCM   Searches for a specific string of text in all documents in a subfolder and replaces that string with another specified string.

■ 8ENVBDR.WCM   Places a graphics border around the mailing address using a helpful dialog box and a choice of 16 exclusive clip art images created specifically for this macro.

NOTE: *This macro uses the following graphics files: ENV4SALE.WPG, ENVBEACH.WPG, ENVCOMP.WPG, ENVDINO.WPG, ENVENVILL.WPG, ENVFALL.WPG, ENVGOLF.WPG, ENVHOTEL.WPG, ENVMAIL.WPG, ENVPETS.WPG, ENVSPORT.WPG, ENVSPRNG.WPG, ENVSUMMR.WPG, ENVSUNFL.WPG, ENVTRAVL.WPG, and ENVWINTR.WPG. Before playing the macro, be sure to copy these graphics files to your default graphics directory.*

■ 8GRAPHIC.WCM   Creates a catalog of your graphics with small, medium or large graphics on each page.

■ 8INDXTAB.WCM   Creates index tabs for hanging file folders.

■ 8INTRUPT.WCM   Adds visual impact to your fliers, brochures, reports, and newsletters by putting a headline right through the top of your text box borders.

■ 8MILES.WCM   Takes a date, an odometer reading, and the number of gallons of gas purchased and then calculates the number of miles driven and the miles per gallon of gas.

■ 8PLANNER.WCM   Creates an annual planning calendar and automatically inserts the name for each month and the date for each day.

■ 8RECIPE.WCM   Uses a WordPerfect file to store recipes. You can find, print, delete, and save recipes to this file.

■ 8RESUME.WCM   Helps you create a customized resume that only takes a few minutes to fill out (assuming you already know what to say).

■ 8TYPETST.WCM   Uses WP 8 to find your typing speed. Not only does it count the number of words you can type per minute, it also finds mistakes and deducts those from the total score.

For more information about IVY International Communications products, go to www.wpmag.com on the Internet.

SSI Macros

These macros from Software Studios are not only useful for automating WordPerfect tasks, they're also a great reference for seeing how to use advanced macro commands. Here are the SSI macros included on the CD:

- Z-AUTOMV.WCM   Automates data entry in a table.

- Z-BOOK.WCM   Prints a document in booklet format.

- Z-BORDER.WCM   Creates a text border around a page.

- Z-BOX.WCM   Creates a check box to a specified size.

- Z-BRAND.WCM   Inserts customized identification in document.

- Z-CAPBOX.WCM   Creates a text box border with caption.

- Z-CARD.WCM   Creates a four-fold greeting card with graphics and a custom message.

- Z-CASE.WCM   Changes the case of the current letter. Recommended to be assigned to a key combination, such as CTRL-SHIFT-C.

- Z-COPY.WCM   Inserts the "COPY" watermark and creates a footer with the path and filename, then prints and closes document.

- Z-COUNT.WCM   Counts the number of times a word or phrase is used in a document.

- Z-DATED.WCM   Places a legal date text string in a document.

- Z-DUP.WCM   Checks a merge data file for duplications.

- Z-EDIT.WCM   Converts punctuation to typesetting format.

- Z-FAX.WCM   Places an identifying fax "stamp" on a document.

- Z-FRACT.WCM   Creates a customized fraction notation.

- Z-JUMP.WCM   Jumps selected text a specified amount above or below the baseline of your sentence.

- Z-LABEL.WCM   Duplicates text (such as address information) onto a specified number of labels.

- Z-LOG.WCM   Helps you create and maintain a daily journal.

- Z-MSG.WCM   Creates a "While-you-were-out" message.

NOTE: *Z-LOG.WCM and Z-MSG.WCM require that you copy Z-SSI.INI to your \Windows directory. You also need to copy Z-LOG.WPD and Z-MSG.WPD to the directory specified to the Z-SSI.INI file.*

- Z-PGNUM.WCM   Spells-out page numbers up to one thousand.

- Z-REVTXT.WCM   Reverses text to white on black or color.

- Z-SECRET.WCM   Protects private documents by converting them into a cryptic code. It also lets you decode previously encoded documents.

- Z-SORT.WCM   Sorts company names alphabetically—including names that begin with "The."

- Z-SPCTAB.WCM   Converts spaces to tabs in your document.

- Z-STAMP.WCM   Inserts a preset identification into a document.

- Z-ZERO.WCM   Converts standard zeros On your document to zeros with a slash.

For more information about Software Studios products, go to www.studio2.com.

PerfectExperts

Corel's PerfectExperts help automate tasks that normally take hours (or longer) to complete. Here are three PerfectExperts that will help you create some great documents with minimal effort.

- PR8AWARDS.ZIP is a slide show expert for Corel Presentations 8 that helps you create an award slide show.

- WP8AWARD.ZIP is a WordPerfect expert that helps you create a great-looking certificate.

- QP8MORTAMOR.ZIP is a Quattro Pro 8 mortgage amortization expert that helps you find payment stream information about a mortgage. (The Quattro Pro mortgage amortization expert was created by KMT Software, Inc. You can learn more about KMT Software by going to KMT's Web site at www.kmt.com. on the Internet.

To use these experts, unzip the files and follow the instructions in the README.TXT file. These experts are from Corel's Web site. Corel periodically offers additional experts free of charge so check Corel's Web site (www.corel.com) for other useful experts.

Book Samples

The CD's Samples directory contains sample files from each of the chapters in this book. By referring to these sample files and utilities while reading each chapter, you'll get hands-on experience that'll speed you on your way to becoming a WordPerfect expert. The following table lists the sample files included on the companion CD, along with a description of the files, and the chapters they're used in. For an explanation of how to use each of these tools, refer to the corresponding chapter.

File	Description	Chapter
ACCOUNT LETTER.FRM	Sample merge form letter that shows how to insert floating cells during a merge with the EmbedMacro merge command	Chapter 2
ACCOUNTS.WB3	Sample Quattro Pro spreadsheet	Chapter 18
ADD LIST.WCM	Sample macro that shows how to use call backs and region commands	Chapter 11
ADDRESS BOOK LABELS.FRM	Sample merge form file that creates labels from your WPWin address book	Chapter 2
ADDRESS BOOK.FRM	Merge form file that creates a printed list of information from your WPWin address book	Chapter 15
BACKUP SETTINGS.WCM	Macro that backs up the default template, project file, QuickCorrect list, and QuickWord list	Chapter 3
BACKUP.WCM	Sample macro that shows how to read and write Registry entries	Chapter 11
BILLING.WCM	Sample macro that shows how to create custom dialog boxes	Chapter 10

BIRTHDAY PS.WPD	Document used with SPECIAL OFFER.FRM to show how to insert documents in a merge	Chapter 2
BRONZE OFFER.FRM	Document used with SPECIAL OFFER.FRM to show how to nest form files in a merge	Chapter 2
CHECKBOOK.WPD	Sample table that includes formulas that keep a running total	Chapter 6
CLASS ROLL.FRM	Sample merge form file that shows how to merge into a table (used with ENROLL.DAT)	Chapter 2
COMPANIES.DAT	Sample merge data file that is used with Company INFO.FRM to show how to perform a merge with two data files	Chapter 2
COMPANY INFO.FRM	Sample merge form file that shows how to perform a merge with two data files (COMPANIES.DAT and NAMES.DAT)	Chapter 2
CONCORDANCE. WPD	Sample concordance file for HANDBOOK.WPD	Chapter 9
CONVERT COMMENTS.WCM	Macro that converts comments to text, moves comments, or deletes comments	Chapter 16
CUSTOMER.DB	Sample Paradox database	Chapter 2
CUSTOMERS.DAT	Merge data file use with ACCOUNT LETTER.FRM and NEW ACCOUNT.FRM	Chapter 2
DATE SORT.WPD	Sample document for sorting by date	Chapter 8
DELETE HYPERLINK.WCM	Macro that deletes a hyperlink from a document after the hyperlink is selected and the original macro has played	Chapter 12
ENROLL.DAT	Merge data file used with CLASS ROLL.FRM to show how to merge into a table	Chapter 2

ENVELOPE GRAPHICS.WCM	Macro that inserts a graphic on an envelope	Chapter 7
GOLD OFFER.FRM	Document used with SPECIAL OFFER.FRM to show how to nest form files in a merge	Chapter 2
HANDBOOK.WPD	Sample document used to show how to create a table of contents and an index	Chapter 9
HANDBOOK2.WPD	Sample document that shows a completed table of contents and index	Chapter 9
HYPERLINK HANDBOOK.WPD	Sample handbook with a hyperlinked table of contents	Chapter 12
ICON VALUES.WPD	Document that contains the icon numbers and descriptions for icons you can use in custom dialog boxes	Chapter 11
INDEX DIVIDER.WCM	Macro that divides an index into alphabetized sections with an initial capital letter at the beginning of each section	Chapter 9
INTERNET LINKS.WPD	Document with sample hyperlinks to Internet sites	Chapter 12
INVOICE FORMULAS.WPD	Sample table used to show how to insert basic table formulas	Chapter 6
INVOICE FORMULAS2.WPD	Table that contains basic table formulas	Chapter 7
INVOICE.WCM	Macro used with INVOICE.WPD to show how to include a macro in a QuickWord	Chapter 3
INVOICE.WPD	Sample document used with INVOICE.WCM to show how to include a macro in a QuickWord	Chapter 3
JOIN OFFER.FRM	Document used with SPECIAL OFFER.FRM to show how to nest form files in a merge	Chapter 2

KEYBOARD MEMO.FRM	Sample keyboard merge file used to create a memo	Chapter 2
LETTER.WPD	Sample letter used to create a letterhead template	Chapter 1
LETTER.WPT	Letterhead template with automated prompts	Chapter 1
LIBRARY.WCM	Library file of macro functions and procedures	Chapter 11
LOAN CALCULATOR. WPD	Table that is used to show how to add financial formulas	Chapter 6
LOAN CALC2.WPD	Table that contains financial formulas	Chapter 6
MACROS TOOLBAR.WPT	Template with a toolbar that includes buttons for main macros on the companion CD	Chapter 13
MEMO MACRO.WCM	Sample of a recorded macro with pauses inserted	Chapter 10
MESSAGE.WPT	Message pad template modified so that you can create more than one message	Chapter 1
MULTILEVEL HYPHEN.STY	Graphics style that sets up multilevel caption numbering in the format 1-1	Chapter 7
MULTILEVEL PERIOD.STY	Graphics style that sets up multilevel caption numbering in the format 1.1	Chapter 7
MULTIMEDIA. WPD	Sample document with sound and video clips	Chapter 17
NAMES.DAT	Sample merge data file that is used with COMPANY INFO.FRM to show how to perform a merge with two data files	Chapter 2
NEW ACCOUNT.FRM	Sample merge file used with CUSTOMERS.DAT to show how to use variables and keyboard prompts in a merge	Chapter 2

NEWSLETTER.WPD	Sample newsletter used to show how to create styles	Chapter 5
NEWSLETTER2.WPD	Sample newsletter that includes styles for formatting	Chapter 5
NUMBER TABLE ROWS.WCM	Macro that automatically numbers table rows with leading zeros	Chapter 6
OPENWPD.WCM	Macro that displays the Open File dialog box showing only files with a WPD extension	Chapter 16
PARAGRAPH NUMBERS.WPD	Sample document with paragraph numbering	Chapter 9
PERSISTVARS.DOF	Delphi file for persistent variable example	Chapter 19
PERSISTVARS.DPR	Delphi file for persistent variable example	Chapter 19
PERSISTVARS.EXE	Sample program for creating and deleting PerfectScript persistent variables	Chapter 19
PERSISTVARS.RES	Delphi file for persistent variable example	Chapter 19
PERSONAL.DAT	Merge data file used with SPECIAL OFFER.FRM	Chapter 2
PERSVARS.DCU	Delphi file for persistent variable example	Chapter 19
PERSVARS.DFM	Delphi file for persistent variable example	Chapter 19
PERSVARS.PAS	Delphi file for persistent variable example	Chapter 19
PHONE MESSAGE.FRM	Sample of a continuous keyboard merge	Chapter 2
POSTCARD.WCM	Sample macro that shows how to interact with the user in a macro	Chapter 10
PROJECT CLEANUP.WCM	Macro that resets the PROJECT.USR file, which contains the project information for the New dialog box	Chapter 1

Q&A.STY	Sample linked styles that help create documents in question-answer format	Chapter 5
REPLACE ATTRIBUTES. WCM	Macro that replaces any font attribute with any other font attribute.	Chapter 4
REPLACE STYLES.WCM	Macro that searches and replaces specific style codes in a document	Chapter 5
ROTATE PAGE NUMBER.WCM	Macro that places a portrait page number on a landscape page	Chapter 4
SEARCH CODE VALUES (ALPHABETICAL). WPD	Alphabetized list of all searchable codes and their values	Chapter 19
SEARCH CODE VALUES (NUMERIC).WPD	List of all searchable WP codes and their values (in numerical order)	Chapter 19
SILVER OFFER.FRM	Document used with SPECIAL OFFER.FRM to show how to nest form files in a merge	Chapter 2
SORT TITLES.WCM	Macro that sorts a list of items that may start with "a," "an," or "the"	Chapter 8
SPECIAL OFFER.FRM	Sample merge form file that show how to use the NestForm merge command	Chapter 2
SPELL REMINDER.WCM	Macro that reminds you to spell check your document before printing or saving	Chapter 1
START MACRO.WCM	Macro that turns on the Macro Toolbar and inserts the Application command	Chapter 10
STUDENT DATA.FRM	Sample merge form file used with STUDENTS.DAT that shows how to use Switch and IfNotBlank commands	Chapter 2

B

STUDENTS.DAT	Sample merge data file used with STUDENT DATA.FRM	Chapter 2
SYMBOL SET.WCM	Macro that changes the symbol set displayed in the Symbols dialog box	Chapter 4
SYSTEM CODES.WCM	Macro that displays useful system variables, such as ?LeftCode and ?RightCode	Chapter 10
TABLE FORMULAS.WPD	Complete alphabetical listing of all WP table formula functions, along with descriptions and examples	Chapter 6
TABLE SORT.WPD	Sample table that shows how to sort dates in a table	Chapter 8
TABLE TOOLS.WCM	Macro that lets you toggle table guidelines, table gridlines, or row and column indicators	Chapter 6
TEMPLATE DATE.WCM	Macro that replaces the date code in a template with date text	Chapter 1
TOOLBAR.WPT	Sample toolbar with buttons for selecting the eight WordPerfect projects installed during a typical WP installation	Chapter 1

Sound, Video, and Java Files

To help you practice inserting multimedia elements in your WordPerfect documents, we've included some fun video and sound files.

HIGHWAY.AVI is an animated clip of a moving stretch of highway (created by Cascom International, Inc.). INDS_07.MID, INTL_16A.MID, NEWA_11A.MID, and SNORE.WAV are sound files from Corel that you can insert in your WordPerfect documents (see Chapter 17 for more information).

CLOCK.ZIP and TICKER.ZIP are shareware Java applets from the Internet Conveyor Ltd. (www.conveyor.com). TICKER.ZIP contains a Java applet that lets you display a scrolling "ticker-tape" message in your Web document and CLOCK.ZIP contains a Java applet that displays the current time in a digital clock in your Web document. See Chapter 14 for more information on adding Java applets to Web documents.

Utilities

The CD's Utilities directory contains three great shareware utilities that will help you save time and money.

- The WINZIP95.EXE file contains WinZip from Nico Mac Computing, Inc. (www.winzip.com). WinZip is one of the leading compression utilities on the market. Since many of the files on the companion CD are zipped (you can tell by the ZIP extension), this is a must-have utility for getting the most out of the CD. This file is a self-extracting executable. You can install it by running the executable and following the instructions.

- DSQUED3.ZIP is a shareware utility (Squedule) that lets you schedule programs to run. Using Squedule, you can launch Windows applications at any time—even if you're away from your computer. Squedule is available at www.bluesquirrel.com.

- NTP300.ZIP (Net Timer Pro) is a shareware utility that automatically tracks the time you spend on the Internet. It includes three timers: one for the current session, one for the current day, and one for the current month. It also includes features such as multiple users and multiple ISP support.

Corel Knowledge Base

The Corel Knowledge Base is a collection of documents (in HTML format) that can answer many of your WordPerfect Suite 8 questions. You can use WordPerfect's QuickFinder or the Windows Find feature to search the Corel Knowledge Base directory on the companion CD for documents containing keywords you specify.

To locate useful documents through the Windows Find feature, choose Start from the Windows taskbar, then choose Find | Files or Folders. In the Named text box type *.*. In the Look In text box, type the path to the Corel Knowledge Base folder on the CD, such as D:\COREL KNOWLEDGE BASE\ (or use the Browse button to select it). Then, select the Advanced tab and type the text you are looking for in the Containing Text text box. Finally, choose Find Now to execute the search. The Find feature displays a list of documents containing the text you specify. Double-click one of the listed documents to open it into your Web browser.